TAXMANN'S SCANNER™

ADVANCED AUDITING & PROFESSIONAL ETHICS

Advanced Auditing & Professional Ethics

Pankaj Garg

9th Edition

Price : ₹ 625

Law stated in this book is as amended upto 31st October, 2019

Published by :
Taxmann Publications (P.) Ltd.

Sales & Marketing :
59/32, New Rohtak Road, New Delhi-110 005 India
Phone : +91-11-45562222
Website : www.taxmann.com
E-mail : sales@taxmann.com

Regd. Office :
21/35, West Punjabi Bagh, New Delhi-110 026 India

Printed at :
Tan Prints (India) Pvt. Ltd.
44 Km. Mile Stone, National Highway, Rohtak Road
Village Rohad, Distt. Jhajjar (Haryana) India
E-mail : sales@tanprints.com

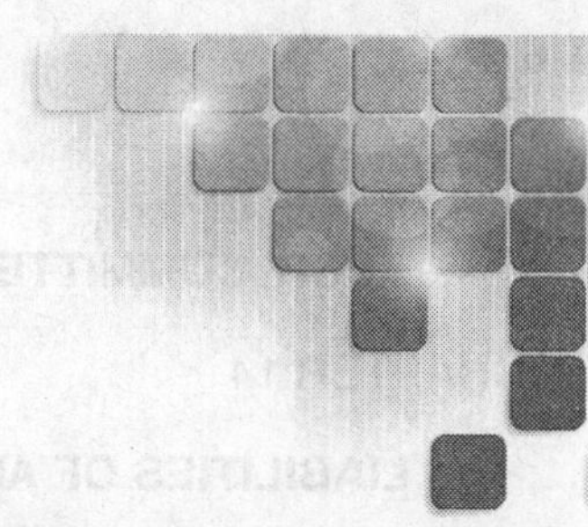

Contents

PAGE

Chapter-wise Marks Distribution

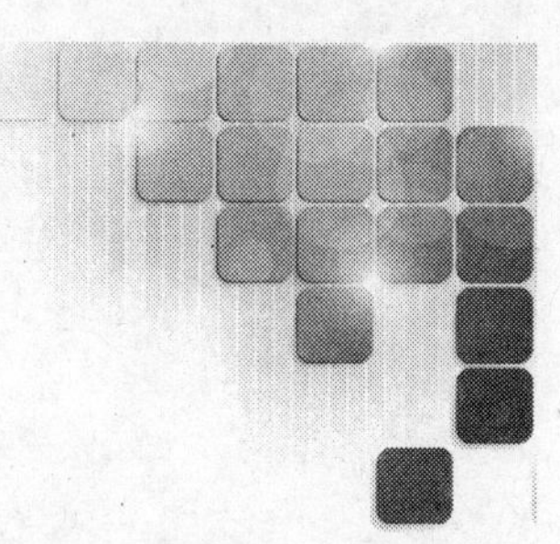

Chapter No.	Chapter Name	New Syllabus				Old Syllabus			
		May 2018	Nov. 2018	May 2019*	Nov. 2019*	May 2018	Nov. 2018	May 2019*	Nov. 2019*
1	Quality Control and Engagement Standards	37	32	19	28	24	24	28	25
2	Audit Planning, Strategy and Execution	-	-	-	5	4	-	-	-
3	Risk Assessment and Internal Control	-	4	5	-	-	-	-	-
4	Audit in an Automated Environment	4	4	5	4	Not in Syllabus			
4A	Audit on CIS Environment	Not in Syllabus				4	3	-	4
4B	SOX Audit	Not in Syllabus				-	-	-	-
5	Professional Ethics	22	18	14	14	20	16	8	12
6	The Company Audit	9	-	8	5	16	12	5	5
7	Audit Reports	4	-	5	-	-	4	-	-
8	CARO, 2016	-	5		-	-	8	-	-
9	Audit of Consolidated Financial Statements	5	5	4	-	4	4	4	4
10	Audit of Dividend	-	5		-	-	-	-	-
11	Audit Committee & Corporate Governance	4	4	6	5	4	4	5	5
12	Liabilities of Auditor	-	4	-	-	-	4	-	-
12A	Cost Audit	Not in Syllabus					4	-	-
13	Internal Audit	-	4	-	-	-	-	5	-
14	Management and Operational Audit	4	5	-	-	4	4	-	-
15	Audit under Fiscal Laws	5	5	4	4	4	4	10	9
16	Due Diligence, Investigation & Forensic Audit	9	-	5	4	4	4	-	5
17	Peer Review and Quality Review	4	4	-	-	4	4	4	-
-	Special Audit Assignments (with Members of S.E.) - Excluded from syllabus from Nov. 19 Exam	-	4	-	-	4	4	5	-
18	Audit of Banks	4	4	4	5	8	4	5	9
19	Audit of NBFC	-	-	-	5	-	4	-	-
20	Audit of Insurance Companies	4	4	5	-	4	-	4	5
20A	Audit of Cooperative Societies	Not in Syllabus				-	-	-	5
21	Audit of PSU	4	4	5	5	4	4	5	-
22	Accounting Standards and Ind-AS	5	5	-	-	-	-	-	-
23	Schedule III of Companies Act, 2013	-	-	-	-	4	5	-	-
Total		124	120	89*	84*	120	120	88*	88*

* For May 19 and Nov. 19 Exams, marks are given only for descriptive questions as MCQs are not issued in public domain.

CHAPTER 1

QUALITY CONTROL AND ENGAGEMENT STANDARDS

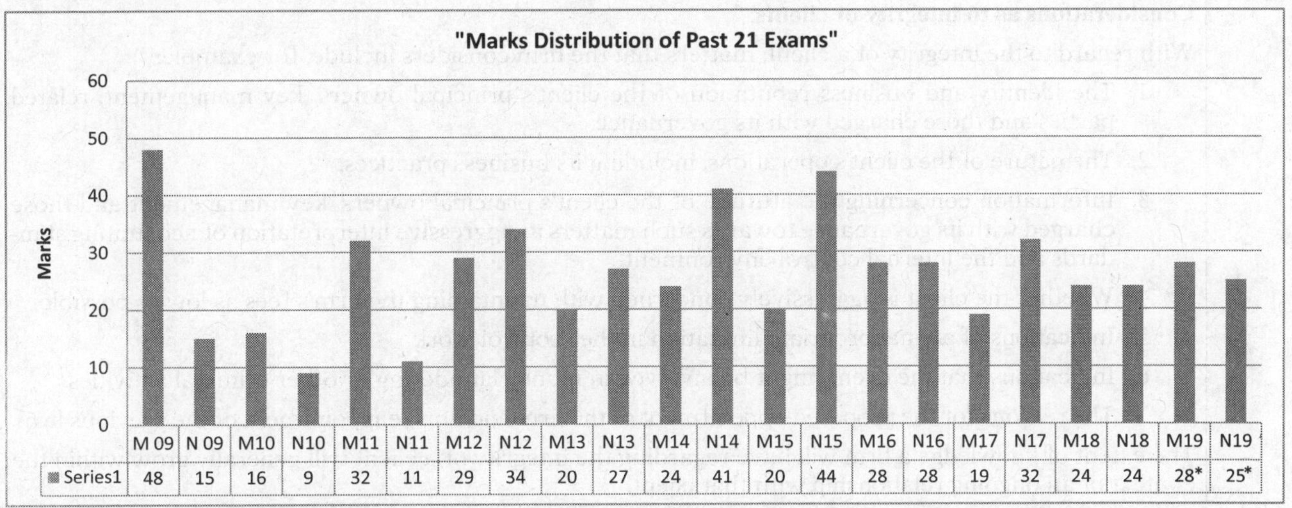

*Only Subjective Questions.

1.1 - SQC 1 "QUALITY CONTROL FOR FIRMS THAT PERFORM AUDITS & REVIEWS OF HISTORICAL FINANCIAL INFORMATION AND OTHER ASSURANCE AND RELATED SERVICES ENGAGEMENTS"

Q.1 **BSS & Associates is a partnership firm of Chartered Accountants which was established five years back. The firm was offering only advisory services at the beginning, however, after audit rotation and advent of GST, firm sees lot of potential in these areas also and started looking for opportunities in these areas also. These services being assurance in nature, the firm required some internal restructuring and set up some policies and procedures for compliance year on year.**

The firm started getting new clients for these new services and is now looking to obtain such information as it considers necessary in the circumstances before accepting an engagement with a new client, when deciding whether to continue an existing engagement, and when considering acceptance of a new engagement with an existing client. Where issues have been identified, and the firm decides to accept or continue the client relationship or a specific engagement, it has been setting up a process to document how the issues were resolved.

The firm is now looking to work with only select clients which are in line with the policies of the firm. The firm understands that the extent of knowledge it will have regarding the integrity of a client will grow within the context of an ongoing relationship with that client. With regard to the integrity of a client, you are required to give some examples of the matters to be considered by the firm as per the requirements of SQC 1. **[RTP-May 19]**

Or

MB & Associates is a partnership firm of the Chartered Accountants which was established seven years back. The firm is getting new clients and has also been offered new engagement services with existing clients. The firm is concerned about obtaining such information as it considers necessary in the circumstances before accepting an engagement with a new client and acceptance of a new engagement with an existing client. The firm is looking to work with only select clients to adhere to the Quality Control Standards. Guide MB & Associates about the matters to be considered with regard to the integrity of a client, as per the requirements of SQC 1. **[Nov. 19 - New Syllabus (4 Marks)]**

Ans. : Considerations as to integrity of clients:

- As per SQC-1 "Quality Control for Firms that Perform Audits and Reviews of Historical Financial Information, and Other Assurance and Related Services Engagements" a firm should establish a system of quality control designed to provide it with reasonable assurance that the firm and its personnel comply with professional standards and regulatory and legal requirements, and that reports issued by the firm are appropriate in the circumstances.
- Accordingly, the firm should obtain such information as it considers necessary in the circumstances before accepting an engagement with a new client, when deciding whether to continue an existing engagement, and when considering acceptance of a new engagement with an existing client. Where issues have been identified, and the firm decides to accept or continue the client relationship or a specific engagement, it should document how the issues were resolved.

Considerations as to integrity of clients:

With regard to the integrity of a client, matters that the firm considers include, for example:

1. The identity and business reputation of the client's principal owners, key management, related parties and those charged with its governance.
2. The nature of the client's operations, including its business practices.
3. Information concerning the attitude of the client's principal owners, key management and those charged with its governance towards such matters as aggressive interpretation of accounting standards and the internal control environment.
4. Whether the client is aggressively concerned with maintaining the firm's fees as low as possible.
5. Indications of an inappropriate limitation in the scope of work.
6. Indications that the client might be involved in money laundering or other criminal activities.
7. The reasons for the proposed appointment of the firm and non-reappointment of the previous firm.

The extent of knowledge a firm will have regarding the integrity of a client will generally grow within the context of an ongoing relationship with that client.

Q.2 **You are an audit senior working for the firm Bohra & Company. You are currently carrying out the audit of Wisdom Ltd., a manufacturer of waste paper bins. You are unhappy with Wisdom Ltd.'s inventory valuation policy and have raised the issue several times with the audit manager. He has dealt with the client for a number of years and does not see what you are making an objection about. He has refused to meet you on site to discuss those issues.**

As the audit manager had dealt with Wisdom Ltd. for so many years, the other partners have decided to leave the audit of Wisdom Ltd. in his capable hands. Comment on the situation outlines above.

Ans. : Quality Control Issues in an engagement:

- SQC - 1 "Quality Control for Firms that perform Audits and Reviews of Historical Financial Information and Other Assurance and Related Services Engagements" requires a firm to establish the policies & procedures for dealing/resolving differences of opinion with in engagement team.
- An engagement partner is usually appointed to each audit engagement undertaken by the firm, to take responsibility for the engagement on behalf of the firm. Assigning the audit to an experienced audit manager is not sufficient.
- SA 220 "Quality Control for an Audit of Financial Statement", requires that the audit engagement partner takes responsibility for settling disputes in accordance with the firm's policy in respect of resolution of difference of opinion required by SQC 1.
- In the present case, partners of the firm have decided to leave the audit in the hands of Audit manager and no engagement partner has been assigned. The lack of an audit engagement partner also means that several of the requirements of SA 220, about ensuring that engagements in relation to independence and directing, supervising and reviewing the audit are not in place.
- Further, the audit manager and senior have conflicting views about the valuation of inventory. This does not appear to have been handled well, with the manager refusing to discuss the issue with the senior.

Conclusion: Failure to resolve the difference of opinion is a breach of the firm's policy under SQC 1. It indicates that the firm does not have a suitable policy concerning such disputes required by SQC 1.

1.2 - SA 200 "OVERALL OBJECTIVES OF THE INDEPENDENT AUDITOR AND CONDUCT OF AN AUDIT IN ACCORDANCE WITH SA"

Q.3 **Discuss with reference to SAs: The auditor is responsible for maintaining an attitude of professional skepticism throughout the audit. Do you agree with the statement?**

Ans. : Professional Skepticism:

(*a*) SA 200 "Overall Objectives of the Independent Auditor and Conduct of Audit in accordance with SAs" requires that the auditor shall plan and perform an audit with professional skepticism.

(*b*) **Meaning of Professional Skepticism**: An attitude that includes a questioning mind, being alert to conditions which may indicate possible misstatement due to error or fraud, and a critical assessment of audit evidence.

(*c*) Professional Skepticism Reduces risk of:

- Overlooking unusual circumstances.
- Over generalising when drawing conclusions from audit observations.
- Using inappropriate assumptions in determining N, T, E of audit procedures & evaluating the results thereof.

(*d*) Professional skepticism includes being alter to:

- Contradictory audit evidence.
- Questions on reliability of documents.
- Conditions indicating possible frauds.
- Circumstances suggesting need for audit procedures in addition to those suggested in SAs.

Q.4 **"An Opinion expressed by the auditor is neither an assurance as to the future viability of the enterprise nor the efficiency or effectiveness with which management has conducted the affairs of the enterprise."**

Ans. : Auditor's responsibility to express an opinion:

- SA 200 "Overall Objectives of the Independent Auditor and Conduct of Audit in accordance with SAs" states that in conducting an audit of financial statements, the auditor is required to express an opinion that whether the F.S. are prepared, in all material respects, in accordance with an applicable FRF.
- The opinion expressed by the auditor is common to all audits of financial statements.
- For this purpose of expressing opinion he is required to obtain reasonable assurance about whether the F.S. as a whole are free from material misstatement, whether due to fraud or error.
- The term reasonable assurance has been defined as higher level of assurance but not absolute.
- The auditor's opinion, therefore, does not assure, the future viability of the entity nor the efficiency or effectiveness with which management has conducted the affairs of the entity.

1.3 - SA 210 "AGREEING THE TERMS OF AUDIT ENGAGEMENT"

Q.5 **Mr. Ram Kapoor, Chartered Accountant, has been appointed as the statutory auditor by XYZ Private Limited for the audit of their financial statements for the year 2018-19. The company has mentioned in the audit terms that they will not be able to provide internal audit reports to Mr. Ram during the course of audit. Further, company also imposed some limitation on scope of Mr. Ram.**

What are the preconditions Mr. Ram should ensure before accepting/refusing the proposal? Also advise, whether Mr. Ram should accept the proposed audit engagement? [RTP-Nov. 19]

Ans. : Preconditions for an audit engagement:

SA 210 "Agreeing the Terms of Engagement" deals with the auditor's responsibilities in agreeing the terms of the audit engagement with management. Before accepting/refusing an audit engagement, to establish whether the preconditions for an audit are present, the auditor shall:

(*a*) Determine whether the financial reporting framework to be applied in the preparation of the financial statements is acceptable; and

(*b*) Obtain the agreement of management that it acknowledges and understands its responsibilities for followings:

(*i*) the preparation of the F.S. in accordance with the applicable FRF.

(ii) exercising necessary internal control to enable the preparation of F.S. that are free from material misstatement, whether due to fraud or error.

(iii) to provide the auditor with:

(a) Access to all relevant information such as records, documentation and other matters;

(b) Additional information that the auditor may request from management for the purpose of the audit; and

(c) Unrestricted access to persons within the entity from whom the auditor determines it necessary to obtain audit evidence.

Q.6 AKJ Ltd. is a small-sized 30 years old company having business of manufacturing of pipes. Company has a plant based out of Dehradun and have their corporate office in Delhi. Recently the company appointed new firm of Chartered Accountants as their statutory auditors.

The statutory auditors want to enter into an engagement letter with the company in respect of their services but the management has contended that since the statutory audit is mandated by law, engagement letter may not be required. Auditors did not agree to this and have shared a format of engagement letter with the management for their reference before getting that signed. In this respect management would like to understand that as per SA 210 (auditing standard referred to by the auditors), if the agreed terms of the engagement shall be recorded in an engagement letter or other suitable form of written agreement, what should be included in terms of agreed audit engagement letter? [MTP-April 19]

Ans. : Agreement on Audit Engagement Terms:

SA 210 "Agreeing the Terms of Audit Engagement" deals with the auditor's responsibilities in agreeing the terms of the audit engagement with management and, where appropriate, those charged with governance. Accordingly,

(1) The auditor shall agree the terms of the audit engagement with management or TCWG, as appropriate.

(2) The agreed terms of the audit engagement shall be recorded in an audit engagement letter or other suitable form of written agreement and shall include:

(a) The objective and scope of the audit of the F.S.;

(b) The responsibilities of the auditor;

(c) The responsibilities of management;

(d) Identification of the applicable FRF for the preparation of the F.S.; and

(e) Reference to the expected form and content of any reports to be issued by the auditor and a statement that there may be circumstances in which a report may differ from its expected form and content.

(3) If law or regulation prescribes in sufficient detail the terms of the audit engagement referred above, the auditor need not record them in a written agreement, except for the fact that such law or regulation applies and that management acknowledges and understands its responsibilities.

Q.7 Comment on the following: "It is not mandatory to send a new engagement letter in recurring audit, but sometimes it becomes mandatory to send new letter." Explain those situations where new engagement letter is to be sent.

Or

R & Co., a firm of Chartered Accountants have not revised the terms of engagements and obtained confirmation from the clients, for last 5 years despite changes in business and professional development. Please elucidate the circumstances that may warrant the revision in terms of engagement.

[May 13 (4 Marks)]

Ans. : Situations in which new engagement letter is required in case of recurring audit:

- SA 210 "Agreeing the Terms of Engagement" deals with the auditor's responsibilities in agreeing the terms of the audit engagement with management. As per SA 210, in case of recurring audits, the auditor shall assess whether circumstances require revision in terms of the audit engagement and whether there is a need to remind the entity of the existing terms of the audit engagement.
- The auditor may decide not to send a new audit engagement letter or other written agreement each period. However, the following factors may make it appropriate to revise the terms of the audit engagement or to remind the entity of existing terms:

1. Any indication that the entity misunderstands the objective and scope of the audit.
2. Any revised or special terms of the audit engagement.
3. A recent change of senior management.
4. A significant change in ownership.
5. A significant change in nature or size of the entity's business.
6. A change in legal or regulatory requirements.
7. A change in the financial reporting framework adopted in the preparation of the F.S.
8. A change in other reporting requirements.

"ICAI Examiner Comments"

Many candidates failed to mention most of the circumstances that may warrant the revision in terms of engagement. Some candidates answered the areas to be changed in the engagement letter.

Q.8 X, a Chartered Accountant was engaged by PQR & Co. Ltd. for auditing their accounts. He sent his letter of engagement to the Board of Directors, which was accepted by the Company. In the course of audit of the company, the auditor was unable to obtain appropriate sufficient audit evidence regarding receivables. The client requested for a change in the terms of engagement. Offer your comments in this regard.

Ans. : Acceptance of changes in Terms of Engagement:

- SA 210 "Agreeing the Terms of Engagement" deals with the auditor's responsibilities in agreeing the terms of the audit engagement with management. As per SA 210, if prior to completing the audit engagement, the auditor is requested to change the audit engagement to an engagement that conveys a lower level of assurance, the auditor shall determine whether there is reasonable justification for doing so.
- The auditor shall not agree to a change in the terms of the audit engagement where there is no reasonable justification for doing so.
- If the terms of the audit engagement are changed, the auditor and management shall agree on and record the new terms of the engagement in an engagement letter or other suitable form of written agreement.
- If the auditor is unable to agree to a change of the terms of the audit engagement and is not permitted by management to continue the original audit engagement, the auditor shall:
  1. Withdraw from the audit engagement where possible under applicable law or regulation; and
  2. Determine whether there is any obligation, either contractual or otherwise, to report the circumstances to other parties, such as TCWG, owners or regulators.

1.4 - SA 220 "QUALITY CONTROL FOR AN AUDIT OF FINANCIAL STATEMENTS"

Q.9 During the audit of FMP Ltd., a listed company, Engagement Partner (EP) completed his reviews and also ensured compliance with independence requirements that apply to the audit engagement. The engagement files were also reviewed by the Engagement Quality Control Reviewer (EQCR) except the independence assessment documentation. Engagement Partner was of the view that matters related to independence assessment are the responsibility of the Engagement Partner and not Engagement Quality Control Reviewer. Engagement Quality Control Reviewer objected to this and refused to sign off the documentation. Please advise as per SA 220. [RTP-May 19]

Ans. : Responsibilities of EP and EQCR in relation to assessment of independence:

- As per SA 220 "Quality control for an Audit of Financial Statements" the engagement partner shall form a conclusion on compliance with independence requirements that apply to the audit engagement. In doing so, the engagement partner shall:
  (*a*) Obtain relevant information from the firm and, where applicable, network firms, to identify and evaluate circumstances and relationships that create threats to independence;
  (*b*) Evaluate information on identified breaches, if any, of the firm's independence policies and procedures to determine whether they create a threat to independence for the audit engagement; and

(c) Take appropriate action to eliminate such threats or reduce them to an acceptable level by applying safeguards, or, if considered appropriate, to withdraw from the audit engagement, where withdrawal is permitted by law or regulation. The engagement partner shall promptly report to the firm any inability to resolve the matter for appropriate action.

- For audits of financial statements of listed entities, the engagement quality control reviewer, on performing an engagement quality control review, shall also consider among other things, the engagement team's evaluation of the firm's independence in relation to the audit engagement.

  Conclusion: View of EP that matters related to independence assessment are the responsibility of the EP and not EQCR is not correct. The independence assessment documentation should also be given to EQCR for his review.

Q.10 **M/s Sureshchandra & Co. has been appointed as an auditor of SC Ltd. for the financial year 2018-19. CA. Suresh, one of the partners of M/s Sureshchandra & Co., completed entire routine audit work by 29th May, 2019. Unfortunately, on the very next morning, while roving towards office of SC Ltd. to sign final audit report, he met with a road accident and died. CA. Chandra, another partner of M/s Sureshchandra & Co., therefore, signed the accounts of SC Ltd., without reviewing the work performed by CA. Suresh.**

State with reasons whether CA. Chandra is right in expressing an opinion on financial statements the audit of which is performed by another auditor.

Ans. : Review of Work performed by others:

- As per SA 220, "Quality Control for an Audit of Financial Statements", the engagement partner shall take responsibility for reviews being performed in accordance with the firm's review policies and procedures. Review procedures consists of the considerations, whether:
  1. the work has been performed in accordance with professional standards and regulatory and legal requirements;
  2. significant matters have been raised for further consideration;
  3. appropriate consultations have taken place and the resulting conclusions have been documented and implemented;
  4. the work performed supports the conclusions reached and is appropriately documented;
  5. the evidence obtained is sufficient and appropriate to support the auditor's report; and
  6. the objectives of the engagement procedures have been achieved.
- When the auditor delegates work to assistants or uses work performed by other auditors/experts he will continue to be responsible for forming and expressing his opinion on the financial statements. However, he will be entitled to rely on the work performed by others, provided he exercises adequate skill and care and is not aware of any reason to believe that he should not have so relied.
- The auditor should carefully direct, supervise and review work delegated to assistants. He should obtain reasonable assurance that work performed by other auditors/experts and assistants is adequate for his purpose.
- In the instant case, Mr. Suresh, a partner of the firm had completed routine audit work and died before signing audit report. Mr. Chandra another partner of the firm has signed the accounts of SC Ltd, relying on the work performed by Mr. Suresh.

  Conclusion: CA. Chandra is allowed to sign the audit report, though, will be responsible for expressing the opinion. He may rely on the work performed by CA. Suresh provided he further exercises adequate skill and due care and review the work performed by him.

Q.11 **Mention any four informations which assists the auditor in accepting and continuing of relationship with the client as per SA 220.**

Ans. : Information assisting auditor in accepting and continuing of relationship with the client:

As per SA 220 "Quality Control for an Audit of F.S." the information which assists the auditor in accepting and continuing of relationship with the client may include the following:

- The Integrity of the principal owners, key management and TCWG of the entity;
- Competency of engagement team to perform the audit engagement and availability of necessary capabilities, including time and resources;
- Compliance with relevant ethical requirements by firm and the engagement team; and
- Significant matters that have arisen during the current or previous audit engagement, and their implications for continuing the relationship.

Q.12 OP & Associates are the statutory auditors of BB Ltd. BB Ltd is a listed company and started its operations 5 years back. The field work during the audit of the financial statements of the company for the year ended March 31, 2019 got completed on May 1, 2019. The auditor's report was dated May 12, 2019. During the documentation review of the engagement, it was observed that the engagement quality control review was completed on May 15, 2019. Engagement partner had completed his reviews in entirety by May 10, 2019. Comment. [MTP-Oct. 18]

Ans. : Review by Engagement Partner:

- As per SA 220, "Quality Control for an Audit of Financial Statements", the engagement partner shall take responsibility for reviews being performed in accordance with the firm's review policies and procedures. For audits of financial statements of listed entities, the engagement partner shall:
  (a) Determine that an engagement quality control reviewer has been appointed;
  (b) Discuss significant matters arising during the audit engagement, including those identified during the engagement quality control review, with the engagement quality control reviewer; and
  (c) Not date the auditor's report until the completion of the engagement quality control review.
- Further, SA 700, "Forming an Opinion and Reporting on Financial Statements", requires the auditor's report to be dated no earlier than the date on which the auditor has obtained sufficient appropriate evidence on which to base the auditor's opinion on the financial statements.
- In the present case, OP & Associates are the statutory auditors of a listed company which started its operations 5 years back. The field work during the audit of the financial statements of the company for the year ended March 31, 2019 got completed on May 1, 2019. The auditor's report was dated May 12, 2019. During the documentation review of the engagement, it was observed that the engagement quality control review was completed on May 15, 2019.

  Conclusion: Signing of auditor's report i.e. on May 12, 2019 which is before the completion of review engagement quality control review i.e. May 15, 2019, is not in order.

1.5 - SA 230 "AUDIT DOCUMENTATION"

Q.13 Mr. A, a practicing Chartered Accountant, has been appointed as an auditor of True Pvt. Ltd. What factors would influence the amount of working papers required to be maintained for the purpose of his audit? [Nov. 15 (5 Marks)]

Ans. : Factors affecting Form, Content and Extent of Audit Documentation:

SA 230 "Audit Documentation" deals with the auditor's responsibility to prepare audit documentation for an audit of financial statements. Accordingly, the various factors that may affect form, content and extent of audit documentation are following:

1. The size and complexity of the entity.
2. The nature of the audit procedures to be performed.
3. The identified risks of material misstatement.
4. The significance of the audit evidence obtained.
5. The nature and extent of exceptions identified.
6. The need to document a conclusion or the basis for a conclusion not readily determinable from the documentation of the work performed or audit evidence obtained.
7. The audit methodology and tools used.

"ICAI Examiner Comments"

Many examinees did not discuss the factors influencing the amount of audit working papers and the answers were general in nature explaining the type of working papers. Also some examinees wrote about the importance of working papers. A few examinees described the need of the working papers which was not required. Some examinees also discussed about current audit file and permanent audit file.

Q.14 Discuss the Auditor's responsibilities to provide access to his audit working papers to Regulators and the third parties. [Nov. 14 (3 Marks)]

Ans. : Access to Working papers to Regulators and Third Parties:

- Clause (1) of Part I of Second Schedule to the Chartered Accountants Act, 1949 states that a CA in practice shall be deemed to be guilty of professional misconduct if he discloses information acquired in the course of his professional engagement to any person other than his client, without the consent of his client or otherwise than as required by law for the time being in force.
- SA 200 on "Overall Objectives of the Independent Auditor and the conduct of an audit in accordance with Standards on Auditing" also reiterates that, "the auditor should respect the confidentiality of the information obtained and should not disclose any such information to any third party without specific authority or unless there is a legal or professional duty to disclose". If there is a request to provide access by the regulator based on the legal requirement, the same has to be complied with after informing the client about the same.
- SQC-1, "Quality Control for Firms that Perform Audits and Reviews of Historical Financial Information, and Other Assurance and Related Services Engagements", provides that, unless otherwise specified by law or regulation, audit documentation is the property of the auditor. He may at his discretion, make portions of, or extracts from, audit documentation available to clients, provided such disclosure does not undermine the validity of the work performed, or, in the case of assurance engagements, the independence of the auditor or of his personnel.
- As per SA 230, Audit documentation serves a number of additional purposes, including the enabling the conduct of external inspections in accordance with applicable legal, regulatory or other requirements.

Conclusion: It is auditor's responsibility to provide access to his audit working papers to Regulators when required by law whereas auditor is under no obligation to provide access to working papers to third parties.

Q.15 As an auditor, how would you deal with the following: The statutory auditor of the Holding Company demands for the working papers of the auditors of the subsidiary company, of which you are the auditor.

Ans. : Access to working papers:

- As per SA 230, "Audit Documentation" working papers are the property of the auditor. The auditor may, at his discretion, make portion of or extracts of his working papers available to his client.
- SA 600 "Using the Work of Another Auditors" also states that an auditor should respect the confidentiality of information acquired during the course of his audit work and should not disclose such information unless there is a legal or professional duty to disclose.
- As per ICAI Guidelines, statutory auditor of an enterprise does not have right of access to the audit working papers of the branch auditor. An auditor can rely on the work of another auditor, without having any right of access to the audit working papers of other auditor.

Conclusion: Statutory auditor of Holding company cannot have access to audit working papers of the subsidiary company's auditor. He can however, ask the auditor to answer certain questions about the manner in which the audit is conducted and certain other clarifications regarding audit.

Q.16 B is the Principal Auditor of ABC Co. Ltd., with 8 branches audited by 8 Branch Auditors. B wanted to ensure that the works of Branch Auditors were adequate for the purpose of his audit. Hence, he insisted on Branch Auditors to get familiar with a check list he prepared for branches and, besides, required them to share the working papers complied by them for his review and return. Is principal auditor within his right in asking for such sharing of working papers? [May 18 - New Syllabus (5 Marks)]

Ans : Principal Auditor's right to review the working papers of branch auditors:

- SA 600 "Using the Work of Another Auditor" guides principal auditor regarding the procedures to be performed when he is using the work of another auditor. As per SA 600, when principal auditor plans to use the work of branch auditor, he should consider the professional competence of the other auditor in the context of specific assignment if the other auditor is not a member of the ICAI. He should perform procedures to obtain sufficient appropriate audit evidence, that the work of the other auditor is adequate for the principal auditor's purposes, in the context of the specific assignment.
- As per SA 230 "Audit Documentation" and SQC 1 "Quality Control for Firms that Perform Audits and Reviews of Historical Financial Information, and Other Assurance and Related Services Engagements", unless otherwise specified by law or regulation, audit documentation is the property of the auditor. The Principal auditors of an enterprise do not have right of access to the audit working papers of the branch auditors.

- In the present case, Mr. B requires the branch auditors to share their working papers with him for the purpose of review.

Conclusion: Considering the requirements of SA 600, SA 230 and SQC 1, principal auditor is not right in asking for sharing of working papers.

1.6 - SA 240 "THE AUDITOR'S RESPONSIBILITIES RELATING TO FRAUD IN AN AUDIT OF FINANCIAL STATEMENTS"

Q.17 In the course of audit, A Ltd you suspect the management has indulged in fraudulent financial reporting? State the possible source of such fraudulent financial reporting. [May 12 (6 Marks)]

Ans. : Possible Sources of Fraudulent Financial Reporting:

SA 240, "The Auditor's responsibilities relating to Fraud in an Audit of Financial Statements", deals with auditor's responsibilities in relation to fraud while performing the audit. Auditor is primarily concerned with those frauds that causes material misstatement in financial statements.

Possible sources of fraudulent financial reporting as stated in SA 240 are:

1. Recording fictitious journal entries, particularly close to the end of an accounting period, to manipulate operating results or achieve other objectives.
2. Inappropriately adjusting assumptions and changing judgments used to estimate account balances.
3. Omitting, advancing or delaying recognition in the financial statements of events and transactions that have occurred during the reporting period.
4. Concealing, or not disclosing, facts that could affect the amounts recorded in the financial statements.
5. Engaging in complex transactions that are structured to misrepresent the financial position or financial performance of the entity.
6. Altering records and terms related to significant and unusual transactions.

"ICAI Examiner Comments"

While some have a good grip over the topic, few have no idea on the practical aspects of possible sources of fraudulent financial reporting.

Q.18 You are appointed as an auditor of Global Ltd. Explain the risk factors relating to misstatements arising from misappropriation of assets. [Nov. 15 (4 Marks)]

Ans. : Risk Factors relating to misstatements arising from misappropriation of Assets:

SA 240, "The Auditor's responsibilities relating to Fraud in an Audit of Financial Statements", deals with auditor's responsibilities in relation to fraud while performing the audit.

Accordingly, various risk factors that relate to misstatements arising from misappropriation of assets are classified according to the below mentioned conditions generally present when fraud exists:

1. **Incentive or pressure to commit fraud**: It may exist when management is under pressure, from sources outside or inside the entity, to achieve an expected (and perhaps unrealistic) earnings target or financial outcome.
2. **A perceived opportunity to do so**: It may exist when an individual believes internal control can be overridden, for example, because the individual is in a position of trust or has knowledge of specific weaknesses in internal control.
3. **Rationalization of the Act**: Individuals may be able to rationalize committing a fraudulent act. Some individuals possess an attitude, character or set of ethical values that allow them knowingly and intentionally to commit a dishonest act. However, even otherwise honest individuals can commit fraud in an environment that imposes sufficient pressure on them.

"ICAI Examiner Comments"

The conditions generally present when fraud exists namely incentives/pressures, opportunities, and attitudes/rationalization are not focused by majority of examinees. Examinees wrote irrelevant answers. Many examinees explained the effect of misappropriation of assets instead of risk factors relating to misstatements arising from misappropriation of assets.

Q.19 Explain briefly duties and responsibilities of an auditor in case of material misstatements resulting from management fraud. [Nov. 09, May 17 (6 Marks)]

or

Cloud Ltd. appointed an auditor for the financial year 2018-19. While going through the audit procedure, the auditor observed that the management has entered into certain transactions which are irregular in nature and the management is personally benefited from such transactions. Explain briefly the duties and responsibilities of an auditor in case of material misstatement resulting from Management Fraud.

Or

Fraud can be committed by management overriding controls using such techniques as engaging in complex transactions that are structured to misrepresent the financial position or financial performance of the entity. In view of the above-mentioned circumstances of management fraud, explain briefly duties and responsibilities of an auditor in case of material misstatement resulting from such Management Fraud.

Ans. : Auditor's duties in case of material misstatement resulting from management fraud:

(*a*) SA 240 "Auditor's Responsibilities relating to fraud in an audit of financial statements" requires that the auditor is responsible for obtaining reasonable assurance that the F.S. taken as a whole are free from material misstatement, whether caused by fraud or error.

(*b*) Management is in a unique position to perpetrate fraud because of management's ability to manipulate accounting records and prepare fraudulent financial statements by overriding controls.

(*c*) When obtaining reasonable assurance, the auditor is responsible for maintaining an attitude of professional skepticism throughout the audit.

(*d*) The auditor should recognize the possibility that a material misstatement due to fraud could exist, notwithstanding his past experience of the honesty and integrity of the entity's management and those charged with governance

(*e*) If conditions cause the auditor to believe that a document may not be authentic or that terms in a document have been modified, the auditor shall investigate further.

(*f*) Where responses to inquiries of management or TCWG are inconsistent, the auditor shall investigate the inconsistencies.

(*g*) Section 143(12) of Companies Act, 2013 requires that if an auditor of a company in the course of the performance of his duties as auditor, has reason to believe that an offence of fraud involving such amount or amounts as may be prescribed, is being or has been committed in the company by its officers or employees, the auditor shall report the matter to the Central Government within such time and in such manner as may be prescribed. For this purpose, Rule 13 of CAAR, 2014 prescribes the amount of ₹ 1 Cr. or more.

(*h*) Para 3(x) of CARO, 2016 also requires the company auditor to report whether any fraud by the company or any fraud on the company by its officers or employees has been noticed or reported during the year. If yes, the nature and the amount involved is to be indicated.

"ICAI Examiner Comments"

Most of the candidates could not write the duties and responsibilities of an auditor in case of material misstatements resulting from management fraud correctly.

Q.20 You notice a misstatement resulting from fraud or suspected fraud during the audit and conclude that it is not possible to continue the performance of audit. As a Statutory Auditor, how would you deal?

Ans. : Auditor's unable to complete the engagement:

SA 240, "The Auditor's responsibilities relating to Fraud in an Audit of Financial Statements", deals with auditor's responsibilities in relation to fraud while performing the audit. Accordingly, if the auditor conclude that it is not possible to continue performing the audit as a result of misstatement resulting from fraud or suspected fraud, the auditor should:

(*a*) Consider the professional and legal responsibilities applicable in the circumstances, including whether there is a requirement for the auditor to report to the person or persons who made the audit appointment or, in some cases, to regulatory authorities;

(*b*) Consider the possibility of withdrawing from the engagement; and

(*c*) If the auditor withdraws:

- Discuss with the appropriate level of management and TCWG, the auditor's withdrawal from the engagement and the reasons for the withdrawal; and
- Determine whether there is a professional or legal requirement to report to the person or persons who made the audit appointment or, in some cases, to regulatory authorities, the auditor's withdrawal from the engagement and the reasons for the withdrawal.

Further, as per section 140(2) of the Companies Act, 2013, the auditor who has resigned from the company shall file within a period of 30 days from the date of resignation, a statement in the Form ADT-3 with the company and the Registrar.

Section 143(12) of Companies Act, 2013 requires that if an auditor of a company in the course of the performance of his duties as auditor, has reason to believe that an offence of fraud involving such amount or amounts as may be prescribed, is being or has been committed in the company by its officers or employees, the auditor shall report the matter to the Central Government within such time and in such manner as may be prescribed. For this purpose, Rule 13 prescribes the amount of ₹ 1 Cr. or more.

Q.21 The Managing Director of the Company has committed a "Teeming and Lading" Fraud. The amount involved has been however subsequently after the year end deposited in the company. As a Statutory Auditor, how would you deal?

Ans. : Fraud Committed by Managing Director:

- SA 240 "Auditor's Responsibilities relating to fraud in an audit of financial statements" requires that the auditor is responsible for obtaining reasonable assurance that the F.S. taken as a whole are free from material misstatement, whether caused by fraud or error.
- Management is in a unique position to perpetrate fraud because of management's ability to manipulate accounting records and prepare fraudulent financial statements by overriding controls.
- In the instant case, Managing Director of the company has committed a "Teeming and Lading" fraud. The fact that the amount involved has been subsequently deposited after the year end is not important because the auditor is required to perform his responsibilities as laid down in SA 240 as stated below:
  (*a*) Consider the impact of fraud on financial statements and its disclosure in the audit report.
  (*b*) Communicate the matter to the Chairman and Board of Directors.
  (*c*) Consider the reliability of audit evidence previously obtained as the fraud has been conducted at a higher level of management which raises a genuine doubt about representations of management.
- Section 143(12) of Companies Act, 2013 requires that if an auditor of a company in the course of the performance of his duties as auditor, has reason to believe that an offence of fraud involving such amount or amounts as may be prescribed, is being or has been committed in the company by its officers or employees, the auditor shall report the matter to the Central Government within such time and in such manner as may be prescribed. For this purpose, Rule 13 prescribes the amount of ₹ 1 Cr. or more.
- Para 3(x) of CARO, 2016 also requires the company auditor to report whether any fraud by the company or any fraud on the company by its officers or employees has been noticed or reported during the year. If yes, the nature and the amount involved is to be indicated.

Q.22 As a Statutory Auditor, how would you deal with the following cases: In the books of account of M/s OPQ Ltd. huge differences are noticed between the control accounts and subsidiary records. The Chief Accountant informs that this is common due to huge volume of business done by the company during the year.

Ans. : Difference between Control Accounts and Subsidiary Records:

- The huge differences found between control accounts and subsidiary records in the books of M/s OPQ Ltd. indicate that there may be material misstatements requiring detailed examination by the auditor to ascertain the cause.
- The contention of Chief Accountant cannot be accepted simply because the company has done huge volume of business. Such a phenomenon indicates that recording of transactions is not being done properly or the accounting system fails to capture all transactions in time.
- Having regard to all these circumstances, it appears from the facts of the case that these differences indicate the possibility of some kind of material misstatements.

- According to SA 240 "The Auditors responsibilities relating to Fraud in an audit of F.S.", when the auditor comes across such circumstances indicating the possible misstatements resulting from entity's procedure, the auditor shall evaluate whether such a misstatement is indicative of fraud.
- In this case, the circumstances indicate the possibility of material misstatements (that might be due to fraud) and accordingly, the auditor must investigate further to consider effect on F.S.
- Section 143(12) of Companies Act, 2013 requires that if an auditor of a company in the course of the performance of his duties as auditor, has reason to believe that an offence of fraud involving such amount or amounts as may be prescribed, is being or has been committed in the company by its officers or employees, the auditor shall report the matter to the Central Government within such time and in such manner as may be prescribed. For this purpose, Rule 13 prescribes the amount of ₹ 1 Cr. or more.
- Para 3(x) of CARO, 2016 also requires the company auditor to report whether any fraud by the company or any fraud on the company by its officers or employees has been noticed or reported during the year. If yes, the nature and the amount involved is to be indicated.

Q.23 While conducting statutory Audit of ABC Ltd., you come across IOUs amounting to ₹ 2 crores as against a cash balance shown in books of ₹ 2.10 crores. You also observe that despite similar high balances throughout the year, small amounts of ₹ 50,000 are withdrawn from the bank to meet day-to-day expenses.

[May 09 (5 Marks)]

Ans. : Auditor's duties in case of suspected fraud:

- SA 240 "Auditor's Responsibilities relating to fraud in an audit of financial statements" requires that the auditor is responsible for obtaining reasonable assurance that the F.S. taken as a whole are free from material misstatement, whether caused by fraud or error.
- When obtaining reasonable assurance, the auditor is responsible for maintaining an attitude of professional skepticism throughout the audit.
- The auditor should recognize the possibility that a material misstatement due to fraud could exist.
- When the auditor comes across such circumstances indicating the possible misstatements resulting from entity's procedure, the auditor shall evaluate whether such a misstatement is indicative of fraud.
- In the present case, the circumstances indicate the possibility of fraud and accordingly, the auditor must investigate further to consider effect on financial statements.
- The Guidance Note on Audit of Cash and Bank balances also mentions that if the entity is maintaining an unduly large balance of cash, he should carry out surprise verification of cash more frequently to ascertain whether it agrees. If cash in hand is not in agreement with the book balance, he should seek explanations and if the same are not satisfactory, he should state this fact appropriately in his Audit Report.

Q.24 M/s Honest Limited has entered into a transaction on 5th March, 2019, near year-end, whereby it has agreed to pay ₹ 5 lakhs per month to Mr. Y as annual retainership fee for "engineering consultation". No amount was actually paid, but ₹ 60 lakhs are provided in books of account as on March 31, 2019. Your inquiry elicits a response that need-based consultation was obtained round the year, but there is no documentary or other evidence of receipt of the service. As the auditor of M/s Honest Limited, what would be your approach?

[Nov. 13 (5 Marks)]

Ans. : Auditor's duties in case of suspected fraud:

- As per SA 240 on "The Auditor's Responsibilities Relating to Fraud in an Audit of Financial Statements", fraud can be committed by management by various means including therein recording of fictitious journal entries, particularly close to the end of an accounting period, to manipulate operating results or achieve other objectives.
- In the given case, Honest Ltd. has entered into an agreement with Mr. Y, at year-end, for engineering consultation. It also provides ₹ 60 lakhs in the books of account, however, no documentary or other evidence of receipt of such service is available. It appears that company has passed fictitious journal entries, near year-end, to manipulate the operating results.
- SA 240 further provides that if, as a result of a misstatement resulting from fraud or suspected fraud, the auditor encounters exceptional circumstances that bring into question the auditor's ability to continue performing the audit, the auditor shall:

(1) Determine the professional and legal responsibilities applicable in the circumstances, including whether there is a requirement for the auditor to report to the person or persons who made the audit appointment or, in some cases, to regulatory authorities;

(2) Consider whether it is appropriate to withdraw from the engagement, where withdrawal from the engagement is legally permitted.

- Further, Sec. 143(12) of the Companies Act, 2013 read with Rule 13 of Companies (Audit & Auditors) Rules, 2014 requires that if an auditor of a company, in the course of the performance of his duties as auditor, has reason to believe that an offence involving fraud is being or has been committed against the company by officers or employees of the company, he shall immediately report the matter to the audit committee within 2 days of his knowledge (as amount involved is less than ₹ 1 Cr.) mentioning the following:
  (*i*) Nature of Fraud with description;
  (*ii*) Approximate amount involved; and
  (*iii*) Parties involved etc.
- Para 3(x) of CARO, 2016 also requires the company auditor to report whether any fraud by the company or any fraud on the company by its officers or employees has been noticed or reported during the year; if yes, the nature and the amount involved is to be indicated.

"ICAI Examiner Comments"

Most of the candidates failed to identify the suspected fraud in the financial statement in accordance with SA 240 and many related it to wrong accounting and creation of provision as per AS-29. Also, some candidates confined themselves to the audit procedures to verify/vouch the transaction and looking for evidence, whereas the question makes it very clear that no evidence is available.

Q.25 Is it appropriate for the auditor to make inquiries of management regarding management's own assessment of the risk of fraud and the controls in place to prevent and detect it? Discuss. [Nov. 16 (5 Marks)]

Ans. : Appropriateness of making inquiries of management regarding assessment of fraud:

SA 240 "Auditor's Responsibilities relating to Fraud in an Audit of Financial Statements" requires the auditor to make inquiries of management regarding:

(*a*) Management's assessment of risk of material misstatement due to fraud;

(*b*) Management's process for identifying & responding to the risks of fraud in the entity, including any specific risks of fraud;

(*c*) Management's communication, if any, to TCWG; and

(*d*) Management's communication, if any, to employees regarding its views on business practices and ethical behaviour.

Management is responsible for the entity's internal control and for the preparation of the financial statements. Accordingly, it is appropriate for the auditor to make inquiries of management regarding management's own assessment of the risk of fraud and the controls in place to prevent and detect it.

The nature, extent and frequency of management's assessment of such risk and controls may vary from entity to entity. In some entities, management may make detailed assessments on an annual basis or as part of continuous monitoring. In other entities, management's assessment may be less structured and less frequent.

The nature, extent and frequency of management's assessment are relevant to the auditor's understanding of the entity's control environment. For example, the fact that management has not made an assessment of the risk of fraud may in some circumstances be indicative of the lack of importance that management places on internal control.

"ICAI Examiner Comments"

Most of the examinees have not understood the topic and failed to answer correctly.

1.7 - SA 250 "CONSIDERATIONS OF LAWS AND REGULATIONS IN AN AUDIT OF FINANCIAL STATEMENTS"

Q.26 Comment on the following: Management is responsible for compliance with Laws and regulations.

Ans. : Management Responsibility for compliance with laws and regulations:

SA 250 "Consideration of Laws and Regulations in an Audit of Financial Statements" states that it is the responsibility of management, with the oversight of TCWG, to ensure that the entity's operations are conducted in accordance with the provisions of laws and regulations.

For this purpose, management may apply the following procedures:

1. Monitoring legal requirements and ensuring that operating procedures are designed to meet these requirements.
2. Instituting and operating appropriate systems of internal control.
3. Developing, publicising and following a code of conduct.
4. Ensuring employees are properly trained and understand the code of conduct.
5. Monitoring compliance with the code of conduct and acting appropriately to discipline employees who fail to comply with it.
6. Engaging legal advisors to assist in monitoring legal requirements.
7. Maintaining a register of significant laws and regulations with which the entity has to comply within its particular industry and a record of complaints.

Q.27 What are the roles and responsibilities of the statutory auditor in relation to compliance with the laws and regulations by the entity. [Nov. 14 (5 Marks)]

Ans. : Role & Responsibilities of Statutory auditor in relation to compliance of Laws and Regulations:

- The auditor shall obtain a general understanding of:
  (*a*) The legal and regulatory framework applicable to the entity and the industry or sector in which the entity operates; and
  (*b*) How the entity is complying with that framework.
- The auditor shall obtain sufficient appropriate audit evidence regarding compliance with the provisions of those laws and regulations generally recognized to have a direct effect on the determination of material amounts and disclosures in the financial statements.
- The auditor shall perform the following audit procedures to identify instances of non-compliance with other laws and regulations that may have a material effect on the financial statements:
  (*a*) Inquiring of management; and
  (*b*) Inspecting correspondence, if any, with the relevant licensing or regulatory authorities.
- During the audit, the auditor shall remain alert to the possibility that other audit procedures applied may bring instances of non-compliance or suspected non-compliance with laws and regulations to the auditor's attention.
- Obtain written representation that all known instances of non-compliance or suspected non-compliance with laws and regulations have been disclosed to the auditor.

"ICAI Examiner Comments"

Very few candidates explained SA 250 and gave general answers. Most of them failed to give the required answer which should be based on the audit procedures to identify instances of non-compliance with other laws and regulations that may have a material effect on the financial statements.

Q.28 As a statutory auditor of a company, comment on the following: While verifying the employee records in a company, it was found that a major portion of the labour employed was child labour. On questioning the management, the auditor was told that it was outside his scope of the financial audit to look into the compliance with other laws. [Nov. 12 (5 Marks)]

Or

CA. Yusuf has been appointed as an auditor of Ajanta Ltd., a textile entity. While going through the employee records of the company, CA. Yusuf identified that most of the labourers employed are of the age between 11-12 years. On enquiring the same, the management argues that there is no such boundation

with regard to employment of such lower age children and contends that it is out of the scope of audit as well to check such compliance. Comment in the context of relevant standard on auditing whether the contention of management is tenable.

Ans. : Auditor's Responsibility for consideration of other Laws:

- SA 250 "Consideration of laws and regulations in an Audit of Financial Statements" requires the auditor to obtain sufficient appropriate audit evidence regarding the compliance with the provisions of those laws and regulations generally recognized to have a direct impact on the determination of material amounts and disclosures in the financial statements including tax and labour laws.
- For the other laws, the auditor's responsibility is limited to undertake specified audit procedures to help identify non-compliance with those laws and regulations that may have a material effect on the financial statements.
- Non-compliance with other laws and regulations may result in fines, litigation or other consequences for the entity, the costs of which may need to be provided for.
- In the instant case, major portion of the labour employed was child labour.

Conclusion: Auditor should ensure the disclosure of above fact and provision of the cost of fines, litigation or other consequences. In case auditor concludes that non-compliance may have a material effect on financial statements, he should modify his opinion accordingly.

Q.29 R & M Co. wants to be alert on the possibility of non-compliance with Laws and Regulations during the course of audit of SRS Ltd. R & M Co. seeks your guidance for identifying the indications of non-compliance with Laws and Regulations. [May 16 (5 Marks)]

Or

As an Auditor of TRP Ltd., you are suspicious that there might be non-compliance with laws and regulations to which the company is subject to. Indicate the possible areas or aspects where you may have to look out for forming an opinion as to whether your suspicion has some based to further inquire. [May 18 - New Syllabus (4 Marks)]

Ans. : Indicators to be considered for verifying compliance with laws and regulations:

SA 250 "Consideration of Laws and Regulations in an audit of Financial Statements" deals with the auditor's responsibilities to consider laws and regulations when performing an audit.

To verify the compliance of laws and regulations, auditor is required to consider the following indicators:

1. Investigation by regulatory organisations Government departments or payment of fines, additional taxes or penalties.
2. Payments for unspecified services or loans to consultants related parties or employees.
3. Sales commission or agent's fees that appear excessive in relation to those ordinarily paid by the entity or in its industry or to the services actually received.
4. Purchases at prices significantly above or below market price.
5. Unusual payments in cash.
6. Unusual payments towards legal and retainer ship fees.
7. Unusual transactions with companies registered in tax havens.
8. Payments for goods or services made other than to the country from which the goods or services originated.
9. Payments without proper exchange control documentation.
10. Existence of an information system which fails to provide an adequate audit trail.
11. Unauthorised transactions or improperly recorded transactions.
12. Adverse media comment.

"ICAI Examiner Comments"

Candidates failed to mention all the important indications correctly. Some of them discussed the reporting requirement by the auditor in the case of non-compliance instead of indications.

Q.30 State the reporting responsibility of an auditor in the context of non-compliance of Law and Regulation in an audit of Financial Statement.

Ans. : Reporting requirements as per SA 250 on Non-Compliance with Laws and regulations:

(*a*) Reporting to Management & TCWG:

- The auditor shall communicate with TCWG matters involving non-compliance with laws and regulations that come to the auditor's attention.
- If, in the auditor's judgment, the non-compliance is believed to be intentional and material, the auditor shall communicate the matter to TCWG as soon as practicable.
- If the auditor suspects that management or TCWG are involved in non-compliance, the auditor shall communicate the matter to the next higher level of authority at the entity, if it exists, such as an audit committee or supervisory board. Where no higher authority exists, the auditor shall consider the need to obtain legal advice.

(*b*) Reporting in Auditor's Report:

- If the auditor concludes that the non-compliance has a material effect on the financial statements, and has not been adequately reflected in the financial statements, the auditor shall, express a qualified or adverse opinion on the financial statements.
- If the auditor is precluded by management or TCWG from obtaining sufficient appropriate audit evidence, the auditor shall express a qualified opinion or disclaim an opinion.
- If the auditor is unable to determine whether non-compliance has occurred because of limitations imposed by the circumstances rather than by management or TCWG, the auditor shall evaluate the effect on the auditor's opinion.

(*c*) Reporting to regulatory and Enforcement Authorities:

If the auditor has identified or suspects non-compliance with laws and regulations, the auditor shall determine whether the auditor has a responsibility to report the identified or suspected non-compliance to parties outside the entity.

1.8 - SA 260 "COMMUNICATION WITH THOSE CHARGED WITH GOVERNANCE"

Q.31 Discuss with reference to SAs: The auditor shall communicate all significant findings with those charged with Governance.

Or

"The auditors should communicate audit matters of governance interest arising from the audit of financial statements with those charged with the governance of an entity". Briefly state the matters to be included in such Communication.

Ans. : Communicating Significant Finding to TCWG:

SA 260 "Communication with Those charged with Governance" deals with auditor's responsibilities to communicate with TCWG in an audit of financial statements.

As per SA 260, auditor should communicate all significant findings with the TCWG, stated as below:

1. The auditor's views about significant qualitative aspects of the entity's accounting practices, including accounting policies, accounting estimates and financial statement disclosures.
2. Significant difficulties, if any, encountered during the audit;
3. Unless all of those charged with governance are involved in managing the entity:
   - Significant matters, arising from the audit that were discussed, or subject to correspondence with management; and
   - Written representations the auditor is requesting;
4. Circumstances that affect the form and content of the auditor's report, if any; and
5. Any other significant matter that in the auditor's professional judgment, are significant to the oversight of the financial reporting process.

Q.32 State the Significant Difficulties encountered during audit with reference to SA 260.

Ans. : Significant Difficulties encountered during audit:

SA 260 "Communication with Those charged with Governance" deals with auditor's responsibilities to communicate with TCWG in an audit of financial statements.

As per SA 260 among other things auditor should communicate significant difficulties to the TCWG. Examples of significant difficulties to be communicated are:

1. Significant delays in management providing required information.
2. An unnecessarily brief time within which to complete the audit.
3. Extensive unexpected effort required to obtain SAAE.
4. Unavailability of expected information.
5. Restrictions imposed on the auditor by management.
6. Scope limitation that leads to modification of auditor's opinion.

Q.33 Write short note on: Factors governing modes of communication of auditor with those charged with governance.

Ans. : Factors affecting mode of Communication:

SA 260 "Communication with Those charged with Governance" deals with auditor's responsibilities to communicate with TCWG in an audit of financial statements. As per SA 260 the various factors affecting mode of communication are:

1. Whether a discussion of the matter will be included in the auditor's report e.g. Key Audit matters?
2. Whether management has previously communicated the matter?
3. The size, operating structure, control environment, and legal structure of the entity.
4. In the case of an audit of special purpose F.S., whether the auditor also audits the entity's general purpose F.S.
5. Legal requirements. In some jurisdictions, a written communication with TCWG is required in a prescribed form by local law.
6. The expectations of TCWG, including arrangements made for periodic meetings or communications with the auditor.
7. The amount of ongoing contact and dialogue the auditor has with TCWG.
8. Whether there have been significant changes in the membership of a governing body.

Q.34 Compare and explain the following: Reporting to Shareholders v. Reporting to TCWG.

[Nov. 14 (3 Marks)]

Ans. : Reporting to Shareholders v. Reporting to those Charged with Governance:

Reporting to Shareholders	Reporting to TCWG
1. SA 700, 701, 705 & 706 & Section 143 of the Companies Act, 2013 deals with the provisions relating to reporting to Shareholders.	1. SA 260 deals with the provisions relating to reporting to those Charged with Governance.
2. Reporting to shareholder generally focuses on true and fair view of financial statements.	2. Reporting to TCWG generally includes auditor's responsibilities, planned scope and timing of audit, significant findings from the audit and independence.
3. Reporting to shareholders is an external report and issued in public domain.	3. Reporting to TCWG is an internal report and not issued in public domain.

"ICAI Examiner Comments"

Most of the candidates discussed only meanings of the topic in general.

1.9 - SA 265 "COMMUNICATING DEFICIENCIES IN INTERNAL CONTROL TO THOSE CHARGED WITH GOVERNANCE"

Q.35 What do you mean by deficiencies in Internal Control? Explain various indicators of Significant deficiencies.

Ans. : Deficiencies in Internal Control:

SA 265 "Communicating Deficiencies in Internal Control to Those Charged with Governance and Management" states that deficiency in internal control exists when:

(*a*) A control is designed, implemented or operated in such a way that it is unable to prevent, or detect and correct, misstatements in the financial statements on a timely basis; or

(*b*) A control necessary to prevent, or detect and correct, misstatements in the financial statements on a timely basis is missing.

Indicators of Significant Deficiencies:

1. Evidence of ineffective aspects of control environment.
2. Entity's Risk assessment process - Absent/ineffective.
3. Ineffective response to identified significant Risks.
4. Correction of prior period misstatements arising due to fraud/error.
5. Management inability to oversee F.S. Preparation.
6. Misstatements detected by the auditor's procedures were not prevented, or detected and corrected by the entity internal control.

Q.36 Write short note on: Written communication in respect of deficiencies of internal control.

Ans : Written communication in respect of deficiencies of internal control:

The auditor shall communicate material weaknesses in internal control identified during the audit on a timely basis to management at an appropriate level of responsibility, and, as required by SA 265 "Communicating Deficiencies in Internal Control to Those Charged with Governance and Management". This communication should be, preferably, in writing through a letter of weakness. Important points with regard to such a letter are as follows:

(*a*) It lists down the area of weaknesses in the internal control system and recommends suggestions for improvement.

(*b*) It should clearly indicate that this letter covers only weaknesses which have come to the attention of the auditor during his evaluation of internal control for the purpose of determining nature, timing and extent of further audit procedures.

(*c*) Letter should clearly indicate that his examination of internal control has not been designed to determine the adequacy of internal control for management.

(*d*) This letter serves as a significant means for management and governing body for the purpose of improving the system and its strict implementation.

(*e*) The letter may also serve to minimize legal liability in the event of a major defalcation or other loss resulting from a weakness in internal control.

1.10 - SA 299 "JOINT AUDIT OF FINANCIAL STATEMENTS"

Q.37 KRP Ltd., at its annual general meeting, appointed Mr. X, Mr. Y and Mr. Z as joint auditors to conduct auditing for the financial year 2017-18. For the valuation of gratuity scheme of the company, Mr. X, Mr. Y and Mr. Z wanted to refer their own known Actuaries. Due to difference of opinion, all the joint auditors consulted their respective Actuaries. Subsequently, major difference was found in the actuary reports. However, Mr. X agreed to Mr. Y's actuary report, though, Mr. Z did not. Mr. X contends that Mr. Y's actuary report shall be considered in audit report due to majority of votes. Now, Mr. Z is in dilemma.

(*i*) You are required to briefly explain the responsibilities of auditors when they are jointly and severally responsible in respect of audit conducted by them and also guide Mr. Z in such situation.

(*ii*) Explain the responsibility of auditors, in case, report made by Mr. Y's actuary, later on, found faulty.

Ans. : Responsibilities of Joint auditors:

SA 299 "Joint Audit of Financial Statements" lays down the principles for effective conduct of joint audit to achieve the overall objectives of the auditor as laid down in SA 200.

Accordingly, in respect of audit work divided among the joint auditors, each joint auditor shall be responsible only for the work allocated to such joint auditor including proper execution of the audit procedures. All the joint auditors shall be jointly and severally responsible for:

a. the audit work which is not divided among the joint auditors and is carried out by all joint auditors;

b. decisions taken by all the joint auditors under audit planning in respect of common audit areas concerning the NTE of the audit procedures to be performed by each of the joint auditors.

c. matters which are brought to the notice of the joint auditors by any one of them and on which there is an agreement among the joint auditors;

d. examining that the F.S. of the entity comply with the requirements of the relevant statutes;

e. presentation and disclosure of the F.S. as required by the applicable FRF;

f. ensuring that the audit report complies with the requirements of the relevant statutes, the applicable Standards on Auditing and the other relevant pronouncements issued by ICAI.

It shall be the responsibility of each joint auditor to determine the NTE of audit procedures to be applied in relation to the areas of work allocated to said joint auditor.

It is the individual responsibility of each joint auditor to study and evaluate the prevailing system of internal control and assessment of risk relating to the areas of work allocated to said joint auditor.

Reporting Responsibilities in case of differences of opinion:

- Joint auditors are required to issue common audit report.
- However, in case of any disagreement among joint auditors with regard to the opinion or any matters to be covered by the audit report, they shall express their opinion in a separate audit report.
- A joint auditor is not bound by the views of the majority of the joint auditors regarding the opinion or matters to be covered in the audit report and shall express opinion formed by the said joint auditor in separate audit report in case of disagreement.
- In case of separate reports, the audit report(s) issued by the joint auditor(s) shall make a reference to the separate audit report(s) issued by the other joint auditor(s). Such reference shall be made under the heading "Other Matter Paragraph" as per SA 706.

In the present case, Mr. Z does not agree with the opinion of Mr. X and Mr. Y, therefore he needs to issue a separate report.

Using the work of an Auditor's Expert: As per SA 620 "Using the Work of an Auditor's Expert", the auditor shall evaluate the adequacy of the auditor's expert's work for the auditor's purposes, including the relevance and reasonableness of that expert's findings or conclusions, and their consistency with another audit evidence.

In the instant case, Mr. X, Mr. Y and Mr. Z, jointly appointed as an auditor of KRP Ltd., referred their own known Actuaries for valuation of gratuity scheme. Mr. Y's referred actuary has provided the gratuity valuation report, which later on found faulty. Further, Mr. Z is not agreed with this report therefore he submitted a separate audit report specifically for such gratuity valuation. In such situation, it was duty of Mr. X, Mr. Y and Mr. Z, before using the gratuity valuation report of Actuary, to ensure the relevance and reasonableness of assumptions and methods used. They were also required to examine the relevance, completeness and accuracy of source data used for such report before expressing their opinion.

Conclusion: Mr. X and Mr. Y will be held responsible for grossly negligence and using such faulty report without examining the adequacy of expert actuary's work whereas Mr. Z will not be held liable for the same due to separate opinion expressed by him.

Q.38 ABC & Co. and DEF & Co. Chartered Accountant firms were appointed as joint auditors of Good Health Care Ltd. for 2017-18. An investigation was conducted under Companies Act, 2013 during March 2019 and observed gross understatement of Revenue. The revenue aspects were looked after by DEF & Co., but there was no documentation for the division of work between the joint auditors.

Or

Dice Ltd. appointed two CA firms MN & Associates and PQ & Co. as joint auditors for conducting audit for the year ended 31st March, 2019. In the course of audit, it has been observed that there is a major understatement in the value of inventory. The inventory valuation work was looked after by MN & Associates but there was no documentation for the division of the work between the joint auditors. Comment on the above situation with regard to responsibilities among joint auditors.

[May 19 - New Syllabus (5 Marks)]

Ans. : Responsibilities of Joint Auditor:

- As per SA 299 "Joint Audit of Financial Statements" where joint auditors are appointed, they should, by mutual discussion, divide the work among themselves.
- After identification and allocation of work among the joint auditors, the work allocation document shall be signed by all the joint auditors and the same shall be communicated to TCWG of the entity.

Documentation of allocation of work helps in avoiding any dispute or confusion which may arise among the joint auditors regarding the scope of work to be carried out by them. Further, the communication of allocation of work to the entity helps in avoiding any dispute or confusion which may arise between the entity and the joint auditors.

- In respect of audit work divided among the joint auditors, each joint auditor is responsible only for the work allocated to him, whether or not he has prepared a separate report on the work performed by him.
- However, for the work not divided, all the joint auditors are jointly and severally responsible.
- In the present case, though the revenue aspects (inventory valuation work) were looked after by DEF & Co. (M N & Associates), but as there is no documentation for division of the work between them, both the joint auditors will be held responsible for it.

Conclusion: Both Joint auditors are jointly and severally responsible.

Note: Conclusion given in Suggested answer of ICAI is different stating that MN & Associates will be held responsible as inventory valuation work was looked after by them. Further, there is a violation of SA 299 as the division of work has not been documented.

Author's view: As the work is not documented, responsibility will be joint and several.

Q.39 P Limited is a limited company and its business activities are divided into three regions. The company appointed PY & Co., KL & Co., and MK & Co., Chartered Accountants to conduct a Joint Audit and report on the financial statements for the Financial year 2018-19. Explain the relationship among the joint auditors for the audit of the financial statements for the year 2018-19. [Nov. 15 (5 Marks)]

Or

Write a short note on: Responsibility of Joint Auditors.

Ans. : Relationship among Joint Auditors:

SA 299 "Joint Audit of Financial Statements" lays down the principles for effective conduct of joint audit to achieve the overall objectives of the auditor as laid down in SA 200.

Accordingly, in respect of audit work divided among the joint auditors, each joint auditor shall be responsible only for the work allocated to such joint auditor including proper execution of the audit procedures. All the joint auditors shall be jointly and severally responsible for:

(*a*) the audit work which is not divided among the joint auditors and is carried out by all joint auditors;

(*b*) decisions taken by all the joint auditors under audit planning in respect of common audit areas concerning the NTE of the audit procedures to be performed by each of the joint auditors.

(*c*) matters which are brought to the notice of the joint auditors by any one of them and on which there is an agreement among the joint auditors;

(*d*) examining that the F.S. of the entity comply with the requirements of the relevant statutes;

(*e*) presentation and disclosure of the F.S. as required by the applicable FRF;

(*f*) ensuring that the audit report complies with the requirements of the relevant statutes, the applicable Standards on Auditing and the other relevant pronouncements issued by ICAI.

It shall be the responsibility of each joint auditor to determine the NTE of audit procedures to be applied in relation to the areas of work allocated to said joint auditor.

It is the individual responsibility of each joint auditor to study and evaluate the prevailing system of internal control and assessment of risk relating to the areas of work allocated to said joint auditor.

"ICAI Examiner Comments"

Most of the examinees explained the topic correctly but few failed to narrate the situations in which the Joint auditors are jointly and severally responsible.

Q.40 Your firm is one of the Joint Auditors of FMP Ltd. Under what circumstances joint auditors are jointly liable for the work in relation to audit of financial statements? Is there any restriction on a joint auditor to communicate a dissenting note differing from the majority opinion of the other joint auditors in the audit report issued under section 143 of the Companies Act, 2013? [Nov. 18-Old Syllabus (5 Marks)]

Ans. : Circumstance in which joint auditors are jointly liable: Refer Answer of Q. No. 39

Restrictions as to communication of dissenting note:

- SA 299 requires the Joint auditors to issue common audit report. However, in case of any disagreement among joint auditors with regard to the opinion or any matters to be covered by the audit report, they shall express their opinion in a separate audit report.
- A joint auditor is not bound by the views of the majority of the joint auditors regarding the opinion or matters to be covered in the audit report and shall express opinion formed by the said joint auditor in separate audit report in case of disagreement.
- In case of separate reports, the audit report(*s*) issued by the joint auditor(*s*) shall make a reference to the separate audit report(*s*) issued by the other joint auditor(*s*). Such reference shall be made under the heading "Other Matter Paragraph" as per SA 706.

Q.41 NMN & Co., LLP and ABC & Associates, LLP are the joint statutory auditors of BHS Ltd. BHS Ltd. is a listed company and has been in existence for the last 50 years. Since beginning this company was audited by MQS & Associates but due to audit rotation, the company had to bring in new auditors. Considering the size of the company, two auditors were appointed as joint auditors. Since the company is new to these auditors and the concept of joint auditors to whom audit work has been divided, management had a discussion and understood that each joint auditor is responsible only for the work allocated to him, whether or not he has prepared a separate report on the work performed by him. Advise.

[MTP-April 19]

Ans. : Reporting in case of Joint Auditors:

- SA 299 "Joint Audit of Financial Statements" lays down the principles for effective conduct of joint audit to achieve the overall objectives of the auditor as laid down in SA 200.
- SA 299 requires the Joint auditors to issue common audit report. However, in case of any disagreement among joint auditors with regard to the opinion or any matters to be covered by the audit report, they shall express their opinion in a separate audit report.
- A joint auditor is not bound by the views of the majority of the joint auditors regarding the opinion or matters to be covered in the audit report and shall express opinion formed by the said joint auditor in separate audit report in case of disagreement.
- In case of separate reports, the audit report(*s*) issued by the joint auditor(*s*) shall make a reference to the separate audit report(*s*) issued by the other joint auditor(*s*). Such reference shall be made under the heading "Other Matter Paragraph" as per SA 706.

Review of work by other joint auditor:

- Each joint auditor is entitled to assume that the other joint auditors have carried out their part of the audit work and the work has actually been performed in accordance with the SAs.
- It is not necessary for a joint auditor to review the work performed by other joint auditors or perform any tests in order to ascertain whether the work has actually been performed in such a manner.
- Each joint auditor is entitled to assume that the other joint auditors have brought to said joint auditor's notice any departure from applicable FRF or significant observations that are relevant to their responsibilities noticed in the course of the audit.
- Before finalizing audit report, the joint auditors shall discuss and communicate with each other their respective conclusions that would form the content of the audit report.

Q.42 Excellent Bank Ltd. is a Public Limited Company. The said Bank has various branches all over India. The Bank appoints 3 Joint Auditors for the financial year ending 31/03/2019. All the 3 Joint Auditors divide the work with mutual consent. Verification of Consolidation, however, remained undivided. All branches and zones were divided amongst the 3 Joint Auditors. During audit of zones, CA. Z, one of the joint auditors expressed a concern about internal control in one of the large corporate branches situated in his zone. The irregularity was not reported in the final accounts as the other 2 Joint Auditors were not in favour of reporting and decision of not reporting the same was taken on the basis of majority. Subsequently, fraud has been detected in the said branch which was audited by CA. Z.

The Bank seeks your advice about the responsibility of the 3 Joint Auditors in the above situation.

[Nov. 19 - Old Syllabus (5 Marks)]

Ans. : Responsibilities of Joint auditors:

SA 299 "Joint Audit of Financial Statements" lays down the principles for effective conduct of joint audit to achieve the overall objectives of the auditor as laid down in SA 200.

Accordingly, in respect of audit work divided among the joint auditors, each joint auditor shall be responsible only for the work allocated to such joint auditor including proper execution of the audit procedures. All the joint auditors shall be jointly and severally responsible for:

(*a*) the audit work which is not divided among the joint auditors and is carried out by all joint auditors;

(*b*) decisions taken by all the joint auditors under audit planning in respect of common audit areas concerning the NTE of the audit procedures to be performed by each of the joint auditors.

(*c*) matters which are brought to the notice of the joint auditors by any one of them and on which there is an agreement among the joint auditors;

(*d*) examining that the F.S. of the entity comply with the requirements of the relevant statutes;

(*e*) presentation and disclosure of the F.S. as required by the applicable FRF;

(*f*) ensuring that the audit report complies with the requirements of the relevant statutes, the applicable Standards on Auditing and the other relevant pronouncements issued by ICAI.

Reporting Responsibilities in case of differences of opinion:

- Joint auditors are required to issue common audit report.
- However, in case of any disagreement among joint auditors with regard to the opinion or any matters to be covered by the audit report, they shall express their opinion in a separate audit report.
- A joint auditor is not bound by the views of the majority of the joint auditors regarding the opinion or matters to be covered in the audit report and shall express opinion formed by the said joint auditor in separate audit report in case of disagreement.
- In case of separate reports, the audit report(s) issued by the joint auditor(s) shall make a reference to the separate audit report(s) issued by the other joint auditor(s). Such reference shall be made under the heading "Other Matter Paragraph" as per SA 706.

In the present case, CA. Z, one of the joint auditors expressed a concern about internal control in one of the large corporate branches situated in his zone. The irregularity was not reported in the final accounts as the other 2 Joint Auditors were not in favour of reporting and decision of not reporting the same was taken on the basis of majority. Subsequently, fraud has been detected in the said branch which was audited by CA. Z.

Conclusion: Mr. Z was required to issue a separate report. He was not bound by the views of other joint auditors. Mr. Z will be held responsible for non-reporting of the matter.

1.11 - SA 300 "PLANNING AN AUDIT OF FINANCIAL STATEMENTS"

Q.43 Comment on the following: Auditor shall establish an overall strategy that sets the scope, timing and direction of the audit, and that guides the development of the audit plan".

Ans. : Establishment of Audit Strategy:

(*a*) SA 300 "Planning an Audit of Financial Statements" requires that the auditor shall establish an overall audit strategy that sets the scope, timing and direction of the audit, and that guides the development of the audit plan.

(*b*) In establishing the overall audit strategy, the auditor shall:

- Identify the characteristics of the engagement that define its scope;
- Ascertain the reporting objectives of the engagement to plan the timing of the audit and the nature of the communications required;
- Consider the factors that are significant in directing the engagement team's efforts;
- Consider the results of preliminary engagement activities and, where applicable, whether knowledge gained on other engagements performed by the engagement partner for the entity is relevant; and
- Ascertain the NTE of procedures necessary to perform.

Q.44 Briefly discuss the following statements in view of SA 300 "Planning an Audit of Financial Statements":

(*a*) For an initial audit, the auditor may need to expand the planning activities.

(*b*) Audit planning is not a discrete phase but a continuous phase.

Ans. : (*a*) Need for expansion of Planning Activities in case of Initial Audit:

As per SA 300 "Planning and Audit of Financial Statements" purpose and objective of planning the audit are the same whether the audit is an initial or recurring engagement. However, for an initial audit, the auditor may need to expand the planning activities because the auditor does not ordinarily have the previous experience with the entity.

For initial audits, additional matters the auditor may consider in establishing the overall audit strategy and audit plan include the following:

- Unless prohibited by law or regulation, arrangements to be made with the predecessor auditor, for example, to review his working papers.
- Any major issues (including the application of accounting principles or of auditing and reporting standards) discussed with management in connection with the initial selection as auditor, the communication of these matters to TCWG and how these matters affect the overall audit strategy and audit plan.
- The audit procedures necessary to obtain SAAE regarding opening balances as prescribed by SA 510 "Initial Engagements-Opening Balances".
- Other procedures required by the firm's system of quality control for initial audit engagements (for example, review of overall audit strategy by senior partner prior to commencing significant audit procedures or to review reports prior to their issuance).

(*b*) Audit Planning - A continuous process:

Planning is not a discrete phase of an audit but rather a continuous process. It often begins shortly after (or in connection with) the completion of the previous audit and continues until the completion of the current audit engagement.

Planning, however, includes consideration of the timing of certain activities and audit procedures that need to be completed prior to the performance of further audit procedures. For example, planning includes the need to consider, prior to the auditor's identification and assessment of the risks of material misstatement, such matters as:

1. The analytical procedures to be applied as risk assessment procedures.
2. Obtaining a general understanding of the legal and regulatory framework applicable to the entity and how the entity is complying with that framework.
3. The determination of materiality.
4. The involvement of experts.
5. The performance of other risk assessment procedures.

Q.45 "The auditor shall document (*i*) The overall audit strategy; (*ii*) The audit plan; and (*iii*) Any significant changes made during the audit engagement to the overall audit strategy or the audit plan, and the reasons for such changes." Explain.

Ans. : Documentation of Audit Strategy and Audit Plan:

- SA 300 "Planning an Audit of Financial Statements" requires that the auditor shall establish an overall audit strategy that sets the scope, timing and direction of the audit, and that guides the development of the audit plan. Accordingly, auditor shall document:
  (*a*) The overall audit strategy;
  (*b*) The audit plan; and
  (*c*) Any significant changes made during the audit engagement to the overall audit strategy or the audit plan, and the reasons for such changes.
- Documentation of the overall audit strategy is a record of the key decisions considered necessary to properly plan the audit and to communicate significant matters to the engagement team.
- Documentation of the audit plan is a record of the planned nature, timing and extent of Risk Assessment procedures and Further Audit Procedures at the assertion level in response to the assessed risks. It also serves as a record of the proper planning of the audit procedures that can be reviewed and approved prior to their performance.
- Record of the significant changes to the overall audit strategy and the audit plan, and resulting changes to the planned NTE of audit procedures, explains why the significant changes were made, and the overall strategy and audit plan finally adopted for the audit.

1.12 - SA 315 "IDENTIFYING AND ASSESSING THE RISK OF MATERIAL MISSTATEMENTS THROUGH UNDERSTANDING THE ENTITY AND ITS ENVIRONMENT"

Q.46 What are the points to be remembered while evaluating the knowledge of the business in the conduct of an audit? [May 09 (8 Marks)]

Or

What are the broad matters to be considered while obtaining knowledge of business for a new audit engagement of a manufacturing concern? [May 10 (4 Marks)]

Ans. : Obtaining an understanding of the entity and its environment:

As per SA 315 "Identifying and Assessing the Risk of Material Misstatements through understanding the entity and its environment" auditor is required to obtain an understating of following as a part of risk assessment procedures:

(*a*) Industry, regulatory, and other external factors including applicable financial reporting framework.

(*b*) The nature of the entity, including:

- its operations;
- its ownership and governance structures;
- the types of investments that the entity is making and plan to make; &
- the way that the entity is structured and how it is financed.

(*c*) The entity's selection and application of accounting policies, including the reasons for changes thereto.

(*d*) The entity's objectives and strategies, and those related business risks that may result in risks of material misstatement.

(*e*) The measurement and review of the entity's financial performance.

The auditor shall also obtain an understanding of internal controls relevant for an audit.

Q.47 Explain the concept of Audit Risk at the level of Financial Statements.

Ans. : Audit Risk at the level of financial statements:

- SA 315 "Identifying and Assessing Risk of Material Misstatements through Understanding the Entity and its Environment" requires the auditor to identify and assess the risks of material misstatement, whether due to fraud or error, at the financial statement and assertion levels.
- Audit risk at the level of financial statements refers to risks of material misstatement that relate pervasively to the financial statements as a whole and potentially affect many assertions.
- Risks at the financial statement level may derive in particular from deficient control environment (although these risks may also relate to other factors, such as declining economic conditions). For example, deficiencies such as management's lack of competence may have a more pervasive effect on the F.S. and may require an overall response by the auditor.
- The auditor's understanding of internal control may raise doubts about the auditability of an entity's financial statements. For example:

  (*i*) Concerns about the integrity of the entity's management may be so serious as to cause the auditor to conclude that the risk of management misrepresentation in the financial statements is such that an audit cannot be conducted.

  (*ii*) Concerns about the condition and reliability of an entity's records may cause the auditor to conclude that it is unlikely that SAAE will be available to support an unqualified opinion on the F.S.

Q.48 In the course of audit of PB Ltd., you observe that there is a likelihood of misstatement in the account balances and disclosures in the financial statements. What should be your considerations as an auditor for "Assessing the Risk of Material Misstatements"? [Nov. 18-Old Syllabus (4 Marks)]

Ans. : Considerations for assessing the Risk of Material Misstatements:

- SA 315 "Identifying and Assessing Risk of Material Misstatements through Understanding the Entity and its Environment" requires the auditor to identify and assess the risks of material misstatement, whether due to fraud or error, at the financial statement and assertion levels.
- As per SA 315, the auditor shall identify and assess the risks of material misstatement at:

  (*a*) the financial statement level; and

(*b*) the assertion level for classes of transactions, account balances, and disclosures; to provide a basis for designing and performing further audit procedures.

- For this purpose, the auditor shall:

(*a*) Identify risks throughout the process of obtaining an understanding of the entity and its environment, including relevant controls that relate to the risks, and by considering the classes of transactions, account balances, and disclosures in the financial statements;

(*b*) Assess the identified risks, and evaluate whether they relate more pervasively to the financial statements as a whole and potentially affect many assertions;

(*c*) Relate the identified risks to what can go wrong at the assertion level, taking account of relevant controls that the auditor intends to test; and

(*d*) Consider the likelihood of misstatement, including the possibility of multiple misstatements, and whether the potential misstatement is of a magnitude that could result in a material misstatement.

"ICAI Examiner Comments"

Examinees correctly quoted concept covered under SA 315 but only few explained what is to be considered by the auditor in this regard.

Q.49 **The identified risks are assessed by auditor as to its significance on account of its likely impact, by way of material misstatement appearing in financial statements or by affecting internal control system. What may be the points of indication that may direct the Auditor to judge that the risks identified may be significant?** **[Nov. 18-New Syllabus (4 Marks)]**

Ans. : Points of indication that direct the Auditor to judge that the risks identified may be significant:

- SA 315 "Identifying and Assessing Risk of Material Misstatements through Understanding the Entity and its Environment" requires the auditor to identify and assess the risks of material misstatement, whether due to fraud or error, at the financial statement and assertion levels.
- As part of the risk assessment, the auditor shall determine whether any of the risks identified are, in the auditor's judgment, a significant risk. In exercising this judgment, the auditor shall exclude the effects of identified controls related to the risk.
- In exercising judgment as to which risks are significant risks, the auditor shall consider at least the following:

(*a*) Whether the risk is a risk of fraud;

(*b*) Whether the risk is related to recent significant economic, accounting, or other developments like changes in regulatory environment, etc., and, therefore, requires specific attention;

(*c*) The complexity of transactions;

(*d*) Whether the risk involves significant transactions with related parties;

(*e*) The degree of subjectivity in the measurement of financial information related to the risk, especially those measurements involving a wide range of measurement uncertainty; and

(*f*) Whether the risk involves significant transactions that are outside the normal course of business for the entity, or that otherwise appear to be unusual.

"ICAI Examiner Comments"

Majority of the examinees have no idea about the topic.

Q.50 **Z Ltd. has its entire operations including accounting computerised. As the audit partner you are concerned about inherent and control risk for material financial statement assertions. What could be the areas you look forward for deficiencies and risk identification.** **[May 11 (4 Marks)]**

Or

Write short note on: Causes of risk at material misstatement in CIS Environment. **[May 14 (4 Marks)]**

Ans. : Risk Assessment in CIS Environment:

SA 315 "Identifying and Assessing the Risks of Material Misstatement through Understanding the Entity and its Environment", requires the auditor to make an assessment of inherent and control risk for material financial statement assertions. In a CIS environment, auditor should look into below mentioned area for risk identification:

TAXMANN®

(*i*) Program Development and maintenance.

(*ii*) System software support.

(*iii*) Operations including processing of data.

(*iv*) Physical CIS security.

(*v*) Control over access to specialized utility program.

"ICAI Examiner Comments"

Majority of the candidates have wrongly referred to all types of controls in a computerized environment. Some of them have wrongly referred to various types of risks.

Q.51 One of the components of an adequate system of internal control is entity's risk assessment process. Risk relevant to reliable financial reporting include external and internal events, transactions or circumstances that may occur and adversely affect an entity's ability to initiate, record, process and report financial data consistent with the assertions of management in the financial statements.

In view of the above. Briefly state any six circumstances of entity's risk assessment Process component under which risks may arise or change.

Or

The Entity's Risk Assessment Process includes how management identifies business risks relevant to the preparation of financial statements in accordance with the entity's applicable financial reporting framework, estimates their significance, assesses the likelihood of occurrence and decides upon actions to respond to and manage them and the results thereof. Elucidate the circumstances in which risks can arise or change.

[Nov. 19 - New Syllabus (5 Marks)]

Ans. : Circumstances of Entity's Risk Assessment Process Component under which risk may arise:

As per SA 315 "Identifying and Assessing the Risks of Material Misstatement through Understanding the Entity and its Environment" the entity's risk assessment process forms the basis for how management determines the risks to be managed. If that process is appropriate to the circumstances, including the nature, size and complexity of the entity, it assists the auditor in identifying RMM. Risk can arise or change due to below mentioned circumstances:

1. Changes in Regulatory or Operating environment.
2. Recruitment of New personnel.
3. New or revamped information systems
4. Significant and rapid expansion of operations
5. Incorporating new technologies into production processes.
6. Entering into business areas or transactions with which an entity has little experience.
7. Corporate restructuring
8. Expansion or acquisition of foreign operations
9. Adoption of new accounting principles or changing accounting principles.

Q.52 IT systems also pose specific risks to an entity's internal control? What are those risks?

[May 10 (4 Marks)]

Or

Enumerate the specific risks that Information Technology (IT) systems can pose to an entity's internal control. [Nov. 17 (5 Marks)]

Ans. : Risk to Internal Control imposed by IT System:

As per SA 315 "Identifying and Assessing the Risks of Material Misstatement through Understanding the Entity and its Environment", IT system also poses specific risks to an entity's Internal Control. These risks are:

(*a*) Reliance on systems or programs that are inaccurately processing data, processing inaccurate data or both.

(*b*) Unauthorised access to data that may result in destruction of data or improper changes to data, including the recording of unauthorized or non-existent transactions, or inaccurate recording of transactions. Particular risk may arise when multiple users access a common database.

(c) The possibility of IT personnel gaining access beyond those necessary to perform their assigned duties thereby breaking down segregation of duties.

(d) Unauthorised changes to data in Master files

(e) Unauthorised changes to systems or programs.

(f) Failure to make necessary changes to systems or programs.

(g) In appropriate manual intervention.

(h) Potential loss of data or inability to access data as required.

"ICAI Examiner Comments"

Many Examinees have not enumerated properly the specific risks that IT system poses to an entity's Internal Control. Only few examinees made a better presentation of the topic. Some examinees wrongly explained the various types of audit risks namely Inherent Risk, Control Risk and Detection Risk while some other examinees wrote general answers like lack of audit trail, segregation of duties, safeguarding of assets, backup, storage etc.

1.13 - SA 320 "MATERIALITY IN PLANNING AND PERFORMING AN AUDIT"

Q.53 Mr. X was appointed as the auditor of M/s Easygo Ltd. and intends to apply the concept of materiality for the financial statements as a whole. Please guide him as to the factors that may affect the identification of an appropriate benchmark for this purpose. [Nov. 13 (4 Marks)]

Ans. : Use of benchmark in determining Materiality:

SA 320 "Materiality in Planning and Performing an Audit" prescribes the use of Benchmarks in determining Materiality for the Financial Statements as a Whole. Accordingly determining materiality involves the exercise of professional judgment. A percentage is often applied to a chosen benchmark as a starting point in determining materiality for the financial statements as a whole.

Factors that may affect the identification of an appropriate benchmark include the following:

(i) The elements of the financial statements (for example, assets, liabilities, equity, revenue, expenses);

(ii) Whether there are items on which the attention of the users of the particular entity's financial statements tends to be focused (for example, for the purpose of evaluating financial performance users may tend to focus on profit, revenue or net assets);

(iii) The nature of the entity, where the entity is at in its life cycle, and the industry and economic environment in which the entity operates;

(iv) The entity's ownership structure and the way it is financed (for example, if an entity is financed solely by debt rather than equity, users may put more emphasis on assets, and claims on them, than on the entity's earnings); and

(v) The relative volatility of the benchmark.

"ICAI Examiner Comments"

Most of the candidates have no idea of the relevant standard and tried to answer the question based on post audit situation rather than pre-audit planning as required in the question. Instead of discussing the factors affecting the identification of appropriate benchmark to apply the concept of materiality, candidates discussed about the concept of materiality, its uses and importance of this concept for audit.

Q.54 As an auditor of RST Ltd. Mr. P applied the concept of materiality for the financial statements as a whole. On the basis of obtaining additional information of significant contractual arrangements that draw attention to a particular aspect of a company's business, he wants to re-evaluate the materiality concept. Please guide him. [May 15 (5 Marks)]

Or

Y & Co., Chartered Accountants have come across in the course of audit of a company that certain machinery had been imported for production of new product. Although the Auditors have applied the concept of materiality for the financial statements as a whole, they now want to re-evaluate the materiality concept for this transaction involving foreign exchange. Give your views in this regard.

[May 18 - New Syllabus (5 Marks)]

Ans. : Re-evaluation of the Materiality Concept:

- SA 320 "Materiality in Planning and Performing an Audit", requires the auditor to determine materiality for the financial statement as a whole, while establishing the overall audit strategy.
- If, in the specific circumstances of the entity, there is one or more particular classes of transactions, account balances or disclosures for which misstatements of lesser amounts than the materiality for the financial statements as a whole could reasonably be expected to influence the economic decisions of users taken on the basis of the financial statements, the auditor shall also determine the materiality level or levels to be applied to those particular classes of transactions, account balances or disclosures.
- The auditor shall revise materiality for the financial statements as a whole and if applicable the materiality levels for particular classes of transactions, account balances or disclosures, in the event of becoming aware of information during the audit that would have caused the auditor to have determined a different amount (or amounts) initially.
- If the auditor concludes a lower materiality for the same, then he should consider the fact that whether it is necessary to revise performance materiality and whether the nature, timing and extent of the further audit procedures remain appropriate.
- In the instant case, Mr. P, auditor of RST Ltd. has applied the concept of materiality for the financial statements as a whole. But he wants to re-evaluate the materiality concept, on the basis of additional information of significant contractual arrangements which draws attention to a particular aspect of the company's business.

Conclusion: Mr. P can re-evaluate the materiality concepts after considering the necessity of such revision.

"ICAI Examiner Comments"

Many candidates erred by writing answers based on SA 330 whereas some of them mentioned SA 320 correctly but failed to explain the required answer.

1.14 - SA 330 "AUDITOR'S RESPONSES TO ASSESSED RISKS"

Q.55 In the course of audit of Z Ltd, its auditor wants to rely on audit evidence obtained in previous audit in respect of effectiveness of internal controls instead of retesting the same during the current audit. As an advisor to the auditor kindly caution him about the factors that may warrant a re-test of controls.

[May 13 (4 Marks)]

Ans. : Factors warranting re-test of controls:

As per SA 330 on "The Auditor's Responses to Assessed Risks", if the auditor plans to use audit evidence from a previous audit about the operating effectiveness of specific controls, he shall establish the continuing relevance of that evidence by obtaining audit evidence about whether significant changes in those controls have occurred subsequent to the previous audit.

The auditor's decision on whether to rely on audit evidence obtained in previous audits for control is a matter of professional judgment.

Factors that may warrant a re-test of controls are—

1. A deficient control environment.
2. Deficient monitoring of controls.
3. A significant manual element to the relevant controls.
4. Personnel changes that significantly affect the application of the control.
5. Changing circumstances that indicate the need for changes in the control.
6. Deficient general IT-controls.

"ICAI Examiner Comments"

Many candidates failed to understand the requirement of the question and discussed mainly the procedure of internal control and reliance on previous auditor rather than the factors that may warrant a retest of controls.

Q.56 While carrying out the statutory audit of a large entity, what are the substantive procedures to be performed to assess the risk of material misstatement? [Nov. 12 (8 Marks)]

Ans. : Substantive Procedures to be performed to assess the risk of material misstatement:

- SA 330, "The Auditor's Response to Assessed Risk", defines substantive procedures as an audit procedure designed to detect material misstatements at the assertion level. They comprise tests of details and substantive analytical procedures.
- **Test of Details**: Irrespective of the assessed risks of material misstatement, the auditor shall design and perform substantive procedures for each material class of transactions, account balance, and disclosure. This requirement reflects the facts that: (i) the auditor's assessment of risk is judgmental and so may not identify all risks of material misstatement; and (ii) there are inherent limitations to internal control, including management override.
- **Substantive Analytical Procedure**: Substantive analytical procedures are generally more applicable to large volumes of transactions that tend to be predictable over time. SA 520, "Analytical Procedures" establishes requirements and provides guidance on the application of analytical procedures during an audit.
- Depending on the circumstances, the auditor may determine that:
  1. Performing only substantive analytical procedures will be sufficient to reduce audit risk to an acceptably low level. For example, where the auditor's assessment of risk is supported by audit evidence from tests of controls.
  2. Only tests of details are appropriate.
  3. A combination of substantive analytical procedures and tests of details are most responsive to the assessed risks.

Q.57 While commencing the statutory audit of B Company Limited, the auditor undertook the risk assessment and found that the detection risk relating to certain class of transactions cannot be reduced to acceptance level. Explain. [May 17 (5 Marks)]

Ans. : Assessment of Risk and Acceptable Level:

- SA 315 "Identifying and Assessing the Risk of Material Misstatement Through Understanding the Entity and its Environment" and SA 330 "The Auditor's Responses to Assessed Risks" establishes standards on the procedures to be followed to obtain an understanding of the accounting and internal control systems and on audit risk and its components.
- SA 315 and SA 330 require that the auditor should use professional judgment to assess risk of material misstatement and to design audit procedures to ensure that it is reduced to an acceptably low level.
- Risk of Material Misstatements comprises of Inherent risk and Control Risk. "Detection risk" is the risk that an auditor's substantive procedures will not detect a misstatement that exists in an account balance or class of transactions that could be material.
- The higher the risk of material misstatement, the more audit evidence the auditor should obtain from the performance of substantive procedures. When both inherent and control risks are assessed as high, the auditor needs to consider whether substantive procedures can provide sufficient appropriate audit evidence to reduce detection risk, and therefore audit risk, to an acceptably low level.
- The auditor should use his professional judgment to assess audit risk and to design audit procedures to ensure that it is reduced to an acceptably low level. If it cannot be reduced to an acceptable level, the auditor should express a qualified opinion or a disclaimer of opinion as may be appropriate.

Q.58 While commencing the statutory audit of ABC Company Limited, what should be the considerations of the auditor to assess Risk of Material Misstatement and his response to such risks? [Nov. 14 (4 Marks)]

Ans. : Considerations of Auditor for Assessing the Risk of Material Misstatement:

SA 315 "Identifying and Assessing the Risk of Material Misstatement through understanding the Entity and its Environment", requires the auditor to identify and assess the risks of material misstatement at the financial statement level; and the assertion level for classes of transactions, account balances, and disclosures to provide a basis for designing and performing further audit procedures. For this purpose, the auditor shall:

(*i*) Identify risks throughout the process of obtaining an understanding of the entity and its environment, including relevant controls;

(*ii*) Assess and evaluate the identified risks;

(*iii*) Relate the identified risks to what can go wrong at the assertion level; and

(*iv*) Consider the likelihood of misstatement.

Auditor's Responses to the Assessed Risk of Material Misstatement:

As per SA 330 "The Auditor's Responses to Assessed Risks", the auditor shall design and implement overall responses to address the assessed risks of material misstatement. In designing the audit procedures to be performed, the auditor shall:

(*i*) Consider the reasons for the assessment given to the risk of material misstatement at the assertion level for each class of transactions, account balance, and disclosure; and

(*ii*) Obtain more persuasive audit evidence for the auditor's assessment of risk.

"ICAI Examiner Comments"

Many candidates failed to mention how the auditor shall identify and assess the risks of material misstatement. Most of the candidates failed to discuss SA 330 on Auditor's response in assessing the risk of material misstatement. Majority of the candidates discussed either SA 315 or SA 330 but not both.

Q.59 "External confirmation procedures frequently are relevant when addressing assertions associated with account balances and their elements, but need not be restricted to these items." Explain.

Or

Point out any eight areas where external confirmation used as an audit evidence.

Ans. : Areas where external confirmations may be used:

As per SA 330 "Responses to Assessed Risks" External confirmation procedures frequently are relevant when addressing assertions associated with account balances and their elements, but need not be restricted to these items.

For example, the auditor may request external confirmation of the terms of agreements, contracts, or transactions between an entity and other parties.

Other situations where external confirmation procedures may provide relevant audit evidence in responding to assessed risks of material misstatement include:

1. Bank balances and other information relevant to banking relationships.
2. Accounts receivable balances and terms.
3. Inventories held by third parties at bonded warehouses for processing or on consignment.
4. Property title deeds held by lawyers or financiers for safe custody or as security.
5. Investments held for safekeeping by third parties, or purchased from stockbrokers but not delivered at the balance sheet date.
6. Amounts due to lenders, including relevant terms of repayment and restrictive covenants.
7. Accounts payable balances and terms.

Q.60 State the factors that may assist the auditor in determining whether external confirmation procedures are to be performed as substantive audit procedures.

Ans. : Factors that may assist in determining use of external confirmations as substantive audit procedures:

As per SA 330 "Responses to Assessed Risks" factors that may assist the auditor in determining whether external confirmation procedures are to be External Confirmations performed as substantive audit procedures include:

1. The confirming party's knowledge of the subject matter - responses may be more reliable if provided by a person at the confirming party who has the requisite knowledge about the information being confirmed.
2. The ability or willingness of the intended confirming party to respond - for example, the confirming party:
   - May not accept responsibility for responding to a confirmation request;
   - May consider responding too costly or time consuming;
   - May have concerns about the potential legal liability resulting from responding;
   - May account for transactions in different currencies; or

- May operate in an environment where responding to confirmation requests is not a significant aspect of day-to-day operations.

In such situations, confirming parties may not respond, may respond in a casual manner or may attempt to restrict the reliance placed on the response.

3. The objectivity of the intended confirming party - if the confirming party is a related party of the entity, responses to confirmation requests may be less reliable.

1.15 - SA 402 "AUDIT CONSIDERATIONS IN AN ENTITY USING SERVICE ORGANISATION"

Q.61 **"As per SA 402, the user auditor shall obtain an understanding of how user entity uses the services of a service organization in the user entity operations." Explain the various matters of which understanding is required.**

Or

A Company gets its accounting data processed by a third party to achieve cost reduction. As a Statutory Auditor of such a company, what are the additional precautions/checks that you would consider for conduct of the audit?

Or

In the course of the audit of R Ltd., the audit manager of ABC & Co. observed that R Ltd. has outsourced certain activities to an outsourcing agency. As the engagement partner guide the audit manager in the assessment of services provided by the outsourcing agency in relation to the audit. [May 11 (4 Marks)]

Or

G Ltd. is a mobile phone operating company. Barring the marketing function, it had outsourced the entire operations like maintenance of mobile infrastructure, customer billing, payroll, accounting functions, etc. Assist the auditor of G Ltd. as to how he can obtain an understanding of how G Ltd. uses the services of the outsourced agency in its operations. [Nov. 13 (5 Marks)]

Or

Durafone Mobile Co. Ltd. have pan India presence and market leader in mobile operation. It has outsourced all its revenue operation including accounting functions to Set Solutions (P) Ltd. As an Auditor of the mobile company, enumerate the factors to be taken into consideration related to its financial reporting.

[May 18 - Old Syllabus (5 Marks)]

Ans. : Matters of which understanding is required by user auditor w.r.t. services of a services organization:

A client may use a service organisation such as one that executes transactions and maintains related accounts or records transactions and processes related data. If a client uses a service organisation, certain policies, procedures and records maintained by the service organisation might be relevant to the audit of the financial statements of the client. Consequently, the auditor would consider the nature and extent of activities undertaken by service organisations so as to determine whether those activities are relevant to the audit and, if so, to assess their effect on audit risk.

SA 402 on "Audit Considerations relating to an Entity Using a Service Organisation" deals with the user auditor's responsibility to obtain sufficient appropriate audit evidence when a user entity uses the services of one or more service organisations. Accordingly, the user auditor is required to obtain an understanding of how user entity uses the services of a service organization in the user entity operation, including:

1. Nature of service provided by the service organization and the significance of those services to the user entity.
2. The nature and materiality of the transactions processed or financial reporting processes affected by service organizations.
3. The degree of interaction between activities of service organizations and those of the user entity.
4. The nature of relationship between user entity and the service organization.

"ICAI Examiner Comments"

Candidates gave only basic idea of gathering knowledge of the outsourced agency but failed to answer specifically as to when obtaining an understanding of the user entity in accordance with SA 315, the user auditor shall obtain an understanding of how a user entity uses the services of a service organization in the user entity's operations. Some candidates have written general audit procedure instead of explaining in terms of SA 402. A few candidates mentioned irrelevant points like visiting the Service Provider's premises and then do the audit/enquiry.

Q.62 In the course of audit of Raja and Rank Ltd., the audit manager of Sharma & Co. observed that Raja and Rank Ltd. has outsourced certain activities to an outsourcing agency:

(*a*) As the engagement partner, guide the audit manager in the assessment of services provided by the outsourcing agency in relation to the audit.

(*b*) Discuss the procedure to be applied in case the user auditor is unable to obtain a sufficient understanding from the user entity?

Ans. :

(*a*) **Assessment of services provided by outsourcing agency:** Refer Answer of Q. No. 61

(*b*) **Procedure to be followed if user auditor is unable to obtain sufficient understanding from user entity:**

- The user auditor shall determine whether a sufficient understanding of nature and significance of services provided by service organization and their effect on the user entity internal control relevant to the audit has been obtained, to provide basis for identification and assessment of risk of Material Misstatement.
- If user auditor is unable to obtain a sufficient understanding from the user entity, the user auditor shall obtain that understanding from one or more of following procedures:

  (*a*) Obtaining a Type 1 or Type 2 Report, if available.

  (*b*) Contacting the service organization, through the user entity, to obtain the sufficient information.

  (*c*) Visiting the service organization.

  (*d*) Using another auditor to perform procedures that will provide the necessary information about the relevant controls at the service organization.

Q.63 When a sub-service organization performs services for a service organization, there are two alternative methods of presenting the description of controls. The service organization determines which method will be used. As a user auditor what information would you obtain about controls at a sub-service organization?

[May 15 (5 Marks)]

Ans. : Information to be obtained w.r.t. controls at a sub-service organisation:

- SA 402 on "Audit Considerations relating to an Entity Using a Service Organisation" deals with the user auditor's responsibility to obtain sufficient appropriate audit evidence when a user entity uses the services of one or more service organisations, which in turn may use a sub-service organisation to provide some of the services provided to a user entity that are part of the user entity's information system relevant to financial reporting.
- If a service organisation uses a subservice organisation, the service auditor's report may either include or exclude the subservice organisation's relevant control objectives and related controls in the service organisation's description of its system and in the scope of the service auditor's engagement. These two methods of reporting are known as the inclusive method and the carve-out method, respectively.
- If the Type 1 or Type 2 report excludes the controls at a sub-service organisation, and the services provided by the sub-service organisation are relevant to the audit of the user entity's financial statements, the user auditor is required to apply the requirements of this SA in respect of the sub-service organisation and accordingly obtain an understanding of the following:

  1. Nature of service provided by the sub-service organization and the significance of those services to the user entity.
  2. The nature and materiality of the transactions processed or financial reporting processes affected by sub-service organizations.
  3. The degree of interaction between activities of sub-service organizations and those of the user entity.
  4. The nature of relationship between user entity and the sub-service organization.

- The nature and extent of work to be performed by the user auditor regarding the services provided by a sub-service organisation depend on the nature and significance of those services to the user entity and the relevance of those services to the audit.

"ICAI Examiner Comments"

Many candidates referred to SA 402 correctly but failed to explain the information that would be obtained by user auditor about controls at sub-service organization.

1.16 - SA 450 "EVALUATION OF MISSTATEMENTS IDENTIFIED DURING THE AUDIT"

Q.64 In the course of audit of T Ltd., the audit team is not sure of the possible source of misstatements in the financial statements. As the audit manager identify the sources of misstatements. [May 11 (4 Marks)]

Or

In audit plan for T Ltd, as the audit partner you want to highlight the sources of misstatements, arising from other than fraud, to your audit team and caution them. Identify the sources of misstatements. [May 13 (4 Marks)]

Ans. : Sources of Misstatement:

SA 450 "Evaluation of Misstatements identified during the Audit", defines the term misstatement as a difference between the amounts, classification, presentation, or disclosure of a reported financial statement item and the amount, classification, presentation, or disclosure that is required for the item to be in accordance with the applicable financial reporting framework. Accordingly, misstatement may cause due to following:

(*i*) An inaccuracy in gathering or processing data from which the financial statements are prepared;

(*ii*) An omission of an amount or disclosure;

(*iii*) An incorrect accounting estimate arising from overlooking, or clear misinterpretation of facts; and

(*iv*) Judgments of management concerning accounting estimates that the auditor considers unreasonable or the selection and application of accounting policies that the auditor considers inappropriate.

"ICAI Examiner Comments"

Candidates, in general, mentioned most of the important sources of misstatements arising from other than fraud but some also wrote about sources of misstatements arising from fraud, which was not required.

Q.65 Discuss the impact of uncorrected misstatements identified during the audit and the auditor's response to the same. [Nov. 14 (4 Marks)]

Or

The auditor of XY & Co. Ltd. has intimated the management that certain misstatements identified during the course of audit need to be corrected. As an auditor, discuss the impact of such misstatements in case the management does not carry out the said corrections. [Nov. 17 (5 Marks)]

Ans. : Impact of uncorrected misstatements identified during the audit:

- SA 450 "Evaluation of Misstatements identified during the audit" deals with the auditor's responsibility to evaluate the effect of identified misstatements on the audit and of uncorrected misstatements, if any, on the financial statements.
- In accordance with SA 450, the auditor shall determine whether uncorrected misstatements are material, individually or in aggregate. In making this determination, the auditor shall consider the size and nature of the misstatements, both in relation to particular classes of transactions, account balances or disclosures and the financial statements as a whole.
- The auditor shall request the management that uncorrected misstatements be corrected. If management refuses to correct some or all of the misstatements communicated by the auditor, the auditor shall obtain an understanding of management's reasons for not making the corrections.
- Prior to evaluating the effect of uncorrected misstatements, the auditor shall reassess materiality determined in accordance with SA 320, to confirm whether it remains appropriate in the context of the entity's actual financial results.
- The auditor shall communicate with TCWG, uncorrected misstatements and the effect that they, individually or in aggregate, may have on the opinion in the auditor's report.
- The auditor shall request a written representation from management and, where appropriate, those charged with governance whether they believe the effects of uncorrected misstatements are immaterial, individually and in aggregate, to the financial statements as a whole.

"ICAI Examiner Comments"

Most of the candidates answered the question in a general manner and failed to explain SA 450 and correlate with the same.

Q.66 **The auditor should take into account the aggregate of all uncorrected misstatements including those involving estimates in his assessment of materiality in audit.**

Ans. : Consideration of uncorrected and unidentified misstatements:

- SA 320 "Materiality in Planning and Performing an Audit" deals with the auditor's responsibility to apply the concept of materiality in planning and performing an audit of financial statements.
- SA 450, "Evaluation of Misstatements identified during the Audit" explains how materiality is applied in evaluating the effect of identified misstatements on the audit and of uncorrected misstatements, if any, on the financial statements.
- SA 450 requires that the auditor shall determine whether the overall audit strategy and audit plan need to be revised if the nature of identified misstatements and the circumstances of their occurrence indicate that other misstatements may exist that, when aggregated with misstatements accumulated during the audit, could be material or the aggregate of misstatements accumulated during the audit approaches materiality determined in accordance with SA 320.
- If the aggregate of misstatements accumulated during the audit approaches materiality determined in accordance with SA 320, there may be a greater risk that possible undetected misstatements, when taken with the aggregate of misstatements accumulated during the audit, could exceed the materiality. Undetected misstatements could exist because of the presence of sampling risk and non-sampling risk.
- In such a situation, auditor may request management to examine a class of transactions, account balance or disclosure in order for management to understand the cause of a misstatement identified by the auditor, perform procedures to determine the amount of the actual misstatement in the class of transactions, account balance or disclosure, and to make appropriate adjustments to the financial statements. Such a request may be made, for example, based on the auditor's projection of misstatements identified in an audit sample to the entire population from which it was drawn.

Q.67 **While auditing accounts of a public limited company for the year ended 31st March, 2016, an auditor found out an error in the valuation of inventory, which affects the financial statement materially - Comment as per standards on auditing.**

Ans. : Errors in Valuation of Inventories and Auditor's Responsibilities:

- SA 450 "Evaluation of Misstatements identified during the audit" deals with the auditor's responsibility to evaluate the effect of identified misstatements on the audit and of uncorrected misstatements, if any, on the financial statements.
- In accordance with SA 450 auditor should consider requesting the management to adjust the financial information or consider extending his audit procedures. If the management refuses to adjust the financial information and the results of extended audit procedures do not enable the auditor to conclude that the aggregate of uncorrected misstatements is not material, the auditor should express a qualified or adverse opinion, as appropriate.

Conclusion: In the instant case, the auditor has detected the material errors affecting the financial statements; the auditor should communicate his findings to the management on a timely basis, consider the implications on true and fair view and also ensure that appropriate disclosures have been made.

1.17 - SA 500 "AUDIT EVIDENCE"

Q.68 **Comment on the following: Z Ltd. had appointed an outside expert to assess accrued gratuity liability of the company. Based on the said report, the company provides ₹ 80 lakhs as gratuity in the financial statements.** **[May 09 (4 Marks)]**

or

What are the procedures to be followed by a statutory auditor for verifying the provision for accrued liability for retirement benefits which is based on a certificate of a reputed actuary? **[May 10 (8 Marks)]**

or

Y Ltd. Engaged an actuary to ascertain its employee cost, gratuity and leave encashment liabilities. As the auditor of Y Ltd. You would like to use the report of actuary as an audit evidence. How do you evaluate the work of actuary. [May 11 (8 Marks), May 16 (4 Marks)]

or

CA. Needle had been appointed as an auditor of M/s Fabric Ltd. in the course of audit, it had been observed that inventory including work-in-process had been valued by management by using experts hired by them. Analyse relevant factors to decide as to whether or not to accept the findings from the work of management expert in valuation of inventories. [May 18 - New Syllabus (5 Marks)]

Ans. : Evaluating the work of Management Expert:

As per SA 500 "Audit Evidence" when information to be used as audit evidence has been prepared using the work of a management's expert, the auditor shall perform the following:

(*i*) **Evaluate the competence, capabilities and objectivity of that expert:**

For this purpose, auditor may consider his qualification, membership of a professional body or industrial association license to practice etc.

(*ii*) **Obtain an understanding of the work of that expert:**

It may include areas of specialty, applicable professional standards and other legal requirements.

(*iii*) **Evaluate the appropriateness of that expert's work:**

With respect to following:

(*a*) **Relevance and reasonableness:** of that expert **findings and conclusion**.

(*b*) **Relevance and reasonableness:** of **assumptions and methods** used; and

(*c*) **Relevance, completeness and accuracy:** of **source data.**

Q.69 As a Statutory Auditor, how would you deal with the following case: M/s LNK's group gratuity scheme's valuation by actuary shows wide variation compared to the previous year's figures.

Ans. : Using the work of Management Expert as an audit evidence:

- SA 500 (Revised), "Audit Evidence" states that the auditor has to evaluate the work of management expert, say, actuary, before adopting the same.
- The work of management expert is required to be evaluated in terms of following:

  (*i*) Relevance and reasonableness of that expert findings and conclusion.

  (*ii*) Relevance and reasonableness of assumptions and methods used; and

  (*iii*) Relevance, completeness and accuracy of source data.
- This becomes more crucial since M/s LNK's group gratuity scheme's valuation by actuary shows wide variation compared to previous year's figures. There is no doubt that appropriateness, reasonableness of assumptions and methods used are the responsibility of the expert, but the auditor has to determine whether they are reasonable based on the auditor's knowledge of the client's business and result of his audit procedures.
- In the present case, the auditor must verify the reasonableness of assumptions made and methods adopted by the actuary in the evaluation particularly with reference to factors such as rate of return on investments, retirement age, number and salary of employees, etc.

Conclusion: In view of provisions of SA 500 as discussed above, the auditor has to satisfy himself whether valuation done by the actuary can be adopted, otherwise he may report on his findings for wide variation.

Q.70 The auditor of SS Ltd. accepted the gratuity liability valuation based on the certificate issued by a qualified actuary. However, the auditor noticed that the retirement age adopted is 65 years as against the existing retirement age of 60 years. The company is considering a proposal to increase the retirement age. Comment. [Nov. 11 (5 Marks)]

Or

For determining the liability for Gratuity, Actuary's Report is produced to the auditor. On examination auditor notices a serious wrong assumption in the report. Auditor challenges the Actuary's report - Comment.

Ans. : Using the work of Management Expert as an audit evidence:

- SA 500 (Revised), "Audit Evidence" states that the auditor has to evaluate the work of management expert, say, actuary, before adopting the same.

- The work of management expert is required to be evaluated in terms of following:
  - (*i*) Relevance and reasonableness of that expert findings and conclusion.
  - (*ii*) Relevance and reasonableness of assumptions and methods used; and
  - (*iii*) Relevance, completeness and accuracy of source data.
- There is no doubt that appropriateness, reasonableness of assumptions and methods used are the responsibility of the expert, but the auditor has to determine whether they are reasonable based on the auditor's knowledge of the client's business and result of his audit procedures.
- In the instant case, a qualified actuary has issued a certificate for gratuity liability valuation, for which retirement age adopted is 65 years against the existing retirement age of 60 years; however, the company is considering a proposal to increase the retirement age.

Conclusion: In view of provisions of SA 500 as discussed above, the assumption made by actuary has no relevance and reasonableness as presently retiring age is of 60 years. Hence the auditor is required to bring out the facts to the notice of management and advice the modification accordingly. In case of failure of compliance of the same the auditor may qualify the report.

Q.71 Y Ltd. Engaged an actuary to ascertain its employee cost, gratuity and leave encashment liabilities. As the auditor of Y Ltd., you would like to use the report of actuary as an audit evidence and for this purpose auditor is required to evaluate the competence, capability and objectivity of the expert. What are the sources from where information about the competence, capability and objectivity of expert may be obtained?

Ans. : Sources of information about competence, capability and objectivity of the expert:

As per SA 500 "Audit Evidence" if any information is prepared by the entity using the work of management expert and auditor has to consider that information as audit evidence, he is required to evaluate the competence, capability and objectivity of that expert. Information regarding the competence, capabilities and objectivity of a management's expert may come from a variety of sources, such as:

1. Personal experience with previous work of that expert.
2. Discussions with that expert.
3. Discussions with others who are familiar with that expert's work.
4. Knowledge of that expert's qualifications, membership of a professional body or industry association, license to practice, or other forms of external recognition.
5. Published papers or books written by that expert.
6. An auditor's expert, if any, who assists the auditor in obtaining sufficient appropriate audit evidence with respect to information produced by the management's expert.

Q.72 Gap Ltd. possesses some investment for which there is no ready market and to assess its fair market value it hires an expert, the result of which it can use in preparing its financial statement. Being an Auditor of the Company, state the matters which may affect the nature, timing and extent of audit procedure to be adopted by you in the instant case. [May 18 - Old Syllabus (5 Marks)]

Ans : Matters affecting NTE of Audit procedures in case of information being produced using work of management expert:

As per SA 500 "Audit Evidence" if any information is prepared by the entity using the work of management expert and auditor has to consider that information as audit evidence, he is required to evaluate the competence, capability and objectivity of that expert. Matters which may affect nature, timing and extent of audit procedures in such a case are:

1. The nature and complexity of the matter to which the management's expert relates.
2. The risks of material misstatement in the matter.
3. The availability of alternative sources of audit evidence.
4. The nature, scope and objectives of the management's expert's work.
5. Whether the management's expert is employed by the entity, or is a party engaged by it to provide relevant services.
6. The extent to which management can exercise control or influence over the work of the management's expert.
7. Whether the management's expert is subject to technical performance standards or other professional or industry requirements.

8. The nature and extent of any controls within the entity over the management's expert's work.
9. The auditor's knowledge and experience of the management's expert's field of expertise.
10. The auditor's previous experience of the work of that expert.

Q.73 "Obtaining Audit Evidence in performing compliance and Substantive procedures." Comment.

Ans. : Methods to obtain audit evidence:

SA 500 "Audit Evidence" requires that the auditor shall design and perform audit procedures that are appropriate in the circumstances for the purpose of obtaining sufficient appropriate audit evidence.

Audit Procedures to obtain audit evidence:

(*a*) Risk assessment Procedures

(*b*) Further Audit procedures: It comprises of

1. Test of Controls, and
2. Substantive Procedures: It consists of Tests of Details and Substantive Analytical Procedures

Nature and timing of audit procedures affected by:

- Availability of audit evidence in electronic form only.
- Availability of audit evidence at certain points/periods in time.

As per SA 500, the auditor can use the following methods while performing compliance and substantive procedures:

(*a*) **Inspection**: It involves examining records or documents, whether internal or external, in paper form, electronic form, or other media, or a physical examination of an asset.

(*b*) **Observation**: It consists of looking at a process or procedure being performed by others, for example, the auditor's observation of inventory counting by the entity's personnel.

(*c*) **External Confirmation**: It represents audit evidence obtained by the auditor as a direct written response to the auditor from a third party (the confirming party), in paper form, or by electronic or other medium.

(*d*) **Recalculation**: It consists of checking mathematical accuracy of documents or records. It may be performed manually or electronically.

(*e*) **Re-performance**: It involves the auditor's independent execution of procedures or controls that were originally performed as part of the entity's internal control.

(*f*) **Analytical Procedures**: It consists of evaluations of financial information made by a study of relationships among both financial and non-financial data.

(*g*) **Inquiry**: It consists of seeking information of knowledgeable persons, both financial and non- financial, within the entity or outside the entity.

Q.74 Write short note on: Inquiry. [Nov. 10 (4 Marks)]

Or

Write short note on: Inquiry as one of the methods of collecting audit evidence. [May 17 (4 Marks)]

Ans. : Inquiry:

- As per SA 500 "Audit Evidence", inquiry is one of the methods to obtain audit evidences. Inquiry consists of seeking information of knowledgeable persons, both financial and non- financial, within the entity or outside the entity.
- Inquiry is used extensively throughout the audit in addition to other audit procedures.
- Inquiries may range from formal written inquiries to informal oral inquiries. However, in case oral inquiries, the auditor may consider it necessary to obtain written representations from management and, where appropriate, TCWG to confirm responses to such inquiries.
- Evaluating responses to inquiries is an integral part of the inquiry process.
- Responses to inquiries may provide the auditor with information not previously possessed or with corroborative audit evidence. Alternatively, responses might provide information that differs significantly from other information that the auditor has obtained. In some cases, responses to inquiries provide a basis for the auditor to modify or perform additional audit procedures.

"ICAI Examiner Comments"

Many candidates mentioned various methods of collecting Auditing Evidence which is not required. Most of them failed to mention about auditor's role in evaluating the Responses to Inquiry; rather they discussed other irrelevant matters without knowing the exact requirements of SA 500, "Audit Evidence".

Q.75 Write short note on: Assessing the reliability of Audit Evidence. [May 09 (4 Marks)]

Ans. : Assessing the reliability of audit evidence:

As per SA 500 "Audit Evidence" the reliability of information to be used as audit evidence, and therefore of the audit evidence itself, is influenced by its source and its nature, and the circumstances under which it is obtained. While recognising that exceptions may exist, the following generalisations about the reliability of audit evidence may be useful:

(*a*) The reliability of audit evidence is increased when it is obtained from independent sources outside the entity.

(*b*) The reliability of audit evidence that is generated internally is increased when the related controls, imposed by the entity are effective.

(*c*) Audit evidence obtained directly by the auditor is more reliable than audit evidence obtained indirectly.

(*d*) Audit evidence in documentary form, whether paper, electronic, or other medium, is more reliable than evidence obtained orally.

(*e*) Audit evidence provided by original documents is more reliable than audit evidence provided by photocopies, or documents that have been filmed, digitised or otherwise transformed into electronic form, the reliability of which may depend on the controls over their preparation and maintenance.

1.18 - SA 501 "AUDIT EVIDENCE - SPECIFIC CONSIDERATIONS FOR SELECTED ITEMS"

Q.76 LMN Ltd. supplies navy uniforms across the country. The company has 4 warehouses at different locations throughout the India and 5 warehouses at the borders. The major stocks are generally supplied from the borders. LMN Ltd. appointed M/s OPQ & Co. to conduct its audit for the financial year 2018-19. Mr. O, partner of M/s OPQ & Co., attended all the physical inventory counting conducted throughout the India but could not attend the same at borders due to some unavoidable reason.

You are required to advise M/s OPQ & Co.:

(*a*) How sufficient appropriate audit evidence regarding the existence and condition of inventory may be obtained?

(*b*) How an auditor is supposed to deal when attendance at physical inventory counting is impracticable?

Or

Crush Ltd. is a dealer in fast moving consumer goods. The Company has warehouses throughout the country where the stocks are stored. The Auditor of the Company normally conduct physical verification of stocks along with the Management at the end of the financial year. However, the Auditor could not be physically present during stock-tacking at two places on account of certain disturbances in the region.

In the light of the above facts:

(*i*) How sufficient appropriate audit evidence regarding the condition and existence of inventory may be obtained?

(*ii*) How an Auditor is supposed to deal when attendance at physical inventory counting is impracticable? [May 18 - Old Syllabus (5 Marks)]

Ans. : (*a*) Auditor's duties to obtain evidences regarding existence and condition of inventory:

SA 501 "Audit Evidence - Specific Considerations for Specific Items", requires from the auditor that when inventory is material to the financial statements, he shall obtain sufficient appropriate audit evidence regarding the existence and condition of inventory by attendance at physical inventory counting, unless impracticable, to:

(*i*) Evaluate management's instructions and procedures for recording and controlling the results of the entity's physical inventory counting;

(*ii*) Observe the performance of management's count procedures;

(*iii*) Inspect the inventory; and

(*iv*) Perform test counts.

Attendance at physical inventory counting involves:

1. Inspecting the inventory to ascertain its existence and evaluate its condition, and performing test counts;
2. Observing compliance with management's instructions and the performance of procedures for recording and controlling the results of the physical inventory count; and
3. Obtaining audit evidence as to the reliability of management's count procedures.

(*b*) Auditor's procedures in case of impractical situations:

- Perform alternative audit procedures to obtain sufficient appropriate audit evidence regarding existence and condition of inventory.
- Alternative Audit Procedure may include inspection of documentation of the subsequent sale of specific inventory items acquired/purchased prior to physical inventory counting.
- If it is not possible to do so, modify the opinion in the auditor's report in accordance with SA 705.

Q.77 You are the auditor of Easy Communications Ltd. for the year 2018-19. The inventory as at the end of the year i.e. 31.03.19 was ₹ 2.25 crores. Due to unavoidable circumstances, you could not be present at the time of annual physical verification. Under the above circumstances how would you ensure that the physical verification conducted by the management was in order? [Nov. 08 (5 Marks)]

Ans. : Auditor's procedures w.r.t. inventory count procedures:

- SA 501 "Audit Evidence - Specific Considerations for Specific Items", requires from the auditor that when inventory is material to the financial statements, he shall obtain sufficient appropriate audit evidence regarding the existence and condition of inventory by attendance at physical inventory counting, unless impracticable, to:
  (*i*) Evaluate management's instructions and procedures for recording and controlling the results of the entity's physical inventory counting;
  (*ii*) Observe the performance of management's count procedures;
  (*iii*) Inspect the inventory; and
  (*iv*) Perform test counts.
- SA 501 further provides that if the auditor is unable to be present at the physical inventory count on the date planned due to unforeseen circumstances, the auditor should take or observe some physical counts on an alternative date and perform audit procedures on intervening transactions to assess whether the changes in inventory between the date of physical count and the period end date are correctly recorded.
- The auditor may also seek management's written representation on (a) the completeness of information provided regarding the inventory, and (b) assurance with regard to adherence to laid down procedures for physical inventory count.

Q.78 "If inventory is material to the financial statements, the auditor shall obtain sufficient appropriate audit evidence regarding the existence of inventory by attending the physical inventory counting unless impracticable." Discusses. [Nov. 15 (5 Marks)]

Ans. : Auditor's procedures w.r.t. inventory count procedures:

- SA 501 "Audit Evidence - Specific Considerations for Specific Items", requires from the auditor that when inventory is material to the financial statements, he shall obtain sufficient appropriate audit evidence regarding the existence and condition of inventory by attendance at physical inventory counting, unless impracticable, to:
  (*a*) Evaluate management's instructions and procedures for recording and controlling the results of the entity's physical inventory counting;
  (*b*) Observe the performance of management's count procedures;
  (*c*) Inspect the inventory; and
  (*d*) Perform test counts;
- Attendance at physical inventory counting involves:
  (*a*) Inspecting the inventory to ascertain its existence and evaluate its condition, and performing test counts;

(*b*) Observing compliance with management's instructions and the performance of procedures for recording and controlling the results of the physical inventory count; and

(*c*) Obtaining audit evidence as to the reliability of management's count procedures.

◆ These procedures may serve as test of controls or substantive procedures depending on the auditor's risk assessment, planned approach and the specific procedures carried out.

"ICAI Examiner Comments"

Examinees failed to highlight the procedure that an auditor would perform to obtain sufficient appropriate audit evidence by attending the physical inventory counting. Irrelevant points on AS-2 and CARO were discussed. Some examinees wrote regarding physical verification which was not required. Also, few examinees discussed about audit of stocks.

Q.79 Your firm has been appointed as the statutory auditors of GBM Private Limited for the financial year 2018-19. While verification of company's inventories as on 31st March, 2019, you found that the significant amount of inventories belonging to the company are held by other parties. However, the company has kept all the records of the inventories maintained by other parties. What is your duty as an auditor in order to ensure that third parties are not such with whom the stock should not be held and the stock as disclosed in company's records actually belongs to them? [RTP-Nov. 19]

Ans. : Inventory under the Custody and Control of a Third Party:

As per SA 501, "Audit Evidence—Specific Considerations for Selected Items" when inventory under the custody and control of a third party is material to the financial statements, the auditor shall obtain sufficient appropriate audit evidence regarding the existence and condition of that inventory by performing one or both of the following:

(*i*) Request confirmation from the third party as to the quantities and condition of inventory held on behalf of the entity.

(*ii*) Perform inspection or other audit procedures appropriate in the circumstances, for example where information is obtained that raises doubt about the integrity and objectivity of the third party, the auditor may consider it appropriate to perform other audit procedures instead of, or in addition to, confirmation with the third party. Examples of other audit procedures include:

◆ Attending, or arranging for another auditor to attend, the third party's physical counting of inventory, if practicable.

◆ Obtaining another auditor's report, or a service auditor's report, on the adequacy of the third party's internal control for ensuring that inventory is properly counted and adequately safeguarded.

◆ Inspecting documentation regarding inventory held by third parties, for example, warehouse receipts.

◆ Requesting confirmation from other parties when inventory has been pledged as collateral.

1.19 - SA 505 "EXTERNAL CONFIRMATION"

Q.80 Write short note on: External Confirmations in audit. [Nov. 09 (4 Marks)]

Ans. : External Confirmations:

◆ As per SA 505 external confirmation may be defined as Audit evidence obtained as a direct written response to the auditor from a third party (the confirming party), in paper form, or by electronic or other medium.

◆ External confirmations are of two types:

(*a*) **Positive confirmation request** - A request that the confirming party respond directly to the auditor indicating whether the confirming party agrees or disagrees with the information in the request, or providing the requested information.

(*b*) **Negative confirmation request** - A request that the confirming party respond directly to the auditor only if the confirming party disagrees with the information provided in the request.

◆ External confirmation procedures frequently are relevant when addressing assertions associated with account balances and their elements, but need not be restricted to these items. For example, the auditor may request external confirmation of the terms of agreements, contracts, or transactions between an entity and other parties.

Q.81 Write short notes on Situations where external confirmations can be used.

Ans. : Situations where external confirmations can be used:

External confirmation procedures frequently are relevant when addressing assertions associated with account balances and their elements, but need not be restricted to these items. For example, the auditor may request external confirmation of the terms of agreements, contracts, or transactions between an entity and other parties.

Other situations where external confirmation procedures may provide relevant audit evidence include:

(*i*) Bank balances and other information relevant to banking relationships.

(*ii*) Accounts receivable balances and terms.

(*iii*) Inventories held by third parties at bonded warehouses for processing or on consignment.

(*iv*) Property title deeds held by lawyers or financiers for safe custody or as security.

(*v*) Investments held for safekeeping by third parties, or purchased from stockbrokers but not delivered at the balance sheet date.

(*vi*) Amounts due to lenders, including relevant terms of repayment.

(*vii*) Accounts payable balances and terms.

Q.82 Mr. Z who is appointed as auditor of Elite Co. Ltd. wants to use confirmation request as audit evidence during the course of audit. What are the factors to be considered by Mr. Z when designing a confirmation request? Also state the effects of using positive external confirmation request by Mr. Z.

[May 16 (5 Marks)]

Ans. : Factors to be considered while designing confirmation requests:

As per SA 505 "External Confirmations" factors to consider when designing confirmation requests include:

(*i*) Assertion being addressed.

(*ii*) Specific identified RMM.

(*iii*) Layout & presentation of request.

(*iv*) Prior experience on the audit of similar engagements.

(*v*) Method of communication.

(*vi*) Management authorisation/encouragement to Confirming Party to respond to auditor.

(*vii*) Ability of Confirming Party to provide/confirm requested information.

Effects of Positive Confirmation Requests:

- A positive external confirmation request asks the confirming party to reply to the auditor in all cases, either by indicating the confirming party's agreement with the given information, or by asking the confirming party to provide information.
- A response to a positive confirmation request ordinarily is expected to provide reliable audit evidence. There is a risk, however, that a confirming party may reply to the confirmation request without verifying that the information is correct.
- The auditor may reduce this risk by using positive confirmation requests that do not state the amount (or other information) on the confirmation request, and ask the confirming party to fill in the amount or furnish other information.

"ICAI Examiner Comments"

Candidates, in general, failed to state all the important factors to be considered while designing the confirmation request and to explain the effect of positive confirmation.

Q.83 The management of S Ltd. Request you not to seek confirmation from its debtors. As the auditor of S Ltd., what can be an appropriate response? [May 11 (6 Marks)]

Or

Never Permit Limited refused to allow you to get direct confirmation of the outstanding balances of trade receivables. You want to ensure on grounds of materiality that atleast outstanding above a threshold limit needs to be confirmed and reconciliation is to be carried out before finalising the audit. If the company does not relent, how will you respond? [May 18 - New Syllabus (4 Marks)]

Ans : Refer Answer of Q. No. 84

Q.84 **The auditor of H Ltd. wanted to obtain confirmation from its creditors. But the management made a request to the auditor not to seek confirmation from certain creditors citing disputes. Can the auditor of H Ltd. accede to this request?** **[May 13 (4 Marks)]**

Or

The accountant of C Ltd. has requested you, not to send balance confirmations to a particular group of trade receivables since the said balances are under dispute and the matter is pending in the Court. As a Statutory Auditor, how would you deal?

Ans. : Management refusal to allow auditor to send confirmation request:

- SA 505, "External Confirmations", establishes standards on the auditor's use of external confirmation as a means of obtaining audit evidence. It requires that the auditor should employ external confirmation procedures in consultation with the management.
- The auditor may come across certain situations in which the management may request him not to seek external confirmation from certain parties because of some reasons, for example, due to a dispute with the particular creditor or debtor.
- If the management refuses to allow the auditor to a send a confirmation request, the auditor shall:
  a. Inquire as to Management's reasons for the refusal, and seek audit evidence as to their validity and reasonableness,
  b. Evaluate the implications of management's refusal on the auditor's assessment of the relevant risks of material misstatement, including the risk of fraud, and on the nature, timing and extent of other audit procedures, and
  c. Perform alternative audit procedures designed to obtain relevant and reliable audit evidence.

If the auditor concludes that management's refusal to allow the auditor to send a confirmation request is unreasonable or the auditor is unable to obtain relevant and reliable audit evidence from alternative audit procedures, the auditor shall communicate with TCWG and also determine its implication for the audit and his opinion.

Q.85 **Moon Limited replaced its statutory auditor for the Financial year 2016-17. During the course of audit, the new auditor found a credit item of ₹ 5 lakhs. On enquiry, the company explained him that it is, a very old credit balance. The creditor had neither approached for the payment nor he is traceable. Under the circumstances, no confirmation of the credit balance is available.** **[Nov. 09 (5 Marks)]**

Ans. : Auditor's duties in case of non-availability of External Confirmation:

- SA 505 "External Confirmations" provides that if the auditor has determined that a response to a positive confirmation request is necessary to obtain sufficient appropriate audit evidence, and alternative audit procedures will not provide the audit evidence the auditor requires, he should determine the implications for the audit and the auditor's opinion in accordance with SA 705.
- In the present case the identities of trade payables are not traceable to confirm the credit balance as appearing in the financial statement of the company. It is also not a case of pending litigation. It might be a case that an income of ₹ 5 lakhs had been hidden in previous year/s.
- The statutory auditor should examine the validity of the credit balance as appeared in the company's financial statements. He should obtain sufficient evidence in support of the balance. He should apply alternative audit procedures to get documentary proof for the transaction/s and should not rely entirely on the management representation. Finally, he should include the matter by way of a qualification in his audit report to the members.

Q.86 **As an auditor how would you deal with the following: When the audit team visited the client to perform substantive audit of debtor, the client produced ledger account of customers and confirmations for the top 10 customers. One of the debtors was more than 5 years old, but it had confirmed his balance.** **[May 10 (5 Marks)]**

Ans. : Auditor's duties in case of doubt over reliability of external confirmations:

- SA 505 "External Confirmations" deals with the auditor's use of external confirmation procedures to obtain audit evidence. External confirmation is the process of obtaining and evaluating audit evidence through a direct communication from a third party in response to a request for information about a particular item affecting assertions made by the management in the financial statements.

- As per SA 505, the auditor is required to maintain a control over the process of selecting those to whom a request will be sent out, the preparation and sending of confirmation requests and responses to those requests. This is because there have been several cases of clients presenting forged confirmation to auditors when such control was absent.
- In the present case, one of the debtors of more than 5 years old had confirmed his balance. The auditor should enquire into the debtor whose dues are outstanding for 5 years or more about his financial abilities and why he has not paid, reasons behind the same, and if found adverse, the client should be advised to provide for "Provision for bad debts" and also to confirm that it is not a forged confirmation.

Q.87 During the course of audit of Star Limited the auditor received some of the confirmation of the balances of trade payables outstanding in the balance sheet through external confirmation by negative confirmation request. In the list of trade payables, there are number of trade payables of small balances except one, old outstanding of ₹ 15 Lacs, of whom, no confirmation on the credit balance received. Comment with respect to Standard of Auditing. [May 14 (5 Marks)]

Ans. : Response to Negative Confirmation Request:

- As per SA 505, "External Confirmation", Negative Confirmation is a request that the confirming party respond directly to the auditor only if the confirming party disagrees with the information provided in the request.
- Negative confirmations provide less persuasive audit evidence than positive confirmations. In case of negative confirmation request, confirming parties may be more likely to respond indicating their disagreement with a confirmation request when the information in the request is not in their favour, and less likely to respond otherwise.
- In the instant case, the auditor sent the negative confirmation requesting the trade payables having outstanding balances in the balance sheet while doing audit of Star Limited. One of the old outstanding of rupees 15 lacs has not sent the confirmation on the credit balance.
- Non-response for negative confirmation request does not mean that there is some misstatement as negative confirmation request itself is to respond to the auditor only if the confirming party disagrees with the information provided in the request.
- In the present case, considering the materiality of the account balance, the auditor may examine subsequent cash disbursements or correspondence from third parties, and other records, such as goods received notes.

Q.88 M/s ABC & Co., LLP are appointed auditors of Sharp Company Ltd. for the year ended 31st March, 2019. As part of the audit process, they want to use confirmation procedures as audit evidence during the course of audit. In view of the fact that positive confirmations are not responded favourably, the firm also intends to use negative confirmation requests. What are the factors to be considered for the same? [May 19 - Old Syllabus (7 Marks)]

Ans. : Use of negative confirmations:

- As per SA 505, "External Confirmation", Negative Confirmation is a request that the confirming party respond directly to the auditor only if the confirming party disagrees with the information provided in the request.
- Negative confirmations provide less persuasive audit evidence than positive confirmations. Accordingly, the auditor shall use negative confirmation requests as the sole substantive audit procedure only when all of the following conditions are present:
  - (*a*) Low Risk of material misstatement and auditor has obtained sufficient appropriate audit evidence regarding the operating effectiveness of controls.
  - (*b*) The population comprises a large number of small, homogeneous, account balances or transactions.
  - (*c*) A very low exception rate is expected.
  - (*d*) The auditor is not aware of circumstances or conditions that would cause recipients of negative confirmation requests to disregard such requests.

Factors to be considered while designing confirmation requests: Refer Answer of Q. No. 82

TAXMANN®

1.20 - SA 510 "INITIAL AUDIT ENGAGEMENTS - OPENING BALANCES"

Q.89 What are Initial Audit Engagement?

Ans. : Initial Audit Engagements:

As per SA 510 "Initial Audit Engagements - Opening Balances", initial audit engagement is an engagement in which either:

(*i*) The financial statements for the prior period were not audited; or

(*ii*) The financial statements for the prior period were audited by a predecessor auditor.

Q.90 Comment on the following: You have been appointed as the auditor of Good Health Ltd. for 2019-20 which was audited by CA Trustworthy in 2018-19. As the Auditor of the company state the steps you would take to ensure that the Closing Balances of 2018-19 have been brought to account in 2019-20 as Opening Balances and the Opening Balances do not contain misstatements. [Nov. 08 (5 Marks)]

Or

What are the procedures to be followed by a Statutory Auditor in the audit of opening balances if the financial statements for the preceding year were audited by another auditor?

Or

You have been appointed as statutory auditor of M/s Moon Ltd. for the financial year 2018-19. As the auditor of the company you want to ensure that closing balances of previous year have been correctly brought forward as opening balances in the current year. State the audit procedures for the same to ensure that there is no misstatement. [Nov. 19 - Old Syllabus (5 Marks)]

Ans. : Audit procedures for verification of opening balances in case of initial audit engagement:

As per SA 510 "Initial Audit Engagements- Opening Balances", the objective of the Auditor while conducting an initial audit engagement with respect to opening balances is to obtain sufficient appropriate audit evidence so that the—

(*i*) opening balances of the preceding period have been correctly brought forward to the current period;

(*ii*) opening balances do not contain any misstatement that materially affect the current period's financial statements; and

(*iii*) appropriate accounting policies reflected in the opening balances have been consistently applied in the current period's financial statements, or changes thereto are properly accounted for and adequately presented and disclosed in accordance with the applicable financial reporting framework.

If the prior period's financial statements were audited by a predecessor auditor, the auditor may be able to obtain sufficient appropriate audit evidence regarding the opening balances by perusing the copies of the audited financial statements including the other relevant documents relating to the prior period financial statements such as supporting schedules to the audited financial statements. Ordinarily, the current auditor can place reliance on the closing balances contained in the financial statements for the preceding period, except when during the performance of audit procedures for the current period the possibility of misstatements in opening balances is indicated.

For current assets and liabilities some audit evidence can ordinarily be obtained as part of audit procedures during the current period. For example, the collection/payment of opening balances of receivables and payables will provide audit evidence as to their existence, rights and obligations, completeness and valuation at the beginning of the period.

In respect of other assets and liabilities such as fixed assets, investments long term debt, the auditor will examine the records relating to opening balances. The auditor may also be able to get confirmation from third parties (e.g., balances of long term loan obtained from banks).

Q.91 In an initial audit engagement, the auditor will have to satisfy about the sufficiency and appropriateness of 'Opening balances' to ensure that they are free from instatements, which may materially affect the current financial statements. Lay down the audit procedure, you will follow, when financial statements are audited for the first time.

If, after performing the procedure, you are not satisfied about the correctness of 'Opening Balances', what approach you will adopt in drafting your audit report? [May 15 (5 Marks)]

Or

Mr. X has been appointed as an auditor of M/s ABC Ltd., Mr. X wants to be satisfied about the sufficiency and appropriateness of 'Opening Balances' to ensure that they are free from misstatements. Lay down the

audit procedure, Mr. X should follow, in the initial audit engagement of M/s ABC Ltd. Also suggest the approach to be followed regarding mention in the audit report if Mr. X is not satisfied about the correctness of 'Opening Balances'? [Nov. 19 - New Syllabus (4 Marks)]

Ans. : Audit procedures for verification of opening balances in case of initial audit engagement:

As per SA 510 "Initial Audit Engagements-Opening Balances", the objective of the Auditor while conducting an initial audit engagement with respect to opening balances is to obtain sufficient appropriate audit evidence so that the:

(*i*) opening balances of the preceding period have been correctly brought forward to the current period;

(*ii*) opening balances do not contain any misstatement that materially affect the current period's financial statements; and

(*iii*) appropriate accounting policies reflected in the opening balances have been consistently applied in the current period's financial statements, or changes thereto are properly accounted for and adequately presented and disclosed in accordance with the applicable financial reporting framework.

When the audit of financial statements is being conducted for the first time, the auditor has to perform auditing procedures to obtain sufficient appropriate audit evidence. Since opening balances represent effect of transaction and events of the preceding period and accounting policies applied in the preceding period, the auditor need to obtain evidence having regard to nature of opening balances, materiality of the opening balances and accounting policies.

Since it will not be possible for auditor to perform certain procedures, e.g., observing physical verification of inventories, etc. the auditor may obtain confirmation, etc. and perform suitable procedures in respect of fixed assets, investments, etc. The auditor can also obtain management representation with regards to the opening balances.

Considerations while drafting Report:

If the auditor is unable to obtain sufficient appropriate audit evidence regarding the opening balances, the auditor shall express a qualified opinion or a disclaimer of opinion, as appropriate. Further, If the auditor concludes that the opening balances contain a misstatement that materially affects the current period's financial statements, and the effect of the misstatement is not properly accounted for or not adequately presented or disclosed, the auditor shall express a qualified opinion or an adverse opinion in accordance with SA 705.

"ICAI Examiner Comments"

Most of the candidates could not write approach for drafting of Audit Report in case of Opening Balance which contains misstatement. Many candidates wrote answer about using previous year audited accounts, while question specifically mentioned that the financial statements were audited for the first time.

Q.92 CA Mr. Jack, a recently qualified practicing Chartered Accountant got his first audit assignment of Futura (P) Ltd. for the financial year 2018-19. He obtained all the relevant appropriate audit evidence for the items related to Statement of Profit and Loss. However, while auditing the Balance Sheet items, CA Jack left out obtaining appropriate audit evidence, say, confirmations, from the outstanding Accounts Receivable amounting ₹ 100 lakhs, continued as it is from the last year, on the affirmation of the management that there is no receipts and further credits during the year. CA Jack, therefore, excluded from the audit programme, the audit of accounts receivable on the understanding that it pertains to the preceding year which was already audited by predecessor auditor. Comment.

Ans. : Audit procedures for verification of opening balances in case of initial audit engagement:

As per SA 510 "Initial Audit Engagements- Opening Balances", the objective of the Auditor while conducting an initial audit engagement with respect to opening balances is to obtain sufficient appropriate audit evidence so that the—

(*i*) opening balances of the preceding period have been correctly brought forward to the current period;

(*ii*) opening balances do not contain any misstatement that materially affect the current period's financial statements; and

(*iii*) appropriate accounting policies reflected in the opening balances have been consistently applied in the current period's financial statements, or changes thereto are properly accounted for and adequately presented and disclosed in accordance with the applicable financial reporting framework.

If the prior period's financial statements were audited by a predecessor auditor, the auditor may be able to obtain sufficient appropriate audit evidence regarding the opening balances by perusing the copies of the audited financial statements including the other relevant documents relating to the prior period financial statements such as supporting schedules to the audited financial statements. Ordinarily, the current auditor can place reliance on the closing balances contained in the financial statements for the preceding period, except when during the performance of audit procedures for the current period the possibility of misstatements in opening balances is indicated.

In the given case, the management of Futura (P.) Ltd. has restrained CA Jack, its auditor, from obtaining appropriate audit evidence for balances of Accounts Receivable outstanding as it is from the preceding year. CA Jack, on believing that the preceding year balances have already been audited and on the statement of the management that there are no receipts and credits during the current year, therefore excluded the verification of Accounts Receivable from his audit programme.

Conclusion: CA Jack was required to obtain from the management a written representation (as covered by SA 580) for their views and expressions; and to perform appropriate procedures on closing balances of Accounts Receivable to ensure its appropriateness. In the present case, CA Jack will be held guilty for professional misconduct for not exercising due diligence in the conduct of his professional duties as per the Code of Ethics.

1.21 - SA 520 "ANALYTICAL PROCEDURES"

Q.93 What are the considerations to be kept in mind while performing analytical procedures on data prepared by the client. [May 09 (6 Marks)]

Ans. : Auditor's considerations while performing analytical procedures:

SA 520 "Analytical Procedures" deals with the auditor's use of analytical procedures as substantive procedures and as procedures near the end of the audit that assist the auditor when forming an overall conclusion on the financial statements.

Accordingly, when the auditor intends to perform analytical procedures on data prepared by the client, he should consider the following:

1. **Determine the suitability of particular substantive analytical procedures** for given assertions, taking account of the assessed risks of material misstatement and tests of details, if any, for these assertions;
2. **Evaluate the reliability of data** from which the auditor's expectation of recorded amounts or ratios is developed, taking account of source, comparability, and nature and relevance of information available, and controls over preparation;
3. **Develop an expectation of recorded amounts or ratios** and evaluate whether the expectation is sufficiently precise to identify a misstatement that, individually or when aggregated with other misstatements, may cause the financial statements to be materially misstated; and
4. **Determine the amount of any difference of recorded amounts from expected values** that is acceptable without further investigation.

Q.94 In the audit of Hotel Great Hay Limited its auditor wants to use the analytical procedure as substantive procedure in respect of room rental income as well as pay roll costs, guide him as to how it can be done? [Nov. 13 (4 Marks)]

Or

You have been appointed as an auditor of M/s Excellent Hotels Ltd. As a senior partner, you want to use analytical procedures in respect of room rentals as well as payroll expenses. Discuss.

[May 19 - Old Syllabus (7 Marks)]

Ans. : Applying analytical procedures as substantive procedures:

- SA 520 "Analytical Procedures" deals with the auditor's use of analytical procedures as substantive procedures and as procedures near the end of the audit that assist the auditor when forming an overall conclusion on the financial statements.
- Accordingly, in some cases, predictive model may be effective as an analytical procedure.
- In case of Payroll cost - Where an entity has a known number of employees at fixed rates of pay throughout the period, it may be possible for the auditor to use this data to estimate the total payroll costs for the period with a high degree of accuracy, thereby providing audit evidence for a significant item in the financial statements and reducing the need to perform tests of details on the payroll.

- In case of Room Rental Income of Hotel, different types of analytical procedures provide different levels of assurance. Analytical procedures involving the prediction of total rental income in case of hotel taking the room tariff rates, the number of rooms and vacancy rates into consideration, can provide persuasive evidence and may eliminate the need for further verification by means of tests of details, provided the elements are appropriately verified.

Q.95 The reliability of data in influenced by its source and nature and is dependent on the circumstances under which it is obtained. Accordingly, what are the relevant criteria which determine whether the data is reliable for the purposes of designing substantive analytical procedures? [Nov. 15 (4 Marks)]

Or

Write short notes on: Relevant Criteria for determining Reliability of Data as per SA 520 'Analytical Procedures'.

Ans. : Criteria for determining the reliability of data used for analytical procedures:

- SA 520 "Analytical Procedures" deals with the auditor's use of analytical procedures as substantive procedures and as procedures near the end of the audit that assist the auditor when forming an overall conclusion on the financial statements.
- Accordingly, when designing and performing substantive analytical procedures, either alone or in combination with tests of details, as substantive procedures in accordance with SA 330, the auditor shall evaluate the reliability of data from which the auditor's expectation of recorded amounts or ratios is developed, considering the following:
  - (*i*) **Source of the information available.** For example, information may be more reliable when it is obtained from independent sources outside the entity;
  - (*ii*) **Comparability of the information available.** For example, broad industry data may need to be supplemented to be comparable to that of an entity that produces and sells specialised products;
  - (*iii*) **Nature and relevance of the information available.** For example, whether budgets have been established as results to be expected rather than as goals to be achieved; and
  - (*iv*) **Controls over the preparation of the information** that are designed to ensure its completeness, accuracy and validity. For example, controls over the preparation, review and maintenance of budgets.

"ICAI Examiner Comments"

Examinees did not explain the relevant criteria when determining whether data is reliable for the purpose of designing substantive analytical procedures. Irrelevant points on AS-18 were discussed. Some examinees wrote wrongly about analytical procedures. Also some examinees answered with respect to source and type of audit evidence instead of reliability of audit evidence.

Q.96 In audit of DEF Limited, the auditor had made use of certain analytical procedures with regard to certain key data in the statement of profit and loss. The results obtained showed inconsistencies with other relevant information. State the course of action that the Auditor should take to ensure that the risk of Material misstatement would be contained to a low level fixed as per materiality level. [Nov. 18-New Syllabus (4 Marks)]

Answer: Investigating Results of Analytical Procedures:

- SA 520 "Analytical Procedures" deals with the auditor's use of analytical procedures as substantive procedures and as procedures near the end of the audit that assist the auditor when forming an overall conclusion on the financial statements.
- As per SA 520, if analytical procedures performed in accordance with this SA 520 identify fluctuations or relationships that are inconsistent with other relevant information or that differ from expected values by a significant amount, the auditor shall investigate such differences by:
  - (*a*) Inquiring of management and obtaining appropriate audit evidence relevant to management's responses; and
  - (*b*) Performing other audit procedures as necessary in the circumstances.
- Audit evidence relevant to management's responses may be obtained by evaluating those responses taking into account the auditor's understanding of the entity and its environment, and with other audit evidence obtained during the course of the audit.

- The need to perform other audit procedures may arise when, for example, management is unable to provide an explanation, or the explanation, together with the audit evidence obtained relevant to management's response, is not considered adequate.

1.22 - SA 530 "AUDIT SAMPLING"

Q.97 Write short note on: Statistical and Non-Statistical Sampling. [May 12 (4 Marks)]

Ans. : Statistical Sampling and Non-Statistical Sampling:

Statistical Sampling

(*i*) Statistical sampling has the following characteristics:

- Random selection of the sample items; and
- The use of probability theory to evaluate sample results, including measurement of sampling risk.

(*ii*) This method is more scientific as it involves use of laws of probability.

(*iii*) This method has reasonably wide application where a population consists of a large number of similar items.

Non-Statistical Sampling

(*i*) A sampling approach that does not have characteristics of random selection and use of probability theory is considered as non-statistical sampling.

(*ii*) In this method, the sample size and its composition are determined on the basis of personal experience and knowledge of the auditor.

(*iii*) This method because of its simplicity in operation was in common application for many years.

Q.98 Write short note on: Sampling Risk.

or

While planning the audit of S Ltd. you want to apply sampling techniques. What are the risk factors you should keep in mind? [May 10 (4 Marks)]

Ans. : Risk Factors while Sampling technique:

- SA 530 deals with the auditor's use of statistical and non-statistical sampling when designing and selecting the audit sample, performing tests of controls and tests of details, and evaluating the results from the sample.
- While using sampling technique, auditor's conclusion based on a sample may be different from the conclusion if the entire population were subjected to the same audit procedure. This is known as sampling risk.
- Sampling risk can lead to two types of erroneous conclusions:
  1. In the case of a test of controls, that controls are more effective than they actually are, or in the case of a test of details, that a material misstatement does not exist when in fact it does.

     The auditor is primarily concerned with this type of erroneous conclusion because it affects audit effectiveness and is more likely to lead to an inappropriate audit opinion.
  2. In the case of a test of controls, that controls are less effective than they actually are, or in the case of a test of details, that a material misstatement exists when in fact it does not.

     This type of erroneous conclusion affects audit efficiency as it would usually lead to additional work to establish that initial conclusions were incorrect.

Q.99 Write short note on: Tolerable Misstatement. [May 14 (4 Marks)]

Or

What is tolerable misstatement and tolerable rate of deviation. [May 17 (4 Marks)]

Ans. : Tolerable Misstatement:

- A monetary amount set by the auditor in respect of which the auditor seeks to obtain an appropriate level of assurance that the monetary amount set by the auditor is not exceeded by the actual misstatement in the population.

- When designing a sample, the auditor determines tolerable misstatement in order to address the risk that the aggregate of individually immaterial misstatements may cause the financial statements to be materially misstated and provide a margin for possible undetected misstatements.
- Tolerable misstatement is the application of performance materiality, as defined in SA 320, to a particular sampling procedure. Tolerable misstatement may be the same amount or an amount lower than performance materiality.

Tolerable Rate of Deviation:

- Rate of deviation from prescribed internal control procedures set by the auditor in respect of which the auditor seeks to obtain an appropriate level of assurance that the rate of deviation set by the auditor is not exceeded by the actual rate of deviation in the population.

"ICAI Examiner Comments"

Many candidates wrongly mixed up Material misstatement with Tolerable Misstatement. Answers were general in nature and many candidates failed to narrate the Tolerable misstatement and Tolerable rate of deviation.

Q.100 Discuss the following: With reference to SA 530, meaning of audit sampling and requirements relating to sample design, sample size & selection of items for testing.

Ans. : Meaning of Audit Sampling, Sample Design, Sample Size and Selection of items for testing:

Audit Sampling: Application of audit procedures to less than 100% of items within a population of audit relevance such that all sampling units have a chance of selection in order to provide the auditor with a reasonable basis on which to draw conclusions about the entire population is known as audit sampling.

Requirement of SA 530 as to Sample Design, Size and Selection of Items for Testing

(*i*) When designing an audit sample, the auditor shall consider the purpose of the audit procedure and the characteristics of the population from which the sample will be drawn.

(*ii*) The auditor shall determine a sample size sufficient to reduce sampling risk to an acceptably low level.

(*iii*) The auditor shall select items for the sample in such a way that each sampling unit in the population has a chance of selection.

Q.101 "In cases where audit sample selection has been done on a random basis, no statistical process for selection of samples needs to be followed". Comment.

Ans. : Selection of Samples on random basis:

- As per SA 530 "Audit Sampling" sampling means application of audit procedures to less than 100% of items within a population of audit relevance such that all sampling units have a chance of selection in order to provide the auditor with a reasonable basis on which to draw conclusions about the entire population.
- Statistical sampling is an approach to sampling that has the following characteristics:
  (*i*) Random selection of the sample items; and
  (*ii*) The use of probability theory to evaluate sample results, including measurement of sampling risk.
- Essential features of statistical sampling are random selection and use of probability theory. Examples of Statistical sampling are Random selection, Systematic Selection and Monetary Unit Sampling.
- Audit sample collection on a random basis ensures that all items within a population have an equal chance of selection by the use of random number tables or random number generators. This method is considered appropriate provided the population to be sampled consists of reasonably similar units and false within a reasonable range.

Conclusion: For application of statistical sampling techniques, one of the prerequisite is selection on random basis, hence in case of selection of an audit sample on random basis, no other statistical process for selection of samples need to be followed.

Q.102 "An Auditor while analyzing the errors in a sample need not consider the qualitative aspects of errors detected." Comment.

Ans. : Consideration of Qualitative Aspects of Errors:

- SA 530 "Audit Sampling" requires the auditor to evaluate the results of the sample and determine whether the use of audit sampling has provided a reasonable basis for conclusions about the population that has been tested.

- If any error or misstatement identified, auditor shall investigate its nature and cause, and evaluate their possible effect on the purpose of the audit procedure and on other areas of the audit.
- In analysing the deviations and misstatements identified, the auditor would also need to consider the qualitative aspects of the misstatements identified by him.
- While evaluating the misstatements, auditor may observe that many have a common feature, for example, type of transaction, location, product line or period of time. In such circumstances, the auditor may decide to identify all items in the population that possess the common feature, and extend audit procedures to those items. In addition, such deviations or misstatements may be intentional, and may indicate the possibility of fraud.

Conclusion: The statement that an auditor while analysing the errors in a sample need not consider the qualitative aspects of errors detected is not correct, as he is required to investigate the nature and causes of the errors identified.

Q.103 Describe the Principal methods of selection of sample. **[Nov. 14 (4 Marks)]**

Or

The auditor should select sample items in such a way that the sample can be expected to be representative of the population. Comment. **[May 17 (5 Marks)]**

Or

In the course of your audit assignment of Indraprastha Ltd., you want to guide your audit assistants in selecting sample items in such a way that sample can be expected to be representative of the population and all items have an opportunity of being selected. Guide your assistants with principal methods of collecting samples. **[May 18 - Old Syllabus (4 Marks)]**

Ans. : Principal Methods of Selection of Samples:

As per SA 530 "Audit Sampling" principal methods of selection of samples are:

1. **Random selection:** This method of sampling ensures that all items within a population stand an equal chance of selection by the use of random number tables or random number generators. The sampling units could be physical items, such as sales invoices or monetary units.
2. **Systematic selection:** The number of sampling units in the population is divided by the sample size to give a sampling interval, for example 50, and having determined a starting point within the first 50, each 50th sampling unit thereafter is selected.
3. **Monetary Unit Sampling:** It is a type of value-weighted selection in which sample size, selection and evaluation results in a conclusion in monetary amounts.
4. **Haphazard selection:** Samples are selected without following a structured technique. Although no structured technique is used, the auditor would nonetheless avoid any conscious bias or predictability. Haphazard selection is not appropriate when using statistical sampling.
5. **Block selection:** It involves selection of a block(s) of contiguous items from within the population. Block selection cannot ordinarily be used in audit sampling because most populations are structured such that items in a sequence can be expected to have similar characteristics to each other, but different characteristics from items elsewhere in the population.

Q.104 Write short note on: Haphazard Sampling.

Ans. : Haphazard Sampling:

- SA 530 "Audit Sampling" recognises haphazard sampling as one of the sample selection method in which samples are selected without following a structured technique.
- Although no structured technique is used, the auditor would nonetheless avoid any conscious bias or predictability (for example, avoiding difficult to locate items, or always choosing or avoiding the first or last entries on a page) and thus attempt to ensure that all items in the population have a chance of selection.
- It may be accepted as alternative to random sampling, provided the auditor attempts to draw a representative sample from the population without any biasness.
- Haphazard selection is not appropriate when using statistical sampling.

Q.105 Write short note on: Block Selection.

Ans. : Block Selection:

- SA 530 "Audit Sampling" recognises block selection as one of the sample selection method in which samples are selected without following a structured technique.

- It involves selection of a block(s) of contiguous items from within the population.
- Block selection cannot ordinarily be used in audit sampling because most populations are structured such that items in a sequence can be expected to have similar characteristics to each other, but different characteristics from items elsewhere in the population.
- In some circumstances, it may be an appropriate audit procedure to examine a block of items, it would rarely be an appropriate sample selection technique when the auditor intends to draw valid inferences about the entire population based on the sample.

Q.106 Describe the principal method of design of the samples and its evaluation. [May 17 (4 Marks)]

Ans. : Principal Method of Design of Samples:

SA 530 "Audit Sampling" deals with the auditor's use of statistical and non-statistical sampling when designing and selecting the audit sample, performing tests of controls and tests of details, and evaluating the results from the sample. Among both methods of designing (Statistical and non-statistical), principal method of design of sample is statistical sampling.

Statistical sampling involves random selection of the sample items and use of probability theory to evaluate sample results, including measurement of sampling risk. This method is more scientific as it involves use of laws of probability. This method has reasonably wide application where a population consists of a large number of similar items.

While applying statistical sampling, auditor may also apply stratification, i.e. the process of dividing a population into sub-populations, each of which is a group of sampling units which have similar characteristics (often monetary value).

Evaluation of Sampling Results:

- SA 530 "Audit Sampling" requires the auditor to evaluate the results of the sample and determine whether the use of audit sampling has provided a reasonable basis for conclusions about the population that has been tested.
- If any error or misstatement identified, auditor shall investigate its nature and cause, and evaluate their possible effect on the purpose of the audit procedure and on other areas of the audit.
- In analysing the deviations and misstatements identified, the auditor would also need to consider the qualitative aspects of the misstatements identified by him.

"ICAI Examiner Comments"

Majority of the candidates seem not to have understood the requirement of the question on the aspects to be considered by auditor in designing the sample and evaluating the results; rather their answers were concentrated mainly on the principal methods of sampling.

1.23 - SA 540 "AUDITING ACCOUNTING ESTIMATES, INCLUDING FAIR VALUE ACCOUNTING ESTIMATES AND RELATED DISCLOSURES"

Q.107 "Accounting estimate means an approximation of a monetary amount in the absence of a precise means of measurement". Discuss explaining the accounting estimates according to SA-540.

Ans. : Accounting Estimates:

SA 540 "Auditing Accounting Estimates, including Fair Value Accounting Estimates and Related Disclosures" defines an accounting estimate as "an approximation of a monetary amount in the absence of a precise means of measurement". This term is used for an amount measured at fair value where there is estimation uncertainty. The degree of estimation uncertainty affects the risks of material misstatement of accounting estimates.

Examples of Accounting Estimates:

1. Allowance for doubtful accounts.
2. Inventory obsolescence.
3. Warranty obligations.
4. Depreciation method or asset useful life.
5. Provision against the carrying amount of an investment.
6. Outcome of long term contracts.
7. Financial Obligations/Costs arising from litigation settlements and judgments.

Examples of Fair Value Accounting Estimates:

1. Complex financial instruments, which are not traded in an active and open market.
2. Share-based payments.
3. Property or equipment held for disposal.
4. Certain assets or liabilities acquired in a business combination, including goodwill and intangible assets.
5. Transactions involving the exchange of assets or liabilities between independent parties without monetary consideration.

Q.108 During the audit of Data Solutions Ltd., a listed company, your audit manager observed that several estimates are made by the Company. He seeks your guidance to know areas of accounting estimates that may give rise to lower level of risk of material misstatement. Guide him with examples.

[Nov. 19 - Old Syllabus (5 Marks)]

Ans. : Areas of accounting estimates that may give rise to lower level of risk of material misstatement:

SA 540 "Auditing Accounting Estimates, including Fair Value Accounting Estimates and Related Disclosures" defines an accounting estimate as "an approximation of a monetary amount in the absence of a precise means of measurement". This term is used for an amount measured at fair value where there is estimation uncertainty. The degree of estimation uncertainty affects the risks of material misstatement of accounting estimates.

Some accounting estimates involve relatively low estimation uncertainty and may give rise to lower risks of material misstatements, for example:

(*a*) Accounting estimates arising in entities that engage in business activities that are not complex.

(*b*) Accounting estimates that are frequently made and updated because they relate to routine transactions.

(*c*) Accounting estimates derived from data that is readily available, such as published interest rate data or exchange-traded prices of securities. Such data may be referred to as "observable" in the context of a fair value accounting estimate.

(*d*) Fair value accounting estimates where the method of measurement prescribed by the applicable financial reporting framework is simple and applied easily to the asset or liability requiring measurement at fair value.

(*e*) Fair value accounting estimates where the model used to measure the accounting estimate is well-known or generally accepted, provided that the assumptions or inputs to the model are observable.

Q.109 "Some accounting estimates involve relatively low estimation uncertainty and may give rise to lower risks of material misstatements whereas for some accounting estimates there may be relatively high estimation uncertainty particularly where they are based on significant assumptions". Explain by giving examples.

Or

With reference to the Standards on Auditing state the example of accounting estimates that may have a high estimation uncertainty. **[Nov. 16 (5 Marks)]**

Ans. : Examples of accounting Estimates having high estimation uncertainty:

SA 540 "Auditing Accounting Estimates, including Fair Value Accounting Estimates and related disclosures" defines an accounting estimate as "an approximation of a monetary amount in the absence of a precise means of measurement". This term is used for an amount measured at fair value where there is estimation uncertainty. The degree of estimation uncertainty affects the risks of material misstatement of accounting estimates.

Some accounting estimates involve relatively low estimation uncertainty and may give rise to lower risks of material misstatements. For some accounting estimates, however, there may be relatively high estimation uncertainty, particularly where they are based on significant assumptions, for example:

1. Accounting estimates relating to the outcome of litigation.
2. Fair value accounting estimates for derivative financial instruments not publicly traded.
3. Fair value accounting estimates for which a highly specialised entity-developed model is used or for which there are assumptions or inputs that cannot be observed in the marketplace.

Additional Examples of Fair Value Accounting Estimates are:

1. Complex financial instruments, which are not traded in an active and open market.
2. Share-based payments.
3. Property or equipment held for disposal.
4. Certain assets or liabilities acquired in a business combination, including goodwill and intangible assets.
5. Transactions involving the exchange of assets or liabilities between independent parties without monetary consideration.

Q.110 While auditing Z Ltd., you observe certain material financial statement assertions have been based on estimates made by the management. As the auditor how do you minimize the risk of material misstatements?

[May 11 (6 Marks)]

Ans. : Evaluation of financial statement assertions based on management estimates:

As per SA 540 "Auditing Accounting Estimates, including Fair Value Accounting Estimates" auditor shall obtain an understanding of the following in order to identify and assess the risks of material misstatement for accounting estimates:

(*a*) The **requirements of the applicable FRF** relevant to accounting estimates.

(*b*) **How management identifies** those transactions, events and conditions that may give rise to the need for accounting estimates.

In obtaining this understanding, the auditor shall make **inquiries of management** about changes in circumstances that may give rise to new, or the need to revise existing accounting estimates.

(*c*) The **estimation making process** adopted by the management including:

(*a*) The method, including where applicable the model used in making the accounting estimates.

(*b*) Relevant controls.

(*c*) Whether management has used an expert.

(*d*) Assumptions underlying the accounting estimates.

(*e*) Whether there has been or ought to have been a change from the prior period in the methods for making the accounting estimates, and if so why.

(*f*) Whether and if so, how the management has assessed the effect of estimation uncertainty.

(*d*) The auditor shall **review the outcome of accounting estimates** included in the prior period financial statements.

Q.111 A Pvt Ltd. is engaged in the business of real estate. The auditor of the company requested the information from the management to review the outcome of accounting estimates (like estimated costs considered for percentage completion etc.) included in the prior period financial statements and their subsequent re-estimation for the purpose of the current period.

The management has refused the information to the auditor saying that the review of prior period information should not be done by the auditor. Please advise.

Ans. : Review of outcome of Accounting Estimates:

- SA 540 "Auditing Accounting Estimates, including Fair Value Accounting Estimates and Related Disclosures" requires the auditor to review the outcome of accounting estimates included in the prior period financial statements, or, where applicable, their subsequent re-estimation for the purpose of the current period.
- The nature and extent of the auditor's review takes account of the nature of the accounting estimates, and whether the information obtained from the review would be relevant to identifying and assessing risks of material misstatement of accounting estimates made in the current period financial statements.
- However, the review is not intended to call into question the judgments made in the prior periods that were based on information available at that time.
- The outcome of an accounting estimate will often differ from the accounting estimate recognised in the prior period financial statements. By performing risk assessment procedures to identify and understand the reasons for such differences, the auditor may obtain:

(*a*) Information regarding the effectiveness of management's prior period estimation process, from which the auditor can judge the likely effectiveness of management's current process.

(*b*) Audit evidence that is pertinent to the re-estimation, in the current period, of prior period accounting estimates.

(*c*) Audit evidence of matters, such as estimation uncertainty, that may be required to be disclosed in the financial statements.

◆ The review of prior period accounting estimates may also assist the auditor, in the current period, in identifying circumstances or conditions that increase the susceptibility of accounting estimates to, or indicate the presence of, possible management bias. The auditor's professional skepticism assists in identifying such circumstances or conditions and in determining the nature, timing and extent of further audit procedures.

Q.112 What are the factors that may influence the degree of estimation uncertainty associated with an accounting estimate?

Ans : Factors Influencing Degree of Estimation Uncertainty:

SA 540 "Auditing Accounting Estimates, including Fair Value Accounting Estimates and Related Disclosures" defines an accounting estimate as "an approximation of a monetary amount in the absence of a precise means of measurement". This term is used for an amount measured at fair value where there is estimation uncertainty. The degree of estimation uncertainty affects the risks of material misstatement of accounting estimates.

The degree of estimation uncertainty associated with an accounting estimate may be influenced by factors such as-

(*i*) The extent to which the accounting estimate depends on judgment.

(*ii*) The sensitivity of the accounting estimate to changes in assumptions.

(*iii*) The existence of recognised measurement techniques that may mitigate the estimation uncertainty (though the subjectivity of the assumptions used as inputs may nevertheless give rise to estimation uncertainty).

(*iv*) The length of the forecast period, and the relevance of data drawn from past events to forecast future events.

(*v*) The availability of reliable data from external sources.

(*vi*) The extent to which the accounting estimate is based on observable or unobservable inputs.

1.24 - SA 550 "RELATED PARTIES"

Q.113 Elaborate how the statutory auditor can verify the existence of related parties for the purpose of reporting under AS 18.

Or

As a statutory auditor, how do you verify the existence of related parties and disclosures of related party transactions. [Nov. 09 (8 Marks)]

Or

In the course of audit of Q Ltd., its statutory auditor wants to be sure of the adequacy of related party disclosures? Kindly guide the auditor in identifying the possible source of related party information. [May 12 (8 Marks)]

Or

As an Auditor, how will you verify the existence of related parties. [Nov. 12 (8 Marks)]

Or

JY & Co. is appointed as auditor of Breeze Ltd. JY & Co. seeks your guidance for reviewing the records and documentation of the company regarding 'related party transactions in the normal course of business'. Describe the steps to be followed. [Nov. 15 (4 Marks)]

Or

The financial statements of Beta Ltd. have been prepared by the Management with due disclosures for related parties and transactions with them. However, as the auditor of the Company, you are not sure of the reliability of the said disclosures. Mention the documents and records that may be helpful in gathering information about related party relationships and transactions. [Nov. 19 - Old Syllabus (5 Marks)]

Ans. : Possible sources of related Party Information:

- As per SA 550 "Related Parties" the auditor shall remain alert, when inspecting records or documents with respect to arrangements or information indicating the existence of related party relationships or transactions, not previously identified or disclosed to the auditor.
- During the audit, the auditor may inspect records or documents that may provide information about related party relationships and transactions, for example:

1. Entity income tax returns.
2. Information supplied by the entity to regulatory authorities.
3. Shareholder registers to identify the entity's principal shareholders.
4. Statements of conflicts of interest from management and TCWG.
5. Records of the entity's investments and those of its pension plans.
6. Contracts and agreements with key management or TCWG.
7. Significant contracts and agreements not in the entity's ordinary course of business.
8. Specific invoices and correspondence from the entity's professional advisors.
9. Life insurance policies acquired by the entity.
10. Significant contracts re-negotiated by the entity during the period.
11. Internal auditors' reports.
12. Documents associated with the entity's filings with a securities regulator (for example, prospectuses).

- Auditor should also obtain further information on significant transactions outside the entity's normal course of business. It enables him to evaluate whether fraud risk factors, if any, are present.
- In addition, the auditor needs to be alert for transactions which appear unusual in the circumstances and which may indicate the existence of previously unidentified related parties. For example: Complex equity transactions such as corporate restructurings or acquisitions, transactions with offshore entities in jurisdictions with weak corporate laws, the leasing of premises etc.
- Finally, the auditor should also obtain a written representation from the management concerning the completeness of information provided regarding the identification of related parties.

"ICAI Examiner Comments"

Examinees did not write about the inspection of various records or documents that may provide information about related party relationships and transactions. Many examinees wrote about related parties transactions and its reporting requirements rather than how to find these.

Q.114 A statutory auditor is required to follow the procedures so as to identify the risk of material misstatement associated with related parties. What are the auditor's duties when he identifies related parties or related party transactions that management not previously disclosed to him?

Ans. : Verification of existence of related parties:

SA 550 "Related Parties" requires the auditor to perform procedures so as to identify the risk of material misstatement associated with related parties. Accordingly, auditor should perform the following:

(*a*) Inquire the management regarding

- Identity of entity's Related Party, changes from prior period.
- Nature of relationships between entity and Related Party.
- Type & purpose of transactions with Related Party during the period.

(*b*) The auditor shall remain alert, when inspecting records or documents, for arrangements or other information that may indicate the existence of related party relationships or transactions that management has not previously identified or disclosed to the auditor.

(*c*) If the auditor identifies related parties or significant related party transactions that management has not previously identified or disclosed to the auditor, the auditor shall:

(*i*) Promptly communicate the relevant information to the other members of the engagement team;

(*ii*) Where the applicable FRF establishes related party requirements:

- Request management to identify all transactions with the newly identified related parties for the auditor's further evaluation; and
- Inquire as to why the entity's controls over related party relationships and transactions failed to enable the identification or disclosure of the related party relationships or transactions;

(*iii*) Perform appropriate substantive audit procedures relating to such newly identified related parties or significant related party transactions;

(*iv*) Reconsider the risk that other related parties or significant related party transactions may exist that management has not previously identified or disclosed to the auditor, and perform additional audit procedures as necessary; and

(*v*) If the non-disclosure by management appears intentional (and therefore indicative of a risk of material misstatement due to fraud), evaluate the implications for the audit.

Q.115 In the course of your audit you have come across a related party transaction which prima facie appears to be biased. How would you deal with this? [Nov. 14 (4 marks)]

Ans. : Related Parties:

As per SA 550 on, "Related Parties", the auditor should review information provided by the management of the entity identifying the names of all known related parties and for this purpose, he may inspect records or documents that may provide information about related party relationships and transactions.

In this case, the auditor is finding a related party transaction which *prima facie* appears to be biased. So, the auditor is required to confirm the same. For identified significant related party transactions outside the entity's normal course of business, the auditor shall inspect the underlying contracts or agreements, if any, and evaluate whether:

(*i*) The business rationale (or lack thereof) of the transactions suggests that they may have been entered into to engage in fraudulent financial reporting or to conceal misappropriation of assets,

(*ii*) The terms of the transactions are consistent with management's explanations; and

(*iii*) The transactions have been appropriately accounted for and disclosed in accordance with the applicable financial reporting framework.

The auditor should also obtain audit evidence that the transactions have been appropriately authorised and approved.

Conclusion: If the auditor concludes that the related party transaction is biased, he should report that the related party relationships and transactions prevent the financial statements from achieving true and fair presentation.

1.25 - SA 560 "SUBSEQUENT EVENTS"

Q.116 Briefly Explain: Audit procedures on subsequent events. [Nov. 09 (4 Marks)]

Or

Briefly describe auditor's responsibility regarding subsequent events.

Ans. : Audit Procedures on subsequent Events:

- SA 560 "Subsequent Events" deals with the auditor's responsibilities relating to subsequent events in an audit of financial statements.
- As per SA 560 the term, Subsequent Events may be defined as the events occurring between the dates of balance sheet and audit report and the facts that become known to the auditor after the date of the auditor's report.
- The auditor shall perform audit procedures designed to obtain sufficient appropriate audit evidence that all events occurring between the date of the financial statements and the date of the auditor's report that require adjustment of, or disclosure in, the financial statements have been identified.
- The auditor's procedures on subsequent events shall include the following:

(*a*) Obtaining an understanding of the procedures through which management has identified subsequent events.

(*b*) Inquiring of management and, TCWG as to occurrence of subsequent events which might affect the financial statements.

(*c*) Reading minutes of management & TCWG meetings that have been held after the date of the financial statements.

(*d*) Reading the entity's latest subsequent interim financial statements, if any.

◆ When, as a result of the procedures performed as required the auditor identifies events that require adjustment of, or disclosure in, the financial statements, the auditor shall determine whether each such event is appropriately reflected in those financial statements.

Q.117 Enquiry from management is helpful for auditor to evaluate subsequent events. Discuss specific enquiries in reference of SA 560, which might have effect on the financial statements.

Or

M/s LMP Associates, Chartered Accountants while conducting the audit of PQR Ltd. want to conduct an inquiry of management and those charged with governance as to whether any subsequent events have occurred which might affect the financial statements. Guide M/s LMP Associates with the matters where specific enquiry may be conducted to evaluate subsequent events. [May 19 - Old Syllabus (7 Marks)]

Ans. : Specific Inquiries having effect on the financial statements:

SA 560 "Subsequent Events" deals with the auditor's responsibilities relating to subsequent events in an audit of financial statements. SA 560 requires from the auditor to conduct inquiry of management and, where appropriate, TCWG as to whether any subsequent events have occurred which might affect the financial statements. The matters where specific inquiry may be conducted are as listed below:

1. Whether new commitments, borrowings or guarantees have been entered into.
2. Whether sales or acquisitions of assets have occurred or are planned.
3. Whether there have been increases in capital or issuance of debt instruments, such as the issue of new shares or debentures, or an agreement to merge or liquidate has been made or is planned.
4. Whether any assets have been appropriated by government or destroyed, for example, by fire or flood.
5. Whether there have been any developments regarding contingencies.
6. Whether any unusual accounting adjustments have been made or are contemplated.
7. Whether any events have occurred or are likely to occur that will bring into question the appropriateness of accounting policies used in the financial statements, as would be the case, for example, if such events call into question the validity of the going concern assumption.
8. Whether any events have occurred that are relevant to the measurement of estimates or provisions made in the financial statements.
9. Whether any events have occurred that are relevant to the recoverability of assets.

Q.118 Comment on the following: A Co. Ltd. has not included in the Balance Sheet as on 31-03-2019 a sum of ₹ 1.50 crores being amount in the arrears of salaries and wages payable to the staff for the last 2 years as a result of successful negotiations which were going on during the last 18 months and concluded on 30-04-2019. The auditor wants to sign the said Balance Sheet and give the audit report on 31-05-2019. The auditor came to know the result of the negotiations on 15-05-2019. [Nov. 10 (5 Marks)]

Ans. : Treatment of subsequent Events:

◆ SA 560 "Subsequent Events" requires that in respect of events occurring between the date of F.S. and date of the Audit Report, the auditor shall perform audit procedures to obtain sufficient & appropriate audit evidence to ensure that events which require adjustments or disclosure in the F.S. have been identified.

◆ If auditor identifies events that require adjustment or disclosure in the F.S., the auditor should determine whether each such event is appropriately reflected in the F.S.

◆ The auditor shall request the management to provide a "Written Representation" that all events occurring subsequent to the date of the F.S. and requires adjustment or disclosure have been adjusted or disclosed.

◆ In the instant case, the amount of ₹ 1.50 crores are a material amount and it is the result of an event, which has occurred after the Balance Sheet date. As per the provisions of AS-4 and AS-29, the obligation requires provision for outstanding expenses.

Conclusion: The facts of the case indicates the event as of adjusting nature as per AS-4 "Contingencies and Events Occurring after the Balance Sheet date" and requires adjustment in assets and liabilities, which has not been made by the management. Auditor should request management to adjust the sum of ₹ 1.50 crores by making provision for expenses. If the management does not accept the request the auditor should qualify the Audit Report.

Q.119 **As a statutory auditor of a company, comment on the following: A fire broke out on 15th May, 2019, in which material worth ₹ 50 lakhs which was lying in inventory since 1st March, 2019 was totally destroyed. The financial statements of the company have not been adopted till the date of fire. The management of the company argues that since the loss occurred in the year, 2019-20, no provision for the loss needs to be made in the financial statements for 2018-19.** **[Nov. 12 (5 Marks)]**

Ans. : Event Occurring after the Balance Sheet Date:

- As per AS- 4 on 'Contingencies and Events Occurring After the Balance Sheet Date', assets and liabilities should be adjusted for events occurring after the balance sheet date that provide additional evidence to assist the estimation of amounts relating to conditions existing at the balance sheet date or that indicate that the fundamental accounting assumption of going concern is not appropriate.
- AS - 4 also requires disclosure of the non-adjusting event, in the report of approving authority.
- Further as per SA 560 "Subsequent Events" the auditor should ensure that all events occurring subsequent to the date of financial statements and for which applicable financial reporting framework requires adjustment or disclosure have been adjusted or disclosed.
- In the instant case, fire took place after the close of the accounting year and does not relate to conditions existing at the balance sheet date.

Conclusion: The event will have no impact on items appearing at the Balance Sheet date and hence not required any adjustment, subject to satisfaction in respect of non-violation of going concern concept. Hence management is correct by not providing provision. However, auditor is required to ensure the proper disclosure in report of approving authority.

Q.120 **Amudhan & Co., are the Auditors of XYZ Company Ltd., for the year ended on 31-03-2019. The Audit Report for that year was signed by the Auditors on 04-05-2019. The Annual General Meeting was decided to be held during the month of August 2019. On 06-05-2019, the Company had received a communication from the Central Government that an amount of Rs. 5800 crore kept pending on account of incentives pertaining to Financial Year 2018-19 had been approved and the amount would be paid to the Company before the end of May 2019. To a query to Chief Financial Officer of the company by the board, it was informed that this amount had not been recognised in the Audited Financial Statements in view of the same not being released before the close of the financial year and due to uncertainty of receipt. Now, having received the amount, the board of Directors wished to include this amount in the Financial Statements of the company for the Financial Year ended on 31.03.2019. On 08.05.2019, the Board amended the accounts, approved the same and requested the Auditor to consider this event and issue a fresh Audit Report for the year ended on 31.03.2019. Analyse the issues involved and give your views as to whether or not the Auditor could accede to the request of the Board of Directors.**

[Nov. 18-New Syllabus (5 Marks)]

Ans. : Event Occurring after the Balance Sheet Date:

(*a*) **Issues Involved:**

1. Whether the Financial statements can be amended after the signing of audit report, but before being issued to stakeholders.
2. What are the disclosure requirements if the financial statements are amended after the signing of the audit report?
3. What are the auditor's duties if the financial statements are revised after signing the audit report?

(*b*) **Responses to issues:**

- As the audit report was signed on 04.05.2019 and financial statements amended on 08.05.2018, it appears that financial statements are not yet been issued to stakeholders. Hence, financial statements may be amended so as to incorporate any significant event which provide evidence of conditions that existed at the end of the reporting period, in accordance with Ind-AS 10 "Events after the Reporting period".

- As required by Ind-AS 10, entity shall disclose the date when the financial statements were approved for issue and who gave that approval. If the entity's owners or others have the power to amend the financial statements after issue, the entity shall disclose that fact.
- As per SA 560, "Subsequent Events", the auditor has no obligation to perform any audit procedures regarding the financial statements after the date of the auditor's report. However, when, after the date of the auditor's report but before the date the financial statements are issued, a fact becomes known to the auditor that, had it been known to the auditor at the date of the auditor's report, may have caused the auditor to amend the auditor's report, the auditor shall
  - (*i*) Discuss the matter with management and, where appropriate, those charged with governance.
  - (*ii*) Determine whether the financial statements need amendment and, if so,
  - (*iii*) Inquire how management intends to address the matter in the financial statements.
- As per SA 560 "Subsequent Events, if management amends the financial statements, the auditor shall:
  - (*a*) Extend the audit procedures to the date of the new auditor's report; and
  - (*b*) Provide a new auditor's report on the amended financial statements.
- It is also provided in SA 560 that when law, regulation or FRF does not prohibit management from restricting the amendment of financial statements to the effect of subsequent events, auditor is permitted to restrict the audit procedures on subsequent events to that amendment. In such case, the auditor shall:
  - (*a*) Amend the Audit report to include an additional date restricted to that amendment.
  - (*b*) Provide a new or amended Audit Report that includes Emphasis of Matter/Other matter Para that conveys that auditor's procedures on subsequent event are restricted solely to amendments of financial statements.

1.26 - SA 570 "GOING CONCERN"

Q.121 ABC Company files a law suit against Unlucky Company for ₹ 5 crores. The Attorney of Unlucky Company feels that the suit is without merit, so Unlucky Company merely discloses the existence of the law suit in the notes accompanying its financial statements. As an auditor of Unlucky Company, how will you deal with the situation? [May 14 (5 Marks)]

Ans. : Evaluating appropriateness of going concern assumption:

- AS 29 "Provisions, Contingent liabilities and Contingent Assets", requires that if any future event may cause a possible obligation, a provision should be made in the accounts to recognize the obligation where there is sufficient evidence that the event will occur.
- SA 570 "Going Concern" requires that the auditor shall consider whether there are events or conditions that may cast significant doubt on the entity's ability to continue as a going concern. Pending legal or regulatory proceedings against the entity that may, if successful, result in claims that the entity is unlikely to be able to satisfy is one of the example of such event.
- When the auditor concludes that the use of the going concern assumption is appropriate in the circumstances but a material uncertainty exists, the auditor shall determine whether the financial statements adequately describe the principal events or conditions that may cast significant doubt on the entity's ability to continue as a going concern and management's plans to deal with these events or conditions.
- In the instant case, ABC Company has filed a law suit against Unlucky Company for ₹ 5 crores. The attorney of Unlucky Company feels that the suit is without merit, so the company merely discloses the existence of law suit in the notes accompanying its financial statements.

Conclusion: Auditor should evaluate the source data on which basis the opinion is formed and evaluate the appropriateness of use of going concern assumption. If the auditor finds the uncertainty, he may request the management to adjust the sum of ₹ 5 crore by making provision for expenses as per AS 29. If the management does not accept the request the auditor should qualify the audit report.

Q.122 A Company's net worth is eroded and creditors are unpaid due to liquidity constraints. The management represents to the statutory auditor that the promoter's wife is expected to give an unsecured loan to meet the liquidity constraints and that negotiations are underway to secure large export orders.

[May 09 (4 Marks)]

Ans. : Appropriateness of Going Concern Assumption:

- SA 570 "Going Concern" requires that the auditor shall consider whether there are events or conditions that may cast significant doubt on the entity's ability to continue as a going concern. Eroded net worth and nonpayment to creditors are one of the examples of such event.
- As per SA 570, when events or conditions have been identified that may cast significant doubt on the entity's ability to continue as a going concern, the auditor shall obtain sufficient appropriate audit evidence to determine whether or not a material uncertainty exists through performing additional audit procedures, including consideration of mitigating factors.
- In the present case, it is subjective, but prima-facie a mere expectation of future cash flows from the promoter's wife without any firm commitment and the possibility of an export order being negotiated, may not that be sufficient appropriate audit evidence of mitigating factors for resolving the going concerns question under SA 570 "Going Concern".

Conclusion: Based on the results of evaluation of appropriateness of going concern assumption, auditor is required to modify the opinion.

Q.123 R & Co. is the statutory auditor of S Ltd. for the financial year ended on 31st March 2019, S Ltd had disclosed in the notes (Note No. X) "The state pollution control board had ordered the closure of the company's only manufacturing plant on the ground that it is environmentally damaging, which the company had challenged in a law suit. Pending the outcome of the law suit the financial statements are prepared on a going concern basis". Further the financial statements prepared by the management of S Ltd include financial statements of certain branches which are audited by other auditors. What are the reporting responsibilities of R & Co?

[May 12 (10 Marks)]

Ans. : Reporting responsibilities of Auditor:

(A) Evaluation of appropriateness of Going Concern Assumption:

- As per SA 570 "Going Concern" auditor is required to obtain sufficient appropriate audit evidence about the appropriateness of management use of going concern assumption in the preparation and presentation of financial statements and to conclude whether there is a material uncertainty about the entity's ability to continue as a going concern.
- When the auditor concludes that the use of the going concern assumption is appropriate in the circumstances but a material uncertainty exists, the auditor shall determine whether the financial statements:
  - (*a*) Adequately describe the principal events that may cast significant doubt on the entity's ability to continue as a going concern and management's plans to deal with these events or conditions; and
  - (*b*) Disclose clearly that there is a material uncertainty related to going concern and, therefore, that it may be unable to realize its assets and discharge its liabilities in the normal course of business.
- If adequate disclosure is made in the financial statements, the auditor shall express an unmodified opinion and the auditor's report shall include a separate section under the heading "**Material Uncertainty Related to Going Concern**".

Conclusion: In the present case, as disclosure is given in financial statements, R & Co. should include a separate section under the heading "**Material Uncertainty Related to Going Concern**".

(B) Reporting of Branches audited by other auditors:

- As per SA 600 "Using the work of Another Auditor", when the principal auditor has to base his opinion on the financial information of an entity as a whole relying upon the statements and reports of the other auditors, his report should state clearly the division of responsibility for the financial information of the entity by indicating the extent to which the financial information of components audited by the other auditors have been included in the financial information of the entity.

Conclusion: R & Co. should include an "Other Matter" paragraph in the audit report on this matter.

Q.124 While examining the going concern assumption of an entity, what important indications should be evaluated and examined?

or

What are the Financial indications to be considered by an auditor for evolution of the going Concern assumption? [Nov. 08 (4 Marks)]

or

Discuss the points and indications to be noted while examining and evaluating the 'Going Concern' assumption for an entity. [Nov. 17 (6 Marks)]

Or

Enumerate the Operating conditions of an entity that may cast significant doubt on the entity's ability to continue as a "Going Concern". [May 19 - Old Syllabus (4 Marks)]

Ans. : Indications to be considered while evaluating Going Concern Assumption:

SA 570 "Going Concern", requires that auditor should obtain sufficient appropriate audit evidence about the appropriateness of management's use of the going concern assumption in the preparation and presentation of the financial statements. Accordingly, when performing risk assessment procedures as required by SA 315, the auditor shall consider whether there are events or conditions that may cast significant doubt on the entity's ability to continue as a going concern. Examples of such events or conditions are:

Financial Indications

1. Net liability or net current liability position.
2. Fixed-term borrowings approaching maturity without realistic prospects of renewal or repayment; or excessive reliance on short-term borrowings to finance long-term assets.
3. Indications of withdrawal of financial support by trade payables.
4. Negative operating cash flows indicated by historical or prospective financial statements.
5. Adverse key financial ratios.
6. Substantial operating losses or significant deterioration in the value of assets used to generate cash flows.
7. Arrears or discontinuance of dividends.
8. Inability to pay trade payables on due dates.
9. Inability to comply with the terms of loan agreements.
10. Change from credit to cash-on-delivery transactions with suppliers.
11. Inability to obtain financing for essential new product development or other essential investments.

Operating Indications

1. Management intentions to liquidate the entity or to cease operations.
2. Loss of key management without replacement.
3. Loss of a major market, key customer(s), franchise, license, or principal supplier(s).
4. Labour difficulties.
5. Shortages of important supplies.
6. Emergence of a highly successful competitor.

Other Indications

1. Non-compliance with capital or other statutory requirements.
2. Pending legal or regulatory proceedings against the entity that may, if successful, result in claims that the entity is unlikely to be able to satisfy.
3. Changes in law or regulation or government policy expected to adversely affect the entity.
4. Uninsured or under insured catastrophes when they occur.

"ICAI Examiner Comments"

Most of the examinees explained only the Financial indications properly and few examinees could not highlight the operating and other indications while examining and valuating the Going concern assumption as per SA 570. Few examinees could not give the breakup of indicators and mixed up the indicators to produce the general answer.

Q.125 Yummy Ltd., dealing in manufacturing and trading of milk butter, has a benchmark in its product for so many years. Tasty Ltd., a rival company to Yummy Ltd., has introduced its new product, peanut butter.

Due to being health conscious, the consumers have shifted from milk butter to peanut butter within few months. This has result into massive loss during the year to Yummy Ltd. due to non-selling of perishable milk products. The company has also started having negative net worth.

It's production head, finance head and marketing head have also left the company. The company has no sound action plan to mitigate these situations. Kindly guide the auditor of Yummy Ltd., how he should deal with the situation.

Or

M/s T K Projects Limited, a manufacturing company in the Steel industry was allegedly involved in some irregularity relating to allotment of coal blocks for which a complaint was lodged against the company by the government. The financial institution stopped additional working capital finance which caused a financial crisis resulting in stoppage of production. The company incurred a massive loss during the year 2018-2019. There were delays in salary and other payments. Certain key managerial personnel including GM Finance and certain other employees left the company. The company has no sound action plan to mitigate these situations. Guide the statutory auditor on how he should deal with this situation.

[Nov. 15 (5 Marks)]

Ans. : Evaluation of appropriateness of Going Concern assumption:

- SA 570 "Going Concern", requires the auditor to obtain sufficient appropriate audit evidence about the appropriateness of management's use of the going concern assumption in the preparation and presentation of the financial statements and to conclude whether there is a material uncertainty about the entity's ability to continue as a going concern.
- The auditor shall evaluate management's assessment of the entity's ability to continue as a going concern. In evaluating management's assessment, the auditor shall consider whether management's assessment includes all relevant information of which the auditor is aware as a result of the audit.
- In the instant case, Yummy Ltd. (TK Projects Ltd.) has suffered massive loss. Company has also started having negative net worth and its key managerial personnel have also left the company. The company has no action plan to mitigate these situations. Thus, there are clear indications that there is danger to entity's ability to continue in future.
- Considering the fact that there is no sound plan of action from the management to mitigate these factors and to recover the company from such situations, the going concern assumption does not seems to be appropriate.

Conclusion: Auditor should ask the management for appropriate disclosure in the financial statement and include the same in his report. However, if the management fails to make adequate disclosure, the auditor should express a qualified or adverse opinion.

"ICAI Examiner Comments"

Although majority of examinees have mentioned that the going concern assumption does not seem appropriate yet some examinees failed to explain the disclosure aspects and the expression of opinion by the auditor. Some examinees wrote about liquidity proceedings. A few examinees explained consequences of fraud and reporting by auditor.

Q.126 Mr. Ram, an auditor, identified some events that cast significant doubt on the entity's ability to continue as a going concern. What are the additional procedures he should perform as per the related Standard on Auditing?

[Nov. 16 (5 Marks)]

Ans. : Additional Procedures required to be performed in case of doubt as to appropriateness of going concern:

As per SA 570 "Going Concern" when events or conditions have been identified that may cast significant doubt on the entity's ability to continue as a going concern, the auditor shall obtain sufficient appropriate audit evidence to determine whether or not a material uncertainty exists through performing additional audit procedures, including consideration of mitigating factors. These procedures shall include:

(*a*) Where management has not yet performed an assessment of the entity's ability to continue as a going concern, requesting management to make its assessment.

(*b*) Evaluating management's plans for future actions, whether the outcome of these plans is likely to improve the situation and whether management's plans are feasible in the circumstances.

(*c*) Where the entity has prepared a cash flow forecast, evaluate the reliability of the underlying data used to prepare the forecast and determine whether there is adequate support for the assumptions underlying the forecast.

(*d*) Considering whether any additional facts or information have become available since the date on which management made its assessment.

(*e*) Requesting WR from management and, where appropriate, TCWG, regarding their plans for future actions and the feasibility of these plans.

"ICAI Examiner Comments"

Though most of the examinees mentioned SA 570 correctly but failed to state the additional audit procedure.

Q.127 Toddle Limited had definite plan of its business being closed within a short period from the close of the accounting year ended on 31st March, 2019. The financial statements for the year ended 31-03-2019 had been prepared on the same basis as it had been in earlier periods with an additional note that the business of the company shall cease in near future and the assets shall be disposed of in accordance with a plan of disposal as decided by the management. The statutory auditors of the company indicated this aspect in Key Audit matters only by a reference as to a possible cessation of business and making of adjustments, if any, thereto to be made at the time of cessation only. Comment on the reporting by the statutory auditor as above. **[May 18 - New Syllabus (5 Marks)]**

Ans : Inappropriate use of Going Concern basis of accounting:

- SA 570 "Going Concern", requires the auditor to obtain sufficient appropriate audit evidence about the appropriateness of management's use of the going concern assumption in the preparation and presentation of the financial statements and to conclude whether there is a material uncertainty about the entity's ability to continue as a going concern.
- If the financial statements have been prepared using the going concern basis of accounting but, in the auditor's judgment, management's use of the going concern basis of accounting in the preparation of the financial statements is inappropriate, the auditor shall express an adverse opinion.
- It is irrelevant whether or not the financial statements include disclosure of the inappropriateness of management's use of the going concern basis of accounting.
- In the present case, company has definite plan of its business being closed within a short period from the close of accounting year. Financial Statements had been prepared on the same basis as it had been in earlier periods i.e. going concern basis. Additional note in the financial statements that business of the company shall cease in near future and the assets shall be disposed of in accordance with a plan of disposal as decided by the management is given. Statutory auditor of the company indicated this aspect in Key Audit Matters.

Conclusion: Reporting made by the statutory auditor is not correct as in this situation, based on the requirements of SA 570, an adverse opinion need to be issued.

Q.128 M/s Airlift Ltd., carrying on the business of Passenger Transportation by air is running into continuous financial losses as well as reduction in Sales due to stiff competition and frequent break down of its own aircrafts. The Financial Statements for the year ended on 31.03.2018 are to be now finalized. The Management is quite uncertain as to its ability to continue in near future and has informed the Auditors that having seized of this matter, it had constituted a committee to study this aspect and to give suggestions for recovery, if any, from this bad situation. Till the study is completed, according to the Management, the issue involves uncertainty as to its ability to continue its business and it informs the Auditor that the fact of uncertainty clamping on the "Going Concern" would suitably be disclosed in notes to accounts. State the reporting requirement if any, in the Independent Auditor's Report in respect of this matter.

[Nov. 18 - New Syllabus (5 Marks)]

Answer: Reporting Requirements in the Independent Auditor's report in respect of Going Concern:

- SA 570 "Going Concern", requires the auditor to obtain sufficient appropriate audit evidence about the appropriateness of management's use of the going concern assumption in the preparation and presentation of the financial statements and to conclude whether there is a material uncertainty about the entity's ability to continue as a going concern.

- When events or conditions have been identified that may cast significant doubt on the entity's ability to continue as a going concern, the auditor shall obtain sufficient appropriate audit evidence to determine whether or not a material uncertainty exists through performing additional audit procedures, including consideration of mitigating factors.
- When the auditor concludes that the use of the going concern assumption is appropriate in the circumstances but a material uncertainty exists, the auditor shall determine whether the financial statements:

  (*a*) Adequately describe the principal events that may cast significant doubt on the entity's ability to continue as a going concern and management's plans to deal with these events or conditions; and

  (*b*) Disclose clearly that there is a material uncertainty related to going concern and, therefore, that it may be unable to realize its assets and discharge its liabilities in the normal course of business.
- If adequate disclosure is made in the financial statements, the auditor shall express an unmodified opinion and the auditor's report shall include a separate section under the heading "Material Uncertainty Related to Going Concern" to:

  (*i*) Draw attention to the note in the financial statements that discloses the matters set out above; and

  (*ii*) State that these events or conditions indicate that a material uncertainty exists that may cast significant doubt on the entity's ability to continue as a going concern and that the auditor's opinion is not modified in respect of the matter.
- In the instant case, the auditor should disclose about the material uncertainty and express an unmodified opinion and in his audit report shall include a separate section under the heading "Material Uncertainty Related to Going Concern" to draw attention to the note in the financial statements that discloses the matters set out above; and state that these events or conditions indicate that a material uncertainty exists that may cast significant doubt on the entity's ability to continue as a going concern and that the auditor's opinion is not modified in respect of the matter.

Q.129 AQP Limited is one of the prominent players in the chemicals industry. The company is a public company domiciled in India and listed on BSE and NSE. The Company was facing extreme liquidity constraints and there were multiple indicators that casted doubt over the company's ability to continue as a going concern.

The Company was led into insolvency proceedings by consortium of banks led by PNB and the NCLT ordered the commencement of corporate insolvency process against the Company on 31 August 2017. The company invited prospective lenders, investors and others to submit their resolution plans to the Resolution Professional (RP) latest by 1 January 2018. The RP reviewed the resolution plans and ensured conformity with Insolvency and Bankruptcy Code, 2016. The compliant plans were presented to Committee on Creditors (CoC) on 2 February 2018 and the resolution plan submitted by PQR Ltd. was evaluated as highest evaluated Compliant Resolution Plan. CoC of AQP Ltd. approved the Resolution Plan submitted by PQR Ltd. on 2 March 2018. The approval of NCLT was finally obtained on 4 May 2018.

PQR Ltd. submitted detailed plans and commitments as part of the resolution plan including clearance of all outstanding debts which were leading to negative cash flows.

Please suggest how would you deal with this situation as the auditors of AQP Ltd. [MTP-March 19]

Ans. : Evaluation of Appropriateness of Going Concern Basis of Accounting:

- As per SA 570 Going Concern, if events or conditions have been identified that may cast significant doubt on the entity's ability to continue as a going concern, the auditor shall obtain sufficient appropriate audit evidence to determine whether or not a material uncertainty exists related to events or conditions that may cast significant doubt on the entity's ability to continue as a going concern (hereinafter referred to as "material uncertainty") through performing additional audit procedures, including consideration of mitigating factors.
- Additional procedures shall include:

  (*i*) Where management has not yet performed an assessment of the entity's ability to continue as a going concern, requesting management to make its assessment.

  (*ii*) Evaluating management's plans for future actions in relation to its going concern assessment, whether the outcome of these plans is likely to improve the situation and whether management's plans are feasible in the circumstances.

(*iii*) Where the entity has prepared a cash flow forecast evaluate the reliability of the underlying data generated to prepare the forecast and determine whether there is adequate support for the assumptions underlying the forecast.

(*iv*) Considering whether any additional facts or information have become available since the date on which management made its assessment.

(*v*) Requesting written representations from management and, where appropriate, those charged with governance, regarding their plans for future actions and the feasibility of these plans.

- The auditor shall evaluate whether sufficient appropriate audit evidence has been obtained regarding, and shall conclude on, the appropriateness of management's use of the going concern basis of accounting in the preparation of the financial statements.
- If events or conditions have been identified that may cast significant doubt on the entity's ability to continue as a going concern but, based on the audit evidence obtained the auditor concludes that no material uncertainty exists, the auditor shall evaluate whether, in view of the requirements of the applicable financial reporting framework, the financial statements provide adequate disclosures about these events or conditions.
- In the instant case, the approval of the resolution plan is a significant mitigating factor to counter the going concern issues of AQP Ltd. PQR Ltd. has submitted a detailed plan and commitments that has been given as part of the resolution plan which includes clearance of all outstanding debts which were leading to negative cash flows.

Conclusion: Events and conditions are mitigated effectively and there is no material uncertainty in relation to the ability of the company to continue as a going concern.

1.27 - SA 580 "WRITTEN REPRESENTATIONS"

Q.130 Explain what is meant by "Written Representations" and indicate to what extent an auditor can place reliance on such representations.

Ans. : Meaning of Written Representation:

- As per SA 580 "Written Representations" it is a written statement by management provided to the auditor to confirm certain matters or to support other audit evidence. Written representations in this context do not include financial statements, the assertions therein, or supporting books and records.
- Written representations are necessary information that the auditor requires in connection with the audit, hence they are recognized as audit evidence as a response to inquiries.
- Although written representations provide necessary audit evidence, they do not provide sufficient appropriate audit evidence on their own about any of the matters with which they deal.
- The written representations shall be in the form of a representation letter addressed to the auditor.

Extent of Reliance:

- If the auditor has concerns about the competence, integrity, ethical values or diligence of management, the auditor shall determine their effect on the reliability of representations (oral or written) and audit evidence in general.
- In particular, if written representations are inconsistent with other audit evidence, the auditor shall perform audit procedures to attempt to resolve the matter.
- If the auditor concludes that the written representations are not reliable, the auditor shall take appropriate actions, including determining the possible effect on the opinion.
- If he claims that there is sufficient doubt about integrity of management, he shall issue a disclaimer of opinion.

Q.131 State briefly the basic elements of Management Representation Letter. [Nov. 11 (2 Marks)]

Ans. : Basic Elements of a Management Representation Letter:

As per SA 580 "Written Representations", some of the basic elements of a Management Representation letter are-

(1) It is a written statement by management provided to the auditor to confirm certain matters or to support other audit evidence.

(2) It does not include financial statements, the assertions therein, or supporting books and records.

(3) The auditor shall request management to provide a written representation that it has fulfilled its responsibility for the preparation of the financial statements in accordance with the applicable financial reporting framework, including where relevant their fair presentation, as set out in the terms of the audit engagement.

(4) The written representations shall be for all financial statements and period(s) referred to in the auditor's report.

(5) The written representations shall be in the form of a representation letter addressed to the auditor.

"ICAI Examiner Comments"

The candidate mentioned the contents of Management Representation Letter instead of basic elements of it.

Q.132 In the course of audit of ABC Ltd. its management refuses to provide written representations. As an auditor what is your duty? [May 10 (4 Marks)]

Ans. : Duty of an Auditor if management refuses to provide written representations:

As per SA 580 "Written Representations", if the management does not provide one or more of the requested written representations, the auditor shall:

(*i*) Discuss the matter with management,

(*ii*) Re-evaluate the Integrity of the management and evaluate the effect that this may have on the reliability of representations (oral or written) and audit evidence in general,

(*iii*) Take appropriate actions, including determining the possible effect on the opinion in the auditor's report, and

(*iv*) Disclaim an opinion on the financial statements in accordance with SA 705 "Modifications to the Opinion in the Independent Auditor's Report".

Q.133 An auditor of Mohan Ltd. was not able to get the confirmation about the existence and value of certain machineries. However, the management gave him a certificate to prove the existence and value of the machinery as appearing in the books of account. The auditor accepted the same without any further procedure and signed the audit report. Is he right in his approach?

Or

The Auditor of PQR Pvt. Ltd. having turnover of ₹ 12 crores, was not able to get the confirmation about the existence and value of certain stock. However, a certificate from the management has been obtained regarding the existence and value of the stock at the year end. The auditor relied on the same and without any further procedure, signed the Audit Report. Is he right in his approach? [Nov. 14 (5 Marks)]

Or

While auditing a lawyer company, Mr. X, the statutory auditor of the company, was unable to get the confirmation about the existence and value of certain books existed in the library worth ₹ 35 lakhs. However, the management gave him a certificate to prove the existence and value of the books as appearing in the books of account. The auditor accepted the same without any further procedure and signed the audit report. Is he right in his approach?

Ans. : Validity of Management Representation:

- The physical verification of fixed assets (Inventory) is the primary responsibility of the management. The auditor, however, is required to examine the verification program adopted by the management. He must satisfy himself about the existence, ownership and valuation of fixed assets (inventory).
- In the case of Mohan Ltd., the auditor has not been able to verify the existence and value of some machinery (inventory) despite the verification procedure followed in routine audit. He accepted the certificate given to him by the management without making any further enquiry.
- As per SA 580 "Written Representation" the representations received from management are recognised as audit evidence, but they do not constitute Sufficient and appropriateness.
- Auditor is required to seek corroborative audit evidence from other sources inside or outside the entity, to evaluate whether such representations are reasonable and consistent with other evidences. Representation received from Management cannot be a substitute for other audit evidence that the auditor could reasonably expect to be available.

- If the auditor is unable to obtain sufficient appropriate audit evidence that he believes would be available regarding a matter, which has or may have a material effect on the financial information, this will constitute a limitation on the scope of his examination even if he has obtained a representation from management on the matter.

Conclusion: The approach adopted by the auditor is not right.

Q.134 PRSH & Co. is the statutory auditor of Make My Journey Ltd. The company is in the business of tours and travels. Annual turnover of the company is INR 2000 crores and profits are INR 190 crores. During the planning meeting of the management and the auditors, it was discussed that the management needs to provide written representation letter to the auditors for the preparation of the financial statements and for the completeness of the information provided to the auditor. At the time of closure of the audit, there has been some confusion about the requirements of the written representation letter. Management argued that representation need not be written, it can also be verbal which has been provided to the audit team during the course of their audit. Auditors have completed their documentation and hence in a way, representation based on verbal discussions with the auditors has also got documented. Auditors explained that this is mandatory to obtain written representation in accordance with the requirements of SA 580. However, still some confusion remains regarding the date and period covered by the written representation. You are required to advise about the date of and period covered by written representation in view of SA 580.

Ans. : Date of and period covered by written representation:

SA 580 "Written Representations" provides the following:

- The date of the written representations shall be as near as practicable to the date of the auditor's report. However, it should not be after the date of auditor's report. The written representations shall be for all financial statements and period(*s*) referred to in the auditor's report.
- In some circumstances it may be appropriate for the auditor to obtain a written representation about a specific assertion in the financial statements during the course of the audit. Where this is the case, it may be necessary to request an updated written representation.
- The written representations are for all periods referred to in the auditor's report because management needs to reaffirm that the written representations it previously made with respect to the prior periods remain appropriate. The auditor and management may agree to a form of written representation that updates written representations relating to the prior periods by addressing whether there are any changes to such written representations and, if so, what they are.
- Situations may arise where current management were not present during all periods referred to in the auditor's report. Such persons may assert that they are not in a position to provide some or all of the written representations because they were not in place during the period. This fact, however, does not diminish such persons' responsibilities for the financial statements as a whole. Accordingly, the requirement for the auditor to request from them written representations that cover the whole of the relevant period(*s*) still applies.

Q.135 In the course of audit of K Ltd., its auditor Mr. 'N' observed that there was a special audit conducted at the instance of the management on a possible suspicion of a fraud and requested for a copy of the report to enable him to report on the fraud aspects. Despite many reminders it was not provided. In absence of the special audit report, Mr. 'N' insisted that he be provided with at least a written representation in respect of fraud on/by the company. For this request also, the management remained silent. Please guide Mr. 'N'.

[May 14 (5 Marks)]

Ans. : Auditors Responsibilities Relating to Fraud:

- As per SA 240, "The Auditor's Responsibilities relating to Fraud in an Audit of Financial Statements", the primary responsibility for the prevention and detection of fraud rests with both those charged with governance of the entity and management. In addition, an auditor conducting an audit in accordance with SAs is responsible for obtaining reasonable assurance that the financial statements taken as a whole are free from material misstatement, whether caused by fraud or error.
- As per SA 580, "Written Representations", if management does not provide the requested written representations, the auditor shall discuss the matter with management; re-evaluate the integrity of management and evaluate the effect that this may have on the reliability of representations (oral or written) and audit evidence in general; and take appropriate actions, including determining the possible effect on the opinion in the auditor's report.
- The auditor shall disclaim an opinion on the financial statements if the auditor concludes that there is sufficient doubt about the integrity of management such that the written representations are not reliable; or management does not provide the written representations.

- In the instant case, in the course of audit of K Ltd., its auditor Mr. N observed that there was a special audit conducted at the instance of the management on a possible suspicion of fraud. Therefore, the auditor requested for special audit report, which was not provided by the management despite of many reminders. Mr. N also insisted for written representation in respect of fraud on/by the company. For this request also, management remained silent.
- Section 143(12) of Companies Act, 2013 requires that if an auditor of a company in the course of the performance of his duties as auditor, has reason to believe that an offence of fraud involving such amount or amounts as may be prescribed, is being or has been committed in the company by its officers or employees, the auditor shall report the matter to the Central Government within such time and in such manner as may be prescribed. For this purpose, Rule 13 prescribes the amount of ₹ 1 Cr. or more.
- Para 3(x) of CARO, 2016 also requires the company auditor to report whether any fraud by the company or any fraud on the company by its officers or employees has been noticed or reported during the year; If yes, the nature and the amount involved is to be indicated.

Conclusion: Auditor is required to state the facts in his report and he should also disclaim an opinion on the financial statements. In exceptional circumstances he may also consider whether it is appropriate to withdraw from engagement.

Q.136 Comment on the following: Statutory auditor of O Ltd. requested the management for a written representation in respect of obsolescence of inventory and warranty obligations recognized by the company in its financial statements. The management denied the representation on the ground that during the course of audit, all the required procedures were performed by the auditor and after obtaining sufficient appropriate audit evidence, auditor has issued a clean report. Please comment. [MTP-March 19]

Ans. : Written Representations as to Accounting Estimates:

- SA 540 "Auditing Accounting Estimates, Including Fair Value Accounting Estimates and Related Disclosures" requires the auditor to obtain written representations from the management and, where appropriate, those charged with governance whether they believe significant assumptions used in making accounting estimates are reasonable.
- Depending on the nature, materiality and extent of estimation uncertainty, written representations about accounting estimates recognised or disclosed in the financial statements may include representations:

  (*a*) About the appropriateness of the measurement processes, including related assumptions and models, used by management in determining accounting estimates in the context of the applicable FRF, and the consistency in application of the processes.

  (*b*) That the assumptions appropriately reflect management's intent and ability to carry out specific courses of action on behalf of the entity, where relevant to the accounting estimates and disclosures.

  (*c*) That disclosure related to accounting estimates are complete and appropriate under the applicable FRF.

  (*d*) That no subsequent event requires adjustment to the accounting estimates and disclosures included in the financial statements.
- For those accounting estimates not recognised or disclosed in the financial statements, written representations may also include representations about:

  (*a*) The appropriateness of the basis used by management for determining that the recognition or disclosure criteria of the applicable financial reporting framework have not been met.

  (*b*) The appropriateness of the basis used by management to overcome the presumption relating to the use of fair value set forth under the entity's applicable financial reporting framework, for those accounting estimates not measured or disclosed at fair value.

Conclusion: Management's contention on the ground that during the course of audit, all the required procedures were performed by the auditor and after obtaining sufficient appropriate audit evidence, auditor has issued a clean report, for not providing written representation is not correct. The management should provide written representations to the auditor.

Duty of the auditor if management refuses to provide written representations: Refer answer of Q. No. 132.

Q.137 **Mr. L while conducting the audit of ABC Ltd., observed that a substantial amount is recognized in respect of obsolescence of inventory and warranty obligation in the financial statements. Mr. L wants to obtain written representation from the management to determine whether the assumptions and estimates used are reasonable.**

Guide Mr. L with reference to the relevant Standard on Auditing. [Nov. 19 - New Syllabus (5 Marks)]

Ans. : Written Representations as to Accounting Estimates:

- SA 540 "Auditing Accounting Estimates, Including Fair Value Accounting Estimates and Related Disclosures" requires the auditor to obtain written representations from the management and, where appropriate, those charged with governance whether they believe significant assumptions used in making accounting estimates are reasonable.
- Depending on the nature, materiality and extent of estimation uncertainty, written representations about accounting estimates recognised or disclosed in the financial statements may include representations:
  (*a*) About the appropriateness of the measurement processes, including related assumptions and models, used by management in determining accounting estimates in the context of the applicable FRF, and the consistency in application of the processes.
  (*b*) That the assumptions appropriately reflect management's intent and ability to carry out specific courses of action on behalf of the entity, where relevant to the accounting estimates and disclosures.
  (*c*) That disclosure related to accounting estimates are complete and appropriate under the applicable FRF.
  (*d*) That no subsequent event requires adjustment to the accounting estimates and disclosures included in the financial statements.
- For those accounting estimates not recognised or disclosed in the financial statements, written representations may also include representations about:
  (*a*) The appropriateness of the basis used by management for determining that the recognition or disclosure criteria of the applicable financial reporting framework have not been met.
  (*b*) The appropriateness of the basis used by management to overcome the presumption relating to the use of fair value set forth under the entity's applicable financial reporting framework, for those accounting estimates not measured or disclosed at fair value.

1.28 - SA 600 "USING THE WORK OF ANOTHER AUDITOR"

Q.138 **"There should be sufficient liaison between a principal auditor and other auditors". Discuss the above statement and state in this context the reporting considerations, when the auditor uses the work performed by other auditor.**

Ans. : Coordination between Principal Auditor and Other Auditor:

SA 600 "Using the work of Another Auditor" applies in situation where an auditor (principal auditor), reporting on the financial information of an entity, uses the work of another auditor (other auditor) with respect to the financial information of one or more components included in the financial information of the entity. To ensure coordination among both of them, SA 600 provides the followings:

1. There should be sufficient liaison between the principal auditor and the other auditor.
2. For this purpose, the principal auditor may find it necessary to issue written communication(s) to the other auditor.
3. The other auditor, knowing the context in which his work is to be used by the principal auditor, should co-ordinate with the principal auditor.
   - Adhering to time-table.
   - Bringing to the attention of PA any significant finding.
   - Compliance with relevant statutory requirements.
   - Respond to detailed questionnaire.

Reporting Considerations:

1. When the principal auditor concludes, based on his procedures, that the work of the other auditor cannot be used and

2. The principal auditor has not been able to perform sufficient additional procedures regarding the financial information of the component audited by the other auditor,
3. The principal auditor should express a qualified opinion or disclaimer of opinion because there is a limitation on the scope of audit.

Q.139 Describe the relevance of SA 600 while auditing consolidation of Financial Statements.

[Nov. 15 (4 Marks)]

Ans. : Audit Procedure when principal auditor is using the work of another auditor:

SA 600 "Using the work of Another Auditor" guides principal auditor regarding the procedures to be performed when he is using the work of another auditor. In case of audit of Consolidated financial statements, principal auditor will used the work of auditor of subsidiary company, associates and joint venture. As per SA 600, auditor of Consolidated Financial Statements is supposed to perform the following:

(*a*) When principal auditor plans to use the work of another auditor, he should consider the professional competence of the other auditor in the context of specific assignment if the other auditor is not a member of the ICAI.

(*b*) The principal auditor should perform procedures to obtain sufficient appropriate audit evidence, that the work of the other auditor is adequate for the principal auditor's purposes, in the context of the specific assignment.

(*c*) The principal auditor should consider the significant findings of the other auditor.

(*d*) The principal auditor should document in his audit working papers the followings:

- Components audited by another;
- Audit procedures adopted and results thereof;
- Conclusion that particular component is not material;
- Manner of dealing with modification in another auditor's report.

(*e*) When the principal auditor concludes, based on his procedures, that the work of the other auditor cannot be used and the principal auditor has not been able to perform sufficient additional procedures regarding the financial information of the component audited by the other auditor, the principal auditor should express a **qualified opinion or disclaimer of opinion** because there is a limitation on the scope of audit.

(*f*) When the principal auditor has to base his opinion on the financial information of the entity as a whole relying upon the statements and reports of the other auditors, his report should state clearly the **division of responsibility** for the financial information of the entity by indicating the extent to which the financial information of components audited by the other auditors have been included in the financial information of the entity.

"ICAI Examiner Comments"

Examinees failed to explain the various aspects the principal auditor would consider while complying with the requirements of SA 600, 'Using the Work of another Auditor'. Many examinees described only consolidation of financial statements rather than using the work of another auditor.

Q.140 B Ltd. is the Subsidiary company of A Ltd. ABC & Associates has been appointed as auditor of A Ltd. for the Financial year 2017-2018 and XYZ & Associates has been appointed as auditor of B Ltd. for the year 2017-18. Explain the role of ABC & Associates and XYZ & Associates as auditors of the parent company and subsidiary respectively. **[Nov. 16 (4 Marks)]**

Ans. : Role of Auditor of Parent Company and Subsidiary Company:

SA 600 "Using the work of Another Auditor" establishes the standard when an auditor, reporting on the financial statements of a group (consolidated financial statements), uses the work of another auditor on the financial information of one or more components included in the financial statements of the entity.

Accordingly, role of auditor of parent company and subsidiary are as follows:

Role of Auditor of Parent Company:

(*a*) Consider the professional competence of Other Auditor, if Other Auditor is not a member of ICAI.

(*b*) Visit component and examine books of account, if essential.

(*c*) Obtain sufficient appropriate evidence, that work of Other Auditor is adequate for Principal Auditor's purposes.

(*d*) Discuss audit procedures applied by Other Auditor.

(*e*) Review a written summary of Other Auditor's procedures and findings through questionnaires/ checklist.

(*f*) Consider significant findings of Other Auditor and discuss audit findings with Other Auditor.

(*g*) Perform supplemental tests if necessary.

Role of Auditor of Subsidiary Company:

The auditor of subsidiary company, knowing the context in which his work is to be used by the principal auditor, should co-ordinate with the principal auditor w.r.t. following:

(*a*) Adhering to time-table.

(*b*) Bringing to the attention of PA any significant finding.

(*c*) Compliance with relevant statutory requirements.

(*d*) Respond to detailed questionnaire.

"ICAI Examiner Comments"

Examinees are not aware of the role of auditor of parent company and subsidiary company.

1.29 - SA 610 "USING THE WORK OF INTERNAL AUDITOR"

Q.141 State the important aspects to be considered by the External auditor in the evaluation of Internal Audit Function. [Nov. 08 (4 Marks)]

Or

You are appointed statutory auditor of X Ltd. X Ltd. has an internal audit system and reports for the same are given to you. Mention the factors you will consider to ensure that the said system of internal audit of X Ltd. is commensurate with the size of the company and nature of its business. [May 09 (8 Marks)]

Or

CA Mr. X, a practicing chartered accountant has been appointed as an internal auditor of Textile Ltd. He conducted the physical verification of the inventory at the year-end and handed over the report of such verification to CA Mr. Y, the statutory auditor of the Company, for his view and reporting. Can CA Mr. Y rely on such report?

Or

In the course of the statutory audit of Z Ltd, its statutory auditors, having determined that the work of internal auditor is likely to be adequate for the purpose of statutory audit, wanted to use the work of internal auditor in respect of physical verification of fixed assets. How an evaluation of this specific work done by the internal auditor can be done? [May 12, Nov. 15 (5 Marks)]

Or

Rajpanth Ltd. appointed you as its statutory auditor for the current financial year. During the course of auditing, you meticulously analysed that the work performed by company's internal auditor is likely to be adequate for the purpose of statutory audit. Consequently, you decided to use the work of internal auditor in respect of physical verification of tangible assets specifically.

State how you would evaluate the specific work performed by internal auditor to determine its adequacy and who would be responsible for expression of opinion on financial statements.

Ans. : Evaluation of Internal Audit function so as to reply on work of Internal Auditor:

SA 610 "Using the work of Internal auditors" deals with the external auditor's responsibilities regarding the work of internal auditors when the external auditor has determined, in accordance with SA 315 that the internal audit function is likely to be relevant to the audit.

For this purpose, external auditor is required to evaluate the following:

A. **Objectivity of Internal Auditor:** Objectivity refers to the ability to perform without allowing bias to override professional judgments. Factors that may affect the external auditor's evaluation include the following:

1. Organizational status of the internal audit function.
2. Conflicting responsibilities.

3. Oversight functions of TCWG w.r.t. employment decisions related to the internal audit function.
4. Constraints or restrictions placed on the internal audit function by management or TCWG.

B. **Level of Competency:** Competence of the internal audit function refers to the attainment of knowledge and skills to enable assigned tasks to be performed diligently. Factors that may affect the external auditor's determination include the following:

1. Policies for hiring, training and assigning internal auditors to internal audit engagements.
2. Adequate of technical training and proficiency in auditing of internal auditors.
3. Knowledge of internal auditors w.r.t. entity's financial reporting and the applicable FRF.
4. Membership of relevant professional bodies that oblige internal auditors to comply with the relevant professional standards.

C. **Systematic and Disciplined Approach:** Factors that may affect the external auditor's determination of whether the internal audit function applies a systematic and disciplined approach include the following:

1. Existence, adequacy and use of documented internal audit procedures.
2. Existence of appropriate quality control policies and procedures for internal audit function.

Conclusion: In the present case, if the statutory auditor is satisfied about the appropriateness of the verification, he can rely on the report but if he finds that the verification is not in order, he has to decide otherwise. The ultimate responsibility to express opinion on the financial statement is that of the statutory auditor.

"ICAI Examiner Comments"

Most of the examinees discussed how to verify fixed assets instead of explaining about evaluation be carried out of specific work done by the internal auditor. Some examinees wrote about the importance of internal audit which was not required.

Q.142 Mr. A was appointed as statutory auditor of X Ltd. X Ltd. has an internal audit system and Mr. A is of the opinion that internal auditors can be used to provide direct assistance for the purpose of statutory audit. Advise Mr. A whether he can take direct assistance of internal auditor and if yes, what are the precautions he need to take.

Or

Moon Ltd. of which you are the statutory auditor, have an internal audit being conducted by an outside agency. State the factors that weigh considerations in opting to make use of direct assistance of the internal auditors for the purpose of statutory audit.
[May 18 - New Course (4 Marks)]

Ans. : Using direct assistance of internal auditor:

As per SA 610 "Using the Work of Internal Auditor" statutory auditor can take direct assistance of internal auditor subject to following conditions:

1. The external auditor is not prohibited by law or regulation from obtaining direct assistance from internal auditors.
2. There are no significant threats to the objectivity of the internal auditor.
3. The internal auditor is sufficient competent to perform the proposed work.

Precautions to be taken while using direct assistance:

1. The external auditor shall not use internal auditors to provide direct assistance to perform procedures that:
   (*a*) Involve making significant judgments in the audit;
   (*b*) Relate to higher assessed risks of material misstatement;
   (*c*) Relate to work with which the internal auditors have been involved; or
   (*d*) Relate to decisions the external auditor makes in accordance with this SA regarding the internal audit function and the use of its work or direct assistance.
2. Prior to using internal auditors to provide direct assistance for purposes of the audit, the external auditor shall:
   (*a*) Obtain written agreement from an authorized representative of the entity that the internal auditors will be allowed to follow the external auditor's instructions, and that the entity will not intervene in the work the internal auditor performs for the external auditor; and

(*b*) Obtain written agreement from the internal auditors that they will keep confidential specific matters as instructed by the external auditor and inform the external auditor of any threat to their objectivity.

3. The external auditor shall direct, supervise and review the work performed by internal auditors on the engagement in accordance with SA 220.

Q.143 Mr. A is appointed as statutory auditor of XYZ Ltd. XYZ Ltd is required to appoint internal auditor as per statutory provisions given in the Companies Act, 2013 and appointed Mr. B as its internal auditor. The external auditor Mr. A asked internal auditor to provide direct assistance to him regarding evaluating significant accounting estimates by the management and assessing the risk of material misstatements.

(*a*) Discuss whether Mr. A, statutory auditor, can ask direct assistance from Mr. B, internal auditor as stated above in view of auditing standards.

(*b*) Will your answer be different, if Mr. A ask direct assistance from Mr. B, internal auditor with respect to external confirmation requests and evaluation of the results of external confirmation procedures?

Ans. : (*a*) Direct Assistance from Internal Auditor:

As per SA 610 "Using the Work of Internal Auditor", the external auditor shall not use internal auditors to provide direct assistance to perform procedures that involve making significant judgments in the audit. The external auditor shall not use internal auditors to provide direct assistance to perform procedures that:

(*a*) Involve making **significant judgments** in the audit;

Significant judgments include the following:

- Assessing the risks of material misstatement;
- Evaluating the sufficiency of tests performed;
- Evaluating the appropriateness of management's use of the going concern assumption;
- Evaluating significant accounting estimates; and
- Evaluating the adequacy of disclosures in the financial statements, and other matters affecting the auditor's report.

(*b*) Relate to higher assessed risks of material misstatement;

(*c*) Relate to work with which the internal auditors have been involved; or

(*d*) Relate to decisions the external auditor makes in accordance with this SA regarding the internal audit function and the use of its work or direct assistance.

In the present case, Mr. A asked internal auditor to provide direct assistance regarding evaluating significant accounting estimates and assessing the risk of material misstatements.

Conclusion: Evaluation of Accounting estimates and assessing Risk of Material Misstatements involve significant judgments, hence Mr. A should not insists for direct assistance in these areas.

(*b*) Direct Assistance from Internal Auditor in case of External Confirmation Procedures:

- SA 610 "Using the Work of Internal Auditor", provide relevant guidance in determining the nature and extent of work that may be assigned to internal auditors.
- In determining the nature of work that may be assigned to internal auditors, the external auditor is careful to limit such work to those areas that would be appropriate to be assigned.
- In accordance with SA 505, "External Confirmation" the external auditor is required to maintain control over external confirmation requests and evaluate the results of external confirmation procedures, it would not be appropriate to assign these responsibilities to internal auditors.

Conclusion: It would not be appropriate to use direct assistance w.r.t. obtaining external confirmation requests and their evaluation. Assistance may be used in assembling information necessary for the external auditor to resolve exceptions in confirmation responses.

Q.144 OPQ Ltd. is in the business of software consultancy. The company has had large balances of accounts receivables in the past years which have been assessed as area of high risk. For the year ended 31 March 2019, in respect of the valuation of accounts receivable, the statutory auditor has assigned the checking of the accuracy of the aging of the accounts receivables and provision based on ageing to the internal auditor providing direct assistance to him. Please advise. [MTP-April 19, RTP-May 19]

Ans. : Direct Assistance from Internal Auditor:

As per SA 610 "Using the Work of Internal Auditor", the external auditor shall not use internal auditors to provide direct assistance to perform procedures that involve making significant judgments in the audit. The external auditor shall not use internal auditors to provide direct assistance to perform procedures that:

(*a*) Involve making significant judgments in the audit;

(*b*) Relate to higher assessed risks of material misstatement;

(*c*) Relate to work with which the internal auditors have been involved; or

(*d*) Relate to decisions the external auditor makes in accordance with this SA regarding the internal audit function and the use of its work or direct assistance.

In the present case, Statutory auditor assigned internal auditor to provide direct assistance regarding checking of the accuracy of the aging of the accounts receivables and provision based on ageing. Valuation of accounts receivable is assessed as an area of higher risk.

Conclusion: Statutory auditor could assign the checking of the accuracy of the aging to an internal auditor providing direct assistance. However, because the evaluation of the adequacy of the provision based on the aging would involve more than limited judgment, it would not be appropriate to assign that latter procedure to an internal auditor providing direct assistance.

1.30 - SA 620 "USING THE WORK OF AUDITOR'S EXPERT"

Q.145 What are the factors that may influence the auditor's decision on whether to use an auditor's expert, when management has used a management's expert in preparing the financial statements?

Ans : Factors influencing the auditor's decision w.r.t. use of auditor's expert when management had used a management expert:

SA 620 "Using the work of an Auditor's Expert" deals with the auditor's responsibilities regarding the use of an individual or organisation's work in a field of expertise other than accounting or auditing, when that work is used to assist the auditor in obtaining sufficient appropriate audit evidence. Accordingly, factors influencing the auditor's decision w.r.t. use of auditor's expert when management had used a management expert are:

1. The nature, scope and objectives of the management's expert's work.
2. Whether the management's expert is employed by the entity, or is a party engaged by it to provide relevant services.
3. The extent to which management can exercise control or influence over the work of the management's expert.
4. The management's expert's competence and capabilities.
5. Whether the management's expert is subject to technical performance standards or other professional or industry requirements.
6. Any controls within the entity over the management's expert's work.

Q.146 While doing audit, Ram, the Auditor requires reports from experts for the purpose of audit evidence. What types of reports/opinions he can obtain and to what extent he can rely upon the same?

[Nov. 10 (4 Marks)]

Ans. : Types of Reports/Opinion:

As per SA 620, "Using the work of an Auditor's Expert", the auditor can obtain the following types of reports, or opinions or statements of an expert for the purpose of audit evidence:

1. The valuation of complex financial instruments, land and buildings, plant and machinery, jewellery, works of art, antiques, intangible assets, assets acquired and liabilities assumed in business combinations and assets that may have been impaired.
2. The actuarial calculation of liabilities associated with insurance contracts or employee benefit plans.
3. The estimation of oil and gas reserves.
4. The valuation of environmental liabilities, and site clean-up costs.
5. The interpretation of contracts, laws and regulations.
6. The analysis of complex or unusual tax compliance issues.

Extent to which Expert work can be relied upon:

When the auditor intends to use the work of an expert, he shall evaluate the adequacy of the auditor's expert's work, w.r.t. the following:

1. **Findings and Conclusions**: To ensure the evaluate the relevance and reasonableness of that expert's findings or conclusions, and their consistency with other audit evidence;
2. **Significant Assumptions and Methods**: If the expert's work involves use of significant assumptions and methods, the relevance and reasonableness of those assumptions and methods should be evaluated;
3. **Source Data used**: Auditor is required to evaluate the relevance, completeness, and accuracy of that source data.

If the auditor determines that the work of the auditor's expert is not adequate for the auditor's purposes, he shall agree with that expert on the nature and extent of further work to be performed by that expert; or perform further audit procedures appropriate to the circumstances.

Q.147 X Ltd had a net worth of INR 1300 crores because of which Ind AS became applicable to them. The company had various derivative contracts - options, forward contracts, interest rate swaps etc. which were required to be fair valued for which company got the fair valuation done through an external third party. The statutory auditors of the company involved an auditor's expert to audit valuation of derivatives. Auditor and auditor's expert were new to each other i.e. they were working for the first time together but developed a good bonding during the course of the audit. The auditor did not enter into any formal agreement with the auditor's expert. Please advise. [MTP-Oct. 18]

Answer: Agreement with Auditor's Expert:

- As per SA 620 "Using work of Auditor's Expert" the auditor shall agree, in writing when appropriate, on the following matters with the auditor's expert:
  1. Nature, scope & objectives of Auditor's Expert work (may include relevant technical standards or other professional and industry requirements).
  2. Respective roles & responsibilities of auditors & Auditor Expert.
  3. Nature, timing & extent of communication, including form of report.
  4. Need for Auditor Expert to observe confidentiality requirements under ethical requirements or Law and regulation.
- In the instant case X Ltd. had various derivative contracts - options, forward contracts, interest rate swaps etc. which were required to be fair valued for which company got the fair valuation done through an external third party. The statutory auditors of the company involved an auditor's expert to audit valuation of derivatives.

Conclusion: Considering the complexity involved in the valuation and volume of derivatives and also due to the fact that the auditor and auditor's expert were new to each other, auditor should have signed a formal agreement/engagement letter with the auditor's expert in respect of the work assigned to him in accordance with SA 620.

Q.148 Mr. Mohan, an auditor of KTEN Limited wants to use the work of an expert. With reference to the Standard on Auditing state the factors which suggest the need for details and written agreement between the auditor and the auditor's expert. [Nov. 16 (5 Marks)]

Ans. : Factors suggesting detailed and written agreement between the auditor and the auditor's expert:

As per SA 620 "Using work of Auditor's Expert" the auditor shall agree, in writing when appropriate, on the following matters with the auditor's expert:

1. Nature, scope & objectives of Auditor's Expert work (may include relevant technical standards or other professional and industry requirements).
2. Respective roles & responsibilities of auditors & Auditor Expert.
3. Nature, timing & extent of communication, including form of report.
4. Need for Auditor Expert to observe confidentiality requirements under ethical requirements or Law and regulation.

Factors suggesting detailed and written agreement between the auditor and the auditor's expert may be listed as follows:

1. The auditor's expert will have access to sensitive or confidential entity information.

2. The respective roles or responsibilities of the auditor and the auditor's expert are different from those normally expected.
3. Multi-jurisdictional legal or regulatory requirements apply.
4. The matter to which the auditor's expert's work relates is highly complex.
5. The auditor has not previously used work performed by that expert.
6. The greater the extent of the auditor's expert's work, and its significance in the context of the audit.

"ICAI Examiner Comments"

Majority of the examinees failed to state the factors necessitating the need for detailed agreement. Resulting in below average performance.

Q.149 State what may be the evaluative or review procedures that the Statutory Auditor may do before concluding as to relevance and reasonableness of Auditor's Expert work for using it for his audit purposes.

[Nov. 18-New Syllabus (5 Marks)]

Or

CA Dabu has been appointed as an auditor of M/s MAP Technocraft Ltd. to conduct statutory audit. While conducting audit, he came across some difficulties which the management could not explain to him properly and, therefore, he decided to take services of Mr. Jay, an engineering consultant. Mr. Jay performed his work and submitted details to CA Dabu. State the specific procedure which CA Dabu should follow to evaluate the adequacy of work performed by Mr. Jay. **[May 19-New Syllabus (5 Marks)]**

Ans.: Evaluation of Work of Auditor's expert:

- As per SA 620 "Using the work of an Auditor's Expert" the auditor shall evaluate the adequacy of the auditor's expert's work for the auditor's purposes, including:
  - (*a*) The **relevance and reasonableness** of that expert's **findings or conclusions**, and their **consistency** with other audit evidence;
  - (*b*) If that expert's work involves use of significant **assumptions and methods**, the **relevance and reasonableness** of those assumptions and methods in the circumstances; and
  - (*c*) If that expert's work involves the use of **source data** that is significant to that expert's work, the **relevance, completeness, and accuracy** of that source data.
- Specific procedures to evaluate the adequacy of the auditor's expert's work for the auditor's purposes may include:
  - (*a*) Inquiries of the auditor's expert.
  - (*b*) Reviewing the auditor's expert's working papers and reports.
  - (*c*) Corroborative procedures, such as:
    - Observing the auditor's expert's work;
    - Examining published data, such as statistical reports from reputable, authoritative sources;
    - Confirming relevant matters with third parties;
    - Performing detailed analytical procedures; and
    - Re-performing calculations.
      - (*a*) Discussion with another expert with relevant expertise when, for example, the findings or conclusions of the auditor's expert are not consistent with other audit evidence.
      - (*b*) Discussing the auditor's expert's report with management.

Q.150 What are the procedures to be followed by a statutory auditor for verifying the provisions for accrued liability for retirement benefits which is based on a certificate of a reputed actuary engaged by the auditor for the purpose.

Or

Explain the procedures to be performed for evaluating the work of auditor's expert.

Ans. : Evaluation of Work of Auditor's expert:

- As per SA 620 "Using the work of an Auditor's Expert" the auditor shall evaluate the adequacy of the auditor's expert's work for the auditor's purposes, including:

(a) The **relevance and reasonableness** of that expert's **findings or conclusions**, and their **consistency** with other audit evidence;

(b) If that expert's work involves use of significant **assumptions and methods**, the **relevance and reasonableness** of those assumptions and methods in the circumstances; and

(c) If that expert's work involves the use of **source data** that is significant to that expert's work, the **relevance, completeness, and accuracy** of that source data.

◆ If the auditor determines that the work of the auditor's expert is not adequate for the auditor's purposes, the auditor shall:

(a) Agree with that expert on the nature and extent of further work to be performed by that expert; or

(b) Perform further audit procedures appropriate to the circumstances.

Q.151 State your views on reference to an expert in the Auditor's report.

Ans. : Reference of Expert in Auditor's Report:

(a) SA 620 "Using the work of an Auditor's Expert" deals with the auditor's responsibilities regarding the use of an individual or organisation's work in a field of expertise other than accounting or auditing, when that work is used to assist the auditor in obtaining sufficient appropriate audit evidence.

(b) With respect to reference of Expert in Auditor's Report, SA 620 provides the following:

- The auditor shall not refer to the work of an auditor's expert in an auditor's report containing an unmodified opinion unless required by law or regulation to do so.
- If such reference is required by law or regulation, the auditor shall indicate in the auditor's report that the reference does not reduce the auditor's responsibility for the audit opinion.

(c) If the auditor makes reference to the work of an auditor's expert in the auditor's report because such reference is relevant to an understanding of a modification to the auditor's opinion, the auditor shall indicate in the auditor's report that such reference does not reduce the auditor's responsibility for that opinion.

Q.152 O Ltd. is in the business of manufacturing of steel. The manufacturing process requires raw material as iron ore for which large stock was maintained by the company at year end - 31 March 2019. The nature of raw material is such that its physical verification requires involvement of an expert. Management hired their expert for stock take and auditors also involved auditor's expert for the stock take.

The auditor observed that the work of the auditor's expert was not adequate for auditor's purposes and the auditor could not resolve the matter through additional audit procedures which included further work performed by both the auditor's expert and the auditor.

Basis above, the auditor concluded that it would be necessary to express a modified opinion in the auditor's report because the auditor has not obtained sufficient appropriate audit evidence. However, the auditor issued a clean report and included the name of the expert in his report to reduce his responsibility for the audit opinion. Comment.

Ans. : Auditor's responsibility in case of use of work of Auditor's Expert:

◆ As per SA 620, "Using the work of an Auditor's Expert", if the auditor concludes that the work of the auditor's expert is not adequate for the auditor's purposes and the auditor cannot resolve the matter through the additional audit, which may involve further work being performed by both the expert and the auditor, or include employing or engaging another expert, it may be necessary to express a modified opinion in the auditor's report in accordance with SA 705 because the auditor has not obtained sufficient appropriate audit evidence.

◆ In addition, the auditor shall not refer to the work of an auditor's expert in an auditor's report containing an unmodified opinion unless required by law or regulation to do so. If such reference is required by law or regulation, the auditor shall indicate in the auditor's report that the reference does not reduce the auditor's responsibility for the audit opinion.

◆ If the auditor makes reference to the work of an auditor's expert in the auditor's report because such reference is relevant to an understanding of a modification to the auditor's opinion, the auditor shall indicate in the auditor's report that such reference does not reduce the auditor's responsibility for that opinion.

Conclusion: The auditor cannot reduce his responsibility by referring the name of auditor's expert and thereby issuing a clean report. Auditor should have issued a modified report and could have given reference to the work of an auditor's expert in that report if such reference was relevant to understanding of a modification to the auditor's opinion but even in that case the auditor should have indicated in his report that such reference of auditor's expert does not reduce his responsibility for that opinion.

1.31 - SA 700 "FORMING AN OPINION AND REPORTING ON FINANCIAL STATEMENTS"

Q.153 Enumerate the basic elements of Audit Report as enshrined in SA 700.

Ans. : Basic Elements of the Auditor's Report:

As per SA 700 "Forming an Opinion and Reporting on Financial Statements", the auditor's report includes the following basic elements:

1. **Title:** Audit Report should have a title clearly stating that it is a report of an independent auditor.
2. **Addressee:** Audit Report is normally addressed to those for whom Audit Report is prepared, i.e. shareholders or TCWG.
3. **Opinion Section:** This section states the auditor's opinion on true and fair view of financial statements. Opinion Section of the Auditor's Report shall also cover the following:
   - Identify the entity whose FS have been audited.
   - State that Financial Statements have been audited.
   - Identify title of each statement that comprises F.S.
   - Refer to the notes, including the summary of significant accounting policies; and
   - Specify date of period covered by each Financial Statement.
4. **Basis for Opinion Section:** The auditor's report shall include a section, directly following the Opinion section, with the heading "Basis for Opinion", that:

   (*a*) States that the audit was conducted in accordance with SA;

   (*b*) Refers to the section of the auditor's report that describes the auditor's responsibilities under the SAs;

   (*c*) Includes a statement that the auditor is independent of the entity in accordance with the relevant ethical requirements relating to the audit, and has fulfilled the auditor's other ethical responsibilities in accordance with these requirements. The statement shall refer to the Code of Ethics issued by ICAI;

   (*d*) States whether the auditor believes that the audit evidence the auditor has obtained is sufficient and appropriate to provide a basis for the auditor's opinion.
5. **Going Concern**: Where applicable, the auditor shall report in accordance with SA 570.
6. **Key Audit matters**: For audits of complete set of general purpose F.S. of listed entities, the auditor shall communicate key audit matters in the auditor's report in accordance with SA 701.
7. **Other Information**: Where applicable, the auditor shall report in accordance with SA 720.
8. **Management's Responsibility for the Financial Statements:** Describe responsibility of Management for preparation of Financial Statements in the manner in which responsibility is described in Terms of Engagement.
9. **Auditor's Responsibility Section:** It shall state the auditor's objectives to obtain reasonable assurance about whether the F.S. as a whole are free from material misstatement, whether due to fraud or error; and to Issue an auditor's report that includes the auditor's opinion. This section also enumerates the auditor's responsibilities as prescribed under different Standards on Auditing.
10. **Other Reporting Responsibilities:** This Section covers reporting over those additional matters on which auditor is required to report under statutory requirements.
11. **Signature of the Auditor:** Audit report to be signed in auditor's personal name. Where firm appointed as auditor, report signed in personal name & in name of audit firm.
12. **Date of Auditor's Report:** It should not be earlier than date on which auditor has obtained Sufficient Appropriate Audit Evidence on which to base auditor's opinion.
13. **Place of signature:** It is ordinarily the city where audit report is signed.

Q.154 What is included in Auditor's Responsibility Paragraph? [May 17 (5 Marks)]

Ans. : Auditor's Responsibility Paragraph:

As per SA 700 "Forming an Opinion and Reporting on Financial Statements", the auditor's responsibility paragraph shall state the following:

(*a*) State that the objectives of the auditor are to obtain reasonable assurance about whether the F.S. as a whole are free from material misstatement, whether due to fraud or error and issue an auditor's report that includes the auditor's opinion.

(*b*) State that reasonable assurance is a high level of assurance, but is not a guarantee that an audit will always detect a material misstatement when it exists.

(*c*) State that misstatements can arise from fraud or error and will be considered when appears material in accordance with the applicable FRF.

(*d*) State that, as part of an audit in accordance with SAs, the auditor exercises professional judgment and maintains professional skepticism throughout the audit.

(*e*) Describe an audit by stating that the auditor's responsibilities are:

(*i*) To identify and assess the Risk of Material Misstatements of the Financial statements, whether due to fraud or error;

(*ii*) To design and perform audit procedures responsive to those risks;

(*iii*) To obtain audit evidence that is sufficient and appropriate to provide a basis for the auditor's opinion.

(*iv*) To obtain an understanding of internal control relevant to the audit in order to design audit procedures that are appropriate in the circumstances.

(*v*) To evaluate the appropriateness of accounting policies used and the reasonableness of accounting estimates and related disclosures made by management.

(*vi*) To conclude on the appropriateness of management's use of the going concern basis of accounting.

"ICAI Examiner Comments"

Many candidates were able to highlight only few matters included in Auditor's Responsibility paragraph. Some candidates unnecessarily discussed about Management's responsibility instead of Auditor's responsibility

Q.155 Write short note on: Unqualified opinion in the context of the Auditor's report. [May 09 (4 Marks)]

Ans. : Unqualified opinion:

SA 700 "Forming an opinion and Reporting on Financial Statements" requires the auditor to express an unqualified opinion when he concludes that the financial statements give a true and fair view in accordance with the financial reporting framework used for preparation and presentation of the financial statements.

An unqualified opinion indicates the following:

1. The financial statements have been prepared using the generally accepted accounting principles and being constantly followed.
2. The financial statements comply with relevant statutory requirements and regulations.
3. All material matters relevant to proper presentation of the financial information, subject to statutory requirement, if applicable, have been adequately disclosed.

Q.156 KPI Ltd. is a company on which International Standards on Auditing are applicable along with Standard on Auditing issued by the ICAI. The company appointed new auditors for the audit of the financial statements for the year ended 31 March, 2020 after doing all appointment formalities. In the auditor's report, auditor referred the International Standard on Auditing in addition to the Standard on Auditing issued by the ICAI.

As an expert, you are required to advise the auditor regarding auditor's report for audits conducted in accordance with both the Standards. [RTP-Nov. 19]

Ans. : Auditor's Report for Audits conducted in accordance with both Standards on Auditing issued by ICAI and International Standards on Auditing:

As per SA 700, "Forming an Opinion and Reporting on Financial Statements", an auditor may be required to conduct an audit in accordance with the International Standards on Auditing, in addition to the Standards on Auditing issued by ICAI. If this is the case, the auditor's report may refer to Standards on Auditing in addition to the International Standards on Auditing, but the auditor shall do so only if:

(*a*) There is no conflict between the requirements in the International Auditing Standards and those in SAs that would lead the auditor:

- to form a different opinion, or
- not to include an Emphasis of Matter paragraph or Other Matter paragraph that, in the particular circumstances, is required by SAs; and

(*b*) The auditor's report includes, at a minimum, each of the elements set out in Auditor's Report Prescribed by Law or Regulation discussed above when the auditor uses the layout or wording specified by the Standards on Auditing.

When the auditor's report refers to both the ISAs and the Standards on Auditing issued by ICAI, the auditor's report shall clearly identify the same including the jurisdiction of origin of the other auditing standards.

1.32 - SA 701 "COMMUNICATING KEY AUDIT MATTERS IN THE INDEPENDENT AUDITOR'S REPORT"

Q.157 Write a short note on: Purpose of communicating key audit matters. [RTP - Nov.18]

Answer: Purpose of communicating key audit matters:

As per SA 701 "Communicating Key Audit matters in the Independent Auditor's Report" Key Audit Matters are those matters that, in the auditor's professional judgment, were of most significance in the audit of the F.S. of the current period. Key audit matters are selected from matters communicated with TCWG.

Various purposes of Key audit matters may be listed as:

1. To enhance the communicative value of the auditor's report by providing greater transparency about the audit that was performed.
2. To provide additional information to intended users of the financial statements to assist them in understanding those matters that, in the auditor's professional judgment, were of most significance in the audit of the F.S. of the current period.
3. To assist intended users in understanding the entity and areas of significant management judgment in the audited F.S.
4. To provide a basis to further engage with management and TCWG about certain matters relating to the entity, the audited F.S. or the audit that was performed.

Q.158 Mr. A was appointed as statutory auditor of X Ltd. While doing audit, Mr. A is required to determine the key audit matters which are required to be mentioned in the audit report. You are required to advise Mr. A about the considerations which Mr. A shall take into account while determining key audit matters.

Or

As an auditor of a listed company for the year ended 31st March, 2019, how would you determine the 'Key Audit Matters'? [May 19 - Old Syllabus (5 Marks)]

Ans. : Considerations to determine Key Audit Matters:

As per SA 701 "Communicating Key Audit matters in the Independent Auditor's Report" Key Audit Matters are those matters that, in the auditor's professional judgment, were of most significance in the audit of the F.S. of the current period. Key audit matters are selected from matters communicated with TCWG.

The auditor shall determine, from the matters communicated with TCWG, those matters that required significant auditor attention in performing the audit. In making this determination, the auditor shall consider the following:

(*a*) Areas of higher assessed RMM, or significant risks identified in accordance with SA 315;

(*b*) Significant auditor judgments relating to areas in the F.S. that involved significant management judgment, including accounting estimates that have been identified as having high estimation uncertainty.

(c) The effect on the audit of significant events or transactions that occurred during the period.

The auditor shall determine which of the matters so determined above were of most significance in the audit of the F.S. of the current period and therefore are the key audit matters.

Q.159 CA. Amar has come across certain key matters while auditing the accounts of PR Ltd. for the financial year 2017-18. He, being the associate of your firm, seeks your advice on "Communicating Key Audit Matters" in the Auditor's report. Guide him.

[Nov. 18-Old Syllabus (5 Marks)]

Answer: Communicating Key Audit Matters:

- As per SA 701 "Communicating Key Audit matters in the Independent Auditor's Report" Key Audit Matters are those matters that, in the auditor's professional judgment, were of most significance in the audit of the F.S. of the current period. Key audit matters are selected from matters communicated with TCWG.
- The auditor shall describe each key audit matter, using an appropriate sub-heading, in a separate section of the auditor's report under the heading "Key Audit Matters".
- The introductory language in this section of the auditor's report shall state that:
  (a) Key audit matters are those matters that, in the auditor's professional judgment, were of most significance in the audit of the financial statements of the current period; and
  (b) These matters were addressed in the context of the audit of the F.S. as a whole, and in forming the auditor's opinion thereon, and the auditor does not provide a separate opinion on these matters.
- The description of each key audit matter in the Key Audit Matters section of the auditor's report shall include a reference to the related disclosure(s), if any, in the F.S. and shall address:
  (a) Why the matter was considered to be one of most significance in the audit and therefore determined to be a key audit matter; and
  (b) How the matter was addressed in the audit.
- The auditor shall describe each key audit matter in the auditor's report unless:
  (i) Law or regulation precludes public disclosure about the matter; or
  (ii) In extremely rare circumstances, the auditor determines that the matter should not be communicated in the auditor's report because the adverse consequences of doing so would reasonably be expected to outweigh the public interest benefits of such communication. This shall not apply if the entity has publicly disclosed information about the matter.
- The auditor shall not communicate a matter in the Key Audit Matters section of the auditor's report when the auditor would be required to modify the opinion in accordance with SA 705 (Revised) as a result of the matter.

Q.160 State the circumstances in which a matter determined to be a key audit matter is not required to be communicated in the Auditor's Report.

Ans. : Circumstances in which key audit matters not required to be communicated:

As per SA 701 "Communicating Key Audit matters in the Independent Auditor's Report" Key Audit Matters are those matters that, in the auditor's professional judgment, were of most significance in the audit of the F.S. of the current period. Key audit matters are selected from matters communicated with TCWG.

The auditor shall describe each key audit matter in the auditor's report unless:

(a) Law or regulation precludes public disclosure about the matter; or

(b) In extremely rare circumstances, the auditor determines that the matter should not be communicated in the auditor's report because the adverse consequences of doing so would reasonably be expected to outweigh the public interest benefits of such communication. This shall not apply if the entity has publicly disclosed information about the matter.

Q.161 The property, plant and equipment of ABC Ltd. included Rs. 25.75 crores of earth removing machines of outdated technology which had been retired from active use and had been kept for disposal after knock down. These assets appeared at residual value and had been last inspected ten years back. As an auditor, what may be your reporting concern as regards matters specified above?

[May 18 - New Syllabus (5 Marks)]

Ans : Reporting Concerns in relation to significant events:

Auditor is required to report under the various requirements of Standards of Auditing, legal and Regulatory provisions. In the present situation, major reporting requirements will be:

(*a*) As per the requirement of SA 260 "Communication with Those Charged with Governance" auditor should communicate significant matters arising during the audit that were discussed, or subject to correspondence, with management.

(*b*) The situation as given in the question appears to be a Key Audit Matter and hence auditor is required to report the situation in the audit report as Key Audit Matter.

(*c*) Further as per requirement of Para 3(i) of CARO, 2016, auditor is required to comment

(*i*) Whether the company is maintaining proper records showing full particulars, including quantitative details and situation of fixed assets

(*ii*) Whether the fixed assets have been physically verified by the management at reasonable intervals. In the present case, physical verification of assets held under disposal.

Conclusion: In the present case, auditor reporting concerns will be as per the requirement of SA 260, SA 701 and Para 3(i) of CARO, 2016.

Alternative Ans : Answer of this question may also be based on the reporting issues like Valuation, Accounting and Disclosures as per the requirements of applicable FRF. In that case, if auditor is not satisfied with the valuation, accounting and disclosures, he may qualify the report as per the requirements of SA 705.

Q.162 AKY Ltd. is a listed company engaged in the business of software and is one of the largest company operating in this sector in India. The company's annual turnover is ₹ 40,000 crores with profits of ₹ 5,000 crores. Due to the nature of the business and the size of the company, the operations of the company are spread out in India as well as outside India. The company's contracts with its various customers are quite complicated and different. During the course of the audit, the audit team spends significant time on audit of revenue - be it planning, execution or conclusion. This matter was also discussed with management at various stages of audit. The efforts towards audit of revenue also involve significant involvement of senior members of the audit team including the audit partner. After completion of audit for the year ended 31 March 2019, the audit partner was discussing significant matters with the management wherein they also communicated to the management that he plans to include revenue recognition as key audit matter in his audit report. The management did not agree with revenue recognition to be shown as key audit matter in the audit report. Comment. [MTP - Oct. 19]

Ans. : Determining Key Audit Matters:

SA 701, "Communicating Key Audit Matters in the Independent Auditor's Report", deals with the auditor's responsibility to communicate key audit matters in the auditor's report. As per SA 701, the auditor shall determine, from the matters communicated with TCWG, those matters that required significant auditor attention in performing the audit. In making this determination, the auditor shall take into account the following:

(*i*) Areas of higher assessed risk of material misstatement, or significant risks identified in accordance with SA 315 Identifying and Assessing the Risks of Material Misstatement through Understanding the Entity and Its Environment.

(*ii*) Significant auditor judgments relating to areas in the financial statements that involved significant management judgment, including accounting estimates that have been identified as having high estimation uncertainty.

(*iii*) The effect on the audit of significant events or transactions that occurred during the period.

The auditor shall determine which of the matters determined in accordance with above were of most significance in the audit of the financial statements of the current period and therefore are the key audit matters.

In the instant case, AKY Ltd., a listed company engaged in the business of software and its contracts with its various customers are also quite complicated and different. Further, the audit team spends significant time on audit of revenue and efforts towards audit of revenue also involve significant involvement of senior members of the audit team including audit partner during audit. This matter was also discussed with management at various stages. After completion of audit, the audit partner communicated the management regarding inclusion of paragraph on revenue recognition as key audit matter in his audit report.

Conclusion: Assessment of the auditor is valid as concerned matter qualifies to be a key audit matter; hence, it should be reported accordingly by the auditor in his audit report.

1.33 - SA 705 "MODIFICATIONS TO THE OPINION IN THE INDEPENDENT AUDITOR'S REPORT"

Q.163 When should an auditor make a disclaimer opinion in his Audit report? [May 09 (5 Marks)]

Ans. : Disclaimer of Opinion:

SA 705 "Modification to the Opinion in the Independent Auditor's Report" requires the auditor to disclaim an opinion

- when the auditor is unable to obtain sufficient appropriate audit evidence on which to base the opinion, and
- the auditor concludes that the possible effects on the financial statements of undetected misstatements, if any, could be both material and pervasive.

If auditor disclaims the opinion auditor is required to add a para in the audit report "Basis for Disclaimer of Opinion Para" describing therein the auditor's inability to collect the sufficient appropriate audit evidence.

Auditor is also required to amend the description of auditor's responsibility para as "Our responsibility is to express an opinion on the financial statements based on conducting the audit in accordance with Standards on Auditing issued by the ICAI. Because of the matter(s) described in the Basis for Disclaimer of Opinion paragraph, however, we were not able to obtain sufficient appropriate audit evidence to provide a basis for an audit opinion".

Q.164 Under the applicable Standards on Auditing, in what circumstances does the report of the statutory auditor require modifications? What are the types of modifications possible to the said report?

[Nov. 12 (8 Marks)]

Or

Explain the circumstances which require a modification to the Auditor's Opinion. [Nov. 17 (6 Marks)]

Or

If financial statements prepared in accordance with the requirements of a fair presentation framework do not achieve fair presentation, the auditor shall discuss the matter with management and, depending on the requirements of the applicable financial reporting framework and how the matter is resolved, shall determine whether it is necessary to modify the opinion in the auditor's report in accordance with SA 705.

Under SA 705, in what circumstances does the report of the statutory auditor require modifications? What are the types of modifications possible in the said report?

Or

ADKS & Co. LLP are the newly appointed statutory auditors of PKK Ltd. During the course of audit, the statutory auditors have come across certain significant observations which they believe could lead to material misstatement of financial statements. Management has a different view and does not concur with the view of the statutory auditors. Considering this the statutory auditors are determining as to how to address these observations in terms of their reporting requirement. Please advise.

Ans. : Circumstances in which a modified opinion may be issued:

As per SA 705 "Modifications to the Opinion in the Independent Auditor's Report" a modified opinion may be expressed in the following circumstances:

(*a*) The auditor concludes that, based on the audit evidence obtained, the *F.S. as a whole are not free from material misstatement,* may be due to following reasons:

- Inappropriate method of selection of Accounting Policies;
- Accounting policies are not consistent with applicable FRF;
- Disclosures as required by FRF are not given.

(*b*) The auditor is unable *to obtain sufficient appropriate audit evidence* to conclude that the financial statements as a whole are free from material misstatement, may be due to following reasons:

- Limitations imposed by management
- Circumstances beyond entity control (For Ex.: Accounting records destroyed by fire)
- Circumstances related to Nature and Timing of auditor's work.

Types of Modified Opinion:

(*a*) **Qualified opinion**: It is issued under following circumstances:

- Financial statements are materially misstated which in the auditor's judgments are not pervasive.
- Auditor is unable to obtain Sufficient and appropriate audit evidence which in the auditor judgment are not pervasive

(*b*) **Adverse Opinion**: It is issued when financial statements are materially misstated which in the auditor's judgments is having pervasive effect.

(*c*) **Disclaimer of Opinion**: It is issued when auditor is unable to obtain Sufficient and appropriate audit evidence which in the auditor judgment are having pervasive effect.

Q.165 After accepting the statutory audit of M/s All in One Ltd., a departmental store, you became aware of the fact that management of the company have imposed certain limitations on the scope of your assurance function which may adversely affect and result in your inability to obtain sufficient appropriate audit evidence to discharge your responsibility required by the statute. Indicate the consequences and your response to the limitations imposed by the management on your scope. [May 19 - New Syllabus (4 Marks)]

Ans. : Limitation after the auditor has accepted the engagement:

- As per SA 705 "Modifications to the Opinion in the Independent Auditor's Report", if, after accepting the engagement, the auditor becomes aware that management has imposed a limitation on the scope of the audit that the auditor considers likely to result in the need to express a qualified opinion or to disclaim an opinion on the financial statements, the auditor shall request that management remove the limitation.
- If management refuses to remove the limitation, the auditor shall communicate the matter to those charged with governance, unless all of those charged with governance are involved in managing the entity, and determine whether it is possible to perform alternative procedures to obtain sufficient appropriate audit evidence.
- If the auditor is unable to obtain sufficient appropriate audit evidence, the auditor shall determine the implications as follows:

  (*a*) If the auditor concludes that the possible effects on the financial statements of undetected misstatements, if any, could be material but not pervasive, the auditor shall qualify the opinion; or

  (*b*) If the auditor concludes that the possible effects on the financial statements of undetected misstatements, if any, could be both material and pervasive so that a qualification of the opinion would be inadequate to communicate the gravity of the situation, the auditor shall:

  (*i*) Withdraw from the audit, where practicable and possible under applicable law or regulation; or

  (*ii*) If withdrawal from the audit before issuing the auditor's report is not practicable or possible, disclaim an opinion on the financial statements.
- If the auditor withdraws, before withdrawing, the auditor shall communicate to those charged with governance any matters regarding misstatements identified during the audit that would have given rise to a modification of the opinion.

Q.166 "When the auditor modifies the audit opinion, the auditor shall use the heading "Qualified Opinion," "Adverse Opinion," or "Disclaimer of Opinion," as appropriate, for the Opinion section." As an expert you are required to brief the special considerations required for expressing:

(*a*) Qualified Opinion;

(*b*) Adverse Opinion and

(*c*) Disclaimer of Opinion. [RTP-Nov. 18]

Ans. : Special Considerations required for modified opinion:

(*a*) Special consideration required for expressing Qualified Opinion:

When the auditor expresses a qualified opinion due to a material misstatement in the financial statements, the auditor shall state that, in the auditor's opinion, except for the effects of the matter(*s*) described in the Basis for Qualified Opinion section:

(*i*) **When reporting in accordance with a fair presentation framework**, the accompanying financial statements present fairly, in all material respects (or give a true and fair view of) [...] in accordance with [the applicable FRF]; or (*ii*) **When reporting in accordance with a compliance framework**, the accompanying financial statements have been prepared, in all material respects, in accordance with [the applicable FRF].

When the modification arises from an inability to obtain sufficient appropriate audit evidence, the auditor shall use the corresponding phrase "except for the possible effects of the matter(*s*) ..." for the modified opinion.

(*b*) **Special consideration needed for expressing Adverse Opinion:**

When the auditor expresses an adverse opinion, the auditor shall state that, in the auditor's opinion, because of the significance of the matter(*s*) described in the Basis for Adverse Opinion section:

(*i*) **When reporting in accordance with a fair presentation framework**, the accompanying financial statements do not present fairly (or give a true and fair view of) [...] in accordance with [the applicable FRF]; or

(*ii*) **When reporting in accordance with a compliance framework**, the accompanying financial statements have not been prepared, in all material respects, in accordance with [the applicable FRF].

(*c*) **Special consideration is required for expressing Disclaimer of Opinion:** When the auditor disclaims an opinion due to an inability to obtain sufficient appropriate audit evidence, the auditor shall:

(*i*) State that the auditor does not express an opinion on the accompanying financial statements;

(*ii*) State that, because of the significance of the matter(*s*) described in the Basis for Disclaimer of Opinion section, the auditor has not been able to obtain sufficient appropriate audit evidence to provide a basis for an audit opinion on the financial statements; and

(*iii*) Amend the statement required in SA 700 (Revised), which indicates that the financial statements have been audited, to state that the auditor was engaged to audit the financial statements.

Unless required by law or regulation, when the auditor disclaims an opinion on the financial statements, the auditor's report shall not include a Key Audit Matters section in accordance with SA 701.

Q.167 **"The Company has been unable to re-negotiate or obtain replacement financing. This situation indicates the existence of a material uncertainty that may cast significant doubt on the Company's ability to continue as a going concern and therefore, the Company may be unable to realize its assets and discharge its liabilities in the normal course of business. The financial statements (and notes thereto) do not fully disclose this fact." You are required to identify the type of opinion and draft the same.**

Ans. : Type of Opinion to be expressed:

As per SA 570 "Going Concern" if adequate disclosure about the material uncertainty is not made in the F.S., the auditor shall:

(*a*) Express a qualified opinion or adverse opinion, as appropriate, in accordance with SA 705; and

(*b*) In the Basis for Qualified (Adverse) Opinion section of the auditor's report, state that a material uncertainty exists that may cast significant doubt on the entity's ability to continue as a going concern and that the F.S. do not adequately disclose this matter.

In the present case, Company has been unable to re-negotiate or obtain replacement financing. This situation indicates the existence of a material uncertainty that may cast significant doubt on the Company's ability to continue as a going concern and therefore, the Company may be unable to realize its assets and discharge its liabilities in the normal course of business. The financial statements (and notes thereto) do not fully disclose this fact. This situation requires the auditor to express a qualified opinion.

Draft Opinion Para:

In our opinion, except for the incomplete disclosure of the information referred to in the Basis for Qualified Opinion paragraph, the financial statements give the information required by the Companies Act, 2013, in the manner so required and give a true and fair view in conformity with the accounting principles generally accepted in India:

a. in the case of the Balance Sheet, of the state of affairs of the company as at March 31, 20X1;

b. in the case of the Profit and Loss Account, of the profit/loss for the year ended on that date; and

c. in the case of the cash flow statement, of the cash flows for the year ended on that date.

Q.168 **"The Company's financing arrangements expired and the amount outstanding was payable on March 31, 20X0. The Company has been unable to re-negotiate or obtain replacement financing and is considering filing for bankruptcy. These events indicate a material uncertainty that may cast significant doubt on the Company's ability to continue as a going concern and therefore it may be unable to realize its assets and discharge its liabilities in the normal course of business. The financial statements (and notes thereto) do not disclose this fact." You are required to identify the type of opinion and draft the same.**

Ans. : Type of Opinion to be expressed:

As per SA 570 "Going Concern" If the financial statements have been prepared using the going concern basis of accounting but, in the auditor's judgment, management's use of the going concern basis of accounting in the preparation of the F.S. is inappropriate, the auditor shall express an adverse opinion.

In the present case, financing arrangements of the company expired and the Company has been unable to re-negotiate or obtain replacement financing and is considering filing for bankruptcy. This indicates that going concern of the entity is not maintainable. Under these situations, auditor is required to express an adverse opinion as per SA 705.

Draft Opinion Para:

In our opinion, because of the omission of the information mentioned in the Basis for Adverse Opinion paragraph, the financial statements do not give the information required by the Companies Act, 2013, in the manner so required and also, do not give a true and fair view in conformity with the accounting principles generally accepted in India:

(*a*) in the case of the Balance Sheet, of the state of affairs of the company as at March 31, 20X0; and

(*b*) in the case of the Profit and Loss Account, of the profit/loss for the year ended on that date; and

(*c*) in the case of the cash flow statement, of the cash flows for the year ended on that date.

Q.169 **As an auditor of ABC Limited, in view of given circumstances, you are required to draft qualified opinion and basis for qualified opinion due to the departure from the applicable Financial Reporting Framework:**

- **Audit of a complete set of financial statements of a company other than a listed company (registered under the Companies Act, 2013) using a fair presentation framework.**
- **The financial statements are prepared by management of the entity in accordance with the Accounting Standards prescribed under section 133 of the Companies Act, 2013 (a general purpose framework).**
- **The terms of the audit engagement reflect the description of management's responsibility for the financial statements in SA 210.**
- **A departure from the applicable financial reporting framework resulted in a qualified opinion.**
- **The relevant ethical requirements that apply to the audit are the ICAI's Code of Ethics and the provisions of the Companies Act, 2013.**
- **Based on the audit evidence obtained, the auditor has concluded that a material uncertainty does not exist related to events or conditions that may cast significant doubt on the entity's ability to continue as a going concern in accordance with SA 570 (Revised).**
- **Between the date of the financial statements and the date of the auditor's report, there was a fire in the entity's production facilities, which was disclosed by the entity as a subsequent event. In the auditor's judgment, the matter is of such importance that it is fundamental to users' understanding of the financial statements. The matter did not require significant auditor attention in the audit of the financial statements in the current period.**
- **The auditor is not required, and has otherwise not decided, to communicate key audit matters in accordance with SA 701.**
- **Those responsible for oversight of the financial statements differ from those responsible for the preparation of the financial statements.**
- **In addition to the audit of the financial statements, the auditor has other reporting responsibilities required under the Companies Act, 2013.**

Answer: Qualified Opinion:

We have audited the standalone financial statements of ABC Limited ("the Company"), which comprise the balance sheet as at March 31, 20X1, and the statement of Profit and Loss, (statement of changes in equity) and the statement of cash flows for the year then ended, and notes to the financial statements, including a summary of significant accounting policies and other explanatory information (in which are included the Returns for the year ended on that date audited by the branch auditors of the Company's branches located at (*location of branches*))2.

In our opinion and to the best of our information and according to the explanations given to us, except for the effects of the matter described in the *Basis for Qualified Opinion* section of our report, the aforesaid financial statements present fairly, in all material respects, or *give a true and fair view* in conformity with the accounting principles generally accepted in India of the state of affairs of the Company as at March 31st, 2XXX and profit/loss, (*changes in equity*) and its cash flows for the year ended on that date.

Basis for Qualified Opinion

The Company's short-term marketable securities are carried in the statement of financial position at xxx. Management has not marked these securities to market but has instead stated them at cost, which constitutes a departure from the Accounting Standards prescribed in section 133 of the Companies Act, 2013. The Company's records indicate that had management marked the marketable securities to market, the Company would have recognized an unrealized loss of Rs. xxx in the statement of comprehensive income for the year. The carrying amount of the securities in the statement of financial position would have been reduced by the same amount at March 31, 20X1, and income tax, net income and shareholders' equity would have been reduced by Rs. xxx, Rs. xxx and Rs. xxx, respectively.

We conducted our audit in accordance with Standards on Auditing (SAs). Our responsibilities under those standards are further described in the *Auditor's Responsibilities for the Audit of the Financial Statements* section of our report. We are independent of the Company in accordance with the ethical requirements that are relevant to our audit of the financial statements under the provisions of the Companies Act, 2013, and we have fulfilled our other ethical responsibilities in accordance with these requirements and the ICAI's Code of Ethics. We believe that the audit evidence we have obtained is sufficient and appropriate to provide a basis for our qualified opinion.

Q.170 **As an auditor of XYZ Limited, in view of given circumstances, you are required to draft Adverse Opinion and basis for adverse opinion due to a Material Misstatement of the Consolidated Financial Statements.**

- **Audit of a complete set of consolidated financial statements of a listed company (incorporated under the Companies Act, 2013) using a fair presentation framework. The audit is a group audit of an entity with subsidiaries (i.e., SA 600 applies).**
- **The consolidated financial statements are prepared by management of the entity in accordance with the Accounting Standards prescribed under section 133 of the Companies Act, 2013 (a general purpose framework).**
- **The terms of the audit engagement reflect the description of management's responsibility for the consolidated financial statements in SA 210.**
- **The consolidated financial statements are materially misstated due to the non-consolidation of a subsidiary. The material misstatement is deemed to be pervasive to the consolidated financial statements. The effects of the misstatement on the consolidated financial statements have not been determined because it was not practicable to do so (i.e., an adverse opinion is appropriate).**
- **The relevant ethical requirements that apply to the audit are the ICAI's Code of Ethics and the provisions of the Companies Act, 2013.**
- **Based on the audit evidence obtained, the auditor has concluded that a material uncertainty does not exist related to events or conditions that may cast significant doubt on the entity's ability to continue as a going concern in accordance with SA 570 (Revised).**
- **SA 701 applies; however, the auditor has determined that there are no key audit matters other than the matter described in the Basis for Adverse Opinion section.**
- **Those responsible for oversight of the consolidated financial statements differ from those responsible for the preparation of the consolidated financial statements.**
- **In addition to the audit of the consolidated financial statements, the auditor has other reporting responsibilities required under the Companies Act, 2013.**

Answer: Adverse Opinion:

We have audited the accompanying consolidated financial statements of XYZ Company Limited (hereinafter referred to as the "Holding Company") and its subsidiaries (the Holding Company and its subsidiaries together referred to as "the Group"), its associates and jointly controlled entities, which comprise the consolidated balance sheet as at March 31, 2XXX, the consolidated statement of profit and Loss, (*consolidated statement of changes in equity*){*where applicable*} and the consolidated statement of cash flows for the year then ended, and notes to the consolidated financial statements, including a summary of significant accounting policies (hereinafter referred to as the "consolidated financial statements").

In our opinion and to the best of our information and according to the explanations given to us, because of the significance of the matter discussed in the *Basis for Adverse Opinion* section of our report, the accompanying consolidated financial statements do not give a true and fair view in conformity with the accounting principles generally accepted in India, of their consolidated state of affairs of the Group, its associates and jointly controlled entities, as at March 31, 20XX, of its consolidated profit/loss, (*consolidated position of changes in equity*) {*where applicable*} and the consolidated cash flows for the year then ended.

Basis for Adverse Opinion

As explained in Note X, the Group has not consolidated subsidiary PQR Company that the Group acquired during 20XX because it has not yet been able to determine the fair values of certain of the subsidiary's material assets and liabilities at the acquisition date. This investment is therefore accounted for on a cost basis. Under the accounting principles generally accepted in India, the Group should have consolidated this subsidiary and accounted for the acquisition based on provisional amounts. Had PQR Company been consolidated, many elements in the accompanying consolidated financial statements would have been materially affected. The effects on the consolidated financial statements of the failure to consolidate have not been determined.

We conducted our audit in accordance with Standards on Auditing (SAs) specified under section 143(10) of the Companies Act, 2013. Our responsibilities under those Standards are further described in the *Auditor's Responsibilities for the Audit of the Consolidated Financial Statements* section of our report. We are independent of the Group, its associates and jointly controlled entities, in accordance with the Code of Ethics and provisions of the Companies Act, 2013 that are relevant to our audit of the consolidated financial statements in India under the Companies Act, 2013, and we have fulfilled our other ethical responsibilities in accordance with the Code of Ethics and the requirements under the Companies Act, 2013. We believe that the audit evidence we have obtained is sufficient and appropriate to provide a basis for our adverse opinion.

Q.171 As an auditor of ABC Limited, in view of given circumstances, you are required to draft disclaimer of opinion and basis for disclaimer of opinion due to the Auditor's Inability to Obtain Sufficient Appropriate Audit Evidence about Multiple Elements of the Financial Statement.

- **Audit of a complete set of financial statements of an entity other than a company incorporated under the Companies Act, 2013, using a fair presentation framework. The audit is not a group audit (i.e., SA 600, does not apply).**
- **The financial statements are prepared by management of the entity in accordance with the Accounting Standards issued by the Institute of Chartered Accountants of India (a general purpose framework).**
- **The terms of the audit engagement reflect the description of management's responsibility for the financial statements in SA 210.**
- **The auditor was unable to obtain sufficient appropriate audit evidence about multiple elements of the financial statements, that is, the auditor was also unable to obtain audit evidence about the entity's inventories and accounts receivable. The possible effects of this inability to obtain sufficient appropriate audit evidence are deemed to be both material and pervasive to the financial statements.**
- **The relevant ethical requirements that apply to the audit are ICAI's Code of Ethics and applicable law/regulation**
- **Those responsible for oversight of the financial statements differ from those responsible for the preparation of the financial statements.**
- **A more limited description of the auditor's responsibilities section is required.**
- **In addition to the audit of the financial statements, the auditor has other reporting responsibilities required under relevant law/regulation.**

Ans. : Disclaimer of Opinion:

We were engaged to audit the financial statements of ABC & Associates ("the entity"), which comprise the balance sheet as at March 31, 20XX, the statement of Profit and Loss, *(the statement of changes in equity)* (*where applicable*) and statement of cash flows for the year then ended, and notes to the financial statements, including a summary of significant accounting policies.

We do not express an opinion on the accompanying financial statements of the entity. Because of the significance of the matters described in the *Basis for Disclaimer of Opinion* section of our report, we have not been able to obtain sufficient appropriate audit evidence to provide a basis for an audit opinion on these financial statements.

Basis for Disclaimer of Opinion

We were not appointed as auditors of the Company until after March 31, 20X1 and thus did not observe the counting of physical inventories at the beginning and end of the year. We were unable to satisfy ourselves by alternative means concerning the inventory quantities held at March 31, 20X0 and 20X1, which are stated in the Balance Sheets at ₹ xxx and ₹ xxx, respectively. In addition, the introduction of a new computerized accounts receivable system in September 20X1 resulted in numerous errors in accounts receivable. As of the date of our report, management was still in the process of rectifying the system deficiencies and correcting the errors. We were unable to confirm or verify by alternative means accounts receivable included in the Balance Sheet at a total amount of ₹ xxx as at March 31, 20X1. As a result of these matters, we were unable to determine whether any adjustments might have been found necessary in respect of recorded or unrecorded inventories and accounts receivable, and the elements making up the statement of Profit and Loss (*and statement of cash flows*) (*Where applicable*).

Q.172 As an auditor of a company registered under section 8 of the Companies Act, 2013 you find that as per the notification of the Ministry of Corporate Affairs regarding applicability of Indian Accounting Standards (Ind-AS), the company has to prepare its financial statements for the year ended 31st March, 2017 under Ind-AS. The management of the company is however of the strong view that being a section 8 company having charitable objects, Ind-AS cannot apply to the company. The financial statements are therefore prepared by the management under the earlier GAAP and a note for the same is given in the financial statements. How would you report on these financial statements?

[Nov. 17 (5 Marks), Nov. 19 - New Syllabus (5 Marks)]

Ans. : Reporting on financial statements:

As per SA 200 "Overall Objectives of the Independent Auditor and Conduct of Audit in accordance with Standards on Auditing" in conducting an audit of financial statements, the overall objectives of the auditor are:

(*a*) To obtain reasonable assurance about whether the F. S. as a whole are free from material misstatement, whether due to fraud or error, thereby enabling the auditor to express an opinion on whether the F.S. are prepared, in all material respects, in accordance with an applicable FRF, and

(*b*) To report on the F.S. and communicate as required by the SAs, in accordance with the auditor's findings.

In all cases when reasonable assurance cannot be obtained and a qualified opinion in the auditor's report is insufficient, the SAs require that the auditor disclaim an opinion or withdraw from the engagement.

In the present case, company was required to prepare its financial statements as per Ind-AS, but the financial statements are being prepared under the earlier GAAP. FRF followed by the company is not acceptable.

Conclusion: Financial reporting framework applied by the management is unacceptable and hence auditor is required to disclaim the opinion in accordance with SA 705 or withdraw from the engagement.

Note: Answer given in Suggested Answer of ICAI is based on the provisions of Sec. 129 and Sec. 133 and specifies that the auditor is required to ensure applicable monetary limits w.r.t. Ind-AS and advise the management to prepare the F.S. as per Ind-AS.

Answer given in suggested answer does not seems to be appropriate as requirement of question was how the auditor report on such financial statements, whereas answer is given on applicability of Ind-AS as per legal requirements of company law.

Examiner comment on this answer was: Examinees did not discuss the requirements of section 133 and section 129 of the Companies Act, 2013, that Companies registered u/s 8 are not exempted from the complying with Ind AS while preparation of their financial statements. Only selected examinees mentioned that the auditor is required to ensure the applicable monetary limits with respect to applicability of Ind-AS. Few examinees answered wrongly in the pretext on applicability of the Accounting standards to Charitable organisation whereas the question is on the applicability of Ind-AS to section 8 companies.

1.34 - SA 706 "EMPHASIS OF MATTER PARAGRAPH AND OTHER PARAGRAPHS IN THE INDEPENDENT AUDITOR'S REPORT"

Q.173 Write short note on: Emphasis of Matter paragraph in Audit Report.

Ans. : Emphasis of Matter Para in Audit Report:

- As per 706 "Emphasis of Matter Paragraphs and Other Matter Paragraphs in the Independent Auditor's Report" Emphasis of Matter is a paragraph which is included in auditor's report to draw users' attention to important matter(s) which are already disclosed in Financial Statements and are fundamental to users' for understanding of Financial Statements.

- EOM is used when there is a uncertainty relating to future outcome of exceptional litigation, regulatory action, etc.; or there is early application (where permitted) of a new accounting standard that has a pervasive effect on the financial statements in advance of its effective date.
- Auditor shall include an Emphasis of Matter paragraph in the auditor's report provided:
  (*a*) The auditor would not be required to modify the opinion in accordance with SA 705 as a result of the matter; and
  (*b*) When SA 701 applies, the matter has not been determined to be a key audit matter to be communicated in the auditor's report.
- When the auditor includes an EOM paragraph in the auditor's report, the auditor shall:
  (*a*) Include the paragraph within a separate section of the auditor's report with an appropriate heading that includes the term "Emphasis of Matter";
  (*b*) Include in the paragraph a clear reference to the matter being emphasized and to where relevant disclosures that fully describe the matter can be found in the financial statements. The paragraph shall refer only to information presented or disclosed in the financial statements; and
  (*c*) Indicate that the auditor's opinion is not modified in respect of the matter emphasized.

Q.174 Beta Limited, is a company registered with SEBI, having five subsidiaries. M/s XYZ, Chartered Accountants, have been appointed as Statutory Auditors for the audit of the Consolidated Financial Statements for the year ending March 31, 2017. Out of five subsidiaries, the audit of one subsidiary was conducted by another auditor, M/s Badnam and Company, Chartered Accountants. The "Opinion" para of audit report furnished by M/s XYZ Chartered Accountants is given below:

Opinion

In Our opinion and to the best of our information and according to the explanations given to us the consolidated financial statements give a true and fair view, except the financial statement of one subsidiary whose accounts were audited by M/s Badnam and company, Chartered Accountants and about the same we are not in a position to express our opinion as the audit has not been performed by us:

(*i*) In the case of the consolidated Balance Sheet, of the state of affairs of the company as at March 31, 2017.

(*ii*) In the case of the consolidated profit and loss account, of the profit/loss for the year ended on that date

Do you find any deficiencies in the opinion para? If yes, you are required to give your suggestions and redraft the opinion para. [Nov. 13 (5 Marks)]

Ans. : Identification of deficiencies in opinion Para:

The opinion para contains the following deficiencies:

1. Out of five subsidiaries, the audit of one subsidiary was conducted by another auditor, M/s Badnam and Company - needs to be reported in other matter para.
2. Opinion regarding cash flow statement has not been covered.

As per SAs 700 & 706 the redrafted opinion para and other matter para are given hereunder:

Opinion Para

In our opinion and to the best of our information and according to the explanations given to us and based on the consideration of the reports of the other auditors on the financial statements of the subsidiaries as noted below, the consolidated financial statements give a true and fair view in conformity with the accounting principles generally accepted in India:

(*a*) in the case of the consolidated Balance Sheet, of the state of affairs of the Company as at March 31, 2017;

(*b*) in the case of the consolidated Profit and Loss Account, of the profit/loss for the year ended on that date; and

(*c*) in the case of the consolidated Cash Flow Statement, of the cash flows for the year ended on that date.

Other Matter Para

We did not audit the financial statements of one subsidiary, whose financial statements reflect total assets (net) of XXXX as at March 31, 2017, total revenues of XXXX and net cash outflows amounting to XXXX for the year then ended. These financial statements have been audited by other auditor's M/s Badnam and Company, Chartered Accountants whose reports have been furnished to us by the Management, and our opinion is based solely on the reports of the other auditors. Our opinion is not qualified in respect of this matter.

Q.175 Compare and Explain the following: Audit Qualification and Emphasis of Matter. [Nov. 14 (3 Marks)]

Ans. : Audit Qualification and Emphasis of Matter:

- SA 705 "Modifications to the Opinion in the Independent Auditor's Report", deals with the provisions relating to Audit Qualification. Audit Qualifications are given when auditor is having reservations on some of the items out of the financial statements.
- It is issued under following circumstances:
  - (*i*) Financial statements are materially misstated which in the auditor's judgments are not pervasive.
  - (*ii*) Auditor is unable to obtain Sufficient and appropriate audit evidence which in the auditor judgment are not pervasive
- As per SA 706 "Emphasis of Matter Paragraphs and Other Matter Paragraphs in the Independent Auditor's Report" Emphasis of Matter is a paragraph which is included in auditor's report to draw users' attention to important matter(s) which are already disclosed in Financial Statements and are fundamental to users' for understanding of Financial Statements.
- EOM is used when there is an uncertainty relating to future outcome of exceptional litigation, regulatory action, etc.; or there is early application (where permitted) of a new accounting standard that has a pervasive effect on the financial statements in advance of its effective date.

Q.176 D Ltd., a Delhi based company having turnover of ₹ 25 crores, has a branch at USA having a turnover of ₹ 10 lakhs (as converted from US dollars). The area where the branch office is located in USA was severely affected by storms and the office along with all accounting records was completely destroyed. Due to the unavailability of records, the financial statements of D Ltd. for the financial year 2018-19 did not include the figures pertaining to the said branch. As the statutory auditor of D Ltd., how will you report on the same? [Nov. 17 (5 Marks)]

Ans. : Reporting on financial statements when information of component is not included:

- As per SA 200 "Overall Objectives of the Independent Auditor and Conduct of Audit in accordance with Standards on Auditing" in conducting an audit of financial statements, the overall objective of the auditor is to obtain reasonable assurance about whether the financial statements as a whole are free from material misstatement, whether due to fraud or error, thereby enabling the auditor to express an opinion on whether the financial statements are prepared, in all material respects, in accordance with an applicable FRF. In all cases when reasonable assurance cannot be obtained and a qualified opinion in the auditor's report is insufficient, the SAs require that the auditor disclaim an opinion or withdraw from the engagement.
- In the present case, D Ltd., a Delhi based company having turnover of ₹ 25 crores, has a branch at USA having a turnover of ₹ 10 lakhs (as converted from US dollars). The area where the branch office is located in USA was severely affected by storms and the office along with all accounting records was completely destroyed. Due to the unavailability of records, the financial statements of D Ltd. for the financial year 2018-19 did not include the figures pertaining to the said branch.
- In the present situation, company is required to make appropriate disclosures in the notes to accounts in this regard. Based on the disclosures made in the financial statements, auditor is required to include an Emphasis of Matter Para in the auditor's report as per requirement of SA 706. If, however no disclosure is made in the financial statements, auditor need to qualify the audit report as turnover of the branch is only ₹ 10 lakhs which does not seems to have pervasive effect as the total turnover of the company is ₹ 25 Crores.

Conclusion: If appropriate disclosures are given in Notes to Accounts, an unmodified opinion with Emphasis of Matter para need to be issued. However, if appropriate disclosures are not given in Notes to Accounts, auditor should qualify the report in accordance with SA 705.

Note: Answer given in Suggested Answer of ICAI is based on the provisions of Sec. 143(8) and specifies who can conduct branch audit.

Answer given in suggested answer does not seems to be appropriate as requirement of question was how the auditor report, whereas content of answer is primarily on the basis of who can conduct branch audit.

In a case where branch records are not available, then there is no logic of mentioning the provisions relating to the concept of branch audit. Answer need to be given from perspective of company auditor, how to deal in such a situation.

Examiner comment on this answer was: Examinees lacked knowledge in applying the required provisions of the Companies Act, 2013 to the given question. Few examinees have misunderstood the question and explained SA 600 on 'Using the Work of Another Auditor'.

Q.177 Enumerate certain important matters which can be included in 'Emphasis of Matter Paragraph' in an Auditor's Report. [Nov. 19 - Old syllabus (5 Marks)]

Ans. : Matters which can be included in Emphasis of Matter Paragraph in Auditor's Report:

- As per 706 "Emphasis of Matter Paragraphs and Other Matter Paragraphs in the Independent Auditor's Report" Emphasis of Matter is a paragraph which is included in auditor's report to draw users' attention to important matter(*s*) which are already disclosed in Financial Statements and are fundamental to users' for understanding of Financial Statements.
- Matters which can be included in 'Emphasis of Matter Paragraph' in an Auditor's Report, may be listed as below:
  (*a*) An uncertainty relating to the future outcome of an exceptional litigation or regulatory action.
  (*b*) A significant subsequent event that occurs between the date of the financial statements and the date of the auditor's report.
  (*c*) Early application (where permitted) of a new accounting standard that has a pervasive effect on the financial statements in advance of its effective date.
  (*d*) A major catastrophe that has had, or continues to have, a significant effect on the entity's financial position.

1.35 - SA 710 "COMPARATIVE INFORMATION - CORRESPONDING FIGURES AND COMPARATIVE FINANCIAL STATEMENTS"

Q.178 Write short note on: Corresponding Figures. [May 13 (4 Marks)]

Ans. : Refer answer of Q. No. 179

Q.179 What are the auditor's responsibilities in respect of corresponding figures? [May 10 (4 Marks)]

Or

Write short notes on the following: Auditor's responsibilities regarding comparatives.

Ans. : Auditor's Procedures in respect of examination of corresponding figures:

1. SA 710 "Comparative Information - Corresponding Figure and Comparative Financial Information" deals with the auditor's responsibilities regarding comparative information in an audit of financial statements.
2. The term Corresponding Figures refers to Comparative information where amounts and other disclosures for the prior period, are included as an ***integral part of current period F.S.***, and are intended to be read only in relation to the amounts and other disclosures relating to the current period.
3. To examine the corresponding figures, auditor is required to perform the following procedures:
   (*a*) Determine whether F.S. include Comparative information required by FRF & whether such information is classified appropriately.
   (*b*) Evaluate the following:
   - Whether the comparative information agrees with the amounts and other disclosures presented in the prior period; and
   - Whether the accounting policies reflected in the comparative information are consistent with those applied in the current period.
   - Whether, changes in accounting policies, if any, have been properly accounted for and adequately presented and disclosed.

(c) In case, auditor has doubt over existence of Possible Material Misstatement, then auditor is required to perform additional audit procedures to obtain sufficient appropriate audit evidence to determine existence of material misstatement.

(d) Obtain Written Representation from management to re-affirm that the Written Representation it previously made with respect to the prior period remain appropriate.

Q.180 The audit report of P Ltd. for the year 2017-18 contained a qualification regarding non-provision of doubtful debts. As the statutory auditor of the company for the year 2018-19, how would you report, if:

(a) The company does not make provision for doubtful debts in 2018-19?

(b) The company makes adequate provision for doubtful debts in 2018-19?

[May 09 (8 Marks), Nov. 14 (5 Marks)]

Or

For the year ended 31st March, 2018, the audit report of Avinash Ltd., contained a qualification regarding non-provision for diminution in the value of investments to the extent of Rs. 50 lacs. As an Auditor of the Company for the year 2018-19, how would you report, if:

(i) The Company does not make provision for diminution in the value of investments in the year 2018-2019.

(ii) The Company makes adequate provision for diminution in the year 2018-2019.

[May 18 – Old Syllabus (5 Marks)]

Ans. : Auditor's responsibilities w.r.t. Corresponding figures:

- As per SA 710, "Comparative Information - Corresponding Figures and Comparative Financial Statements" When the auditor's report on the prior period, as previously issued, included a modified opinion and the matter which gave rise to the modified opinion is resolved and properly accounted for or disclosed in the financial statements in accordance with the applicable FRF, the auditor's opinion on the current period need not refer to the previous modification.
- SA 710 further states that if the auditor's report on the prior period, as previously issued, included a modified opinion and the matter which gave rise to the modification is unresolved, the auditor shall modify the auditor's opinion on the current period's financial statements.
- In the Basis for Modification paragraph in the auditor's report, the auditor shall either:

  (i) Refer to both the current period's figures and the corresponding figures in the description of the matter giving rise to the modification when the effects or possible effects of the matter on the current period's figures are material; or

  (ii) In other cases, explain that the audit opinion has been modified because of the effects or possible effects of the unresolved matter on the comparability of the current period's figures and the corresponding figures.

Conclusion:

(a) If P Ltd. does not make provision for doubtful debts the auditor will have to modify his report for both current and previous year's figures as mentioned above.

(b) If however, the provision is made, the auditor need not refer to the earlier year's modification.

Q.181 Mr. A, a practicing Chartered Accountant, audited the financial statements of C Ltd. for the previous year 2017-18 and expressed an unmodified opinion. C Ltd. was of the view that Mr. A is not conducting the audit properly and therefore, for the current year 2018-19, it appointed Ms. B, a leading practicing Chartered Accountant to conduct the audit and present Comparative Financial Statements. Ms. B, while performing the auditing procedures, found that C Ltd. has undercharged the wages of ₹ 10 lakhs during the previous year resulting in overstatement of profits. What are the further procedures, Ms. B is required to pursue?

Ans. : Auditor's Procedures in respect of examination of comparative F.S.:

1. SA 710 "Comparative Information - Corresponding Figure and Comparative Financial Information" deals with the auditor's responsibilities regarding comparative information in an audit of financial statements.
2. To examine the comparative information, auditor is required to perform the following procedures:
   - Determine whether F.S. include Comparative information required by FRF & whether such information is classified appropriately?

- Evaluate whether the comparative information agrees with the amounts and other disclosures presented in the prior period; and

3. In the present case, auditor identified material misstatement for the previous year, financial statements of which are audited by Mr. A. Ms. B Current Auditor is required to discuss the matter with the management and issue suitable report based on the action taken by the management in this regard.

Conclusion: Ms. B is required to communicate the matter to the management and request them to inform the same to Mr. A. After revision or non-revision of the prior period's financial statements, Ms. B may report accordingly.

Q.182 It was observed from the modified audit report of the financial statements of AS Ltd. for the year ended 31st March, 2017 that depreciation of Rs. 2.50 crore for the year 2016-17 had been charged off to the statement of Profit and Loss instead of including it in "Carrying value of asset under construction". State in relation to the audit for the year ended 31st March 2018, whether such modification in the previous year's audit report would have any audit implication for the current year and if yes, how would you deal with it in your audit report? [Nov. 18-Old Syllabus (5 Marks)]

Answer: Impact of Modification in the predecessor auditor's report:

- SA 710 "Comparative Information - Corresponding Figure and Comparative Financial Information deals with the auditor's responsibilities regarding comparative information in an audit of financial statements.
- As per SA 710, if the auditor's report on the prior period, as previously issued, included a modified opinion and the matter which gave rise to the modification is unresolved, the auditor shall modify the auditor's opinion on the current period's financial statements. In the Basis for Modification paragraph in the auditor's report, the auditor shall either:
  - (*a*) Refer to both the current period's figures and the corresponding figures in the description of the matter giving rise to the modification when the effects or possible effects of the matter on the current period's figures are material; or
  - (*b*) In other cases, explain that the audit opinion has been modified because of the effects or possible effects of the unresolved matter on the comparability of the current period's figures and the corresponding figures.
- Further, if the financial statements of the prior period were audited by a predecessor auditor and the auditor is permitted by law or regulation to refer to the predecessor auditor's report on the corresponding figures and decides to do so, the auditor shall state in an Other Matter paragraph in the auditor's report:
  - (*a*) That the financial statements of the prior period were audited by the predecessor auditor;
  - (*b*) The type of opinion expressed by the predecessor auditor and, if the opinion was modified, the reasons therefore; and
  - (*c*) The date of that report.
- In the instant case, it was observed from the modified audit report of the financial statements of AS Ltd. for the year ended 31st March, 2017 that depreciation of Rs. 2.50 crore for the year 2016-17 had been charged off to the statement of Profit and Loss instead of including it in "Carrying value of asset under construction".

Conclusion: Modification in the predecessor audit report will impact the current period audit report and auditor shall deal in accordance with SA 710 as mentioned above.

1.36 - SA 720 "THE AUDITOR'S RESPONSIBILITIES RELATING TO OTHER INFORMATION."

Q.183 SA 720 requires the auditor to read and consider the other information because other information that is materially inconsistent with the F.S. or the auditor's knowledge obtained in the audit may indicate that there is a material misstatement of the F.S. or that a material misstatement of the other information exists, either of which may undermine the credibility of the F.S. and the auditor's report thereon. Explain the meaning of the term Other Information and state the requirements of SA 720 as to obtaining and considering the other information.

Ans. : Other Information and Requirements of SA 720:

SA 720 "The Auditor's Responsibilities relating to Other Information" deals with the auditor's responsibilities relating to Other Information, whether financial or non-financial information included in an entity's annual report. SA 720 defines the term other information as Financial or non-financial information (other than F.S. and the auditor's report thereon) included in an entity's annual report.

Requirements of SA 720 as to obtaining the other information:

The auditor shall:

(*a*) Determine, through discussion with management, which documents comprises the annual report, and the entity's planned manner and timing of the issuance of such documents;

(*b*) Make appropriate arrangements with management to obtain in a timely manner and, if possible, prior to the date of the auditor's report, the final version of the documents comprising the annual report; and

(*c*) When some or all of the documents determined above will not be available until after the date of the auditor's report, request management to provide a written representation that the final version of the documents will be provided to the auditor when available, and prior to its issuance by the entity, such that the auditor can complete the procedures required by this SA.

Requirements of SA 720 as to considering the Other information:

The auditor shall read the other information and, in doing so shall:

(*a*) Consider whether there is a material inconsistency between the other information and the financial statements. As the basis for this consideration, the auditor shall, to evaluate their consistency, compare selected amounts or other items in the other information (that are intended to be the same as, to summarize, or to provide greater detail about, the amounts or other items in the financial statements) with such amounts or other items in the financial statements; and

(*b*) Consider whether there is a material inconsistency between the other information and the auditor's knowledge obtained in the audit, in the context of audit evidence obtained and conclusions reached in the audit.

While reading the other information, the auditor shall remain alert for indications that the other information not related to the financial statements or the auditor's knowledge obtained in the audit appears to be materially misstated.

Q.184 Comment on the following: While reading the other information, auditor finds certain misstatement of other information. Explain the requirement of relevant SA w.r.t. Auditor's responses in such a situation.

Ans. : Auditor's responses on a material misstatement in the Other Information:

- SA 720 "The Auditor's Responsibilities relating to Other Information" deals with the auditor's responsibilities relating to Other Information, whether financial or non-financial information included in an entity's annual report.
- If the auditor concludes that a material misstatement of the other information exists, the auditor shall request management to correct the other information. If management:

  (*a*) Agrees to make the correction, the auditor shall determine that the correction has been made; or

  (*b*) Refuses to make the correction, the auditor shall communicate the matter with TCWG and request that the correction be made.
- If the auditor concludes that a material misstatement exists in other information obtained prior to the date of the auditor's report, and the other information is not corrected after communicating with TCWG, the auditor shall take appropriate action, including:

  (*a*) Considering the implications for the auditor's report and communicating with TCWG about how the auditor plans to address the material misstatement in the auditor's report,

  (*b*) Withdrawing from the engagement, where withdrawal is possible under applicable law or regulation.
- If the auditor concludes that a material misstatement exists in other information obtained after the date of the auditor's report, the auditor shall:

  (*a*) If the other information is corrected, perform the procedures necessary in the circumstances; or

  (*b*) If the other information is not corrected after communicating with TCWG, take appropriate action considering the auditor's legal rights and obligations, to seek to have the uncorrected material misstatement appropriately brought to the attention of users for whom the auditor's report is prepared.

Q.185 LMP Associates, Chartered Accountants, conducting the audit of PQR Ltd., a listed Company for the year ended 31st March, 2019 is concerned with the auditor's responsibilities relating to other information, both financial and non-financial, included in the Company's annual report. While regarding other information, LMP Associates considers whether there is a material inconsistency between other. Information and the financial statements. As a basis for the consideration the auditor shall evaluate their consistency, compare selected amounts or other items in the other information with such amounts or other items in the financial statements. Guide LMP Associates with examples of "Amounts" or "other items" that may be included in the "other information" with reference to SA 720. [Nov. 19 - New Syllabus (5 Marks)]

Ans. : Reading and considering the Other information:

- SA 720 "The Auditor's Responsibilities relating to Other Information" deals with the auditor's responsibilities relating to Other Information, whether financial or non-financial information included in an entity's annual report. SA 720 defines the term other information as Financial or non-financial information (other than F.S. and the auditor's report thereon) included in an entity's annual report.
- The auditor shall read the other information and, in doing so shall consider whether there is a material inconsistency between the other information and the financial statements. As the basis for this consideration, the auditor shall, compare selected amounts or other items in the other information (that are intended to be the same as, to summarize, or to provide greater detail about, the amounts or other items in the financial statements) with such amounts or other items in the financial statements.
- Other information may include amounts or other items that are intended to be the same as, to summarize, or to provide greater detail about, the amounts or other items in the financial statements. Examples of such amounts or other items may include:

  (*a*) Tables, charts or graphs containing extracts of the financial statements.

  (*b*) A disclosure providing greater detail about a balance or account shown in the financial statements, such as "Revenue for 20X1 comprised ₹ XXX million from product X and ₹ YYY million from product Y."

  (*c*) Descriptions of the financial results, such as "Total research and development expense was ₹ XXX in 20X1."

AUDIT STRATEGY, PLANNING AND PROGRAMMING

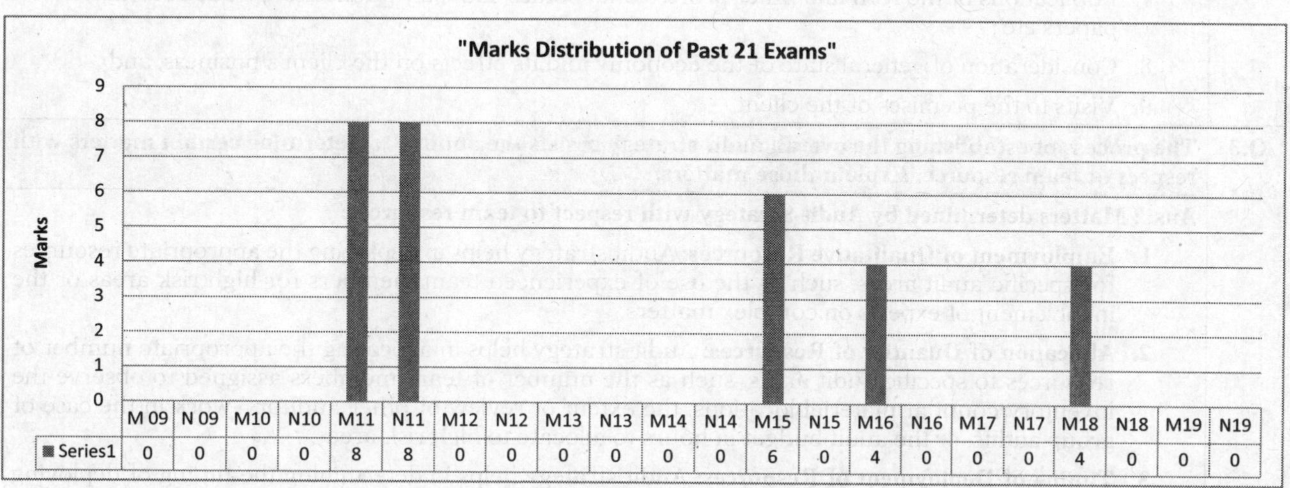

	M 09	N 09	M10	N10	M11	N11	M12	N12	M13	N13	M14	N14	M15	N15	M16	N16	M17	N17	M18	N18	M19	N19
Series1	0	0	0	0	8	8	0	0	0	0	0	0	6	0	4	0	0	0	4	0	0	0

2.1 AUDIT STRATEGY

Q.1 Designing an Audit Strategy is the back bone of the "Audit planning" process. Discuss.

Ans. : Designing an Audit Strategy:

Audit strategy is concerned with designing optimised audit approaches that seek to achieve the necessary audit assurance at the lowest cost within the constraints of the information available.

SA 300 "Planning an Audit of Financial statements" requires the auditor to establish an audit strategy that sets the scope, timing and direction of the audit.

Audit strategy is designed by following the various activities:

1. **Obtaining knowledge of business**: SA 315 requires the auditor to obtain sufficient knowledge of the business to enable him to identify and understand the events, transactions and practices that, in his judgment, may have a significant effect on the financial statements or audit report.
2. **Performing analytical procedures at initial stages**: The use of analytical procedures during the planning stage requires the extensive use of accounting and business knowledge and experience to assess the potential for material misstatement in the financial statements as a whole.
3. **Evaluating inherent risks**: To assess inherent risk, the auditor should evaluate numerous factors, having regard to his experience of the entity from previous audit engagements of the entity, controls established by management and his knowledge of any significant changes which might have taken place since his last assessment.
4. **Evaluating internal control system for strategy purposes**: For strategy purposes the auditor should obtain a sufficient understanding of the control environment. The auditor needs an understanding of the accounting systems, regardless of whether the audit strategy will involve an extended assessment of internal accounting controls.

Q.2 What are the major sources of obtaining information about the client's business.

Ans. : Major Sources of Obtaining information about Client's business:

1. Annual Reports circulated among the shareholders;
2. Minutes of meetings of shareholders, directors and their committees;
3. Internal reports over financial aspects for current and previous periods, including budgets;
4. Working Papers of previous year audits;
5. Policy and procedures Manual of the Client;
6. Discussions with the client;
7. Publications of the ICAI and other professional bodies, industry publication, trade Journals, newspapers etc.;
8. Consideration of general state of the economy and its effects on the client's business; and
9. Visits to the premises of the client.

Q.3 The process of establishing the overall audit strategy assists the auditor to determine certain matters with respect of team resource. Explain those matters.

Ans. : Matters determined by Audit Strategy with respect to team resources:

1. **Employment of Qualitative Resources:** Audit strategy helps in deploying the appropriate resources for specific audit areas, such as the use of experienced team members for high risk areas or the involvement of experts on complex matters.
2. **Allocation of Quantity of Resources:** Audit strategy helps in allocating the appropriate number of resources to specific audit areas, such as the number of team members assigned to observe the inventory count at material locations, the extent of review of other auditors' work in the case of group audits, or the audit budget in hours to allocate to high risk areas.
3. **Timing of Deployment of Resources:** Audit strategy helps in determining the timing of deploying the resources, such as whether at an interim audit stage or at key cut-off dates.
4. **Management of Resources:** Audit strategy helps in managing, directing, supervising the resources, such as when team briefing and debriefing meetings are expected to be held, how engagement partner and manager reviews are expected to take place (for example, on-site or off-site), and whether to complete engagement quality control reviews.

Q.4 You have been appointed as an auditor of Bahubali Ltd. for the first time. Enumerate the factors to be considered while establishing an overall audit strategy and its benefits. [May 18 – Old Course (4 Marks)]

Ans : Factors to be considered in establishing audit strategy:

SA 300 "Planning an Audit of Financial Statements" requires that the auditor shall establish an overall audit strategy that sets the scope, timing and direction of the audit, and that guides the development of the audit plan. In establishing the overall audit strategy, the auditor shall:

- Identify the characteristics of the engagement that define its scope;
- Ascertain the reporting objectives of the engagement to plan the timing of the audit and the nature of the communications required;
- Consider the factors that are significant in directing the engagement team's efforts;
- Consider the results of preliminary engagement activities and, where applicable, whether knowledge gained on other engagements performed by the engagement partner for the entity is relevant; and
- Ascertain the NTE of procedures necessary to perform.

Benefits of Audit Strategy: Refer answer of Q. No. 3

Q.5 As an auditor of garment manufacturing company for the last five years you have observed that new venture of online shopping has been added by the company during current year. As an auditor what factors would be considered by you in formulating the audit strategy of the company? [May 15 (6 Marks)]

Ans. : Factors to be considered in formulating audit strategy: Refer answer of Q. No. 4

Specific Factors of audit strategy for online shopping:

1. Nature of transactions significant to the financial statements;

TAXMANN®

2. Procedures, within both information technology and manual systems, by which transactions are initiated, recorded, processed, corrected (if necessary), transferred to the general ledger and reported in the financial statements;
3. System by which the information system captures events and conditions, other than transactions, that are significant to the financial statements;
4. Controls used to record non-recurring, unusual transactions or adjustments.

"ICAI Examiner Comments"

Candidates have not focused on factors to be considered in formulating audit strategy and instead they elaborated the areas of audit and answers were general in nature. They could not write general and specific factors of audit strategy for online shopping.

2.2 AUDIT PLANNING

Q.6 Write short notes on: Usefulness of careful and adequate audit planning. [May 09 (4 Marks)]

Ans. : Objectives of audit planning:

(*i*) **To ensure that appropriate attention is devoted to important areas of the audit**: This is done through formal written audit plan, laying down the objectives and the procedures to be followed in order to meet those objectives.

(*ii*) **To facilitate review**: Work should be delegated to staff with the appropriate level of experience. All work should be properly supervised and reviewed by a senior member of staff.

(*iii*) **To ensure that potential problems are identified**: The auditor must ensure that resources are directed towards material/high risk areas.

(*iv*) **To assist in the proper assignment of work**: This may be to members of the audit team or to experts or other auditors. It helps the audit to proceed in a timely and efficient manner.

(*v*) **Coordination of work done by auditors of components and experts.**

Q.7 A & Co. was appointed as auditor of Great Airways Ltd. As the audit partner what factors shall be considered in the development of overall audit plan? [May 11 (8 Marks)]

Ans. : Factors to be considered in development of overall audit plan:

1. Terms of his engagement and any statutory responsibilities.
2. Nature and timing of reports or other communications.
3. Applicable Legal or Statutory requirements.
4. Accounting policies adopted by the clients and changes, if any, in those policies.
5. The effects of new accounting and auditing pronouncement on the audit.
6. Identification of significant audit areas.
7. Setting of materiality levels for the audit purpose.
8. Conditions requiring special attention such as the possibility of material error or fraud or involvement of parties in whom directors or persons who are substantial owners of the entity are interested and with whom transactions are likely.
9. Degree of reliance to be placed on the accounting system and internal control.
10. Possible rotation of emphasis on specific audit areas.
11. Nature and extent of audit evidence to be obtained.
12. Work of the internal auditors and the extent of reliance on their work, if any in the audit.
13. Involvement of other auditors in the audit of subsidiaries or branches of the client and involvement of experts.
14. Allocation of works to be undertaken between joint auditors and the procedures for its control and review.
15. Establishing and coordinating staffing requirements.

(Note: Any eight points may be answered)

Q.8 Discuss the relationship between Audit strategy and Audit Plan. **[Nov. 16 (4 Marks)]**

Ans. : Relationship between Audit Strategy and Audit Plan:

- Audit strategy and audit plan are inter-related to each other because change in one would result into change in the other.
- The audit strategy is prepared before the audit plan. The audit plan contains more details than the overall audit strategy.
- The audit strategy provides the guidelines for developing the audit plan.
- Audit strategy establishes the scope, timing and direction of the audit and thereby works as basis for developing a detailed audit plan.
- Detailed audit plan would include the nature, timing and extent of the audit procedures so as to obtain sufficient appropriate audit evidence.

2.3 AUDIT PROGRAMMING

Q.9 As an internal auditor for a large manufacturing concern, you are asked to verify whether there are adequate records for identification and value of Plant and Machinery, tools and dies and whether any of these items have become obsolescent and not in use. Draft a suitable audit programme for the above.

Ans. : Audit Programme to determine adequacy of records w.r.t. Plant and Machinery:

The Internal Audit Programme for verification of adequate records for identification and value of plant and machinery may cover the following:

1. **Examination of Internal Control System Aspects**: with respect to following:
   - Maintenance of separate register for fully owned assets, jointly owned assets hired assets and leased asset
   - Periodic inspection of fixed asset.
   - Proper authorisation and recording for purchase, repair and disposal of fixed assets.
2. **Examination of Assets Register**: To ensure whether the registers are showing clearly the date of purchase, cost price, location, depreciation charged, etc. for each plant and machinery.
3. **Examination of Measurement of Cost**: Verify the items which have been capitalised.
4. **Examination of Code Register**: To ensure that each item of plant and machinery has been given a distinct code number.
5. **Physical Verification**: Ensure that physical verification has been conducted by management at frequent intervals.
6. **Disposal of Assets**: Examine whether assets have been disposed off after proper technical and financial advice and is properly authorised.
7. **Spare Parts Register**: To examine the system of control over the various tools and spare parts to be used for each plant and machinery.
8. **Review of Maintenance**: Examine the programme for an periodical servicing and overhauling of machines.

Q.10 As an internal auditor of a Cement Manufacturing Company, draft an audit programme for verification of transportation charges for dispatches from the factory.

Ans. : Audit Programme for verification of transportation charges:

1. Examine the agreement to note down the rates contracted with transporters for carriage of goods.
2. Examine whether the rates charged in the invoice is as per the contract. In case of any discrepancy, ensure whether the same is authorized by the appropriate authority.
3. Examine whether the transporter's invoice includes a delivery challan bearing the customers stamp indicating the receipt of goods. In case there is no stamp on the delivery challan, check whether the goods are received back and there is a corresponding inward note.
4. Check whether all the goods to be dispatched have a transport booking order reference.
5. Check whether invoice of transporter's mentions the transport booking order reference.
6. Check whether the transport booking orders have corresponding transporters names and transport booking orders are pre-numbered.

7. Ensure correct recording of amount stated in the invoice.
8. Examine whether service-tax on the transporters is properly correctly calculated and accounted.
9. Check whether TDS has been deducted at appropriate rate and deposited with the government in time.

Q.11 You have been appointed as the auditor of a Multiplex Cinema House. Draw an audit programme in respect of its Revenue and Expenditure. **[Nov. 08 (8 Marks)]**

Or

Cineplex, a movie theatre complex, is the foremost theatre located in Delhi. Along with the sale of tickets over the counter and online booking, the major proportion of income is from the cafe, shops, pubs etc. located in the complex. It's other income includes advertisements exhibited within/outside the premises such as hoardings, banners, slides, short films etc. The facility for parking of vehicles is also provided in the basement of the premises.

Cineplex appointed your firm as the auditor of the entity. Being the head of the audit team, you are therefore required to draw an audit programme initially in respect of its revenue and expenditure considering the above-mentioned facts along with other relevant points relating to a complex.

[Nov. 19 - New Syllabus (5 Marks)]

Ans. : Audit Programme for Revenue and Expenditure of Multiplex:

1. Study the MOA and AOA of the entity so as to ensure that the object clause of MOA permits the entity to engage in this business.
2. In respect of **income from sale of tickets,** perform the following:—
   (*a*) Examine the internal control system to ensure proper accounting of sale of tickets.
   (*b*) Examine the system of on line booking and realization of money.
   (*c*) Examine the system of reconciliation of collections with the number of seats available.
3. Examine the existence and effectiveness of internal control system relating to the **income from cafes shops, pubs etc.**, located within the multiplex.
4. Examine the control exercised relating to the **income receivable from advertisements** exhibited within the premises.
5. Examine the system of **collection from the parking areas.**
6. Examine the system of **payment to the distributors** which may be either through out right payment or percentage of collection.
7. Examine the system of **payment of salaries and other benefits to the employees** and ensure compliance of statutory requirements.
8. Examine the expenses incurred in respect of the **maintenance of the building.**

Q.12 XY Ltd. is a manufacturing company, provided following details of wastages of raw materials in percentage, for various months. You have been asked to enquire into causes of abnormal wastage of raw materials. Draw out an audit plan. Wastage percentage are:

July 2019 -1.5% **Aug 2019 - 1.7%**

Sep. 2019 - 1.4% **Oct 2019 - 4.1%** **[Nov. 11 (8 Marks)]**

Ans. : Audit Plan to inquire causes of abnormal wastage of raw material:

Before planning for detailed investigation, the auditor is required to understand the manufacturing operations from the initial stage of purchase of materials, issue of material, consumption of material and conversions into finished goods. To locate the reasons for the abnormal wastage, the audit plan may include the following:

1. Obtain a list of raw materials used in the production process mentioning therein the names and detailed characteristics of each raw material.
2. Ascertain the basis of computation of normal wastage figures and its consistency as compared to previous months.
3. Obtain internal control reports, in respect of manufacturing costs incurred with reference to predetermined standards or budgets.
4. Examine the stock records so as to determine the raw material purchased, material issued to production.

5. Examine the production records so as to determine the material received from the stores and actual material consumed in the production and waste produced in the production process.
6. Study the Maintenance Programme of machinery to ensure that the machinery does not consume more raw material and quality of goods manufacture is not of sub-standard nature.
7. Ascertain whether employees engaged in production are properly trained and working efficiently.
8. Determine the existence and effectiveness of quality control techniques employed in the entity.
9. Examine inventory controls in respect of storage, pilferage, issues etc.
10. Obtain a statement showing break up of wastage figures in storage, handling and production for the period under reference and compare the results of the analysis for each of the month.
11. Consider the existence of following situations that may also cause the abnormal wastage:
    (*a*) Purchase of poor quality of raw materials.
    (*b*) Machinery breakdown or power failure.
    (*c*) High rate of rejections of finished goods
    (*d*) Deterioration of raw material lying in godowns
    (*e*) Abnormal wastages in storage and handling.
    (*f*) Commencing new production line.

RISK ASSESSMENT AND INTERNAL CONTROL

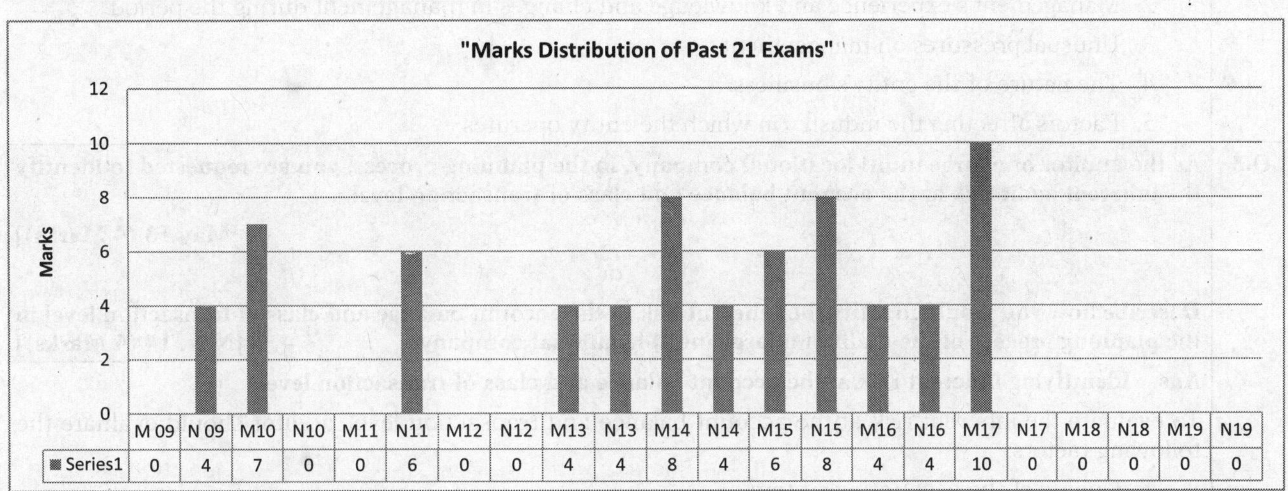

	M 09	N 09	M10	N10	M11	N11	M12	N12	M13	N13	M14	N14	M15	N15	M16	N16	M17	N17	M18	N18	M19	N19
Series1	0	4	7	0	0	6	0	0	4	4	8	4	6	8	4	4	10	0	0	0	0	0

3.1 AUDIT RISK

Q.1 Write short note on: Audit Risk

Ans. : Audit Risk:

- As per SA 200 "Overall Objectives of the Independent Auditor and the Conduct of an Audit in Accordance with Standards on Auditing", audit risk is a function of the risks of material misstatement and detection risk.
- Audit risk may be defined as the risk that the auditor gives an inappropriate audit opinion when the financial statement are materially misstated. Thus, it is the risk that the auditor may fail to express an appropriate opinion in an audit assignment.
- An auditor may consider audit risk both at overall level as well as at the level of individual account balances or classes of transactions. At overall level the auditor applies their professional judgment to determine the extent of risk which he considers to be an acceptable level. At account balance level, audit risk refers to the risk that error in monetary terms exists beyond a tolerable error limit in the account balances or class of transaction which the auditor fails to detect.
- Audit Risk has three components: Inherent Risk, Control Risk and Detection Risk. Inherent Risk and Control Risk are collectively known as Risk of Material Misstatement.
- Inherent Risk is the susceptibility of an account balance or class of transaction to a material misstatement, assuming that there were no internal controls.
- Control Risk is the risk that material misstatement will not be prevented or detected and corrected on a timely basis by the internal control system.
- Detection Risk is the risk that the substantive procedures performed by the auditor fails to detect material misstatement.

Q.2 **In the audit planning process of X Ltd., you would like to consider audit risk at the financial statement level. What are the factors can influence your decision?** **[May 10 (3 Marks)]**

or

Write Short note on: Evaluation of Inherent Risk at the Level of Financial Statements. **[May 14 (4 Marks)]**

or

Explain the concept of Audit Risk at the Level of Financial Statements.

Ans. : Factors to be evaluated to assess inherent risk at the level of financial statements:

1. Integrity of management.
2. Management's experience and knowledge and changes in management during the period.
3. Unusual pressures on management.
4. The nature of the entity's business.
5. Factors affecting the industry in which the entity operates.

Q.3 **As the auditor of a large multi locational company, in the planning process, you are requested to identify the inherent audit risk at the account balance and class of transaction level.** **[May 13 (4 Marks)]**

or

Describe how you would identify the inherent risk at the account balance and class of transaction level in the planning process of the audit of a large multi-locational company. **[Nov. 14 (4 Marks)]**

Ans. : Identifying inherent risk at the account balance and class of transaction level:

To evaluate the inherent risk at the account balance and transaction level, auditor should evaluate the following factors:

1. Quality of the accounting system.
2. Susceptibility of Financial statements to misstatement.
3. The complexity of underlying transactions and other events which might require using the work of an expert.
4. The degree of judgment involved in determining account balances.
5. Susceptibility of assets to loss or misappropriation.
6. The completion of unusual and complex transactions, particularly at or near period end.
7. Transactions not subjected to ordinary processing.

"ICAI Examiner Comments"

Question not clearly understood by majority of candidates and answered in general manner. In fact, most of the candidates showed lack of understanding of the topic on inherent risk and discussed control risk and detection risk which was not required in the question.

Q.4 **Write short note on: Factors relevant in evaluation of inherent risk.**

Ans. : Refer Answer of Q. Nos. 2 & 3

Q.5 **While commencing the statutory audit of B Company Limited, the auditor undertook the risk assessment and found that the detection risk relating to certain class of transactions cannot be reduced to acceptance level. Explain.** **[May 17 (5 Marks)]**

Ans. : Assessment of Risk and Acceptable Level:

- SA 315 "Identifying and Assessing the Risk of Material Misstatement Through Understanding the Entity and its Environment" and SA 330 "The Auditor's Responses to Assessed Risks" establishes standards on the procedures to be followed to obtain an understanding of the accounting and internal control systems and on audit risk and its components.
- SA 315 and SA 330 require that the auditor should use professional judgment to assess risk of material misstatement and to design audit procedures to ensure that it is reduced to an acceptably low level.

- Risk of Material Misstatements comprises of Inherent risk and Control Risk. "Detection risk" is the risk that an auditor's substantive procedures will not detect a misstatement that exists in an account balance or class of transactions that could be material.
- The higher the risk of material misstatement, the more audit evidence the auditor should obtain from the performance of substantive procedures. When both inherent and control risks are assessed as high, the auditor needs to consider whether substantive procedures can provide sufficient appropriate audit evidence to reduce detection risk, and therefore audit risk, to an acceptably low level.
- The auditor should use his professional judgment to assess audit risk and to design audit procedures to ensure that it is reduced to an acceptably low level. If it cannot be reduced to an acceptable level, the auditor should express a qualified opinion or a disclaimer of opinion as may be appropriate.

Q.6 Compute the overall Audit Risk if looking to the nature of business there are chances that 40% bills of services provided would be defalcated, inquiring on the same matter management has assured that internal control can prevent such defalcation to 75%. At his part the Auditor assesses that the procedure he could apply in the remaining time to complete Audit gives him satisfaction level of detection of frauds & error to an extent of 60%. Analyse the Risk of Material Misstatement and find out the overall Audit Risk.

[MTP-April 19]

Ans. : Determination of Audit Risk:

- As per SA-200, "Overall Objectives of the Independent Auditor and the Conduct of an Audit in Accordance with Standards on Auditing", the Audit Risk is a risk that Auditor will issue an inappropriate opinion while Financial Statements are materially misstated.
- Audit Risk is a function of two components: Risk of material Misstatement and Detection Risk, i.e. **Audit Risk = Risk of material Misstatement X Detection Risk**
- Risk of Material Misstatement is anticipated risk that a material Misstatement may exist in Financial Statement before start of the Audit. It has two components Inherent risk and Control risk. The relationship can be defined as **Risk of material Misstatement = Inherent risk X control risk**
- Inherent risk is the susceptibility of an assertion about account balance; class of transaction, disclosure towards misstatements which may be either individually or collectively with other Misstatement becomes material before considering any related internal control. Inherent Risk in the given case is 40%.
- Control Risk is the risk that material misstatement will not be prevented or detected and corrected on a timely basis by the internal control system. Control risk in the given case is 25% (100%-75%).
- Risk of material Misstatement = 40% X 25% = 10%
- Detection risk is the risk that the substantive procedures performed by the auditor fails to detect material misstatement. Detection Risk in the given case is 100-60 = 40%
- Overall Audit Risk = Risk of Material Misstatement X Detection Risk = 10 × 40% = 4%

3.2 RISK BASED AUDIT

Q.7 What are the General Steps in the conduct of Risk Based Audit? [May 16 (4 Marks)]

Or

What are the main phases in the conduct of risk based audit. [May 17 (4 Marks)]

Or

ST Ltd. is a growing company and currently engaged in the business of manufacturing of tiles. The company is planning to expand and diversify its operations. The management has increased the focus on the internal controls to ensure better governance. The management had a discussion with the statutory auditors to ensure the steps required to be taken so that the statutory audit is risk based and focused on areas of greatest risk to the achievement of the company's objectives. Please advise the management and the auditor on the steps that should be taken for the same. [MTP-March 19, RTP-May 19]

Ans. : Steps to be followed while conducting Risk Based Audit:

Risk Based audit is an audit approach that analyzes audit risks, sets materiality thresholds based on audit risk analysis, and develops audit programmes that allocate a larger portion of audit resources to high-risk areas.

Stages in Risk Based Audit:

1. **Understanding the auditee operations:** Auditor should understand the auditee operations in order to identify and prioritize the risks that impact audit of financial statements. Auditor should obtain understanding of the following:
   - Environment in which entity operates;
   - Framework of operations;
   - Operational performances;
   - Information process framework etc.
2. **Determination of Residual Risk:** Auditor should assess entity management strategies and controls so as to determine how the controls are designed within the entity.
3. **Manage Residual Risk:** It requires design and execution of a risk reduction approach so as to bring the residual audit risk to an acceptable level. More resources should be allocated to areas of high audit risks.
4. **Reporting to Auditee:** The auditor should communicate to the auditee immediately his significant observation w.r.t. following:
   - weaknesses in the internal control system,
   - deficiencies in the design and operation of internal controls that affect the organization's ability to record, process, summarize and report financial data.

"ICAI Examiner Comments"

Candidates lacked conceptual knowledge of the topic and instead of explaining the steps in conducting Risk based audit, mentioned and explained types of risk.

3.3 INTERNAL CONTROL

Q.8 Pasta Ltd., a manufacturing concern want to develop internal control system. You are an expert in developing the internal control system, hereby called to brief about the same. In view of above, you are required to brief about internal control system and inherent limitations of the internal control?

Ans. : Internal Control System and its Inherent Limitations:

SA 315 "Identifying and Assessing the Risk of Material Misstatement Through Understanding the Entity and its Environment" defines internal control as the process designed, implemented and maintained by TCWG, management and other personnel to provide reasonable assurance about the achievement of an entity's objectives with regard to:

(*a*) reliability of financial reporting;

(*b*) effectiveness and efficiency of operations;

(*c*) safeguarding of assets; and

(*d*) compliance with applicable laws and regulations.

Inherent Limitations of Internal Control System:

(*a*) Management's consideration that a control should be cost-effective.

(*b*) The fact that the most controls do not tend to be directed at transactions of unusual nature.

(*c*) Potential for human error.

(*d*) Possibility of circumvention of controls through collusion with parties outside the entity or with employees of entity.

(*e*) Possibility that a person responsible for exercising control could abuse that authority.

(*f*) Possibility that procedures may become inadequate due to changes in conditions and compliance with procedures may deteriorate.

(*g*) Manipulations by management with respect to transactions or estimates and judgments required in the preparation of financial statements.

Q.9 **XYZ Hospital Private Ltd. is engaged in running a hospital of 200 Beds since last 20 years. Revenue Track of the hospital for last 3 years is as under:**

2015-16 : ₹ 20 Crores

2016-17 : ₹ 25 Crores

2017-18 : ₹ 35 Crores

Hospital has its own Pharmacy, Laboratory, Blood Bank, Radiology & General Stores. Its management suspects that leakages/theft is happening in Pharmacy, Radiology, Laboratory and General Stores departments. It seeks advice of RST & Co., Internal Auditors of the Company, as to how it can Institute/Improve its Internal Control. In this context, Management wants to understand the concept of components of Internal Control Structure in detail. Advise. **[MTP-Aug. 18]**

Answer: Key components of Internal Control Structure:

Internal Control structure in an organization is referred to as the policies and procedures established by the entity to provide reasonable assurance that the objectives are achieved.

The control structure in an organization basically has the following components:

1. **Control Environment** - Control environment covers the effect of various factors like management attitude; awareness and actions for establishing, enhancing or mitigating the effectiveness of specific policies and procedures.
2. **Accounting System** - Accounting system means the process by which transactions are processed for maintaining financial records. Accounting system identifies, assemble, analyze, calculate, classify, record, summarize and report transactions and other events.
3. **Control Procedure** - Policies and procedures means those policies and procedures in addition to the control environment and accounting systems which the management has established to achieve the entity's specific objectives. Such Policies and Procedures cover the followings:
    - Segregation of duties.
    - Authorisation of Transactions.
    - Adequacy of records and documents.
    - Accountability and safeguarding of assets.
    - Independent checks.

Q.10 **As auditor of Z Ltd., you would like to limit your examination of account balance tests. What are the control objectives you would like the accounting control system to achieve to suit your purpose?** **[May 10 (4 Marks)]**

Ans. : Control Objectives:

The objectives of internal control systems are determined by the management, after considering the nature of business, scale of operations, the extent of professionalism of the management etc. The objectives of internal controls relating to the accounting system are:

(*i*) Transactions are executed through general or specific management authorization.

(*ii*) All transactions are promptly recorded in an appropriate manner to permit the preparation of financial information and to maintain accountability of assets.

(*iii*) Assets and records are safeguarded from unauthorized access, use or disposition.

(*iv*) Assets are verified at reasonable intervals and appropriate action is taken with regard to the discrepancies.

Precisely, the control objectives ensure that the transactions processed are complete, valid and accurate. The basic accounting control objectives which are sought to be achieved by any accounting control system are:

(*a*) whether all transactions are recorded;

(*b*) whether recorded transactions are real;

(*c*) whether all recorded transactions are properly valued;

(*d*) whether all transactions are recorded timely;

(*e*) whether all transactions are properly posted;

(*f*) whether all transactions are properly classified and disclosed;

(*g*) whether all transactions are properly summarized.

Q.11 As an auditor, during your interim visit at Marathon Ltd. you observed that internal controls were not in use throughout the period covered under audit. What are the controls objectives you would like to consider to achieve your purpose?

[May 15 (6 Marks)]

Ans. : Control Objectives to be considered for Audit Purpose:

The objectives of internal control systems are determined by the management, after considering the nature of business, scale of operations, the extent of professionalism of the management etc. Auditor's knowledge about the existence of control activities assists the auditor in determining whether it is necessary to devote additional attention to obtaining an understanding of control activities.

To ensure whether the internal control were in use throughout the period or not, the auditor may consider the following control objectives:

1. Existence and effective implementation of policies and procedures so as to ensure orderly and efficient conduct of business.
2. Safeguarding of assets.
3. Prevention and detection of frauds and errors.
4. Accuracy and completeness of the accounting records.
5. Timely preparation of reliable financial information.
6. Compliance with applicable laws and regulations.
7. Verification of assets at reasonable intervals.
8. Proper authorization of transactions.
9. Monitoring of accounting/financial controls.
10. Reviews of performance.
11. Segregation of duties.

"ICAI Examiner Comments"

Most of the candidates could not describe the control objectives as required in the question.

Q.12 In the use of standardized Internal Control Questionnaire (ICQ), certain basic assumptions about elements of a good internal control system are taken into account. List down few such assumptions.

[Nov. 18-New Syllabus (4 Marks)]

Answer: Assumptions presumed about elements of good control while using standardized internal control questionnaire:

1. Certain procedures in general used by most business concerns are essential in achieving reliable internal control. For example, deposits into bank of the entire receipts of a day or daily balancing of the cash book and ledgers or periodic reconciliation with the control accounts
2. Extensive division of duties and responsibilities within the organisation.
3. Separation of accounting function with the custodial function.
4. No single person is entrusted with the responsibility of completing a transaction all by himself.
5. There should always be evidence to identify the person who has done the work whether involving authorisation, implementation or checking.
6. The work performed by each one is expected to come under review of another in the usual course of routine.
7. There is proper documentation and recording of the transactions.

"ICAI Examiner Comments"

Examinees failed to point out the basic assumptions about elements of good control in case of standardized internal control questionnaire.

Q.13 Explain briefly the Flow Chart technique for evaluation of the Internal Control system.

[Nov. 09 (4 Marks)]

Ans. : Flow Chart Technique for evaluation of Internal Control System:

1. It is a graphic presentation of internal controls in the organisation and is normally drawn up to show the controls in each section or sub-section.

2. It provides the most concise and comprehensive way for reviewing the internal controls and the evaluator's findings.
3. A flow chart is a diagram full with lines and symbols and if judicious use of them can be made, it is probably an effective way of presenting the state of internal controls in the client's organisation.
4. A properly drawn up flow chart can provide a neat visual picture of the whole activities of the section or department involving flow of documents and activities. More specifically it can show—
    - at what point a document is raised internally or received from external sources;
    - the number of copies in which a document is raised or received;
    - the intermediate stages set sequentially through which the document and the activity pass;
    - distribution of the documents to various sections, department or operations;
    - checking authorisation and matching at relevant stages;
    - filing of the documents; and
    - final disposal by sending out or destruction.

Q.14 Briefly discuss the compliance procedures and their use in evaluation of internal controls.

Ans. : Compliance Procedures:

Compliance procedures are tests designed to obtain reasonable assurance that those internal controls on which audit reliance is to be placed are in effect. Obtaining audit evidence from compliance procedures is intended to reasonably assure the auditor in respect of the following assertions:

- Existence - that the internal control exists.
- Effectiveness - that the internal control is operating effectively.
- Continuity - that the internal control has so operated throughout the period of intended reliance.

Compliance procedures (also known as Tests of control) may include:

(*a*) Inspection of documents supporting transactions and other events to gain audit evidence that internal controls have operated properly.

(*b*) Inquiries about and observation of internal controls which leave no audit trail.

(*c*) Re-performance of internal controls.

(*d*) Testing of internal controls operating on specific computerised applications.

The auditors' objective in studying and evaluating internal controls is to establish the reliance he can place thereon in determining the nature, timing and extent of his substantive auditing procedures. Based on the results of his compliance procedures, the auditor evaluates whether the internal controls are adequate for his purpose. If based on the results of the compliance procedures, the auditor concludes that it is not appropriate to rely on a particular internal control to the degree previously contemplated, he should ascertain whether there is another control which would satisfy his purpose and on which he might rely (after applying appropriate compliance procedures). Alternatively, he may modify the nature, timing or the extent of his substantive audit procedures.

Q.15 "Surprise Checks" help the auditors to ascertain whether the internal control system is operating effectively in a company or not. Discuss.

Ans. : Importance of Surprise checks in ascertain operating effectiveness of internal control:

- SA 315 "Identifying and Assessing the Risk of Material Misstatement through Understanding the Entity and its Environment" requires the auditor to obtain an understanding of the entity and its environment including internal control. SA 330 "The Auditor's Responses to Assessed Risks" requires the auditor to design and perform tests of controls to obtain sufficient appropriate audit evidence as to the operating effectiveness of internal controls.
- The understanding of the internal control system can be obtained in several ways including inspection of documents and making inquires of management and TCWG, observation of activities, etc. In this context, surprise checks intend to ascertain whether the system of internal control is operating effectively and whether the accounting and other records are prepared concurrently and kept up-to-date.
- Surprise checks are a useful method of determining whether or not errors exist and where they exist, to bring the matter promptly to the attention of the management so that corrective action is taken immediately.
- As per the ICAI Recommendations, Surprise checks are a part of the normal audit and the results of such checks are important primarily to the auditor himself in deciding the scope of his audit and submitting his report thereon.

- The need for and frequency of surprise checks is a matter to be decided having regard to the circumstances of each audit. It would depend upon the extent to which the auditor considers the internal control system as adequate, the nature of the clients' transaction, the locations from which he operates and the relative importance of items like cash, investments, stores etc.
- However, wherever feasible a surprise check should be made at least once in the course of an audit.
- If this surprise checks reveals any weaknesses in the system of internal control or any fraud or error or the fact that any book or register has not been properly maintained or kept up-to-date, the auditor should communicate the same to the management and ensure that action is taken on the matters communicated by him. It does not necessarily follow that all or any of the matters communicated to the management should form part of the auditor's report on the accounts.

Conclusion: "Surprise checks" help the auditors, during the course of their audit, to ascertain whether the internal control is operating effectively in a company or not.

Q.16 **A newly qualified professional has received his first appointment as auditor of a large company and is very much concerned about the effectiveness of internal control and wants to assess and evaluate the control environment as part of his audit program. Towards achieving his objective, he seeks your help in knowing the Standard Operating Procedures (SOPs) of assessment and evaluation of control.**

[May 19 - New Syllabus (5 Marks)]

Ans. : Standard Operating Procedures (SOPs) of assessment and evaluation of control:

1. **Enterprise Risk Management:** Organization having robust processes to identify & mitigate risks across the entity & its periodical review will assist in early identification of weaknesses in internal control and taking effective control measures. In such entities, surprises of failures in controls is likely to be few.
2. **Segregation of Job Responsibilities:** Segregation of duties is an important element of control which ensures that no two commercial activities should be conducted by the same person.
3. **Job Rotation in Sensitive Areas:** In key commercial functions, job rotation is regularly followed to avoid degeneration of controls.
4. **Documents of delegation of Financial Powers**: Document on delegation of powers allows controls to be clearly operated without being dependant on individuals.
5. **IT based Controls**: In an IT Environment, it is much easier to embed controls through the system instead of being human dependant. The failure rate for IT embedded controls is likely to be low, is likely to have better audit trail & is thus easier to monitor.

Q.17 **Y Co. Ltd. has five entertainment centers to provide recreational facilities for public especially for children and youngsters at 5 different locations in the peripheral of 200 kilometers. Collections are made in cash. Specify the adequate system towards collection of money.**

[Nov. 11 (6 Marks)]

Ans. : System towards collection of money:

(*a*) **Printing of tickets:** Tickets should be serially numbered and pre-printed Serial numbers should not be repeated during a reasonable period, say a month or year depending on the turnover.

(*b*) **Sale of Tickets:** Tickets should be sold from the Central ticket office at each of the 5 centers, preferably through machines.

(*c*) **Reconciliation of daily cash:** Cash collection at each office should be reconciled with the number of tickets sold.

(*d*) **Banking of daily cash collection:** Daily collection should be deposited in the bank on next working day of the bank. Till that time, the cash should be in the custody of properly authorized person.

(*e*) **Cancellation of Entrance ticket:** Entrance tickets should be cancelled at the entrance gate when public enters the centre.

(*f*) **Advance booking:** If advance booking of facility is made available, the system should ensure that all advance booked tickets are paid for.

(*g*) **Discounts and free pass:** The discount policy should be such that the concessional rates should be properly authorized and signed forms for such authorization should be preserved.

(*h*) **Surprise checks:** Internal audit system should carry out periodic surprise checks for cash counts, daily banking, reconciliation and stock of unsold tickets etc.

Q.18 During the course of his audit, the auditor noticed material weaknesses in the internal control system and he wishes to communicate the same to the management. You are required to elucidate the important points the auditor should keep in mind while drafting the letter of weaknesses in internal control system. [Nov. 15 (4 Marks)]

Ans. : Points to be considered while drafting letter of weaknesses:

As per SA 265, "Communicating Deficiencies in Internal Control to those who Charged with Governance and Management", the auditor shall include in the written communication of significant deficiencies in internal control –

(*a*) A description of the deficiencies and an explanation of their potential effects; and

(*b*) Sufficient information to enable those charged with governance and management to understand the context of the communication.

This communication should be, preferably, in writing through a letter of weakness. Important points with regard to such a letter are as follows:

(*a*) It lists down the area of weaknesses in the internal control system and recommends suggestions for improvement.

(*b*) It should clearly indicate that this letter covers only weaknesses which have come to the attention of the auditor during his evaluation of internal control for the purpose of determining nature, timing and extent of further audit procedures.

(*c*) Letter should clearly indicate that his examination of internal control has not been designed to determine the adequacy of internal control for management.

(*d*) This letter serves as a significant means for management and governing body for the purpose of improving the system and its strict implementation.

(*e*) The letter may also serve to minimize legal liability in the event of a major defalcation or other loss resulting from a weakness in internal control.

"ICAI Examiner Comments"

Examinees failed to point out the important points to be included in letter of weakness.

3.4 INTERNAL CHECK

Q.19 Write short note on: Objectives of Internal Check System. [May 14 (4 Marks)]

Ans. : Objectives of Internal Check System:

1. To detect error and frauds with ease.
2. To avoid and minimize the possibility of commission of errors and fraud.
3. To increase the efficiency of the staff working within the organization.
4. To locate the responsibility area or the stages where actual fraud and error occurs.
5. To protect the integrity of the business by ensuring that accounts are always subject to proper scrutiny and check.
6. To prevent and avoid the misappropriation or embezzlement of cash and falsification of accounts.

Q.20 The Auditor of S Limited has just commenced the statutory audit. What should be considerations for the effectiveness of a system of internal check? [Nov. 13 (4 Marks)]

Or

State the considerations on which effectiveness of an efficient system of internal check depends. [Nov. 16 (4 Marks)]

Ans. : Considerations for effectiveness of a system of internal check:

1. No single person should have an independent control over any important aspect of the business.
2. The duties of members of the staff should be changed from time to time without any previous notice so that the same officer or subordinate does not, without a break, perform the same function for a considerable length of time.
3. Every member of the staff should be encouraged to go on leave at least once in a year.
4. Persons having physical custody of assets must not be permitted to have access to the books of account.

5. To prevent loss or misappropriation of cash, mechanical devices, such as the automatic cash register, should be employed.
6. Budgetary control would enable the management to review from time to time the progress of trading activities.
7. The financial and administrative powers should be distributed very judiciously among different officers and the manner in which these are actually exercised should be reviewed periodically.
8. Procedures should be laid down for periodical verification and testing of different sections of accounting records to ensure that they are accurate.
9. Accounting procedures should be reviewed periodically, for, even well-designed and carefully installed procedures, in course of time, cease to be effective.

Q.21 New life Hospital is a multi-specialty hospital which has been facing a lot of pilferage and troubles regarding their inventory maintenance and control. On investigation into the matter it was found that the person in charge of inventory inflow and outflow from the store house is also responsible for purchases and maintaining inventory records. According to you, which basic system control has been violated? Also list down the other general conditions pertaining to such system which needs to be maintained and checked by the management. [Nov. 15 (4 Marks)]

Ans. : Deficiencies in Internal Control System:

An organisation is required to segregate the responsibilities of its employees in such a manner that no single person should have an independent control over any important aspect of the business. In the present case, person in charge of inventory is not only responsible for inflow an outflow of inventory from store house but also responsible for purchase and maintaining inventory records. So in this case, one of the essential of internal check system that independent and complete control should not be given to a single person has been violated.

General Conditions pertaining to internal check: Refer the considerations specified in Q. No. 20.

"ICAI Examiner Comments"

Examinees did not discuss the general conditions pertaining to the internal check system. The answers were general. Many examinees applied internal control instead of internal check. Also, some examinees wrote about stock audit.

Q.22 BSF Limited is engaged in the business of trading leather goods. You are the internal auditor of the company for the year 2018-19. In order to review internal controls of the Sales Department of the company, you visited the Department and noticed the work division as follows:

(1) An officer was handling the sales ledger and cash receipts.

(2) Another official was handling dispatch of goods and issuance of Delivery challans.

(3) One more officer was there to handle customer/debtor accounts and issue of receipts.

As an internal auditor, you are required to briefly discuss the general condition pertaining to the internal check system prevalent in internal control system. Do you think that there was proper division of work in BSF Limited? If not, why? [MTP-Oct. 19, RTP-Nov. 19]

Ans. : General Conditions pertaining to internal check:

Refer the considerations specified in Q. No. 20.

In the given scenario, Company has not done proper division of work as:

(*i*) the receipts of cash should not be handled by the official handling sales ledger and

(*ii*) delivery challans should be verified by an authorised official other than the officer handling despatch of goods.

SPECIAL AUDIT TECHNIQUES

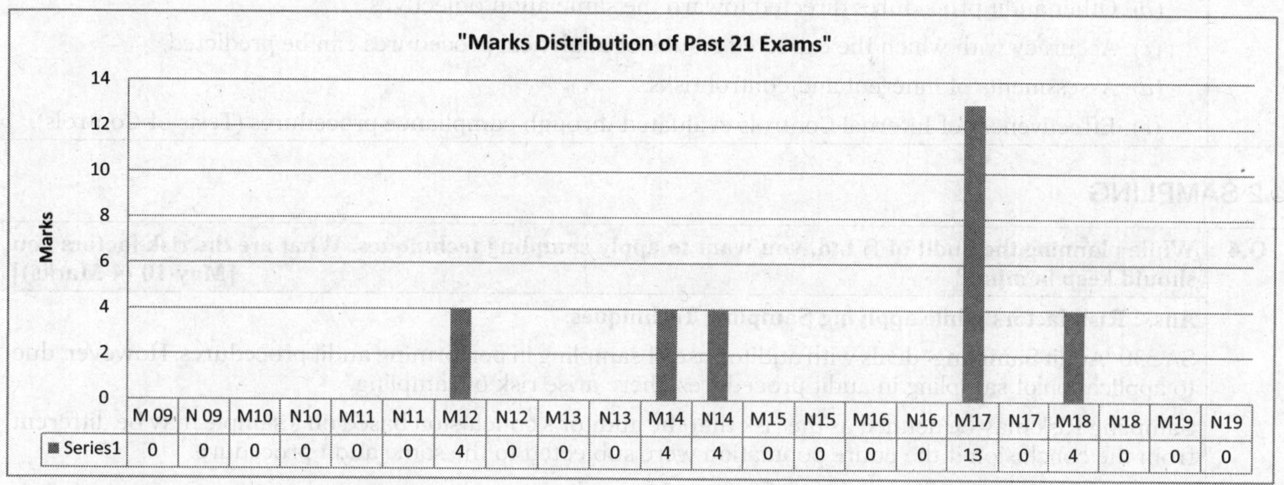

4.1 ANALYTICAL PROCEDURES

Q.1 Write short note on: Analytical Procedure in planning an audit.

Ans. : Analytical Procedures in Planning an Audit:

In planning stage, analytical procedures assist the auditor in the following:

- Understanding the client's business
- Identifying areas of potential risk
- Determining the nature, timing and extent of his other audit procedures.

Analytical procedures in planning an audit use both financial data and non-financial information, such as number of employees, machine hours, number of goods produced and similar information.

Q.2 Write short note on: Purposes for which analytical procedures are used.

Ans. : Purposes for which analytical procedures are used:

Analytical Procedures means evaluations of financial information through analysis of relationships among both financial and non-financial data. It also encompass such investigation as is necessary of identified fluctuations or relationships that are inconsistent with other relevant information or that differ from expected values by a significant amount. The analytical procedures may be used for following purposes:

1. To assist the auditor in planning the nature, timing and extent of audit procedures.
2. As a substantive procedures when their use can be more effective or efficient than tests of details in reducing detection risk for specific F.S. assertions; and
3. As an overall review of the F.S. in the final review, stage of the audit.

Q.3 Write short note on: Extent on Reliance on Analytical procedures.

Ans. : Extent of reliance on analytical procedures (SA-520)

The application of analytical procedures is based on the expectation that relationships among data exist and continue in the absence of known conditions to the contrary. The presence of these relationships provides audit evidence as to the completeness, accuracy and validity of the data produced by the accounting system.

However, reliance on the results of analytical procedures will depend on the auditor's assessment of the risk that the analytical procedures may identify relationships as expected when, in fact, a material misstatement exists. The extent of reliance that the auditor places on the results of analytical procedures depends on the following factors:

(*a*) Materiality of the items involved.

(*b*) Other audit procedures directed toward the same audit objectives.

(*c*) Accuracy with which the expected results of analytical procedures can be predicted.

(*d*) Assessments of inherent and control risks.

(*e*) Effectiveness of Internal Controls evaluated through compliance procedures (Tests of Controls).

4.2 SAMPLING

Q.4 While planning the audit of S Ltd. you want to apply sampling techniques. What are the risk factors you should keep in mind? [May 10 (4 Marks)]

Ans. : Risk factors while applying Sampling Techniques:

SA 530 "Audit Sampling" deals with auditor use of sampling in performing audit procedures. However, due to application of sampling in audit procedures, there arise risk of sampling.

Sampling Risk may be defined as the risk that the auditor's conclusion based on a sample may be different from the conclusion if the entire population were subjected to the same audit procedure.

Sampling risk can lead to two types of erroneous conclusions:

(*i*) In the case of a test of controls, that controls are more effective than they actually are, or in the case of a test of details, that a material misstatement does not exist when in fact it does. The auditor is primarily concerned with this type of erroneous conclusion because it affects audit effectiveness and is more likely to lead to an inappropriate audit opinion.

(*ii*) In the case of a test of controls, that controls are less effective than they actually are, or in the case of a test of details, that a material misstatement exists when in fact it does not. This type of erroneous conclusion affects audit efficiency as it would usually lead to additional work to establish that initial conclusions were incorrect.

Q.5 Write short note on: Statistical and Non-Statistical Sampling. [May 12 (4 Marks)]

Ans. : Statistical Sampling and Non-Statistical Sampling:

Statistical Sampling

(*i*) Statistical sampling has the following characteristics:

- Random selection of the sample items; and
- The use of probability theory to evaluate sample results, including measurement of sampling risk.

(*ii*) This method is more scientific as it involves use of laws of probability.

(*iii*) This method has reasonably wide application where a population consists of a large number of similar items.

Non-Statistical Sampling

(*i*) A sampling approach that does not have characteristics of random selection and use of probability theory is considered as non-statistical sampling.

(*ii*) In this method, the sample size and its composition are determined on the basis of personal experience and knowledge of the auditor.

(*iii*) This method because of its simplicity in operation was in common application for many years.

Q.6 Write short note on: Tolerable Misstatement. **[May 14 (4 Marks)]**

Or

What is tolerable misstatement and tolerable rate of deviation. **[May 17 (4 Marks)]**

Ans. : Tolerable Misstatement:

- A monetary amount set by the auditor in respect of which the auditor seeks to obtain an appropriate level of assurance that the monetary amount set by the auditor is not exceeded by the actual misstatement in the population.
- When designing a sample, the auditor determines tolerable misstatement in order to address the risk that the aggregate of individually immaterial misstatements may cause the financial statements to be materially misstated and provide a margin for possible undetected misstatements.
- Tolerable misstatement is the application of performance materiality, as defined in SA 320, to a particular sampling procedure. Tolerable misstatement may be the same amount or an amount lower than performance materiality.

Tolerable Rate of Deviation:

Rate of deviation from prescribed internal control procedures set by the auditor in respect of which the auditor seeks to obtain an appropriate level of assurance that the rate of deviation set by the auditor is not exceeded by the actual rate of deviation in the population.

Q.7 "An Auditor while analyzing the errors in a sample need not consider the qualitative aspects of errors detected." Comment.

Ans. : Consideration of Qualitative Aspects of Errors:

- SA 530 "Audit Sampling" requires the auditor to evaluate the results of the sample and determine whether the use of audit sampling has provided a reasonable basis for conclusions about the population that has been tested.
- If any error or misstatement identified, auditor shall investigate its nature and cause, and evaluate their possible effect on the purpose of the audit procedure and on other areas of the audit.
- In analysing the deviations and misstatements identified, the auditor would also need to consider the qualitative aspects of the misstatements identified by him.
- While evaluating the misstatements, auditor may observe that many have a common feature, for example, type of transaction, location, product line or period of time. In such circumstances, the auditor may decide to identify all items in the population that possess the common feature, and extend audit procedures to those items. In addition, such deviations or misstatements may be intentional, and may indicate the possibility of fraud.

Conclusion: The statement that an auditor while analysing the errors in a sample need not consider the qualitative aspects of errors detected is not correct, as he is required to investigate the nature and causes of the errors identified.

Q.8 Describe the Principal methods of selection of sample. **[Nov. 14 (4 Marks)]**

Or

The auditor should select sample items in such a way that the sample can be expected to be representative of the population. Comment. **[May 17 (5 Marks)]**

Or

In the course of your audit assignment of Indraprastha Ltd., you want to guide your audit assistants in selecting sample items in such a way that sample can be expected to be representative of the population and all items have an opportunity of being selected. Guide your assistants with principal methods of collecting samples. **[May 18 (4 Marks)]**

Ans. : Principal Methods of Selection of Samples:

As per SA 530 "Audit Sampling" principal methods of selection of samples are:

1. **Random selection:** This method of sampling ensures that all items within a population stand an equal chance of selection by the use of random number tables or random number generators. The sampling units could be physical items, such as sales invoices or monetary units.
2. **Systematic selection:** The number of sampling units in the population is divided by the sample size to give a sampling interval, for example 50, and having determined a starting point within the first 50, each 50th sampling unit thereafter is selected.

3. **Monetary Unit Sampling:** It is a type of value-weighted selection in which sample size, selection and evaluation results in a conclusion in monetary amounts.
4. **Haphazard selection:** Samples are selected without following a structured technique. Although no structured technique is used, the auditor would nonetheless avoid any conscious bias or predictability. Haphazard selection is not appropriate when using statistical sampling.
5. **Block selection:** It involves selection of a block(s) of contiguous items from within the population. Block selection cannot ordinarily be used in audit sampling because most populations are structured such that items in a sequence can be expected to have similar characteristics to each other, but different characteristics from items elsewhere in the population.

Q.9 Write short note on: Haphazard Sampling.

Ans. : Haphazard Sampling:

- SA 530 "Audit Sampling" recognises haphazard sampling as one of the sample selection method in which samples are selected without following a structured technique.
- Although no structured technique is used, the auditor would nonetheless avoid any conscious bias or predictability (for example, avoiding difficult to locate items, or always choosing or avoiding the first or last entries on a page) and thus attempt to ensure that all items in the population have a chance of selection.
- It may be accepted as alternative to random sampling, provided the auditor attempts to draw a representative sample from the population without any biasness.
- Haphazard selection is not appropriate when using statistical sampling.

Q.10 Write short note on: Block Selection. [MTP-Aug. 16]

Ans. : Block Selection:

- SA 530 "Audit Sampling" recognises block selection as one of the sample selection method in which samples are selected without following a structured technique.
- It involves selection of a block(s) of contiguous items from within the population.
- Block selection cannot ordinarily be used in audit sampling because most populations are structured such that items in a sequence can be expected to have similar characteristics to each other, but different characteristics from items elsewhere in the population.
- In some circumstances, it may be an appropriate audit procedure to examine a block of items, it would rarely be an appropriate sample selection technique when the auditor intends to draw valid inferences about the entire population based on the sample.

Q.11 Describe the principal method of design of the samples and its evaluation. [May 17 (4 Marks)]

Ans. : Principal Method of Design of Samples:

SA 530 "Audit Sampling" deals with the auditor's use of statistical and non-statistical sampling when designing and selecting the audit sample, performing tests of controls and tests of details, and evaluating the results from the sample. Among both methods of designing (Statistical and non-statistical), principal method of design of sample is statistical sampling.

Statistical sampling involves random selection of the sample items and use of probability theory to evaluate sample results, including measurement of sampling risk. This method is more scientific as it involves use of laws of probability. This method has reasonably wide application where a population consists of a large number of similar items.

While applying statistical sampling, auditor may also apply stratification, i.e. the process of dividing a population into sub-populations, each of which is a group of sampling units which have similar characteristics (often monetary value).

Evaluation of Sampling Results:

- SA 530 "Audit Sampling" requires the auditor to evaluate the results of the sample and determine whether the use of audit sampling has provided a reasonable basis for conclusions about the population that has been tested.
- If any error or misstatement identified, auditor shall investigate its nature and cause, and evaluate their possible effect on the purpose of the audit procedure and on other areas of the audit.
- In analysing the deviations and misstatements identified, the auditor would also need to consider the qualitative aspects of the misstatements identified by him.

SOX AUDIT

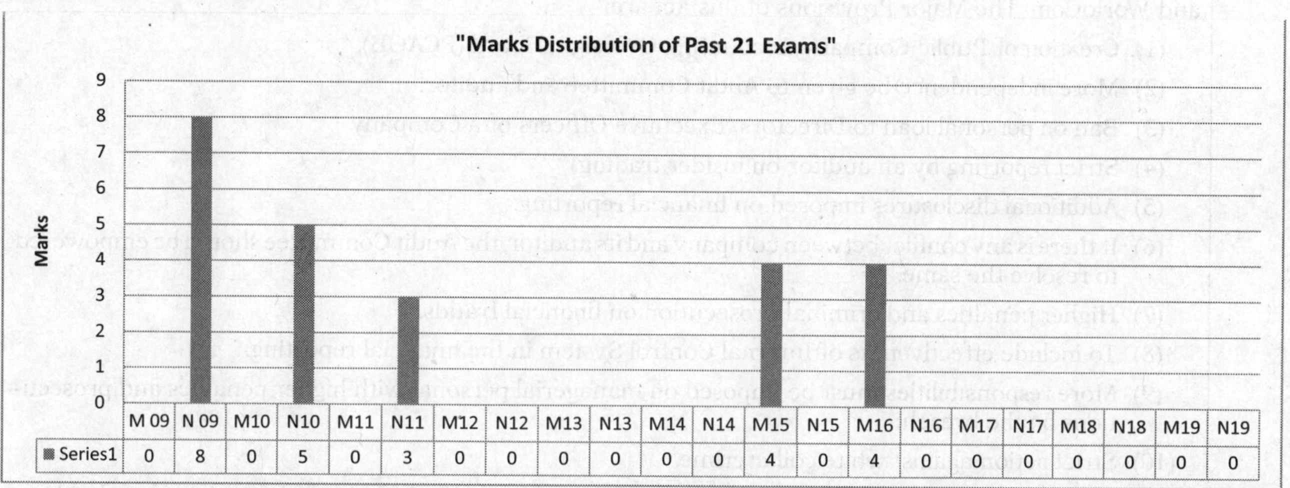

Q.1 Highlight the provisions relating to corporate responsibility under Sarbanes Oxley Act of 2002.

[Nov. 08 (4 Marks)]

or

Corporate responsibility as envisaged under Sarbanes-Oxley Act of 2002. Briefly Explain.

[Nov. 11 (3 Marks)]

or

Write short note on - Corporate Responsibility under Sarbanes and Oxley Act. [May 15 (4 Marks)]

Ans. : Corporate Responsibility under Sarbanes Oxley Act, 2002:

The Sarbanes-Oxley Act of 2002, also known as the Public Company Accounting Reform and Investor Protection Act of 2002 is a United States federal law passed in response to a number of major corporate and accounting scandals including those affecting Enron, Tyco International, and World Com. The Corporate Responsibility as stated in the law are:

(*i*) The audit committee to be more independent through enhancement of their over sight responsibilities and one of the Audit committee members to be financial expert.

(*ii*) Requires CEO & CFO to issue certification of the quarterly financial results and annual reports to SEC as part of compliance.

(*iii*) Provides rules of conduct for companies managerial and their officers regarding Pension matters.

(*iv*) To Comply with SEC rules requiring attorneys to report violation of securities to the company's CEO or Chief Legal Counsel and to Audit Committee if no action is taken.

"ICAI Examiner Comments"

Most of the candidates described general points of audit committee and CSR under Companies Act, 2013 instead of Corporate Responsibility under Sarbanes Oxley Act as required in the question.

Q.2 State briefly eight provisions of the Sarbanes-Oxley Act of 2002, which shall, if strictly applied to Indian Corporates, get fruitful results. **[Nov. 09 (8 Marks)]**

or

"Corporate accountability and civil and criminal penalties for white collar crimes". Comment on the major provisions of Sarbanes-Oxley Act. **[Nov. 10 (5 Marks)]**

Ans. : Major Provisions of Sarbanes-Oxley Act:

The Sarbanes-Oxley Act of 2002 established corporate accountability and civil and criminal penalties for white - collar crimes. This act also known as the Public Company Accounting Reform and Investor Protection Act of 2002 and commonly called SOX or Sarbox; is a United States federal law passed in response to a number of major corporate and accounting scandals including those affecting Enron, Tyco International, and WorldCom. The Major Provisions of this Act are:

(1) Creation of Public Company Accounting Oversight Board (PCAOB).

(2) More independence be given to Audit Committee and auditor.

(3) Ban on personal loan to Directors/Executive Officers of a Company

(4) Strict reporting by an auditor on insider trading.

(5) Additional disclosures imposed on financial reporting.

(6) If there is any conflict between company and its auditor, the Audit Committee should be empowered to resolve the same.

(7) Higher penalties and criminal prosecution on financial frauds.

(8) To include effectiveness of Internal Control System in the financial reporting.

(9) More responsibilities must be imposed on managerial personal with higher penalties and prosecutions on the breach.

(10) Strict action against white collar crime.

(11) Disclosures of the % of shareholdings by Directors, Executive Officers and principal shareholders.

Q.3 State the key requirements of auditing standards of Public Company Accounting over sight board. **[May 16 (4 Marks)]**

Ans. : key requirements of Auditing Standards of Public Company Accounting over sight Board:

Auditing Standards of the Public Company Accounting Oversight Board (PCAOB) has the following key requirements:

1. The design of controls-relevant assertions related to all significant accounts and disclosures in the financial statements;
2. Information about how significant transactions are initiated, authorized, supported, processed, and reported;
3. Enough information about the flow of transactions to identify where material misstatements due to error or fraud could occur;
4. Controls designed to prevent or detect fraud, including who performs the controls and the regulated segregation of duties;
5. Controls over the period-end financial reporting process;
6. Controls over safeguarding of assets;
7. The results of management's testing and evaluation.

"ICAI Examiner Comments"

Very few candidates attempted this question and those attempted lacked knowledge about requirement of the question and discussed only irrelevant points of Sarbanes-Oxley Act.

Q.4 The SEC identifies the COSO framework by name as a methodology for achieving compliance. The COSO framework defines five areas, which when implemented, can help support the requirements as set forth in the Sarbanes-Oxley legislation. Briefly explain these five areas and their impacts for the IT department.

Ans. : Areas defined by COSO Framework:

PCAOB suggests considering the Committee of Sponsoring Organizations of the Tread way Commission (COSO) framework in management/auditor assessment of controls. The COSO framework defines five areas, which when implemented, can help support the requirements as set forth in the Sarbanes-Oxley legislation. These five areas and their impacts for the IT Department are as follows:

1. **Risk Assessment** - Before the necessary controls are implemented, IT management must assess and understand the areas of risk affecting the completeness and validity of the financial reports.
2. **Control Environment** - An environment in which the employees take ownership for the success of their projects will encourage them to escalate issues and concerns, and feel that their time and efforts contribute to the success of the organization. This is the foundation on which the IT organization will thrive.
3. **Control Activities** - Design, implementation and quality assurance testing teams should be independent. ERP and CRM systems that collect data, but feed into manual spreadsheets are prone to human error. The organization will need to document usage rules and create an audit trail for each system that contributes financial information.
4. **Monitoring** - Auditing processes and schedules should be developed to address the high risk areas within the IT organization. IT personnel should perform frequent internal audits.
5. **Information and Communication** - Without timely, accurate information, it will be difficult for IT management to proactively identify and address areas of risk. They will be unable to react to issues as they occur. IT management must demonstrate to company management an understanding of what needs to be done to comply with Sarbanes-Oxley.

6 CHAPTER

AUDIT IN CIS ENVIRONMENT

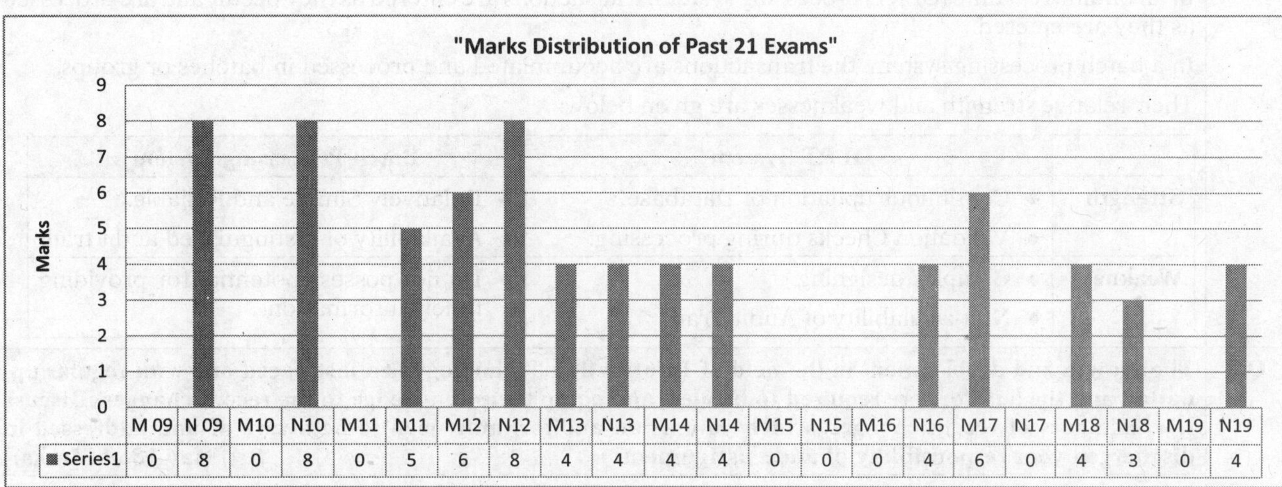

	M 09	N 09	M10	N10	M11	N11	M12	N12	M13	N13	M14	N14	M15	N15	M16	N16	M17	N17	M18	N18	M19	N19
■ Series1	0	8	0	8	0	5	6	8	4	4	4	4	0	0	0	4	6	0	4	3	0	4

6.1 TYPES OF ACCOUNTING SYSTEMS

Q.1 What are the characteristics of On-line Computer system.

Ans. : Characteristics of OLRT Processing system:

1. **Validation Checks:** When data are entered on-line, they are usually subject to immediate validation checks. Data failing this validation would not be accepted and a message may be displayed on the terminal screen, providing the user with the ability to correct the data and re-enter the valid data immediately.
2. **On-Line Access:** Users may have on-line access to the system that enables them to perform various functions. The extent of this access will depend upon such things as the design of the particular application and the implementation of software designed to control access to the system.
3. **Transaction Trail:** An on-line computer system may be designed in a way that does not provide supporting documents for all transactions entered into the system. However, the system may provide details of the transactions on request.
4. **Programmer Access:** Programmers may have on-line access to the system that enables them to develop new programs and modify existing programs. Unrestricted access provides the programmer with the potential to make unauthorised changes to programs and obtain unauthorised access to other parts of the system.

Q.2 You have been approached by an organization to suggest a system where the user wants to access data immediately. What would be your suggestions if they want to process it after validation?

Ans. : Suggestion for File Processing System:

- **System through which data can be accessed immediately**: If the user wants to access date immediately, the On-line real time (OLRT) systems can serve the purpose. In this system transactions are entered as they occur and are processed as they are entered. This system enables the users to access data and programmes directly through terminal devices. The individual transactions are entered at terminal devices, validated and used to update related computer files immediately. This system forms the heart of management information system.

- **System which process date after validation**: If the user wants to process the data after validation then the on-line batch processing system may be used.

In on-line batch processing system, individual transactions are entered at a terminal device subject to certain validation checks and added to a transaction file that contains other transactions entered during the period. The transaction file may be validated further during every processing cycle and relevant master file is updated. Transactions are accumulated and grouped for the day and processed as a group. They do not process transaction as quickly as on-line real time system does.

Q.3 **"On-line real time processing system and batch processing system have their inherent strengths and weaknesses." Please comment.**

Ans. : Strength and Weaknesses of OLRT and Batch Processing System:

In an on-line real time (OLRT) processing system, transactions are entered as they occur, and are processed as they are entered.

In a batch processing system, the transactions are accumulated and processed in batches or groups.

Their relative strength and weaknesses are given below:

	OLRT System	Batch Processing System
Strength	◆ Continuous updation of Database. ◆ Validation Checks during processing.	◆ Relatively Simple and Reliable. ◆ Availability of distinguished audit trail.
Weakness	◆ Complex designing. ◆ Non-availability of Audit Trail	◆ Do not possess potential for providing timely information.

Q.4 **The growth and development in the field of Information Technology is a fast paced one with regular updation and the auditors are required to be alert and equip their knowledge to the recent changes. Discuss few instances of recent changes, which you, as an auditor, may need to be aware of and addressed in discharged your responsibility of audit assignment.** **[May 18 (4 Marks)]**

Ans : Recent Changes with which auditor must be aware of:

1. Substitution of mini/micro users by Mainframes.
2. Shift from basic operating system to more universal ones like UNIX, LINUX, etc.
3. Increasing use of Relational Data Base Management (RDBMS).
4. Use of Computer Aided Software Engineering for systems development.
5. Increased use of End user computing.
6. Increase in need for data communication and networking.
7. Replacement of common business documents by paperless electronic data interface (EDI).
8. Data entry by use of scanner, digitized image processes, voice recognition system etc.

Q.5 **Superior Limited wants to shift its accounting process from manual to electronic medium. Discuss the primary effect of such changes.** **[Nov. 16 (4 Marks)]**

Ans. : Primary Effect of changes from manual accounting to electronic medium:

1. **Process of recording transactions:** In a CIS Environment, order of recording transaction from supporting document to prime books and then to ledgers may not be followed strictly in sequential from as is observed in manual system.
2. **Form of accounting records:** Mechanisation often results in the abandonment in whole or in part of the primary records.
3. **Use of loose-leaf stationeries:** CIS system is characterized by use of loose-leaf machine written records in electronic medium as against bound hand written records in manual accounting processes. This requires proper control over such records to prevent their unauthorised use, destruction or substitution.
4. **Use of accounting code:** In CIS system, codes are extensively used to represent names and description. Accountants and Auditors need to get themselves familiarised with these codes to understand the various transactions.
5. **Absence of link between transaction (Loss of Audit Trail):** In a CIS environment, cross-reference between the basic documents, primary records and the principal records may be absent which creates problem to the auditors in tracing a transaction from start to finish.

6.2 CHARACTERISTICS OF CIS ENVIRONMENT

Q.6 Enumerate the risk and internal control characteristics in an audit conducted in a CIS Environment.

Or

"When the computer information systems are significant, the auditor should obtain an understanding of the CIS environment and whether it may influence the assessment of inherent and control risk". What factors an auditor has to consider in such risk assessment?

Ans. : Characteristics of CIS Environment:

1. **Lack of transaction trails**: It increases the risk of auditor as errors embedded in an application's program logic may be difficult to detect on a timely basis by manual procedures.
2. **Uniform processing of transactions**: It eliminates clerical errors ordinarily associated with manual processing, but programming or other systematic errors may arise.
3. **Lack of segregation of function**: Many control procedures that would ordinarily be performed by separate individuals in manual systems may become concentrated in a CIS environment. Thus, an individual who has access to computer programs, processing or data may be in a position to perform incompatible functions.
4. **Potential for errors and irregularities**: Potential for human error in the development, maintenance and execution of CIS may be greater than in manual system.
5. **Automatic execution of transactions**: CIS may include the capability to execute certain types of transactions automatically. Management's authorization of these transactions may be implicit in CIS design.
6. **Dependence of other controls over computer processing**: Computer processing may produce reports and other output that are used in performing manual control procedures. The effectiveness of these manual control procedures can be dependent on the effectiveness of controls over the completeness and accuracy of computer processing.
7. **Potential for increased management supervision:** CIS can offer management a variety of analytical tool that may be used to review, supervise and enhance entire internal control structure.
8. **Potential for the use of CAAT**: Processing and analysis of large quantity of data using computers, may require the use of specialized computer audit techniques and tools in the execution of audit tests.

Q.7 Q Ltd. operates in an ERP environment. Its auditor requires your assistance on the aspects that are needed to be looked into in respect of control over input and output of transactions. Kindly help him.

[Nov. 13 (4 Marks)]

Ans. : Control over Input and Output:

(A) Control over input: Following aspects to be considered with respect to control over input:

(*i*) Transactions are properly authorised before being processed by the computer.

(*ii*) Transactions are accurately converted into machine readable form and recorded in the computer data files.

(*iii*) Transactions are not lost, added, duplicated or improperly changed.

(*iv*) Incorrect transactions are rejected, corrected and if necessary, resubmitted on a timely basis.

(B) Control over Output: Following aspects to be considered with respect to control over input:

(*i*) Results of processing are accurate.

(*ii*) Access to output is restricted to authorised personnel.

(*iii*) Output is provided to appropriate authorised personnel on a timely basis.

Q.8 Discuss some problems that will encountered in CIS Environment in implementation of internal control.

Ans. : Problems that may arise due to implementation of internal control in CIS:

1. **Separation of duties:** In a manual system, separate individuals are responsible for initiating transactions, recording transactions and custody of assets. Due to automation in the system, such controls are not possible in a computer system.
2. **Delegation of Authority and responsibility:** Due to use of resources by multiple user, it becomes difficult to delegate authority and responsibility in a precise manner. For example, as many users access the database, it may not be possible to trace the person making unauthorized changes in it.

3. **Competent and Trustworthy persons:** Organisations find it difficult to find and retain competent and trustworthy personnel to take charge of their CIS set up.
4. **System of authorisation:** As against the manual system, automation of the authorization procedure is an important feature of CIS System. For example, the computer system may determine the price to be charged to customers. Thus the auditor has to verify the veracity of computer processing.
5. **Adequate documents & records:** In computer systems, documents may not be used to support the initiation execution and recording of some transactions. Thus, no visible audit trail may be available.
6. **Physical control over assets and records:** As the data processing assets and records are concentrated at a place, the risk of loss and unauthorized access is high.
7. **Adequate management supervision:** In computer systems, data communications may be used to enable the employees to be closer to the customer they service. Thus supervision of employees may have to be carried out remotely.
8. **Comparing records with physical assets:** Unlike in manual system, the records may be automatically reconciled with the assets. Thus unauthorized modifications to programs or data files that these programs use, may be difficult to detect.

6.3 CONTROLS TO BE EVALUATED BY AUDITOR IN CIS ENVIRONMENT

Q.9 Different types of controls which operate over date moving into, through and out of the computer. Auditor is required to review such control. Comment. [Nov. 10 (8 Marks)]

Ans. : Review of Controls operating over data:

1. **Organisation structure and control:** Examine the responsibilities of each job position w.r.t. CIS function and ensure that the person understands the duties, authority and responsibilities. The duties have to be separated to ensure the internal control is established.
2. **Documentation Control:** Ensure existence of proper and adequate documentation for approval of system flowcharts, Programme flowcharts, Programme changes, etc. Changes made in the above are also documented & approved by authorized persons.
3. **Access Control:** Ensure that the system restricts the persons to access restricted data. Ensure that the system denies access to unauthorized persons.
4. **Input controls:** Ensure that only properly authorized and approved data goes in the input. Examine validation controls.
5. **Processing controls:** These controls are must for integrity of data. Processing validation checks should be applied.
6. **Recording Controls:** To enable the records to be kept free of errors.
7. **Storage Controls:** Examine Back-up and recovery facilities to ensure the proper data availability to the management.
8. **Output controls:** The data processed must go to the authorized person in the required manner. Examine whether the audit trail relating to output is provided.

Q.10 The auditor must evaluate major clauses of control used in a Computerised Information system to enhance its reliability - Comment. [Nov. 08 (8 Marks)]

Or

While auditing in a (CIS) Environment, the reliability of a component is a function of control that acts on the component. There are certain types of controls used to enhance component reliability which the auditor must evaluate. You are required to briefly explain those controls.

Ans. : Clauses of controls to be evaluated:

In a computer system the following are the major types of controls that are used to enhance component reliability which the auditor must evaluate:

1. **Authenticity Control:** They are exercised to verify the identity of the individuals or process involved in a system. For example: use of Password, Digital Signature etc.
2. **Accuracy Control:** It ensures the correctness of the data and processes in a system (Validation Check).
3. **Completeness Control:** This ensures that no data is missing and all processing is carried through.

4. **Privacy Control:** This ensures the protection of data from unauthorised disclosure.
5. **Audit Trail Controls:** This ensures the traceability of all events occurred in a system.
6. **Redundancy Control:** It ensures that processing of data is done only once.
7. **Existence Control:** It attempts to ensure the on going availability of all system resources.
8. **Asset Safeguarding controls:** It attempts to ensure that all resources within a system are protected from destruction or corruption.
9. **Effectiveness Control:** It attempts to ensure that the system achieves its goals.
10. **Efficiency Control:** It attempts to ensure that a system uses minimum resources to achieve its goals.

Q.11 You are a member of an audit team of B & C Associates, auditors of a multinational company YB Co. Ltd. The company is working in CIS environment. The partner in charge of B & C Associates asked you to draw out the audit plan for evaluating the reliability of controls.

[Nov. 11 (5 Marks)]

Or

ABC Co. Ltd. a company having trans-national operations, conducts its entire operations in a Computerised Information Systems (CIS) environment. As the audit partner of M/s. XYZ & Co., draw out the audit plan evaluating the reliability of controls. **[May 17 (6 Marks)]**

Ans. : Audit Plan for Evaluating the reliability of controls:

In evaluating the effects of a control, the auditor needs to assess the reliability by considering the various attributes of a control. Accordingly, audit plan should cover the followings:

1. Whether the control is in place and is functioning as desired.
2. Generality versus specificity of the control with respect to the various types of errors and irregularities that might occur.
3. Whether the control acts to prevent, detect or correct errors. The auditor focuses here on
   a. **Preventive controls**: Controls which stop errors or irregularities from occurring.
   b. **Detective controls**: Controls which identify errors and irregularities after they occur.
   c. **Corrective controls**: Controls which remove the effects of errors and irregularities after they have been identified.
4. The number of components used to execute the control: Multi-component controls are more complex and more error prone but they are usually used to handle complex errors and irregularities.

Q.12 What are the considerations which an auditor should consider while evaluating the reliability of the accounting and internal control systems in a CIS Environment? **[Nov. 12 (8 Marks)]**

Ans. : Considerations in evaluating the reliability of accounting and internal control system:

While evaluating the reliability of the accounting and internal control system, the auditor should consider whether the CIS System provides the following:

(*i*) Availability of authorized, correct and complete data for processing.
(*ii*) Timely detection and correction of errors
(*iii*) Existence of data recovery arrangement and back-up system.
(*iv*) Adequate data security against fire and other calamities, wrong processing etc.
(*v*) Prevention of unauthorized amendments to the program.
(*vi*) Provision for Offsite processing in the event of disaster.
(*vii*) Safe custody of source code of application software and data files.
(*viii*) Accuracy and completeness of output.
(*ix*) Prevention of loss of data in case of interruption in the work due to power, mechanical or processing failure.

6.4 AUDIT APPROACHES IN CIS ENVIRONMENT, AUDIT TRAIL & CAATS

Q.13 Explain the factors to be considered to examine the impact of computerisation on audit approach.

Ans. : Factors to be considered to examine the impact of computerisation on audit approach:

1. **High speed:** High speed of CIS Environment enables the auditor to extend their substantive procedures for collection of more evidence in support of their judgment.
2. **Low clerical error:** Due to systematic and sequential programmed processing, the chances of commission of error are considerably reduced.
3. **Concentration of duties:** In a CIS Environment, computer programs perform more than one set of activities at a time thereby concentrating the duties of several personnel involved in the work.
4. **Shifting of internal control base:** In a CIS Environment, internal control focus shifts to IT systems primarily in relation to Application systems development control and Systems software control
5. **Disappearance of Manual Reasonableness:** In CIS Environment, many stages required under manual operations are either deleted or managed to create a focused computer system. In such creative effort, the manual reasonableness may be missing.
6. **Impact of poor system:** If system analysis and designs falls short of expected standard of performance, a CIS environment may do more harm to integrated business operation than good.
7. **Exception reporting:** It is a part of Management information system. Exception Reporting is a departure from straight reporting of all variables. Here the value of a variable is only reported if it lies outside some pre-determined normal range.
8. **Man-machine interface:** Man-machine interface ensures maximum effectiveness of the information system. It is required to determine what information was necessary to achieve through a careful analysis of the job or task for which the user needed the information.

Q.14 What is audit trail? State the reasons for non-existence of audit trail in CIS Environment.

Ans. : Audit Trail:

Audit trail refers to the facility to trace individual transactions through system from source to completion. In the manual system of accounting, the audit trail is distinct and can be followed by the auditor through the distinct stages of accounting process. However, in computerized system audit trail is often missing or is sketchy. A proper audit trail ensures audit checking for proper processing and accumulation of data.

Reasons for non-existence of audit trail in CIS

1. Source documents once transcribed in machine readable form are not retained in a manner that permits subsequent access.
2. Master files may replace ledger summaries.
3. Transaction listing is often not provided.
4. Reports may be only on exceptions.

Remedies for non-existence of audit trail

The auditor may adopt below mentioned techniques to verify computerized data in case of loss of audit trail:

1. Examination of computer Program
2. Use of test packs, and
3. Use of computer audit programs for different audit purposes.

Q.15 What is an Audit Trail? Briefly describe the special audit techniques using the computer as an audit tool.

Ans. : Audit Trail: Refer Answer of Q. No. 14

Special Audit Techniques using computer as an audit tool:

The lack of visible audit trail may require the use of Computer Assisted Audit Techniques (CAATs). The effectiveness and efficiency of auditing procedures may be enhanced through the use of CAATs. Popularly, two common types of CAATs are in vogue, viz., test packs or test data and audit software or computer audit programmes.

1. **Audit Software:** Audit software consists of computer program used by the auditor as a part of his auditing procedure to process data of audit significance. It may consist of:
   (*a*) **Package programs:** These are generalised computer programs designed to perform data processing which includes reading computer files, selecting information, performing calculations, creating data files and printing reports in a format as specified by the auditor.

(*b*) **Purpose written programs:** These are computer programs designed to perform audit tasks in specific circumstances. These programs may be prepared by the auditor, by the organisation or by an programmer engaged by the auditor.

(*c*) **Utility programs:** These are used by the organisation to perform common data processing functions, such as sorting, creating and printing files. These programs are generally not designed for audit purposes.

2. **Test Data:** Test data techniques are used in conducting audit procedures by entering data into the entity computer system and comparing the results obtained with pre-determined results.

Test data used to test **specific controls** in computer programs, such as, on line password and data access controls. Test **transactions selected from previously processed transactions** preferably historical data or data treated by the auditor to test specific processing characteristics of the organisation's computer system. Such transactions are generally processed separately from the entity's normal processing.

Q.16 In the audit of K Ltd., its auditor wants to use CAATs for performing various audit procedures. Guide him as to what procedures can be performed using CAATs. [May 12 (6 Marks)]

Or

E & Co. a firm of chartered Accountants, requires your help in identifying the audit procedures that can be performed using CAATs. Please guide them. [May 13 (4 Marks)]

Ans. : Procedures that can be performed through CAAT:

CAATs can be used for both compliance and substantive testing. CAATs may be used in performing various auditing procedures, including:

(*i*) **Tests of details of transactions and balances** - for example, the use of audit software to test all (or a sample) of the transactions in a computer file.

(*ii*) **Analytical review procedures** - for example, the use of audit software to identify unusual fluctuations of items.

(*iii*) **Sampling programs** - to extract data for audit testing.

(*iv*) **Re-performing calculations** - performed by the entity accounting systems.

(*v*) **Compliance test of general IT controls** - for example, the use of test data to test access procedures to the program libraries.

(*vi*) **Compliance tests of IT application controls** - for example, the use of test data to test the functioning of a programmed procedure.

Q.17 "Use of Audit Software would increase the probability of detecting frauds". Comment. [May 08 (6 Marks)]

Ans. : Uses of CAAT in Fraud Detection:

- CAATs may be used in performing various auditing procedures, including the following:
  1. Tests of details of transactions and balances.
  2. Analytical review procedures.
  3. Sampling programs.
  4. Re-performing calculations.
  5. Compliance test of general IT controls.
  6. Compliance tests of IT application controls.
- In a CIS Environment, auditor is required to plan his work by exercising reasonable skill and care so as to detect material misstatement in the financial statements resulting from fraud or error.
- Errors are intentional and fraud are intentional. Uses of CAAT while performing audit may highlight some frauds, but there is no evidence to prove the assertion that use of audit software has unearthed the well concealed frauds.
- Hence, it cannot be concluded that uses of audit software increase the probability of detection of fraud.

Q.18 Write short note on: Test Pack

Or

Explain how "Test Data" is used as an audit technique to test specific controls in computer programs. [Nov. 18 (3 Marks)]

Ans. : Test Data:

Test data techniques are used in conducting audit procedures by entering data into the computer system of the organisation and comparing the results obtained with pre-determined results. For example:

- Test data used to test specific controls in computer programs, such as, on line password and data access controls.
- Test transactions selected from previously processed transactions preferably historical data or data treated by the auditor to test specific processing characteristics of the organisation's computer system. Such transactions are generally processed separately from the entity's normal processing.
- Test transactions used in an integrated test facility where a 'dummy' unit is established and to which test transactions are posted during the normal processing.

When test data is processed with the organisation's normal processing the auditor should ensure that the test transactions are subsequently eliminated from accounting records of the organisations.

Q.19 Write short notes on: Factors to consider in determining the use of CAAT. [May 07 (4 Marks)]

Or

In determining whether to use Computer Assisted Auditing Techniques (CAATs), what are the factors that a statutory auditor has to consider?

Or

What are the factors that an auditor has to be consider while using CAAT?
[Nov. 19-Old Syllabus (4 Marks)]

Ans. : Considerations in the Use of CAAT:

1. **Availability of sufficient IT knowledge & expertise**: It is essential that members of the audit team should possess sufficient knowledge and experience to plan, execute and use the results of CAAT.
2. **Incompatibility between CAATs and computer facilities:** Auditor may plan to use other computer facilities when the use of CAATs on an entity's computer is uneconomical or impractical, e.g. incompatibility between audit program and entity's computer.
3. **Impracticability of manual tests:** Some audit procedures may not be possible to perform manually because they rely on complex processing (for example, advanced statistical analysis) or involve amounts of data that would overwhelm any manual procedure.
4. **Impact on effectiveness & efficiency in extracting a data:** It includes selection of samples, applying analytical procedures, time involved in application of CAAT, etc.
5. **Time constraints:** In certain data, transaction details, are often kept for a short time and may not be available in machine-readable form by the time auditor wants them. Thus, the auditor will need to make arrangements for the retention of data required, or may need to alter the timing of the work that requires such data.

Q.20 Indicate the control procedures which the auditor should adopt in applying CAAT (Computer Assisted Audit Technique) in an audit under CIS environment.

Ans. : Control Procedures to be adopted in applying CAAT:

(A) Control Procedures for Audit Software Application:

1. Participating in the design and testing of the computer programmes.
2. Checking the coding of the programme.
3. Requesting the entity's computer staff to review the operating system instructions to ensure that the software will run in the entity's computer.
4. Running the audit software on small test files before running on the main data files.
5. Ensuring that the correct files were used.
6. Obtaining evidence that the audit software functioned as planned.
7. Establishing appropriate security measures to safeguard against manipulations of the entity's data files.

(B) Control Test Data Application:

1. Controlling the sequence of submissions of test data where it spans several processing cycles.
2. Performing test runs containing small amounts of test data before submitting the main audit test data.

3. Predicting the results of the test data and comparing it with the actual test data output, for the individual transactions and in total.
4. Confirming that the answered version of the programmes was used to process the test data.
5. Obtaining reasonable assurance that the programmes used to process the test data were used by the entity throughout the applicable audit period.

Q.21 State the important characteristics of an effective system of Computer Audit Programme.
[Nov. 06 (8 Marks)]

Ans. : Characteristics of Computer Audit Program

1. **Simplicity**: The system should be simple to use & eliminate the need for remembering countless details normally required in writing computer programs.
2. **Understandability**: The system should be readily understandable by members of the audit staff, even those with little computer expertise. The capabilities of the system should be known & should be easy to use.
3. **Adaptability**: The system should be capable of writing computer audit programs for the various types of computers used in the company or expected to be acquired.
4. **Vendor technical support**: w.r.t. Initial installation, Adequate documentation, Training to audit staff and Provision for future revisions in the programs.
5. **Statistical sampling capability** w.r.t. Selection of items on a random basis, determination of sample size, and evaluation of results at different confidence levels.
6. **Acceptability**: System should be acceptable to both - auditors and computer centres. For the auditors the programs should be easily carried to the site and practical to use. For the computer centre the programs should be compatible with the system and be capable of minimum interference with normal routines.
7. **Processing Capabilities**: Program must have ability to process many different types of applications, capability for extended data selection and stratification and ability to operate under multiprogramming situations.
8. **Report Writing**: Program must have ability to prepare multiple reports in a single program run and generate flexible output report formats.

6.5 COLLECTION AND EVALUATION OF AUDIT EVIDENCES IN CIS ENVIRONMENT

Q.22 The role of an auditor in collecting audit evidences under CIS system is more complex than under the manual system - Discuss. **[Nov. 09 (8 Marks)]**

Or

How would the method of collecting audit evidence relating to effectiveness of controls and evaluating the same change under a computerized environment. **[Nov. 14 (4 Marks)]**

Or

"The method of collecting Audit evidence and evaluating the same changes drastically under CIS Environment". - Comment.

Ans. : Collection and Evaluation of audit Evidences in CIS Environment:

(A) Collection of Audit Evidences: Collecting evidence on the reliability of a computer system is often more complex than collecting evidence on the reliability of a manual system due to the following reasons:

1. Existence of diverse and complex range of internal control technology that did not exist in manual system.
2. Rapid developments in Hardware and Software technology.
3. Cryptographic controls to protect the privacy of data.
4. Collection of audit evidence through manual means is not possible.

With these limitations, auditors have to run through computer system themselves if they are to collect the necessary evidence. Though generalized audit softwares are available, the development of these tools cannot be relied upon due to lack of information. Hence auditors are forced to compromise in some way when performing the evidence collection.

(B) Evaluation of Audit Evidences: In an CIS environment it becomes more difficult for the auditors to evaluate the evidences due to following reasons:

1. Increasing complexity of computer systems and control technology.
2. In a shared data environment a single input transaction may update multiple data item used by various users may be difficult to understand.
3. Consequence of errors in a computer system is a serious matter as errors in computer system tend to be deterministic, i.e., an erroneous program will always execute data incorrectly.
4. Errors are generated at high speed & the cost and effort to correct and re-run program may be high.

Under these circumstances, there is requirement of internal controls that ensure high quality computer systems should be designed implemented and operated upon. The auditors must ensure that these control are sufficient to maintain assets safeguarding, data integrity, system effectiveness and system efficiency and that they are in position and functioning.

7 CHAPTER

PROFESSIONAL ETHICS

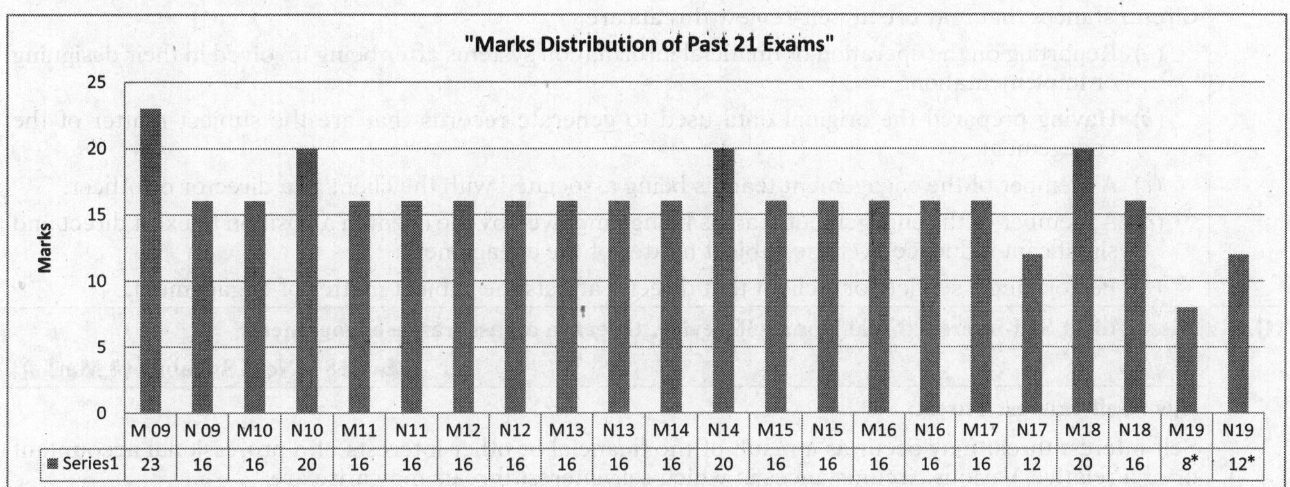

*Only Subjective Questions.

7.1 - FUNDAMENTAL PRINCIPLES TO BE FOLLOWED BY AN ACCOUNTANT

Q.1 **What are the fundamental principles as per code of ethics of ICAI? What are the threats involved while complying with the fundamental principles? [Nov. 16 (4 Marks)]**

Ans. : Fundamental Principles as per Code of Ethics:

1. **Integrity:** A professional accountant should be straightforward and honest in all professional and business relationships.
2. **Objectivity**: A professional accountant should not allow bias, conflict of interest or undue influence of others to override professional judgments.
3. **Professional Competence and Due Care**: A professional accountant has a continuing duty to maintain professional knowledge and skill at the level required to ensure that a client or employer receives competent professional service based on current developments in practice, legislation and techniques. A professional accountant should act diligently and in accordance with applicable technical and professional standards while providing professional services.
4. **Confidentiality**: A professional accountant should respect the confidentiality of information acquired as a result of professional and employment relationships and should not disclose any such information to third parties without proper and specific authority unless there is a legal or professional right or duty to disclose.
5. **Professional Behaviour**: A professional accountant should comply with relevant laws and regulations and should avoid any action that discredits the profession.

Threats involves in compliance:

1. **Self-interest threats:** It may occur as a result of the financial or other interests of a professional accountant or of a relative
2. **Self-review threats:** It may occur when a previous judgment needs to be re-evaluated by the professional accountant responsible for that judgment.

3. **Advocacy threats**: It may occur when a professional accountant promotes a position or opinion to the point that subsequent objectivity may be compromised.
4. **Familiarity threats**: It may occur when, because of a relationship, a professional accountant becomes too sympathetic to the interests of others.
5. **Intimidation threats**: It may occur when a professional accountant may be deferred from acting objectively by threats, actual or perceived.

Q.2 What is self-review threat. List the circumstances that may create self-review threats.

Ans. : Self-review Threats:

As per Section 100 of Code of Ethics, self-review threats occur when a previous judgment needs to be re-evaluated by the professional accountant responsible for that judgment.

Circumstances that may create self-review threats are:

(*a*) Reporting on the operation of financial information systems after being involved in their designing or implementation.

(*b*) Having prepared the original data used to generate records that are the subject matter of the engagement.

(*c*) A member of the engagement team is being associated with the client as a director or officer.

(*d*) A member of the engagement team is being employed by the client in a position to exert direct and significant influence over the subject matter of the engagement.

(*e*) Performing a service for a client that directly affects the subject matter of engagement.

Q.3 Distinguish: Self-interest threat from self-review threat in an assurance engagement.

[May 18 - New Syllabus (4 Marks)]

Ans : Self Interest Threat:

Self-interest threat may occur as a result of the financial or other interests of a professional accountant or of a relative. Various circumstances in which self-interest threats may arise are:

(*a*) A financial interest in a client or jointly holding a financial interest with a client.

(*b*) Undue dependence on total fees from a client.

(*c*) Having a close business relationship with a client.

(*d*) Concern about the possibility of losing a client.

(*e*) Potential employment with a client

(*f*) A loan to or from an assurance client or any of its directors or officers.

Self-Review Threats: Refer Answer of Q. No. 2.

Q.4 A professional accountant in public practice is always subject to various threats in compliance with fundamental principles of his profession and you, as a professional accountant, is worried about engagement specific threat in your audit assignment of M/s Soft Ltd. and want to implement some measures to eliminate and reduce the same. Enumerate some engagement specific safeguards which you may introduce in your work environment to ward off such threats. [May 19 - New Syllabus (5 Marks)]

Ans. : Engagement-specific safeguards in the work environment:

(*a*) Involving an additional professional accountant to review the work done or otherwise advise as necessary.

(*b*) Consulting an independent third party, such as a committee of independent directors, a professional regulatory body or another professional accountant.

(*c*) Discussing ethical issues with TCWG of the client.

(*d*) Disclosing to TCWG of the client the nature of services provided and extent of fees charged.

(*e*) Rotating senior assurance team personnel.

7.2 - RELEVANT PROVISIONS OF CA ACT, 1949

Q.5 Comment on the following with reference to the Chartered Accountants Act, 1949, Code of Ethics and Schedules to the Act: P, a Chartered Accountant in practice provides management consultancy and other services to his clients. During 2017-18, looking to the growing needs of his clients to invest in the stock markets, he also advised them on Portfolio Management Services whereby he managed portfolios of some of his clients.

Or

Mr. P, a Chartered Accountant in practice, provides guidance on post-issue activities to his clients e.g. follow up steps which include listing of instruments, dispatch of certificates and refunds etc. with the various agencies connected with the work. During the year 2017-18, looking to the growing needs of his clients to invest in the stock markets, he also started advising them on Portfolio Management Services whereby he managed portfolios of some of his clients.

Ans. : Advising on Portfolio Management Services:

- The Council of the ICAI pursuant to Section 2(2)(*iv*) of the CA Act, 1949 has passed a resolution permitting "Management Consultancy and other Services" by a CA in practice.
- A clause of the aforesaid resolution allows CAs in practice to act as advisor or consultant to an issue of securities including such matters as drafting of prospectus, filing of documents with SEBI, preparation of publicity budgets, advice regarding selection of brokers, etc.
- It is, however, specifically stated that CAs in practice are not permitted to undertake the activities of broking, underwriting and portfolio management Services. Thus, a CA in practice is not permitted to manage portfolios of his clients.

Conclusion: P would be guilty of misconduct under the Chartered Accountants Act, 1949 as a practicing CA is not permitted to render portfolio management services.

Q.6 **Comment on the following with reference to the Chartered Accountants Act, 1949 and Schedules thereto: Mr. A, a practicing Chartered Accountant agreed to select and recruit personnel, conduct training programmes for and on behalf of a client.** **[Nov. 07 (5 Marks), May 15 (4 Marks)]**

Ans. : Selection and Recruitment of Personnel:

- Under Section 2(2)(*iv*) of the CA Act, 1949, a member of the Institute shall be deemed "to be in practice" when individually or in partnership with CAs in practice, he, in consideration of remuneration received or to be received renders such other services as, in the opinion of the Council, are or may be rendered by a CA in practice.
- Pursuant to Section 2(2)(*iv*) above, the Council has passed a resolution permitting a CA in practice to render entire range of "Management Consultancy and other Services".
- The definition of the expression "Management Consultancy and other Services" includes Personnel recruitment and selection.
- Personnel Recruitment and selection includes, development of human resources including designing and conduct of training programmes, work study, job description, job evaluation and evaluations of workloads.

Conclusion: There is no misconduct on part of Mr. A, as personnel recruitment and selection is covered under management consultancy and other services.

Q.7 **Mr. S, a practicing Chartered Accountant agreed to provide "Portfolio management Services" to his client M/s. D Limited. Comment with reference to the Chartered Accountants Act, 1949.** **[Nov. 15 (4 Marks)]**

Ans. : Advising on Portfolio Management Services:

- The Council of the ICAI pursuant to Section 2(2)(*iv*) of the CA Act, 1949 has passed a resolution permitting "Management Consultancy and other Services" by a CA in practice.
- A clause of the aforesaid resolution allows CAs in practice to act as advisor or consultant to an issue of securities including such matters as drafting of prospectus, filing of documents with SEBI, preparation of publicity budgets, advice regarding selection of brokers, etc.
- It is, however, specifically stated that CAs in practice are not permitted to undertake the activities of broking, underwriting and portfolio management Services. Thus, a CA in practice is not permitted to manage portfolios of his clients.

Conclusion: S would be guilty of misconduct under the Chartered Accountants Act, 1949 as a practicing CA is not permitted to render portfolio management services.

"ICAI Examiner Comments"

Examinees failed to point out that Chartered Accountants in practice are not permitted to undertake the activities of broking, underwriting and portfolio management services as per resolution of the Council pursuant to Section 2(2)(*iv*) of the Chartered Accountants Act, 1949 regarding "Management Consultancy and other Services."

Q.8 **CA Natraj, in practice, accepted an assignment as advisor and consultant to the public issue of shares by his client M/s Super Ltd. Besides helping the company as an advisor, he also underwrote the public issue of the company to the extent of 25% at a commission of 1%. Remaining shares were underwritten by banks and other financial institutions at the same rate of commission. He contends that above assignments are**

part of management consultancy work permitted by the council of the Institute. Do you agree with the view of CA Natraj? Decide in the light of applicable code of conduct.

[May 19 - New Syllabus (4 Marks)]

Ans. : Advising on Portfolio Management Services:

- The Council of the ICAI pursuant to Section 2(2)(*iv*) of the CA Act, 1949 has passed a resolution permitting "Management Consultancy and other Services" by a CA in practice.
- A clause of the aforesaid resolution allows CAs in practice to act as advisor or consultant to an issue of securities including such matters as drafting of prospectus, filing of documents with SEBI, preparation of publicity budgets, advice regarding selection of brokers, etc.
- It is, however, specifically stated that CAs in practice are not permitted to undertake the activities of broking, underwriting and portfolio management Services. Thus, a CA in practice is not permitted to render underwriting services to his clients.

Conclusion: CA Natraj would be guilty of misconduct under the Chartered Accountants Act, 1949 as a practicing CA is not permitted to render underwriting services.

Q.9 **Discuss the following with reference to the CA Act, 1949 and schedules thereto: Mr. A, CA in practice has been suspended from practice for a period of 6 months & he had surrendered his COP for the said period. During the said period of suspension, though he did not undertake any audit assignments, he undertook representation assignments for income tax whereby he would appear before the tax authorities in his capacity as a CA.** **[Nov. 02, Nov. 11 (4 Marks)]**

Ans. : Undertaking Tax Representation Work:

- Sec. 6 of CA Act, 1949, requires that no member of the Institute shall be entitled to practice unless he has obtained from the Council a certificate of practice.
- In case a person has been suspended from practice for a period, he remains a member of ICAI and abide by the provisions of CA Act and its regulations.
- Such a member cannot take up in any other capacity, any practice separable from his capacity to practices as a member of the Institute. If he appears before the taxation and related authorities, he is only doing so in his capacity as a CA and a member of the Institute.
- The particulars of this case are similar to case of A.C. Kaher, wherein COP has been cancelled by High Court for 6 months and ICAI informed the member that he continued to be member of the Institute but he was only suspended from practice under the order of the High Court for a period of six months, and that he should comply with the provision of the Act and the Regulations in so far as they were applicable to member of the Institute.

Conclusion: A would not be allowed to represent before the income tax authorities for the period he remains suspended. Accordingly, in the present case, he is guilty of professional misconduct.

Q.10 **Mr. Dice, a practicing Chartered Accountant was ordered to surrender his certificate of practice and he was suspended for one year on certain professional misconduct against him. During the period of suspension, Mr. Dice, designating himself as GST consultant, did the work of filing GST returns and made appearance as a consultant before various related authorities. He contended that there is nothing wrong in it as he, like any other GST consultant, could take such work and his engagement as such in no way violate the order of suspension inflicted on him. Is he right in his contention?** **[May 18 - New Syllabus (4 Marks)]**

Answer: Undertaking Tax Representation Work:

- Sec. 6 of CA Act, 1949, requires that no member of the Institute shall be entitled to practice unless he has obtained from the Council a certificate of practice.
- In case a person has been suspended from practice for a period, he remains a member of ICAI and abide by the provisions of CA Act and its regulations.
- Such a member cannot take up in any other capacity, any practice separable from his capacity to practices as a member of the Institute. If he appears before the taxation and related authorities, he is only doing so in his capacity as a CA and a member of the Institute.
- However, if a member of ICAI, is doing so in any other capacity such as GST Consultant wherein his capacity is not chartered accountant in practice, he will not be held guilty for misconduct.
- In the instant case, Mr. Dice was a practicing chartered accountant and he was ordered to surrender his certificate of practice and was suspended for one year. Mr. Dice is doing the work of filing GST returns and has appeared as a consultant before various related authorities as GST Consultant

which is not in capacity of a practicing chartered accountant rather in capacity of authorized representative. Any person who has been authorized to act as a GST Practitioner on behalf of the concerned registered person can become authorized representative. Thus, filing GST return and appearing as GST Consultant by Mr. Dice is not professional misconduct.

Conclusion: Contention of Mr. Dice is correct as long as he is not working in his capacity as a CA, during the period he was suspended from practice as CA.

Q.11 **Is there any misconduct on the part of a Chartered Accountant in the following circumstances: Mr. G, a Chartered Accountant in practice as a sole proprietor has an office in Mumbai near Church Gate. Due to increase in professional work, he opens another office in a suburb of Mumbai which is approximately 80 kilometres away from the municipal limits of the city. For running the new office, he employs three retired Income-tax Officers.**

Ans. : Maintenance of Branch office:

- In terms of Section 27 of the CA Act, 1949 if a chartered accountant in practice has more than one office in India, each one of these offices should be in the separate charge of a member of the Institute.
- There is however an exemption for the above if the second office is located in the same premises, in which the first office is located; or the second office is located in the same city, in which the first office is located; or the second office is located within a distance of 50 kms. from the municipal limits of a city, in which the first office is located.

Conclusion: As the second office is situated beyond 50 kms. of municipal limits of Mumbai city, Mr. G would be liable for committing a professional misconduct and provisions of Clause 1, Part II, Second Schedule will be attracted.

Q.12 **Comment on the following with reference to the Chartered Accountants Act, 1949 and Schedules thereto: XY & Co., a firm of Chartered Accountant having 2 partners X & Y, one in charge of Head Office and another in charge of Branch at a distance of 80 kms., puts up a name-board of the firm in both premises and also in their respective residences.**

Ans. : Putting up of name Board:

- The council of the Institute has decided that with regard to the use of the name-board, there will be no bar to the putting up of a name-board in the place of residence of a member with the designation of chartered accountant, provided, it is a name-plate or board of an individual member and not of the firm.
- In the given case partners of X Y & Co., put up a name board of the firm in both offices and also in their respective residences.

Conclusion: The chartered accountants are guilty of misconduct, as name board of the firm cannot be put in place of residence.

Q.13 **Give your comments with reference to the Chartered Accountants Act, 1949 and Schedules thereto: K, Chartered Accountant in practice as a sole proprietor at Chennai has an office in the suburbs of Chennai. Due to increase in the income tax assessment work, he opens another office near the income tax office. For running the new office, he has employed a retired Income Tax Commissioner. [Nov. 12 (4 Marks)]**

Ans. : Maintenance of Branch office:

- In terms of Section 27 of the CA Act, 1949 if a chartered accountant in practice has more than one office in India, each one of these offices should be in the separate charge of a member of the Institute.
- There is however an exemption from the above if the second office is located in the same premises, in which the first office is located; or the second office is located in the same city, in which the first office is located; or the second office is located within a distance of 50 kms. from the municipal limits of a city, in which the first office is located.

Conclusion: Assuming that the distance between new office and municipal limits of Suburbs (area where existing office is situated) is greater than 50 Km., Mr. K would be liable for committing a professional misconduct.

Q.14 **Mr. K, Chartered Accountant in practice as a sole proprietor at Chennai has an office in the suburbs of Chennai. Due to increase in the income tax assessment work, he opens another office near the income tax office, which is within the city and at a distance of 30 kms. from his office in the suburb. For running the new office, he has employed a retired Income Tax Commissioner who is not a Chartered Accountant. Comment. [Nov. 15, May 18 - Old Syllabus (4 Marks)]**

Ans. : Maintenance of Branch office:

- In terms of Section 27 of the CA Act, 1949 if a chartered accountant in practice has more than one office in India, each one of these offices should be in the separate charge of a member of the Institute.
- There is however an exemption from the above if the second office is located in the same premises, in which the first office is located; or the second office is located in the same city, in which the first office is located; or the second office is located within a distance of 50 kms. from the municipal limits of a city, in which the first office is located.

Conclusion: As the distance between new office and municipal limits of Suburbs (area where existing office is situated) is less than 50 km., Mr. K would not be liable for any misconduct.

Q.15 M & Co., a sole proprietary Chartered Accountant firm in practice with an office in a busy belt of a city, had great difficulty in regularly attending to the consultancy needs of his client who are mostly located in an industrial cluster in a nearby outskirt which is situated at a distance of 26 kms from the office of the firm. To mitigate the difficulty and to have ease of business, a facilitation centre was opened in the industrial cluster. The proprietor managed both the office and the facilitation centre, by himself. No intimation was made to the institute of chartered accountants of India. Examine whether there is any professional misconduct in this respect. **[May 18 - New Syllabus (5 Marks)]**

Ans: Maintenance of Separate office:

- In terms of Section 27 of the CA Act, 1949 if a chartered accountant in practice has more than one office in India, each one of these offices should be in the separate charge of a member of the Institute.
- There is however an exemption from the above if the second office is located in the same premises, in which the first office is located; or the second office is located in the same city, in which the first office is located; or the second office is located within a distance of 50 kms from the municipal limits of a city, in which the first office is located.
- Regulation 189 of CA Regulations, 1988 requires that a CA in practice or a firm of such CAs shall inform the Council within one month of the opening or closing of a branch office.
- In the present case, a CA in practice has opened a new office with 26 Kms from the existing office and managing both offices by himself. However, no intimation was made to the ICAI.

Conclusion: Though there is no problem in managing both the offices, but misconduct arises due to non-intimation to Council of ICAI.

7.2A - FIRST SCHEDULE PART I - PROFESSIONAL MISCONDUCT IN RELATION TO MEMBERS IN PRACTICE

Q.16 CA Sant, a newly qualified professional with certificate of practice, approached CA Pant, the auditor of his father's company M/s Max Ltd., to allow him to have some practical and professional knowledge and experience in his firm before he can set up his own professional practice. CA Pant allowed him to sit in his office for 6 months and allotted a small chamber with other office infrastructure facility. In the course of his association with CA Pant's office, he used to provide tax consultancy independently to the client of the firm and also filed few IT and GST return and represented himself before various tax authorities on behalf of the firm although no documents were signed by him. During his association in CA Pant's office he did not get any salary or share of profit or commission but only re-imbursement of usual expenses like conveyance, telephone etc. was made to him. After the end of the agreed period, he was given a lump sum amount of Rs. 3,00,000 by CA Pant for his association out of gratitude.

Examine the case in the light of code of professional misconduct. **[May 19 - New Syllabus (5 Marks)]**

Ans. : Allowing Others to use firm's name:

- As per Clause (1) of Part 1 of First Schedule to the Chartered Accountants Act, 1949, a CA in Practice is deemed to be guilty of professional Misconduct if he allows any person to practice in his name as a Chartered Accountant, unless such person is also a Chartered Accountant in practice, and is in partnership with, or employed by himself.
- This clause ensures that the work of the accountant will be carried out by a Chartered Accountant who may be his partner, or his employee and would work under his control and supervision.
- In the present case, CA Pant allowed Mr. Sant, another Chartered Accountant, holding Certificate of Practice to practice in his firm for a period of 6 months, whereas Mr. Sant is not a partner or employee. Further after expiry of six months, Mr. Pant also gives Mr. Sant a lump sum amount of Rs. 3,00,000 for his association out of gratitude.

	Conclusion: Mr. Pant will be guilty of professional misconduct by virtue of Clause 1 of Part I of First Schedule as he allows another practice to practice in his firm name, whereas other person (Mr. pant) is neither a partner nor an employee.
Q.17	**A CA obtained a loan from a finance company for purchase of office building agreeing to pay interest at 6% p.a. and 10% of his gross professional receipts till the loan is repaid. [May 94 (5 Marks)]**
	Ans. : Sharing Professional Receipts with others: As per Clause (2) of Part I of the First Schedule to the Chartered Accountants Act, 1949, a CA in practice is deemed to be guilty of professional misconduct if he pays or allows or agrees to pay or allow, directly or indirectly, any share, commission or brokerage in the fees or profits of his professional business, to any person other than ◆ A member of the Institute or ◆ A partner or ◆ A retired partner or ◆ The legal representative of a deceased partner, ◆ Or a member of any other professional body or ◆ With such other persons having such qualification as may be prescribed, for the purpose of rendering such professional services from time to time in or outside India. In the given case in substance the CA has agreed to share his receipt with a finance company from whom he has taken a loan, which is not permitted. **Conclusion**: Mr. K will be deemed to be guilty of professional misconduct under Clause 2 of Part I of First Schedule.
Q.18	**Comment on the following with reference to the Chartered Accountants Act, 1949 and Schedules thereto: A CA Firm pays share of profits to widow of deceased partner. [May 09 (4 Marks)]**
	Ans. : Sharing of Profits with widow of deceased Partner: As per Clause (2) of Part I of the First Schedule to the Chartered Accountants Act, 1949, a CA in practice is deemed to be guilty of professional misconduct if he pays or allows or agrees to pay or allow, directly or indirectly, any share, commission or brokerage in the fees or profits of his professional business, to any person other than ◆ a member of the Institute or ◆ a partner or ◆ a retired partner or ◆ the legal representative of a deceased partner, ◆ or a member of any other professional body or ◆ with such other persons having such qualification as may be prescribed, for the purpose of rendering such professional services from time to time in or outside India. However, it is further decided by the Council of the ICAI that widow or legal representative of a deceased partner can continue to receive a share of profit where the partnership agreement provides the same. **Conclusion:** If the agreement so provides, there would not be any professional misconduct on part of the firm, otherwise, it amounts to professional misconduct.
Q.19	**Give your comments with reference to the Chartered Accountants Act, 1949 and Schedules thereto: K, a practicing Chartered Accountant gave 50% of the audit fees received by him to L, who was not a Chartered Accountant, under the nomenclature of office allowance and such an arrangement continued for a number of years. [May 12 (4 Marks)]**
	Ans. : Sharing Fees with Employees: As per clause (2) of Part I of the First Schedule to the Chartered Accountants Act, 1949, a CA in practice is deemed to be guilty of professional misconduct if he pays or allows or agrees to pay or allow, directly or indirectly, any share, commission or brokerage in the fees or profits of his professional business, to any person other than ◆ a member of the Institute or ◆ a partner or ◆ a retired partner or ◆ the legal representative of a deceased partner,

- or a member of any other professional body or
- with such other persons having such qualification as may be prescribed,

for the purpose of rendering such professional services from time to time in or outside India.

In the given case in substance the CA has shared his profit and therefore, is guilty of professional misconduct under the clause. It is not the nomenclature to a transaction that is material but it is the substance of the transaction, which has to be looked into.

Conclusion: Mr. K will be deemed to be guilty of professional misconduct under Clause 2 of Part I of First Schedule.

Q.20 Mr. X who passed his CA examination of ICAI on 18th July, 2017 and started his practice from August 15, 2017. On 16th August 2017, one female candidate approached him for articleship. In addition to monthly stipend, Mr. X also offered her 1% profits of his CA firm. She agreed to take both 1% profits of the CA firm and stipend as per the rate prescribed by the ICAI. The Institute of Chartered Accountants of India sent a letter to Mr. X objecting the payment of 1% profits. Mr. X replies to the ICAI stating that he is paying 1% profits of his firm over and above the stipend to help the articled clerk as the financial position of the articled clerk is very weak. Is Mr. X liable to professional misconduct.

[Nov. 13 (4 Marks)]

Or

Mr. X, who passed his CA examination of ICAI on 18th July, 2017 had started his practice from 15th August, 2017. On 16th August, 2017 one candidate approached him for article ship. Mr. X decided to give her 1% profits of his CA firm in addition to monthly stipend. She agreed to take both 1% of profits and prescribed stipend. The ICAI had sent a letter to Mr. X objecting the payment of 1% profits.

Mr. X replied stating that sharing 1% profits is over and above the stipend to help the articled clerk to overcome her financial crisis.

Is Mr. X liable for Professional misconduct? [May 16 (4 Marks)]

Ans. : Sharing Profits with Articled Clerks:

As per clause (2) of Part I of the First Schedule to the Chartered Accountants Act, 1949, a CA in practice is deemed to be guilty of professional misconduct if he pays or allows or agrees to pay or allow, directly or indirectly, any share, commission or brokerage in the fees or profits of his professional business, to any person other than

- a member of the Institute or
- a partner or
- a retired partner or
- the legal representative of a deceased partner,
- or a member of any other professional body or
- with such other persons having such qualification as may be prescribed,

for the purpose of rendering such professional services from time to time in or outside India.

Conclusion: Mr. X will be guilty of professional misconduct in terms of clause 2 of part I of First Schedule and reply of Mr. X that he is paying 1% profits over and above the stipend to help the article clerk is not tenable.

Q.21 Give your comments with reference to the Chartered Accountants Act, 1949 and Schedules thereto: A Chartered Accountant who was in practice since last 20 years died in a road accident. His widow sold the practice to another Chartered Accountant in practice for ₹ 30 lakhs. The price also included the right to use the firm name. [Nov. 12 (4 Marks)]

or

Mr. Qureshi, Chartered Accountant, in practice died in a road accident. His widow proposes to sell the practice of her husband to Mr. Pardeshi, Chartered Accountant, for ₹ 5 lakhs. The price also includes right to use the firm name-Qureshi and Associates. Can widow of Qureshi sell the practice and can Mr. Pardeshi continue to practice in that name as a proprietor? [Nov. 04 (4 Marks)]

Ans. : Sale of Practice by widow of deceased member:

With reference to Clause 2 of Part I of First Schedule to CA Act, 1949, in case of sole proprietorship firm, the Council of ICAI has resolved that the sale/transfer of goodwill shall be permitted in respect of cases where the death of the proprietor occurred on or after 30-8-1998 provided:

- ICAI's permission to practice in the deceased's firm name is sought within a year of death. (In such a case, name of the firm is kept in abeyance till one year from the date of death).
- In case there exist a dispute as to the legal heir of the deceased proprietor, information as to the existence of the dispute is received by the Institute within a year of the death. (In such a case, name of the firm is kept in abeyance till one year from the date of settlement of dispute).

Conclusion: Widow of deceased member can sell the goodwill provided sale is completed within one year from the death of member and permission of ICAI is obtained.

Q.22 **Mr. X is a practicing Chartered Accountant. Mr. Y is a practicing Advocate representing matters in the court of law. X and Y decided to help each other in the matters involving their professional expertise. Accordingly, Mr. X recommends Mr. Y in all litigation matters in the court of law and Y consults X in all matters relating to finance and other related matters, which comes to him in arguing various cases. Consequently, they started sharing profits of their professional work. Is Mr. X liable for professional misconduct?**

[May 16 (4 Marks)]

Ans. : Sharing Fees with Advocate or of Advocate:

- As per clause (2) of Part I of the First Schedule to the Chartered Accountants Act, 1949, a CA in practice is deemed to be guilty of professional misconduct if he pays or allows or agrees to pay or allow, directly or indirectly, any share, commission or brokerage in the fees or profits of his professional business, to any person other than a member of the Institute or a partner or a retired partner or the legal representative of a deceased partner, or a member of any other professional body or with such other persons having such qualification as may be prescribed, for the purpose of rendering such professional services to time in or outside India.
- As per Clause 3 of Part I of the First Schedule to the CA Act, 1949, a CA in Practice is deemed to be guilty of professional Misconduct if he accepts or agrees to accept any part of the profits of the professional work of a person who is not a member of the Institute. However, such a restriction does not apply in respect of member of any other professional bodies or with such other persons having prescribed qualifications.
- For the purpose of Clauses 2 & 3, Regulation 53A of CA Regulations 1988 allows sharing of profit with an advocate.

Conclusion: Mr. X will not be deemed to be guilty of professional misconduct as Clauses 2 & 3 permits a CA in practice for profit sharing with members of any other professional bodies or with such other persons having prescribed qualifications and advocates are prescribed under Regulation 53A.

"ICAI Examiner Comments"

Handful of candidates failed to mention the exception and concluded wrongly.

Q.23 **CA. P is a newly qualified Chartered Accountant in practice and in order to increase his professional practice and client base, entered into an agreement with Mr. A, a qualified and experienced registered valuer to share 20% professional fees for all cases of valuation referred to him by CA. P. Based on this, CA. P received ₹ 1,20,000 during the year 2018-19 from Mr. A. Is CA. P guilty of misconduct under the Chartered Accountants Act, 1949?** **[Nov. 19 - Old Syllabus (4 Marks)]**

Ans. : Sharing Fees of professional work of others:

- As per Clause 3 of Part I of the First Schedule to the Chartered Accountants Act, 1949, a CA in Practice is deemed to be guilty of professional Misconduct if he accepts or agrees to accept any part of the profits of the professional work of a person who is not a member of the Institute. However, such a restriction does not apply in respect of member of any other professional bodies or with such other persons having prescribed qualifications.
- Regulations 53A and 53B of CA Regulations, 1988 prescribes the qualifications of persons with whom profits can be shared.
- In this case, CA. P a practicing Chartered Accountant entered into an agreement with Mr. A, a qualified and experienced registered valuer to share 20% professional fees for all cases of valuation referred to him by CA. P. Based on this, CA. P received ₹ 1,20,000 during the year 2018-19 from Mr. A.

Conclusion: Mr. P will be deemed to be guilty of professional misconduct by virtue of Clause 3, Part I of First Schedule as he accepts professional fees from a person who is not a member of ICAI. Further, registered valuers are not recognised for profit sharing purpose under Regulations 53A and 53B.

Q.24 **Comment on the following with reference to the Chartered Accountants Act, 1949 and Schedules thereto: Mr. P, a Chartered Accountant in practice entered into a partnership with Mr. L, an advocate for sharing of fees for work sent by one to the other. However, due to some disputes, the partnership was dissolved after 1 month without any fees having been received.** **[Nov. 05 (4 Marks)]**

Ans. : Partnership with an Advocate:

As per Clause 4, Part I of First Schedule, a CA in Practice is deemed to be guilty of professional Misconduct if he enters into partnership in or outside India with any person other than the following:

- C.A. in practice, or
- Member of any other professional body having prescribed qualifications, or
- A person who but for his residence abroad would be entitled to be registered as member, or
- A person whose qualifications are recognized by CG or Council for the purpose of permitting such partnerships.

As per Regulations 53A and 53B of Chartered Accountant Regulations, 1988, a member is permitted to enter into partnership with an advocate, member of Bar Council of India, besides other qualified persons and members of other professional bodies.

Conclusion: Mr. P will not be deemed to be guilty of professional misconduct as clause 4 permits a CA in practice for entering into partnership with members of any other professional bodies or with such other persons having prescribed qualifications and members of bar council of India and persons having Bachelor of Law are prescribed.

Q.25 **Can a practicing CA be held guilty of professional misconduct under the following circumstance: Z, a Chartered Accountant wrote several letters to Government Department, pointing out seniority of his firm, sending his life sketch and stating that he had a glorious record of service to the country as well as to the organisation of accountancy profession with a view to get the audit work.** **[Nov. 03 (4 Marks)]**

Ans. : Soliciting work directly or indirectly:

- As per Clause 6 of Part I of First Schedule to the Chartered Accountants Act, 1949 a member shall be held guilty if a Chartered Accountant in practice solicits clients or professional work either directly or indirectly by circular, advertisement, personal communication or interview or by any other means.
- As per Council Guidelines for Advertisement for the members in practice, a member is not permitted to claim any superiority over any other Member(s)/Firm(s) or to include the names of the clients in any write up.
- In the present case, Mr. Z, a practicing Chartered Accountant sent the letter to government departments, pointing out his seniority and stating his record of serving the nation, which seems to be indirect methods to adventure their professional practice with a view to solicit professional work.

Conclusion: Mr. Z will be deemed to be guilty of professional misconduct as per clause 6 of part I of First Schedule of the Chartered Accountants Act, 1949.

Note: Alternatively, answer may be based on Clause 7, Part I to First Schedule referring to advertisement of professional attainments.

Q.26 **Comment on the following with reference to the Chartered Accountants Act, 1949 and Schedules thereto: M/s XYZ, a firm of Chartered Accountants created a website "www.xyzindia.com". The website besides containing details of the firm and bio-data of the partners also contains the photographs of all the partners of the firm.** **[May 05 (5 Marks)]**

Ans. : Hosting Details on Website:

- As per guidelines of the ICAI laid down in Clause (6) of Part I of the First Schedule to the Chartered Accountants Act, 1949, a firm of chartered accountant can create its own website using any format subject to guidelines.
- However, the website should be so designed that it does not solicit clients or professional work and should not amount to direct or indirect advertisement.
- The guidelines of the ICAI allows a firm to put up the details of the firm, bio-data of partners and display of a passport size photograph.

Conclusion: M/s XYZ had complied with all the guidelines and there does not appear any violation of the Chartered Accountants Act, 1949 and its Regulations.

Q.27 Comment on the following with reference to the Chartered Accountants Act, 1949 and Schedules thereto: Mr. S, a Chartered Accountant published a book and gave his personal details as the author. These details also mentioned his professional experience and his present association as partner with M/s RST, a firm. [Nov. 05 (5 Marks)]

Ans. : Solicitation of Professional Work:

- As per clause 6 of Part I of the First Schedule to the Chartered Accountants Act, 1949 a CA in practice will be deemed to be guilty of professional misconduct if he solicits client or professional work either directly or indirectly, by circular, advertisement, personal communication or interview or by any other means.
- While elaborating forms of soliciting work, the Council has specified that a member is not permitted to indicate in a book or an article, published by him, the association with any firm of chartered accountants.
- In the present case, Mr. S a Chartered Accountant published the book and mentioned his professional experience and his association as a partner with M/s RST, a firm of chartered accountants.

Conclusion: Mr. S has violated the restriction imposed under Clause 6 of Part I of First Schedule and hence held to be guilty of professional misconduct.

Q.28 Comment on the following with reference to the Chartered Accountants Act, 1949, Code of Ethics and Schedules to the Act: XYZ & Associates, a firm with 5 partners developed a website www.xyzassociates.com. The website also contained a link to "All India Chartered Accountants Association", a voluntary association where X, a partner of the firm is currently the Vice-president. [May 06 (4 Marks)]

Ans. : Hosting Details on Website:

- As per guidelines of the ICAI laid down in Clause (6) of Part I of the First Schedule to the Chartered Accountants Act, 1949, a chartered accountant or the firm of chartered accountants can create its own website using any format subject to guidelines.
- As per guidelines, a website may provide a link to website of ICAI, its regional councils, branches and government departments and other professional bodies like AICPA, ICAEW etc.
- In the present case, website provide a link to the "All India Chartered Accountants Association" which is not permitted.

Conclusion: The firm is guilty of professional misconduct by virtue of Clause 6 of Part I of First Schedule.

Q.29 Comment on the following with reference to the Chartered Accountants Act, 1949, Code of Ethics and Schedules to the Act: M/s LMN, a firm of Chartered Accountants responded to a tender from a State Government for computerization of land revenue records. For this purpose, the firm also paid ₹ 50,000 as earnest deposit as part of the terms of the tender. [May 06 (4 Marks)]

Ans. : Solicitation of Work:

- Clause 6 of Part I of First Schedule allows solicitation of client or professional work through responding to tenders.
- Further Guidelines are being issued by Council allowing therein a member to respond to tenders where minimum fees of the assignment is prescribed in the tender document itself or where the areas are open to other professionals along with Chartered Accountants.
- Further, in respect of a non-exclusive area, members are permitted to pay reasonable amount towards earnest money/security deposits.
- In the present case, since computerisation of property records does not fall within exclusive areas for Chartered Accountants, M/s LMN can respond to tenders as well as deposit ₹ 50,000 as earnest deposit and shall not have committed any professional misconduct.

Conclusion: There is no professional misconduct on part of M/s LMN.

Q.30 Comment on the following with reference to the Chartered Accountants Act, 1949 and Schedules thereto: A chartered Accountant in practice created his own website in attractive format and colours and circulated information contained in the website through E-mail. [May 07 (5 Marks)]

Or

Comment on the following with reference to the Chartered Accountants Act, 1949 and schedules thereto: Mr. Brilliant, a chartered accountant in practice, created his own website in attractive format and highlighted the contents in blue colour. He also circulated the information contained in the website through E-mail to acknowledge public at large about his expertise. However, due to shortage of time, he could not intimate his website address to the Institute.

Ans. : Solicitation of work through website:

- As per Clause 6 of Part I of the First Schedule to the Chartered Accountants Act, 1949, a CA in practice shall be deemed to be guilty of misconduct if he solicits clients or professional work either directly or indirectly by a circular, advertisement, personal communication or interview or by any other means.
- Guidelines issued by the ICAI under Clause 6 of Part I of First Schedule to the CA Act 1949, for development of website by members in practice does not prescribe any standard format or restriction on use of colours.
- However, it is a requirement that none of the information contained in the website be circulated on their own or through E-mail or by any other mode except on a specific pull request.
- Further, there is no requirement to intimate the website address to the Institute. Members are only required to comply with the website guidelines issued by Council of ICAI.
- In the present case, information is circulated through e-mail, hence it is a violation of guidelines.

Conclusion: Member would be held guilty of professional misconduct for circulation of information through e-mail.

Q.31 **CA. S and CA. M are two partners of the CA firm SM & Co. Being very pious, CA. S organised a religious ceremony at his home for which he instructed his printing agent to add his designation "Chartered Accountant" with his name in the invitation cards. Later on, the invitations were distributed to all the relatives, close friends and clients of both the partners.**

Ans. : Using designation "Chartered Accountant" on marriage invitation cards:

- As per Clause 6, Part I of First Schedule of Chartered Accountants Act, 1949, a CA in practice shall be deemed to be guilty of professional misconduct if he solicits clients or professional work either directly or indirectly, by circular, advertisement, personal communication or interview or by any other means.
- Guidelines issued by the Council of ICAI under Clause 6 allowed a member to use designation "Chartered Accountant" as well as name of firm in greeting cards, invitations for marriages and religious ceremonies and any invitation for opening or inauguration of office, or letters regarding change in office premises or telephone numbers provided these are sent only to clients, relatives and close friends of concerned member.
- In the present case, CA. S is adding the designation Chartered Accountant with his name on invitation cards and these cards were distributed to his and his partner's relatives, close friends and clients.

Conclusion: CA. S shall be deemed to be guilty of professional misconduct for sending the invitation cards using designation chartered accountant to partner's relatives, close friends and clients.

Q.32 **Comment on the following with reference to the Chartered Accountants Act, 1949, and Schedules thereto: Mr. X, a CA in practice, provides part-time tutorship under the coaching organization of the Institute. On 30th June, 2017, he was awarded 'Best Faculty of the year' as gratitude from the Institute. Later on, he posted his framed photograph on his website wherein he was receiving the said award from the Institute.**

Ans. : Posting other than passport size photo on website:

- As per Clause 6, Part I of First Schedule of Chartered Accountants Act, 1949, a CA in practice shall be deemed to be guilty of professional misconduct if he solicits clients or professional work either directly or indirectly, by circular, advertisement, personal communication or interview or by any other means.
- As per guidelines of the ICAI laid down in Clause (6) of Part I of the First Schedule to the Chartered Accountants Act, 1949, a chartered accountant or the firm of chartered accountants can create its own website using any format subject to guidelines.
- As per the guidelines, a member is not permitted to display any photograph on the website, other than passport size photograph.
- In the present case, Mr. X displayed his framed photograph on website wherein he was receiving "Best faculty of the year" award from the Institute.

Conclusion: Mr. X will be guilty of professional misconduct because as per the guidelines for the website issued under Clause 6 of Part I of First Schedule, no photograph of any sort (except passport size photograph of member) is permitted to be displayed on website.

Q.33 Comment on the following with reference to the CA Act, 1949, and Schedules thereto: A special notice has been issued for a resolution at 6th AGM of F Ltd. providing expressly that CA. S shall not be reappointed as an auditor of the company. Consequently, CA. S submitted a representation in writing to the company as provided under section 140(4)(iii) of the Companies Act, 2013. In the representation, CA. S incorporated his independent working as a professional throughout the term of office and also indicated his willingness to continue as an auditor if reappointed by the shareholders of the Company.

Ans. : Sending representation to solicit the professional work:

- As per Clause 6, Part I of First Schedule of Chartered Accountants Act, 1949, a CA in practice shall be deemed to be guilty of professional misconduct if he solicits clients or professional work either directly or indirectly, by circular, advertisement, personal communication or interview or by any other means.
- Guidelines issued by the Council of ICAI under Clause 6 allowed a member to send representation to the company provided right of Representation should not be used to secure needless publicity. It need to be set out in a dignified manner how he has been acting independently through his term of office and his willingness to continue as an auditor if reappointed by shareholders.
- In the present case, CA. S has submitted the representation u/s 140(4)(*iii*) of Companies Act, 2013 in the proper manner.

Conclusion: No misconduct arises on Part of CA. S as guidelines issued under Clause 6 of Part I of First Schedule allows a CA in practice to make the representation u/s 140(4) of Companies Act, 2013 which is not used by the auditor to secure needless publicity.

Q.34 Comment on the following with reference to the Chartered Accountants Act, 1949, and its Schedules to the Act: CA. N, in practice, started project consultancy work as a part of his practice and to advance the same, sent mail to all the CAs in the country informing them of his services and for securing professional work.

Ans. : Soliciting the professional work from another chartered accountant:

- As per Clause 6 of Part I of the First Schedule to the Chartered Accountants Act, 1949, a Chartered Accountant in practice shall be deemed to be guilty of misconduct if he solicits clients or professional work either directly or indirectly by a circular, advertisement, personal communication or interview or by any other means.
- However, it is specifically provided under Clause 6, that noting contained in Clause 6 shall be construed as preventing or prohibiting any chartered accountant from applying or requesting for or inviting or securing professional work from another chartered accountant in practice.
- In the present case, CA. N sent mail to all the CAs in the country informing them of his services and for securing professional work.

Conclusion: There is no misconduct on Part of CA. N as exceptions to Clause 6 of Part I of First Schedule allows a CA in practice to secure professional work from another CA in practice.

Q.35 M/s LMN & Associates, a firm of Chartered Accountants responded to a tender issued exclusively for Chartered Accountants by an organisation in the area of tax audit. However, no minimum fee was prescribed in the tender document.

Ans. : Responding to tenders in exclusive area:

- Clause 6 of Part I of First Schedule allows solicitation of client or professional work through responding to tenders.
- Further Guidelines are being issued by Council allowing therein a member to respond to tender where minimum fees of the assignment is prescribed in the tender document itself or where the areas are open to other professionals along with Chartered Accountants.
- In the present case, M/s LMN & Associates responded to a tender of tax audit which is exclusively reserved for Chartered Accountants even though no minimum fee was prescribed in the tender document.

Conclusion: LMN & Associates shall be guilty of professional misconduct as responding to tenders in exclusive area in which minimum fees is not prescribed amounts to solicitation of work.

Q.36 Discuss the following with reference to the Chartered Accountants Act, 1949 and the Schedules thereto: M/s XYZ a firm of Chartered Accountants in practice develops a website "XYZ.com". The colour chosen for the website was a very bright green and the website was to run on a "push" technology where the name of the partners of the firm and the major clients were to be displayed on the website without any disclosure obligation from any regulator.

Ans. : Hosting Details on Website:

- As per guidelines of the ICAI laid down in Clause (6) of Part I of the First Schedule to the Chartered Accountants Act, 1949, a chartered accountant of the firm can create its own website using any format subject to guidelines.
- However, the website should be so designed that it does not solicit clients or professional work and should not amount to direct or indirect advertisement.
- As per guidelines, there is no restriction on the use of colours. However, the website is required to run on a "pull" technology and not on "push" technology; and the name of clients and fees charged from them is not permitted to be appear on the website.
- Disclosure of names of clients and/or fees charged, on the website is permissible only where it is required by a regulator, whether or not constituted under a statute, in India or outside India, provided that such disclosure is only to the extent of requirement of the regulator.
- In the present case, M/s XYZ, a firm of Chartered Accountants in practice develops a website "XYZ.com". The colour chosen for the website was a very bright green and the website was to run on a "push" technology where the name of the partners of the firm and the major clients were to be displayed on the website without any disclosure obligation from any regulator.

Conclusion: The firm would be liable for professional misconduct due to running website on Push Technology and displaying name of clients on website without any requirement of regulator.

Q.37 **Give your comments with reference to the Chartered Accountants Act, and Schedules thereto: An advertisement was published in a Newspaper containing the photograph of Mr. X, a member of the institute wherein he was congratulated on the occasion of the opening ceremony of his office.**

[Nov. 09 (4 Marks)]

Ans. : Solicitation of Client or Professional Work:

- As per Clause 6 of Part I of the First Schedule to the Chartered Accountants Act, 1949, a Chartered Accountant in practice shall be deemed to be guilty of misconduct if he solicits clients or professional work either directly or indirectly by a circular, advertisement, personal communication or interview or by any other means.
- In the given case, Mr. X published an advertisement in a Newspaper containing his photograph on the occasion of the opening ceremony of his office.
- This kind of advertisement will amount to soliciting professional work by advertisement directly or indirectly.

Conclusion: Mr. X would be guilty under Clause 6 of Part I of the First Schedule to the Chartered Accountants Act, 1949.

Q.38 **Give your comments with reference to the Chartered Accountants Act, and Schedules thereto: Mr. X, a Chartered Accountant and the proprietor of X & Co., wrote several letters to the Assistant Registrar of Co-operative Societies stating that though his firm was on the panel of auditors, no audit work was allotted to the firm and further requested him to look into the matter.** **[Nov. 09 (4 Marks)]**

Ans. : Soliciting Professional Work:

- As per Clause 6 of Part I of the First Schedule to the Chartered Accountants Act, 1949, a Chartered Accountant in practice shall be deemed to be guilty of misconduct if he solicits clients or professional work either directly or indirectly by a circular, advertisement, personal communication or interview or by any other means.
- In the given case, Mr. X, a Chartered Accountant and proprietor of M/s X and Co., wrote several letters to the Assistant Registrar of Co-operative Societies, requesting for allotment of audit work.
- The writing of continuous letter to ascertain the reasons for not getting the work is quite alright but request for allowing the work does not appears to be correct.

Conclusion: Mr. X would be held guilty under clause 6 of Part I of First Schedule of the CA Act, 1949.

Q.39 **Comments with reference to the Chartered Accountants Act, 1949 and Schedules thereto: PQR and Associates, Chartered Accountants have their website and on the letterhead of the firm it is mentioned that "Visit our website: www.pqr.com". In the website the nature of assignments handled, names of prominent clients and fees charged is also displayed without any disclosure obligation by any regulator.**

[Nov. 10 (4 Marks)]

Ans. : Website Particulars:

- The Council of the ICAI has issued guidelines for posting the particulars on Website by CA in practice and firms of CA in practice under Clause (6) of Part I of First Schedule to the CA Act, 1949.
- According to the guidelines the details in the website should be so designed that it does not amount to soliciting client or professional work. It is permitted to mention the website address on letterhead but soliciting people to visit website is not permitted.
- PQR and Associates letterhead invites to people to visit their website. Similarly, the website mentions the nature of assignments, names of the prominent clients and fees charged. The nature of assignments is permitted for display only on specific 'Pull' request, and the name of clients, the fees charged is not permitted at all.
- Disclosure of names of clients and/or fees charged, on the website is permissible only where it is required by a regulator, whether or not constituted under a statute, in India or outside India, provided that such disclosure is only to the extent of requirement of the regulator.

Conclusion: PQR & Associates will be held guilty of Professional Misconduct under Clause 6 of Part I of First Schedule to the Chartered Accountants Act, 1949.

Q.40 Give your comments with reference to the Chartered Accountants Act, 1949 and Schedules thereto: Mr. Sodhi, a Chartered Accountant in practice, who is proposed to be removed as the auditor of a company makes unsubstantiated and derogatory remarks against the management of the company in his representation u/s 140 of the Companies Act, 2013. [May 11 (4 Marks)]

Ans. : Use of Right to representation u/s 140:

- As per Clause 6 of Part I of the First Schedule to the CA Act, 1949, a CA in practice is deemed to be guilty of professional misconduct if he solicits clients or professional work, directly or indirectly, by circular, advertisement, personal communication or by other means.
- Using unsubstantiated and derogatory remarks against the Management of the Company in his representation u/s 140 of the Companies Act, 2013 tantamount to securing professional work by undignified means.
- The Council of the Institute has clarified that the right to make a representation u/s 140 of the Companies Act, 2013 does not mean that an auditor has any prescriptive right on a lien to an audit. The wording of this representation should be such that, apart from the opportunity not being abused to secure needless publicity, it does not tantamount directly or indirectly to canvassing or soliciting for his continuance as an auditor.
- The letter should merely set out in a dignified manner how he has been acting independently and conscientiously through the terms of office and may, in addition, indicate if he so chooses, his willingness to continue as an auditor if reappointed by the shareholder.

Conclusion: In the present case, Mr. Sodhi is guilty of professional misconduct.

Q.41 Give your comments with reference to the Chartered Accountants Act, 1949 and Schedules thereto: A letter is sent by a Chartered Accountant in practice to the Ministry of Finance inquiring whether a panel of auditors is being maintained by the Ministry and if so to include his name in the panel (CV enclosed). [May 11 (4 Marks)]

Or

A CA firm M/s GST & Associates, has sent a letter to the Goods and Service Tax Council stating that the firm has 2 partners who specialize in the law of Goods and Service Tax and asked the said Council to include their name in the panel, whenever formed, for providing advisory to the Chartered Accountants Act, 1949. [Nov. 17 (4 Marks)]

Ans. : Roving Enquiries:

- As per Clause 6 of Part I of the First Schedule to the CA Act, 1949, a CA in practice shall be deemed to be guilty of misconduct if he solicits clients or professional work either directly or indirectly by a circular, advertisement, personal communication or interview or by any other means.
- Such a restraint has been put so that the members maintain their independence of judgment and may be able to command respect from their prospective clients.
- In case of making an application for the empanelment for the allotment of audit and other professional work, the Council has opined that, "where the existence of such a panel is within the knowledge of the member, he is free to write to the concerned organization with a request to place his name on the panel.

- However, it would not be proper for the member to make roving inquiries by applying to any such organization for having his name included in any such panel."

Conclusion: The member is guilty of misconduct in terms of the above provision as he has solicited professional work by making roving inquiries about the panel.

"ICAI Examiner Comments"

Majority of the examinees made correct reference of the relevant clause but few examinees wrongly concluded that the firm and its partners are not guilty. Some examinees failed to discuss the council's opinion that "where the existence of such a panel is within the knowledge of the member, he is free to write to the concerned organization with a request to place his name on the panel.

Q.42 **Give your comments with reference to the Chartered Accountants Act, 1949 and Schedules thereto: M, a practicing Chartered Accountant sent a letter to another firm of Chartered Accountants, claiming himself to be a pioneer in liaisoning with Central Government Ministries and its allied Departments for getting various Government clearances for which he had claimed to have expertise and had given a list of his existing clients and details of his staff etc.** **[May 12 (4 Marks)]**

Ans. : Soliciting work directly or indirectly:

- As per Clause 6 of Part I of First Schedule to the Chartered Accountants Act, 1949 a member shall be held guilty if a Chartered Accountant in practice solicits clients or professional work either directly or indirectly by circular, advertisement, personal communication or interview or by any other means.
- As per Council Guidelines for Advertisement for the members in practice, a member is not permitted to claim any superiority over any other Member(s)/Firm(s) or to include the names of the clients in any write up.
- In the present case, Mr. M, a practicing Chartered Accountant sent the letter to another firm of Chartered Accountants, claiming himself to be a pioneer in liaisoning with Central Government Ministries and its allied Departments for getting various Government clearances for which he had claimed to have expertise and had also given a list of his existing clients and details of his staff etc. which seems to be indirect methods to adventure their professional practice with a view to gain publicity and thereby solicit clients or professional work.

Conclusion: Mr. M was guilty of professional misconduct as per clause 6 of part I of First Schedule of the Chartered Accountants Act, 1949.

Q.43 **Mr. Honest, a Chartered Accountant in practice, wrote two letters to M/s XY Chartered Accountants a firm of CA's; requesting them to allot him some professional work. As he did not have a significant practice or clients, he also wrote a letter to M/s ABC, a firm of Chartered Accountants for securing professional work. Mr. Clever, another CA, informed ICAI regarding Mr. Honest's approach to secure the professional work. Is Mr. Honest wrong in soliciting professional work?** **[Nov. 13 (4 Marks)]**

Ans. : Solicitation of professional work from another CA:

- As per Clause 6 of Part I of the First Schedule to the Chartered Accountants Act, 1949 a Chartered Accountant in practice shall be deemed to be guilty of misconduct if he solicits clients or professional work either directly or indirectly by a circular, advertisement, personal communication or interview or by any other means.
- However, nothing in clause 6 shall be construed as preventing or prohibiting any Chartered Accountant from applying or requesting for or inviting or securing professional work from another chartered accountant in practice.
- In the given case, Mr. Honest wrote letters only to other Chartered Accountants, M/s XY and M/s ABC requesting them to allot some professional work to him, which is not prohibited under clause 6.

Conclusion: Mr. Honest is not wrong in soliciting professional work from another CA, hence there is no professional misconduct.

Q.44 **During the opening ceremony of a new branch office of CA. Young, his friend CA. Old introduced to CA. Young, his friend and client Mr. Rich, the owner of an Export House whose accounts had been audited by CA. Old for more than 15 years. After few days, Mr. Rich approached CA. Young and offered a certification work which hitherto had been done by CA. Old CA. Young undertook the work for a fee which was not less than fee charged by CA. Old in earlier period.**

Comment whether CA. Young had done any professional misconduct.

[Nov. 18 - New Syllabus (5 Marks)]

Answer: Soliciting work directly or indirectly:

- As per Clause 6 of Part I of First Schedule to the Chartered Accountants Act, 1949 a member shall be held guilty if a Chartered Accountant in practice solicits clients or professional work either directly or indirectly by circular, advertisement, personal communication or interview or by any other means.
- As per Council Guidelines for Advertisement for the members in practice, acceptance of original professional work emanating from a client introduced by another member is not permitted.
- In the present case, during the opening ceremony of a new branch office of CA. Young, his friend CA. Old introduced to CA. Young, his friend and client Mr. Rich, the owner of an Export House whose accounts had been audited by CA. Old for more than 15 years. After few days, Mr. Rich approached CA. Young and offered a certification work which hitherto had been done by CA. Old CA. Young undertook the work for a fee which was not less than fee charged by CA. Old in earlier period.

Conclusion: Mr. Young will be deemed guilty of professional misconduct under clause 6, Part I of First Schedule.

Q.45 **Comment with reference to the Chartered Accountants Act, 1949 and schedules thereto:**

A special notice has been issued for a resolution at 3rd AGM of LED Ltd., providing expressly that CA. Anoop shall not be re-appointed as an auditor of the company. Consequently, CA. Anoop submitted a representation in writing to the company with a request to circulate to the members. In the detailed representation, CA. Anoop included the contributions made by him in strengthening the control procedures of the company during his association with the company and also indicated his willingness to continue as an auditor if reappointed by the shareholders of the company. [Nov. 19 - New Syllabus (4 Marks)]

Ans. : Right of representation:

- Section 140(4) of the Companies Act, 2013 permits an auditor to make a representation in writing (not exceeding a reasonable length) to the company. The proposition of the partner to highlight contributions made by the firm in strengthening the control procedures in the representation is not acceptable because the representation letter should not be prepared in a manner so as to seek publicity.
- The Code of Ethics issued by the Institute makes it amply clear that the right to make representation does not mean that an auditor has any prescriptive right or a lien on an audit.
- The wording of his representation should be such that, apart from the opportunity not being abused to secure needless publicity, it does not tantamount directly or indirectly to canvassing or soliciting for his continuance as an auditor. The letter should merely set out in a dignified manner how he has been acting independently and conscientiously through the term of office and may in addition, indicate if he so chooses his willingness to continue as auditor if re-appointed by the shareholders.

Conclusion: Mr. Anoop will be guilty of professional misconduct under Clause (6) of Part I of the First Schedule to the Chartered Accountants Act, 1949, as including contributions made by him in strengthening the control procedures of the company, amounts to solicitation of work which is not permitted.

Q.46 **Comment on the following with reference to the Chartered Accountants Act, 1949, Code of Ethics and Schedules to the Act: B, a Chartered Accountant in practice is a partner in 3 firms. While printing his personal letter heads, B gave the names of all the firms in which he is a partner. [May 09 (4 Marks)]**

Or

Mr. B, a Chartered Accountant in practice, is a partner of 4 firms. While printing his personal letter heads, Mr. B gave the names of all the firms in which he is a partner. Comment. [Nov. 15 (4 Marks)]

Ans. : Mentioning Firm's Name on Letter Heads:

- Clause 7 of Part 1 of First Schedule to the CA Act, 1949 provides that a CA in practice is deemed to be guilty of professional misconduct if he (i) advertises his professional attainments or services or (ii) uses any designation or expressions other than "Chartered Accountant" on professional documents, visiting cards, letter heads or sign boards.
- However, a degree of a university established by law in India or recognized by the Central Government or a title indicating membership of the ICAI or of any other institution that has been recognized by the Central Government or may be recognized by the council is permitted to be mentioned.

- There is no prohibition for printing names of all firms on the personal letter heads in which a member holding certificate of practice is a partner.

Conclusion: Mr. B is not guilty of any professional misconduct in the above case.

"ICAI Examiner Comments"

Many examinees wrongly referred to clause (6) of Part I of First Schedule to the Chartered Accountant Act, 1949, and wrongly concluded that by printing names of all 4 firms on the personal letter heads in which a member holding certificate of practice is a partner is guilty of any professional misconduct in the given case.

Q.47 Give your comments with reference to Chartered Accountants Act, 1949 and schedules thereto: Mr. B, a practicing Chartered Accountant as well as a qualified lawyer, was permitted by the bar council to practice as a lawyer also. He printed his visiting card where he mentioned his designation as Chartered Accountant and Advocate. [May 13 (4 Marks)]

Ans. : Using designation other than Chartered Accountant:

- As per clause 7 of Part 1 of First Schedule, a CA in practice is deemed to be guilty of professional misconduct if he (i) advertises his professional attainments or services or (ii) uses any designation or expressions other than "Chartered Accountant" on professional documents, visiting cards, letter heads or sign boards unless it be a degree of a university established by law in India or recognized by the Central Government or a title indicating membership of the ICAI or of any other institution that has been recognized by the Central Government or may be recognized by the council.
- Members of the Institute in practice who are otherwise eligible may practice as advocates subject to the permission of the Bar Council but in such case, they should not use designation "chartered accountant" in respect of the matters involving the practice as an advocate.
- In respect of other matters, they should use the designation 'chartered accountant' but they should not use the designation 'chartered accountant' and 'advocate' simultaneously.
- In the present case, Mr. B has printed his visiting card where he mentioned his designation as Chartered Accountant and Advocate which is prohibited under the clause 7.

Conclusion: Mr. B is guilty of professional misconduct due to use of designation of advocate in addition to Chartered Accountant.

Q.48 Mr. Nigal, a Chartered Accountant in practice, delivered a speech in the national conference organized by the Ministry of Textiles. While delivering the speech, he told to the audience that he is a management expert and his firm provides services of taxation and audit at reasonable rates. He also requested the audience to approach his firm of chartered accountants for these services and at the request of audience he also distributed his business cards and telephone number of his firm to those in the audience. Comment. [Nov. 13 (4 Marks)]

Ans. : Solicitation of Professional Work and Advertisement:

- Clause 6 of Part I of the First Schedule to the Chartered Accountants Act, 1949 states that a Chartered Accountant in practice shall be deemed to be guilty of misconduct if he solicits clients or professional work either directly or indirectly by a circular, advertisement, personal communication or interview or by any other means.
- Section 7 of the Chartered Accountants Act, 1949 read with Clause 7 of Part I of the First Schedule to the said Act prohibits advertising of professional attainments or services of a member. It also restrains a member from using any designation or expression other than that of a Chartered Accountant in documents through which the professional attainments of the member would come to the notice of the public.
- Guidelines issued under clauses 6 & 7 permits a practicing member to give lectures at forums and may give their names and describe themselves as Chartered Accountants, but no reference should be made, to the name and address or services of his firm.
- In the present case, Mr. Nigal uses the designation of "Management Expert" and also made reference to the services provided by his firm of Chartered Accountants at reasonable rates and distribute business cards to audience.

Conclusion: Mr. Nigal will be held guilty of professional misconduct under clauses 6 & 7 of Part I of First Schedule to the CA Act, 1949 due to solicitation of professional work and advertisement of services rendered by his firm.

Q.49 Comment with respect to Chartered Accountant Act, 1949: Mr. SP, a Chartered Accountant obtains registration as category IV merchant banker under the SEBI's Rules and Regulations and act as Advisor to a capital issue of MB Co. Ltd. He designated himself under the caption "Merchant banker" in client offer documents and 'Advisor to issue' in his own letterheads, visiting cards and professional documents.
[May 15 (4 Marks)]

Ans. : Using designation other than Chartered Accountant:

- As per clause 7 of Part 1 of First Schedule, a CA in practice is deemed to be guilty of professional misconduct if he (i) advertises his professional attainments or services or (ii) uses any designation or expressions other than "Chartered Accountant" on professional documents, visiting cards, letter heads or sign boards unless it be a degree of a university established by law in India or recognized by the Central Government or a title indicating membership of the ICAI or of any other institution that has been recognized by the Central Government or may be recognized by the council.
- A Chartered Accountant is allowed to act as advisor to a capital issue and offer document of client company may specify the name of address of chartered accountant under the caption "Advisor to issue". However, it is specifically prohibited that member concerned should not use the designation either "Merchant Banker" or "Advisor to issue" in their own letterheads, visiting cards and professional documents.
- In the present case, Mr. SP designated himself under the caption "Merchant banker" in client offer documents and 'Advisor to issue' in his own letterheads, visiting cards and professional documents.

Conclusion: Mr. SP is guilty of Professional Misconduct under Clause 7 of Part I of First Schedule due to use of designation other than Chartered Accountant.

Q.50 Mr. M, a chartered accountant in practice, has printed visiting cards which besides other details also carries a Quick Response (QR) code. The visiting card as well the QR code contains his name, office and residential address, contact details, e-mail id and name of the firm's website. Comment with reference to the Chartered Accountants Act, 1949 and schedules thereto. **[May 17 (4 Marks)]**

Ans. : Printing of Visiting Cards and using QR Code:

- As per clause 7 of Part 1 of First Schedule, a CA in practice is deemed to be guilty of professional misconduct if he (i) advertises his professional attainments or services or (ii) uses any designation or expressions other than "Chartered Accountant" on professional documents, visiting cards, letter heads or sign boards unless it be a degree of a university established by law in India or recognized by the Central Government or a title indicating membership of the ICAI or of any other institution that has been recognized by the Central Government or may be recognized by the council.
- As per guidelines issued under Clause 7, printing photograph on the visiting cards is not permissible. However Quick Response Code may be printed on visiting card provided that the Code does not contain information that is not otherwise permissible to be printed in their visiting card.
- In the present case, Mr. M, a chartered accountant in practice, has printed visiting cards which besides other details also carries a Quick Response (QR) code. The visiting card as well the QR code contains his name, office and residential address, contact details, e-mail id and name of the firm's website.

Conclusion: No misconduct arises on part of Mr. M as information printed on visiting card and information contained in QR Code are permissible.

"ICAI Examiner Comments"

Candidates wrongly mentioned Clause (6) Part I of First Schedule instead of Clause (7) of Part I of First Schedule to the Chartered Accountants Act, 1949.

Q.51 Comment on the following with reference to the Chartered Accountants Act, 1949 and schedules thereto: A Chartered Accountant in practice, empanelled as IP (Insolvency Professional) has mentioned the same on his visiting cards, letter heads and other communications also. Mr. A, who is residing in his neighbourhood has filed a complaint for professional misconduct against the said member for such mention of insolvency professional on circulations. **[RTP-Nov. 18, May 19-Old Syllabus (4 Marks)]**

Answer: Using designation other than Chartered Accountant:

- As per clause 7 of Part 1 of First Schedule, a CA in practice is deemed to be guilty of professional misconduct if he (*i*) advertises his professional attainments or services or (*ii*) uses any designation or expressions other than "Chartered Accountant" on professional documents, visiting cards, letter heads or sign boards unless it be a degree of a university established by law in India or recognized by the Central Government or a title indicating membership of the ICAI or of any other institution that has been recognized by the Central Government or may be recognized by the council.

- In the present case, a Chartered Accountant in practice, empanelled as IP (Insolvency Professional) has mentioned the same on his visiting cards, letter heads and other communications also. Mr. A, who is residing in his neighbourhood has filed a complaint for professional misconduct against the said member for such mention of insolvency professional on circulations.

Conclusion: A Chartered Accountant empanelled as IP (Insolvency Professional) can mention 'Insolvency Professional' on his visiting cards, Letter heads and other communication, as this is a title recognised by the Central Government in terms of Clause-7 of Part-1 of First Schedule to the Chartered Accountants Act, 1949. Thus, complaint of neighbour is not enforceable/valid.

Q.52 **Comment with the reference to the Chartered Accountants Act, 1949 and schedules thereto: R, a practicing Chartered Accountant, is a Director in X Ltd; a Public Company. The prospectus of X Ltd. mentions the name of Mr. R as a director along with his various professional attainments, his areas of specialization and expertise in the fields of international taxation.** **[Nov. 18-Old Syllabus (4 Marks)]**

Answer: Advertisements of professional attainments:

- As per clause 7 of Part I of First Schedule, a CA in practice is deemed to be guilty of professional misconduct if he (*i*) advertises his professional attainments or services or (*ii*) uses any designation or expressions other than 'Chartered Accountant" on professional documents, visiting cards, letter heads or sign boards unless it be a degree of a university established by law in India or recognized by the Central Government or a title indicating membership of the ICAI or of any other institution that has been recognized by the Central Government or may be recognized by the council.
- As per guidelines issued under Clause 7, name of CA acting as director in the company is permissible to appear in the prospectus of the company, however descriptions regarding his expertise, specialisation and knowledge in any particular field is not permitted.
- In thc present case, R, a practicing Chartered Accountant, is a Director in X Ltd. a Public Company. The prospectus of X Ltd. mentions the name of Mr. R as a director along with his various professional attainments, his areas of specialization and expertise in the fields of international taxation.

Conclusion: Mr. R will be deemed to be guilty of professional misconduct under Clause 7, Part I of First Schedule.

Q.53 **Mr. X a chartered Accountant accepted his appointment as tax auditor of a firm under Sec. 44AB of the Income Tax Act and commenced the tax audit within two days of his appointment since the client was in a hurry to file return of income before the due date. After commencing the audit, Mr. X realised his mistake of accepting this tax audit without sending any communication to the previous tax auditor. In order to rectify his mistake, before signing the tax audit report, he sent a registered post to the previous auditor and obtained the postal acknowledgement. Will Mr. X be held guilty under the CA Act?**

Ans. : Prior Communication with the previous auditor:

- As per Clause 8 of Part I of First Schedule to the CA Act, 1949, a chartered accountant in practice is deemed to be guilty of professional misconduct if he accepts a position as auditor previously held by another chartered accountant without first communicating with him in writing.
- This requirement would apply to all types of audit i.e. statutory audit, tax audit, internal audit, concurrent audit, etc.
- It is further provided that if time schedule given for the assignment is such that there is no time to wait for the reply from the retiring auditor, the incoming auditor may give conditional acceptance of the appointment and can commence the work immediately after he has sent the communication to the retiring auditor.
- In the present case, Mr. X has commenced his work and thereafter he sent the letter to the predecessor auditor.

Conclusion: Mr. X is guilty of professional misconduct by virtue of clause 8 of Part I of First Schedule.

Q.54 **Can a practicing Chartered Accountant be held guilty of professional misconduct under the following circumstance: W, a chartered Accountant has sent letters under certificate of posting to the previous auditor informing him his appointment as an auditor before the commencement of audit by him.**

Ans. : Prior Communication with the previous auditor:

- As per Clause 8 of Part I of First Schedule to the CA Act, 1949, a chartered accountant in practice is deemed to be guilty of professional misconduct if he accepts a position as auditor previously held by another chartered accountant without first communicating with him in writing.
- This requirement would apply to all types of audit i.e. statutory audit, tax audit, internal audit, concurrent audit, etc.
- It is further provided that incoming auditor is required to send his communication by Registered post acknowledgement due or by hand against an acknowledgement in writing. Mere posting of a letter under certificate of posting is not sufficient to establish communication.
- In the present case, Mr. W has sent letter under Certificate of posting.

Conclusion: Mr. W will be Guilty of professional misconduct by virtue of clause 8 of Part I of first schedule in accordance with which communication need to be sent "Registered Post Acknowledgement Due" or by "hand against a written acknowledgement".

Q.55 **Comment on the following with reference to the Chartered Accountants Act, 1949 and schedules thereto: BC & Co, a firm of Chartered Accountants, accepted an assignment for audit under CGST Act, without any prior communication with the previous auditor.**

Ans. : Prior Communication with the previous auditor:

- As per Clause 8 of Part I of First Schedule to the CA Act, 1949, a chartered accountant in practice is deemed to be guilty of professional misconduct if he accepts a position as auditor previously held by another chartered accountant or a certified auditor who has been issued certificate under the Restricted Certificates Rules, 1932, without first communicating with him in writing.
- In the present case, BC & Co. accepted VAT Audit under State Level Act, carried out by another firm of chartered accountants in the previous year, without prior communication with the previous auditor.
- A communication is mandatory requirement for all types of audit, if the previous auditor is a chartered accountant.

Conclusion: BC & Co., the firm is guilty of professional misconduct due to non-compliance of requirement as stated in Clause 8 of Part I of First Schedule.

Q.56 **M/s CD & Co., a firm of Chartered Accountants, accepted an assignment for audit under State level VAT Act and communicated the same over phone to the previous auditor, M/s AB & Co., Chartered Accountants. Comment.**

Ans. : Prior Communication with the previous auditor:

- As per Clause 8 of Part I of First Schedule to the CA Act, 1949, a chartered accountant in practice shall be deemed to be guilty of professional misconduct if he accepts a position as auditor previously held by another chartered accountant without first communicating with him in writing.
- This requirement would apply to all types of audit i.e. statutory audit, tax audit, internal audit, concurrent audit, VAT audit etc.
- It is further provided that incoming auditor is required to send his communication by Registered post acknowledgement due or by hand against an acknowledgement in writing.
- In the present case, incoming auditor communicate his appointment to predecessor auditor over the phone.

Conclusion: M/S CD & Co. is guilty of professional misconduct, as they are required to send his communication by Registered post acknowledgement due or by hand against an acknowledgement in writing. Mere communication over phone is not sufficient to establish written communication.

Q.57 **Comment on the following with reference to the Chartered Accountants Act, 1949 and schedules thereto: Mr. B was appointed as auditor of XYZ Ltd. in place of Mr. A. Mr. B had send a letter of communication to Mr. A under certificate of posting and proceeds to conduct the audit. A makes a complaint to the Institute on the basis of non-receipt of communication.**

Ans. : Prior Communication with the previous auditor:

- As per Clause 8 of Part I of First Schedule to the CA Act, 1949, a chartered accountant in practice is deemed to be guilty of professional misconduct if he accepts a position as auditor previously held by another chartered accountant without first communicating with him in writing.

- This requirement would apply to all types of audit i.e. statutory audit, tax audit, internal audit, concurrent audit, etc.
- It is further provided that incoming auditor is required to sent his communication by Registered post acknowledgement due or by hand against an acknowledgement in writing. Mere posting of a letter under certificate of posting is not sufficient to establish communication.
- In the present case, Mr. B has sent letter under Certificate of posting.

Conclusion: Mr. B will be Guilty of professional misconduct by virtue of clause 8 of Part I of First Schedule in accordance with which communication need to be sent "Registered Post Acknowledgement Due" or by "hand against a written acknowledgement".

Q.58 Comment on the following with reference to the Chartered Accountants Act, 1949 and its Schedules: CA. T, in practice, was appointed to carry out internal audit of a stock broker, listed with BSE. However, he failed to intimate his appointment to the statutory auditors of the company. The statutory auditor feels this is violation of professional ethics.

Ans. : Prior Communication with the previous auditor:

- As per Clause 8 of Part I of First Schedule to the CA Act, 1949, a chartered accountant in practice is deemed to be guilty of professional misconduct if he accepts a position as auditor previously held by another chartered accountant without first communicating with him in writing.
- This requirement would apply to all types of audit i.e. statutory audit, tax audit, internal audit, concurrent audit, etc.
- Further the requirement of Clause 8 is applicable in situation of replacing of one auditor by another auditor and not in case of parallel positions.
- In the present case, CA T was appointed as Internal Auditor, he owes no duty towards statutory auditor for prior communication.

Conclusion: There is no violation of professional ethics as Clause 8 of Part I of First Schedule applies in case of replacement positions and not in case of parallel positions.

Q.59 Can a practicing Chartered Accountant be held guilty of professional misconduct under the following circumstance: P, a Chartered Accountant had accepted appointment as an auditor of QRS Company limited without ascertaining from the company whether the requirements of Secs. 139 and 140 of the Companies Act, 2013 had been complied with. However, he realised this defect only after acceptance.

Ans. : Non-observance of compliance of Sections 139 & 140 of Companies Act, 2013:

- As per Clause 9 of Part I of First Schedule to Chartered Accountant Act, 1949, a CA in practice shall be deemed to be guilty of professional misconduct if he accepts an appointment as auditor of a company, without ascertaining whether requirements of Secs. 224 & 225 of Companies Act, 1956 (Secs. 139 & 140 of Companies Act, 2013), in respect of such appointment have been duly complied with.
- In the present case, P, a Chartered Accountant had accepted appointment as an auditor of QRS Company limited without ascertaining from the company whether the requirements of Secs. 139 and 140 of the Companies Act, 2013 had been complied with.

Conclusion: P will be held to be guilty of professional misconduct under clause 9 of Part I of First Schedule to the Chartered Accountants Act, 1949. Realisation of defect subsequent to acceptance of audit is immaterial.

Q.60 Comment on the following with reference to the C. A. Act, 1949 and schedules thereto: CA X was appointed as the Auditor of ABC Ltd. for 2018-19. Since he declined to accept the appointment, the Board of Directors appointed CA Y as the auditor in the place of CA X, which was also accepted by CA Y.

[Nov. 08 (4 Marks)]

Ans. : Violation of Clause 9:

- Clause (9) of Part I of the First Schedule to the Chartered Accountants Act, 1949, provides that a member in practice shall be deemed to be guilty of professional misconduct if he accepts an appointment as auditor of a company without first ascertaining from it whether the requirements of Sections 224 and 225 of the Companies Act, 1956 (now Sections 139 and 140 read with Section 141 of the Companies Act, 2013), in respect of such appointment have been duly complied with.
- Board of Directors has been given powers u/s 139(6) and u/s 139(8)(*i*) to appoint first auditors and to fill casual vacancy respectively. The non-acceptance of appointment by CA. X does not constitute a casual vacancy to be filled by the Board. In this case, it will be deemed that no auditor was appointed in the AGM.

- As per Sec. 139(10) of the Companies Act, 2013 when at any AGM, no auditor is appointed or re-appointed, the existing auditor shall continue to be the auditor of the company. Hence, the appointment of the auditor by the Board is not valid in law.

Conclusion: CA. Y is guilty of professional misconduct as per clause 9 of the First Schedule as he accepted the appointment without verification of statutory requirements.

Q.61 XYZ Ltd. appoints you as the auditor of the company. You observe that previous auditor's A & Co., resigned. Also Balance Sheet as at 31-03-2017 shows an audit fee payable of ₹ 25,000. What precautions you will take before commencing the audit work? [Nov. 10 (4 Marks)]

Ans. : Precautions before Commencing the Audit Work:

(*i*) Check whether a statement, in the prescribed form, has been filed by the resigning auditor within a period of 30 days from the date of resignation, to the company and the registrar, indicating the reasons and other facts as may be relevant with regard to the resignation, for the compliance of Section 140(2) of the Companies Act, 2013.

(*ii*) Ascertain that the appointment of new Auditor is in compliance with Section 139(8) of the Act as mentioned above i.e. the resolution appointing the new auditor has been approved by the company in the general meeting as it is case of casual vacancy by resignation.

(*iii*) The auditor should also refer the resignation statement file by the previous auditor and communicate with him (previous auditor) to ascertain the circumstances which led up him to retire.

(*iv*) The auditor must ascertain whether there exist any circumstances on account of which he should not accept the appointment. As per Section 139 of the Act, the auditor must ensure that before any appointment or reappointment of auditors is made at an AGM, a written certificate has been provided by him to the company that his appointment is in accordance with the limits specified in Section 141(3)(g).

(*v*) He should also satisfy himself that the notice provided for under Sections 139 and 140 has been effectively served on the outgoing auditor.

(*vi*) Further, Clause (8) of Part I of the First Schedule to the Chartered Accountants Act, 1949, provides that a member in practice shall be deemed to be guilty of professional misconduct if he accepts a position as auditor previously held by another chartered accountant without first communicating with him in writing.

(*vii*) Moreover, Clause (9) of Part I of the same Schedule, provides that a member in practice shall be deemed to be guilty of professional misconduct if he accepts an appointment as auditor of a company without first ascertaining from it whether the requirements of Sections 224 and 225 of the Companies Act, 1956 (now Sections 139 and 140 of the Companies Act, 2013), in respect of such appointment have been duly complied with.

Q.62 Comment with reference to the CA Act, 1949 and schedules thereto: CA D, a Chartered Accountant prepared a project report for one of his clients to obtain bank finance (long-term) of ₹ 50 lakhs from a Commercial Bank. Consequent to the sanction of the loan by the bank CA. D raised a bill for his services @ 2% of the loan sanctioned. [Nov. 08 (4 Marks)]

Ans. : Charging fees on %age basis:

- Clause 10 of Part I to First Schedule to the CA Act, 1949 prohibits a CA in practice to charge, or offers to charge, accept or offers to accept in respect of any professional employment, fees which are based on a percentage of profits or which are contingent upon the findings or results of such employment.
- However, this restriction is not applicable where such payment is permitted by the regulations made in this behalf. The Council of the Institute has framed regulation 192 which exempts certain professional services from the operation of clause 10.
- Charging fees on %age of fund raised is covered under Regulation 192.

Conclusion: No misconduct arises on part of Mr. D by charging fees as a %age of loan sanctioned.

Note: It is assumed that Bank finance is covered within the meaning of fund-raising service. Alternatively, if it is presumed that bank finance is not covered within the meaning of fund-raising services, charging fees on a %age of loan sanctioned will amount to professional misconduct.

Q.63 Comment on the following with reference to the Chartered Accountants Act, 1949 and Schedules thereto: An auditor of a cooperative society has agreed to charge fees @ 5% of the profits of the society.

Ans. : Charging Fees on Percentage Basis:

- Clause 10 of Part I of First schedule to CA Act, 1949, prohibits a CA in practice to charge or offer to charge, accept or offer to accept in respect of any professional work, fees which are based on a percentage of profits or which are contingent upon the findings or result of work.
- However, this restriction is not applicable where such payment is permitted by the regulations made in this behalf. The Council of the Institute has framed regulation 192 which exempts certain professional services from the operation of clause 10.
- As per Regulation 192, in the case of an audit of a co-operative society, fees may be charged on a percentage of the paid up capital or the working capital or the gross or net income or profits.

Conclusion: Audit of Co-operative society is included in the exceptions stated in regulation 192, the auditor is not guilty of any professional misconduct.

Q.64 **Comment on the following with reference to the Chartered Accountants Act, 1949 and Schedules thereto: PQR Pvt Ltd. approached CA. Whai, a Chartered Accountant in Practice, for debt recovery services. CA Whai accepted the work and insisted for fees to be based on 2% of the debt recovered.**

Ans. : Charging Fees on Percentage Basis:

- Clause 10 of Part I of First Schedule to CA Act, 1949, prohibits a CA in practice to charge or offer to charge, accept or offer to accept in respect of any professional work, fees which are based on a percentage of profits or which are contingent upon the findings or result of work.
- However, this restriction is not applicable where such payment is permitted by the regulations made in this behalf. The Council of the Institute has framed regulation 192 which exempts certain professional services from the operation of clause 10.
- As per Regulation 192, in the case of debt recovery services, fees may be charged on a percentage of amount of debt recovered.

Conclusion: Charging fees on a percentage of debt recovered in case of debt recovery services is included in the exceptions stated in regulation 192, Hence CA. Whai is not guilty of any professional misconduct.

Q.65 **Comment with respect to Chartered Accountant Act, 1949: Mr. P a practicing chartered accountant acting as liquidator of AB & Co. charged his professional fees on percentage of the realization of assets.**

[May 15 (4 Marks)]

Ans. : Charging Fees on Percentage Basis:

- Clause 10 of Part I of First schedule to CA Act, 1949, prohibits a CA in practice to charge or offer to charge, accept or offer to accept in respect of any professional work, fees which are based on a percentage of profits or which are contingent upon the findings or result of work.
- However, this restriction is not applicable where such payment is permitted by the regulations made in this behalf. The Council of the Institute has framed regulation 192 which exempts certain professional services from the operation of clause 10.
- As per Regulation 192, in case of a receiver or a liquidator, the fees may be charged on a percentage of the realisation or disbursement of the assets.

Conclusion: No Misconduct arises on part of Mr. P under Clause 10 of Part I to First schedule as charging fees as a percentage of realisation of assets while acting as a liquidator is permitted by Regulation 192.

"ICAI Examiner Comments"

Few candidates were not aware of the exception granted under Regulation to liquidator to charge fees on percentage basis on realization.

Q.66 **Efficient Ltd. is running into losses and in order to optimize resource utilization and cost reduction, approaches you to carry out the assignment and offers a fee of 5% of benefits derived from the suggestions made by you. Comment with respect to Chartered Accountants Act, 1949 and Regulations there to.**

[May 18 - Old Syllabus (4 Marks)]

Ans. : Charging Fees on Percentage Basis:

- Clause 10 of Part I of First schedule to CA Act, 1949, prohibits a CA in practice to charge or offer to charge, accept or offer to accept in respect of any professional work, fees which are based on a percentage of profits or which are contingent upon the findings or result of work.
- However, this restriction is not applicable where such payment is permitted by the regulations made in this behalf. The Council of the Institute has framed regulation 192 which exempts certain professional services from the operation of clause 10.

- As per Regulation 192, in the case of services related to cost optimization, fees may be charged on the basis of percentage of benefit derived.

Conclusion: No Misconduct arises under Clause 10 of Part I to First schedule as charging fees as a percentage of benefit derived while providing services related to cost optimisation is permitted by Regulation 192.

Q.67 Mr. J started his practice as Chartered Accountant in 2013. During 2018, he got an offer for the post of Chief Accountant of a Software Development Company, as a fulltime employee for a salary of ₹ 60,000 p.m. On accepting the offer, Mr. J converted his practice into a partnership firm by taking a fresh Chartered Accountant as his partner. Mr. J neither intimated the Institute nor obtained permission from the Institute about his employment. Will Mr. J be held guilty under the CA Act?

Ans. : Engagement in other occupations:

- Clause 11 of Part 1 of First Schedule to the CA Act, 1949 prohibits a member in practice to engage in any business or occupation other than the profession of chartered accountants unless permitted by the Council so to engage.
- It does not prohibit a CA from being a director of a company, except MD or a whole-time director. But if any of the partners is interested in such company as an auditor then he cannot be director of the said company.
- In the present case Mr. J has accepted the full-time employment of a software company which requires prior approval from the council of ICAI.

Conclusion: Mr. J will be held guilty of professional misconduct by virtue of Clause 11 of Part I of First schedule, as he has accepted the employment in addition to the practice without obtaining permission of the Institute.

Q.68 Comment on the following with reference to the Chartered Accountants Act, 1949 and schedules thereto: Mr. J.J. a practicing Chartered Accountant engages himself as part time finance manager of Quick Return Securities Ltd. He is of the view that as both functions are independent, he need not take permission from the Institute.

Ans. : Engagement in other occupations:

- Clause 11 of Part 1 of First Schedule to the CA Act, 1949 prohibits a member in practice to engage in any business or occupation other than the profession of chartered accountants unless permitted by the Council so to engage.
- It does not prohibit a CA from being a director of a company, except MD or a whole-time director. But if any of the partners is interested in such company as an auditor then he cannot be director of the said company.
- In the present case Mr. JJ has accepted the part time employment of Quick Return Securities Ltd. which requires prior approval from the council of ICAI.

Conclusion: Mr. JJ will be held guilty of professional misconduct by virtue of Clause 11 of Part I of First schedule, as he has accepted the employment in addition to the practice without obtaining permission of the Institute.

Q.69 Comment on the following with reference to the Chartered Accountants Act, 1949 and schedules thereto: A chartered accountant in practice takes up the appointment as managing director of a public limited company.

Ans. : Engagement in other occupations:

- Clause 11 of Part 1 of First Schedule to the CA Act, 1949 prohibits a member in practice to engage in any business or occupation other than the profession of chartered accountants unless permitted by the Council so to engage.
- It does not prohibit a CA from being a director of a company, except MD or a whole-time director. But if any of the partners is interested in such company as an auditor then he cannot be director of the said company. To accept the position of MD in a company, member is required to obtain prior permission from Council of ICAI.
- In the present case, a CA in practice has taken up the appointment as managing director of a public limited company.

Conclusion: Appointment requires prior and specific approval from Council. In absence of such approval, member will be held to be guilty of professional misconduct (by virtue of clause 11 of Part I of First Schedule and Regulation 190A), otherwise not.

Q.70 Comment on the following with reference to the Chartered Accountants Act, 1949 and schedules thereto: M, a Chartered Accountant in practice, is the Statutory Auditor of S Ltd. for the year ended 31st March 2018. In January 2018, he was appointed as a Director in H Ltd., which is the holding Compony of S Ltd.

Ans. : Appointment as Auditor in Holding Company:

- As per clause 11 of Part I of the First Schedule to the CA Act, 1949, a CA in practice can be a director of a company wherein he or any of his partners is not interested in such company as auditor.
- In the present case, Mr. M is statutory auditor of S Ltd. whereas he is appointed as director in H Ltd. which is holding of S Ltd. Such an appointment is not restricted under Clause 11 of Part I of First Schedule.
- However, public conscience is expected to be ahead of law and to ensure and reflect independence, members should thus not place themselves in position which may affect their independence.

Conclusion: Auditor of a subsidiary should not accept the position as a director in holding company as it might affect his independence.

Q.71 Comment on the following with reference to the Chartered Accountants Act, 1949 and Schedules thereto Mr. A, a Chartered Accountant in practice has been appointed editor of a monthly journal which analyses performance of the Stock Market and Mutual Fund Schemes.

Ans. : Engagement in other occupations:

- Clause 11 of Part 1 of First Schedule to the CA Act, 1949 prohibits a member in practice to engage in any business or occupation other than the profession of chartered accountants unless permitted by the Council so to engage.
- It does not prohibit a CA from being a director of a company, except MD or a whole-time director. But if any of the partners is interested in such company as an auditor then he cannot be director of the said company.
- General permission is granted under Regulation 190A for being appointed as editor of professional journal.
- In the present case Mr. A has accepted the appointment as editor of a monthly journal which analyses the stock performance.

Conclusion: Clause 11 permits editorship of professional journals, but in the instant case journal related to performance analysis of stock market and mutual fund schemes cannot be treated as professional journal hence, Mr. A would be held guilty of professional misconduct by virtue of Clause 11 of Part I of First Schedule.

Q.72 Comment on the following with reference to the Chartered Accountants Act, 1949, and Schedules thereto: CA. Sufi is practicing since 2008 in the field of company auditing. Due to his good practical knowledge, he was offered editorship of a 'Company Audit' Journal which he accepted. However, he did not take any permission from the council regarding such editorship.

Ans. : Engagement in other occupations:

- Clause 11 of Part 1 of First Schedule to the CA Act, 1949 prohibits a member in practice to engage in any business or occupation other than the profession of chartered accountants unless permitted by the Council so to engage.
- It does not prohibit a CA from being a director of a company, except MD or a whole-time director. But if any of the partners is interested in such company as an auditor then he cannot be director of the said company.
- General permission is granted under Regulation 190A for being appointed as editor of professional journal.
- In the present case CA Sufi has accepted the appointment as editor of a "Company Audit", which is a professional journal.

Conclusion: Clause 11 permits editorship of professional journals, hence no misconduct arises on part of Mr. Sufi.

Q.73 CA. Preeti is a leading Income Tax Practitioner in Delhi. She is very much fond of cooking. Due to this passion of her, she also wrote a cookery book "Delight your tummy" during the year. But, she didn't take any permission from the Council of the Institute for engaging herself into authorship of such book. Comment.

Ans. : Engagement in other occupations:

- Clause 11 of Part 1 of First Schedule to the CA Act, 1949 prohibits a member in practice to engage in any business or occupation other than the profession of chartered accountants unless permitted by the Council so to engage.
- It does not prohibit a CA from being a director of a company, except MD or a whole time director. But if any of the partners is interested in such company as an auditor then he cannot be director of the said company.
- General permission is granted under Regulation 190A for authorship of any book or article.
- In the present case CA. Preeti has authored a cookery book for which no specific permission is required.

Conclusion: Clause 11 permits authorship of any book, hence no misconduct arises on part of CA. Preeti.

Q.74 Give your comments with reference to CA Act and schedules thereto: Mr. A, a practicing CA, took over as the executive Chairman of a software company on 01.04.2018. On 10.04.2018 he applied to the council for permission. [May 10 (4 Marks)]

Ans. : Engagements in other occupations:

- As per Clause 11 of Part I of First Schedule of the Chartered Accountants Act, 1949, a Chartered Accountant in practice will be deemed to be guilty of professional misconduct if he engages in any business or occupation other than the profession of Chartered Accountant unless permitted by the Council so to engage.
- In the instant case, Mr. A took over as the executive chairman on 01.04.2018 and applied for permission on 10.04.2018.
- On the basis of these facts, he was engaged in other occupation between the period 01.04.2018 and 10.04.2018, without the permission of the Council.

Conclusion: Mr. A is guilty of professional misconduct in terms of Clause 11 of Part I of First Schedule of the Chartered Accountants Act, 1949 as he accepted the employment without obtaining permission from Council.

Q.75 Give your comments with reference to the Chartered Accountants Act, 1949 and schedules thereto: Mr. B is a practising Chartered Accountant holding a valid certificate of practice. He accepted the appointment as Director of the Green World Co. Ltd. Mr. C, a partner of Mr. B is statutory auditor of the said company. [Nov. 10 (4 Marks)]

Ans. : Engagement in other occupations:

- Clause 11 of Part 1 of First Schedule to the CA Act, 1949 prohibits a member to engage in any business or occupation other than the profession of chartered accountants unless permitted by the Council so to engage.
- It does not prohibit a CA from being a director of a company, except MD or a whole-time director. But if any of the partners is interested in such company as an auditor then he cannot be director of the said company.
- In the present case Mr. B has accepted the directorship in a Company where his partner Mr. C is an auditor without obtaining specific permission of the council.
- As per Clause 4 of Part I of the Second Schedule to the CA Act, 1949, expressing an opinion on F.S. of any entity in which the auditor, his firm or a partner of his firm has a substantial interest would constitute misconduct.
- Sec. 141(3)(c) of the Companies Act, 2013 also disqualifies a person to be appointed as an auditor if he is a partner of an officer of the company. Sec. 141(4) of the Companies Act, 2013 requires the appointed auditor to vacate his office if he incurs any of the disqualifications mentioned under Sec. 141(3).

Conclusion: Mr. B will be held for Professional Misconduct under Clause 11 of Part 1 of First Schedule to the Chartered Accountants Act, 1949.

Mr. C, a partner of Mr. B, should vacate the office as per requirement of Sec. 141(4) of Companies Act, 2013, being disqualified u/s 141(3)(*c*).

Q.76 **C.A Z, is a leading income tax practitioner and consultant for derivative products. He resides in Mumbai near to the ABC commodity stock exchange and does trading in commodity derivatives. Everyday, he invests nearly 50% of his time settle the commodity transactions. Is CA Prabhu liable for professional misconduct?** **[Nov. 13 (4 Marks)]**

Or

Comment on the following with reference to the Chartered Accountants Act, 1949 and schedules there to: CA Z who is a leading Income Tax Practitioner and consultant in Jaipur is also trading in derivatives. **[Nov. 08 (4 Marks)]**

Or

Z, a Chartered Accountant holding Certificate of Practice, is a leading Income Tax Practitioner in Gurugram. He is also trading in derivatives. Comment with reference to the Chartered Accountant Act, 1949 and schedules thereto. **[May 17 (4 Marks)]**

Ans. : Engagement into other occupation:

- As per clause 11 of Part I of First Schedule of CA Act, 1949, a Chartered Accountant is deemed to be guilty of professional misconduct if he "engages in any business or occupation other than the profession of Chartered Accountant unless permitted by the Council so to engage".
- However, the Council has granted general permission to the members to engage in certain specific occupation. In respect of all other occupations specific permission of the Institute is necessary.
- In this case CA Z is engaged in the occupation of trading in commodity derivatives which is not covered under the general permission, hence specific permission of the Institute has to be obtained.

Conclusion: If Mr. Z has obtained specific permission of the council, then there is no misconduct, otherwise he will be deemed to be guilty of professional misconduct under clause 11 of Part I of First Schedule of CA Act, 1949.

Q.77 **Comment with respect to Chartered Accountants Act, 1949: A Chartered Accountant having COP entered into partnership with persons, who are not the members of the institute, for the purpose of carrying on business. The share of the chartered account in the profit and losses was 25%. He was to take part in the business and was entitled to represent the firm before Govt. authorities etc. he was operating the bank account of the firm was receiving moneys from the customers and was also looking after the affairs of the partnership.** **[May 15 (4 Marks)]**

Ans. : Entering into partnership with others and engagement into other occupation:

- As per Clause 4 of Part I of First Schedule a CA in Practice shall be deemed to be guilty of professional Misconduct if he enters into partnership in or outside India with any person other than C.A. in practice or other recognised person.
- As per Clause 11 of Part I of First Schedule of CA Act, 1949, a CA in practice shall be deemed to be guilty of professional misconduct if he "engages in any business or occupation other than the profession of Chartered Accountant unless permitted by the Council so to engage".
- In the present case, A CA entered into partnership with persons who are not covered under Clause 4 for the purpose of carrying on a business activity for which specific and prior permission of Council was required.

Conclusion: CA shall be guilty of Professional Misconduct by virtue of clauses 4 & 11 of Part I of First Schedule due to entering into partnership with persons other than prescribed under Clause 4 and carrying on a business without obtaining permission from Council of ICAI.

Q.78 **CA Raghu is practicing in the field of Income - tax over a period of 12 years. He has gained experience in this domain over others.**

Sam, a student of Chartered Accountancy Course is very much impressed with the knowledge of CA Raghu. He approached CA Raghu to take guidance on some topics of Income-tax related to his course. Ca Raghu, on request decided to spare time and started providing private tutorship to Sam and some of his friends along with. However, he forgot to take specific permission from the ICAI, for such private tutorship,

Is CA Raghu, professionally liable for misconduct? **[May 16 (4 Marks)]**

Ans. : Engagement into other occupation:

- As per clause 11 of Part I of First Schedule of CA Act, 1949, a Chartered Accountant is deemed to be guilty of professional misconduct if he "engages in any business or occupation other than the profession of Chartered Accountant unless permitted by the Council so to engage".

- However, the Council has granted general permission to the members to engage in certain specific occupation. In respect of all other occupations specific permission of the Institute is necessary.
- In this case CA Raghu is engaged in the occupation of private tutorship which is covered under the general permission, hence specific permission of the Institute is not required.

Conclusion: Mr. Raghu will not be liable for professional misconduct as for imparting private tutorship no specific permission is required to be obtained from Council of ICAI as provided under Regulation 190A.

"ICAI Examiner Comments"

Some of the candidates failed to differentiate specific and general permission and thus concluded wrongly.

Q.79 **Comment on the following with reference to the Chartered Accountants Act, 1949 and schedules thereto: S a practicing chartered accountant gives power of attorney to an employee chartered accountant to sign reports and financial statements, on his behalf.**

Ans. : Delegation of Certification work:

- As per clause 12 of Part I of the First Schedule of the Chartered Accountants Act, 1949, a Chartered Accountant in practice is deemed to be guilty of professional misconduct "if he allows a person not being a member of the Institute in practice or a member not being his partner to sign on his behalf or on behalf of his firm, any balance sheet, profit and loss account, report or financial statements".
- This clause should be read in conjunction with Section 26 of Chartered Accountants Act, 1949 which stipulates that no person other than a member of the Institute shall sign any document on behalf of a chartered accountant in practice or a firm of such chartered accountants in his or its professional capacity
- In this case CA 'S' gives power of attorney to an employee to sign reports and financial statements on his behalf, which is not permitted as such.

Conclusion: S is guilty of professional misconduct under clause 12 of Part I of First Schedule.

Q.80 **Give your comments with reference to the Chartered Accountants Act, 1949 and Schedules thereto: CA Smart, a practicing Chartered Accountant was on Europe tour between 15-09-17 and 25-09-17. On 18-09-17 a message was received from one of his clients requesting for a stock certificate to be produced to the bank on or before 20-09-17. Due to urgency, CA Smart directed his assistant, who is also a Chartered Accountant to sign and issue the stock certificate after due verification, on his behalf.**

[May 11 (4 Marks)]

Ans. : Signing of Stock Certificate:

- As per clause 12 of Part I of the First Schedule of the C.A. Act, 1949, a CA in practice is deemed to be guilty of professional misconduct "if he allows a person not being a member of the Institute in practice or a member not being his partner to sign on his behalf or on behalf of his firm, any balance sheet, profit and loss account, report or financial statements".
- In this case CA Smart allowed his assistant who is not a partner but a member of the ICAI to sign stock certificate on his behalf and thereby commits misconduct.

Conclusion: CA Smart is guilty of professional misconduct under clause 12 of Part I of First Schedule of the CA Act, 1949.

Q.81 **Mr. 'A' is a practicing Chartered Accountant working as proprietor of M/s A & Co. He went abroad for 3 months. He delegated the authority to Mr. 'Y' a Chartered Accountant his employee for taking care of routine matters of his office. During his absence Mr. 'Y' has conducted the under mentioned jobs in the name of M/s A & Co.**

(*i*) He issued the audit queries to client which were raised during the course of audit.

(*ii*) He issued production certificate to a client under GST Laws.

(*iii*) He attended the Income Tax proceedings for a client as authorized representative before Income Tax Authorities.

Please comment on eligibility of Mr. 'Y' for conducting such jobs in name of M/s A & Co. and liability of Mr. 'A' under the Chartered Accountants Act, 1949. **[May 14 (5 Marks)]**

Ans. : Delegation of Certification work:

- As per clause 12 of Part I of the First Schedule of the Chartered Accountants Act, 1949, a Chartered Accountant in practice is deemed to be guilty of professional misconduct "if he allows a person not being a member of the Institute in practice or a member not being his partner to sign on his behalf or on behalf of his firm, any balance sheet, profit and loss account, report or financial statements".

- In this case CA 'A' proprietor of M/s A & Co., went to abroad and delegated the authority to another Chartered Accountant Mr. Y, his employee, for taking care of routine matters of his office who is not a partner but a member of the Institute of Chartered Accountants.
- The Council has clarified that the power to sign routine documents on which a professional opinion or authentication is not required to be expressed, may be delegated and such delegation will not attract provisions of clause 12. Examples of such instances are issue of audit queries, asking for information or issue of questionnaire, attending to routing matters in tax practice etc.

Conclusion:

(*i*) Issuing audit queries during the course of audit falls under routine work, which can be delegated by the auditor. Therefore, there is no misconduct in this case.

(*ii*) Issuance of production certificate to a client under GST Laws by Mr. "Y" is not a routine work and it is outside his authorities. Thus, CA 'A' is guilty of professional misconduct under clause 12 of Part I of First Schedule of the Chartered Accountants Act, 1949.

(*iii*) Attending Income tax proceedings for a client as authorized representative before Income Tax Authorities falls under routine work, hence Mr. Y, the employee of M/s A & Co. can attend to routine matter in tax practice. Therefore, there is no misconduct in this case.

Q.82 **Mr. 'K', a practicing Chartered Accountant is the proprietor of M/s K & Co. since 1995. He went abroad in the month of December 2018. He delegated the authority to Mr. 'Y' a Chartered Accountant, his employee for taking care of the important matters of his office.**

During his absence Mr. 'Y' has conducted the under mentioned jobs in the name of M/s K & Co.

(*i*) He issued Net worth certificate to a client for furnishing to a Bank.

(*ii*) He attended the GST proceedings for a client as authorized representative before GST Authorities.

Please comment on eligibility of Mr. 'Y' for conducting such jobs in name of M/s K & Co. and liability of Mr. 'K' under the Chartered Accountants Act, 1949. [Nov. 19 - New Syllabus (5 Marks)]

Ans. : Delegation of Certification work:

- As per clause 12 of Part I of the First Schedule of the Chartered Accountants Act, 1949, a Chartered Accountant in practice is deemed to be guilty of professional misconduct "if he allows a person not being a member of the Institute in practice or a member not being his partner to sign on his behalf or on behalf of his firm, any balance sheet, profit and loss account, report or financial statements".
- In this case CA 'K' proprietor of M/s K & Co., went abroad and delegated the authority to another Chartered Accountant Mr. Y, his employee, for taking care of routine matters of his office.
- The Council has clarified that the power to sign routine documents on which a professional opinion or authentication is not required to be expressed, may be delegated and such delegation will not attract provisions of clause 12. Examples of such instances are issue of audit queries, asking for information or issue of questionnaire, attending to routing matters in tax practice etc.

Conclusion:

(*i*) Issuance of Net Worth Certificate to a client for furnishing to Bank by Mr. "Y" is not a routine work and it is outside his authorities. Thus, CA 'K' is guilty of professional misconduct under clause 12 of Part I of First Schedule of the Chartered Accountants Act, 1949.

(*ii*) Attending GST proceedings for a client as authorized representative before GST Authorities falls under routine work, hence Mr. Y, the employee of M/s K & Co. can attend to routine matter in tax practice. Therefore, there is no misconduct in this case.

7.3 - FIRST SCHEDULE, PART II-PROFESSIONAL MISCONDUCT IN RELATION TO MEMBERS IN SERVICE

Q.83 **Give your comments with reference to Chartered Accountants Act, 1949 and Schedules thereto: Mr. 'C', a Chartered Accountant holds a certificate of practice while in employment also, recommends a particular lawyer to his employer in respect of a case. The lawyer, out of the professional fee received from employer paid a particular sum as referral fee to Mr. 'C'. [May 14 (4 Marks)]**

Ans. : Referral Fee from Lawyer:

- As per Clause 2 of Part II of First Schedule of the Chartered Accountant Act, 1949, a member of the Institute (other than a member in practice) shall be guilty of professional misconduct, if he being an employee of any company, firm or person accepts or agrees to accept any part of fee, profits or gains from a lawyer, a chartered accountant or broker engaged by such company, firm or person or agent or customer of such company, firm or person by way of commission or gratification.

- In the present case, Mr. C who besides holding a certificate of practice, is also an employee and by referring a lawyer to the company in respect of a case, he receives a particular sum as referral fee from the lawyer out of his professional fee.

Conclusion: Mr. C is guilty of professional misconduct by virtue of clause 2 of Part II of First Schedule for accepting referral fees from the lawyer of his employer.

Q.84 **Mr. 'C', a Chartered Accountant employed as Senior executive in charge of Tax in a company, and not holding certificate of practice recommends a particular lawyer to his employer in respect of a case. The lawyer, out of the professional fee received from the employer of Mr. 'C' paid a particular sum as referral fee to Mr. 'C'. Comment with reference to the Chartered Accountants Act, 1949 and schedules thereto.** **[Nov. 19 - New Syllabus (5 Marks)]**

Or

C, a member of the Institute of Chartered Accountants of India, not holding certificate of practice, is employed with a firm of Chartered Accountants. He recommends a particular lawyer to his firm for some client related litigation being handled by the firm. The lawyer, out of the professional fee received by him from the said client, paid a certain sum as referral fee to C. Is A guilty of misconduct under the Chartered Accountants Act, 1949? **[Nov. 19 - Old Syllabus (4 Marks)]**

Ans. : Referral Fee from Lawyer:

- As per Clause 2 of Part II of First Schedule of the Chartered Accountants Act, 1949, a member of the Institute (other than a member in practice) shall be guilty of professional misconduct, if he being an employee of any company, firm or person accepts or agrees to accept any part of fee, profits or gains from a lawyer, a chartered accountant or broker engaged by such company, firm or person or agent or customer of such company, firm or person by way of commission or gratification.
- In the present case, Mr. C, a Chartered Accountant is working in capacity of an employee and by referring a lawyer to the employer in respect of a case, he receives a particular sum as referral fee from the lawyer out of his professional fee.

Conclusion: Mr. C is guilty of professional misconduct by virtue of clause 2 of Part II of First schedule for accepting referral fees from the lawyer of his employer.

7.4 - FIRST SCHEDULE, PART III - PROFESSIONAL MISCONDUCT IN RELATION TO MEMBERS GENERALLY

Q.85 **Give your comments with reference to CA Act and schedules thereto: Mr. X, a Chartered accountant, employed as a paid assistant with a Chartered Accountant firm. On 31st Dec. 2017, he leaves the services of the firm. Despite many reminders from ICAI he fails to reply regarding the date of leaving of the services of the firm.** **[May 10 (4 Marks)]**

Ans. : Failed to supply information called for:

- Clause 2 of Part III of the First Schedule to the Chartered Accountants Act, 1949, a member, whether in practice or not, will be deemed to be guilty of professional misconduct if he does not supply the information called for, or does not comply with the requirements asked for, by the Institute, Council or any of its Committees, Director (Discipline), Board of Discipline, Disciplinary Committee, Quality Review Board or the Appellate authority.
- In the given case, Mr. X has failed to reply to the letters of the Institute asking him to confirm the date of leaving the service as a paid assistant.

Conclusion: Mr. X is held guilty of professional misconduct as per Clause 2 of Part III of the First Schedule to the Chartered Accountants Act, 1949.

Q.86 **Give your comments with reference to Chartered Accountants Act, 1949 and Schedules thereto: Mr. 'G', while applying for a certificate of practice, did not fill in the columns which solicit information about his engagement in other occupation or business, while he was indeed engaged in a business.** **[May 14 (3 Marks)]**

Ans. : Disclosure of Information:

- As per Clause 2 of Part III of First Schedule to the Chartered Accountants Act, 1949 a member shall be held guilty if a Chartered Accountant, in practice or not, does not supply the information called for, or does not comply with the requirements asked for, by the Institute, Council or any of its Committees, Director (Discipline), Board of Discipline, Disciplinary Committee, Quality Review Board or the Appellate Authority;
- In the given case, Mr. "G", a Chartered Accountant while applying for a certificate of practice, did not fill in the columns which solicit information about his engagement in other occupation or business, while he was indeed engaged in a business.
- Details of engagement in business need to be disclosed while applying for the certificate of practice as it was the information called for in the application, by the Institute.

Conclusion: Mr. G will be held guilty for professional misconduct under the clause 2 of Part III of First Schedule for not providing the information to the Institute.

Q.87 XYZ Associates, a Chartered Accountants Firm is having a relationship with a multi-national accounting firm in India. The ICAI required that all firms having networking relationship with any other entity need to furnish information online within the stipulated time. XYZ Associated failed to respond. Comment on this with reference to professional misconduct, if any. [Nov. 18-New Syllabus (4 Marks)]

Ans. : Failed to supply information called for:

- Clause 2 of Part III of the First Schedule to the Chartered Accountants Act, 1949, a member, whether in practice or not, will be deemed to be guilty of professional misconduct if he does not supply the information called for, or does not comply with the requirements asked for, by the Institute, Council or any of its Committees, Director (Discipline), Board of Discipline, Disciplinary Committee, Quality Review Board or the Appellate authority.
- In the given case, XYZ Associates, a Chartered Accountants Firm is having a relationship with a multi-national accounting firm in India. The ICAI required that all firms having networking relationship with any other entity need to furnish information online within the stipulated time. XYZ Associated failed to respond.

Conclusion: XYZ Associates will be deemed to be guilty of professional misconduct as per Clause 2 of Part III of the First Schedule to the Chartered Accountants Act, 1949.

7.5 - FIRST SCHEDULE, PART IV - OTHER MISCONDUCT IN RELATION TO MEMBERS GENERALLY

Q.88 Write a short note on - Other Misconduct. [Nov. 10 (4 Marks)]

Or

A Chartered Accountant is liable for disciplinary action under section 21 of CA Act, 1949, if he is found guilty of any professional or other misconduct.

Explain the meaning of other misconduct with the help of two illustrative example.

[Nov. 16 (4 Marks)]

Ans. : Other Misconduct:

As per Part IV of First Schedule to Chartered Accountant Act, 1949, a member of the Institute, whether in practice or not, shall be deemed to be guilty of other misconduct, if he

1. is held guilty of any civil or criminal court for an offence which is punishable with imprisonment for a term not exceeding six months.
2. In the opinion of the Council brings disrepute to the profession or the Institute as a result of his action whether or not related to his professional work.

As per Part III of Second Schedule to Chartered Accountant Act, 1949, a member of the Institute, whether in practice or not, shall be deemed to be guilty of other misconduct, if he is held guilty of any civil or criminal court for an offence which is punishable with imprisonment for a term exceeding six months.

Some illustrative examples, where a member may be found guilty of "Other Misconduct", under the aforesaid provisions rendering, himself unfit to be member are:

(*i*) Where a chartered accountant retains the books of account and documents of the client and fails to return these to the client on request without a reasonable cause.

(*ii*) Where a chartered accountant makes a material misrepresentation.

(*iii*) Where a chartered accountant uses the services of his articled or audit clerk for purposes other than professional practice.

(*iv*) Misappropriation by office-bearer of a Regional Council of the Institute, of a large amount and utilisation thereof for his personal use.

(*v*) Non-replying within a reasonable time and without a good cause to the letter of the public authorities.

(*vi*) Where a chartered accountant had adopted coercive methods on a bank for having a loan sanctioned to him.

Q.89 **CA D, a chartered accountant in practice availed of a loan against his personal investments from a bank. He issued 2 cheques towards repayment of the said loan as per the instalments due. However, both the cheques were returned back by the bank with the remarks "Insufficient funds". Comment with reference to the Chartered Accountants Act, 1949. [Nov. 17 (4 Marks)]**

Ans. : Bringing disrepute to the profession:

- As per Clause 2 of Part IV of First Schedule to the Chartered Accountants Act, 1949, a member of the Institute, whether in practice or not, shall be deemed to be guilty of other misconduct, if in the opinion of the council, that member brings disrepute to the profession or the Institute, as a result of his action, whether or not related to his professional work.
- Accordingly, a Chartered Accountant is also expected to maintain the highest standards and integrity even in his personal affairs and any deviation from these standards calls for disciplinary action.
- In the present case, two cheques were dishonoured and returned back with the remarks "Insufficient Funds". Issuing cheques without having sufficient balance in the account is punishable offence under the Negotiable Instruments Act, 1881.

Conclusion: As the cheques were dishonoured due to insufficiency of funds, the drawer will be held guilty of offence under Negotiable Instruments Act, 1881 and consequently he would be held guilty of "Other Misconduct".

"ICAI Examiner Comments"

Examinees answered the question referring to the relevant clause, but only few examinees explained that as per Negotiable Instruments Act, 1881, where a cheque is dishonoured for insufficiency of funds the drawer of such a cheque shall be deemed to commit an offence.

Q.90 **Comment on the following with reference to the Chartered Accountants Act, 1949 and Schedules thereto: Mr. P, CA, proprietor of M/s P & Co. requests the manager of a Bank branch to sanction him a loan for ₹ 10 lakhs. He also offers free services to the manager and the staff for filing Income-tax returns for 3 years.**

or

Comment on the following: Mr. P, a Chartered Accountant in practice approached Manager of a Nationalised Bank for a loan of ₹ 25 lakhs. He has also informed the Manager that if the loan is sanctioned, the Income Tax return of the Manager and staff will be filed without charging any fees, as quid Pro quo for the loan sanctioned. [Nov. 11 (4 Marks)]

Ans. : Coercive Method for Sanction of Loan:

- Clause 2 of Part IV of First Schedule to the Chartered Accountants Act, 1949 states that member of the Institute, whether in practice or not, shall be deemed guilty of other misconduct, if he in the opinion of the Council, brings disrepute to the profession or to the Institute as a result of his action whether or not related to his professional work.
- Accordingly, a Chartered Accountant is also expected to maintain the highest standards and integrity even in his personal affairs and any deviation from these standards calls for disciplinary action.
- In the present case, the action of Mr. P, a Chartered Accountant in practice offering free service in return to sanction of loan brings disrepute to the profession of a Chartered Accountant.

Conclusion: Mr. P will be held guilty of other misconduct under Clause 2 of Part IV of the First Schedule of the Chartered Accountants Act, 1949.

Q.91 **Give your comments with reference to the Chartered Accountants Act, 1949 and schedules thereto: YKS & Co., a proprietary firm of Chartered Accountants was appointed as concurrent auditor of a bank. YKS used his influence for getting some cheques purchased and thereafter failed to repay the loan/overdraft. [Nov. 10 (4 Marks)]**

Ans. : Bringing disrepute to profession:

- Clause 2 of Part IV of First Schedule to the Chartered Accountants Act, 1949 states that member of the Institute, whether in practice or not, shall be deemed guilty of other misconduct, if he in the opinion of the Council, brings disrepute to the profession or to the Institute as a result of his action whether or not related to his professional work.
- Accordingly, a Chartered Accountant is also expected to maintain the highest standards and integrity even in his personal affairs and any deviation from these standards calls for disciplinary action.
- In the present case YKS & Co, being a concurrent auditor used his position to obtain the funds and failed to repay the same to the bank. This brings disrepute to the profession of a Chartered Accountant.

Conclusion: YKS & Co. will be held guilty of other misconduct under clause 2 of Part IV of First Schedule of the Chartered Accountants Act, 1949.

Q.92 Give your comments with reference to Chartered Accountants Act, 1949 and schedules thereto: Mr. A, a practicing Chartered Accountant, failed to return the books of account and other documents of a client despite many reminders from the client. The client had settled his entries fees dues also. [May 13 (4 Marks)]

Ans. : Non-return of Client's Books:

- As per Part IV of the First Schedule to the Chartered Accountants Act, a member of the Institute, whether in practice or not, shall be deemed to be guilty of other misconduct, if he
  (1) is held guilty by any civil or criminal court for an offence which is punishable with imprisonment for a term not exceeding six months;
  (2) in the opinion of the Council, brings disrepute to the profession or the Institute as a result of his action whether or not related to his professional work.
- A member may be found guilty of "Other Misconduct", as per clause 2, if he retains the books of account and documents of the client and fails to return these to the client on request without a reasonable cause.
- In the given case, Mr. A failed to return the books of account and other documents of his client without any reasonable cause.

Conclusion: Mr. A would be guilty of Other Misconduct under Part IV of First Schedule and liable to disciplinary action under Section 21.

Q.93 Comment on the following with reference to the Chartered Accountants Act, 1949 and schedules thereto: CA Kumar who is contesting Central Council Elections of Institute, engages his Articled Assistant for his election campaigning promising him that he will come in contact with influential people which will help to enhance his career after completion of his training period. [RTP-Nov. 18]

Ans. : Engaging Articled Assistance for personal work:

- As per Part IV of the First Schedule to the Chartered Accountants Act, a member of the Institute, whether in practice or not, shall be deemed to be guilty of other misconduct, if he
  (1) is held guilty by any civil or criminal court for an offence which is punishable with imprisonment for a term not exceeding six months;
  (2) in the opinion of the Council, brings disrepute to the profession or the Institute as a result of his action whether or not related to his professional work.
- A member may be found guilty of "Other Misconduct", as per clause 2, if he uses the services of articles for personal work.
- In the given case, CA Kumar who is contesting Central Council Elections of Institute, engages his Articled Assistant for his election campaigning promising him that he will come in contact with influential people which will help to enhance his career after completion of his training period.

Conclusion: CA. Kumar would be guilty of Other Misconduct under Part IV of First Schedule and liable to disciplinary action under Section 21.

7.6 - SECOND SCHEDULE, PART I "PROFESSIONAL MISCONDUCT IN RELATION TO MEMBERS IN PRACTICE"

Q.94 **A CA in practice was engaged by a businessman to represent him before the tax authorities on current matters and in the course of such employment he came across certain documents pointing of tax frauds in the preceding years for which the client was not represented by him.**

Is the member liable to disclose the existence and contents of the documents to tax authorities?

Ans. : Disclosure of confidential information:

- Clause (1) of Part I of the Second Schedule to the Chartered Accountants Act, 1949 states that a chartered accountant in practice shall be deemed to be guilty of professional misconduct if he discloses information acquired in the course of his professional engagement to any person other than his client, without the consent of the client or otherwise than as required by law for the time being in force.
- In respect of taxation matters, the code of conduct recommends that "If the fraud discovered by the member, relates to the accounts or tax matters of the client for past year(s) for which the client was not represented by the member the client should be advised to make a disclosure. The member may however, continue to act for the client in respect of current matter, but is under no obligation so to continue.

Conclusion: Member is not liable to disclose the existence and contents of the documents to tax authorities.

Q.95 **XYZ Co. Ltd. has applied to a bank for loan facilities. The bank on studying the financial statements of the company notices that you are the auditor and requests you to call at the bank for a discussion. In the course of discussions, the bank asks for your opinion regarding the company and also asks for detailed information regarding few items in the financial statements. The information is available in your working paper file. What should be your response and why?**

Ans. : Disclosure of Confidential Information:

- Clause (1) of Part I of the Second Schedule to the Chartered Accountants Act, 1949 states that a chartered accountant in practice shall be deemed to be guilty of professional misconduct if he discloses information acquired in the course of his professional engagement to any person other than his client, without the consent of the client or otherwise than as required by law for the time being in force.
- In the instant case, the bank has asked the auditor for detailed information regarding few items in the financial statements available in his working papers. Having regard to the position stated earlier, the auditor cannot disclose the information in his possession without specific permission of the client.
- As far as working papers are concerned, SA 230 on "Documentation" states "working papers are the property of the auditor. The auditor may, at his discretion, make portions of or extracts from his working papers available to his client".

Conclusion: There is no requirement compelling the auditor to divulge information obtained in the course of audit and included in the working papers to any outside agency except as and when required by any law.

Q.96 **Give your comments with reference to Chartered Accountants Act, 1949 and schedules thereto: Mr. C, a practicing Chartered Accountant, in the course of the audit of a listed company discovered serious violations of the provisions of the Companies Act, 2013, informed the registrar of companies out of public interest.** **[May 13 (4 Marks)]**

Ans. : Disclosure of Confidential Information:

- As per Clause 1 of Part I of the Second Schedule to the Chartered Accountants Act, 1949 a member in practice will be guilty of professional misconduct if he discloses information acquired in the course of his professional engagement to any person other than his client so engaging him without the consent of his client or otherwise than as required by any law for the time being in force.
- Further, Sec. 143(12) of Companies Act, 2013 requires that if an auditor of a company, in the course of the performance of his duties as auditor, has reason to believe that an offence involving fraud is being or has been committed against the company by officers or employees of the company, he shall immediately report the matter to the Central Government within 60 days of his knowledge and after following the prescribed procedure.
- In the given case, Mr. C has disclosed serious violations of the provisions of the Companies Act, 2013 to Registrar of Companies without the consent of the client under the impression that it would be

in public interest. It is not clear from the questions whether the violations of provisions involve fraud being committed by officers or employees of the company.

- Hence, in the present case, instead of disclosing the violations to the ROC directly, auditor should mention the violations in his report in due compliance of SA 250 "Consideration of Laws and regulations in an audit of financial statements".

Conclusion: Mr. C will be guilty of professional misconduct covered by clause 1 of Part I of Second Schedule to the Chartered Accountants Act, 1949.

Q.97 **Comment on the following: Mr. Z, a Chartered Accountant was invited by the Chamber of Commerce to present a paper in a symposium on the issues facing Indian Leather Industry. During the course of his presentation he shared some of the vital information of his client's business under the impression that it will help the Nation to compete with other countries at international level. [Nov. 14 (4 Marks)]**

Or

Mr. B, a chartered accountant in practice was invited to deliver a seminar on GST which was attended by professionals as well as by representatives of various industry to which it pertains. Mr. B enthusiastically explained the issue and elaborated how he actually solved this for his client facing the same issue with worked out examples from the computer storage device using the actual data of one of his clients with full identification of client details being displayed to the group for the sake giving clarity on a topic in a real life situation. Comment his acts in the light of code of conduct. [May 18 - New Syllabus (4 Marks)]

Ans. : Disclosure of Client's Information:

- Clause 1 of Part I of the Second Schedule to the CA Act, 1949 deals with the professional misconduct relating to the disclosure of information by a CA in practice relating to the business of his clients to any person other than his client without the consent of his client or otherwise than as required by any law for the time being in force would amount to breach of confidence.
- The Code of Ethics further clarifies that such a duty continues even after completion of the assignment. The CA may, however, disclose the information in case it is required as a part of performance of his professional duties.
- In the given case, Mr. Z has disclosed vital information of his client's business without the consent of the client under the impression that it will help the nation to compete with other countries at International level.

Conclusion: Disclosing the client's information without obtaining consent of client amounts to professional misconduct under clause 1 of Part I of Second Schedule to the CA Act, 1949.

Q.98 **Comment on the following with reference to the Chartered Accountants Act, 1949 and schedules thereto: As a Chartered Accountant in practice, you are asked to conduct a review of the "Profit Forecast" prepared by a Company in connection with its application for a Term loans from a bank.**

Ans. : Review of Profit Forecast:

- As per Clause 3 of Part I, Second schedule to the CA Act, Chartered Accountant in practice shall be deemed to be guilty of professional misconduct if he permits his name or the name of the firm to be used in connection with the estimates of earnings, contingent upon future transactions, in a manner which may lead to the belief that he vouches for the accuracy of the forecast.
- Further SAE 3400 "The Examination of Prospective Financial Information", provides that the management is responsible for the preparation and presentation of the prospective financial information, including the identification and disclosure of the sources of information, the basis of forecasts and the underlying assumptions.
- The auditor may be asked to examine and report on the prospective financial information to enhance its credibility, whether it is intended for use by third parties or for internal purposes. While making report on projection, the auditor need to mention that his responsibility is to examine the evidence supporting the assumptions and other information in the prospective financial information, his responsibility does not include verification of the accuracy of the projections, therefore, he does not vouch for the accuracy of the same.

Conclusion: Offer of review of profit forecast can be accepted subject to compliance of conditions as stated in SAE 3400, otherwise it amounts to professional misconduct.

Q.99 **L, a chartered accountant prepares and certifies projected financial statements of his client Abacus Ltd. Abacus Ltd. forwarded the same to their banks to secure some loans and bank, on that basis sanctioned a loan. Comment with reference to the Chartered Accountants Act, 1949 and schedules thereto.**

[May 17 (4 Marks)]

Ans. : Certification of Financial forecast:

- As per Clause 3 of Part I, Second Schedule to the CA Act, 1949 Chartered Accountant in practice shall be deemed to be guilty of professional misconduct if he permits his name or the name of the firm to be used in connection with the estimates of earnings, contingent upon future transactions, in a manner which may lead to the belief that he vouches for the accuracy of the forecast.
- Further SAE 3400 "The Examination of Prospective Financial Information", provides that the management is responsible for the preparation and presentation of the prospective financial information, including the identification and disclosure of the sources of information, the basis of forecasts and the underlying assumptions.
- The auditor may be asked to examine and report on the prospective financial information to enhance its credibility, whether it is intended for use by third parties or for internal purposes. Thus, while making report on projection, the auditor need to mention that his responsibility is to examine the evidence supporting the assumptions and other information in the prospective financial information, his responsibility does not include verification of the accuracy of the projections, therefore, he does not vouch for the accuracy of the same.
- In the given case, Mr. L, a chartered accountant **prepares and certifies** projected financial statements of his client Abacus Ltd. Abacus Ltd. forwarded the same to their banks to secure some loans and bank, on that basis sanctioned a loan.
- Preparing as well as certifying projected financial statements by the same chartered accountant is not in order.

Conclusion: Mr. L will be deemed to be guilty of professional misconduct under clause 3 of Part I of Second Schedule assuming that conditions stated in SAE 3400 not being fulfilled.

Q.100 Give your comments with reference to Chartered Accountants Act, 1949 and Schedules thereto: Mr. 'E', a practicing Chartered Accountant, was requested by one of his client to prepare a projection for next five years and also a report on the same. Mr. 'E' after having prepared the same stated in his report 'The sources of information, the basis of forecasts and also the major assumptions made in arriving at the forecasts. He also stated that he does not vouch for the accuracy of the forecasts. [May 14 (4 Marks)]

Ans. : Certification of Financial Forecast:

- As per Clause 3 of Part I of Second Schedule to the Chartered Accountants Act, 1949, a chartered accountant in practice is deemed to be guilty of professional misconduct if he permits his name or the name of his firm to be used in connection with an estimate of earnings contingent upon future transactions in a manner which may lead to the belief that he vouches for the accuracy of the forecast.
- Further SAE 3400 "The Examination of Prospective Financial Information", provides that the management is responsible for the preparation and presentation of the prospective financial information, including the identification and disclosure of the sources of information, the basis of forecasts and the underlying assumptions.
- In the given case, Mr. E is being engaged by the client to prepare and report the projection. Mr. E is required to ensure that the requirements of SAE 3400 have been fulfilled. Mr. E after having prepared the projections for next five years stated in his report, "the sources of information, the basis of forecasts and also the major assumptions made in arriving at the forecasts." He also stated that he does not vouch for the accuracy of the forecasts.

Conclusion: There is no violation of the Chartered Accountants Act, 1949 and its Regulations.

Q.101 Comment with the reference to the Chartered Accountants Act, 1949 and schedules thereto: D, a practicing Chartered Accountant examined and reported on the prospective financial statements for one of his clients to obtain a cash credit facility of Rs.75 lakhs from a Private Bank. The bank has sanctioned the cash credit facility for Rs. 60 lakhs to his client. Consequent to the sanction of loan by Bank, he charged a fees of Rs. 60,000 based on 1% of the credit facility sanctioned. [Nov. 18-Old Syllabus (4 Marks)]

Ans. : Certification of Financial Forecast and charging fees on a %age basis:

- As per Clause 3 of Part I of Second Schedule to the Chartered Accountants Act, 1949, a chartered accountant in practice is deemed to be guilty of professional misconduct if he permits his name or the name of his firm to be used in connection with an estimate of earnings contingent upon future transactions in a manner which may lead to the belief that he vouches for the accuracy of the forecast.

- Further SAE 3400 "The Examination of Prospective Financial Information", provides that the management is responsible for the preparation and presentation of the prospective financial information, including the identification and disclosure of the sources of information, the basis of forecasts and the underlying assumptions.
- The auditor may be asked to examine and report on the prospective financial information to enhance its credibility, whether it is intended for use by third parties or for internal purposes. Thus, while making report on projection, the auditor need to mention that his responsibility is to examine the evidence supporting the assumptions and other information in the prospective financial information, his responsibility does not include verification of the accuracy of the projections, therefore, he does not vouch for the accuracy of the same.
- Clause 10 of Part I to First Schedule to the CA Act, 1949 prohibits a CA in practice to charge, or offers to charge, accept or offers to accept in respect of any professional employment, fees which are based on a percentage of profits or which are contingent upon the findings or results of such employment.
- However, this restriction is not applicable where such payment is permitted by the regulations made in this behalf. The Council of the Institute has framed regulation 192 which exempts certain professional services from the operation of clause 10. Charging fees on %age of bank finance sanctioned is not covered under Regulation 192.

Conclusion: Mr. D will be deemed to be guilty of professional misconduct by virtue of clause 10 of part I of First schedule as he charges fees on %age of credit facility sanctioned.

Q.102 **Comment on the followings: A firm of chartered accountants were appointed by a company to evaluate the costs of the various products manufactured by it for their operation system. One of the partners of the firm of chartered accountants was a non-executive director of the company. [Nov. 14 (4 Marks)]**

Or

AP & Co., a firm of Chartered Accountants, was appointed by D Ltd., to evaluate the cost of a new product manufactured by it for their information system and fixation of fair market price. Partner 'P' of the CA firm is a non-executive director of the Company. Comment with reference to Chartered Accountants Act, 1949 and Regulations thereto. [May 18 - Old Syllabus (4 Marks)]

Ans. : Evaluation of Cost structure:

- Clause 4 of Part I of the Second Schedule to the Chartered Accountants Act, 1949 desists a chartered accountant in practice to express opinion on financial statements of an enterprise in which he, his firm or a partner in his firm has a substantial interest.
- In the present case, the firm has been appointed to evaluate the costs of the various products manufactured by it for their operation system, not for expressing opinion on financial statements, so it cannot be construed to be misconduct, as it is a verification of facts and no opinion is expressed.

Conclusion: There is no professional misconduct in evaluating the costs of a company in which one of the partners of firm is a non-executive director.

Q.103 **Comment on the following with reference to the Chartered Accountants Act, 1949 and schedules thereto: Mr. A was appointed by H Ltd. to audit the PF trust maintained by the company. While conducting the audit he noticed that large number of loans have been given out of the trust to the employer company in contravention of the rules of the PF Trust. He disclosed the irregularities to the trustees and to the company but not to the individual subscribers of the PF. When queried on his omission to disclose, he explained that he owed no duty to the individual members.**

Ans. : Failure to Disclose Material Facts:

- As per Clause (5) of Part I of Second Schedule to the CA Act, 1949, a CA in practice will be held liable for misconduct if he fails to disclose a material fact known to him, which is not disclosed in the financial statements but disclosure of which is necessary to make the financial statements not misleading.

- In this case, Mr. A has noticed that large numbers of loans were given out of the trust to the employer company in contravention of the rules of the PF Trust.
- Mr. A has disclosed the irregularities to the trustees, but not to the subscribers. Mr. A was required to disclose such facts to beneficiaries of a fund just like he gives his report to the shareholders of a company.

Conclusion: Mr. A will be attracted by the provisions of professional misconduct under clause (5) of Part I of Second Schedule to the Chartered Accountants Act, 1949.

Q.104 Comment on the following with reference to Chartered Accountants Act, 1949 and schedules thereto: Mr. J, a Chartered Accountant has identified that ABC Ltd. has taken a loan of ₹ 15 lakhs from Provident Fund Account, during the course of audit. The said loan was not reflected in the books of account and statements were prepared ignoring the same. [Nov. 11 (4 Marks)]

Or

In the course of his assignment in M/s Bailey Ltd, CA J came to know that the company, due to financial crunch and unable to meet employees salary, has taken a loan of ₹ 50 lacs from Employees Gratuity Fund. The said loan was not reflected in the books of account of the company and the auditor ignored this transaction in his report.

Comment with reference to the Chartered Accountants Act, 1949 and Regulations thereto.

[May 18 - Old Course (4 Marks)]

Ans. : Failure to Disclose Material Facts:

- As per Clause (5) of Part I of Second Schedule to the CA Act, 1949, a CA in practice will be held liable for misconduct if he fails to disclose a material fact known to him, which is not disclosed in the financial statements but disclosure of which is necessary to make the financial statements not misleading.
- In this case, Mr. J has come across an information that a loan of ₹ 15 lakhs has been taken by the company from Employees PF and the said loan has not been reflected in the books of account and hence not disclosed in the financial statements.

Conclusion: If Mr. J fails to disclose the fact stated above in his report, he will be attracted by the provisions of professional misconduct under Clause (5) of Part I of Second Schedule to the Chartered Accountants Act, 1949. However, if he discloses the fact in his report, there will not be any misconduct.

Q.105 Comment on the following with reference to the Chartered Accountants Act, 1949 and schedules thereto: The superannuation-cum-pension fund for the employees of a company was under a separate 'trust'. Both the company and the trust were under the same management. The auditor, who was auditing the accounts of the company as well as the trust noted some irregularities in the operation of the trust and commented upon these irregularities in the confidential report given to the trustees, but did not mention about these irregularities in his report on the Annual accounts of the Trust.

Or

Comment with the reference to the Chartered Accountants Act, 1949 and schedules thereto: ENI Ltd; a company registered under the Companies Act, 2013 has created a separate Trust "ENI Employees Gratuity Fund Trust". Both the Company and Trust are under the same management. Mr. A is the auditor of both the entities. Mr. A has observed that some part of the expenditure was not applied towards the objects of the Trust. He informed the matter to the Board of Trustees through a separate report but did not qualify the Audit Report of the Trust. [Nov. 18-Old Syllabus (4 Marks)]

Ans. : Non-disclosure of irregularities:

- A Chartered Accountant in practice is deemed to be guilty of professional misconduct under clause 5 of Part I of the Second Schedule if he "fails to disclose a material fact known to him which is not disclosed in a financial statement but disclosure of which is necessary to make the financial statement not misleading".
- In this case, the Chartered Accountant was aware of the contraventions and irregularities committed by the trust as these were referred to in the confidential report given by the Chartered Accountant to the trustees of the company. However, he had issued the annual accounts without any qualification.
- On similar facts it was held by the Supreme Court in *Kishorilal Dutta* v. *P. K. Mukherjee* that it was the duty of the Chartered Accountant to have disclosed the irregularities and contravention to the beneficiaries of the fund in the statement of accounts signed by him.

Conclusion: Chartered Accountant is guilty of professional misconduct if the amount of irregularities is proved material.

Q.106 Answer the following: Loans were given out of the funds of an Employees Provident Fund to the employer company in contravention of the applicable rules. As the auditor of the said Provident Fund, M discloses the contraventions to the Trustees of the fund, but failed to do so to the members of the fund. Comment. [May 09 (5 Marks)]

Ans. : Failure to disclose the material facts:

- As per clause 5 of Part I of Second Schedule to the Chartered Accountants Act, 1949, a member in practice will be deemed to be guilty of professional misconduct if he fails to disclose a material fact known to him which is not disclosed in a financial statement, but disclosure of which is necessary to make the financial statement not misleading, where he is concerned with that financial statement in a professional capacity.
- In the given Case, it is the duty of Mr. M to disclose material facts known to him so that the financial statement does not become misleading. Auditor should disclose such facts to beneficiaries of a fund just like he gives his report to the shareholders of a company.

Conclusion: Mr. M is guilty of professional misconduct.

Q.107 Mr. X partner of X & Co. Chartered Accountants, has compiled and signed the balance sheet of False Limited., for submission to the bankers of the said company. Mr. X has also compiled and signed at the request of the company another balance Sheet inflating the value of assets by 20%, for submission to a term lending institution. Both the Balance Sheets were not in conformity with the books of account maintained by the company as they were not up-to-date. Comment on Mr. X liability.

Ans. : Failure to disclosure the material irregularities:

- As per clause 5 of Part I of Second Schedule to the Chartered Accountants Act, 1949, a member in practice will be deemed to be guilty of professional misconduct if he fails to disclose a material fact known to him which is not disclosed in a financial statement, but disclosure of which is necessary to make the financial statement not misleading, where he is concerned with that financial statement in a professional capacity.
- As per clause 6 of Part I of Second Schedule, a member in practice will be deemed to be guilty of professional misconduct if he fails to report a material misstatement known to him to appear in a financial statement with which he is concerned in a professional capacity.
- In the present case, Mr. X partner of X & Co. Chartered Accountants, has compiled and signed the balance sheet of False Limited., for submission to the bankers of the said company. Mr. X has also compiled and signed at the request of the company another balance Sheet inflating the value of assets by 20%, for submission to a term lending institution. Both the Balance Sheets were not in conformity with the books of account maintained by the company as they were not up-to-date.

Conclusion: Mr. X would be held guilty under clauses 5 and 6 of Part I of Second Schedule to the CA Act, 1949 as Mr. X had compiled the two different balance sheets for the same date without reference to the actual books of account, but on instructions of the client. As per clause 5 he has failed to disclose material fact known to him and further, as per clause 6 he has also failed to report a material misstatement known to him.

Q.108 Comment on the following with reference to the Chartered Accountants Act, 1949 and schedules thereto: A practicing Chartered Accountant was appointed to represent a company before the tax authorities. He submitted on behalf of his client's certain information and explanations to the authorities, which were found to be false and misleading.

Or

D, a Chartered Accountant in practice was appointed by Realty Limited to represent its cases before GST Authorities under a duty executed power of representation. In the course of proceedings, he submitted certain statements - written as well as oral - which later found to be false and materially misleading. Comment this in the light of Professional Code. [Nov. 18-New Syllabus (4 Marks)]

Ans. : Failure to disclose the material facts:

- As per clause 5 of Part I of Second Schedule, a member in practice will be deemed to be guilty of professional misconduct if he fails to disclose a material fact known to him which is not disclosed in a financial statement, but disclosure of which is necessary to make the financial statement not misleading, where he is concerned with that financial statement in a professional capacity.

- As per clause 6 of Part I of Second Schedule, a member in practice will be deemed to be guilty of professional misconduct if he fails to report a material misstatement known to him to appear in a financial statement with which he is concerned in a professional capacity.
- In given case, the Chartered Accountant had submitted the statements before the taxation authorities. These statements are based on the data provided by the management of the company. Although the statements prepared were based on incorrect facts and misleading, the Chartered Accountant had only submitted them acting on the instructions of his client as his authorized representative.

Conclusion: The Chartered Accountant would not be held liable for professional misconduct.

Q.109 Mr. Fair a practicing CA, was appointed to carry out a Balance Sheet Audit of a Non-Profit Organisation. The Internal Auditors detected certain irregularities at one of the branches of the organization which Mr. Fair had failed to detect.

Ans. : Auditor's Responsibilities in relation to branch audit:

- As per clause 7 of Part I of Second Schedule of Chartered Accountants Act, 1949, a Chartered Accountant in practice is deemed to be guilty of professional misconduct if he "does not exercise due diligence or is grossly negligent in the conduct of his professional duties".
- In the present case, internal auditor detected certain irregularities at one of the branches of the organisation which the statutory auditor Mr. Fair had failed to detect. Lance sheet audit
- Statutory auditor has been appointed to carry out the balance sheet audit, he is not required to check the matters relating to branch in depth.

Conclusion: There is no professional misconduct on part of Mr. Fair.

Q.110 A search under section 132 of Income Tax Act in the premises of a leading merchant led to the discovery of two sets of account books - one set to record all the income correctly and second to record only limited income. A CA has issued audit report on the basis of second set of books. What would be your answer if the first set of account books carried evidence of checking by the CA?

Ans. : Auditor's negligence in performance of duties:

- As per clause 7 of Part I of Second Schedule of Chartered Accountants Act, 1949, a Chartered Accountant in practice is deemed to be guilty of professional misconduct if he "does not exercise due diligence or is grossly negligent in the conduct of his professional duties".
- In the present case, it has been found that client has maintained two sets of account books - one set to record all the income correctly and second to record only limited income. CA has issued audit report on the basis of second set of books. In this case, there will not be any misconduct on part of CA if the auditor is not aware of the first set of books.
- However, if there exist evidences that auditor is aware of first set of books also, then he will be deemed to be guilty of professional misconduct being grossly negligent in performance of his duties.

Conclusion: In the first case, he would not be deemed to be guilty of misconduct. But in the second case, he would be deemed to be guilty of misconduct.

Q.111 Mr. X, a CA in practice and statutory auditor of True Ltd., advised the Managing Director of the company to include in sales, "Orders under negotiation" to reflect a better financial position for obtaining bank loan. Mr. X, thereafter, gave clean reports on the balance sheet prepared accordingly without examining the accounts.

Ans. : Auditor's negligence in performance of duties:

- As per clause 7 of Part I of Second Schedule of Chartered Accountants Act, 1949, a Chartered Accountant in practice is deemed to be guilty of professional misconduct if he "does not exercise due diligence or is grossly negligent in the conduct of his professional duties".
- In the present case, Mr. X, a partner of X & Co., advised the M.D. of True Ltd. to include in sales, orders under negotiations to reflect a better financial position for obtaining bank loan.

Conclusion: Mr. X is guilty of professional misconduct under Clause 7 of Part I, Second Schedule to the CA Act, 1949, as he has acted in a negligent manner.

He will also be deemed guilty of other misconduct under Clause (2) of part IV of First Schedule for advising unethical practice to the client.

Q.112 The Cashier of a company committed a fraud and absconded with the proceeds thereof. This happened during the course of the accounting year. The Chief Accountant of the company also did not know about fraud.

In the course of the audit, at the end of the year, the auditor failed to discover the fraud. After the audit was completed, however, the fraud was discovered by the Chief Accountant. Investigation made at that time indicate that the auditor did not exercise proper skill and care and performed his work in a desultory and haphazard manner. With this background, the Directors of the company intend to file disciplinary proceedings against the auditor. Discuss the position of the auditor with regard to the disciplinary proceedings.

Or

You were the statutory auditor of Speed Ltd., a PSU, for the year 2016-17. In the course of your audit, you did not observe any fraud having been committed during that year. However, the C & AG audit staffs during their routine inspection found that chief cashier of the Company have committed a fraud in Debtor's ledger and absconded with the amount. Investigation made in the fraud revealed that the Auditor did not exercise proper skill and care and performed his work in an improper way.

Director of the Company, intends to file disciplinary proceeding against the Auditor with the ICAI. Discuss the position of the auditor with regard to the disciplinary proceeding under Chartered Accountants Act, 1949 and Regulations thereto. [May 18 - Old Course (4 Marks)]

Ans. : Failure to Exercise Reasonable Care and Skill:

- As per clause 7 of Part I of Second Schedule of Chartered Accountants Act, 1949, a Chartered Accountant in practice is deemed to be guilty of professional misconduct if he "does not exercise due diligence or is grossly negligent in the conduct of his professional duties".
- In the present case, it appears that the auditor did not exercise proper skill and care and he performed his work in a desultory and haphazard manner. Cash is a very significant item in any situation and the fact that the cashier had left during the year without notice should have placed the auditor on alert as regards the cash book. In fact, the very fact that the cashier was absconding, i.e., left without any notice constituted sufficient circumstances to excite suspicion of the auditor to probe to the bottom.
- Thus, having regard to this and a fraud has actually taken place during the year, committed by the absconding cashier, it is reasonable to think that *prima facie* there is a case against the auditor for gross negligence. Thus, such instances require reference to Disciplinary Committee of the Council of the Institute.

Q.113 Comment on the following with reference to the Chartered Accountant Act, 1949 and schedules there to: Mr. B a practicing CA expressed his opinion on the financial statements of M/s ABC Ltd. For the year ended on 31st March 2018. It was later found that the closing stock was valued arbitrarily by Management which was accepted by him without verification and large amount of revenue expenditure was capitalized.

Ans. : Auditor's negligence in performance of duties:

- As per clause 7 of Part I of Second Schedule of Chartered Accountants Act, 1949, a Chartered Accountant in practice is deemed to be guilty of professional misconduct if he "does not exercise due diligence or is grossly negligent in the conduct of his professional duties".
- In the present case, Mr. B a practicing CA expressed his opinion on the financial statements of M/s ABC Ltd. and it was found later that the closing stock was valued arbitrarily by Management which was accepted by him without verification and large amount of revenue expenditure was capitalized.
- Thus, having regard to this, it is reasonable to think that *prima facie* there is a case against the auditor for gross negligence.

Conclusion: Mr. B is guilty of gross negligence by virtue of clause 7 of Part I of second schedule.

Q.114 Give your comments with reference to Chartered Accountants Act, 1949 and schedules thereto: Mr. D, a practicing Chartered Accountant, did not complete his work relating to the audit of the accounts of a company and had not submitted his audit report in due time to enable the company to comply with the statutory requirements. [May 13 (4 Marks)]

Ans. : Failure to exercise due diligence:

- As per clause 7 of Part I of Second Schedule of Chartered Accountants Act, 1949, a Chartered Accountant in practice is deemed to be guilty of professional misconduct if he "does not exercise due diligence or is grossly negligent in the conduct of his professional duties".
- Where a Chartered Accountant had not completed his work relating to the audit of the accounts a company and had not submitted his audit report in due time to enable the company to comply with the statutory requirement in this regard, it can be said that the work is carried out with gross negligence.

Conclusion: Mr. D is guilty of professional misconduct by virtue of clause 7 of Part I of Second Schedule to the CA Act, 1949.

Q.115 Comment on the following with reference to the Chartered Accountant Act, 1949 and schedules there to: CA Z who conducted ABC audit of a Marathi daily 'New Era' certified the circulation figures based on Management Information System Report (M.I.S Report) without examining the books of Account.

[Nov. 08 (4 Marks)]

Or

Give your comments with reference to CA Act and schedules thereto: Mr. Z, a practicing Chartered Accountant, issued a circulation certificate for a periodical on the basis of outward memos, which was later found to be false. **[May 10 (4 Marks)]**

Or

Give your comments with reference to the Chartered Accountants Act, 1949 and schedules thereto: Mr. Mohan is a practicing Chartered Accountant. He issued a certificate of consumption which did not reflect the correct factual position of the consumption of raw material by the concerned entity. It is found that the certificate is given on the basis of data appearing in the minutes of meeting of the Board of Directors. **[Nov. 10 (4 Marks)]**

Or

Comment on the following with reference to Chartered Accountants Act, 1949 and schedules thereto: Mr. Z, a Chartered Accountant certified the circulation of a weekly magazine without examining the records and relevant documents. **[Nov. 11 (4 Marks)]**

Or

Give your comments with reference to the Chartered Accountants Act, 1949 and Schedules thereto: Z, a practicing Chartered Accountant issued a certificate of circulation of a periodical without going into the most elementary details of how the circulation of a periodical was being maintained i.e. by not looking into the financial records, bank statements or bank pass books, by not examining evidence of actual payment of printers bills and by not caring to ascertain how many copies were sold and paid for.

[May 12 (4 Marks)]

Ans. : Failure to exercise due diligence and to obtain necessary information:

- Clause 2 of Part I of Second Schedule of CA Act, 1949 states that a CA in practice shall be guilty of professional misconduct if he Certifies or submits in his name or in the name of his firm a report of an examination of financial statements unless the examination of such statements and the related records has been made by him or by a partner or an employee in his firm or by another CA in practice.
- Clause 7 of Part I of Second Schedule of CA Act, 1949 states that a CA in practice shall be deemed to be guilty of professional misconduct if he "does not exercise due diligence or is grossly negligent in the conduct of his professional duties".
- Clause 8 of Part I of Second Schedule to CA Act, 1949 states that if a CA in practice fails to obtain sufficient information to warrant the expression of an opinion or its exceptions are sufficient material to negate the expression of an opinion, the CA shall be deemed to be guilty of a professional misconduct.
- In the present case, Mr. Z, did not exercise due diligence and is grossly negligent in the conduct of his professional duties since he certified the circulation figures without the examination of records and other required documents. He should not express his opinion before obtaining the required data and information.
- As an auditor, Mr. Z ought to have verified the basic records such as print order, printer's bill, number of copies sold and paid for, number of copies returned unsold to ensure the correctness of circulation figures.

Conclusion: Mr. Z will be held guilty of professional misconduct as per clauses 2, 7 and 8 of Part I of Second Schedule of Chartered Accountants Act, 1949.

Q.116 Give your comments with reference to the Chartered Accountants Act, and schedules thereto: Mr. A, a Chartered Accountant was the auditor of 'A Limited'. During the financial year 2017-18, the investment appeared in the Balance Sheet of the company of ₹ 10 lakhs and was the same amount as in the last year. Later on, it was found that the company's investments were only ₹ 25,000, but the value of investments was inflated for the purpose of obtaining higher amount of Bank loan. **[Nov. 09 (4 Marks)]**

Ans. : Negligence in performance of duties:

- As per Clause 2 Part I of Second Schedule to the Chartered Accountants Act, 1949, a CA in practice shall be deemed to be guilty of professional misconduct, if he, certifies or submits in his name or in the name of his firm, a report of an examination of financial statements unless the examination of such statements and the related records has been made by him or by a partner or an employee in his firm or by another chartered accountant in practice.
- As per Clause 7 of Part I of Second Schedule to the Chartered Accountants Act, 1949, a CA in practice shall be guilty of professional misconduct if does not exercise due diligence, or is grossly negligent in the conduct of his professional duties.
- As per Clause 8 of Part I of Second Schedule, a CA in practice will be deemed to be guilty of professional misconduct if he fails to obtain sufficient information which is necessary for expression of an opinion or its exceptions are sufficiently material to negate the expression of an opinion.
- The primary duty of physical verification and valuation of investments is of the management. However, the auditor's duty is also to verify the physical existence and valuation of investments placed, at least on the last day of the accounting year.
- In the instant case, it appears that auditors failed to confirm the value of investments from any proper source and he simply relied on the management's representation.

Conclusion: Mr. A, will be held liable for professional misconduct under Clauses 2, 7 and 8 of Part I of the Second Schedule to the Chartered Accountants Act, 1949.

Q.117 **Comment on the following with reference to Chartered Accountants Act, 1949 and schedules thereto: A charitable institution entrusted ₹ 10 lakhs with its auditor's M/s Ram and Co., a Chartered Accountant firm, to invest in a profitable portfolio. The auditors pending investment of the money, deposited it in their Savings bank account and no investment was made in the next three months.**

Ans. : Deposit of Client's Money in Separate Bank account:

- As per Clause 10 of Part I of Second Schedule to the Chartered Accountants Act, 1949, a Chartered Accountant in practice will be deemed to be guilty of professional misconduct if he fails to keep moneys of his client other than the fees or remuneration or money meant to be expended in a separate banking account or to use such moneys for purposes for which they are intended within a reasonable time.
- The term reasonable time would depend upon the circumstances of the case. Moneys which are intended to be spent within a reasonably short time need not be put in a separate bank account.
- In the instant case, M/s Ram & Co. should have deposited the amount into a separate bank account. Further, they are not permitted to provide the service of portfolio management to the client.

Conclusion: M/s Ram & Co. will be held guilty of professional misconduct as he deposited the client money in his saving bank account.

Q.118 **Comment on the following with reference to the Chartered Accountants Act, 1949 and schedules thereto: M/s XYZ a firm of Chartered Accountants received ₹ 2 lakhs in January, 2018 on behalf of one of their clients, who has gone abroad and deposited the amount in their Bank account, so that they can return the money to the client in July, 2018, when he is due to return to India.**

Ans. : Deposit of Client's Money in Separate Bank account:

- As per Clause 10 of Part I of Second Schedule to the Chartered Accountants Act, 1949, a Chartered Accountant in practice will be deemed to be guilty of professional misconduct if he fails to keep moneys of his client other than the fees or remuneration or money meant to be expended in a separate banking account or to use such moneys for purposes for which they are intended within a reasonable time.
- The term reasonable time would depend upon the circumstances of the case. Moneys which are intended to be spent within a reasonably short time need not be put in a separate bank account.
- In the instant case, M/s XYZ should have kept the amount in a separate bank account.

Conclusion: M/s XYZ will be deemed to be guilty of professional misconduct by virtue of clause 10 of Part I of Second Schedule as the money is required to be kept in a separate bank account.

Q.119 **Mr. Ram, a Chartered Accountant in practice, received ₹ 15,00,000 on 15th December, 2017 on behalf of one of his clients, who has gone to USA. Mr. Ram deposited the said amount in his saving bank account (SB Account). As per instruction of the client, the said amount is to be returned to the client on March 31, 2018 when he will return to India. On the occasion of birthday of his wife Sita, Mr. Ram withdrew**

₹ 5,00,000 and spent on Birthday party. He re-deposited ₹ 5,00,000 in the said SB account on 25th March, 2018 and then returned the entire amount of ₹ 15,00,000 to the client on March 31, 2018.

Ans. : Deposit of Client's Money in Separate Bank account:

- As per Clause 10 of Part I of Second Schedule to the Chartered Accountants Act, 1949, a Chartered Accountant in practice shall be deemed to be guilty of professional misconduct if he fails to keep moneys of his client other than the fees or remuneration or money meant to be expended in a separate banking account or to use such moneys for purposes for which they are intended within a reasonable time.
- The term reasonable time would depend upon the circumstances of the case. Moneys which are intended to be spent within a reasonably short time need not be put in a separate bank account.
- In the instant case, Mr. Ram should have deposited the amount into a separate bank account. Further, he was not supposed to spent the amount for personal purposes.

Conclusion: Mr. Ram will be guilty of professional misconduct for his failure to keep the client money in separate bank account and using the client money for personal purposes.

Q.120 **Give your comments with reference to CA Act and schedules thereto: Mr. Z, a practicing Chartered Accountant received a sum of ₹ 1 lac on 01.09.2017 from a client who intends to leave abroad for a period of year, with a request that his advance tax liabilities to be paid over the three instalments, on 15th Sep., 2017, 15th Dec. 2017 and 15.03.2018. After remitting the 1st instalment of advance tax on 15.09.2017, Z did not keep the money in a separate bank account and he is of the opinion that he will remit the money within reasonable time as per schedule of advance tax. [May 10 (4 Marks)]**

Ans. : Deposit of Client's Money in Separate Bank account:

- As per Clause 10 of Part I of Second Schedule to the Chartered Accountants Act, 1949, a Chartered Accountant in practice will be deemed to be guilty of professional misconduct if he fails to keep moneys of his client other than the fees or remuneration or money meant to be expended in a separate banking account or to use such moneys for purposes for which they are intended within a reasonable time.
- The term reasonable time would depend upon the circumstances of the case. Moneys which are intended to be spent within a reasonably short time need not be put in a separate bank account.
- In the instant case, Mr. Z should have kept the balance money after remitting the first instalment of advance tax into a separate bank account.

Conclusion: Mr. Z is guilty of professional misconduct as per Clause 10 of Part I of Second Schedule of the Chartered Accountants Act, 1949.

Q.121 **Comment: M/s. ABC, a firm of Chartered Accountants received ₹ 2 lakhs in March, 2018 from a client to pay the Advance Tax. However, the firm has used that money for its own purpose and later on adjusted the same with the outstanding fee payable. [Nov. 14 (4 Marks)]**

Ans. : Deposit of Client's Money in separate Bank account:

- Clause 10 of Part I of Second Schedule to the Chartered Accountants Act, 1949 states that a Chartered Accountant in practice shall be deemed to be guilty of professional misconduct if "he fails to keep money of his clients other than fees or remuneration or money meant to be expended in separate banking account or to use such money for the purpose for which they are intended".
- In the present case, M/s. ABC received the money in March, 2015 for payment of the advance tax; hence it should be deposited in a separate bank account. However, firm has used that money for its own purposes.

Conclusion: Since M/s. ABC have failed to keep the sum of ₹ 2 lakhs received on behalf of their client in a separate Bank Account, it amounts to professional misconduct under clause 10 of part I of Second Schedule.

Q.122 **A film artist who was going abroad for long shooting, deposited a sum of ₹ 20 lakhs with his tax consultant Mr. G, a practicing chartered accountant for payment of GST monthly when they were due. Mr. G duly remitted all but one instalment. He utilized the amount of instalment which he did not pay, to remit his own advance of income tax. However, while filing return of GST of the film artist, he duly remitted on her behalf the tax payable with interest due for late payment of GST out of money lying with him. He also bore for himself the interest due to short fall in remittance of tax of his client. Comment on the above in the light of Code of Conduct. [May 18 - New Course (4 Marks)]**

Ans : Deposit of Client's Money in separate Bank account:

- Clause 10 of Part I of Second Schedule to the Chartered Accountants Act, 1949 states that a Chartered Accountant in practice shall be deemed to be guilty of professional misconduct if "he fails to keep money of his clients other than fees or remuneration or money meant to be expended in separate banking account or to use such money for the purpose for which they are intended".

- In the present case, a film artist who was going abroad, deposited a sum of ₹ 20 lakhs with Mr. G, a practicing chartered accountant for payment of GST monthly when they were due. Mr. G duly remitted all but one instalment. He utilized the amount of instalment which he did not pay, to remit his own advance of income tax. However, while filing return of GST of the film artist, he duly re-mitted on her behalf the tax payable with interest due for late payment of GST out of money lying with him.

Conclusion: Since Mr. G uses the client money for payment of personal taxes, he will be deemed to be guilty of professional misconduct under clause 10 of part I of Second Schedule.

7.7 - SECOND SCHEDULE, PART II "PROFESSIONAL MISCONDUCT IN RELATION TO THE MEMBERS OF THE INSTITUTE GENERALLY"

Q.123 **Comment on the following with reference to the Chartered Accountants Act, 1949 and schedules thereto: Mr. Dheeraj, an aspiring student of ICAI, approached Mr. Murli, a practicing CA, for the purpose of articleship. Mr. Murli, the principal, offered him stipend at the rate of ₹ 2,000 p.m. to be paid every 6th month along with interest at the rate of 10% p.a. compounded monthly to compensate such late payment on plea that cycle of professional receipts from clients is 6 months. Mr. Dheeraj agreed for such late payment in the hope of getting extra stipend in the form of interest. Mr. Murli, however, used to disburse salary to all of his employees on time.**

Or

CA X is a chartered accountant in practice. He has an articled trainee H. X has informed H that since his practice and receipt of fees is seasonal, the stipend would not be paid in the months of April to December, but would be paid from January to March and the shortfall for the earlier 9 months will be made good in these 3 months along with interest @ 5% p.a. Comment with reference to the Chartered Accountants Act, 1949. **[Nov. 17 (4 Marks)]**

Ans. : Contravening Provisions of the Act/Regulations:

- As per Clause (1) of Part II of the Second Schedule to the Chartered Accountants Act, 1949, a member of the Institute, whether in practice or not, shall be deemed to be guilty of professional misconduct under, if he contravenes any of the provisions of this Act or the regulations made thereunder or any guidelines issued by the Council.
- Regulation 48 of Chartered Accountants Regulations, 1988 requires that payment to articled clerks to be made on monthly basis.
- In the present case, Chartered Accountant has failed to make the payments of stipend to articled assistant every month in accordance with Regulation 48. The fact that the articled assistant will be compensated with extra sum in the form of interest on late payment and the plea that his receipts are seasonal is of no relevance and hence not acceptable.

Conclusion: Regulation 48 of CA Regulations, 1988 has been violated, hence chartered accountant would be guilty of professional misconduct under Clause 1, Part II of Second Schedule.

Q.124 **Comment on the following with reference to the Chartered Accountants Act, 1949 and schedules thereto: The manager of ABC (P) Ltd. approached CA. X in the need of a certificate in respect of a consumption statement of raw material. Without having certificate of practice (COP), CA. X issued the certificate to the manager of the company, acting as a CA in Practice and applied for the COP to the Institute on very next day to avoid any dispute.**

Ans. : Contravening Provisions of the Act:

- As per Clause (1) of Part II of Second Schedule to the Chartered Accountants Act, 1949, a member of the Institute, whether in practice or not, shall be deemed to be guilty of professional misconduct, if he contravenes any of the provisions of this Act or the regulations made thereunder or any guidelines issued by the Council.
- Section 6 of Chartered Accountants Act, 1949 provides that no member of the Institute shall be entitled to practice (whether in India or elsewhere) unless he has obtained from the Council a certificate of practice.
- In the given case, CA. X has issued a certificate in respect of a consumption statement of raw material to the manager of ABC (P) Ltd., as a Chartered Accountant in practice when he had not

even applied for the COP to the Institute, thereby contravening the provisions of Section 6 of the Chartered Accountants Act, 1949.

Conclusion: Mr. X has violated the provisions of Sec. 6 of CA Act, 1949 and hence would be guilty of professional misconduct under Clause 1, Part II of Second Schedule.

Q.125 **Comment on the following with reference to the Chartered Accountants Act, 1949 and schedules thereto: PQ & Co., a firm of Chartered Accountants, included the name of R as a partner while filing an application for empanelment as auditor for Public Sector bank branches. It was subsequently noticed that on the date of application, P was not a partner with AB & Co. [Nov. 07 (4 Marks)]**

Or

CA P and CA Q are running a firm of chartered accountants in the name of M/s. PQ & Co. On 21.06.2017 they included the name of CA R a practicing CA, without his knowledge, as a partner while submitting an application for empanelment as auditors for public sector banks branches to the institute.

Whether CA P and CA Q are professionally liable for misconduct? [May 16 (4 Marks)]

Or

Mr. P and Mr. Q are running a firm of Chartered Accountants in the name of M/s AB & Co. On 23.05.2017, they included the name of Mr. R, a practicing Chartered Accountant, without his knowledge, as a partner while submitting an application for empanelment as auditor for Public Sector Bank branches to the Institute. However, they added Mr. R as a partner to their firm offering a share of 25% of the profits, on 25.05.2017.

Ans. : Providing False information to ICAI:

- As per clause 3 of Part II of second schedule, a Chartered Accountant whether in practice or not is guilty of professional misconduct if he includes in any information, statement, return or form to be submitted to the Institute, Council or any of its committees, Directors (Discipline), Board of Discipline, Disciplinary Committee, Quality Review Board or the Appellate Authority any particulars knowing them to be false.
- In the instant case PQ & Co. included another Chartered Accountant name as partner in his firm, in his application for empanelment as Auditor of branches of Public Sector Banks submitted to the Institute. In fact such a member was not a partner of the said firm on the date of application.

Conclusion: CA P & CA Q will be held guilty of professional misconduct as per Clause 3, Part II of Second Schedule for submitting false information with the Institute.

"ICAI Examiner Comments"

Most of the candidates failed to mention the correct clause and explain the same properly.

Q.126 **Mr. Brilliant, a practicing CA received a major professional assignment. To complete the said assignment, he was required to buy four computers. Due to his inability to provide funds for acquiring the same he borrowed money from a firm, where one of the articled clerk's and his father were interested. What will be the Chartered Accountants Liability.**

Ans. : Non-compliance of CA Regulations:

- As per Clause 1 of Part II of Second Schedule to the Chartered Accountants Act, 1949 a member shall be held guilty of professional misconduct if he contravenes any of the provisions of the Act or the regulations made thereunder or any guidelines issued by the Council.
- Regulation 47 of CA Regulations, 1988 provides that "No amount shall be charged from, or be payable by, an articled clerk or any other person on his behalf, directly or indirectly whether by way of premium or as loan or deposit or in any other form in connection with his engagement as an articled clerk.
- Accepting a loan from an articled clerk in case of an engagement of an article clerk is prohibited under the Regulations. But, in the present case, it appears from the facts that the articled clerk is already been engaged and serving under him.

Conclusion: Mr. Brilliant will not be held guilty of professional misconduct under Clause 1 of Part II of Second Schedule of CA Act, 1949.

Q.127 **Give your comments with reference to the Chartered Accountants Act, 1949 and Schedules thereto: X, a practicing Chartered Accountant in an application for permission to study submitted by his Articled Assistant to the council had confirmed that the normal working hours of his office were from 11 A.M. to 6 P.M. and the hours during which the Articled Assistant was required to attend classes are 7.00 A.M. to**

9:30 A.M. According to the information from College, the Articled Assistant attended the Collage from 10 A.M. to 1.55 P.M. on all week days. About the Articled Assistant attending the classes even during office hours, X pleaded ignorance. [May 12 (4 Marks)]

Ans. : Failure to Observe the Regulations:

- As per Clause 1 of Part II of Second Schedule to the Chartered Accountants Act, 1949 a member shall be held guilty of professional misconduct if he contravenes any of the provisions of the Act or the regulations made thereunder or any guidelines issued by the Council.
- As per Clause 3 of Part II of Second Schedule to the CA Act, 1949, a member is deemed to be guilty of professional misconduct if he includes in any information, statement, return or form to be submitted to the Institute, Council or any of its Committees, Director (Discipline), Board of Discipline, Disciplinary Committee, Quality Review Board or the Appellate Authority any particulars knowing them to be false.
- The chartered accountant, as per Regulations also, is expected to impart proper practical training. There is a specific circular issued which guides on timing for training for articleship.
- In the instant case, the articled clerk must have not been attending office on a regular basis and the explanation of the Chartered Accountant cannot be accepted. It is also quite likely that the articled clerk would be availing leave quite often and coming late to the office. X knew about the college timing of his articled assistant and he had given information to the institute knowing them to be false.

Conclusion: Mr. X will be deemed to be guilty of professional misconduct under Clause 1 of Part II of Second Schedule for contravention of regulations of the Institute and under Clause 3 of Part II of Second Schedule for submission of false information to the ICAI.

Q.128 Comment on the following with reference to the Chartered Accountants Act, 1949 and schedules thereto: A Chartered Accountant in practice certified in requisite Form that an articled assistant was undergoing training with him, whereas, he was also employed in a company between 10 a.m. and 6 p.m. on a monthly salary of ₹ 17,000 and attended the office of the Chartered Accountant thereafter until 7 p.m. The Chartered Accountant pleaded that the articled assistant was on audit of the company.

Ans. : Failure to Observe Regulations:

- As per Clause 1 of Part II of Second Schedule to the Chartered Accountants Act, 1949, a member shall be held guilty of professional misconduct if he contravenes any of the provisions of the Act or the regulations made thereunder or any guidelines issued by the Council. The chartered accountant, as per Regulations also, is expected to impart proper practical training.
- As per Clause 3 of Part II of Second Schedule to the CA Act, 1949, a member is deemed to be guilty of professional misconduct if he includes in any information, statement, return or form to be submitted to the Institute, Council or any of its Committees, Director (Discipline), Board of Discipline, Disciplinary Committee, Quality Review Board or the Appellate Authority any particulars knowing them to be false.
- In the instant case, the articled assistant is not attending office on timely basis and the explanation of the Chartered Accountant that the articled assistant was on audit of the company cannot be accepted particularly in view of the fact that articled assistant is getting monthly salary from that company.

Conclusion: Chartered Accountant will be deemed to be guilty of professional misconduct under Clause 1 of Part II of Second Schedule for contravention of regulations of the Institute and under Clause 3 of Part II of Second Schedule for submission of false information to the ICAI.

Q.129 Comment: M/s. XYZ, a firm of Chartered Accountants has taken a loan for acquiring a home from a company whose Managing Director's son is an Articled Assistant with A, a partner of M/s. XYZ. The Articled Assistant had no direct interest in the Company and the loan was not related to his engagement. [Nov. 14 (4 Marks)]

Ans. : Premium from Articled Clerks:

- As per Clause 1 of Part II of Second Schedule to the Chartered Accountants Act, 1949, a chartered accountant is deemed to be guilty of professional misconduct if he contravenes any of the provisions of Chartered Accountants Act, 1949 or Regulations made thereunder.
- Regulation 47 of the Chartered Accountant's Regulations, 1988, prohibits a member from accepting any premiums or loans or any deposit in any form from an articled clerk directly or indirectly.

- In the present case, M/s XYZ has taken loan from a company whose Managing Director happens to be father of articled clerk with Mr. A, a partner of M/s XYZ. However, the articled trainee has no direct interest in that company and the loan was not related to his engagement.

Conclusion: There will no professional misconduct on part of M/s XYZ as articles trainee had no interest in the company and the loan was not related to engagement.

7.8 - COUNCIL GENERAL GUIDELINES, 2008

Q.130 Comment on the following with reference to Chartered Accountants Act, 1949 and schedules thereto: Mr. Shah, a Chartered Accountant certified the financial statements of a company in which his wife is a Director holding substantial interest.

Ans. : Certification of Financial Statement of a related entity:

- Clause (4) of Part I of Second Schedule to the CA Act, 1949 states that if an auditor expresses his opinion on the financial statements of any business in which he, his firm or a partner in his firm has substantial interest, he is committing professional misconduct.
- Chapter IV of Council General Guidelines, 2008 further provides that a member of the Institute shall not express his opinion on financial statements of any business or enterprise in which one or more persons who are his "relatives" within the meaning of AS 18 has/have, either by themselves or in conjunction with such member, a substantial interest in the said business or enterprise. As per AS 18, the term 'Relative' includes husband and wife. Violation of Council Guidelines amounts to professional misconduct under Clause 1 of Part II of Second Schedule.
- Sec. 141(3)(*f*) of the Companies Act, 2013, requires that a person shall not be eligible for appointment as an auditor of a company whose relative is a director or is in the employment of the company as director or key managerial personnel.
- Non-compliance of Secs. 139, 140 & 141 amounts to professional misconduct under Clause 9 of Part I of First schedule.
- In the given case Mr. Shah, Chartered Accountant, has certified the financial statements of a company in which his wife is a director with substantial interest.

Conclusion: Mr. Shah is guilty of professional misconduct under various clauses as mentioned above.

Q.131 Comment with reference to the Chartered Accountants Act, 1949 and Schedules thereto: P, a Chartered Accountant in practice, accepts appointment as statutory auditor for LMN Pvt. Ltd. Q, brother of P has substantial interest in LMN Pvt. Ltd. [May 09 (5 Marks)]

Ans. : Appointment as Company Auditor:

- As per Clause (4) of Part I of Second Schedule to the CA Act, 1949, a CA is deemed to be guilty of professional misconduct if he expresses his opinion on financial statements in which his firm or a partner has substantial interest.
- Chapter IV of Council General Guidelines 2008 further provides that a member of the Institute shall not express his opinion on financial statements of any business or enterprise in which one or more persons who are his "relatives" within the meaning of AS 18 has/have, either by themselves or in conjunction with such member, a substantial interest in the said business or enterprise. As per AS 18, the term 'Relative' includes brother. Violation of Council Guidelines amounts to professional misconduct under Clause 1 of Part II of Second Schedule.
- Further, as per Section 141(3)(*d*) of the Companies Act, 2013, a person shall not be eligible for appointment as an auditor of a company if his relative is holding shares in the company for face value exceeding ₹ 1 Lac. Non-compliance of Secs. 139, 140 & 141 amounts to professional misconduct under Clause 9 of Part I of First Schedule. Face Value of the shares held by brother is not given in the question. It may be assumed that it exceeds ₹ 1 Lac.
- In the instant case, since Q, a relative has a substantial interest in LMN Pvt. Ltd, P cannot conduct the audit.

Conclusion: Mr. P will be guilty of professional misconduct under various clauses as mentioned above.

Q.132 Give your comments with reference to the Chartered Accountants Act, and schedules thereto: Mrs. M is a Director of XYZ Private Limited, having 15% share-holdings in the company. During 2017, the company appointed C.A. Mr. N, Mrs. M spouse, as its statutory auditor. On Mr. N's advice, the company issued fresh equity shares in 2017-18, in the ratio of one share for every two shares held by the shareholders of the company. Mr. N used to deliver audit report for subsequent years without any comments or disclosures, thereupon. [Nov. 09 (4 Marks)]

Ans. : Auditor's disqualifications:

- Clause 4 of Part I of Second Schedule to the Chartered Accountants Act, 1949 states that if an auditor expresses his opinion on the financial statements of any business or enterprises in which he, his firm or a partner in his firm has substantial interest, he is committing professional misconduct.
- Chapter IV of Council General Guidelines 2008 further provides that a member of the Institute shall not express his opinion on financial statements of any business or enterprise in which one or more persons who are his "relatives" within the meaning of AS 18 has/have, either by themselves or in conjunction with such member, a substantial interest in the said business or enterprise. As per AS 18, the term 'Relative' includes husband and wife. Violation of Council Guidelines amounts to professional misconduct under Clause 1 of Part II of Second Schedule.
- Sec. 141(3)(*f*) of the Companies Act, 2013, requires that a person shall not be eligible for appointment as an auditor of a company whose relative is a director or is in the employment of the company as director or key managerial personnel. Non-compliance of Secs. 139, 140 & 141 amounts to professional misconduct under Clause 9 of Part I of First Schedule.
- In the present case, Mrs. M is a Director of XYZ Private Limited and the company has appointed Mr. N, Chartered Accountant, Mrs. M's spouse, as its statutory auditor. Though Mrs. M do not hold substantial interest in the company Mr. N should not accept the appointment as statutory auditor of the company, where his wife M is director.

Conclusion: Mr. N is guilty of professional misconduct under Clause 9 of Part I of First Schedule.

Q.133 Give your comments with reference to the Companies Act, 2013 and the Chartered Accountants Act, 1949 and Schedules thereto: Mr. A has been appointed statutory auditor of a private limited company where his spouses' sister' husband is having 75% ownership. [Nov. 12 (4 Marks)]

Ans. : Appointment as an Auditor in a concern in which relative has substantial interest:

- Clause 4 of Part I of Second Schedule to the Chartered Accountants Act, 1949 states that if an auditor expresses his opinion on the financial statements of any business or enterprises in which he, his firm or a partner in his firm has substantial interest, he is committing professional misconduct.
- Council General Guidelines, 2008, specifies that a member of the Institute shall not express his opinion on financial statements of any business or enterprise in which one or more persons who are his "relatives" within the meaning of AS 18 has/have, either by themselves or in conjunction with such member, a substantial interest in the said business or enterprise.
- As per AS 18 "Related Parties" the term relative, in relation to an individual, means the spouse, son, daughter, brother, sister, father and mother who may be expected to influence, or be influenced by, that individual in his/her dealings with the reporting enterprise.
- As per Sec. 141(3)(*d*) of Companies Act, 2013, a person who, or his relative or partner is holding any security of or interest in the company or its subsidiary, or of its holding or associate company or a subsidiary of such holding company, is also disqualified to be appointed as auditor of company. However relative may hold security or interest in the company of face value not exceeding ₹ 1,000 or such sum as may be prescribed (₹ One Lac has been prescribed under the Rules). The term relative as defined u/s 2(77) of Companies Act, 2013, does not include spouse sister husband.
- In the present case, Mr. A has been appointed as auditor of private limited company in which spouse' sister' husband is having substantial interest. This relationship is not covered under AS 18 and Sec. 2(77) of Companies Act, 2013 and consequently no disqualification arises.

Conclusion: Mr. A is qualified to be appointed as auditor.

Q.134 Comment on the following with reference to the Chartered Accountants Act, 1949 and Schedules thereto: Mr. P, a Chartered Accountant, did not maintain any books of account on the ground that his income did not exceed the limits prescribed u/s 44AA of the Income-tax Act, 1961.

Or

Comment on the following with reference to the CA Act, 1949, and Schedules thereto: CA. Ajit registered his proprietorship firm last year and started practicing in the name of "M/s Ajit & Co.". He is of the view that a professional need to maintain books of account only if his earnings exceed the minimum prescribed limit as per Sec. 44AA of the Income Tax Act, 1961. Therefore, he decided not to maintain his books of account as his earnings are below the prescribed limit given u/s 44AA of the said Act.

Or

Mr. P, a CA in practice runs his proprietorship firm as "M/s P & Co.". His annual gross receipts are in excess of ₹ 50 Lakhs. He maintains a small pocket diary in which he writes the fees received from various clients. Based on his record, he prepares and files his income tax return.

Ans. : Maintenance of Books of Account:

- As per Clause 1 of Part II of Second Schedule, a member of the Institute will be held guilty of professional misconduct if he contravenes any of the provisions of this act or the regulations made there under or any guidelines issued by the council.
- Chapter V of the Council General Guidelines, 2008 specifies that a member of the Institute in practice or the firm of Chartered Accountants of which he is a partner shall maintain and keep in respect of his/its professional practice, proper books of account including the following:

  (*i*) a Cash Book

  (*ii*) a Ledger
- In the instant case, Chartered Accountant being in practice was required to maintain the books of account, but he does not maintain the books and writes the fees received from various clients in small pocket diary. A small pocket diary maintained by him cannot be books of account.

Conclusion: Mr. P will be held guilty for professional misconduct for violation of Council General Guidelines, 2008.

Q.135 Mr. X, a Chartered Accountant in Practice filed his income tax return for the Assessment Year 2018-19 u/s 44ADA of the Income Tax Act, 1961, declaring his income on presumptive basis. In a disciplinary proceeding alleged against him for an alleged misuse of funds of his clients, it was asked that he should submit his books of account for the financial year ended on 31.03.2018. Mr. X refused to submit books of account on the ground that he had not maintained any books and even for income tax purposes, he submitted his Return of Income on a presumptive basis. Is he right in putting such a defence? Analyse the issue in the lights of Professional Code, if any. [Nov. 18-New Syllabus (5 Marks)]

Ans. : Maintenance of Books of Account:

- As per Clause 1 of Part II of Second Schedule, a member of the Institute will be held guilty of professional misconduct if he Contravenes any of the provisions of this act or the regulations made there under or any guidelines issued by the council.
- Chapter V of the Council General Guidelines, 2008 specifies that a member of the Institute in practice or the firm of Chartered Accountants of which he is a partner shall maintain and keep in respect of his/its professional practice, proper books of account including the following:

  (*a*) a Cash Book

  (*b*) a Ledger
- In the instant case, Mr. X, a Chartered Accountant in Practice filed his income tax return for the u/s 44ADA of the income Tax Act, 1961, declaring his income on presumptive basis. In a disciplinary proceeding alleged against him for an alleged misuse of funds of his clients, it was asked that he should submit his books of account for the financial year ended on 31.03.2018. Mr. X refused to submit books of account on the ground that he had not maintained any books and even for income tax purposes, he submitted his Return of Income on a presumptive basis.

Conclusion: Defence of Mr. X is not admissible and he will be held guilty of professional misconduct by virtue of Clause 1 of Part II of Second Schedule, due to contravention of Chapter V of Council General Guidelines, 2008 for non-maintenance of books of account.

Q.136 A member of the institute shall not accept in a year more than the specified number of tax audits under section 44AB of the Income Tax Act.

Mr. Gaurav is a partner in M/s XYZ & Co., a firm of Chartered Accountants with 6 partners.

During the assessment year 2017-18, Mr. Gaurav alone had signed 290 tax audit reports consisting of both corporate and non-corporate assessees. [Nov. 16 (4 Marks)]

Ans. : Signing of Tax Audit Report:

- As per Chapter VI of Council General Guidelines 2008, a member of the Institute in practice shall not accept, in a financial year, more than the "specified number of tax audit assignments" u/s 44AB of the Income-tax Act, 1961.
- In the case of a firm of CAs in practice, the "specified number of tax audit assignments" shall be construed as the specified number of tax audit assignments for every partner of the firm.
- The specified number of tax audit assignments in the case of firm of CAs in practice, 60 tax audit assignments per partner in the firm, in a financial year, whether in respect of corporate or non-corporate assessees.

- It is further clarified by the Council of ICAI that tax audit report accepted by the firm of Chartered Accountants can be signed by any partner on the behalf of the firm.
- In the present case, there are six partners in the firm and hence the firm can accept 360 tax audit assignment and any partner can sign the tax audit report on the behalf of the firm.

Conclusion: Mr. Gaurav can sign the 290 tax audit reports on behalf of the firm.

Q.137 M/S PQR & Co. is a partnership firm of 3 partners P, Q and R. All partners are exclusively associated with the firm in practice and are not doing practice in individual capacity. For the year ended 31st March, 2019, the partners have undertaken audits and signed audit reports under section 44AB/44AD of the Income Tax Act, 1961 as under:

	Under Section 44AB	Under Section 44AD
P	10	15
Q	60	5
R	100	5

Discuss whether there is any professional misconduct by the firm in regard to the aforesaid audits.

[Nov. 19 - Old Syllabus (4 Marks)]

Ans. : Signing of Tax Audit Report:

- As per Chapter VI of Council General Guidelines, 2008, a member of the Institute in practice shall not accept, in a financial year, more than the "specified number of tax audit assignments" u/s 44AB of the Income-tax Act, 1961.
- In the case of a firm of CAs in practice, the "specified number of tax audit assignments" shall be construed as the specified number of tax audit assignments for every partner of the firm.
- The specified number of tax audit assignments in the case of firm of CAs in practice, 60 tax audit assignments per partner in the firm, in a financial year, whether in respect of corporate or non-corporate assessees.
- The audits conducted under Sections 44AD, 44AE, 44AF of the Income Tax Act, 1961 shall not be taken into account for the purpose of reckoning the "specified number of tax audit assignments".
- It is further clarified by the Council of ICAI that tax audit report accepted by the firm of Chartered Accountants can be signed by any partner on the behalf of the firm.
- In the present case, there are three partners in the firm and hence the firm can accept 180 tax audit assignment and any partner can sign the tax audit report on the behalf of the firm. Firm has accepted 170 tax audit assignments other than the audit under section 44AD.

Conclusion: No Misconduct arises on part of Firm or partners.

Q.138 Mr. Z accepted the statutory audit of a sick unit - NCT Limited for the year ending 31.03.2017. During course of audit it was noticed by the statutory auditor that company's net worth was negative for year ended 31.03.2016 and there was also a liability of tax audit fees of ₹ 35,000 in favour of the previous auditors. Comment. **[Nov. 16 (4 Marks)]**

Ans. : Accepting Appointment as an Auditor:

- As per Clause 1 of Part II of Second Schedule, a member of the Institute will be held guilty of professional misconduct if he contravenes any of the provisions of this act or the regulations made there under or any guidelines issued by the council.
- As per Chapter VII of Council General Guidelines 2008, a member of the Institute in practice shall not accept the appointment as auditor of an entity in case the undisputed audit fee of another Chartered Accountant for carrying out the statutory audit under the Companies Act, 1956 or various other statutes has not been paid. As per the proviso, such prohibition shall not apply in case of a sick unit where a sick unit is defined to mean "where the net worth is negative".
- In the present case, Mr. Z accepted the audit of M/s PSU Ltd., though the undisputed fees of previous auditor remain unpaid.

Conclusion: Mr. Z would still not be guilty of professional misconduct since the M/s PSU Ltd. is a sick unit having negative net worth for the year 2015-16.

Q.139 Write short note on: Record of Audit assignments.

Ans. : Record of Audit Assignments:

Chapter 8 of Council General Guidelines, 2008 requires a Chartered Accountant in practice as well as firm of Chartered Accountants in practice to maintain a record of the audit assignments accepted by him or by the firm of Chartered Accountants, or by any of the partners of the firm in his individual name or as a partner of any other firm, as far as possible, in the following format:

S. No.	Name of the Company	Registration No.	Date of Appointment	Date of Acceptance	Date on which Form ADT-1 Filed with ROC
1	2	3	4	5	6

Q.140 J, a practicing Chartered Accountant has not maintained the records of audit assignments of the companies on the ground that he is conducting lesser number of audits prescribed under Section 141(3)(*g*) of the Companies Act, 2013. [Nov. 18-Old Syllabus (4 Marks)]

Ans. : Record of Audit Assignments:

- As per Clause 1 of Part II of Second Schedule, a member of the Institute will be held guilty of professional misconduct if he Contravenes any of the provisions of this act or the regulations made there under or any guidelines issued by the council.
- Chapter VIII of Council General Guidelines, 2008 requires a Chartered Accountant in practice as well as firm of Chartered Accountants in practice to maintain a record of the audit assignments accepted by him or by the firm of Chartered Accountants, or by any of the partners of the firm in his individual name or as a partner of any other firm, as far as possible, in the following format:

S. No.	Name of the Company	Registration No.	Date of Appointment	Date of Acceptance	Date on which Form ADT-1 Filed with ROC
1	2	3	4	5	6

- In the present case, J, a practicing Chartered Accountant has not maintained the records of audit assignments of the companies on the ground that he is conducting lesser number of audits prescribed under Section 141(3)(*g*) of the Companies Act, 2013.

Conclusion: Ground of Mr. J is not admissible and he will be held guilty of professional misconduct by virtue of Clause 1 of Part II of Second Schedule, due to contravention of Chapter VIII of Council General Guidelines, 2008 for not maintaining of record of audit assignments.

Q.141 Comment on the following with reference to the Chartered Accountants Act, 1949 and schedules thereto: A is the auditor of Z Ltd., which has a turnover of ₹ 200 crores. The audit fee for the year is fixed at ₹ 50 lakhs. During the year, the company offers A an assignment of management consultancy within the meaning of Section 2(2)(iv) of the CA Act, 1949 for a remuneration of ₹ 1 crore. A seeks your advice on accepting the assignment.

or

Comment on the following with reference to the Chartered Accountants' Act, 1949 and schedules thereto: Mr. Moon is the auditor of M/s Sun Ltd., which has a turnover of ₹ 100 crores. The audit fee for the year is fixed at ₹ 25 lakhs. During the year the company offers Mr. Moon an assignment of Management Consultancy for a remuneration of ₹ 50 lakhs.

Ans. : Appointment as a statutory auditor of a PSUs'/Govt. company/listed company and other public company:

- As per Clause 1 of Part II of Second Schedule, a member of the Institute will be held guilty of professional misconduct if he Contravenes any of the provisions of this act or the regulations made there under or any guidelines issued by the council.
- Council General Guidelines 2008, specifies that a member of the Institute in practice shall be deemed to be guilty of professional misconduct if he accepts the appointment as a statutory auditor of a

	PSUs'/Govt. companies/listed companies and other public company having a turnover of ₹ 50 crores or more in a year and accepts any other work(s) or assignment(s) or service(s) in regard to same undertaking(s) on a remuneration which in total exceeds the fee payable for carrying out the statutory audit of the same undertaking. **Conclusion**: In view of the above position it would be a misconduct on A's part if he accepts the management consultancy assignment. **Note: Applicability of Chapter IX of Council General Guidelines, 2008 seems to be redundant in case of companies, because as per Section 144 of the Companies Act, 2013, auditor of a company cannot render management services to the company, its holding company or subsidiary company, directly or indirectly.**
Q.142	**Comment with reference to the Chartered Accountants Act, 1949 and Schedules thereto: D, who conducts the tax audit u/s 44AB of the Income Tax Act, 1961 of M/s ABC, a partnership firm, has received the entire audit fees of ₹ 25,000 in April, 2018 in respect of the tax audit for the year ended 31.3.2018. The audit report was, however, signed on 25.05.2018.** **What will be your answer if fees were recovered on progressive basis? [May 09 (4 Marks)]**
	Ans. : Appointment of an auditor when he is indebted to the concern: ◆ As per Clause 1 of Part II of Second Schedule, a member of the Institute will be held guilty of professional misconduct if he Contravenes any of the provisions of this act or the regulations made there under or any guidelines issued by the council. ◆ Council General Guidelines, 2008 specifies that a member of the Institute in practice or a partner of a firm in practice or a firm shall not accept appointment as auditor of a concern while indebted to the concern or given any guarantee or provided any security in connection with the indebtedness of any third person to the concern, for limits fixed in the statute and in other cases for amount exceeding ₹ 10,000. ◆ As per explanation to Sec. 288 to Income Tax Act, 1961, an individual who, or his relative or partner is indebted to the assessee cannot conduct tax audit, provided that the relative may be indebted to the assessee for an amount not exceeding ₹ 1,00,000. ◆ In the instant Case, D is appointed to conduct a tax audit u/s 44AB of the Income Tax Act, 1961. In view of the above-mentioned provision, D is disqualified to be appointed as tax auditor of the company being indebted to the assessee. **Conclusion**: Mr. D will be held guilty of professional misconduct by virtue of clause I of Part II of Second Schedule.. However, if fees were recovered on progressive basis, no professional misconduct arises.
Q.143	**Give your comments with reference to the Companies Act, 2013 and the Chartered Accountants Act, 1949 and Schedules thereto: Mr. E, proprietor of M/s. E & Co. is the statutory auditor of a company which owns a store dealing in computer equipment. During the year 2017-18, E purchased a computer from the store costing ₹ 25,000 for his son.** **He did not make any payment for the same, but asked the company to adjust the same against the audit fees payable of ₹ 50,000. [Nov. 12 (4 Marks)]**
	Ans. : Auditor indebtedness: ◆ As per Sec. 141(3)(*d*)(*ii*) of Companies Act, 2013 a person who, or his relative or partner is indebted to the company, or its subsidiary or its holding or associate company or a subsidiary of such holding company for an amount exceeding ₹ 5 Lacs is disqualified to be appointed as auditor of that company. ◆ Further, it has been provided by Council General Guidelines 2008 that a member of the Institute in practice or a partner of a firm in practice or a firm shall not accept appointment as auditor of a concern while indebted to the concern or given any guarantee or provided any security in connection with the indebtedness of any third person to the concern, for limits fixed in the statute and in other cases for amount exceeding ₹ 10,000/- ◆ The audit fees can be received on progressive basis, but not as an advance. Any advance received from the client amounts to indebtedness and brings disqualification. **Conclusion**: Mr. E is permitted to continue the office as his indebtedness does not exceed ₹ 5 Lacs.

Q.144 M/s ASKS, a firm of Chartered Accountants, having three partners accepts an audit assignment of a private limited company for a fee of ₹ 4,000 only. Comment. [May 09 (5 Marks), Nov. 15 (4 Marks)]

Ans. : Minimum Audit Fees:

- Council of ICAI has prescribed minimum audit fees for the practicing members. However, prescribed minimum audit fee is recommendatory, not mandatory in nature.
- Therefore, acceptance of audit assignment by M/s ASKS, a firm of Chartered Accountants having 5 partners of a newly formed private limited company for audit fees of ₹ 5,000 is not violation of any provisions.

Conclusion: M/s ASKS will not be held liable for guilty of misconduct.

"ICAI Examiner Comments"

Some examinees related it to number of companies in which a CA can be appointed as an auditor.

Q.145 Comment on the following with reference to the Chartered Accountants Act, 1949, and Schedules thereto: M (P) Ltd. appointed CA. P for some professional assignments like company's ROC work, preparation of minutes, statutory register etc. For this, CA. P charged his fees depending on the complexity and the time spent by him on each assignment.

Later on, M (P) Ltd. filed a complaint against CA. P to the ICAI that he has charged excessive fees for the assignments comparative to the scale of fees recommended by the Committee as well as duly considered by the Council of ICAI.

Ans. : Charging Excess Fees:

- Prescribed scale of fees for the professional assignments done by the chartered accountants is recommendatory in nature. Fees in any professional assignment depend upon the mutual agreement and understanding between the member and the client.
- Charging fee more than the fees recommended for a professional assignment does not constitute any misconduct in the context of the provisions of the Chartered Accountants Act, 1949 and regulation made thereunder.
- In the given case, CA. P has charged excess fees comparative to the scale of fees recommended by the Committee as well as duly considered by the Council of ICAI.

Conclusion: Scale of fees recommended by the Committee as well as duly considered by the Council of ICAI is only recommendatory and not mandatory, hence no misconduct arise on part of Mr. P.

7.9 - SELF REGULATORY MEASURES

Q.146 Write short note on: Self-Regulatory Measures as recommended by Council of ICAI.

Ans. : Recommended Self-Regulatory Measures:

1. **Branch Audits:** The branch audits of a company should not be conducted by its statutory auditors consisting of ten or more members, but should be conducted by the local firms of auditors consisting of less than ten members. This should not be understood to mean any restriction on the right of the statutory auditors to have access over branch accounts conferred under the Companies Act, 2013.
2. **Joint Audit:** In the case of large companies the practice of associating a practicing firm with less than five members as Joint auditors should be encouraged. Where a client desires to appoint such a firm as joint auditor, the senior firm should not object to the same.
3. **Ratio Between Qualified and Unqualified Staff:** In the Council's view, a practicing firm of Chartered Accountants engaged in audit work should have at least one member for every five non-qualified members of the staff, excluding articled and audit clerks, typists, peons and other persons not engaged directly in such professional work.
4. **Disclosure of Interest by Auditors in other Firms:** The Council has decided that as a good and healthy practice, auditors should make a disclosure of the payments received by them for other services through the medium of a different firm or firms in which the said auditor may be either a partner or proprietor.

7.10 - KYC NORMS

Q.147 Write short note on: KYC norms for a Chartered Accountant in practice.

[May 18 - Old Course (4 Marks)]

Ans : KYC Norms for a Chartered Accountant in Practice:

A Chartered Accountant is required to observe certain KYC norms, in accordance with which he need to maintain certain details about his clients. Details required as per KYC norms are:

(A) **Individual Client:**

General Information: Name of the Individual, PAN No. or Aadhaar Card No. of the Individual, Business Description and Copy of last Audited Financial Statement

Engagement Information: Type of Engagement

(B) **Corporate Entity:**

General Information: Name and Address of the Entity, Business Description, Name of the Parent Company in case of Subsidiary, Copy of last Audited Financial Statement

Engagement Information: Type of Engagement

Regulatory Information: Company PAN No., Company Identification No., Directors' Names & Addresses, Directors' Identification No.

(C) **Non- Corporate Entity:**

General Information: Name and Address of the Entity, Copy of PAN No., Business Description, Partner's Names & Addresses (with their PAN/Aadhaar Card/DIN No.), Copy of last Audited Financial Statement

Engagement Information: Type of Engagement.

Importance of KYC Norms: Refer Answer of Q. No. 148.

Q.148 Write short note on: Importance of KYC requirements for a Chartered Accountant's practice.

[Nov. 14 (4 Marks)]

Ans. : Importance of KYC Norms for a practicing CA:

- The financial services industry globally is required to obtain information of their clients and comply with KYC norms.
- Keeping in mind the highest standards of Chartered Accountancy profession in India, the Council of ICAI recommended such norms to be observed by the members of the profession who are in practice.
- Considering the spirit underlying these measures, it is expected that every Chartered Accountant carrying out attest function is encouraged to follow them and implementation of these measures would go a long way in ensuring equitable flow of work among the members and would also further enhance the prestige of the profession in the society.
- These Know Your Client (KYC) Norms are also important in order to ensure a healthy growth of the profession and an equitable flow of professional work among the members.

7.11 - EXERCISE QUESTIONS

Q.149 A Chartered Accountant in service agrees to entrust the work of investment broker to Mr. X on the specific understanding that 20% of commission Mr. X earns would be paid to him.

Ans. : Sharing other's emoluments by a CA in Service:

- As per Clause 2 of Part II of First Schedule of the Chartered Accountant Act, 1949, a member of the Institute (other than a member in practice) shall be guilty of professional misconduct, if he being an employee of any company, firm or person accepts or agrees to accept any part of fee, profits or gains from a lawyer, a chartered accountant or broker engaged by such company, firm or person or agent or customer of such company, firm or person by way of commission or gratification.
- In the present case, a CA in service agrees to entrust the work of investment broker to Mr. X on the specific understanding that 20% of commission Mr. X earns would be paid to him.

Conclusion: Concerned CA will be deemed to be guilty of professional misconduct by virtue of clause 2 of Part II of First Schedule.

Q.150 Discuss whether the following action by a Chartered Accountant would amount to misconduct or not: A practising Chartered Accountant uses a visiting card in which he designates himself, besides as Chartered Accountant, as (a) Tax Consultant (b) Cost Accountant.

Ans. : Using designation other than Chartered Accountant:

- Clause 7 of Part 1 of First Schedule to the CA Act, 1949 provides that a CA in practice is deemed to be guilty of professional misconduct if he (i) advertises his professional attainments or services or (ii) uses any designation or expressions other than "Chartered Accountant" on professional documents, visiting cards, letter heads or sign boards.
- As per Section 7 of Chartered Accountants Act, 1949, every member of the Institute in practice shall use the designation of a chartered accountant.
- However, a degree of a university established by law in India or recognized by the Central Government or a title indicating membership of the ICAI or of any other institution that has been recognized by the Central Government or may be recognized by the council is permitted to be mentioned.
- In the given case, a practising Chartered Accountant uses a visiting card in which he designates himself, besides as Chartered Accountant, as Tax Consultant/Cost Accountant.

Conclusion: Concerned CA shall be held guilty of professional misconduct as per Clause (7) of Part I of First Schedule to the Chartered Accountants Act, 1949.

Q.151 As a Practising CA do you approve the following: In a representation to be submitted to a company u/s 140(4) of the Companies Act, 2013, the partner of the firm of auditors wants to include the contributions made by the firm in strengthening the control procedures of the company during their association with the company. If not, why?

Ans. : Right of representation:

- Section 140(4) of the Companies Act, 2013 permits an auditor to make a representation in writing (not exceeding a reasonable length) to the company. The proposition of the partner to highlight contributions made by the firm in strengthening the control procedures in the representation is not acceptable because the representation letter should not be prepared in a manner so as to seek publicity.
- The Code of Ethics issued by the Institute makes it amply clear that the right to make representation does not mean that an auditor has any prescriptive right or a lien on an audit.
- The wording of his representation should be such that, apart from the opportunity not being abused to secure needless publicity, it does not tantamount directly or indirectly to canvassing or soliciting for his continuance as an auditor. The letter should merely set out in a dignified manner how he has been acting independently and conscientiously through the term of office and may in addition, indicate if he so chooses his willingness to continue as auditor if re-appointed by the shareholders.

Conclusion: Action proposed by a partner could not be approved since, it would lead to his being held guilty of professional misconduct under Clause (6) of Part I of the First Schedule to the Chartered Accountants Act, 1949.

Q.152 As a practising chartered accountant do you approve the following: The Chairman of an Audit Committee of a Bluechip Company, who is a Chartered Accountant asked the firm in which he was previously a partner to quote their fee on a success fee basis so as to ensure that a professional work is assigned to such firm.

Ans. : Charging fees on %age basis:

- Clause 10 of Part I to First Schedule to the CA Act, 1949 prohibits a CA in practice to charge, or offers to charge, accept or offers to accept in respect of any professional employment, fees which are based on a percentage of profits or which are contingent upon the findings or results of such employment.
- However, this restriction is not applicable where such payment is permitted by the regulations made in this behalf. The Council of the Institute has framed regulation 192 which exempts certain professional services from the operation of clause 10.
- In the present case, the Chairman of an Audit Committee of a Bluechip Company, who is a Chartered Accountant asked the firm in which he was previously a partner to quote their fee on a success fee basis so as to ensure that a professional work is assigned to such firm.

Conclusion: Such quotation cannot be approved as it will amount to professional misconduct by virtue of clause 10 of Part I of First Schedule.

Q.153 Is there any misconduct on the part of a Chartered Accountant in the following circumstances: The offer document of a listed company in which Mr. D, a practising Chartered Accountant is a director mentions the name of Mr. D as a director along with his various professional attainments and spheres of specialisation.

Ans. : Clauses 6 & 7 of Part I of First Schedule:

If a public Company, in which a CA in practice is a Director issues a prospectus or gives any announcement that gives descriptions about the CA's expertise, specialization and knowledge in any particular field, it will attract professional misconduct under clauses 6 & 7. In the given case, the CA is guilty of professional misconduct.

Q.154 X & Co. Chartered Accountants were informed by True & Co. Ltd. that they have been appointed as auditor of the company in place of ABC & Co. who have been removed, subject however to the approval of the shareholders in the ensuing AGM. X & Co. accepted the appointment and commenced the work without their appointment being approved by the shareholders of the company.

Ans. : Non-observance of compliance of Sections 139 & 140 of Companies Act, 2013:

- As per Clause 9 of Part I of First Schedule to Chartered Accountant Act, 1949, a CA in practice shall be deemed to be guilty of professional misconduct if he accepts an appointment as auditor of a company, without ascertaining whether requirements of Secs. 224 & 225 of Companies Act, 1956 (Secs. 139 & 140 of Companies Act, 2013), in respect of such appointment have been duly complied with.
- In the present case, X & Co. Chartered Accountants were informed by True & Co. Ltd. that they have been appointed as auditor of the company in place of ABC & Co. who have been removed, subject however to the approval of the shareholders in the ensuing AGM. X & Co. accepted the appointment and commenced the work without their appointment being approved by the shareholders of the company.
- Commencing the work without being appointed as auditor in the AGM is clearly a non-compliance of Sec. 139.

Conclusion: X & Co. will be held to be guilty of professional misconduct under clause 9 of Part I of First Schedule to the Chartered Accountants Act, 1956.

Q.155 Mr. X, a practicing Chartered Accountant, accepts appointment as a valuer of goodwill of a business for the purpose of taxation laws on the condition that he would be paid 5% of the value of the goodwill so determined as his fees.

Ans. : Charging Fees on Percentage Basis:

- Clause 10 of Part I of First schedule to CA Act, 1949, prohibits a CA in practice to charge or offer to charge, accept or offer to accept in respect of any professional work, fees which are based on a percentage of profits or which are contingent upon the findings or result of work.
- However, this restriction is not applicable where such payment is permitted by the regulations made in this behalf. The Council of the Institute has framed regulation 192 which exempts certain professional services from the operation of clause 10.
- As per Regulation 192, in the case of a valuer, for the purposes of direct taxes and duties, fees may be charged on a percentage of the value of property valued.

Conclusion: Charging fees on %age basis in the capacity of valuer for the purposes of taxation laws is included in the exceptions stated in regulation 192, Mr. X is not guilty of any professional misconduct.

Q.156 Is there any misconduct on the part of a Chartered Accountant in the following circumstances: Mr. X has charged a fee for representing his client in an income tax appeal based on the expected relief as a result of the appeal.

Ans. : Charging fees on %age basis:

- Clause 10 of Part I to First Schedule to the CA Act, 1949 prohibits a CA in practice to charge, or offers to charge, accept or offers to accept in respect of any professional employment, fees which are based on a percentage of profits or which are contingent upon the findings or results of such employment.
- However, this restriction is not applicable where such payment is permitted by the regulations made in this behalf. The Council of the Institute has framed regulation 192 which exempts certain professional services from the operation of clause 10.
- The services rendered by X are not covered by any of exemptions provided under regulation 192.

Conclusion: Mr. X is guilty of professional misconduct.

Q.157 A CA in practice, inspite of repeated requests from the secretary of the Institute, fails to submit Form 18. Is he liable for misconduct. [May 17 (4 Marks)]

Ans. : Failure to supply information called for:

- Clause 2 of Part III of the First Schedule to the Chartered Accountants Act, 1949, a member, whether in practice or not, will be deemed to be guilty of professional misconduct if he does not supply the information called for, or does not comply with the requirements asked for, by the Institute, Council or any of its Committees, Director (Discipline), Board of Discipline, Disciplinary Committee, Quality Review Board or the Appellate authority.
- In the given case, concerned CA has failed to submit form No. 18 inspite of several requests from Secretary of the Institute.

Conclusion: Concerned CA is held guilty of professional misconduct as per Clause 2 of Part III of the First Schedule to the Chartered Accountants Act, 1949.

Q.158 Discuss the following with reference to the Chartered Accountants Act, 1949 and schedules thereto: Mr. R, a Chartered Accountant in practice has been elected as the treasurer of a Regional Council of the Institute. The Regional Council had organized an international tour through a tour operator during the year for its members. During the audit of the Regional Council, it was found that Mr. R had received a personal benefit of ₹ 50,000 from the tour operator.

Ans. : Bringing disrepute to profession:

- Clause 2 of Part IV of First Schedule to the Chartered Accountants Act, 1949 states that member of the Institute, whether in practice or not, shall be deemed guilty of other misconduct, if he in the opinion of the Council, brings disrepute to the profession or to the Institute as a result of his action whether or not related to his professional work".
- Accordingly, a Chartered Accountant is also expected to maintain the highest standards and integrity even in his personal affairs and any deviation from these standards calls for disciplinary action.
- In the present case, Mr. R (treasurer of regional council) had received a personal benefit of ₹ 50,000 from a tour operator who organised an international tour of the Regional Council. This brings disrepute to the profession of a Chartered Accountant.

Conclusion: Mr. R will be held guilty of other misconduct under clause 2 of Part IV of First Schedule of the Chartered Accountants Act, 1949.

Q.159 Comment on the following with reference to the Chartered Accountants Act, 1949 and Schedules thereto: L, a Chartered Accountant, certifies a financial forecast of his client which was forwarded to the client's bank based on which the bank sanctioned a loan to the client.

Ans. : Certification of Financial forecast:

- As per Clause 3 of Part I, Second Schedule to the CA Act, 1949 Chartered Accountant in practice shall be deemed to be guilty of professional misconduct if he permits his name or the name of the firm to be used in connection with the estimates of earnings, contingent upon future transactions, in a manner which may lead to the belief that he vouches for the accuracy of the forecast.
- SAE 3400 "The Examination of Prospective Financial Information" allows to a member to participate in the preparation of profit or financial forecasts and can review them subject to following conditions:
  (*a*) He indicates the source of information.
  (*b*) He indicates the basis of forecasts.
  (*c*) He gives in his report the major assumptions made in arriving at the forecasts.
  (*d*) He does not vouch for the accuracy of the forecasts.
- In the given case, L, a Chartered Accountant, certifies a financial forecast of his client which was forwarded to the client's bank based on which the bank sanctioned a loan to the client.

Conclusion: Mr. L will be guilty of professional Misconduct by virtue of clause 3 of Part I of Second Schedule, if he has certified the financial forecast without taking adequate safeguards as specified in SAE 3400.

Q.160 A chartered accountant holding certificate of practice and having four articled clerks registered under him accepts appointment as a full-time lecturer in a college. Also, he becomes a partner with his brother in a business. Examine his conduct in the light of CA. Act, 1949 and the regulations thereunder.

Ans. : Partnership with a relative and entering into business:

As per Clause 4, part I of First Schedule, a CA in Practice is deemed to be guilty of professional Misconduct if he enters into partnership in or outside India with any person other than the following:

- C.A. in practice, or
- Member of any other professional body having prescribed qualifications, or
- a person who but for his residence abroad would be entitled to be registered as member, or
- a person whose qualifications are recognized by CG or Council for the purpose of permitting such partnerships.

As per Clause 11 of Part 1 of First Schedule to the CA Act, 1949 a member in practice is prohibited to engage in any business or occupation other than the profession of chartered accountants unless permitted by the Council so to engage.

In the present case, A CA in practice entered into partnership with his brother in a business. And accepts appointment as a full time lecturer in a college which requires prior approval from the Council of the ICAI.

Conclusion: A CA in practice cannot engage in any business or occupation other than the profession of Chartered Accountant unless permitted by the council so to engage. Hence the CA will be guilty under clauses 4 & 11.

Q.161 Comment on the following with reference to CA Act, 1949 and schedules thereto: A is a partner of 2 firms, M/s ABC & Company and M/s A & Associates. For most of the audits handled by him, the appointment is in the name of M/s ABC & Company. The visiting cards of A carries the names of both the firms.

Ans. : Mentioning Firm's Name on Letter Heads:

- Clause 7 of Part 1 of First Schedule to the CA Act, 1949 provides that a CA in practice is deemed to be guilty of professional misconduct if he (i) advertises his professional attainments or services or (ii) uses any designation or expressions other than "Chartered Accountant" on professional documents, visiting cards, letter heads or sign boards.
- However, a degree of a university established by law in India or recognized by the Central Government or a title indicating membership of the ICAI or of any other institution that has been recognized by the Central Government or may be recognized by the council is permitted to be mentioned.
- There is no prohibition for printing names of all firms on the personal letter heads in which a member holding certificate of practice is a partner.

Conclusion: Mr. A is not guilty of any professional misconduct in the above case.

Q.162 Bahadur was an auditor of a firm M/s Manmeet Corporation. He retained the books of account and voucher files and failed to hand over them to the firm regardless of their repeated requests. Is he guilty of professional misconduct.

Ans. : Non-return of Client's Books:

- As per Part IV of the First Schedule to the Chartered Accountants Act, a member of the Institute, whether in practice or not, shall be deemed to be guilty of other misconduct, if he
  1. is held guilty by any civil or criminal court for an offence which is punishable with imprisonment for a term not exceeding six months;
  2. in the opinion of the Council, brings disrepute to the profession or the Institute as a result of his action whether or not related to his professional work.
- A member may be found guilty of "Other Misconduct", as per clause 2, if he retains the books of account and documents of the client and fails to return these to the client on request without a reasonable cause.
- In the given case, Mr. Bahadur failed to return the books of account and other documents of his client without any reasonable cause.

Conclusion: Mr. Bahadur would be guilty of Other Misconduct under Part IV of First Schedule and liable to disciplinary action under Section 21.

Q.163 Ajay is a practising Chartered Accountant. Vijay is a practising Advocate representing matters in courts of law. Ajay and Vijay agree to help each other in matters involving their professional expertise. Accordingly, Ajay recommends Vijay in all tax litigations in courts of law. Vijay consults Ajay on all matters relating to finance and related matters, which come to him for arguing in various courts of law. Ajay seeks your advice on how he and Vijay should

(*i*) remunerate each other (ii) 'share' the remuneration.

Ans. : Sharing Fees with Advocate or of Advocate:

- As per clause (2) of Part I of the First Schedule to the Chartered Accountants Act, 1949, a CA in practice is deemed to be guilty of professional misconduct if he pays or allows or agrees to pay or allow, directly or indirectly, any share, commission or brokerage in the fees or profits of his professional business, to any person other than a member of the Institute or a partner or a retired partner or the legal representative of a deceased partner, or a member of any other professional body or with such other persons having such qualification as may be prescribed, for the purpose of rendering such professional services to time in or outside India.
- As per Clause 3 of Part I of the First Schedule to the CA Act, 1949, a CA in Practice is deemed to be guilty of professional Misconduct if he accepts or agrees to accept any part of the profits of the professional work of a person who is not a member of the Institute. However, such a restriction does not apply in respect of member of any other professional bodies or with such other persons having prescribed qualifications.
- For the purpose of Clauses 2 & 3, Regulation 53A of CA Regulations, 1988 allows sharing of profit with an advocate.

Conclusion: Ajay and Vijay can share the remuneration with each other with or without being entered into partnership as sharing of profits as well as partnership with Advocates are permitted by clauses 2, 3 and 4 of Part I of First Schedule.

Q.164 A CA in practice entered into partnership with his uncle in Textile business, which, however, did not take off. Will he be held guilty of professional misconduct?

Ans. : Partnership with a relative and entering into business:

As per Clause 4, part I of First Schedule, a CA in Practice is deemed to be guilty of professional Misconduct if he enters into partnership in or outside India with any person other than the following:

- C.A. in practice, or
- Member of any other professional body having prescribed qualifications, or
- a person who but for his residence abroad would be entitled to be registered as member, or
- a person whose qualifications are recognized by CG or Council for the purpose of permitting such partnerships.

As per Clause 11 of Part 1 of First Schedule to the CA Act, 1949 a member in practice is prohibited to engage in any business or occupation other than the profession of chartered accountants unless permitted by the Council so to engage.

In the present case, A CA in practice entered into partnership with his uncle in Textile business.

Conclusion: A CA in practice cannot engage in any business or occupation other than the profession of Chartered Accountant unless permitted by the council so to engage. Even if the agreement is not acted upon, the mere fact that he entered into partnership by such an agreement would constitute misconduct. Hence the CA will be guilty under clauses 4 & 11.

Q.165 A CA in practice appearing on television on budget proposals was introduced to the viewers, on the basis of the bio-data furnished by him, as the Senior most partner of M/s Tick & Tag a leading firm of CA's established in Delhi in 1978. See whether there is any professional misconduct in this case.

Ans. : Solicitation of Professional Work and Advertisement:

- Clause 6 of Part I of the First Schedule to the Chartered Accountants Act, 1949 states that a Chartered Accountant in practice shall be deemed to be guilty of misconduct if he solicits clients or professional work either directly or indirectly by a circular, advertisement, personal communication or interview or by any other means.
- Section 7 of the Chartered Accountants Act, 1949 read with Clause 7 of Part I of the First Schedule to the said Act prohibits advertising of professional attainments or services of a member. It also restrains a member from using any designation or expression other than that of a chartered accountant in documents through which the professional attainments of the member would come to the notice of the public.
- Guidelines issued under clauses 6 & 7 permits a practicing member to give lectures at forums and may give their names and describe themselves as Chartered Accountants, but no reference should be made, to the name and address or services of his firm.

- In the given case - (1) Reference to name of the firm, (2) Use of adjective expressions such as "a leading firm of CA's and Senior Most Partner", and (3) Reference to the date of establishment of firm, violate of the code of conduct.

Conclusion: Concerned CA will be guilty of professional misconduct.

Q.166 Z, a Chartered Accountant wrote several letters to Government Department, pointing out seniority of his firm, sending his life sketch and stating that he had a glorious record of service to the country as well as to the organization of accountancy profession with a view to get the audit work.

Ans. : Refer Q. No. 25.

Q.167 X & Co., CAs informed selected multinational organizations, who are not their clients that Mr. Y, the former Partner - in - charge of taxation of one of the largest accounting firms of the world, had joined them as a partner. Is this action liable for professional misconduct?

Ans. : Solicitation of Professional Work and Advertisement:

- Clause 6 of Part I of the First Schedule to the Chartered Accountants Act, 1949 states that a Chartered Accountant in practice shall be deemed to be guilty of misconduct if he solicits clients or professional work either directly or indirectly by a circular, advertisement, personal communication or interview or by any other means.
- Section 7 of the Chartered Accountants Act, 1949 read with Clause 7 of Part I of the First Schedule to the said Act prohibits advertising of professional attainments or services of a member. It also restrains a member from using any designation or expression other than that of a chartered accountant in documents through which the professional attainments of the member would come to the notice of the public.

Conclusion: Issuing circular to persons who are not clients but may likely requires services of a CA would tantamount to advertisements since it is solicitation of professional work by making roving enquiries. Usage of the words "one of the largest accounting firms of the world" and the specification of specialization in Taxation would amount to advertisement and thus, constitute professional misconduct.

Q.168 A junior CA in practice requests in writing to a senior member of his profession who is over-burdened with professional work to divert some of his work to him on profit sharing basis. Is there any offence in seeking professional work by a member from another member/Give reason for your answer?

Ans. : Solicitation of professional work from another CA:

- As per Clause 6 of Part I of the First Schedule to the Chartered Accountants Act, 1949 a Chartered Accountant in practice shall be deemed to be guilty of misconduct if he solicits clients or professional work either directly or indirectly by a circular, advertisement, personal communication or interview or by any other means.
- However, nothing in clause 6 shall be construed as preventing or prohibiting any Chartered Accountant from applying or requesting for or inviting or securing professional work from another chartered accountant in practice.
- In the given case, junior CA request to senior member to allot some professional work to him, which is not prohibited under clause 6.

Conclusion: There is nothing wrong in soliciting professional work from another CA, hence there is no professional misconduct.

Q.169 T, a practicing CA uses the designation, 'Municipal Councillor' apart from the expression 'FCA' on his visiting card. Comment.

Ans. : Using designated other than CA:

- As per clause (7) of Part I of the First Schedule to the CA Act, 1949, a CA in practice is deemed to be guilty of professional misconduct if he Advertises his professional attainments or services, or uses any designation or expressions other than the CA on professional documents, visiting cards, letter heads or sign boards.
- However, a recognized degree of university or title indicating membership of ICAI or other recognized institution may be used.
- It also restrains a member from using any designation or expression other than that of a CA in documents through which the professional attainments of the member would come to the notice of the public.

Conclusion: A member is not permitted to use the designation such as 'Member of Parliament', 'Municipal Councillor' or any other functionary in addition to that of CA. Therefore under this clause T is guilty of professional misconduct.

Q.170 Comment on the following with reference to the Chartered Accountants Act, 1949 and Schedules thereto: M/s ABC, a partnership firm carrying on business has complained to the Institute of Chartered Accountants of India (ICAI) that Mr. M, a Chartered Accountant has charged the firm excessive fees for a professional assignment.

Ans. : Excessive Fees:

- The matter of fixation of actual fees charged in individual cases, depends upon the mutual agreements and understanding between chartered accountant and client. The scales of fees recommended by the council of the Institute is only recommendatory.
- In the circumstances, the contention of the client of Mr. M that he has charged an excessive fee for a professional assignment, does not constitute professional misconduct in the context of the provisions of Chartered Accountants Act, 1949 and regulations made thereunder.

Conclusion: In view of the above Mr. M is not liable for any professional misconduct under the Chartered Accountants Act, 1949.

Q.171 Comment on the following with reference to CA Act, 1949 and schedules thereto: M/s PQR a firm of Chartered Accountants responded to a tender from a State Government department for switching over to double entry system of accounting. For the purposes the firm also paid ₹ 20,000 as earnest money deposits as per the terms of the tender.

Ans. : Responding to tenders:

- Clause 6 of Part I of First Schedule to the Chartered Accountants Act, 1949 prohibits solicitation of work either directly or indirectly by circular, advertisement, personal communication or interview or by any other means, would constitute professional misconduct.
- However, a member is permitted to respond to tenders or inquiries raised by various users of professional services or organizations.
- Guidelines are being issued by Council under Clause 1 of Part II of Second Schedule allowing therein a member to respond to tenders where minimum fees of the assignment is prescribed in the tender document itself or where the areas are open to other professionals along with Chartered Accounts.
- Further, in respect of a non-exclusive area, members are permitted to pay reasonable amount towards earnest money/security deposits.
- In the present case, tenders were issued by State Government for switching over double entry system of accounting, which does not fall within exclusive areas for CAs, hence M/s LMN can respond to tenders as well as deposit ₹ 50,000 as earnest deposit.

Conclusion: M/S PQR have not committed any professional misconduct.

Q.172 Comment on the following with reference to the Chartered Accountants Act, 1949 and schedules thereto: A Partner of a firm of Chartered Accountants during a T.V. interview handed over a bio-data of his firm to the Chairperson. Such bio-data detailed the standing with International firm and also his achievements and recognition as an expert in the field of Taxation. The bio-data was read out during the said interview.

Ans. : Prohibition on solicitation of work

- Clause 6 of Part I of First Schedule to the Chartered Accountants Act, 1949 prohibits solicitation of work either directly or indirectly by circular, advertisement, personal communication or interview or by any other means, would constitute professional misconduct.
- In the present case, partner of a firm handed over bio data of firm which was read out during interview. The bio data contains personal recognition and achievements of the partner as an expert in the field of taxation. Such an act would lead to the promotion of his name and publicity thereof to the firm.

Conclusion: Partner is guilty of professional misconduct under Clause 6 of Part I of the First Schedule to the Chartered Accountants Act, 1949.

Q.173 Comment on the following with reference to CA Act, 1949 and schedules thereto: X was appointed statutory auditor in ABC Ltd. On inquiry X found that his wife had acquired before a few years, 100 shares in the said company. She was holding the shares with the name of X as joint holder. Can X accept the appointment?

Ans. : Certification of Financial Statement of a related entity:

- Clause (4) of Part I of Second Schedule to the CA Act, 1949 states that if an auditor expresses his opinion on the financial statements of any business in which he, his firm or a partner in his firm has substantial interest, he is committing professional misconduct.
- Chapter IV of Council General Guidelines 2008 further provides that a member of the Institute shall not express his opinion on financial statements of any business or enterprise in which one or more persons who are his "relatives" within the meaning of AS 18 has/have, either by themselves or in conjunction with such member, a substantial interest in the said business or enterprise. As per AS 18, the term 'Relative' includes husband and wife.
- Sec. 141(3)(*d*) of the Companies Act, 2013, disqualifies a person to be appointed as auditor of the company in which he or his partner or relative is holding shares of the same company. However relative may hold shares of face value upto ₹ 1,00,000.
- In the given case Mr. X is joint shareholder in ABC Ltd and disqualify to be appointed as auditor.

Conclusion: X should decline the acceptance, as being disqualified u/s 141(3).

Q.174 Is there a professional misconduct in the following case in the context to CA Act and its regulations: Mr. X, a CA in practice and a lawyer agree to pay to each other 12% of the gross fees received by them from clients referred to each other. It is agreed that both of them will maintain a record in respect of such clients and the account will be settled at the end of year. However, at the end of first year, CA refuses to pay the referral fees as per the agreement and tells the lawyer that the agreement stands terminated.

Ans. : Sharing Fees with Advocate or of Advocate:

- As per clause (2) of Part I of the First Schedule to the Chartered Accountants Act, 1949, a CA in practice is deemed to be guilty of professional misconduct if he pays or allows or agrees to pay or allow, directly or indirectly, any share, commission or brokerage in the fees or profits of his professional business, to any person other than a member of the Institute or a partner or a retired partner or the legal representative of a deceased partner, or a member of any other professional body or with such other persons having such qualification as may be prescribed, for the purpose of rendering such professional services to time in or outside India.
- As per Clause 3 of Part I of the First Schedule to the CA Act, 1949, a CA in Practice is deemed to be guilty of professional misconduct if he accepts or agrees to accept any part of the profits of the professional work of a person who is not a member of the Institute. However, such a restriction does not apply in respect of member of any other professional bodies or with such other persons having prescribed qualifications.
- For the purpose of Clauses 2 & 3, Regulation 53A of CA Regulations, 1988 allows sharing of profit with an advocate.

Conclusion: Mr. X will not be deemed to be guilty of professional misconduct as clauses 2 & 3 permits a CA in practice for profit sharing with members of any other professional bodies or with such other persons having prescribed qualifications and members of bar council of India and persons having Bachelor of Law are prescribed.

Q.175 Comment on the following with reference to the Chartered Accountants Act, 1949 and schedules thereto: Mr. Rahul, a locally based CA, accepted an audit assignment at a fee lower than that charged by the previous auditor, who was stationed in another town and had to spend a lot of money on travel for which he did not charge separately.

Ans. : Undercutting of Fees:

- Council of ICAI has prescribed minimum audit fees for the practicing members. However, prescribed minimum audit fee is recommendatory, not mandatory in nature.
- Fees in any professional assignment depend upon the mutual agreement and understanding between the member and the client.
- In considering whether variation in fees charged would constitute undercutting, the quantum of work; incidental and out of pocket expenses and other terms of appointment should be considered.
- In this case, Mr. Rahul is a locally based Chartered Accountant, accepted an audit assignment at a fee lower than that charged by the previous auditor, who was outstation based Chartered Accountant and had to spend a lot of money on travel which was included in his audit fee and was not charged by him separately.

- It appears that the motive of Mr. Rahul was not to get the work from previous auditor by accepting the audit assignment on lower fee i.e. undercutting of fee since the previous auditor was stationed in another town and therefore, had to incur higher cost on account of conveyance, and the previously the fee was decided on a composite basis inclusive of travelling expenses of the auditor.

Conclusion: No misconduct arises on part of Mr. Rahul towards undercutting of fees as it appears from the fact of the case that fees charged by previous auditor is inclusive of travel expenses.

Q.176 Comment on the following with reference to the Chartered Accountants Act, 1949 and schedules thereto: Alora Pvt. Ltd. approached CA. Neha, a practicing Chartered Accountant since 1998, for recovery of debts amounting ₹ 20 crores. CA Neha accepted the work and requested to charge fees @ 1.5% of the debt recovered. Later on, she raised a bill for debts recovered and charged ₹ 27 lacs for recovering 90% of the debts.

Ans. : Charging Fees on Percentage Basis:

- Clause 10 of Part I of First schedule to CA Act, 1949, prohibits a CA in practice to charge or offer to charge, accept or offer to accept in respect of any professional work, fees which are based on a percentage of profits or which are contingent upon the findings or result of work.
- However, this restriction is not applicable where such payment is permitted by the regulations made in this behalf. The Council of the Institute has framed regulation 192 which exempts certain professional services from the operation of clause 10.
- As per Regulation 192, **in the case of debt recovery services, fees may be charged** on a percentage of amount of debt recovered.

Conclusion: Charging fees on a percentage of debt recovered in case of debt recovery services is included in the exceptions stated in regulation 192, Hence CA. Neha is not guilty of any professional misconduct.

Q.177 Comment on the following with reference to the Chartered Accountants Act, 1949 and schedules thereto: CA. Aman, a practicing Chartered Accountant, took over as the executive chairman of Signora IT Ltd. on 01.04.2018. However, realizing about obtaining prior approval from the Council of the ICAI for engaging into other business, he applied to Council for permission within 10 days.

Ans. : Engagements in other occupations:

- As per Clause 11 of Part I of First Schedule of the Chartered Accountants Act, 1949, a Chartered Accountant in practice will be deemed to be guilty of professional misconduct if he engages in any business or occupation other than the profession of Chartered Accountant unless permitted by the Council so to engage.
- In the instant case, CA. Aman took over as the executive chairman of Signora IT Ltd. on 01.04.2018 and applied for permission thereafter though within 10 days.
- On the basis of these facts, he was engaged in other occupation between the period 01.04.2018 and 10.04.2018, without the permission of the Council.

Conclusion: CA. Aman will be deemed to be guilty of Professional Misconduct under Clause 11 of Part I of First Schedule as he accepts the position of chairman of a company for which prior permission from Council is required.

Q.178 Comment on the following with reference to the Chartered Accountants Act, 1949 and schedules thereto: INFRO Foundation decided to review its historical financial statements. For this, it proposed a tender exclusively for Chartered Accountants to obtain assurance, primarily by performing inquiry, and analytical procedures about whether the financial statements as a whole are free from material misstatement. However, the foundation did not prescribe the minimum fee in the tender document. M/s Soni & Sons, a Chartered Accountant firm, responded to such tender

Ans. : Responding to tenders in exclusive area:

- Clause 6 of Part I of First Schedule allows solicitation of client or professional work through responding to tenders.
- Further Guidelines are being issued by Council allowing therein a member to respond to tender where minimum fees of the assignment is prescribed in the tender document itself or where the areas are open to other professionals along with Chartered Accountants.
- In the present case, M/s Soni & Sons responded to a tender of review of its historical financial statements which is exclusively reserved for Chartered Accountants even though no minimum fee was prescribed in the tender document.

Conclusion: Firm will be deemed to be guilty of Professional Misconduct under Clause 6 of Part I of First Schedule as responding to tender in exclusive area in which minimum fees is not prescribed is not permitted.

Q.179 Comment on the following with reference to the Chartered Accountants Act, 1949 and schedules thereto: CA. Raagi, a practicing Chartered Accountant, certifies a financial forecast of Capex Ltd. one of her clients, which was forwarded to the company's bank based on which the bank sanctioned a loan amounting ₹ 2.5 crore to the company. CA. Raagi, however, mentioned in the report that her responsibility is to examine the evidence supporting the assumptions and other information in the Prospective financial information, her responsibility does not include verification of the accuracy of the projections, therefore, she does not vouch for the accuracy of the same.

Ans. : Certification of Financial Forecast:

- As per Clause 3 of Part I of Second Schedule to the Chartered Accountants Act, 1949, a chartered accountant in practice is deemed to be guilty of professional misconduct if he permits his name or the name of his firm to be used in connection with an estimate of earnings contingent upon future transactions in a manner which may lead to the belief that he vouches for the accuracy of the forecast.
- Further SAE 3400 "The Examination of Prospective Financial Information", provides that the management is responsible for the preparation and presentation of the prospective financial information, including the identification and disclosure of the sources of information, the basis of forecasts and the underlying assumptions.
- In the given case, CA Raagi is being engaged by the client to certify a financial forecast. CA Raagi is required to ensure that the requirements of SAE 3400 have been fulfilled. CA. Raagi, mentioned in the report that her responsibility is to examine the evidence supporting the assumptions and other information in the Prospective financial information, her responsibility does not include verification of the accuracy of the projections, therefore, she does not vouch for the accuracy of the same.

Conclusion: No misconduct arises on part of CA. Raagi for certifying financial forecast under clause 3 of Part I of Second Schedule as she certifies the forecast in compliance of SAE 3400.

Q.180 Comment on the following with reference to the Chartered Accountants Act, 1949 and schedules thereto: Mr. Raj, a renowned practicing CA, decided to tie his knot with Ms. Anjali. While giving order for marriage invitation cards, Mr. Raj instructed to add his designation "Chartered Accountant" with his name. Later on, the cards were distributed to all his relatives, close friends and clients.

Ans. : Using designation "Chartered Accountant" on marriage invitation cards:

- As per Clause 6, Part I of First Schedule of Chartered Accountants Act, 1949, a CA in practice shall be deemed to be guilty of professional misconduct if he solicits clients or professional work either directly or indirectly, by circular, advertisement, personal communication or interview or by any other means.
- Guidelines issued by the Council of ICAI under Clause 6 allowed a member to use designation "Chartered Accountant" as well as name of firm in greeting cards, invitations for marriages and religious ceremonies and any invitation for opening or inauguration of office, or letters regarding change in office premises or telephone numbers provided these are sent only to clients, relatives and close friends of concerned member.
- In the present case, Mr. Raj is adding the designation Chartered Accountant with his name on marriage invitation cards and these cards were distributed to his relatives, close friends and clients.

Conclusion: No misconduct arises on part of Mr. Raj.

Q.181 Comment on the following with reference to the Chartered Accountants Act, 1949 and schedules thereto: WCP & Co. LLP are the internal auditors of DEF Ltd. WCP & Co. LLP also agreed to undertake Goods and Services Tax (GST) Audit of DEF Ltd. simultaneously. [RTP-May 19]

Ans. : Accepting GST Audit by Internal Auditors:

- The Council of the ICAI, while considering the issue whether an internal auditor of an entity can also undertake Tax Audit of the same entity as required under the Income-Tax Act, 1961, decided, that internal auditor, whether working as employee or external to the organisation, cannot be appointed as his Tax auditor (under the Income-Tax Act, 1961).
- Upon consideration, the Council decided that based on the conflict in roles as statutory and internal auditor simultaneously, the bar on internal auditor of an entity to accept tax audit (under Income-Tax Act, 1961) will also be applicable to GST Audit (under the CGST Act, 2017).
- In the instant case, WCP & Co. LLP are the internal auditors of DEF Ltd. and it also agreed to undertake Goods and Services Tax (GST) Audit of DEF Ltd simultaneously.

Conclusion: WCP & Co. LLP will be held guilty for misconduct as Internal Auditor of an entity cannot undertake GST Audit of the same entity.

CHAPTER 8
COMPANY AUDIT

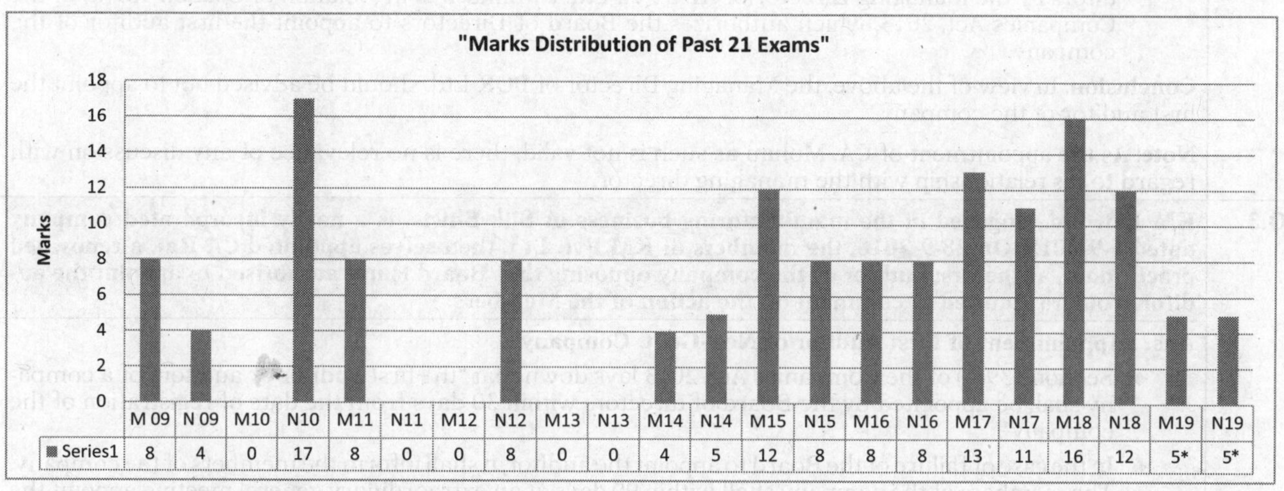

*Only Subjective Questions.

8.1 - APPOINTMENT OF AUDITORS

Q.1 **CA. X is a partner in M/s AB & Associates and M/s MN & Associates simultaneously. M/s AB & Associates has completed its tenure of 10 years as an auditor in XYZ Ltd. immediately preceding the current financial year. It may be noted that the provisions for applicability of rotation of auditors are applicable to XYZ Ltd. Now, the company wants to appoint M/s MN & Associates as auditor for 5 years.**

(*a*) Whether M/s MN & Associates is allowed to accept the appointment as auditor of XYZ Ltd.?

(*b*) Would your answer be different from above if CA. X, being in-charge of M/s AB & Associates and certifying authority of financial statements of XYZ Ltd., retires from the partnership in M/s AB & Associates and joins M/s MN & Associates?

Ans. : Appointment of Firm as auditor having common Partner:

- As per Second Proviso to sec. 139(2) of Companies Act, 2013, as on the date of appointment no audit firm having a common partner or partners to the other audit firm, whose tenure has expired in a company immediately preceding the financial year, shall be appointed as auditor of the same company for a period of five years.
- In the present case, CA X is common partner in the firm AB & Associates and MN & associates.

Conclusion: MN & Associates is disqualified for appointment as auditor of XYZ Ltd. for a period of 5 years.

Appointment of firm as auditor having one of partner was in-charge in previous audit firm:

- As per *Explanation* given in Rule 6 of Companies (Audit & auditors) rules, 2014 if a partner, who is in charge of an audit firm and also certifies the financial statements of the company, retires from the said firm and joins another firm of chartered accountants, such other firm shall also be ineligible to be appointed for a period of five years.
- In the present case, CA. X was incharge of M/s AB & Associates and certifying authority of financial statements of XYZ Ltd. Retires from the M/s AB 7 associates and joins MN & Associates.

Conclusion: MN & Associates is disqualified for appointment as auditor of XYZ Ltd. for a period of 5 years.

Q.2 **ABC Pvt. Ltd., a new company, incorporated on 1-7-2017 is engaged in the manufacturing business. On 30-7-2017, the Managing Director of ABC Pvt. Ltd. himself appointed CA Mohan, his daughter's husband, as the first auditor of the company. You are required to—**

(*i*) State the provisions of the Companies Act, 2013 relating to appointment of first auditor.

(*ii*) Comment on the action of the Managing Director.

Ans. : Appointment of First Auditor of Non-Govt. Company:

- Section 139(6) of the Companies Act, 2013 lays down that "the first auditor or auditors of a company shall be appointed by the Board of directors within 30 days from the date of registration of the company".
- In the instant case, the appointment of CA Mohan, a practicing Chartered Accountant as first auditors by the Managing Director of ABC Pvt. Ltd. by himself is in violation of Section 139(6) of the Companies Act, 2013, which authorizes the Board of Directors to appoint the first auditor of the company.

Conclusion: In view of the above, the Managing Director of PQR Ltd. should be advised not to appoint the first auditor of the company.

Note: As the appointment of CA. Mohan as such is not valid, there is no relevance of any discussion with regard to his relationship with the managing director.

Q.3 **KM Pvt. Ltd., engaged in the manufacturing business of Silk Shirts, is a newly incorporated company dated 1-9-2018. On 28-9-2018, the members of KM Pvt. Ltd. themselves appointed CA Raj, a renowned practitioner, as the first auditor of the company opposing that Board is not authorised to appoint the auditor. You are required to comment on the action of the Members.**

Ans. : Appointment of First Auditor of Non-Govt. Company:

- Section 139(6) of the Companies Act, 2013 lays down that "the first auditor or auditors of a company shall be appointed by the Board of directors within 30 days from the date of registration of the company".
- In the case of failure of the Board to appoint the auditor, it shall inform the members of the company. The members of the company shall within 90 days at an extraordinary general meeting appoint the auditor. Appointed auditor shall hold office till the conclusion of the first annual general meeting.
- In the instant case, the appointment of CA Raj, a practicing Chartered Accountant as first auditors by the members of the company, opposing that Board is not authorised to appoint the auditor, is not in order

Conclusion: Appointment of CA Raj as first auditor, within 30 days of registration by the members of the company is not in order.

Q.4 **The first auditor of M/s Healthy Wealthy Ltd., a Government company, was appointed by the Board of Directors.**

Ans. : Appointment of First Auditor of Govt. Company

- Section 139(7) of the Companies Act, 2013 lays down that in the case of a Government company or any other company owned or controlled, directly or indirectly, by the CG, or by any SG, or SGs, or partly by the CG and partly by one or more SGs, the first auditor shall be appointed by the CAG of India within 60 days of registration of the company.
- In case the CAG of India does not appoint such auditor within the said period, the BOD of the company shall appoint such auditor within the next 30 days.
- In the case of failure of the Board to appoint such auditor within the next 30 days, it shall inform the members of the company who shall appoint such auditor within the 60 days at an EGM.
- Hence in the case of M/s Healthy Wealthy Ltd., being a government company, the first auditors shall be appointed by the CAG of India.

Conclusion: The appointment of first auditors made by the Board of Directors of M/s Healthy Wealthy Ltd., is null and void.

Q.5 **Nick Ltd. is a subsidiary of Ajanta Ltd., whose 20% shares have been held by Central Government, 25% by Uttar Pradesh Government and 10% by Madhya Pradesh Government. Nick Ltd. appointed Mr. P as statutory auditor for the year.**

Ans. : Appointment of Auditor of Govt. Company:

- As per Sec. 2(45) of the Companies Act, 2013, a Government company is defined "as any company in which not less than 51% of the paid-up share capital is held by the Central Government or by any State Government or Governments or partly by the Central Government and partly by one or more State Governments and includes a company which is a subsidiary of a Government Company as thus defined".

- Sec. 139(7) requires that the auditors of a government company shall be appointed or reappointed by the Comptroller and Auditor General of India.
- In the given case Ajanta Ltd. is a government company as its 20% shares have been held by Central Govt., 25% by U.P. State Government and 10% by M.P. State Govt. Total 55% shares have been held by Central and State governments.
- Nick Ltd. will also be a government company, being subsidiary company of Ajanta Ltd. and hence the Auditor of Nick Ltd. can be appointed only by C & AG.

Conclusion: Appointment of 'P' is invalid and 'P' should not give acceptance to the Directors of Nick Ltd.

Q.6 **At the AGM of ICI Ltd., Mr. X was appointed as the statutory auditor. He, however, resigned after 3 months since he wanted to give up practice and join industry. State, how the new auditor will be appointed by ICI Ltd. and the conditions to be complied for.**

Ans. : Filling of Casual vacancy:

- As per Sec. 139(8) of the Companies Act, 2013, any casual vacancy in the office of an auditor may be filled by Board of Directors within thirty days.
- However, if casual vacancy has been created by the resignation of the auditor, such appointment shall also be approved by the company at a general meeting convened within three months of the recommendation of the board.
- The auditor so appointed shall hold office till the conclusion of the next annual general meeting.

Conclusion: In this case, the casual vacancy has been created on account of resignation. Therefore, Board of Directors will have to fill the vacancy within thirty days and such appointment shall be approved by the company at the general meeting within three months of the recommendations of the board. The new auditor so appointed shall hold office only till the conclusion of the next AGM.

Q.7 **Due to the resignation of the existing auditor(s), the Board of directors of X Ltd. appointed Mr. Hari as the auditor. Is the appointment of Hari as auditor valid?**

Ans. : Board's Powers to Appoint an Auditor:

- As per Sec. 139(8) of the Companies Act, 2013, any casual vacancy in the office of an auditor may be filled by Board of Directors within thirty days.
- However, if casual vacancy has been created by the resignation of the auditor, such appointment shall also be approved by the company at a general meeting convened within three months of the recommendation of the board.
- The auditor so appointed shall hold office till the conclusion of the next annual general meeting.

Conclusion: Appointment of Hari by Board of Directors will be Valid if it is made within 30 days of casual vacancy and such appointment is approved by the company at a general meeting within three months of the recommendations of the Board.

Q.8 **At an AGM of a listed company, Mr. R a retiring auditor after completing the tenure of 5 consecutive years of his service claims that he has been reappointed automatically, as the intended resolution of which a notice had been given to appoint Mr. P, could not be proceeded with, due to Mr. P's death.**

Ans. : Restrictions over tenure of Auditor (Rotation of Auditor)

- As per Sec. 139(2) of the Companies Act, 2013, listed companies and other prescribed class of companies shall not appoint or reappoint an individual as auditor for more than one term of five consecutive years.
- Sec. 139(10) of Companies Act, 2013 provides that if no auditor is appointed or reappointed at AGM, existing auditor will continue.
- In the given case, notice has been given of an intended resolution to appoint some person or persons in the place of a retiring auditor, and by reason of the death, incapacity or disqualification of that person or of all those persons, as the case may be, the resolution cannot be proceeded with.
- In the instant case, if Sec. 139(10) of the Companies Act, 2013 is invoked, it results into violation of Sec. 139(2). Hence, Mr. R cannot continue as auditor due to restrictions of Sec. 139(2).

Conclusion: Mr. R cannot continue as auditor of the company due to rotation provisions. Companies Act, 2013 does not provide any provision for such kind of situation, hence it can be concluded that vacancy arises in the office of auditor which need to be filled by company in EGM.

Q.9 **No AGM was held for the year ended 31st March, 2018, in XYZ Ltd., Mr. X is the auditor for the previous 3 years, whether he should continue to hold office for current year or not.**

Ans. : Auditor's position if no AGM is held:

- Sec. 139(1) of the Companies Act, 2013 provides that every company shall, at the first AGM appoint an individual or a firm as an auditor who shall hold office from the conclusion of that meeting till the conclusion of its 6th AGM and thereafter till the conclusion of every 6th meeting.

- In case the AGM is not held within the period prescribed, the auditor will continue in office till the AGM is actually held and concluded.

Conclusion: Mr. X shall continue to hold office till the conclusion of the AGM.

Q.10 **M/s Young & Co., a Chartered Accountant firm, and Statutory Auditors of Old Ltd., is dissolved on 1.4.2018 due to differences of opinion among the partners. The Board of Directors of Old Ltd. in its meeting on 6-4-2018 appointed another firm M/s Sharp & Co. as their new auditors for one year.**

Ans. : Filling of Casual Vacancy:

- As per Sec. 139(8) of the Companies Act, 2013, any casual vacancy in the office of an auditor may be filled by Board of Directors within thirty days.
- However, if casual vacancy has been created by the resignation of the auditor, such appointment shall also be approved by the company at a general meeting convened within three months of the recommendation of the board.
- The auditor so appointed shall hold office till the conclusion of the next annual general meeting.

Conclusion: In the instant case the action of the board of directors in appointing M/s Sharp & Co. to fill up the casual vacancy due to dissolution of M/s Young & Co., is correct.

However, the board of directors are not correct in giving them appointment for one year. M/s Sharp & Co. can hold office until the conclusion of next AGM only.

Q.11 **X Ltd. is an unlisted public company. Its balance sheet shows paid up share capital of ₹ 7.5 crore and public deposits of ₹ 70 crores. The company appointed M/s ABC & Co., a CA firm, as the statutory auditor in its AGM held at the end of September 2018 for 11 years. Comment.**

Ans. : Rotation of Auditor & Cooling Off Period Provisions:

- As per Section 139(2) of the Companies Act, 2013, no listed company or a company belonging to such class or classes of companies as prescribed, shall appoint or re-appoint-
- an individual as auditor for more than one term of five consecutive years; and
- an audit firm as auditor for more than two terms of five consecutive years.
- Rule 5 of Companies (Audit and Auditors) Rules, 2014, prescribes the following classes of companies (Excluding OPC and small companies) for the purpose of rotation:
  - *a.* all unlisted public companies having paid up share capital of ₹ 10 crore or more;
  - *b.* all private limited companies having paid up share capital of ₹ 50 crore or more;
  - *c.* all companies having paid up share capital of below threshold limit mentioned above, but having public borrowings from financial institutions, banks or public deposits of ₹ 50 crores or more.
- In the given case, X Ltd. is an unlisted public company having paid up share capital of ₹ 7.50 crore and public deposits of ₹ 70 Crore, the provisions relating to rotation of auditor will be applicable.

Conclusion: X Ltd. cannot appoint the auditor for more than two terms of five consecutive years each, *i.e.* M/s ABC & Co. shall hold office from the conclusion of this meeting upto conclusion of 6th AGM to be held in the year 2023 and thereafter can be re-appointed as auditor for one more term of five years *i.e.* upto year 2028. The appointment shall be subject to ratification by members at every AGM of the company. As a result, the appointment of M/s ABC & Co. made by X Ltd. for 11 years is void.

Q.12 **While auditing, CA Mr. X, the statutory auditor of Y Ltd. encounters exceptional circumstances that bring into question his ability to continue performing the audit. Considering it appropriate, CA Mr. X resigned from the office of auditor of Y Ltd. Due to the resignation of the existing auditor, the Board of Directors of Y Ltd. itself appointed CA Mr. Y, a practicing Chartered Accountant, as the statutory auditor till the conclusion of 6th meeting.**

You are required to state the provisions related to filling of casual vacancy as per the Companies Act, 2013 and comment upon the validity of appointment made by the Board.

Ans. : Filling of Casual Vacancy:

- As per Section 139(8) of the Companies Act, 2013, any casual vacancy in the office of an auditor shall–
  - (*i*) In the case of a non-government company, be filled by the Board of Directors within 30 days. But, if such casual vacancy is as a result of the resignation of an auditor, such appointment shall also be approved by the company at a general meeting convened within 3 months of the recommendation of the Board and the auditor so appointed shall hold the office till the conclusion of the next AGM.

(*ii*) In the case of a government company, the casual vacancy be filled by the CAG of India within 30 days. But if the CAG does not fill the vacancy within the said period the Board of Directors shall fill the vacancy within next 30 days.

- In the given case, CA Mr. X, the statutory auditor of Y Ltd. has resigned from the office of auditor. Therefore, such casual vacancy can be filled by the Board of Directors subject to approval by the company at a general meeting convened within 3 months of the recommendation of the Board.

Conclusion: The appointment of CA Mr. Y made by the Board of Directors without the approval of the company at a general meeting is invalid and further, if appointment is approved by the company, CA Mr. Y can hold office only till the conclusion of the next AGM.

Q.13 C.A. Ashwin was appointed as auditor of Bristol Ltd. for the year 2018-19. Since he declined to accept the appointment, the Board of Directors appointed CA John as the Auditor in place of C.A. Ashwin and the appointment was accepted by C.A. John. Discuss. [May 15 (4 Marks)]

Ans. : BOD Powers to fill the Vacancy:

- Board of Directors of the company has been empowered to appoint the auditor other than first auditor in the following cases:

  Sec. 139(2) - Appointment of auditor is not ratified by the members of the company in AGM.

  Sec. 139(8) - Any casual vacancy arises in the office of auditor.
- The present case does not fall under any of the circumstances; hence BOD does not have power to fill up the vacancy.
- Under the circumstances, it may be deemed that no auditor appointed at AGM and provisions of Sec. 139(10) may be invoked which provides that where at any AGM, no auditor is appointed or re-appointed, the existing auditor shall continue to be the auditor of the company.
- Further, Clause (9) of Part I of the First Schedule to the Chartered Accountants Act, 1949 provides that a member in practice shall be deemed to be guilty of professional misconduct if he accepts an appointment as auditor of a company without first ascertaining from it whether the requirements of Sections 139 and 140 of the Companies Act, 2013, in respect of such appointment have been duly complied with.
- In the present case, appointment of Mr. John by Board of Directors is not in line with the provisions of Sec. 139 of Companies Act, 2013.
- Vacancy so remains due to non-acceptance by Mr. Ashwin can only be filled by the Company in General Meeting.

Conclusion: Board of Directors are not authorised to fill up the vacancy in case the auditors appointed at the AGM refuse to accept the appointment.

Mr. John will be guilty of professional misconduct by virtue of clause (9) of Part 1 of First Schedule of Chartered Accountants Act, 1949.

"ICAI Examiner Comments"

Candidates have not touched upon Clause (9) of Part I of the First Schedule to the Chartered Accountants Act, 1949 regarding professional misconduct for accepting the audit without complying with the provisions of Companies Act, 2013.

Q.14 M/s IO Ltd. is registered with Registrar of Companies on 1st of May 2018. The company's 27% of paid up share capital is held by Central Government; 28% by State Government and the remaining 45% by public. The Board of Directors appointed RMG, Chartered Accountants as statutory auditors for the financial year 2018-19 by passing a resolution at the Board Meeting held on 25th May, 2018. Comment whether appointment is valid or not. [May 16 (4 Marks)]

Ans. : Appointment of First Auditor of Government Company:

- As per Sec. 2(45) of the Companies Act, 2013, a Government company is defined "as any company in which not less than 51% of the paid-up share capital is held by the Central Government or by any State Government or Governments or partly by the Central Government and partly by one or more State Governments and includes a company which is a subsidiary of a Government Company as thus defined".
- As per Sec. 139(7) of Companies Act, 2013, in the case of a Government company or any other company owned or controlled, directly or indirectly, by the CG, or by any SG, or SGs, or partly by the CG and partly by one or more SGs, the first auditor shall be appointed by the CAG of India, within 60 days of registration of company.

- In case the CAG of India does not appoint such auditor within the said period, the BOD of the company shall appoint such auditor within next 30 days; In the case of failure of the Board to appoint such auditor within the next 30 days, it shall inform the members of the company who shall appoint such auditor within 60 days at an EGM.
- In the present case, 55% of share capital is held by Central Government and State Government, hence it is a case of Government Company and the first auditor need to be appointed by CAG within 60 days of registration of company.

Conclusion: Appointment of First Auditor within 60 days of registration of government company by Board of Directors is not valid.

Q.15 M/s. ABC & Co. is an audit firm having partners Mr. A, Mr. B and Mr. C, whose tenure as statutory auditor in R Ltd. a listed entity, has expired as per the Companies Act, 2013. M/s XY is another audit firm which is appointed as the statutory auditor of R Ltd. for the subsequent year. Mr. A joins M/s. XY as partner, 3 months after it was appointed as the statutory auditor of R Ltd. Comment. [May 17 (5 Marks)]

Ans. : Applicability of Rotation provisions:

- Sec. 139(2) of Companies Act, 2013 provides that no listed company or **other prescribed companies**, shall appoint or re-appoint an audit firm as auditor for more than two terms of five consecutive years
- An audit firm which has completed its term, shall not be eligible for re-appointment as auditor in the same company for five years from the completion of such term:
- It is also provided that as on the date of appointment no audit firm having a common partner or partners to the other audit firm, whose tenure has expired in a company immediately preceding the financial year, shall be appointed as auditor of the same company for a period of five years.
- In the present case, on completion of tenure of M/s ABC & Co, retiring auditor, company has appointed M/s XY as their auditor. After three months of appointment of XY Ltd. as auditor, Mr. A, joins M/X XY as partner. As per provisions of Sec. 139(2), incoming auditor shall not be eligible for appointment in case of common partner as on date of appointment. But in this case, there were no common partner as on date of appointment. Mr. A joins after 3 months of appointment.

Conclusion: Applying the provisions of Sec. 139(2), no issue arises as there were no common partners as on date of appointment.

Note: Interpretation of this provision appears to be against the intention of law, which intends for the cooling off period of retiring auditor for a period of 5 years in case of listed and other prescribed companies.

8.2 - REMOVAL OF AUDITOR

Q.16 Comment: "M/s. PQR, audit firm has been re-appointed as sole statutory auditor of a listed company in the AGM, where till last year M/s. LMN, audit firm was also one of the joint auditors along with M/s. PQR. One tenure of consecutive five years of both the firms get completed in the mentioned AGM. Mention the steps that should be taken by M/s. PQR before commencing the audit".

Ans. : Appointment of Sole Auditor:

When one of the joint auditors of the previous years is considered for ratification by the members as the sole auditor for the next year, it is similar to non-re-appointment of one of the retiring joint auditors. As per Sec. 140(4) of the Companies Act, 2013, special notice shall be required for a resolution at an AGM appointing as auditor a person other than a retiring auditor, or providing expressly that a retiring auditor shall not be re-appointed, except where the retiring auditor has completed a consecutive tenure of five years or, as the case may be, ten years, as provided u/s 139(2).

Accordingly, provisions of the Companies Act, 2013 to be complied with are as under:

1. **Special Notice**: Ascertain that special notice u/s 140(4) of the Companies Act, 2013 was received by the company from requisite number of members (1% of total voting power or paid up capital not less than ₹ 5 Lacs) at least 14 days before the AGM date.
2. **Sending copy of notice**: Check whether the said notice has been sent to all the members at least 7 days before the date of the AGM.
3. **Contents of Notice**: Verify that the notice contains an express intention of a member for proposing the resolution for appointing a sole auditor in place of both the joint auditors who retire at the meeting but are eligible for re-appointment.

4. **Notice to Auditor**: Ensure that the notice has also been sent to the retiring auditor.
5. **Sending the Representation**: Verify whether any representation, received from the retiring auditor was sent to the members of the company.
6. **Consideration of representation**: Verify from the minutes book whether the representation received from the retiring joint auditor was considered at the AGM.

In addition to requirements of Companies Act, 2013, auditor is required to ensure compliance of Clauses 8 and 9 of Part I of First Schedule to Chartered Accountants Act, 1949.

Q.17 PQR Company Ltd. removed their first auditor by passing a resolution in the meeting of the Board of Directors for his removal without obtaining prior approval from the Central Government. Offer your comments in this regard.

Ans. : Removal of first Auditor:

- As per Sec. 140(1) of the Companies Act, 2013, an auditor appointed u/s 139 may be removed from his office before the expiry of his term only by a special resolution of the company, after obtaining the prior approval of the Central Government.
- For this purpose, an application to the Central Government for removal of auditor shall be made in Form ADT-2 and shall be accompanied with prescribed fees.
- The application shall be made to the Central Government within thirty days of the resolution passed by the Board.
- The company shall hold the general meeting within sixty days of receipt of approval of the Central Government for passing the special resolution.
- In the instant case the first auditor appointed by the Board of Directors was removed by a resolution in the meeting of the Board of Directors inspite of the Special resolution of the Company and without the prior approval of the Central Government in that behalf.

Conclusion: Removal of Auditor is Invalid as Special Resolution has not been passed and approval of Central Govt. not obtained.

Q.18 What are the professional obligations of the auditor who has resigned from the audit before completion of his term due to non-co-operation of the Management in completing certain audit procedures?

[Nov. 14 (5 Marks)]

Ans. : Professional Obligations in case of resignation by auditor:

- Section 140(2) of Companies Act, 2013 requires that the auditor who has resigned from the company shall file within a period of 30 days from the date of resignation, a statement in the prescribed form (ADT-3) with the company and the Registrar.
- In case of Government companies, such statement is also required to be filed with the Comptroller and Auditor-General of India.
- Statement must indicate the reasons and other facts as may be relevant with regard to his resignation.
- Section 140(3) of Companies Act, 2013 provides that if the auditor does not comply with Sec. 140(2), he shall be punishable with fine of ₹ 50,000 or the remuneration of the auditor, whichever is less but it may extend to ₹ 5,00,000.

Q.19 Elucidate the power of tribunal to change the auditor of a company if found acted in a fraudulent manner as provided under sub-section (5) of section 140 of the Companies Act, 2013.

Or

Write short note on: Direction by Tribunal in case auditor acted in a fraudulent manner.

[May 18 - Old Syllabus (4 Marks)]

Or

The Auditor of M/s Quick Limited succumbed to the pressure of the Management in Certifying the financials with an over stated figure of turnover by not adhering to the cut-off principles of the time scale for the transaction of the year. On taking cognizance of this act of the Auditor, the Tribunal under the Companies Act, 2013 initiated the proceedings against him. Briefly list the powers of the Tribunal in this respect including those relating to making orders against the auditor found to be guilty.

[May 18 - New Syllabus (4 Marks)]

Or

Anvisha Ltd. is a company engaged in the business of software development. It is one of the largest companies in this sector with a turnover of ₹ 25,000 crores. The operations of the company are increasing constantly, however, the focus of the management is more on cost cutting in the coming years to improve its profitability. In respect of the financial statements of the company which are used by various stakeholders, some fraud was observed in respect of assets reported therein due to which those stakeholders suffered damages. As a result, those stakeholders applied to Tribunal for change of auditor on the basis that auditor is colluded in the fraud.

Elucidate the power of tribunal to change the auditor of a company if found acted in a fraudulent manner as provided under sub-section (5) of section 140 of the Companies Act, 2013.

[MTP-Oct. 19, RTP-Nov. 19]

Or

On the advice of Management of M/s Quick Ltd., the auditor of the Company overlooked and did not report on shifting of certain current year's sales transactions to the next year. The National Company Law Tribunal (NCLT) wants to take action against you. Describe the powers of the NCLT under Section 140(5) of the Companies Act, 2013 for such action and consequences to the auditor.

[Nov. 19 - Old Syllabus (5 Marks)]

Ans. : Power of Tribunal in case Auditor acted in a Fraudulent Manner:

- Sec. 140(5) of the Companies Act, 2013, provides that the Tribunal either *suo motu* or on an application made to it by the Central Government or by any person concerned, if it is satisfied that the auditor of a company has, whether directly or indirectly, acted in a fraudulent manner or abetted or colluded in any fraud by, or in relation to, the company or its directors or officers, it may, by order, direct the company to change its auditors.
- However, if the application is made by the Central Government and the Tribunal is satisfied that any change of the auditor is required, it shall within 15 days of receipt of such application, make an order that he shall not function as an auditor and the Central Government may appoint another auditor in his place.
- It may be noted that an auditor, whether individual or firm, against whom final order has been passed by the Tribunal under this section shall not be eligible to be appointed as an auditor of any company for a period of five years from the date of passing of the order and the auditor shall also be liable for action under section 447 of the said Act.
- It is hereby clarified that the case of a firm, the liability shall be of the firm and that of every partner or partners who acted in a fraudulent manner or abetted or colluded in any fraud by, or in relation to, the company or its director or officers.

8.3 - QUALIFICATIONS AND DISQUALIFICATIONS OF AUDITOR (SEC. 141)

Q.20 **"Mr. A", a practicing Chartered Accountant, is holding securities of "XYZ Ltd." having face value of ₹ 900. Whether Mr. A is qualified for appointment as an Auditor of "XYZ Ltd."?**

Would your answer be different, if instead of Mr. A, Mr. B the step father of Mr. A is holding the securities.

Ans. : Disqualification as to Security:

As per section 141(3)(*d*)(*i*) an auditor is disqualified to be appointed as an auditor if he, or his relative or partner holding any security of or interest in the company or its subsidiary, or of its holding or associate company or a subsidiary of such holding company.

However, the relative of the auditor may hold the securities or interest in the company of face value not exceeding ₹ 1,00,000.

Conclusion: In the present case, Mr. A. is holding security of ₹ 900 in the XYZ Ltd., therefore he is not eligible for appointment as an Auditor of "XYZ Ltd".

However, in second case, Mr. A is eligible, as relative may hold securities of face value upto ₹ 1 Lac.

Q.21 **"Mr. P" is a practicing Chartered Accountant and "Mr. Q", the relative of "Mr. P", is holding securities of "ABC Ltd." having face value of ₹ 90,000. Whether "Mr. P" is Qualified from being appointed as an Auditor of "ABC Ltd."?**

Or

Mr. P, a practicing Chartered Accountant, has been offered for appointment as an auditor of ABC Ltd., a leading company. Later on, Mr. Q, the step-brother of Mr. P, purchased securities of the company having face value of ₹ 90,000. Comment, whether Mr. P may accept the offer of appointment as an auditor?

Ans. : Disqualifications as to Securities:

- As per section 141(3)(d)(i) an auditor is disqualified to be appointed as an auditor if he, or his relative or partner holding any security of or interest in the company or its subsidiary, or of its holding or associate company or a subsidiary of such holding company.
- However, the relative of the auditor may hold the securities or interest in the company of face value not exceeding ₹ 1,00,000.

Conclusion: In the present case, Mr. Q (relative of Mr. P, an auditor), is having securities of ₹ 90,000 face Value in the ABC Pvt. Ltd., which is as per requirement of proviso to section 141(3)(d)(i), Therefore, Mr. P will not be disqualified to be appointed as an auditor of ABC Ltd.

Q.22 **"BC & Co." is an Audit Firm having partners "Mr. B" and "Mr. C", and "Mr. A" the relative of "Mr. C", is holding securities of "MWF Ltd." having face value of ₹ 1,01,000. Whether "BC & Co." is qualified from being appointed as an Auditor of "MWF Ltd."?**

Ans. : Disqualifications as to security:

- As per section 141(3)(d)(i) an auditor is disqualified to be appointed as an auditor if he, or his relative or partner holding any security of or interest in the company or its subsidiary, or of its holding or associate company or a subsidiary of such holding company.
- However, the relative of the auditor may hold the securities or interest in the company of face value not exceeding of ₹ 1,00,000.

Conclusion: In the instant case BC & Co., will be disqualified for appointment as an auditor of MWF Ltd. as the relative of Mr. C *i.e.* partner of BC & Co., is holding the securities in MWF Ltd. which is exceeding the limit mentioned in proviso to section 141(3)(d)(i).

Q.23 **A, a chartered accountant has been appointed as auditor of Laxman Ltd. in the AGM of the company held in Sep. 2018, which assignment he accepted. Subsequently in January, 2019 he joined B, another chartered accountant, who is the Manager Finance of Laxman Ltd., as partner.**

Ans. : Disqualification as to partner of employee:

- Section 141(3)(c) of the Companies Act, 2013 prescribes that any person who is a partner or in employment of an officer or employee of the company will be disqualified to act as an auditor of a company.
- Sec. 141(4) provides that an auditor who becomes subject, after his appointment, to any of the disqualifications specified in Sec. 141(3), he shall be deemed to have vacated his office as an auditor.

Conclusion: In the present case, A, an auditor of M/s Laxman Ltd., joined as partner with B, who is Manager Finance of M/s Laxman Limited, will be disqualified by Sec. 141(3)(c) and, therefore, he shall be deemed to have vacated office of the auditor of M/s Laxman Limited.

Q.24 **An auditor purchased goods worth ₹ 501,500 on credit from a company being audited by him. The company allowed him one month's credit, which it normally allowed to all known customers.**

Ans. : Disqualification as to indebtedness:

- Section 141(3)(d) of the Companies Act, 2013 specifies that a person shall be disqualified to act as an auditor if he is indebted to the company for an amount exceeding ₹ 5 Lacs.
- Where an auditor purchases goods or services from a company audited by him on credit, he is definitely indebted to the company and if the amount outstanding exceeds ₹ 5 Lacs, he is disqualified for appointment as an auditor of the company.
- It will not make any difference if the company allows him the same period of credit as it allows to other customers on the normal terms and conditions of the business.

Conclusion: In instant case, auditor has become indebted to the company and consequently he has deemed to have vacated his office.

Q.25 **Ram and Hanuman Associates, Chartered Accountants in practice have been appointed as Statutory Auditor of Krishna Ltd. for the accounting year 2018-2019. Mr. Hanuman holds 100 equity shares of Shiva Ltd., a subsidiary company of Krishna Ltd.**

Ans. : Auditor holding securities of a company:

- As per Sec. 141(3)(d) of the Companies Act, 2013, a person shall not be eligible for appointment as an auditor of a company, who, or his relative or partner is holding any security of or interest in the company or its subsidiary, or of its holding or associate company or a subsidiary of such holding company.
- In the present case, Mr. Hanuman, Chartered Accountant, a partner of M/s Ram and Hanuman Associates, holds 100 equity shares of Shiva Ltd. which is a subsidiary of Krishna Ltd.

Conclusion: The firm, M/s Ram and Hanuman Associates would be disqualified to be appointed as statutory auditor of Krishna Ltd., which is the holding company of Shiva Ltd., because one of the partner Mr. Hanuman is holding equity shares of its subsidiary.

Q.26 Mr. Amar, a Chartered Accountant, bought a car financed at ₹ 7,00,000 by Chaudhary Finance Ltd., which is a holding company of Charan Ltd. and Das Ltd. He has been the statutory auditor of Das Ltd. and continues to be even after taking the loan.

Ans. : Disqualification as to indebtedness:

- As per Sec. 141(3)(d)(ii) of the Companies Act, 2013, a person is not eligible for appointment as auditor of any company, If he is indebted to the company, or its subsidiary, or its holding or associate company or a subsidiary of such holding company, in excess of rupees ₹ 5 Lacs.
- In the given case Mr. Amar is disqualified to act as an auditor u/s 141(3)(*d*)(*ii*)) as he is indebted to M/s Chaudhary Finance Ltd. for more than ₹ 5 Lacs.
- Further he cannot act as an auditor of any subsidiary of Chaudhary Finance Ltd. *i.e.* he is also disqualified to work in Charan Ltd. & Das Ltd.
- Further Sec. 141(4) provides that a person appointed as auditor incurs any of the disqualification mentioned u/s 141(3) after his appointment, he shall vacate the office immediately and it will be treated a casual vacancy.

Conclusion: Mr. Amar should vacate his office immediately and Das Ltd. must have to appoint any other CA as an auditor of the company.

Q.27 Praveen, a member of the ICAI, does not hold a Certificate of practice. Is his appointment as an auditor valid?

Ans. : Qualifications of an Auditor:

- As per Sec. 141(1) a person shall be qualified for appointment as an auditor of a company, only if he is a Chartered Accountant within the meaning of the Chartered Accountants Act, 1949.
- Under the Chartered Accountants Act, 1949, only a Chartered Accountant holding the certificate of practice can engage in public practice.

Conclusion: Mr. Praveen does not hold a certificate of practice and hence cannot be appointed as an auditor of a company.

Q.28 'B' owes ₹ 5,01,000 to 'C' Ltd., of which he is an auditor. Is his appointment valid? Will it make any difference, if the advance is taken for meeting-out travelling expenses?

Ans. : Indebtedness to the Company:

- As per Section 141(3)(d)(ii) of the Companies Act, 2013, a person who, or his relative or partner is indebted to the company, or its subsidiary, or its holding or associate company, or a subsidiary of its holding company, for an amount exceeding ₹ 5 Lacs, then he is not qualified for appointment as an auditor of a company.
- Even if the advance was taken for meeting out travelling expenses particularly before commencement of audit work, his appointment is not valid because in such a case also the auditor shall be indebted to the company. The auditor is entitled to recover fees on a progressive basis only.

Conclusion: B's appointment is not valid and he is disqualified as the amount of debt exceeds ₹ 5,00,000.

Q.29 Mr. Aditya, a practising chartered accountant is appointed as a "Tax Consultant" of ABC Ltd., in which his father Mr. Singhvi is the Managing Director.

Ans. : Appointment of relative as tax consultant:

- Sec. 141(3)(f) of Companies Act, 2013 disqualifies a person to be appointed as auditor whose relative is a director or is in employment of the company as director or key managerial personnel.
- However, no such disqualification is prescribed under the law for appointing a person as a tax consultant. therefore sec. 141(3)(f) will not be attracted.

Conclusion: Mr. Aditya can be appointed as tax consultant irrespective that his father is the managing director of the company.

Q.30 **Mr. Ram, a relative of a Director was appointed as an auditor of the company. Comment.**

[Nov. 10 (6 Marks)]

Ans. : Appointment of director's relative as auditor:

- Section 141(3)(f) explicitly disqualifies a person from being appointed as an auditor of a company whose relative is a director or is in the employment of the company as director or key managerial personnel.
- The term relative has been defined u/s 2(77) of and explained under Rule 4 of the Companies (Specification of Definitions Details) Rules, 2014. As per Sec. 2(77) the term relative with reference to any person, means who anyone who is related to another, if they are members of HUF; they are husband and wife; or related to the other in prescribed manner. Rule 4 provides that a person shall be deemed to be relative of another, if he or she is related to another as father, mother, son, son's wife, daughter, daughter's husband, brother or sister.

Conclusion: Assuming that Mr. Ram falls within the above-mentioned relations, he should not accept the appointment as an auditor of that company.

Q.31 **Comment on the following: Sri & Company, a firm of Chartered Accountants was appointed as statutory auditors of Aaradhana Company Ltd. Aaradhana Company Ltd. holds 51% shares in Sarang Company Ltd. Mr. Sri, one of the partners of Sri & Company, owed ₹ 1,500 as on the date of appointment to Sarang Company Ltd. for goods purchased in normal course of business.**

Ans. : Disqualification as to indebtedness:

- As per Section 141(3)(d)(ii) of the Companies Act, 2013, a person who, or his relative or partner is indebted to the company, or its subsidiary, or its holding or associate company, or a subsidiary of its holding company, for an amount exceeding ₹ 5,00,000 then he is not qualified for appointment as an auditor of a company.

Conclusion: Mr Sri is not disqualified to be appointed as auditor of the company as he is indebted to the company for an amount not exceeding ₹ 5,00,000, consequently, Sri & Co., is not disqualified to be appointed as an auditor of Aaradhana Company Ltd.

Q.32 **Dabloo Ltd. offered appointment as its auditor to Mr. Bee, a practicing Chartered Accountant. Later on, Mr. Dee, the step-brother of Mr. Bee, purchased securities of the company having face value of ₹ 4,99,000. Comment, whether Mr. Bee may accept the offer of appointment as an auditor?**

Ans. : Disqualification as to holding of security by relatives:

- **As per** section 141(3)(d)(i) of the Companies Act, 2013 read with Rule 10 of the Companies (Audit and Auditors) Rules, 2014, a person is disqualified to be appointed as an auditor if he, or his relative or partner holding any security of or interest in the company or its subsidiary, or of its holding or associate company or a subsidiary of such holding company.
- However, the relative of the auditor may hold the securities or interest in the company of face value not exceeding of ₹ 1,00,000. The term "relative" as defined under the Companies Act, 2013 includes step-brother.
- In the present situation, Mr. Dee, the step-brother of Mr. Bee, is holding the securities having face value of ₹ 4,99,000 in Dabloo Ltd. Thus, holding of securities in Dabloo Ltd. by Mr. Dee having face value exceeding ₹ 1,00,000, will disqualify Mr. Bee from being appointed as an auditor of Dabloo Ltd.

Conclusion: Mr. Bee may not accept the offer of appointment as an auditor of Dabloo Ltd.

Q.33 **M/s Duster & Co., Chartered Accountants, appointed as a statutory auditor of R Ltd. for the financial year 2018-19. The company is also in need of some actuarial services. Consequently, the Board of Directors of the company offered the same to M/s Srivastava & Co., an associate to M/s Duster & Co., which has been duly accepted by the firm. Comment.**

Ans. : Services not to be rendered By Auditor:

- Section 141(3)(i) of the Companies Act, 2013 disqualify a person who directly or indirectly renders any service referred to in sec. 144 to the company or its holding company or its subsidiary company.
- Section 141(4) of the Act provides that where a person appointed as an auditor of a company incurs any of the disqualifications mentioned in sec. 141(3) after his appointment, he shall vacate his office as such auditor and such vacation shall be deemed to be a casual vacancy in the office of the auditor.

- As per Section 144 of Companies Act, 2013 an auditor appointed under this Act shall not provide certain service, directly or indirectly to the company or its holding company or subsidiary company. List of such services include actuarial services.
- In the given case, M/s Duster & Co., Chartered Accountants, was appointed as an auditor of R Ltd. and, the company offered actuarial services to M/s Srivastava & Co., an associate to M/s Duster & Co., which has also been duly accepted by the firm.

Conclusion: M/s Duster & Co. is disqualified to hold office as an auditor of R Ltd. u/s 141(3)(i), as its associate is involved in providing such services, to R Ltd., as mentioned in Sec. 144. Subsequently, M/s Duster & Co. shall have to vacate the office of auditor of R Ltd.

Q.34 X & Associates, a Chartered Accountant firm, has been appointed as Statutory Auditor of H Ltd. for the financial year 2018-2019. Mr. Y, the relative of Mr. X, a partner in X & Associates, is indebted for ₹ 5,50,000 to S Ltd., a subsidiary company of H Ltd. Comment.

Ans. : Disqualification as to indebtedness to the Subsidiary Company:

- Section 141(3)(d)(ii) of the Companies Act, 2013 provides that a person shall not be eligible for appointment as an auditor of a company, if he, or his relative or partner is indebted to the company, or its subsidiary, or its holding or associate company or a subsidiary of such holding company, in excess of ₹ 5 lakhs.
- Section 141(4) of the Companies Act, 2013 provides that where a person appointed as an auditor of a company incurs any of the disqualifications mentioned in Section 141(3) after his appointment, he shall vacate his office as such auditor and such vacation shall be deemed to be a casual vacancy in the office of the auditor.
- In the present case, Mr. Y, the relative of Mr. X, a partner in X and Associates, has been indebted to S Ltd., a subsidiary company of H Ltd., for ₹ 5,50,000.

Conclusion: X & Associates would be disqualified to be appointed as statutory auditor of H Ltd. as per section 141(3)(d)(ii), which is the holding company of S Ltd., because Mr. Y, the relative of Mr. X, a partner in X and Associates, has been indebted to S Ltd. for an amount exceeding ₹ 5 Lacs.

Q.35 R and M is an audit firm having partners CA R, CA M and CA G. Mr. S is the relative of CA R holding shares of STP Ltd. having a face value of ₹ 1,51,000 Whether CA R and CA M are qualified to be appointed as auditors of STP Ltd.? [May 15 (4 Marks)]

Ans. : Disqualifications as to security:

- As per section 141(3)(d)(i) a person is disqualified to be appointed as an auditor if he, or his relative or partner holding any security of or interest in the company or its subsidiary, or of its holding or associate company or a subsidiary of such holding company.
- However, the relative of the auditor may hold the securities or interest in the company of face value not exceeding of ₹ 1,00,000.
- In the instant case Mr. S relative of CA R, is holding the securities in STP Ltd. which is exceeding the limit mentioned in proviso to section 141(3)(d)(i). Therefore Audit firm is disqualified for appointment as an auditor of STP Ltd.

Conclusion: CA R and CA M are not qualified to be appointed as auditor of STP Ltd.

Q.36 CA Mr. X was indebted to ABC Ltd. for a sum of ₹ 5,50,000 as on 1-4-2018. However, Mr. X having come to know that he might be appointed as auditor of the company, he squared up the amount on 10-7-2018. Later on, he was appointed as an auditor of the company at the Annual General Meeting held on 16-7-2018. Subsequently, one of the shareholders complains that the appointment of Mr. X as an auditor is invalid because he incurred disqualification under section 141 of the Companies Act, 2013. Comment.

[Nov. 16 (4 Marks)]

Ans. : Auditor's Disqualifications as to Indebtedness:

- Section 141(3)(d)(ii) of the Companies Act, 2013 provides that a person who is indebted to the company for an amount exceeding ₹ 5,00,000 shall be disqualified to act as an auditor of such company.
- However, where the person proposed to be appointed as auditor, liquidated the debt before the date of appointment, no disqualification arises as to appointment.
- In the given case, CA Mr. X was indebted to ABC Ltd. for a sum of ₹ 5,50,000 as on 1-4-2018. He repaid the loan amount fully to the company on 10-7-2018. He was appointed as an auditor of the company at the Annual General Meeting held on 16-7-2018. At the time of appointment, he was not indebted to the company hence, not disqualified.

Conclusion: The appointment of CA Mr. X as an auditor is valid and the shareholder's complaint is not acceptable.

Q.37 Comment on the validity of the appointments of Mr. A as an auditor of ABC Ltd. in the following situations:

(i) **Mr. B, a partner of Mr. A held shares of face value of Rs. 1,00,000 in DEF Ltd., the holding company of ABC Ltd. Mr. B has sold the securities after a period of 45 days from the date of appointment of Mr. A as an auditor of ABC Ltd.**

(ii) **Mrs. A, wife of Mr. A had given a financial guarantee for the principal amount of a debt owed by Mr. X to ABC Ltd. for Rs. 6 lakhs. Mr. X has repaid Rs. 5 lakhs to ABC Ltd. 2 days before the date of appointment of Mr. A as an auditor of the company. [Nov. 18-Old Syllabus (6 Marks)]**

Ans. : Validity of Appointments:

(i) **Auditor's disqualifications as to security:**

- As per section 141(3)(*d*)(*i*) a person is disqualified to be appointed as an auditor if he, or his relative or partner holding any security of or interest in the company or its subsidiary, or of its holding or associate company or a subsidiary of such holding company.
- However, the relative of the auditor may hold the securities or interest in the company of face value not exceeding of Rs. 1,00,000. It is also provided that in the event of acquiring and security or interest by a relative above the threshold limit, the corrective action to maintain the limits as specified above shall be taken by the auditor within 60 days of such acquisition or interest.
- In the present case, Mr. B, a partner of Mr. A held shares of face value of Rs. 1,00,000 in DEF Ltd., the holding company of ABC Ltd. Mr. B has sold the securities after a period of 45 days from the date of appointment of Mr. A as an auditor of ABC Ltd.

  Conclusion: Appointment of Mr. A as auditor in ABC Ltd. is not valid as he is disqualified by virtue of provisions as stated in Sec. 141(3)(*d*)(*i*). Subsequent sale of securities by the partner is of no relevance in this case.

(ii) **Auditor's disqualifications as to security:**

- As per section 141(3)(*d*)(*iii*) a person is disqualified to be appointed as an auditor if he, or his relative or partner has given a guarantee or provided any security in connection with the indebtedness of any third person to the company, or its subsidiary, or its holding or associate company or a subsidiary of such holding company, in excess of ₹ 1 Lac.
- These disqualifications need to be examined as at the time of appointment.
- In the present case, Mrs. A, wife of Mr. A had given a financial guarantee for the principal amount of a debt owed by Mr. X to ABC Ltd. for Rs. 6 lakhs. Mr. X has repaid Rs. 5 lakhs to ABC Ltd. 2 days before the date of appointment of Mr. A as an auditor of the company.

  Conclusion: Appointment of Mr. A as auditor in ABC Ltd. is valid as the amount of guarantee given by the Mrs. A for indebtedness of Mr. X in the company does not exceed Rs. 1 lac as on date of appointment.

Q.38 Mr. Y, a practicing Chartered Accountant, has been appointed as an auditor of M/s Z Ltd. on 12th June, 2018 for the year ended 31st March, 2019. Following persons have done following transactions in securities of M/s Z Ltd.:

- **Daughter of Mr. Y: Purchase of Securities on 10th September, 2018 of face value of Rs. 45,000 (market value Rs. 90,000)**
- **Husband of daughter of Mr. Y: Purchase of Securities on 10th December, 2018 of face value of Rs. 90,000 (Market value Rs. 1,90,000).**

All the above securities were sold on 10th March, 2019 for Rs. 3,00,000. Discuss the implications of the above on the appointment of Mr. Y. [May 19 - Old Syllabus (5 Marks)]

Ans. : Auditor's disqualifications as to security:

- As per section 141(3)(*d*)(*i*) of Companies Act, 2013, a person is disqualified to be appointed as an auditor if he, or his relative or partner holding any security of or interest in the company or its subsidiary, or of its holding or associate company or a subsidiary of such holding company.
- As per Rule 10 of Companies (Audit and Auditor's) Rules, 2014, the relative of the auditor may hold the securities or interest in the company of face value not exceeding of Rs. 1,00,000. It is also provided that in the event of acquiring and security or interest by a relative above the threshold limit, the corrective action to maintain the limits as specified above shall be taken by the auditor within 60 days of such acquisition or interest.

- The term relative as defined in Sec. 2(77) includes daughter and daughter's husband.
- In the present case, Mr. Y, has been appointed as an auditor of M/s Z Ltd. on 12th June, 2018 for the year ended 31st March, 2019. His daughter purchases securities of Z Ltd. on 10th Sep., 2018 of face value of Rs. 45,000, whereas husband of daughter of Mr. Y purchases securities of Z Ltd. on 10th Dec., 2018 of face value of Rs. 90,000. Aggregate face value of securities held by relatives of Mr. Y amounts to Rs. 1,35,000. Mr. Y was required to take corrective action within 60 days of 10th Dec. 2018 to bring the value of securities held by relatives to Rs. 1,00,000. However, securities were sold on 10th March, 2019 after expiry of 60 days from 10th Dec. 2018.

Conclusion: Mr. Y becomes disqualified on expiry of 60 days from 10th Dec. 2018 as he fails to take corrective action so as to bring the shareholding of relatives within prescribed limit of ₹1 Lac (face Value).

Q.39 **PQ and Co. is an audit firm with P and Q as partners. For the financial year 2018-19, the firm has been appointed as statutory auditor of M/s Mango Orchards Hotel Ltd. The audit firm is a regular customer of the hotel and the partners usually stay in the same hotel at various locations in the course of travelling for their various professional assignments. Normally, payments for such stay are settled against quarterly bills raised by the company. Give you comment with respect to the Companies Act, 2013.**

[May 19 - New Syllabus (4 Marks)]

Ans. : Auditor's disqualifications as to business relationship:

- As per Sec. 141(3)(*d*)(*ii*) of the Companies Act, 2013 read with Rule 10 of Companies (Audit and Auditor's) Rules, 2014, a person who is indebted to the company for an amount exceeding ₹ 5 Lacs shall be disqualified to be appointed as auditor.
- As per section 141(3)(*e*) of Companies Act, 2013, a person or a firm who, whether directly or indirectly, has business relationship with the company, or its subsidiary, or its holding or associate company or subsidiary of such holding company or associate company of such nature as may be prescribed, is disqualified to be appointed as auditor of that company.
- As per Rule 10 of Companies (Audit and Auditor's) Rules, 2014, the term "business relationship" shall be construed as any transaction entered into for a commercial purpose, except:
    - commercial transactions which are in the nature of professional services permitted to be rendered by an auditor or audit firm under the Act and the Chartered Accountants Act, 1949 and the rules or the regulations made under those Acts;
    - commercial transactions which are in the ordinary course of business of the company at arm's length price - like sale of products or services to the auditor, as customer, in the ordinary course of business, by companies engaged in the business of telecommunications, airlines, hospitals, hotels and such other similar businesses.
- In the present case, audit firm is a regular customer of the client running a hotel and the partners usually stay in the same hotel at various locations in the course of travelling for their various professional assignments. Normally, payments for such stay are settled against quarterly bills raised by the company.

Conclusion: No disqualification arises as the services availed are in ordinary course of business of client and cannot be considered as business relationship.

8.4 - CEILING ON NUMBER OF AUDITS [SEC. 141(3)(G)]

Q.40 **"ABC & Co." is an Audit Firm having partners "Mr. A", "Mr. B" and "Mr. C", Chartered Accountants. "Mr. A", "Mr. B" and "Mr. C" are holding appointment as an Auditor in 4, 6 and 10 Companies respectively.**

(*i*) Provide the maximum number of Audits remaining in the name of "ABC & Co."

(*ii*) Provide the maximum number of Audits remaining in the name of individual partner i.e. Mr. A, Mr. B and Mr. C.

(*iii*) Can ABC & Co. accept the appointment as an auditor in 60 private companies having paid-up share capital less than ₹ 100 Cr. which has not committed default in filing its financial statements u/s 137 or annual return u/s 92 of Companies Act with the Registrar 2 small companies and 1 dormant company?

(*iv*) Would your answer be different, if out of those 60 private companies, 45 companies are having paid-up share capital of ₹ 110 crore each?

Ans. : Ceiling on Number of Audit:

As per section 141(3)(g) of the Companies Act, 2013, a person shall not be eligible for appointment as an auditor if he is in full time employment elsewhere or a person or a partner of a firm holding appointment as its auditor, if such person or partner is at the date of such appointment or reappointment holding appointment as auditor of more than twenty companies other than one person company, dormant companies, small companies and private companies having paid up share capital less than ₹ 100 Crores, which has not committed default in filing its financial statements u/s 137 or annual return u/s 92 of Companies Act with the Registrar.

As per section 141(3)(g), this limit of 20 company audits is per person. In the case of an audit firm having 3 partners, the overall ceiling will be 3 × 20 = 60 company audits. Sometimes, a chartered accountant is a partner in a number of auditing firms. In such a case, all the firms in which he is partner or proprietor will be together entitled to 20 company audits on his account.

Conclusion:

(*i*) ABC & Co. can hold appointment as an auditor of 40 more companies as computed below:

Total Number of Audits available to the Firm	= 20*3	= 60
Number of Audits already taken by all the partners In their individual capacity	= 4+6+10	= 20
Remaining number of Audits available to the Firm		= 40

(*ii*) Mr. A can hold: 20 - 4 = 16 more audits.

Mr. B can hold 20-6 = 14 more audits and

Mr. C can hold 20-10 = 10 more audits.

(*iii*) M/s ABC & Co. can hold appointment as an auditor in all the 60 private companies having paid-up share capital less than ₹ 100 crores, 2 small companies and 1 dormant company as these are excluded from the ceiling limit of company audits given under section 141(3)(g) of the Companies Act, 2013.

(*iv*) M/s ABC & Co. can also accept the appointment as an auditor for 2 small companies, 1 dormant company, 15 private companies having paid-up share capital less than ₹ 100 crores and 40 private companies having paid-up share capital of ₹ 110 crore each in addition to above 20 company audits already holding.

Q.41 KBC & Co. a firm of Chartered Accountants has three partners, K, B & C; K is also in whole time employment elsewhere. The firm is offered the audit of ABC Ltd. and is already holding audit of 40 companies. Comment

Ans. : Ceiling on Number of Company Audits:

- As per section 141(3)(g) of the Companies Act, 2013, a person shall not be eligible for appointment as an auditor if he is in full time employment elsewhere or a person or a partner of a firm holding appointment as its auditor, if such person or partner is at the date of such appointment or reappointment holding appointment as auditor of more than twenty companies.
- In the firm of KBC & Co., K is in whole-time employment elsewhere, therefore, he will be excluded in determining the number of company audits that the firm can hold.
- If B and C do not hold any audits in their personal capacity or as partners of other firms, the total number of company audits that can be accepted by KBC & Co., is forty, and in the given case company is already holding forty audits.

Conclusion: KBC & Co. can't accept the offer for audit of ABC Ltd.

Q.42 What are the steps to be taken by a firm of Chartered Accountant to ensure that its appointment as Statutory Auditor of a Company is valid?

Ans. : Validity of appointment as a statutory auditor:

To ensure that the appointment is valid, the incoming auditor should take the following steps before accepting his appointment:

1. **Ceiling limit**: Ensure that a certificate has been issued u/s 139 of the Companies Act, 2013 so that the total number of company audits held by the firm (including the new appointment) will not exceed the specified number.

2. **Resolution at AGM**: Verify that, a proper resolution is passed at AGM of the Company. For this purpose, minutes book of general meeting may be inspected.
3. **Compliance with law**: Ensure compliance of provisions of sections 139 and 140 of the Companies Act 2013, relating to appointment of auditor and removal of existing auditor.
4. **Code of conduct**: Ensure compliance of Clause 8 of Part I of First schedule of Chartered Accountants Act, 1949 requiring communication with the previous auditor, in writing, to ascertain whether there are any professional reasons for not accepting the appointment.

Q.43 KSY & Co. Chartered Accountants is an audit firm having two partners CA K and CA Y. KSY & Co. is already holding appointment as auditors of 36 public companies.

KSY & Co. seeks your advice in the following situations:

(*i*) KSY & Co. has been offered the appointment as Auditors of 7 more Private Limited Companies. Of the seven, one is a company with a paid-up share capital of 150 crores, five are "small companies" as per the Act and one is a "Dormant Company".

(*ii*) Would your answer be different, if out of those 7 Private Companies, 3 Companies have paid up capital of ₹ 90 crores each? [May 16 (4 Marks)]

Note: None of the private companies has committed default in filing its financial statements under section 137 or annual return under section 92 of the Companies Act with the Registrar.

Ans. : Ceiling on Number of Audits:

- Section 141(3)(g) of Companies Act, 2013 provides that a person is not eligible to be appointed as auditor of a company if he at the date of such appointment or reappointment holding appointment as auditor of more than 20 Companies other than one-person company, dormant companies, small companies and private companies having paid up share capital less than 100 Crores which has not committed default in filing its financial statements u/s 137 or annual return u/s 92 of Companies Act with the Registrar;
- In the case of firm of auditors, it has been further provided that specified number of companies shall be construed as the number of companies specified for every partner of the firm who is not in full time employment elsewhere.
- In the present case, KSY & Co. has two partners and hence eligible for audit of 40 Companies. Firm is already holding audit of 36 Public companies. It can accept the audit of 4 more companies other than One-person company, dormant companies, small companies and private companies having paid up share capital less than 100 Crores.

Conclusion:

(*i*) KSY & Co. can accept audit of all 7 Private companies, because 5 small companies and one dormant company will not be considered for the purpose of ceiling limit. Total number of audit after acceptance of all seven audits remains at 37.

(*ii*) Answer will remain same, as the private companies having paid up capital less than 100 Crores are not considered for the purpose of ceiling limit. Total number of audit after acceptance of all seven audits remains at 40 assuming that other four companies having paid up capital in excess of ₹ 100 Crores.

Q.44 M/s ABC and Co., a firm of Chartered Accountants, comprising of three partners A, B, and C are Statutory Auditors of 50 Companies as per details given below:

(*i*) Small Companies - 10

(*ii*) Private Companies having paid up share capital of less than ₹ 100 Crores - 20

(*iii*) Private Companies having paid up share capital of more than ₹ 100 Crores - 15

(*iv*) Public Companies - 5

Mr. A signs the Balance Sheet of 10 Small Companies and 10 Private Companies having paid up share capital of less than ₹ 100 Crores. Mr. B signs the Balance Sheet of 10 Private Companies having paid up share capital of less than ₹ 100 Crores and 5 private Companies having paid up share capital of more than ₹ 100 Crores. Mr. C signs the Balance Sheet of 10 Private Companies having paid up share capital of more than ₹ 100 crores and 5 Public Companies.

What is the maximum number of audits that the firm as a whole can accept and what is the maximum number of audits each individual partner can accept? [May 18 - Old Syllabus (6 Marks)]

Note: None of the private companies has committed default in filing its financial statements under section 137 or annual return under section 92 of the Companies Act with the Registrar.

Ans : Ceiling on Number of Audit:

As per section 141(3)(g) of the Companies Act, 2013, a person shall not be eligible for appointment as an auditor if he is in full time employment elsewhere or a person or a partner of a firm holding appointment as its auditor, if such person or partner is at the date of such appointment or reappointment holding appointment as auditor of more than twenty companies other than one person company, dormant companies, small companies and private companies having paid up share capital less than ₹ 100 Crores which has not committed default in filing its financial statements u/s 137 or annual return u/s 92 of Companies Act with the Registrar.

As per section 141(3)(g), this limit of 20 company audits is per person. In the case of an audit firm having 3 partners, the overall ceiling will be $3 \times 20 = 60$ company audits.

Conclusion:

- Firm can accept 40 more audits of Public companies and private companies having paid up capital of more than ₹ 100 Crores. Audit of Small companies and private companies having paid up share capital less than ₹ 100 cr. are not considered for the purpose of ceiling.
- Partner A can accept 20 audits of Public companies and private companies having paid up capital of more than ₹ 100 Crores. Partner B can accept 15 audits of Public companies and private companies having paid up capital of more than ₹ 100 Crores. Partner C can accept 5 audits of Public companies and private companies having paid up capital of more than ₹ 100 Crores. Audit of Small companies and private companies having paid up share capital less than ₹ 100 cr. are not considered for the purpose of ceiling.

8.5 - POWERS AND DUTIES OF AUDITOR - SEC. 143, SEC. 144, SEC. 145, SEC. 146

Q.45 CA. G, was appointed by DP Ltd., as Statutory Auditor. While doing the audit of DP Ltd., CA. G observed that certain loans and advances were made without proper securities; certain trade receivables and trade payables were adjusted inter se; and personal expenses were charged to revenue. As a company auditor comment on the reporting responsibilities of CA. G. [Nov. 19 - New Syllabus (5 Marks)]

Ans. : Inquiry into Propriety Matters u/s 143(1):

- Section 143(1) of the Companies Act, 2013 requires the auditor to conduct inquiry into certain matters and if the auditor finds answer of any of these matters in adverse, auditor is required to report, otherwise no reporting is required. In relation to observations stated in the question, auditor should inquire as follows:
  1. Clause (a) of Section 143(1) requires the auditor to inquire "Whether loans and advances made by the company on the basis of security have been properly secured and whether the terms on which they have been made are prejudicial to the interests of the company or its members".
  2. Clause (b) of section 143(1), requires the auditor to inquire "whether transactions of the company which are represented merely by book entries are prejudicial to the interests of the company".
  3. Clause (e) of section 143(1) requires the auditor to inquire "Whether personal expenses have been charged to revenue account".
- If the auditor finds that the loans and advances have not been properly secured, he may enter an adverse comment in the report without modifying opinion on financial statements if the loans and advances are properly described and presented in terms of Part I of Schedule III to the Companies Act.
- If relation to his observation regarding *inter se* adjustment of trade receivables and trade payables, being a book entry, auditor should have inquired into the legitimate interests of the company. If appears prejudicial, he may enter adverse comment in the report.
- Regarding charging of personal expenses to revenue account auditor should inquire whether such expenses are incurred on the basis of the company's contractual obligations, or in accordance with accepted business practice. If personal expenses incurred by the company are not covered by contractual obligations or by accepted business practice and charged to revenue account, it would be the duty of the auditor to report thereon.

Conclusion: In the instant case, Mr. X, the statutory auditor of ABC Ltd., needs to enquire in light of above provisions, as a result of the enquiries if he is satisfied then there is no further duty to report on these matters.

Q.46 As an auditor, how would you deal with the following: In the audit of ABC Private Limited, auditor came across cases of payments to Directors, whereby, expenses of a personal nature were reimbursed.

Ans. : Personal Expenses of Directors:

- All payments to Directors as remuneration or perquisites whether in the case of a public or private company need to be authorised in accordance with the Companies Act as well as Articles of Association of the company.
- If the terms of appointment of a Director include payment of expenses of a personal nature, then such expenses can be incurred by the company; otherwise, no such expense can be incurred or reimbursed by the company.
- In the instant case the auditor has to ensure that the payment is authorized by the Articles of Association and the same has been covered by terms of appointment.
- Further as this payment is also covered u/s 143(1), and hence auditor is also required to inquire into the matter and make a disclosure in his report accordingly.

Q.47 Director of T Ltd. draws an advance of US$ 200 per day in connection with the foreign trip undertaken on behalf of the company. On his return he files a declaration stating that entire advance was expended without any supporting or evidence. T Ltd. books the entire expenses on the basis of such declaration. As the auditor of T Ltd. how do you deal with this? [May 11 (8 Marks)]

Ans. : Personal Expenses Charged to revenue Account:

- Section 143(1)(e) of the Companies Act, 2013 requires an auditor to inquire and report whether personal expenses have been charged to revenue account.
- SA 500 "Audit Evidence" states that an auditor should obtain sufficient appropriate audit evidence to be able to draw reasonable conclusions on which to base his option.
- All payments to Directors as remuneration or perquisites whether in the case of a public or private company need to be authorised in accordance with the Companies Act as well as Articles of Association of the company.
- In the present case, company has booked foreign trip expenses of director in its revenue account. In the context, auditor is required to inquire whether the payment made by the company for the foreign trip is personal expense or not and collect the necessary supporting evidences.
- If it appears to be personal expense, auditor is required to ascertain whether such expense is properly authorized or not. If not authorized, auditor should state the matter in his report.

Q.48 What are the statements of facts that an auditor has to report u/s 143 of the Companies Act, 2013.

Ans. : Statement of Facts to be reported u/s 143:

Section 143(3) of Companies Act, 2013 requires the auditor the comment on the following in addition to opinion on true and fair view of financial statements:

(*a*) Whether he has sought and obtained all the information and explanations which to the best of his knowledge and belief were necessary for the purpose of his audit and if not, the details thereof and the effect of such information on the financial statements;

(*b*) Whether, in his opinion, proper books of account as required by law have been kept by the company so far as appears from his examination of those books and proper returns adequate for the purposes of his audit have been received from branches not visited by him;

(*c*) Whether the report on the accounts of any branch office of the company audited u/s 143(8) by a person other than the company's auditor has been sent to him under the proviso to that sub-section and the manner in which he has dealt with it in preparing his report;

(*d*) Whether the company's balance sheet and profit and loss account dealt with in the report are in agreement with the books of account and returns;

(*e*) Whether, in his opinion, the financial statements comply with the accounting standards;

(*f*) The observations or comments of the auditors on financial transactions or matters which have any adverse effect on the functioning of the company;

(*g*) Whether any director is disqualified from being appointed as a director under sub-section (2) of section 164;

(*h*) any qualification, reservation or adverse remark relating to the maintenance of accounts and other matters connected therewith;

(*i*) whether the company has adequate internal financial controls with reference to financial statements in place and the operating effectiveness of such controls;

(*j*) such other matters as may be prescribed.

Further, Rule 11 of the Companies (Audit and Auditors) Rules, 2014 prescribes the other matters to be included in auditor's report. The auditor's report shall also include their views and comments on the following matters, namely:

(*a*) whether the company has disclosed the impact, if any, of pending litigations on its financial position in its financial statement;

(*b*) whether the company has made provision, as required under any law or accounting standards, for material foreseeable losses, if any, on long term contracts including derivative contracts;

(*c*) whether there has been any delay in transferring amounts, required to be transferred, to the Investor Education and Protection Fund by the company.

Q.49 While conducting the audit of a limited company for the year ended 31st March, 2019, the auditor wanted to refer to the Minute Books. The Board of Directors refused to show the Minute Books to the auditor.

Ans. : Right of Access to Books of Account:

- Sec. 143(1) of the Companies Act, 2013 grants powers to the auditor that every auditor has a right of access, at all times, to the books of account and vouchers of the company.
- The term books of account include all books which have any bearing or are likely to have any bearing on the accounts, whether these be the usual financial books or the statutory or statistical books.
- In order to verify actions of the company and to vouch and verify some of the transactions of the company, it is necessary for the auditor to refer to the decisions of the shareholders and/or the directors of the company.
- It is, therefore, essential for the auditor to refer to the Minute Books. In the absence of the Minute Books, the auditor may not be able to vouch/verify certain transactions of the company.

Conclusion: In case the directors have refused to produce the Minute Books, the auditor may consider extending the audit procedure as also consider qualifying his report in any appropriate manner.

Q.50 The auditor of X Ltd. did not report on the matters, specified u/s 143(1) of the Companies Act, 2013, on which he inquired into, because of the reason that he was satisfied. But the management of the company wanted the auditor to report on those matters so that the members can also be aware of the true position of the company. Comment as to whether the auditor is required to report the matters, specified under the Act, he inquired into and whether the contention of the management is sustainable.

Ans. : Reporting of Matters contained under Section 143(1) of the Companies Act, 2013:

- Sec. 143(1) of the Act deals with the duties of an auditor requiring him to make an inquiry in respect of specified propriety matters.
- The matters in respect of which the inquiry has to be made by the auditor are relating to loans and advances on the basis of security, transactions represented merely by book entries, investments sold at less than cost price, loans and advances shown as deposits, personal expenses charged to revenue account etc.
- The law requires the auditor to make an inquiry, the Research Committee of the Institute opined that the auditor is not required to report on these matters unless he has any special comments to make on any of the items referred to therein. If the auditor is satisfied as a result of the inquiries, he has no further duty to report that he is so satisfied.
- Therefore, it could be said that the auditor should make a report to the members in case he finds answer to any of these matters in adverse.

Conclusion: The auditor of X Ltd. is correct in non-reporting on the matters specified in Sec. 143(1) of the Act and hence, the contention of the management is not sustainable.

Q.51 M/s XYZ & Co., auditors of Goodwill Education Foundation, a recognised non-profit organisation feels that the standards on auditing need not to be applied as Goodwill Education Foundation is a non-profit making concern.

Ans. : Compliance with Standards on Auditing:

- As per Sec. 143(9) of the Companies Act, 2013, every auditor shall comply with the auditing standards. Further as per Sec. 143(10), the Central Government may prescribe the standards of auditing or any addendum thereto, as recommended by the ICAI, in consultation with and after examination of the recommendations made by the NFRA.
- However, until any auditing standards are notified, standards of auditing specified by the ICAI shall be deemed to be the auditing standards.
- Further, the Preface to Standards on Auditing requires that while discharging their attest function; it is the duty of the Chartered Accountant to ensure that SAs are followed in the audit of financial information covered by their audit reports.

Conclusion: In the given case, even though the client is a non-profit oriented entity the SAs shall apply and the auditor is required to ensure their compliance. In case he fails to discharge his duty he shall be guilty of professional misconduct.

Q.52 An auditor became aware of a matter regarding a company, only after he had issued his audit opinion. Had he become aware of the same prior to his issuing the audit report, he would have issued a different opinion.

Ans. : Auditor's duties w.r.t. subsequent events:

- Sec. 146 of the Companies Act, 2013 requires the auditors of a company to attend the general meeting of the company unless otherwise exempted by the company.
- Auditor shall have the right to be heard at such meeting on any part of the business which concerns him as auditors.
- The discovery of a fact after issuance of the financial statements that existed at the date of the audit report which would have caused the revision of the audit report, requires the auditor to bring this to the notice of shareholders.
- Further SA 560 "Subsequent Event" also prescribes the procedures which the auditor is required to perform.

Conclusion: It will be advisable for the auditor to attend the meeting with a view to bringing to the notice of the shareholders the matter which came to his knowledge subsequent to his signing the report and perform procedures as per the requirement of SA 560.

Q.53 Y, is the auditor of X Pvt. Ltd. in which there are four shareholders only, who are also the Directors of the company. On account of bad trade and for reducing the expenses in all directions, the directors asked Y to accept a reduced fee and for that he has been offered not to carry out such full audit as he has done in the past. Y accepted the suggestions of the directors.

Ans. : Restricting Scope of Audit:

- Auditor's duties are governed by the provisions of Sec. 143 of Companies Act, 2013, which cannot be restricted either by the director or even by the entire body of shareholders.
- Further, remuneration is a matter of arrangement between the auditor and the shareholders. Section 142 specifies the remuneration of an auditor, shall be fixed by the company in general meeting or in such manner as the company in general meeting may determine.
- Duties of auditor may not necessarily commensurate with his remuneration.

Conclusion: Y, should not accept the suggestions of the directors regarding the scope of the work to be done. If he accepts the suggestions of the directors regarding the scope of work to be done, it would not reduce his responsibility as an auditor under the law and he will be violating the provisions of the Companies Act, 2013.

Q.54 At the Annual General Meeting of the Company, a resolution was passed by the entire body of shareholders restricting some of the powers of the Statutory Auditors. Whether powers of the Statutory Auditors can be restricted?

Ans. : Restrictions on Powers of Statutory Auditors:

- Section 143 of the Companies Act, 2013 provides that an auditor of a company shall have right of access at all times to the books and account and vouchers of the company whether kept at the Head Office or other places and shall be entitled to require from the offices of the company such information and explanations as the auditor may think necessary for the purpose of his audit.

- These specific rights have been conferred by the statute on the auditor to enable him to carry out his duties and responsibilities prescribed under the Act, which cannot be restricted or abridged in any manner.
- Further it was held in the case of **Newton vs. Birmingham Small Arms Co.** that any resolution even if passed by entire body of shareholders which preclude the auditors from availing themselves of all the information for which they are entitled to under the Company Law are inconsistent with the Act and therefore null and void.

Conclusion: Any resolution restricting the scope of statutory right of auditor even if passed by entire body of shareholders is *ultra vires* and therefore void.

Q.55 Mr. Rajendra, a fellow member of the Institute of Chartered Accountants of India, working as Manager of Shrivastav and Co., a Chartered Accountant firm, signed the audit report of Om Ltd. on behalf of Shrivastav & Co.

Ans. : Signature on Audit Report:

- Section 145 of the Companies Act, 2013 requires that the person appointed as an auditor of the company shall sign the auditor's report or sign or certify any other document of the company in accordance with the provisions of Sec. 141(2), *i.e.* where a firm including a LLP is appointed as an auditor of a company, only the partners who are CAs shall be authorized to act and sign on behalf of the firm.
- In the present case, Mr. Rajendra, a fellow member of the Institute and a manager of M/s Shrivastav & Co., Chartered Accountants, cannot sign on behalf of the firm in view of the specific requirements of the Companies Act, 2013. If any auditor's report or any document of the company is signed or authenticated otherwise than in conformity with the requirements of Section 145, the auditor concerned and the person, if any, other than the auditor who signs the report or signs or authenticates the document shall, if the default is wilful, be punishable with a fine.

Q.56 The members of C. Ltd. preferred a complaint against the auditor stating that he has failed to send the auditor's report to them.

Ans. : Dispatch of Auditor's Report to Shareholders:

- Section 143 of the Companies Act, 2013 lays down the powers and duties of auditor. As per provisions of the law, it is no part of the auditor's duty to send a copy of his report to members of the company.
- The auditor's duty concludes once he forwards his report to the company. It is the responsibility of company to send the report to every member of the company.
- In case of Allen Graig and Company (London) Ltd., it was held that duty of the auditor after having signed the report to be annexed to a balance sheet is confined only to forwarding that report to the secretary of the company. It will be for the secretary or the director to convene a general meeting and send the balance sheet and report to the members (or another person) entitled to receive it.

Conclusion: Auditor cannot be held liable for the failure to send the report to the shareholders.

Q.57 What are the duties of an auditor regarding disqualifications of directors under section 164(2) of Companies Act, 2013. [May 09 (8 Marks)]

Ans. : Auditor's duties w.r.t. Director's disqualifications:

- Section 143(3)(g) of the Companies Act, 2013 imposes a specific duty on the auditor to report whether any director is disqualified from being appointed as directors under section 164(2) of the Companies Act, 2013.
- As per Section 164(2) of Companies Act, 2013, no person who is or has been a director of a company which
  - (*a*) has not filed financial statements or annual returns for any continuous period of three financial years; or
  - (*b*) has failed to repay the deposits accepted by it or pay interest thereon or to redeem any debentures on the due date or pay interest due thereon or pay any dividend declared and such failure to pay or redeem continues for one year or more,

  shall be eligible to be re-appointed as a director of that company or appointed in other company for a period of five years from the date on which the said company fails to do so.

- Rule 14(1) of Companies (Appointment and Qualification of Directors) Rules, 2014 requires every director to inform to the company concerned about his disqualification under Sec. 164(2), if any, in Form DIR-8 before he is appointed or re-appointed.
- The auditor is required to ensure whether the director has submitted DIR-8 to the company at the time of appointment or reappointment.
- Auditor may also request for the inspection of DIR-8 available with the company and obtain a copy of the same for the purpose of his record.

Q.58 One of the directors of Hitech Ltd. is attracted by the disqualification under Section 164(2) of the Companies Act, 2013.

Ans. : Disqualification of a Director under section 164(2) of the Companies Act, 2013:

- Section 143(3)(g) of the Companies Act, 2013 imposes a specific duty on the auditor to report whether any director is disqualified from being appointed as directors under section 164(2) of the Companies Act, 2013.
- The auditor has to ensure that written representation have been obtained by the Board from each director that one is not hit by Section 164(2).

Conclusion: In this case, one of the director is attracted by disqualification u/s 164(2) of the Act, the auditor shall state in his report as per Sec. 143 about the disqualification of the particular director.

Q.59 The Board of Directors of a company have filed a complaint with the ICAI against their statutory auditors for their failing to attend the AGM of the Shareholders in which audited accounts were considered.

Ans. : Auditor's Attendance at Annual General Meeting:

- Section 146 of the Companies Act, 2013 requires the auditor of a company to attend either by himself or through his qualified authorised representative to attend the general meeting, unless exempted.
- The said section provides that all notices and other communications relating to any general meeting of a company shall also be forwarded to the auditor.
- Further, it has been provided that the auditor shall have right to be heard at such meeting on any part of the business which concerns him as an auditor.

Conclusion: Complaint filed by the Board of Directors is valid if the auditor was not being exempted by the company.

Q.60 Mr. X, a Director of M/s KP Private Ltd., is also a Director of another company viz., M/s GP Private Ltd., which has not filed the financial statements and annual return for last three years 2015-16 to 2017-18. Mr. X is of the opinion that he is not disqualified u/s 164(2) of the Companies Act, 2013, and auditor should not mention disqualification remark in his audit report.

Ans. : Disqualification of a Director under section 164(2) of the Companies Act, 2013:

- Section 143(3)(g) of the Companies Act, 2013 imposes a specific duty on the auditor to report whether any director is disqualified from being appointed as director u/s 164(2) of the Companies Act, 2013.
- As per provisions of Section 164(2), if a director is already holding a directorship of a company which has not filed the financial statements or annual returns for any continuous period of 3 financial years shall not be eligible to be reappointed as a director of that company or appointed in other company for a period of five years from the date on which the said company fails to do so.

Conclusion: In this case, Mr. X is a director of M/s KP Private Ltd. as well as of M/s GP Private Ltd., And, M/s GP Private Ltd., has not filed the financial statements and annual return for last three years. Hence the provisions of section 164(2) are applicable to him and as such he is disqualified from directorship of both the companies. Therefore, the auditor shall report about the disqualification u/s 143(3)(g) of the Companies Act, 2013.

Q.61 Comment: Contravene Ltd. appointed CA Innocent as an auditor for the company for the current financial year. Further the company offered him the services of actuarial, investment advisory and investment banking which was also approved by the Board of Directors.

Ans. : Services not to be Rendered by the Auditor:

Section 144 of the Companies Act, 2013 prescribes certain services not to be rendered by the auditor. An auditor appointed under this Act shall provide to the company only such other services as are approved by the Board of Directors or the audit committee, as the case may be, but which shall not include any of the following services (whether such services are rendered directly or indirectly to the company or its holding company or subsidiary company), namely:

(i) accounting and book keeping services;
(ii) internal audit;
(iii) design and implementation of any financial information system;
(iv) actuarial services;
(v) investment advisory services;
(vi) investment banking services;
(vii) rendering of outsourced financial services;
(viii) management services; and
(ix) any other kind of services as may be prescribed.

Further section 141(3)(i) of the Companies Act, 2013 also disqualify a person for appointment as an auditor of a company who, directly or indirectly, renders any service referred to in Sec. 144 to the company or its holding company or its subsidiary company.

In the given case, CA Innocent was appointed as an auditor of Contravene Ltd. He was offered additional services of actuarial, investment advisory and investment banking which was also approved by the Board of Directors.

Conclusion: The auditor is advised not to accept the services as these services are specifically notified in the services not to be rendered by him as an auditor as per section 144 of the Act.

Q.62 When can a company be said to have 'Not maintained' proper books of account? What is the role of the statutory auditor for the same?

or

The auditor report of company states that proper books of account as required by law have been maintained by the company. What is the role of statutory auditor of the company, when a company be said to have not maintained proper books of account? [May 15 (4 Marks)]

Or

Write short note on: Proper Books of Account as per Companies Act, 2013 [May 17 (4 Marks)]

Ans. : Auditor's duties in case of non-maintenance of proper books of account:

- Section 143(3)(b) of Companies Act, 2103 requires that the auditor's report shall state whether, in his opinion, proper books of account as required by law have been kept by the company so far as appears from his examination of those books and proper returns adequate for the purposes of his audit have been received from branches not visited by him.
- As per Section 128 of the Companies Act, 2013, every company shall prepare and keep at its registered office books of account and other relevant books and papers and financial statement for every financial year which give a true and fair view of the state of the affairs of the company, including that of its branch office or offices, if any.
- Such books shall be kept on accrual basis and according to the double entry system of accounting.

Conclusion: The Auditor is required to check that the company has complied with all the provisions related to maintenance of books of account prescribed under section 128. If the statutory auditor finds that the books are not maintained properly, he will have to modify his report and shall state the reasons for the same.

"ICAI Examiner Comments"

Many Candidates failed to explain the provisions of section 143(3)(b). Few candidates laid stress on various books of account, records and document as per section 2(13).

Q.63 Write short note on: Obligation of the statutory auditor to report frauds to the Central Government during the audit carried out under the Companies Act, 2013. [Nov. 15 (4 Marks)]

or

An auditor observed a fraud committed by an employee of the company. State the manner and timing of reporting of the fraud by the auditor. [Nov. 16 (4 Marks)]

or

You have been appointed statutory auditor of a company for the financial year ended 31st March, 2018 in place of the retiring auditor. During the course of audit, you observe that a fraud had been committed by a general manager who retired in March 2018. While going into further details, it was found that the

fraud was going on since last 2-3 years and the total amount misappropriated was likely to exceed ₹ 100 lakhs. As statutory auditor, what would be your reporting responsibilities to the government?

[Nov. 17 (5 Marks)]

Ans. : Auditor's duties to report fraud to the Central Government:

- Section 143(12) of Companies Act, 2013 requires that if an auditor of a company in the course of the performance of his duties as auditor, has reason to believe that an offence of fraud involving such amount or amounts as may be prescribed, is being or has been committed in the company by its officers or employees, the auditor shall report the matter to the Central Government within such time and in such manner as may be prescribed. For this purpose, Rule 13 prescribes the amount of ₹ 1 Cr. or more.
- However, in case of a fraud involving lesser than the specified amount, *i.e.* below ₹ 1 Cr., the auditor shall report the matter to the audit committee constituted u/s 177 or to the Board in other cases within such time and in such manner as may be prescribed:
- The companies, whose auditors have reported frauds to the audit committee or the Board but not reported to the Central Government, shall disclose the details about such frauds in the Board's report in such manner as may be prescribed.
- Rule 13 of Companies (Audit and Auditors) Rules, 2014 prescribes the manner of Reporting of Frauds in various cases. Accordingly:

(1) If an auditor of a company, in the course of the performance of his duties as statutory auditor, has reason to believe that an offence of fraud, which involves or is expected to involve individually an amount of ₹ 1 Cr. or above, is being or has been committed against the company by its officers or employees, the auditor shall report the matter to the CG.

(2) The auditor shall report the matter to the CG as under:

(*a*) the auditor shall report the matter to the Board or the Audit Committee, as the case may be, immediately but not later than 2 days of his knowledge of the fraud, seeking their reply or observations within 45 days;

(*b*) on receipt of such reply or observations, the auditor shall forward his report and the reply or observations of the Board or the Audit Committee along with his comments (on such reply or observations of the Board or the Audit Committee) to the CG within 15 days from the date of receipt of such reply or observations;

(*c*) in case the auditor fails to get any reply or observations from the Board or the Audit Committee within the stipulated period of 45 days, he shall forward his report to the CG along with a note containing the details of his report that was earlier forwarded to the Board or the Audit Committee for which he has not received any reply or observations;

(*d*) the report shall be sent to the Secretary, Ministry of Corporate Affairs in a sealed cover by Registered Post with Acknowledgement Due or by Speed Post followed by an e-mail in confirmation of the same;

(*e*) the report shall be on the letter-head of the auditor containing postal address, e-mail address and contact telephone number or mobile number and be signed by the auditor with his seal and shall indicate his Membership Number; and

(*f*) the report shall be in the form of a statement as specified in Form ADT-4.

(3) In case of a fraud involving amount less than ₹ 1 Cr., the auditor shall report the matter to Audit Committee constituted u/s 177 or to the Board immediately but not later than 2 days of his knowledge of the fraud and he shall report the matter specifying the following:

(*a*) Nature of Fraud with description;

(*b*) Approximate amount involved; and

(*c*) Parties involved.

(4) The following details of each of the fraud reported to the Audit Committee or the Board under sub-rule (3) during the year shall be disclosed in the Board's Report:—

(*a*) Nature of Fraud with description;

(*b*) Approximate Amount involved;

(*c*) Parties involved, if remedial action not taken; and

(*d*) Remedial actions taken.

"ICAI Examiner Comments"
The procedures to be followed as per Companies (Audit and Auditors) Rules, 2014 to report frauds have not been properly explained by examinees.

Q.64 **RX Ltd. is a sugar manufacturing company. The company appointed Mr. Suresh, a practicing cost accountant, to conduct cost audit of its cost records under section 148 of the Companies Act, 2013. While conducting audit, Mr. Suresh found some misstatement resulting into fraud committed by the officers of the company amounting ₹ 1.5 crore. However, he did not report the matter to the Central Government believing that liability for such reporting lies only with statutory auditor of the company. Advise.**

Ans. : Reporting of Fraud u/s 142(12) by a Cost Accountant:

- Sec. 143(12) of the Companies Act, 2013 along with Rule 13 of the Companies (Audit and Auditors) Rules, 2014 provides that if auditor of a company, in the course of the performance of his duties as statutory auditor, has reason to believe that an offence of fraud, which involves or is expected to involve individually an amount of ₹ 1 crore or above, is being or has been committed against the company by its officers or employees, the auditor shall report the matter to the Central Government as per the prescribed procedure.
- Sec. 143(14) of Companies Act, 2013 provides that the provisions related to reporting of fraud shall also apply, *mutatis mutandis,* to a cost accountant conducting cost audit u/s 148 of the Companies Act, 2013.
- In the present case, Mr. Suresh, being the cost auditor of RX Ltd., found misstatement resulting into fraud amounting ₹ 1.5 crore committed by the officers of the company. He was required to report the fraud to the Central Government.

Conclusion: Mr. Suresh failed to perform his duties to report the fraud to C.G.

Q.65 **Write short note on: Auditor's right to Lien as per Companies Act, 2013.** **[May 17 (4 Marks)]**

Ans. : Auditor's Right of Lien:

- Lien refers to the right of a person for lawful possession of somebody's else property on which he has worked. Right of lien is exercised for non-payment of his dues for the work done.
- The auditors can exercise right of lien on the client's books and documents in his possession for non-payment of fees by the client, for the work done on the books and documents.
- In respect of auditor exercising the lien, The Institute of Chartered Accountants of England and Wales has expressed a similar view subject to the following conditions:
  - (*i*) Documents must belong to the client who owes the money,
  - (*ii*) These documents must come to the possession of the auditor on the client's authority.
  - (*iii*) The auditor can retain such documents, only if he has done work on such documents, on which fees have not been paid.

Note: As per Ethical Standard Board of ICAI, a chartered accountant cannot exercise lien over the client documents/records for non-payment of his fees.

"ICAI Examiner Comments"
Many candidates explained Right of Lien of Auditors in a general manner but most of the candidates failed to explain the Auditor's Right to Lien in the context of Companies Act, 2013. Few candidates wrongly mentioned Rights of an auditor which was not required.

8.6 - COST AUDIT AND COMPANIES (COST RECORDS AND AUDIT) RULES, 2014

Q.66 **Sugar Ltd. is a top sugar manufacturer and exporter in India operating from Noida Specific Economic Zone, Uttar Pradesh. Its revenue from sale/export for the immediate preceding year is given below:**

Sale within India	**₹ 1157 lakhs**
Sale outside India (Export)	**₹ 1353 lakhs**
Total Revenue	**₹ 2510 lakhs**

Mr. X, the statutory auditor of Sugar Ltd., is of the view that the company is mandatorily required to include cost records in their books of account and consequently conduct cost audit. He also suggested the

name of his friend, who is a Cost Accountant in Practice, for the purpose of such cost audit. However, the management is of the view that the company neither required including cost records in their books of account nor conduct cost audit.

Being an expert in cost records and audit rules, you are required to guide the management in this regard.

Ans. : Applicability of Provisions related to Cost Records and Audit:

- The provisions relating to cost records and audit are governed by section 148 of the Companies Act, 2013 read with the Companies (Cost Records and Audit) Rules, 2014. The audit conducted under this section shall be in addition to the audit conducted under section 143.
- Rule 3 of the Companies (Cost Records and Audit) Rules, 2014 provides the classes of companies (including Foreign Companies) required to include cost records in their books of account if they are having turnover ₹ 35 Cr. or more during immediately preceding financial year. The said rule has also divided the list of companies into regulated sectors and non-regulated sectors. Company belonging to sugar industry is one of the types of companies prescribed under the regulated sectors.
- Rule 4 of Companies (Cost Records and Audit) Rules, 2014 requires audit of cost records in case of regulated sector industries if annual turnover from all products and services in immediately preceding financial year is ₹ 50 Cr. or more and the turnover of individual product or service is ₹ 25 Cr. or more.
- Rule 4 further provides that requirement of cost audit shall not apply to a company whose revenue from exports in foreign exchange exceeds 75% of total revenue or which is operating from a SEZ.
- In the given case, Sugar Ltd., a sugar manufacturer and exporter in India, is operating from Noida Specific Economic Zone, Uttar Pradesh and its turnover for the immediate preceding year is just ₹ 25.10 Cr.

Conclusion: Sugar Ltd. is not required to include cost records in their books of account in accordance with Rule 3 of the Companies (Cost Records and Audit) Rules, 2014 and no Cost audit is required.

Q.67 XYZ Ltd., having place of business in Delhi, is engaged in the production, trading, import and export of orthopaedic implants and pacemaker. The company's revenue from export is usually in foreign currency. Its total revenue classification for the immediate preceding financial year is as below:

Intra-State Sale	**₹ 1400 lakhs**
Inter-State Sale	**₹ 1550 lakhs**
Export to US	**₹ 4900 lakhs**
Export to UK	**₹ 6900 lakhs**
Total Revenue	**₹ 14750 lakhs**

The management of the company is of the opinion that the company is not required to maintain cost records in their books of account. Consequently, there is no need to appoint cost auditor and conduct cost audit. Comment.

Ans. : Applicability of Provisions Related to Cost Records and Audit:

- The provisions relating to cost records and audit are governed by section 148 of the Companies Act, 2013 read with Companies (Cost Records and Audit) Rules, 2014. The audit conducted under this section shall be in addition to the audit conducted under section 143.
- Rule 3 of the Companies (Cost Records and Audit) Rules, 2014 provides the classes of companies (including Foreign Companies) required to include cost records in their books of account if they are having turnover ₹ 35 Cr. or more during immediately preceding financial year.
- Rule 4 of Companies (Cost Records and Audit) Rules, 2014 requires audit of cost records in case of non-regulated sector industries if annual turnover from all products and services in immediately preceding financial year is ₹ 100 Cr. or more and the turnover of individual product or service is ₹ 35 Cr. or more.
- Rule 4 further provides that requirement of cost audit shall not apply to a company whose revenue from exports in foreign exchange exceeds 75% of total revenue or which is operating from a SEZ.
- In the given case, XYZ Ltd. is a foreign company and its total revenue for the immediate preceding financial year is ₹ 14750 lakhs, out of which, export, in foreign currency, comprises ₹ 11800 lakhs (₹ 4900 lakhs + ₹ 6900 lakhs). The proportion of the company's export to its total revenue is 80% [(₹ 11800 lakhs/₹ 14750 lakhs)×100].

Conclusion: XYZ Ltd. is required to include cost records in their books of account in accordance with Rule 3 of the Companies (Cost Records and Audit) Rules, 2014.

However, the company is not required to conduct cost audit as its revenue from exports, in foreign exchange, exceeds 75 per cent of its total revenue.

Q.68 Electro Ltd. is engaged in generation of electricity for captive consumption through Captive Generating Plant. The Company also maintain cost records in their books of account as required under Cost Records and Audit Rules. Mr. X, friend of Managing Director of the company, suggested name of his brother, who is a Cost Accountant in Practice, for the purpose of cost audit. However, the statutory auditor of the company, is of the view that the company is not legally required to conduct cost audit. Now, the Managing Director is in dilemma about the requirement of cost audit.

Being an expert in cost records and audit rules, you are required to guide in this regard.

Ans. : Applicability of Provisions related to Cost Records and Audit:

Provisions relating to cost records and audit are governed by section 148 of the Companies Act, 2013 read with the Companies (Cost Records and Audit) Rules, 2014.

Rule 3 of the Companies (Cost Records and Audit) Rules, 2014 provides the classes of companies, engaged in the production of goods or providing services, required to include cost records in their books of account. However, the requirement for cost audit under these rules shall not be applicable to a company which is covered under Rule 3, and,

(*i*) whose revenue from exports, in foreign exchange, exceeds 75 per cent of its total revenue; or

(*ii*) which is operating from a special economic zone.

(*iii*) which is engaged in generation of electricity for captive consumption through Captive Generating Plant.

In the given case, Electro Ltd. is engaged in generation of electricity for captive consumption through Captive Generating Plant. Electro Ltd. is not required to conduct cost audit as it is falling under the exemption criteria.

Conclusion: The opinion of statutory auditor of the company regarding non-applicability of cost audit is correct and the management should follow the same.

Q.69 X Ltd. is engaged in the production of Iron and Steel. A CA Firm 'M/s M & Co.' was appointed as the statutory auditor of X Ltd. for the current financial year. During the year, the management of the company realized that the company is required to maintain cost records in their books of account and get it audited. Therefore, in a general meeting, the members of the company appointed M/s M & Co. as the cost auditor of the company. You are required to examine the validity of appointment of M/s M & Co. as the cost auditor.

Ans. : Appointment of Statutory Auditor as Cost Auditor:

As per Section 148(3) of the Companies Act, 2013 read with Rule 6 of Companies (Cost Records and Audit) Rules, 2014—

(*i*) in the case of companies which are required to constitute an audit committee, the Board shall appoint an individual, who is a cost accountant in practice, or a firm of cost accountants in practice, as cost auditor on the recommendations of the Audit committee;

(*ii*) in the case of other companies which are not required to constitute an audit committee, the Board shall appoint an individual who is a cost accountant in practice or a firm of cost accountants in practice as cost auditor.

Sec. 148(3) also provides that no person appointed under section 139 as an auditor of the company shall be appointed for conducting the audit of cost records.

In the given case, the members of X Ltd. in general meeting appointed M/s M & Co., the statutory auditor of the company, as the cost auditor.

Therefore, the appointment of the CA firm as cost auditor made by the company is not valid.

Conclusion: Appointment is not valid as a CA firm cannot be appointed as cost auditor. The Board shall appoint a cost accountant in practice or a firm of cost accountants in practice to conduct such cost audit.

Q.70 On 30-8-2017, the Board of SRE Ltd. proposed to appoint Mr. Elex, a Cost Accountant in practice, for conducting cost audit for the financial year 2017-18. The management came to know about the certificate which needs to be obtained from the auditor before such appointment is made. However, the management is unaware about what certification is required from the auditor. Please guide.

Ans. : Certificate to be obtained from Cost Auditor:

As per Rule 6 of Companies (Cost Records and Audit) Rules, 2014, Companies required to get the cost records audited, shall within 180 Days of the commencement of every financial year, appoint a cost auditor. Before such appointment is made, the written consent of cost auditor to such appointment and a certificate from him or it shall be obtained.

The Cost Auditor appointed shall submit certificate that—

(*a*) the individual or the firm, as the case may be, is eligible for appointment and is not disqualified for appointment under the Act, the Cost and Works Accountants Act, 1959 and the Rules or regulations made thereunder.

(*b*) the individual or the firm, as the case may be, satisfies the criteria provided in Sec. 141, so far as may be applicable.

(*c*) the proposed appointment is within the limits laid down by or under the authority of the Act.

(*d*) the list of proceedings against the cost auditor or audit firm or any partner of the audit firm pending with respect to professional matters of conduct, as disclosed in the certificate, is true and correct.

Q.71 Elucidate the provisions relating to submission of Cost Audit Report - To the Board and the Central Government as per the Companies Act, 2013.

Ans. : Submission of Cost Audit Report:

- Sec. 148(5) of Companies Act, 2013 requires the cost auditor to submit the report on the audit of cost records to the Board of Directors of the company. Sec. 148(6) provides that the company shall within **30** days from the date of receipt of a copy of the cost audit report furnish the Central Government with such report along with full information and explanation on every reservation or qualification contained therein.
- Sec. 148(7) of Companies Act, 2013 provides that if, after considering the cost audit report and the information and explanation furnished by the company, the Central Government is of the opinion that any further information or explanation is necessary, it may call for such further information and explanation and the company shall furnish the same within such time as may be specified by that Government.
- Rule 6 of Companies (Cost Records and Audit) Rules, 2014 provides the following in this regard:
  a. Every cost auditor, who conducts an audit of the cost records of a company, shall submit the cost audit report along with his or its reservations or qualifications or observations or suggestions, if any, in Form CRA-3.
  b. Every cost auditor shall forward his report to the Board of Directors of the company within a period of 180 days from the closure of the financial year to which the report relates and the Board of Directors shall consider and examine such report particularly any reservation or qualification contained therein.
  c. Every company covered under these rules shall, within a period of thirty days from the date of receipt of a copy of the cost audit report, furnish the Central Government with such report along with full information and explanation on every reservation or qualification contained therein, in Form CRA-4 along with specified fees.

Q.72 Pearl Ltd. is an exporter of precious and semi-precious stones. The turnover of the company is Rs. 150 crores, out of which Rs. 105 crores are from export business and remaining Rs. 45 crores from domestic sales. Amount received from export business is all in foreign currency. Directors of Pearl Ltd. is of the opinion that cost audit is not applicable to their company as maximum revenue has been generated from export business. Give you opinion. [May 19 - New Syllabus (4 Marks)]

Ans. : Applicability of Cost Audit:

- Provisions relating to cost audit are governed by section 148 of the Companies Act, 2013 read with the Companies (Cost Records and Audit) Rules, 2014.
- Rule 4 of Companies (Cost Records and Audit) Rules, 2014 requires audit of cost records in case of non-regulated sector industries if annual turnover from all products and services in immediately preceding financial year is Rs. 100 Cr. or more and the turnover of individual product or service is Rs. 35 Cr. or more.
- Rule 4 further provides that requirement of cost audit shall not apply to a company whose revenue from exports, in foreign exchange, exceeds 75 per cent of its total revenue.
- In the present case, the turnover of the company is Rs. 150 crores, out of which Rs. 105 crores are from export business and remaining Rs. 45 crores from domestic sales. Amount received from export business is all in foreign currency. Revenue from exports in foreign exchange amounts to 70% of total revenue.

Conclusion: Opinion of the Directors that cost audit is not applicable to their company as maximum revenue has been generated from export business is not valid as total revenue from exports in foreign exchange is less than 50% of total revenue. Hence company is required to get its cost records audited.

Note 1 : It is assumed that figures of revenue are given for immediately preceding financial year.

Note 2 : Suggested Answer of ICAI refer Rule 3 instead of Rule 4. Rule 3 is related to applicability of cost records. Provisions related with Cost Audit are covered in Rule 4.

8.7 - BRANCH AUDIT

Q.73 **As a Statutory Auditor, how would you deal with the following: P Ltd. of whom you are the Statutory Auditor appoints M/s XYZ as Branch Auditors for one of its branches. M/s XYZ conducted the audit of the branch without visiting the branch and instead getting the books at the H.O. M/s XYZ has submitted their Branch Audit Report to you.**

Ans. : Duties of Company Auditor w.r.t. Branches not audited by him:

- As per Sec. 143(8) of the Companies Act, 2013, the accounts of a branch office of a company may be audited either by the company's auditor or by any other person qualified for appointment as auditor of the company.
- The branch auditor shall prepare a report on the accounts of the branch examined by him and send it to the auditor of the company who shall deal with it in his report in the manner as he considers necessary.
- It is however not necessary for branch auditor to visit the branch and conduct the audit only at branch's premises. It is a matter of professional judgment for the branch auditor to decide as to whether he needs to visit the branch.
- As per SA 600 "Using the work of another auditor", the principal auditor is not required to evaluate professional competence because branch auditor happens to be member of ICAI. The statutory auditor is also required to deal with the Branch Auditor's report in the manner, he considers necessary.
- Under the present circumstances the statutory auditor is entitled to rely on the work of branch auditor unless there are special circumstances to make it essential for him to visit the branch and examine the books of account and voucher records.

Conclusion: The statutory auditor is required to deal with branch auditor's report in the manner it considers fit under the circumstances.

Q.74 **X Ltd. has a branch office in Malaysia. The company has appointed Mr. X, who is qualified to audit accounts as per Malaysian laws. Mr. Z, the statutory auditor objects to the same, contending that he alone can audit the branch office accounts. Discuss.**

Ans. : Eligibility criteria for appointment as Branch Auditor

- As per Sec. 143(8) of the Companies Act, 2013, where the branch office is situated in a country outside India, the accounts of the branch office shall be audited either by the company's auditor or by an accountant or by any other person duly qualified to act as an auditor of the accounts of the branch office in accordance with the laws of that country.
- Hence, a company can appoint as auditor of a foreign branch an accountant duly qualified to act as an auditor in accordance with the laws of the foreign country.

Conclusion: Mr. Z contention that he alone can audit the branch office accounts is not valid.

Q.75 **Bhishm Limited decided to appoint Mr. Rajvir, chartered accountant, as the branch auditor for the audit of its Lucknow branch accounts for the year 2019-20. The decision to appoint branch auditor was taken by way of Board Resolution in the meeting of Board of Directors of the company, held in April 2018, subject to shareholders' approval in AGM of the company scheduled to be held in June 2018. Meanwhile, the Principal Auditor of the company raised an objection that the branch auditor cannot be appointed without his consent. Advise, whether the objection raised by company auditor is valid. [RTP-Nov. 19]**

Ans. : Appointment of Branch Auditor:

- As per Sec. 143(8) of the Companies Act, 2013, where the branch office is situated in a country outside India, the accounts of the branch office shall be audited either by the company's auditor or by an accountant or by any other person duly qualified to act as an auditor of the accounts of the branch office in accordance with the laws of that country.

- In the instant case, Bhishm Limited decided to appoint Mr. Rajvir, chartered accountant, as the branch auditor for the audit of its Lucknow branch accounts and the decision to appoint branch auditor was taken by way of Board Resolution in the meeting of Board of Directors of the company subject to shareholders' approval in AGM of the company.

Conclusion: Objection raised by company auditor is not valid as per section 143(8) of the Companies Act, 2013 and the Board has authority to appoint branch auditor but should be approved by shareholders in General Meeting.

Q.76 **M/s. Seeman & Co. had been the company auditor for Amudhan Company Limited for the year 2017-18. The company had three branches located at Chennai, Delhi and Mumbai. The audits of branches-Chennai, Delhi were looked after by the company auditors themselves. The audit of Mumbai branch had been done by another auditor M/s Vasan & Co., a local auditor situated at Mumbai. The branch auditor had completed the audit and had given his report too. After this, but before finalization, the company auditor wanted to visit the Mumbai branch and have access to the inventory records maintained at the branch. The management objects to this on the grounds of the company auditor is transgressing the scope of audit areas agreed. Comment.**

Ans. : Right of Access of Company Auditor for Branch Records:

- As per Sec. 143(8) of the Companies Act, 2013 the audit of the branches can be done by the company auditor himself or by another auditor. Even where, the branch accounts are audited, the company auditor has right to visit the branch if he deems it necessary to do so for the performance of his duties as auditor.
- Company Auditor has also right of access at all times to the books and account and vouchers of the company maintained at the branch office. He can appropriately deal with the report of the branch auditor in framing his main report. He will disclose how he had dealt with the branch audit report.
- In this case, the audits of two branches were done by the company auditor and one branch was done by a separate branch auditor.

Conclusion: Management's objection that the company auditor is transgressing the scope of audit areas agreed, is absolutely, wrong. The right of company auditor in visiting and accessing the records of branch cannot be forfeited. Even where the branch accounts are audited by another local auditor, the company auditor has right to visit the branch and can have access to the books and vouchers of the company maintained at the branch office.

Q.77 **A company has a branch office which recorded a turnover of ₹ 1,90,000 in the financial year 2018-19. No audit of the branch has been carried out. The statutory auditor of the company has made no reference of the above branch in his report. The total turnover of the company is ₹ 10 crores for the year 2018-19. Comment.**

Or

A Ltd. is a Chennai based company. The total turnover of the company is ₹ 10 crores for the year 2017-18. The company has a branch office at an area which was recently affected by flood. The transportation services are not available due to destruction caused by flood. The branch office recorded turnover of ₹ 1,50,000 in the Financial Year 2018-19. No audit of branch has been carried out. The statutory auditor of the company has made no reference of the above branch in his report. Comment.

[May 14 (4 Marks)]

Ans. : Requirement of Branch Audit:

- As per section 143(8) of the Companies Act, 2013 if a company has a branch office, the accounts of that office shall be audited either by the auditor appointed for the company or by any other person qualified for appointment as an auditor of the company, or where the branch office is situated in a country outside India, the accounts of the branch office shall be audited either by the company's auditor or by an accountant or by any other person duly qualified to act as an auditor of the accounts of the branch office in accordance with the laws of that country.
- Therefore, if any office is described by the company as branch office, the company has to get its branch audited by a person specified u/s 143(8).
- In case accounts of the branch has not been audited, company's auditor is required to mention this fact in the audit report and deal appropriately.

Conclusion: Company's auditor is required to state the fact of non-audit of branch office in his report and deal appropriately.

Q.78 **Lakshya Ltd. has a branch office located outside India. Company is in the process of appointment of non-Chartered Accountant as an auditor but otherwise qualified person from country where the branch office is situated. Statutory auditor is of the opinion that non-Chartered Accountant cannot be appointed as branch auditor. Comment.**

You are also required to discuss the applicability of SA 600 using the work of another auditor by the head office auditor in regard to branch located outside India, if non-Chartered Accountant is appointed.

Ans. : Eligibility criteria for appointment as Branch Auditor

- As per Sec. 143(8) of the Companies Act, 2013, where the branch office is situated in a country outside India, the accounts of the branch office shall be audited either by the company's auditor or by an accountant or by any other person duly qualified to act as an auditor of the accounts of the branch office in accordance with the laws of that country.
- Hence, a company can appoint as auditor of a foreign branch an accountant duly qualified to act as an auditor in accordance with the laws of the foreign country.

Conclusion: Contention of statutory auditor that non-Chartered Accountant cannot be appointed as auditor is not valid.

Applicability of SA 600:

SA 600 "Using the work of another Auditor" deals with the principal auditor's responsibility in relation to his use of the work of the other auditor. SA 600 provides the following:

- When planning to use the work of another auditor, the principal auditor should consider the professional competence of the other auditor in the context of specific assignment if the other auditor is not a member of the ICAI.
- The principal auditor should perform procedures to obtain sufficient appropriate audit evidence, that the work of the other auditor is adequate for the principal auditor's purposes, in the context of the specific assignment.
- The principal auditor should consider the significant findings of the other auditor.
- When the principal auditor has to base his opinion on the financial information of the entity as a whole relying upon the statements and reports of the other auditors, his report should state clearly the division of responsibility for the financial information of the entity by indicating the extent to which the financial information of components audited by the other auditors have been included in the financial information of the entity, *e.g.*, the number of divisions/branches/subsidiaries or other components audited by other auditors.

8.8 - GUIDANCE NOTE ON INTERNAL FINANCIAL CONTROL OVER FINANCIAL REPORTING

Q.79 **Explain the terms:**

(*i*) 'Internal Financial Control' and

(*ii*) 'Internal Financial Control' over 'Financial Reporting'. **[Nov. 18-Old Syllabus (6 Marks)]**

Answer: Internal Financial Control and Internal Financial Control over Financial Reporting:

(*i*) Internal Financial Control:

Explanation to Sec. 134(5) of Companies Act, 2013 defines the term Internal Financial Controls as the policies and procedures adopted by the company for ensuring:

- Orderly and efficient conduct of its business, including adherence to Company's policies,
- Safeguarding of its assets,
- Prevention and detection of frauds and errors,
- Accuracy and completeness of the accounting records, and
- Timely preparation of reliable financial information.

(*ii*) Internal Financial Control over Financial reporting:

Guidance Note on Internal Financial Control over Financial Reporting provides the guidance as to the concept of Internal financial control over financial reporting. Accordingly,

- Internal Financial Control over Financial Reporting is a Process designed to provide reasonable assurance regarding the reliability of financial reporting and the preparation of financial statements for external purposes in accordance with generally accepted accounting principles.

- A Company's internal financial control over financial reporting includes those policies and procedures which pertain to the maintenance of the records that, in reasonable detail, accurately and fairly reflect the transactions and dispositions of the assets of the company.
- It provides reasonable assurance that transactions are recorded as necessary to permit preparation of financial statement in accordance with generally accepted accounting principles, and those receipts and expenditures of the company are being made only in accordance with authorizations of management and director of the company.
- It provides reasonable assurance regarding prevention or timely detection of unauthorized acquisition, use or disposition of the company's assets that could have a material effects of the financial statement.

8.9 - MISCELLANEOUS

Q.80 X Ltd. issued 10,000 shares of face value of ₹ 10 each at a premium of ₹ 450 each in May, 2018. The company received the stated minimum amount in the prospectus and transferred a sum equal to the aggregate amount of the premium received on shares (i.e. ₹ 45 lakhs) to the 'Securities Premium Account'. Unfortunately, in the month of July, the godown of the company caught fire and stock worth ₹ 40 lakhs burnt to ashes. Now, the management desires to adjust the loss due to fire against the said premium account. Comment.

Or

X Ltd. is a sick company and has accumulated losses of ₹ 10 crores. The company has ₹ 12 crores in its share Premium Account. The Management desires to adjust the accumulated losses against the share premium balance. Advise the company giving your reasons.

Ans. : Application of Share Premium Account:

- As per Section 52 of the Companies Act, 2013, where a company issues shares at a premium, whether for cash or otherwise, a sum equal to the aggregate amount of the premium received on those shares shall be transferred to an account called "Securities Premium Account".
- The securities premium account may be applied by the company
  1. towards the issue of unissued shares of the company to the members of the company as fully paid bonus shares;
  2. in writing off the preliminary expenses of the company;
  3. in writing off the expenses of, or the commission paid or discount allowed on, any issue of shares or debentures of the company;
  4. in providing for the premium payable on the redemption of any redeemable preference shares or of any debentures of the company; or
  5. for the purchase of its own shares or other securities under section 68.
- In view of these provisions of the Companies Act, 2013, it is not permitted to adjust its losses against the securities premium account.

Conclusion: X Ltd. is not permitted to adjust its loss against the securities premium account by virtue of provisions of Section 52 of Companies Act, 2013.

Q.81 Mr. X is a whole-time director of Manthan Ltd. who has a very good relation with the Director (Operations) of the company. Consequently, he entered into a purchase contract for supply of goods of ₹ 5,00,000 with the company without obtaining prior consent of the Board. What is the responsibility of the auditor in relation to the Companies Act, 2013?

Ans. : Auditor's Responsibility in relation to Director's contract with companies:

- As per Section 188 of the Companies Act, 2013, no company shall enter into any contract or arrangement with a related party with respect to sale, purchase or supply of any goods or materials, except with the consent of the Board of Directors given by a resolution at a Board Meeting.
- First proviso to Sec. 188 provides that in the case of a company having specified paid-up share capital, or transactions exceeding prescribed sum, no contract or arrangement shall be entered into except with the prior approval of the company by a resolution.
- Third proviso to Sec. 188 provides that Sec. 188 is not applicable to any transactions entered into by the company in ordinary course of business other than transactions which are not on an arm's length price.

- Sec. 189 of Companies Act, 2013 requires that particulars of such contracts or arrangements shall be maintained in one or more registers.
- Section 184 of the Companies Act, 2013 requires every director who is in any way whether directly or indirectly interested in a contract or proposed contract shall disclose the nature of his interest at the meeting of the Board in which such contract is discussed and shall not participate in such meeting.
- In the present case one of the director of the company has entered into a contract for supply of goods worth ₹ 5,00,000 without obtaining consent of the Board. Auditor is required to determine whether the transactions is in ordinary course of business or entered on arm's length price.

Conclusion: Auditor is required to ensure compliance of Sections 184, 188 & 189 of Companies Act, 2013. In case of any violation, auditor is required to state the fact in his audit report accordingly.

Q.82 Mr. X, Director of ABC Ltd. made a purchase contract for ₹ 10,00,000 with the company. Comment. [Nov. 10 (5 Marks)]

Ans. : Auditor's duties in case of director's contract with the company:

- Section 184 of the Companies Act, 2013 requires every director who is in any way whether directly or indirectly interested in a contract or proposed contract shall disclose the nature of his interest at the meeting of the Board in which such contract is discussed and shall not participate in such meeting.
- As per Section 188 of the Companies Act, 2013, no company shall enter into any contract or arrangement with a related party with respect to sale, purchase or supply of any goods or materials, except with the consent of the Board of Directors given by a resolution at a Board Meeting.
- First proviso to Sec. 188 provides that in the case of a company having specified paid-up share capital, or transactions exceeding prescribed sum, no contract or arrangement shall be entered into except with the prior approval of the company by a resolution.
- Third proviso to Sec. 188 provides that Sec. 188 is not applicable to any transactions entered into by the company in ordinary course of business other than transactions which are not on an arm's length price.
- Sec. 189 of Companies Act, 2013 requires that particulars of such contracts or arrangements shall be maintained in one or more registers.
- In the present case one of the director of the company has entered into a purchase contract worth ₹ 10,00,000 with the company. Auditor is required to determine whether the transactions is in ordinary course of business or entered on arm's length price.

Conclusion: Auditor is required to ensure compliance of Sections 184, 188 & 189 of Companies Act, 2013. In case of any violation, auditor is required to state the fact in his audit report accordingly.

Q.83 M/s IT Limited has prepared the financial statements for the year 2018-19 and mentioned in the significant accounting policies that depreciation on tangible fixed assets is provided on the straight-line method over the useful lives of the assets as estimated by the management. The company has ignored the useful lives of assets mentioned in Schedule II of the Companies Act, 2013. As statutory auditor of the company how would you deal with this? [Nov. 15 (4 Marks)]

Ans. : Consideration of useful lives estimated by management:

- Schedule II to the Companies Act, 2013 defines the useful life of an asset is the period over which an asset is expected to be available for use by an entity or the number of production or similar units expected to be obtained from the asset by the entity.
- The useful life of an asset shall not be longer that the useful life specified in the Part C of Schedule II. If, however where a company uses a different useful life justification for the difference shall be disclosed in the financial statement with justification supported by technical device.
- In the present case, auditor is required to examine the appropriateness of disclosures made in the financial statements with respect to difference in estimated useful life. If appropriate not given in the financial statements, auditor need to qualify his report stating the appropriate facts.

Conclusion: Company may use different useful lives, but disclosure is required in financial statements with justification supported by technical advice.

"ICAI Examiner Comments"

Many examinees have not referred to Section 129 of the Companies Act, 2013. They also failed to mention that if the justification has not been disclosed by the management for consideration of different useful life, then the auditor should qualify his report accordingly. Some examinees were not aware about Schedule II of the Companies Act, 2013.

Q.84 **As an auditor of DEF Ltd., you notice certain differences in the figures between the books of account and the 'Offer document' for the proposed issue of securities. The company explains that the same is due to certain adjustments as per the SEBI (Disclosure and Investor Protection) Guidelines. What are such disclosures and adjustments to be incorporated in the financial statements included in the 'Offer document'? [Nov. 17 (6 Marks)]**

Ans. : Disclosures and Adjustments to be incorporated in the financial statements included in the Offer Document:

(A) Disclosures:

1. Principal terms of loan and assets charged as security: Brief terms and conditions of the term loans including re-schedulement, prepayment, penalty, default, etc.
2. Age-wise analysis of sundry debtors.
3. Aggregate book value of quoted investments as well as aggregate market value of quoted investments.
4. All significant accounting policies and standards followed in the preparation of the financial statements
5. Auditors' qualifications.

(B) Adjustments:

Statements of Assets and Liabilities and Profit and Loss or any other financial information shall be incorporated after making the following adjustments, wherever quantification is possible:

1. Adjustments/rectification for all incorrect accounting practices or failures to make provisions or other adjustments which resulted in audit qualifications.
2. Material amounts relating to adjustments for previous years shall be identified and adjusted in arriving at the profits of the years to which they relate irrespective of the year in which the event triggering the profit or loss occurred.
3. Where there has been a change in accounting policy, the profits or losses of the earlier years (required to be shown in the offer document) and of the year in which the change in the accounting policy has taken place shall be recomputed to reflect what the profits or losses of those years would have been if a uniform accounting policy was followed in each of these years.
4. If an incorrect accounting policy is followed, the re-computation of the financial statements shall be in accordance with correct accounting policies.
5. Statement of profit or loss shall disclose the profit or the loss arrived at before considering extraordinary items and after considering the profit or loss from extraordinary items.
6. The statement of assets and liabilities shall be prepared after deducting the balance outstanding on revaluation reserve account from both fixed assets and reserves and the net worth arrived at after such deductions.

Note: SEBI (DIP) Guidelines replaces by SEBI (ICDR) Regulations in the year 2009. Answer is given on the basis of SEBI (ICDR) Regulations, 2009

"ICAI Examiner Comments"

Majority of the examinees have not attempted this question and those who attempted were not aware of the topic. Examinees were not aware of the adjustments to be incorporated in the Financial Statements included in the Offer Document as per SEBI Guidelines. Few examinees have misunderstood the question and answered in the context of SAE 3420.

Q.85 **Beneath Minerals Limited is a Public-Sector company engaged in extraction of minerals from land. It has to pump out water in the first layer of the soil if the minerals are to be excavated. The company pumps out water and diverts the water through a water course constructed by it to nearby villages and the water is allowed to be used by villagers for drinking purposes. The cost of construction of water course amounted to 5.25 crores and the company had disclosed this amount as CSR expenses in the statement of profit and loss. Comment. [May 18 - New Syllabus (5 Marks)]**

Ans : Treatment of expenses in normal course of business as CSR Expense:

- As per Section 135 of Companies Act, 2013, the Board of directors of every company referred to in Sec. 135(1), sub-section (1), shall ensure that the company spends, in every financial year, at least two per cent of the average net profits of the company made during the three immediately preceding financial years, in pursuance of its Corporate Social Responsibility Policy.
- For this purpose, Schedule VII of Companies Act, 2013 prescribes the activities which may be included in CSR Activities. Ministry of Corporate Affairs also time to time, through various notifications provide clarification as to what kind of expenses will be covered in CSR activities.
- However, any expense which is incurred by a company in the normal course of its business activities cannot be considered as CSR Expense.
- In the present case, company pump out the water from the soil and construct a water course so as to divert the water to nearby villages and water is being used by villagers for drinking purposes. This kind of expenditure cannot be treated as expenditure incurred for CSR as the expense is being incurred as incidental to its business activities.

Conclusion: Though expenditure incurred in arranging drinking facilities qualifies as CSR expense, but any expenditure incurred in the normal course of business activity is not classified as CSR Expense. In the present case, pumping out the water is an essential part of business activity and for its disposal, a water course is being constructed. So, expenditure cannot be classified as CSR Expense and hence auditor should state the fact in the report and qualify the report.

Note: Alternative answer is possible with different assumptions.

9 CHAPTER

AUDIT REPORTS

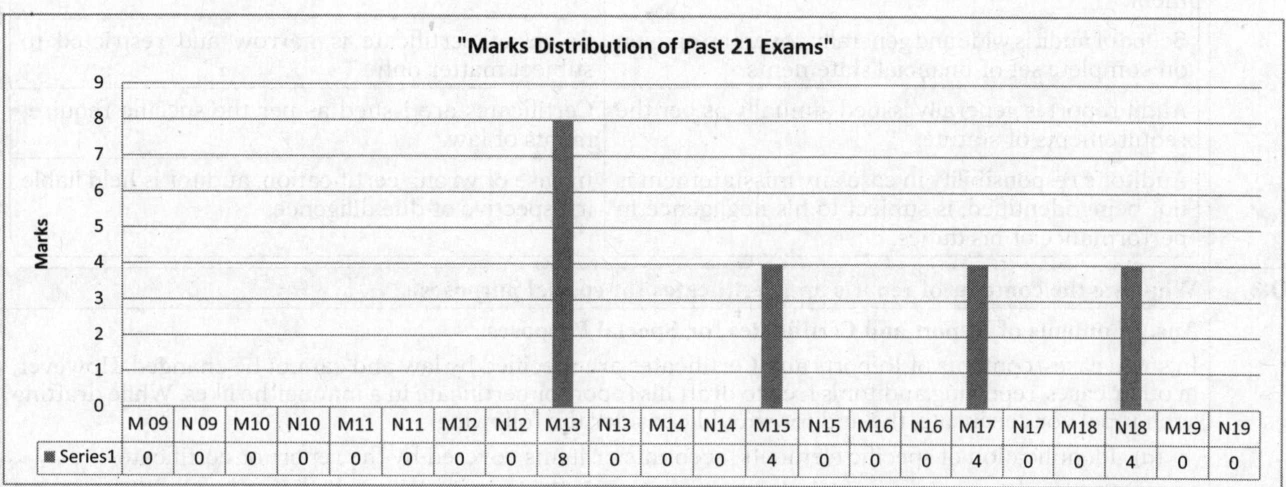

9.1 - AUDIT REPORTS

Q.1 Distinguish between Notes on Accounts and Qualifications.

Ans. : Notes on Accounts vs. Qualifications

Notes on Accounts	Qualifications
Notes represents management's stand on a matter and assessment on all matters involving difference of opinion between them and the auditors.	Qualification represents auditor disagreement on the matters with Management.
Notes of a qualificatory nature appear in the accounts and forms part of Financial Statements.	Qualifications are stated by auditor in the auditor's report
Management may insist upon the auditor for not modifying his audit opinion considering the management has disclosed full facts and assessment of the matter through notes on the F.S.	Auditor needs to exercise his professional judgment to determine whether the disclosures in the notes alone would suffice or a qualification is needed in audit report.
Notes on accounts includes information which is necessary to make the financial statements understandable by the users.	Qualification must be expressed by the Auditor in a clear and unambiguous manner.

9.2 - REPORT VS. CERTIFICATE

Q.2 Write a short note on Certificate for Special Purpose vs. Audit Report.

Or

Differentiate between audit report and audit certificate. **[May 17 (4 Marks)]**

Ans. : Report and Certificate:

Audit Report: An audit report is a formal statement usually made after an enquiry, examination or review of specified matters under report and includes the reporting auditor's opinion thereon.

While issuing an audit report, auditor is responsible to ensure that his opinion is in due accordance with facts, and that it is arrived at by the application of due care and skill.

Meaning of Certificate: A certificate is a written confirmation of the accuracy of the facts stated therein and does not involve any estimate or opinion. Such certificates are often required by Government authorities in support of statements or other information prepared by an enterprise. Such certificates represent that the auditor has verified certain figures and is satisfied about their accuracy.

Report	Certificate
It is an expression of opinion on true and fair view of financial statements and books of account.	It is a confirmation of correctness and accuracy of subject matter for which certificate is being issued.
Report is based on practitioner professional judgment.	Certificate is based on actual facts and figures.
Scope of audit is wide and generally covers an opinion on complete set of financial statements.	Scope of certificate is narrow and restricted to subject matter only.
Audit report is generally issued annually as per the requirements of statute.	Certificates are issued as per the specific requirements of law.
Auditor's responsibility in case any misstatement is not being identified, is subject to his negligence in performance of his duties.	In case of wrong certification, auditor is held liable irrespective of due diligence.

Q.3 What are the contents of reports and certificates for special purposes.

Ans. : Contents of Report and Certificates for Special Purposes:

In some cases, contents of Reports and Certificates are specified by law and cannot be changed. However, in other cases, reporting auditor is free to draft his report or certificate in a manner he likes. While drafting such report or certificate, the auditor should consider the following:

(*a*) Identification of specific elements, accounts or items covered by the report or certificate.

(*b*) Stating the manner in which the audit was conducted, e.g., by the application of generally accepted auditing practices, or any other specific tests.

(*c*) limitation on scope, if any, should be clearly mentioned.

(*d*) Fundamental Assumptions on which the special purpose statement is based should be clearly indicated.

(*e*) Information and explanations obtained during the course of work should be included.

(*f*) The title of the report or certificate should clearly indicate its nature.

(*g*) Extent to which reliance has been placed on the report of other auditor, who have carried out audit of general purpose financial statements.

(*h*) Where a report requires the interpretation of statute, the reporting auditor should clearly indicate the fact that he is merely expressing his opinion in the matter.

(*i*) An audit report or certificate should ordinarily be a self-contained document and should not confine itself to a mere reference to another report or certificate.

(*j*) Extent of responsibility assumed by the reporting auditor should be clearly indicated.

Q.4 Draft an audit report under following circumstances:

(*i*) Under the Payment of Bonus Act, 1965, a 'report' on the computation of bonus payables.

(*ii*) Auditor's Report in accordance with Regulation 55 of the SEBI (Mutual Fund) Regulations, 1996.

[May 15 (4 Marks)]

Ans. : Draft Audit Report Under the Payment of Bonus Act, 1965, a 'report' on the computation of bonus payables.

"We have reviewed the figures in the above computation in comparison with the books and records produced to us, the audit of which has already been completed by us and report that subject to the notes given on face of the computation in our opinion, and to the best of our knowledge and belief and according to the information and explanation given to us, the above computation is in due accordance therewith and has been made on a basis reasonably consistent with the provisions of the Payment of Bonus Act, 1965."

Place: For AB & Co.

Date: Chartered Accountants

Auditor's Report in accordance with Regulation 55 of the SEBI (Mutual Fund) Regulations, 1996.

All Mutual funds shall be required to get their accounts audited in terms of a provision to that effect in their trust deeds. The Auditor's Report shall form a part of the Annual Report.

The auditor shall state whether:

1. He has obtained all information and explanations which, to the best of his knowledge and belief, were necessary for the purpose of his audit.
2. The Balance Sheet and the Revenue Account are in agreement with the books of account of the fund.

The auditor shall give his opinion as to whether:

1. The Balance Sheet gives a true and fair view of the scheme wise state of affairs of the fund as at the balance sheet date, and
2. The Revenue Account gives a true and fair view of the scheme wise surplus/deficit of the fund for the year/period ended at the balance sheet date.

"ICAI Examiner Comments"

Candidates were lacking knowledge in drafting of Auditor's Report in accordance with Regulation 54 of the SEBI (Mutual Fund) Regulations, 1993.

9.3 - MISCELLANEOUS

Q.5 Distinguish: Reasonable assurance engagement from limited assurance engagement.

[May 18 – New Syllabus (4 Marks)]

Or

List out the key differences between "Reasonable Assurance" and "Limited Assurance" engagements.

[Nov. 18-Old Syllabus (4 Marks)]

Ans. : Limited and Reasonable Assurance:

- Guidance Note on Reports or certificates for special purpose defines the term assurance engagement as "An engagement in which a practitioner aims to obtain sufficient appropriate evidence in order to express an opinion/conclusion, designed to enhance the degree of confidence of the intended users, other than the responsible party about the subject matter information (that is, the outcome of the measurement or evaluation of an underlying subject matter against criteria)".
- Each assurance engagement is classified on two dimensions: either a reasonable assurance engagement or a limited assurance engagement.
- **Reasonable assurance engagement:** An assurance engagement in which the practitioner reduces engagement risk to an acceptably low level in the circumstances of the engagement, as the basis for the practitioner's opinion. The practitioner's opinion is expressed in a form that conveys the practitioner's opinion on the outcome of the measurement or evaluation of the underlying subject matter against the criteria.
- **Limited assurance engagement:** An assurance engagement in which the practitioner reduces engagement risk to a level that is acceptable in the circumstances of the engagement but where that risk is greater than for a reasonable assurance engagement, as the basis for expressing a conclusion in a form that conveys whether, based on the procedures performed and evidence obtained, a matter(s) has(have) come to the practitioner's attention to cause the practitioner to believe that the subject matter information is materially misstated.
- The NTE of procedures performed in a limited assurance engagement is limited compared with that necessary in a reasonable assurance engagement but is planned to obtain a level of assurance that is, in the practitioner's professional judgment, meaningful.

Q.6 A professional accountant is often required to give certificates or report for special purposes required by various authorities and statute and he needs to take careful evaluation of such engagement. However, issuing such special purpose certificates or reports has some inherent limitations which could limit his review and evaluation. Enumerate some of the limitations associated with such special purpose report or certificates. **[May 19-New Syllabus (4 Marks)]**

Ans. : Limitations associated with such special purpose report or certificates:

Whenever a practitioner is required to give a "certificate" or a "report" for special purpose, the practitioner needs to undertake a careful evaluation of the scope of the engagement, i.e., whether the practitioner would be able to provide reasonable assurance or limited assurance on the subject matter. A practitioner is expected to provide either a reasonable assurance or a limited assurance, since it is difficult to reduce engagement risk to zero due to inherent limitations.

The inherent limitations could arise from:

(*a*) the nature of financial reporting;

(*b*) the use of selective testing;

(*c*) the inherent limitations of internal controls;

(*d*) the fact that much of the evidence available to the practitioner is persuasive rather than conclusive;

(*e*) the nature of procedures to be performed in a specific situation;

(*f*) the use of professional judgment in gathering and evaluating evidence and forming conclusions based on that evidence;

(*g*) in some cases, the characteristics of the underlying subject matter when evaluated or measured against the criteria; and

(*h*) the need for the engagement to be conducted within a reasonable period of time and at a reasonable cost.

Q.7 XYZ Ltd. has significant operations in a foreign country. Due to civil and political unrest in that country physical verification of inventory and fixed assets could not carried out and you are not in a position to obtain audit evidence through other audit procedures also. The value of fixed assets and inventory forms part of 80% of the asset value of the company. As the auditor of XYZ Ltd. what factors do you consider in your reporting responsibility. Also draft a suitable report that will be incorporated in the main audit report (Reporting under CARO need not be considered). [May 13 (8 Marks)]

Ans. : Factors to be considered in Audit reporting;

Auditor is required to consider the following factors:

1. Inventories and the Fixed Assets constitute 80% of the assets and hence having a pervasive effect.
2. Auditor is not being able to attend physical verification of the inventories and fixed assets due to civil and political unrest in the foreign country, where the inventory and fixed assets are located.
3. Auditor failed to obtain proper and sufficient audit evidence, even by alternative audit procedures.

Relevant Draft to be incorporated in the main audit report:

"Our responsibility is to express an opinion on these financial statements based on our audit in accordance with the Standards on Auditing issued by the Institute of Chartered Accountants of India. Because of the matters described in the Basis for Disclaimer of Opinion paragraph, however, we were not able to obtain sufficient appropriate audit evidence to provide a basis for an audit opinion.

Basis for Disclaimer of Opinion

We were appointed as auditors of the Company and we report that we could not observe the counting of physical inventories and physical verification of fixed assets due to civil and political unrest in foreign country where the company has significant operation. We were also unable to satisfy ourselves by alternative means concerning the inventory quantities and fixed assets of the company held at March 31st 20XX, which are stated in the Balance Sheet at ₹ XXX and ₹ XXX, respectively.

Disclaimer of Opinion

Because of the significance of the matters described in the Basis for Disclaimer of Opinion paragraph, we have not been able to obtain sufficient appropriate audit evidence to provide a basis for an audit opinion. Accordingly, we do not express an opinion on the financial statements.

Report on Other Legal and Regulatory Requirements

As required by section 143(3) of the Companies Act, 2013, we report that:

As described in the Basis for Disclaimer of Opinion paragraph, we were unable to obtain all the information and explanations which to the best of our knowledge and belief were necessary for the purpose of our audit.

CARO, 2016

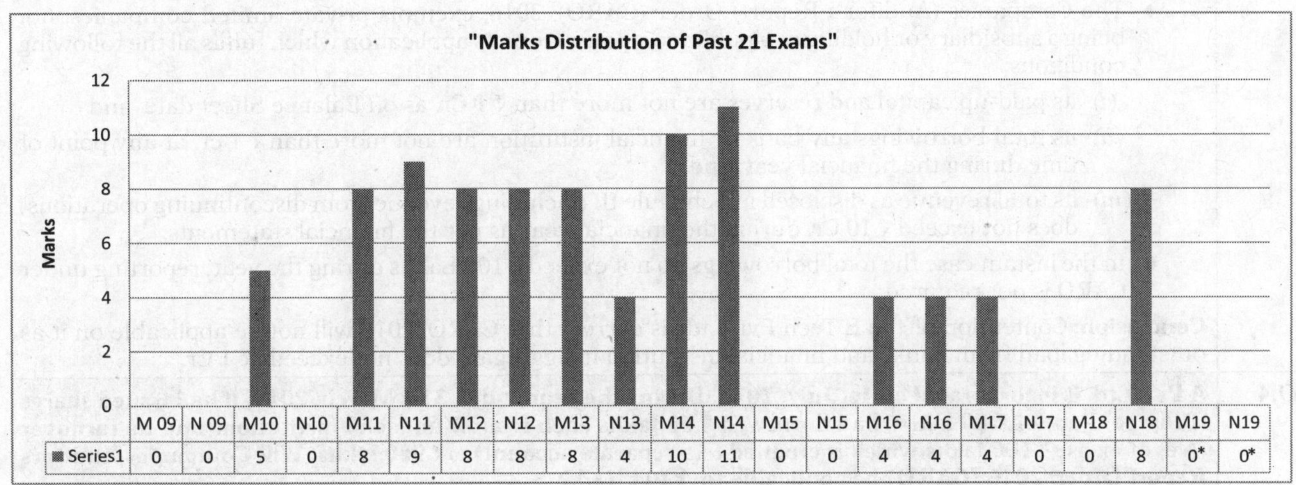

*Only Subjective Questions.

10.1 - APPLICABILITY OF CARO, 2016

Q.1 ABC Pvt. Ltd. is a holding company of XYZ Ltd. Whether CARO is applicable to ABC Pvt. Ltd.?

Ans. : Applicability of CARO over a Private company (holding of public company):

- The Companies (Auditor's Report) Order, 2016, exempts private limited companies, not being a subsidiary or holding of a public company, from its application which fulfils all the following conditions:
  - (*i*) its paid-up capital and reserves are not more than ₹ 1 Cr. as on Balance Sheet date, and
  - (*ii*) its total borrowings any bank or financial institution are not more than ₹ 1 cr. at any point of time during the financial year; and
  - (*iii*) its total revenue as disclosed in Schedule III (including revenue from discontinuing operations) does not exceed ₹ 10 Cr. during the financial year as per the financial statements.
- In the present case, ABC Pvt. Ltd. is a holding company of XYZ Ltd., hence reporting under CARO is required.

Conclusion: CARO is applicable.

Q.2 Astha Pvt. Ltd. has fully paid capital of ₹ 140 lakh. During the year, the company had borrowed ₹ 15 lakh each from a bank and a financial institution independently. It has the turnover (Net of excise ₹ 50 lakh which is credited to a separate account) of ₹ 475 lakh. Will Companies (Auditor's Report) Order, 2016 be applicable to Astha Pvt. Ltd.?

Ans. : Applicability of CARO over a Private Company:

- The Companies (Auditor's Report) Order, 2016, exempts private limited companies, not being a subsidiary or holding of a public company, from its application which fulfils all the following conditions:
  - (*i*) its paid-up capital and reserves are not more than ₹ 1 Cr. as on Balance Sheet date, and
  - (*ii*) its total borrowings any bank or financial institution are not more than ₹ 1 cr. at any point of time during the financial year; and

(*iii*) its total revenue as disclosed in Schedule III (including revenue from discontinuing operations) does not exceed ₹ 10 Cr. during the financial year as per the financial statements.

- In the present case, paid-up capital of the company exceeds ₹ 1 Cr., hence reporting under CARO is required.

Conclusion: CARO is applicable over the company.

Q.3 **E-Tech Pvt. Ltd., which has an aggregate outstanding loan of ₹ 20 lakhs from Banks and ₹ 30 lakhs from Financial Institutions, defaulted in repayment thereof to the extent of 50%. The company holds that it being a private limited company, the Companies (Auditor's Report) Order, 2016 is not applicable.**

You are required to state the list of companies to which CARO is not applicable and state how would you deal with the given situation as an auditor of the company.

Ans. : Applicability of CARO, 2016:

- The Companies (Auditor's Report) Order (CARO), 2016, exempts private limited companies, not being a subsidiary or holding of a public company, from its application which fulfils all the following conditions:

  (*i*) its paid-up capital and reserves are not more than ₹ 1 Cr. as on Balance Sheet date, and

  (*ii*) its total borrowings any bank or financial institution are not more than ₹ 1 cr. at any point of time during the financial year; and

  (*iii*) its total revenue as disclosed in Schedule III (including revenue from discontinuing operations) does not exceed ₹ 10 Cr. during the financial year as per the financial statements.

- In the instant case the total borrowings do not exceed ₹ 100 Lakhs during the year, reporting under CARO is not required.

Conclusion: Contention of the E Tech Pvt. Ltd., is correct that CARO, 2016 will not be applicable on it as outstanding loan from banks and financial institution in aggregate does not exceeds ₹ 1 Cr.

Q.4 **A Pvt. Ltd. is incorporated on 1st July, 2018. During the year ended 31st March, 2019, it had issued shares (fully paid up) of ₹ 80 lakhs, had borrowed ₹ 60 lakhs each from 2 financial institutions and its turnover (Net of excise ₹ 100 lakhs which is credited to a separate account) is ₹ 950 lakhs. Will Companies Auditors Report Order, 2016 (CARO) be applicable to A Pvt. Ltd.?**

Ans. : Applicability of CARO, 2016:

- The Companies (Auditor's Report) Order (CARO), 2016, exempts private limited companies, not being a subsidiary or holding of a public company, from its application which fulfils all the following conditions:

  (*i*) its paid-up capital and reserves are not more than ₹ 1 Cr. as on Balance Sheet date, and

  (*ii*) its total borrowings any bank or financial institution are not more than ₹ 1 cr. at any point of time during the financial year; and

  (*iii*) its total revenue as disclosed in Schedule III (including revenue from discontinuing operations) does not exceed ₹ 10 Cr. during the financial year as per the financial statements.

- In the present case paid-up capital is ₹ 80 lakhs, turnover is less than ₹ 10 Crores but its borrowings from banks and financial institution is ₹ 120 Lakhs.
- While computing revenue, excise duty will not be considered as per the requirements of Schedule III.
- While computing borrowings from banks and financial statements, loans are to be taken cumulatively not individually.

Conclusion: Contention of the A Pvt. Ltd. is not correct as total borrowings exceeds ₹ 1 Cr., hence reporting under CARO, 2016 will be required.

Q.5 **As an auditor, how would you deal with the following: L Private Ltd., which has outstanding loan of more than ₹ 100 lakhs from Financial Institution defaulted in repayment thereof to the extent of 50%. The company holds that it being a private limited company, the Companies Auditors Report Order (CARO) is not applicable.**

Ans. : Applicability of CARO, 2016:

- The Companies (Auditor's Report) Order (CARO), 2016, exempts private limited companies, not being a subsidiary or holding of a public company, from its application which fulfils all the following conditions:

  (*i*) its paid-up capital and reserves are not more than ₹ 1 Cr. as on Balance Sheet date, and

  (*ii*) its total borrowings any bank or financial institution are not more than ₹ 1 cr. at any point of time during the financial year; and (*iii*) its total revenue as disclosed in Schedule III (including revenue from discontinuing operations) does not exceed ₹ 10 Cr. during the financial year as per the financial statements.

- In the instant case the total borrowings exceed ₹ 100 Lakhs out of which company defaults in re-payment to the extent of 50%. As borrowings exceeds ₹ 1 Cr. during the year, reporting under CARO is required.
- Para 3 (viii) of CARO, 2016 requires the auditor to comment whether the company has defaulted in repayment of loans or borrowings to a financial institution, bank, government or debenture holders? If yes, the period and amount of default to be reported.

Conclusion: Contention of L Pvt. Ltd. is not correct as borrowings from financial institution exceeds ₹ 1 Cr., and auditor is required to report the period and amount of default in repayment of dues under Para 3(viii) of CARO, 2016.

Q.6 **T Pvt. Ltd.'s paid up Capital & Reserves are less than ₹ 1 cr. and it has no outstanding loan exceeding ₹ 1 Cr. from any bank or financial institution. Its sales are ₹ 12 crores before deducting Trade discount ₹ 20 lakhs and Sales returns ₹ 1.90 Cr. The services rendered by the company amounted to ₹ 20 lakhs. The company contends that reporting under Companies Auditor's Reports Order (CARO) is not applicable. Discuss.**

Ans. : Applicability of CARO, 2016:

- The Companies (Auditor's Report) Order (CARO), 2016, exempts private limited companies, not being a subsidiary or holding of a public company, from its application which fulfils all the following conditions:

  (*i*) its paid-up capital and reserves are not more than ₹ 1 Cr. as on Balance Sheet date, and

  (*ii*) its total borrowings any bank or financial institution are not more than ₹ 1 cr. at any point of time during the financial year; and

  (*iii*) its total revenue as disclosed in Schedule III (including revenue from discontinuing operations) does not exceed ₹ 10 Cr. during the financial year as per the financial statements.
- As per Schedule III, revenue from operations shall consists of revenue from sale of products, sale of services, and other operating revenues.
- While computing total revenue, trade discount as well as sales returns are required to be deducted.
- In the present case the turnover of the company including value of service rendered after deducting trade discount and sales returns amounts to ₹ 10.10 crores (*i.e.* 12 - 0.20 - 1.90 + 0.20 crore).

Conclusion: Contention of the company that CARO is not applicable is not correct, as Total Revenue exceeds ₹ 10 Cr.

Q.7 **A Private limited company reports the following position as on 31st March 2019:**

Paid-up capital	**60 Lacs**
Revaluation reserves	**20 Lacs**
Capital reserves	**22 Lacs**
P & L A/c (Dr. Balance)	**4 Lacs**

The management of the company contends that CARO, 2016 is not applicable to it.

Ans. : Applicability of CARO, 2016:

- The Companies (Auditor's Report) Order (CARO), 2016, exempts private limited companies, not being a subsidiary or holding of a public company, from its application which fulfils all the following conditions:

  (*i*) its paid-up capital and reserves are not more than ₹ 1 Cr. as on Balance Sheet date, and

  (*ii*) its total borrowings any bank or financial institution are not more than ₹ 1 cr. at any point of time during the financial year; and

  (*iii*) its total revenue as disclosed in Schedule III (including revenue from discontinuing operations) does not exceed ₹ 10 Cr. during the financial year as per the financial statements.
- As per Guidance Note on CARO, 2016 issued by ICAI, while computing paid-up capital and reserves, capital reserves, revenue reserves, revaluation reserves and credit balance of Profit and loss account are to be considered in aggregate as reduced by debit balance in the profit and loss account, if any.
- In the present case, paid-up capital and reserves after deducting debit balance of Profit & Loss Account amounts to ₹ 98 Lacs (60 + 20 + 22 - 4).

Conclusion: CARO is not applicable as paid-up capital and reserves does not exceed ₹ 1 Cr. (assuming that other conditions as to borrowings and revenue also satisfied).

Q.8 **Under CARO 2016, how as a statutory auditor would you comment on the following: X Pvt. Ltd. is a subsidiary of a listed entity. The management of the company believes that since X Pvt. Ltd. is a private company and satisfies all conditions under CARO 2016, reporting under CARO is not applicable.**

Ans. : Applicability of CARO, 2016:

- The Companies (Auditor's Report) Order (CARO), 2016, applies to all companies including foreign companies except certain companies which are specifically exempted.
- CARO, 2016 exempts private limited companies not being a subsidiary or holding of a public company, from its application which fulfils certain conditions.
- In the present case M/s X Pvt. Ltd. is a subsidiary of a listed entity and its management believes that the company satisfies all conditions as required under CARO, 2016.

Conclusion: Exemption from CARO is not available to a private company which is a subsidiary of a public company. Hence contention of the management that company being a private limited company and satisfies all the conditions required for exemption, is not correct.

Q.9 **H Private Ltd. (not a small company) had taken overdrafts from two banks with a limit of ₹ 40 lacs each against the security of fixed deposit it had with those banks and an unsecured overdraft from a financial institution of ₹ 36 lacs. The said loans were outstanding as at 31st March 2019. The paid-up capital and reserves of the company as at that date was ₹ 80 lacs and its revenue during the financial year ended on 31st March, 2019 was ₹ 6 crores. The management of the company is of the opinion that CARO, 2016 is not applicable to it because turnover and paid-up capital were within the limits prescribed and loans taken against the fixed deposits cannot be considered. The company further contended that loan limit is to be reckoned per bank or financial institution and not cumulatively. Comment.** **[May 13 (4 Marks)]**

Ans. : Applicability of CARO, 2016:

- The Companies (Auditor's Report) Order (CARO), 2016, exempts private limited companies, not being a subsidiary or holding of a public company, from its application which fulfils all the following conditions:
  - (*i*) its paid-up capital and reserves are not more than ₹ 1 Cr. as on Balance Sheet date, and
  - (*ii*) its total borrowings any bank or financial institution are not more than ₹ 1 cr. at any point of time during the financial year; and
  - (*iii*) its total revenue as disclosed in Schedule III (including revenue from discontinuing operations) does not exceed ₹ 10 Cr. during the financial year as per the financial statements.
- In the present case paid-up capital is less than ₹ 1 Cr., Revenue is less than ₹ 10 Crores but its total borrowings from banks and financial institution is ₹ 1.16 Cr.
- As per Guidance Note of CARO, 2016 issued by ICAI, while computing total borrowings from banks and financial statements, loans against Fixed deposits are to be taken into consideration. Further loans from banks and financial institutions are to be taken cumulatively not individually.

Conclusion: Contention of H Ltd. is not correct as total borrowings exceeds ₹ 1 Cr., hence reporting under CARO, 2016 will be required.

Q.10 **A Private Limited Company reports the following position as on 31st March, 2019:**

Paid-up Capital	**₹ 70 Lacs**
Revaluation Reserve	**₹ 24 Lacs**
Capital Reserve	**₹ 20 Lacs**
Profit & Loss (Dr.) Balance	**₹ 24 Lacs**

The Management of the Company contends that CARO, 2016 is not applicable to it. Comment.

Ans. : Applicability of CARO, 2016:

- The Companies (Auditor's Report) Order (CARO), 2016, exempts private limited companies, not being a subsidiary or holding of a public company, from its application which fulfils all the following conditions:
  - (*i*) its paid-up capital and reserves are not more than ₹ 1 Cr. as on Balance Sheet date, and
  - (*ii*) its total borrowings any bank or financial institution are not more than ₹ 1 cr. at any point of time during the financial year; and
  - (*iii*) its total revenue as disclosed in Schedule III (including revenue from discontinuing operations) does not exceed ₹ 10 Cr. during the financial year as per the financial statements.
- As per Guidance Note on CARO, 2016 issued by ICAI, while computing paid up capital and reserves, capital reserves, revenue reserves, revaluation reserves and credit balance of Profit and loss account are to be considered in aggregate as reduced by debit balance in the profit and loss account, if any.

◆ In the present case, paid-up capital and reserves after deducting debit balance of Profit & Loss Account amounts to ₹ 90 Lacs (70 + 24 + 20 - 24).

Conclusion: CARO is not applicable as paid-up capital and reserves does not exceed ₹ 1 Cr. (assuming that other conditions as to borrowings and revenue also satisfied).

10.2 - MATTERS TO BE REPORTED UNDER CARO, 2016

Q.11 **X Ltd. closed its manufacturing operations and sold all its manufacturing fixed assets during the financial year ended 31st March, 2019. However, it intends continue its operations as a trading company. In respect of other fixed assets, the company carried out a physical verification as at the end of 31st March, 2019 and found a material discrepancy to the tune of ₹ 1 lac, which was written off and is disclosed separately in the profit and loss account. Kindly incorporate the above in your audit report. [Nov. 13 (4 Marks)]**

Ans. : Reporting w.r.t. Fixed Assets:

- Para 3(*i*) of CARO, 2016 requires the auditor to comment whether the fixed assets have been physically verified by the management at reasonable intervals; whether any material discrepancies were noticed on such verification and if so, whether the same have been properly dealt with in the books of account.
- SA 570 "Going Concern" requires the auditor to perform appropriate procedures so as to ensure appropriateness of going concern assumption.
- In the present case, X ltd. had closed its manufacturing operations and sold all its manufacturing fixed assets, but it intends continue its operations as a trading company. Hence auditor is required to examine management plans for continuation of the company and appropriateness of going concern assumption by performing appropriate procedures.
- Further, in respect of other fixed assets, company has carried out physical verification and found a material discrepancy of ₹ 1 Lacs which was written off and disclosed separately in the profit and loss account. In respect of this, auditor should incorporate the below mentioned para in his report:

"As per AS-1, "Disclosure of Accounting Policies", "the enterprise is normally viewed as a going concern, that is as continuing its operation for the foreseeable future. It is assumed that the enterprise has neither the intention nor the necessity of liquidation or of curtailing materially the scale of its operations." Although the company has disposed off its manufacturing fixed assets during the financial year ending on 31-3-2019, it is still a going concern in the form of a trading company.

We also report that on physical verification of other fixed assets, a material discrepancy to the tune of ₹ 1 Lac was noticed and that the same has been properly dealt with in the books of account".

Q.12 **Under CARO, 2016, as a statutory auditor, how would you report: NSP Limited has its factory building, appearing as fixed assets in its financial statements in the name of one of its director who was overlooking the manufacturing activities.**

Ans. : Audit procedures w.r.t. reporting over title deeds of immovable properties under CARO:

- Para 3(*i*)(*c*) of CARO, 2016 requires the auditor to comment whether title deeds of immovable properties are held in the name of the company. If not, provide details thereof.
- The Order is silent as to what constitutes 'title deeds'. In general, title deeds mean a legal deed or document constituting evidence of a right, especially to the legal ownership of the immovable property.
- Title deeds of the immovable property may be Registered sale deed/transfer deed/conveyance deed, etc. of land, land & building together, etc. purchased, allotted, transferred by any person including any government, government authority/body/agency/corporation, etc. to the company.
- Reporting under this clause, where the title deeds of the immovable property are not held in the name of the Company, may be made incorporating following details, in the form of a table or otherwise:

(*a*) **In case of land:**

- total number of cases,
- whether leasehold/freehold,
- gross block and net block, (as at Balance Sheet date), and
- remarks, if any.

(*b*) **In case of Buildings:**

- total number of cases,
- gross block & net block, (as at Balance Sheet date) and
- remarks, if any.

Q.13 ABC Ltd. owns a piece of Land and Building situated at IP road, Mumbai which was purchased before 30 years. The title deeds for the same are deposited with State Bank of India for obtaining credit facilities by the company.

As the statutory auditor of the company for the year ended 31st March, 2018, what are the audit procedures to be followed and what is the reporting under CARO, 2016? [May 17 (4 Marks)]

Ans. : Audit procedures w.r.t. reporting over title deeds of immovable properties under CARO:

- Para 3(i)(c) of CARO, 2016 requires the auditor to comment whether title deeds of immovable properties are held in the name of the company. If not, provide details thereof.
- The Order is silent as to what constitutes 'title deeds'. In general, title deeds mean a legal deed or document constituting evidence of a right, especially to the legal ownership of the immovable property.
- Title deeds of the immovable property may be Registered sale deed/transfer deed/conveyance deed, etc. of land, land & building together, etc. purchased, allotted, transferred by any person including any government, government authority/body/agency/corporation, etc. to the company.
- Where the title deeds of the immovable property have been mortgaged with the Banks/Financial Institutions, etc., for securing the borrowings and loan raised by the company, a confirmation about the same should be sought from the respective institution to this effect. The auditor may also consider verifying this information from the online records, if available, of the relevant State.
- Reporting under this clause, where the title deeds of the immovable property are not held in the name of the Company, may be made incorporating following details, in the form of a table or otherwise:

  (*a*) **In case of land:**
  - total number of cases,
  - whether leasehold/freehold,
  - gross block and net block, (as at Balance Sheet date), and
  - remarks, if any.

  (*b*) **In case of Buildings:**
  - total number of cases,
  - gross block & net block, (as at Balance Sheet date) and
  - remarks, if any.

"ICAI Examiner Comments"

Majority of the Candidates failed to discuss the audit procedures and manner of reporting even though they have mentioned the relevant clause of CARO, 2016.

Q.14 The Property, Plant and Equipment of Amir Ltd. included Rs. 25.75 crores of earth removing machines of outdated technology which had been retired from active use and had been kept for disposal after knock down. These assets appeared at residual value and had been last inspected ten years back. As an Auditor, what may be your reporting concern in view of CARO, 2016 on matters specified above? [MTP-Aug.18]

Answer: Reporting w.r.t. Fixed Assets:

- Para 3(*i*) of CARO 2016 requires the auditor to comment
  - whether the fixed assets have been physically verified by the management at reasonable intervals;
  - whether any material discrepancies were noticed on such verification and if so,
  - whether the same have been properly dealt with in the books of account.
- In the present case, the Property, Plant and Equipment of Amir Ltd. included Rs. 25.75 crores of earth removing machines of outdated technology which had been retired from active use and had been kept for disposal after knock down. These assets appeared at residual value and had been last inspected ten years back.
- Inspection of above-mentioned machine was done 10 years back. Though it is a retired machine, however value is ₹ 25.75 crores which is a significant amount, requires physical verification at regular intervals.

Conclusion: Auditor is required to state the fact about discrepancies in system of physical verification of machineries held for disposal.

Q.15 What are the reporting requirements for closing stock in the CARO, 2016.

Ans. : Reporting Requirement for Closing Stock under CARO:

Para 3(*ii*) of CARO, 2016 requires the auditor to comment on the following:

(*a*) whether physical verification of inventory has been conducted at reasonable intervals by the management; and

(*b*) whether any material discrepancies were noticed on physical verification and if so, whether the same have been properly dealt with in the books of account.

Q.16 As the statutory auditor of B Ltd. to whom CARO, 2016 is applicable, how would you report in the following situations: Physical verification of only 50% (in value) of items of inventory has been conducted by the company. The balance 50% will be conducted in next year due to lack of time and resources.

Ans. : Physical verification of Inventory:

- Para 3(*ii*) of CARO, 2016 requires the auditor to state in his report whether physical verification of inventory has been conducted at reasonable interval by the management.
- Physical verification of inventory is the responsibility of the management which should verify all material items at least once in a year and more often in appropriate cases.
- What constitutes "reasonable intervals" depends on circumstances of each case. The periodicity of the physical verification of inventories depends upon the nature of inventories, their location and the feasibility of conducting a physical verification. The management of a company normally determines the periodicity of the physical verification of inventories considering these factors.
- Normally, wherever practicable, all the items of inventories should be verified by the management of the company at least once in a year.
- The auditor in order to satisfy himself about verification at reasonable intervals should examine the adequacy of evidence and record of verification.
- In the given case, physical verification of 50% of the items has not been conducted by the management during the year.

Conclusion: Auditor should point out the fact regarding inadequacies in the physical verification procedures of inventory in his report.

Q.17 In the course of audit of Y Ltd., as the auditor of the company you observe the following: The company has advanced a loan to a firm in which a director was interested at a rate lower than the prevailing market rate as well as there was no agreement on terms of repayment.

How auditor will report in CARO, 2016? [May 14 (6 Marks)]

Ans. : Reporting requirement under CARO, 2016:

- As per Para 3 (*iii*) the auditor has to report whether the company has granted any loans, secured or unsecured to companies, firms, LLPs or other parties covered in the register maintained u/s 189 of the Act. If so, auditor is required to comment upon following:

  (*a*) Whether the terms and conditions of the grant of such loans are not prejudicial to the company's interest;

  (*b*) Whether the schedule of repayment of principal and payment of interest has been stipulated and whether the repayments or receipts are regular;

  (*c*) If the amount is overdue, state the total amount overdue for more than 90 days, and whether reasonable steps have been taken by the company for recovery of the principal and interest.

- In the present case, company has granted a loan to a firm in which a director is interested, the terms and conditions of which are prejudicial to the company interest, hence auditor may report as under:

  "According to the information and explanations given to us and based on the audit procedures conducted by us, we are of the opinion that the terms and conditions of loans granted by the company to a firm covered in the register maintained u/s 189 of the Companies Act, 2013, (total loan amount granted ₹ -- -- and balance outstanding as at balance sheet date ₹ -------) are prejudicial to the company's interest on account of the fact that the loans have been granted at an interest rate of ____% per annum which is significantly lower than the cost of funds to the company and also lower than the prevailing yield of government security close to the tenor of the loan".

TAXMANN®

◆ In case of non-stipulation of schedule of repayment of principal & payment of Interest, the auditor should state the fact and may report that he is unable to make specific comment on the regularity of repayment of principal & payment of interest, in such cases.

Q.18 H Ltd. granted unsecured loan of ₹ 1 crore @ 15% p.a. to two of its subsidiaries during the Financial Year 2017-18. Before the year end both the companies repaid the loan. The management of H Ltd. is of the opinion that since no balance is outstanding as on 31st March 2018, these loans are not required to be reported in CARO, 2016. Comment and draft a suitable report. [May 14 (4 Marks)]

Ans. : Reporting requirement under CARO, 2016:

◆ As per Para 3 (*iii*) the auditor has to report whether the company has granted any loans, secured or unsecured to companies, firms, LLPs or other parties covered in the register maintained under section 189 of the Act. If so, auditor is required to comment upon following:

(*a*) Whether the terms and conditions of the grant of such loans are not prejudicial to the company's interest;

(*b*) Whether the schedule of repayment of principal and payment of interest has been stipulated and whether the repayments or receipts are regular;

(*c*) If the amount is overdue, state the total amount overdue for more than 90 days, and whether reasonable steps have been taken by the company for recovery of the principal and interest.

◆ As per Guidance Note on CARO, 2016, the clauses (*b*) & (*c*) covers not only the loan granted during the year but covers all loans including opening balances. Therefore, while examining the loans, the auditor should also take into consideration the loan transactions that have been squared-up during the year and report such transactions under the clause.

◆ In the given case, H Ltd. has granted unsecured loan of ₹ 1 crore @15% p.a. to two of its subsidiaries during the Financial Year 2015-16. During the year, both the companies have repaid its loan. Therefore, the auditor need to consider the transaction and comment as follows:

"The Company has granted loan of ₹ 1 Crore @ 15% p.a. to 2 of its subsidiaries covered in the register maintained under Section 189 of the Companies Act, 2013 during the Financial Year 2017-18. The maximum amount involved during the year was ₹ 1.00 crore and the year-end balance of such loans was Nil".

Q.19 ABC Ltd. has granted a loan of ₹ 20 crores to its associate XYZ (P.) Ltd. at the beginning of the financial year and it remain outstanding at the year end. How the auditor should report the fact?

Ans. : Reporting requirement under CARO, 2016:

◆ As per Para 3 (*iii*) the auditor has to report whether the company has granted any loans, secured or unsecured to companies, firms, LLPs or other parties covered in the register maintained under section 189 of the Act. If so, auditor is required to comment upon following:

(*a*) Whether the terms and conditions of the grant of such loans are not prejudicial to the company's interest;

(*b*) Whether the schedule of repayment of principal and payment of interest has been stipulated and whether the repayments or receipts are regular;

(*c*) If the amount is overdue, state the total amount overdue for more than 90 days, and whether reasonable steps have been taken by the company for recovery of the principal and interest.

◆ In the given case, ABC Ltd. has granted a loan of ₹ 20 crores to its associates at the beginning the Financial Year and it remain outstanding at year end.

Conclusion: Auditor is required to report the matters as required under Para 3(*iii*) of CARO, 2016.

Q.20 As a Company auditor you noticed that there is an inter-corporate loan granted by the company. What are the reporting requirements as regard the matters concerning terms of interest on the inter-corporate loan? [Nov. 18-Old Syllabus (4 Marks)]

Ans. : Reporting requirements as to inter-corporate loan granted by the company:

◆ As per Para 3(*iv*) the auditor is required to report, in respect of loans, investments, guarantees, and security whether provisions of Sections 185 and 186 of the Companies Act, 2013 have been complied with. If not, provide details thereof.

◆ For this purpose of ensuring compliance of Sec. 186, the auditor should:

◆ Obtain the details of, loans given to any person or other body corporate, guarantee given or security provided in connection with a loan to any other body corporate or person and securities acquired of any other body corporate by way of subscription, purchase or otherwise, made during the year as well as the outstanding balances as at the beginning of the year.

- Check whether rate of interest is not lower than the prevailing yield of one year, three-year, five years or ten-year government security closest to the tenor of the loan granted.
- Check if the company is in default in the repayment of any deposits accepted or in payment of interest thereon, then the company is not allowed to give any loan or guarantee or any security or an acquisition till such default is subsisting.
- Non-compliance of Sec. 186 with respect to interest on the intercorporate loan may be reported incorporating following details:

S. No.	Non-compliance of Section 186	Name of Company/ Party	Amount Involved	Balance as at Balance Sheet Date	Remarks, if any
1	Loan given at rate of interest lower than prescribed				
2	Any other default				

Q.21 **CARO, 2016 requires the auditor of the company to report whether maintenance of cost records has been specified by the Central Government under section 148 of the Companies Act, 2013 and whether such accounts and records have been so made and maintained.**

You are required to briefly explain the audit procedure to be followed by the auditor and suggest the reporting pattern.

Ans. : Reporting requirement under CARO, 2016:

- Para 3(*vi*) of CARO, 2016 requires the auditor to comment "whether maintenance of cost records has been specified by the CG u/s 148(1) of the Companies Act, 2013 and whether such accounts and records have been so made and maintained".
- The word "made" applies in respect of cost accounts (or cost statements) and the word "maintained" applies in respect of cost records relating to materials, labour, overheads, etc.
- The auditor has to report under the clause irrespective of whether a cost audit has been ordered by the central government.
- The auditor should obtain a written representation from the management stating
  - (*a*) whether cost records are required to be maintained for any product(s) or services of the company u/s 148 of the Act, and the Companies (Cost Records and Audit) Rules, 2014; and
  - (*b*) whether cost accounts and records are being made and maintained regularly.
- The auditor should also obtain a list of books/records made and maintained in this regard.
- The Order does not require a detailed examination of such records. The auditor should, therefore, conduct a general review of the cost records to ensure that the records as prescribed are made and maintained. He should, of course, make such reference to the records as is necessary for the purposes of his audit.
- It is necessary that the extent of the examination made by the auditor is clearly brought out in his report. The following wording is, therefore, suggested:

"We have broadly reviewed the books of account maintained by the company pursuant to the Rules made by the Central Government for the maintenance of cost records under section 148 of the Act, and are of the opinion that *prima facie,* the prescribed accounts and records have been made and maintained."

Q.22 **As a statutory auditor, how would you deal with the following case: During the course of audit of ABC Ltd. it is noticed that out of ₹ 12 Lacs of provident fund contribution accounted in the books, only ₹ 2 Lacs has been remitted to the authorities during the year. On enquiry the Chief Accountant informed that due to financial problems they have not remitted but will remit the same as and when the position improves.**

Or

During the course of Audit of M/s CT Ltd. for the financial year 2017-18, it has noticed that ₹ 2.00 lakhs of employee contribution and ₹ 9.50 lakhs of employer contribution towards employee state insurance contribution have been accounted in the books of account in respective heads. Whereas, it was found that ₹ 4.00 lakhs only have been deposited with ESIC department during the year ended 31st March, 2018. The Finance Manager informed that auditor that due to financial crunch they have not deposited the amount due, but will deposit the amount overdue along with interest as and when financial position improves. Comment as a statutory auditor. **[May 16 (4 Marks)]**

TAXMANN®

Ans. : Reporting Requirement under CARO w.r.t. payment of statutory dues:

- Para 3(*vii*)(*a*) of CARO, 2016 requires the auditor to comment whether the company is regular in depositing undisputed statutory dues including Provident Fund, Employees State Insurance (ESI), Income-tax, Sales-tax, Wealth tax, Service tax, Duties of Customs, Duty of Excise, Value Added Tax, cess and any other statutory dues with the appropriate authorities and if not, the extent of the arrears of outstanding statutory dues as at the last day of the financial year concerned for a period of more than six months from the date they became payable.
- SA 250 "Consideration of Laws and Regulations in an audit of financial statements, also requires the auditor to obtain sufficient appropriate audit evidence regarding compliance with the provisions of those laws and regulations generally recognised to have a direct effect on the determination of material amounts and disclosures in the financial statements.
- A company is required to deposit provident fund and Employees State Insurance dues to appropriate authorities with in the period prescribed under the EPF Act and the Rules governing it.
- In the present case company is not regular in depositing the provident Fund/ESI Contributions. The reason put forward by the Chief Accountant that the amount has not been deposited due to financial problems faced by the Company is no excuse for not remitting the PF/ESI Contributions.

Conclusion: Non-payment of PF/ESI contribution needs to be disclosed by the auditor in his audit report as per requirement of Para 3(*vii*)(*a*) of CARO, 2016.

"ICAI Examiner Comments"

Most of the candidates failed to explain reporting requirement both as per SA 250 and clause (vii) (a) of Para-3 of CARO, 2016. Some of the candidates explained such non-compliance as per Section 43B of Income Tax Act, 1961.

Q.23 As a Statutory Auditor, how would you deal with the following: PQR Ltd. has not deposited Provident Fund contribution of ₹ 10 lakhs with the authorities till the year-end.

Ans. : Reporting Requirement under CARO w.r.t. payment of statutory dues:

- Para 3(*vii*)(*a*) of CARO, 2016 requires the auditor to comment whether the company is regular in depositing undisputed statutory dues including Provident Fund, Employees State Insurance (ESI), Income-tax, Sales-tax, Wealth tax, Service tax, Duties of Customs, Duty of Excise, Value Added Tax, cess and any other statutory dues with the appropriate authorities and if not, the extent of the arrears of outstanding statutory dues as at the last day of the financial year concerned for a period of more than six months from the date they became payable.
- SA 250 "Consideration of Laws and Regulations in an audit of financial statements, also requires the auditor to obtain sufficient appropriate audit evidence regarding compliance with the provisions of those laws and regulations generally recognised to have a direct effect on the determination of material amounts and disclosures in the financial statements.
- A company is required to deposit provident fund and Employees State Insurance dues to appropriate authorities with in the period prescribed under the EPF Act and the Rules governing it.
- In the present case company is not regular in depositing the provident Fund.

Conclusion: Non-payment of PF needs to be disclosed by the auditor in his audit report as per requirement of Para 3(*vii*)(*a*) of CARO, 2016.

Q.24 Comment on the following: Is the company regular in depositing undisputed statutory dues including Provident Fund, Employees State Insurance, Income Tax, Sales Tax, Wealth Tax, Customs duty, Excise duty, Value added Tax, Cess and any other statutory dues with the appropriate authorities and if not, the extent of arrears of outstanding statutory dues as at the last day of the financial year concerned for a period of more than six months from the date they became payable shall be indicated by the auditor.

[Nov. 08 (4 Marks)]

Ans. : Reporting on Regularity of payment of statutory dues:

- Para 3(*vii*)(*a*) of CARO, 2016 requires the auditor to comment
  - (*i*) whether the company is regular in depositing undisputed statutory dues including Provident Fund, Employees State Insurance, Income-tax, Sales Tax, Service Tax, Duties of Customs, duty of Excise, Value added Tax, Cess and any other statutory dues with the appropriate authorities and
  - (*ii*) if not, the extent of arrears of outstanding statutory dues as at the last day of the financial year concerned for a period of more than six months from the date they became payable shall be indicated by the auditor.

◆ Implication of Para 3(*vii*)(*a*) are as follows:

(*i*) Auditor is required to comment upon regularity in depositing undisputed statutory dues.

(*ii*) Payment includes all statutory dues payable by the company. The amount payable will include the interest/penalty payable under the respective laws.

(*iii*) If the company is not regular in depositing the undisputed statutory dues the auditor is required to state the extent of outstanding statutory dues as at the last day of the financial year from a period of more than six months from the date they became payable.

(*iv*) The auditor has to get a written representation from the management indicating the details of disputed claims, undisputed but have remained outstanding for more than six months and a statement as to the completeness of the information provided by the management.

Q.25 Big and Small Ltd. received a show cause notice from central excise department intending to levy a demand of ₹ 25 lakhs in December 2018. The company replied to the above notice in January 2019 contending that it is not liable for the levy. No further action was initiated by the central excise department upto the finalization of the audit for the year ended on 31st March, 2019. As the auditor of the company, what is your role in this? [May 11 (4 Marks), Nov. 14 (3 Marks)]

Ans. : Reporting in case of Statutory dues:

◆ Para 3(*vii*)(*b*) of CARO, 2016 requires that in case dues of Income tax/Sales tax/Service tax/Custom duty/Excise duty/Value Added Tax or cess have not been deposited on account of any dispute, auditor is required to state in his report the amounts involved and the forum where dispute is pending.

◆ A mere representation to the Department shall not constitute the dispute.

◆ In the present case issuance of show cause notice by Excise Department does not tantamount to demand payable by the Company. In as much as the Company has replied to the notice and no further correspondence was received from the Department, it has to be construed that there is no demand.

Conclusion: The auditor needs not to report on this.

Q.26 XYZ Pvt. Ltd. has submitted the financial statements for the year ended 31-3-18 for audit. The audit assistant observes and brings to your notice that the company's records show following dues:

◆ **Income Tax relating to Assessment Year 2014-15 ₹ 125 lacs - Appeal is pending before Hon'ble ITAT since 30-9-15.**

◆ **Customs duty ₹ 85 lakhs - Demand notice received on 15-9-17 but no action has been taken to pay or appeal.**

As an auditor, how would you bring this fact to the members? [Nov. 11 (5 Marks)]

Ans. : Reporting under CARO w.r.t. Statutory Dues:

◆ Para 3(*vii*)(*a*) CARO, 2016 requires the auditor to comment whether the company is regular in depositing undisputed statutory dues including Provident Fund, Employees State Insurance, Income-tax, Sales-tax, Service tax, Duties of Customs, Duty of Excise, Value Added Tax, cess and any other statutory dues with the appropriate authorities and if not, the extent of the arrears of outstanding statutory dues as at the last day of the financial year concerned for a period of more than six months from the date they became payable, shall be indicated by the auditor.

◆ Para 3(*vii*)(*b*) of CARO, 2016 requires that in case dues of Income tax/Sales tax/Service tax/Custom duty/Excise duty/Value Added Tax or cess have not been deposited on account of any dispute, auditor is required to state in his report the amounts involved and the forum where dispute is pending.

◆ The auditor should also obtain a management representation about the disputed dues, the amounts involved and the forum where the dispute is pending. The auditor should carry out necessary audit procedures to verify the information provided by the management.

◆ In the present case, there is Income Tax demand of ₹ 125 Lacs and the company has gone for an appeal, it should be brought to notice of members by reporting under Para 3(vii)(b) of CARO, 2016 as below:

S. No.	Name of the Statute	Nature of Dues	Amount (in Lacs)	Period to which amount relates	Forum where dispute is pending
1	Income-tax Act, 1961	Income-tax	125.00	AY 2014-15	ITAT

◆ In reference to demand notice received for Custom Duty of ₹ 85 Lacs on 15-9-2017 for which company has not taken any action and is outstanding for more than 6 months, it leads to the irregularity which should be brought to notice of members by reporting under Para 3(vii)(b) of CARO, 2016.

Q.27 OK Ltd. has taken a term loan from a nationalized bank in 2012 for ₹ 200 lakhs repayable in five equal instalments of ₹ 40 lakhs from 31st March, 2013 onwards. It had repaid the loans due in 2013 & 2014, but defaulted in 2015, 2016 & 2017. As the auditor of OK Ltd. what is your responsibility assuming that company has sought re-schedulement of loan? [May 11 (4 Marks)]

Ans. : Reporting w.r.t. repayment of dues:

◆ As per Para 3(*viii*) of CARO, 2016 auditors of a company are required to comment in his report whether the Company has defaulted in repayment of loans or borrowings to a financial institution, bank, government or debentures holders and if yes, the period and amount of default to be reported. In case of defaults of banks, financial institutions and government, lender wise details to be provided.

◆ As per the general instructions for preparation of Balance Sheet, provided under Schedule III to the Companies Act, 2013, terms of repayment of term loans and other loans is required to be disclosed in the notes to accounts. It also requires disclosure of period and amount of continuing default as on the balance sheet date in repayment of loans and interest, separately in each case.

◆ As per Guidance Note on CARO, 2016, submission of application for re-schedulement/restructuring does not mean that no default has occurred.

◆ In this case OK Ltd. has defaulted in repayment of dues for three years. Application for rescheduling will not change the default position.

Conclusion: The auditor has to report in his audit report that the Company has defaulted in its repayment of dues to the bank to the extent of ₹ 120 lakhs.

Particulars	Amount of default as at the balance sheet date	Period of default
(*i*) Name of the Lenders: In case of: Bank Financial Institution & Government		
(*ii*) Debentures		

Q.28 R Ltd. as at 31st March 2018 defaulted in the repayment of interest and principal due to a financial institution. The due date was 28th February 2018. However, the defaulted amount was paid on 5th April 2018. The company's management is of the opinion that since the default is set right before the audit completion these need not be reported in CARO 2016. Comment and draft a suitable report.

[May 13 (4 Marks)]

Or

C Limited has defaulted in repayments of dues to a financial institution during the financial year 2016-17 and the same remained outstanding as at March 31, 2018. However, the Company settled the total outstanding dues including interest in April, 2018 subsequent to the year end and before completion of the audit. Discuss how you would deal with this matter and draft a suitable Auditor's Report.

[Nov. 14 (4 Marks)]

Ans. : Reporting w.r.t. repayment of dues:

◆ As per Para 3(*viii*) of CARO, 2016 auditors of a company is required to comment in his report whether the Company has defaulted in repayment of loans or borrowings to a financial institution, bank, government or dues to debenture holders? If yes, the period and amount of default to be reported (In case of defaults of banks, financial institutions and government, lender wise details to be provided).

◆ As per the general instructions for preparation of Balance Sheet, provided under Schedule III to the Companies Act, 2013, terms of repayment of term loans and other loans is required to be disclosed in the notes to accounts. It also requires disclosure of period and amount of continuing default as on the balance sheet date in repayment of loans and interest, separately in each case.

◆ In the given case, company has defaulted in repayments of dues to a financial institution during the financial year 2017-18 which remain outstanding as at March 31, 2018. However, the company has settled the total outstanding dues including interest in April, 2018 but, the dues were outstanding as at March 31, 2018.

Conclusion: The auditor is required to state in his report the default of the company in respect of repayment of its dues and report as under:

"The company has defaulted in repayment of principal and interest to the financial institution amounted to ₹ ...., that become due on 28th Feb, 2018. However, the outstanding sum was settled by the company on 5th April, 2018.

Q.29 Under CARO how, as a statutory auditor how would you comment on the following: A Term Loan was obtained from a bank for ₹ 75 lakhs for acquiring R&D equipment, out of which ₹ 12 lakhs were used to buy a car for use of the concerned director, who was overlooking the R&D activities.

[Nov. 12 (4 Marks)]

Ans. : Utilisation of Term Loans:

- Para 3(*ix*) of CARO, 2016 requires the auditor to comment whether moneys raised by way of initial public offer or further public offer (including debt instruments) and term loans were applied for the purposes for which those are raised. If not, the details together with delays or default and subsequent rectification, if any, as may be applicable, be reported.
- For this purpose, auditor should examine the terms and conditions of the term loan with the actual utilisation of the loans. If the auditor finds that the fund has not been utilized for the purpose for which they were obtained, the report should state the fact.
- In the instant case, term loan was taken for the purpose of purchase of Research & Development equipment, but a part of it has been utilized for purchase of vehicle for the use of Director.
- Purchase of vehicle for use by Director who was incharge of the R&D activities, cannot be considered as purchase of Research & Development equipment.

Conclusion: Auditor is required to report the fact in his audit report. Reporting may be as follows:

"In our opinion and according to the information and explanations given to us, the Company has utilized the money raised by way of IPO/FPO (including debt instruments) and the term loans during the year for the purposes for which they were raised, except for:

Nature of the fund Raised	Details of default (Reason/ Delay)	Amount (₹)	Subsequently rectified (Yes/No) and details

Q.30 As a Statutory Auditor, how would you deal with the following: LM Ltd. had obtained a Term Loan of ₹ 300 lakhs from a bank for the construction of a factory. Since there was a delay in the construction activities, the said funds were temporarily invested in short term deposits.

Ans. : Utilisation of Term Loans:

- Para 3(ix) of CARO, 2016 requires the auditor to comment whether moneys raised by way of initial public offer or further public offer (including debt instruments) and term loans were applied for the purposes for which those are raised. If not, the details together with delays or default and subsequent rectification, if any, as may be applicable, be reported.
- For this purpose, auditor should examine the terms and conditions of the term loan with the actual utilisation of the loans. If the auditor finds that the fund has not been utilized for the purpose for which they were obtained, the report should state the fact.
- As per Guidance Note on CARO, 2016, sometimes, companies, may, temporarily invest the surplus funds pending utilization for the purpose for which funds were arranged. In such cases, the auditor should mention the fact that pending utilisation of the funds raised through Initial Public Offer or Further Public Offer (including debt instruments) or term loans for the stated purpose, the funds were temporarily used for the purpose other than for which they were raised but were ultimately utilised for the stated end-use.
- In the instant case, term loan was taken for the purpose of construction of a factory, but said funds were invested in short term deposits due to delay in construction activities.

Conclusion: Auditor is required to report the fact that the pending utilisation of term loan, the funds are temporarily invested in short term deposits, in his audit report as per requirement of paragraph 3(ix) of CARO, 2016.

Q.31 During the financial year ended on 31/03/2018, LM Private Limited had borrowed from a Nationalized Bank, a term loan of Rs. 120 lakhs consisting of Rs. 100 lakhs for purchase of a machinery for the new plant and Rs. 20 lakhs for erection expenses. As on the date of 31st March, 2018, the total of capital and

free reserves of the Company was Rs. 50 lakhs and turnover for the year 2017-18 was Rs. 750 lakhs. The Bank paid Rs. 100 lakhs to the vendor of the Company for the supply of machinery on 31/12/2017. The machinery had reached the yard of the Company. On 28/02/2018, the Company had drawn the balance of loan viz. Rs. 20 lakhs to the credit of its current account maintained with the Bank and utilized the full amount for renovating its administrative office building. The machinery had been kept as capital stock under construction. Comment as to reporting issues, if any, that the Auditor should be concerned with for the financial year ended on 31/03/2018, in this respect. [Nov. 18-New Syllabus (5 marks)]

Answer: Reporting as to mis-utilisation of Term Loans:

- Reporting under CARO, 2016 is applicable in case of a private limited company if the total borrowings exceed ₹ 1 Cr. from any bank or financial institution at any point of time during the financial year.
- As per Para 3(*ix*) of CARO, 2016 requires the auditor to comment whether moneys raised by way of initial public offer or further public offer (including debt instruments) and term loans were applied for the purposes for which those are raised. If not, the details together with delays or default and subsequent rectification, if any, as may be applicable, be reported.
- In the present case, LM Private limited had borrowed from a Nationalized Bank, a term loan of Rs. 120 lakhs consisting of Rs. 100 lakhs for purchase of a machinery for the new plant and Rs. 20 lakhs for erection expenses. The Bank paid Rs. 100 lakhs to the vendor of the Company for the supply of machinery on 31/12/2017. The machinery had reached the yard of the Company. On 28/02/2018, the Company had drawn the balance of loan viz. Rs. 20 lakhs to the credit of its current account maintained with the Bank and utilized the full amount for renovating its administrative office building.
- Auditor of LM Private Limited is under obligation to report on matters covered under CARO, 2016 as total borrowings exceed ₹ 1 Cr. LM Private Limited had taken term loan for erection purposes, but utilized the funds for renovation of administrative office building.

Conclusion: As per requirement of Para 3(*ix*) of CARO, 2016, auditor is required to report the fact that out of the term loan obtained for machinery purchase and erection, ₹ 20 Lacs was not utilized for the purpose of erection of machinery.

Q.32 As a statutory auditor, how would you report on the following under CARO: ABC Pvt. Ltd. is an manufacturer of jewellery. A senior employee of the Company informed you that the Company does not properly disclose the purity of gold used on the jewellery.

Ans. : Reporting under CARO w.r.t. Fraud:

- Para 3(x) of CARO 2016 requires the auditor to comment whether any fraud by the company or any fraud on the Company by its officers/employees has been noticed or reported during the year; If yes, the nature and the amount involved is to be indicated.
- In the present case if purity of gold is not properly disclosed on the jewellery it amounts to defrauding the customers. It implies that the management is deceiving customers to obtain an illegal advantage.
- As per SA 240 "The Auditor's responsibilities in relation to an audit of Financial Statements" the auditor is concerned with fraudulent acts that cause a material misstatement in financial statements. Hence as long as books of account are not falsified arising out of difference in the purity of gold, *i.e.*, actual cost of the gold and the sale price of gold, it has no implication for the auditor.

Conclusion: From the view point of reporting on frauds under CARO, 2016, there is no implication for misstatement in the financial statements. Hence, no reporting is necessary for non-proper disclosure of purity of gold on the jewellery.

Q.33 What are the reporting requirements in the audit report under the Companies Act, 2013/CARO, 2016 for the following situations?

(*a*) A fraud has been committed against the company by an officer of the company.

(*b*) A fraud has been committed against the company by a vendor of the company.

(*c*) The company has committed a major fraud on its customer and the case is pending in the court.

(*d*) A fraud has been reported in the cost audit report but not noticed by statutory auditors in his audit.

[Nov. 18-Old Syllabus (4 Marks)]

Answer: Reporting under Companies Act, 2013/CARO, 2016 w.r.t. Fraud:

- Section 143(12) of Companies Act, 2013 requires that if an auditor of a company in the course of the performance of his duties as auditor, has reason to believe that an offence of fraud involving such amount or amounts as may be prescribed, is being or has been committed in the company by its officers or employees, the auditor shall report the matter to the Central Government within such time and in such manner as may be prescribed. For this purpose, Rule 13 prescribes the amount of Rs. 1 Cr. or more.
- However, in case of a fraud involving lesser than the specified amount, i.e. below Rs. 1 Cr., the auditor shall report the matter to the audit committee constituted u/s 177 or to the Board in other cases within such time and in such manner as may be prescribed:
- Para 3(*x*) of CARO 2016 requires the auditor to comment whether any fraud by the company or any fraud on the Company by its officers/employees has been **noticed or reported** during the year; If yes, the nature and the amount involved is to be indicated.
- Accordingly, reporting requirements will be:

S. No.	Situation	Reporting under Companies Act, 2013	Reporting under CARO, 2016
1	**A fraud has been committed against the company by an officer of the company**	Reporting required to C.G. if amount of fraud exceeds ₹ 1 Cr.	Nature of Fraud and amount involved need to be reported under Para 3(*x*).
2	**A fraud has been committed against the company by a vendor of the company.**	No reporting required.	No reporting required.
3	**The company has committed a major fraud on its customer and the case is pending in the court.**	Effect of such fraud on financial statements need to be reported.	Nature of Fraud and amount involved need to be reported under Para 3(*x*).
4	**A fraud has been reported in the cost audit report but not noticed by statutory auditors in his audit.**	Effect of such fraud on financial statements need to be reported.	Para 3(*x*) requires reporting of fraud that has been noticed or reported during the year.

Q.34 CARO, 2016 has made several significant changes and has introduced many new reporting requirements vis-à-vis CARO 2015.

In view of the above, describe the relevant clause relating to Nidhi Companies - compliance with net owned funds to deposit requirements and the relevant provisions.

What audit procedures are to be adopted for verification and reporting on the same?

[Nov. 16 (4 Marks)]

Ans. : Clause relating to NIDHI Companies under CARO, 2016:

Clause (*xii*) of Para 3 of CARO, 2016 requires the auditor to report certain matters relating to Nidhi Companies. The matters on which auditor is required to report are:

- Whether the Nidhi Company has complied with the Net Owned Fund to Deposits in the ratio of 1: 20 to meet out the liability and
- Whether the Nidhi Company is maintaining 10% unencumbered term deposits as specified in the Nidhi Rules, 2014 to meet out the liability.

Audit Procedures for Verification and Reporting:

- Ministry of Corporate Affairs on 31st March 2014, *vide* its Notification No. GSR 258(E) notified the 'Nidhi Rules 2014', which came into force on the first day of April 2014.
- As per Rule 3(d) Net Owned Funds are defined as the aggregate of paid up equity share capital and free reserves as reduced by accumulated losses and intangible assets appearing in the last audited balance sheet. Provided that, the amount representing the proceeds of issue of preference shares, shall not be included for calculating Net Owned Funds.
- A Nidhi company can accept fixed deposits, recurring deposits and savings deposits from its members in accordance with the directions notified by the Central Government. The aggregate of such deposits is referred to as "deposit liability".

- The auditor should ask the management to provide the computation of the deposit liability and net owned funds on the basis of the requirements mentioned above. This would enable him to verify that the ratio of deposit liability to net owned funds is in accordance with the requirements prescribed in this regard.

Q.35 RNT Ltd. has entered into non-cash transactions with Mr. Ram, son of one of the directors of the company, which is an arrangement by which the RNT Ltd. is in process to acquire assets for consideration other than cash. Under CARO, 2016, as a statutory auditor, how would you report?

Ans. : Reporting under CARO, 2016:

- Pare 3(xv) of CARO, 2016 requires the auditor to comment "whether the company has entered into any non-cash transactions with directors or persons connected with him and if so, whether provisions of Section 192 of Companies Act, 2013 have been complied with".
- Section 192 of the Companies Act, 2013 of the Act deals with restriction on non-cash transactions involving directors or persons connected with them. The section prohibits the company from entering into following types of arrangements unless it meets the conditions laid out in the said section:
  - (*i*) An arrangement by which a director of the company or its holding, subsidiary or associate company or a person connected with such director acquires or is to acquire assets for consideration other than cash, from the company.
  - (*ii*) An arrangement by which the company acquires or is to acquire assets for consideration other than cash, from such director or person so connected.
- The reporting requirements under this clause are in two parts. The first part requires the auditor to report on whether the company has entered into any non-cash transactions with the directors or any persons connected with such director/s. The second part of the clause requires the auditor to report whether the provisions of section 192 of the Act have been complied with. Therefore, the second part of the clause becomes reportable only if the answer to the first part is in affirmative.
- Suggested paragraph on reporting:

"According to the information and explanations given to us, the Company has entered into non-cash transactions with one of the directors/person connected with the director during the year, by the acquisition of assets by assuming directly related liabilities, which in our opinion is covered under the provisions of Section 192 of the Act, and for which approval has not yet been obtained in a general meeting of the Company."

Q.36 Whilst the Audit team has identified various matters, they need your advice to include the same in your audit report in view of CARO 2016:

(*a*) The long-term borrowings from the parent has no agreed terms and neither the interest nor the principal has been repaid so far.

(*b*) The Company is in the process of selling its office along with the freehold land available at Chandigarh and is actively on the lookout for potential buyers. Whilst the same was purchased at ₹25 Lakhs in 2008, the current market value is ₹250 Lakhs.

This property is pending to be registered in the name of the Company, due to certain procedural issues associated with the Registration though the Company is having a valid possession and has paid its purchase cost in full. The Company has disclosed this amount under Fixed Assets though no disclosure of non-registration is made in the notes forming part of the accounts.

(*c*) An amount of ₹3.25 Lakhs per month is paid to M/s. WE CARE Associates, a partnership firm, which is a 'related party' in accordance with the provisions of the Companies Act, 2013 for the marketing services rendered by them. Based on an independent assessment, the consideration paid is higher than the arm's length pricing by ₹0.25 Lakhs per month. Whilst the transaction was accounted in the financial statements based on the amounts' paid, no separate disclosure has been made in the notes forming part of the accounts highlighting the same as a 'related party' transaction.

(*d*) The Internal Auditor of the Company has identified a fraud in the recruitment of employees by the HR department wherein certain sums were alleged to have been taken as kick-back from the employees for taking them on board with the Company. After due investigation, the concerned HR Manager was sacked. The amount of such kick-backs is expected to be in the range of ₹12 Lakhs. [MTP-March 19, RTP-May 19]

Ans. : Reporting under CARO, 2016

(*a*) Auditor is required to report the matter as per Para 3(xiii) of CARO 2016 which requires him to report "whether all transactions with the related parties are in compliance with sections 177 and 188 of Companies Act, 2013 where applicable and the details have been disclosed in the Financial Statements etc., as required by the applicable accounting standards".

(*b*) Auditor is required to report the matter as per Para 3(*i*)(*c*) of CARO 2016 which requires him to report, "whether the title deeds of immovable properties are held in the name of the company. If not, provide the details thereof."

Reporting under this clause, where the title deeds of the immovable property are not held in the name of the Company, may be made incorporating following details, in the form of a table or otherwise in case of land:

- total number of cases,
- whether leasehold/freehold,
- gross block and net block, (as at Balance Sheet date), and
- remarks, if any.

(*c*) Auditor is required to report the matter as per Para 3(xiii) of CARO 2016 which requires him to report "whether all transactions with the related parties are in compliance with sections 177 and 188 of Companies Act, 2013 where applicable and the details have been disclosed in the Financial Statements etc., as required by the applicable accounting standards".

Reporting is required, as one of related party transaction amounting ₹ 3.25 lakhs per month *i.e.* in lieu of marketing services has been noticed of which amount ₹ 0.25 lakh per month is exceeding the arm's length price has not been disclosed highlighting the same as related party transactions as per AS 18.

(*d*) Auditor is required to report the matter as per Para 3(*x*) of CARO 2016 which requires him to report, "whether any fraud by the company or any fraud on the Company by its officers or employees has been noticed or reported during the year; If yes, the nature and the amount involved is to be indicated."

Reporting is required, as a fraud has been identified in recruitment of employees by the HR Department wherein certain sums were alleged to have been taken as kickback from the employees of company amounting to ₹12 Lakhs approx.

AUDIT OF CONSOLIDATED FINANCIAL STATEMENTS

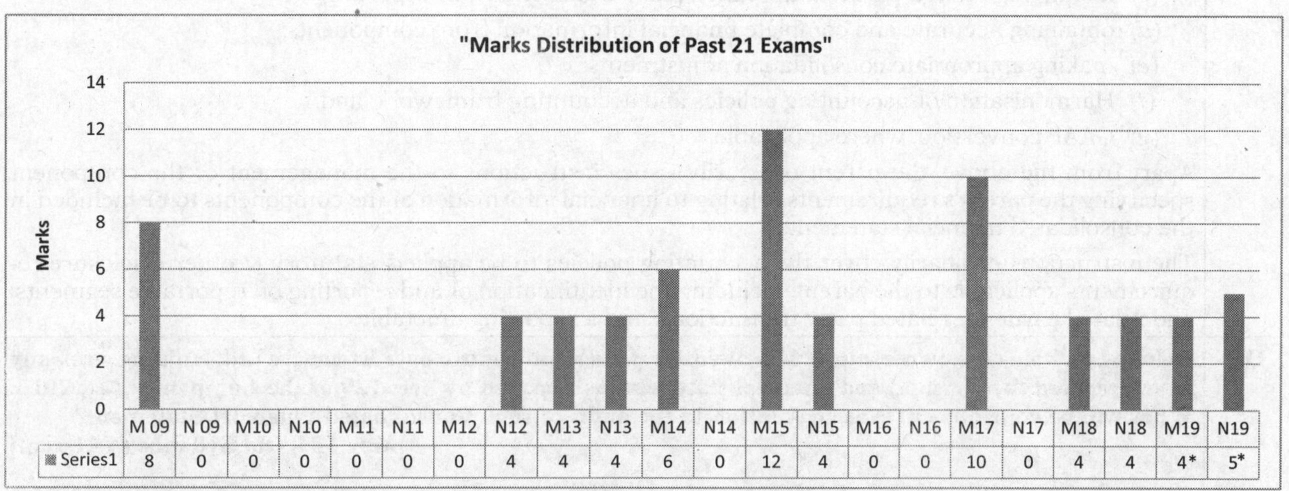

	M 09	N 09	M10	N10	M11	N11	M12	N12	M13	N13	M14	N14	M15	N15	M16	N16	M17	N17	M18	N18	M19	N19
Series1	8	0	0	0	0	0	0	4	4	4	6	0	12	4	0	0	10	0	4	4	4*	5*

*Only Subjective Questions.

Q.1 **ANC Ltd., having two subsidiaries but did not have any holding company, is a company whose securities are not listed on any stock exchange, whether in India or outside India. The CEO of the ANC Ltd. says that since it is an unlisted company therefore consolidation of financial statement is not applicable. Comment on the contention of the CEO.**

Ans. : Preparation of Consolidated Financial Statement:

As per section 129(3) of the Companies Act, 2013, where a company has one or more subsidiaries or associate companies, it shall, in addition to its own financial statements prepare a consolidated financial statement of the company and of all the subsidiaries and associate companies in the same form and manner as that of its own and in accordance with the applicable accounting standards.

However, by virtue of second proviso to Rule 6 of Companies (Accounts) Rules, 2014, the requirement related to preparation of consolidated financial statements shall not apply to a company if it meets the following conditions:

(*i*) it is a wholly-owned subsidiary, or is a partially-owned subsidiary of another company and all its other members, including those not otherwise entitled to vote, having been intimated in writing and for which the proof of delivery of such intimation is available with the company, do not object to the company not presenting consolidated financial statements;

(*ii*) it is a company whose securities are not listed or are not in the process of listing on any stock exchange, whether in India or outside India; and 5

(*iii*) its ultimate or any intermediate holding company files consolidated financial statements with the Registrar which are in compliance with the applicable Accounting Standards.

In the given case, ANC Ltd. is a holding company of two subsidiaries and not a subsidiary company.

Conclusion: Contention of the CEO of the company is not tenable and the company needs to prepare consolidated financial statements.

Q.2 **Write short note on: Responsibility of holding company for preparation of Consolidated Financial Statements.** **[Nov. 12 (4 Marks)]**

Ans. : Responsibility of holding company for preparation of Consolidated Financial Statements:

As per section 129(3) of the Companies Act, 2013, where a company has one or more subsidiaries or associate companies, it shall, in addition to its own financial statements prepare a consolidated financial statement of the company and of all the subsidiaries and associate companies in the same form and manner as that of its own and in accordance with the applicable accounting standards.

The responsibility for the preparation and presentation of consolidated financial statements, among other things, is that of the management of the parent. This includes:

(*a*) identifying components, and including the financial information of the components to be included in the consolidated financial statements;

(*b*) where appropriate, identifying reportable segments for segmental reporting;

(*c*) identifying related parties and related party transactions for reporting;

(*d*) obtaining accurate and complete financial information from components;

(*e*) making appropriate consolidation adjustments;

(*f*) Harmonisation of accounting policies and accounting framework; and

(*g*) GAAP conversion, where applicable.

Apart from the above, the parent ordinarily issues instructions to the management of the component specifying the parent's requirements relating to financial information of the components to be included in the consolidated financial statements.

The instructions ordinarily cover the accounting policies to be applied, statutory & other disclosure requirements applicable to the parent, including the identification of and reporting on reportable segments, and related parties & related party transactions, and a reporting timetable.

Q.3 Deluxe Ltd. holds the ownership of 51% of voting power and control over Executive Ltd. Holding company have prepared the consolidated financial statement as required by Sec. 129 of the Companies Act, 2013. What will be your objective, as an Auditor, in the audit of such Consolidated Financial Statement?

[May 18 - Old Syllabus (4 Marks)]

Or

Write a short note on: Auditor's objectives in an audit of consolidated financial statements.

[RTP-Nov. 19]

Ans : Objectives of Auditor while auditing the Consolidating Financial Statements:

The auditor of the CFS is responsible for expressing an opinion on whether the CFS are prepared, in all material respects, in accordance with the FRF under which the parent prepares the CFS.

Therefore, the auditor's objectives in an audit of CFS are:

(*a*) to satisfy himself that the consolidated financial statements have been prepared in accordance with the requirements of applicable financial reporting framework;

(*b*) to enable himself to express an opinion on the true and fair view presented by the consolidated financial statements;

(*c*) to enquire into the matters as specified in section 143(1) of the Companies Act, 2013;

(*d*) to report on the matters given in the clauses (a) to (i) of section 143(3) of the Companies Act, 2013; for other matters under section 143(3)(j) read with rule 11 of the Companies (Audit and Auditors) Rules, 2014; and

(*e*) The auditor should also validate the requirement of preparation of CFS for the company as per applicable FRF.

Q.4 While doing the audit of consolidated financial statements, which current period consolidation adjustments are to be taken into account.

[May 09 (8 Marks)]

Or

X Limited is the holding company of Y Limited and Z Limited. Explain the nature of current period consolidation adjustments which will be taken into account for the preparation of Consolidated Financial Statements.

[May 14 (6 Marks)]

Or

You have been appointed to audit consolidated financial statements of Xerna Ltd. for the financial year 2018-19 while vouching, you observed that Intra Group Transactions have not been eliminated

You are, therefore, required to guide the management by explaining what are current period adjustments and list out the same.

Ans. : Current Period Consolidation Adjustment

These are those adjustments which are made in the accounting period for which Consolidated Financial Statements are prepared.

These adjustments primarily relate to elimination of intra-group transactions and account balances including:

(*a*) intra-group interest paid and received or management fees, etc;

(*b*) unrealised intra-group profits on assets acquired/transferred from/to other subsidiaries;

(*c*) intra-group indebtedness;

(*d*) adjustments relating to harmonising the different accounting policies being followed by the parent and its components;

(*e*) adjustments to the F.S. (of the parent and the components being consolidated) for recognized subsequent events or transactions that occur between the balance sheet date and the date of the auditor's report on the consolidated F.S. of the group.

(*f*) adjustments for the effects of significant transactions or other events that occur between date of components balance sheet and not already recognised in its F.S. and the date of the auditor's report on the group's consolidated F.S. when the financial statements of the component to be used for consolidation are not drawn upto the same balance sheet date as that of the parent;

(*g*) In case of a foreign component, adjustments to convert a component's audited F.S. prepared under the component's local GAAP to the GAAP under which the consolidated F.S. are prepared.

(*h*) determination of movement in equity attributable to the minorities interest since the date of acquisition of the subsidiary.

(*i*) adjustments of deferred tax on account of temporary differences arising out of elimination of profit and losses resulting from intra-group transactions and undistributed profits of the component in case of consolidated F.S. prepared under Ind AS.

Q.5 Write short note on: Permanent Consolidation adjustments. [May 13, Nov. 15 (4 Marks)]

Ans. : Permanent Consolidation Adjustments:

Permanent consolidation adjustments are those adjustments that are made only on the first occasion or subsequent occasions in which there is a change in the shareholding of a particular entity which is consolidated. These adjustments are:

(*i*) Determination of Goodwill or Capital Reserve as per applicable AS.

(*ii*) Determination of the amount of equity attributable to minority.

Verification Points

- Auditor should verify that the adjustment of goodwill or capital reserve and minority interest have been made appropriately.
- The auditor should pay particular attention to the determination of pre-acquisition reserves of the components. Date(s) of investment in components assumes importance in this regard.
- Examine whether the pre-acquisition reserves have been allocated appropriately between the parent and the minority of the subsidiary.
- Verify the changes that might have taken place in permanent consolidation adjustments on account of subsequent acquisition of shares in the components, disposal of the components in the subsequent years.

"ICAI Examiner Comments"

Most of the examinees referred to irrelevant points on AS-21 and temporary adjustment.

Q.6 H Limited, a company registered with SEBI, has three subsidiaries and one associate. While doing the audit of Consolidated Financial Statement (CFS) of H Limited you have come to know that the associate entity had made a provision dividend in its financial statement. H Limited computed its share of the results of operations of the associate after taking into account the proposed dividend. Comment.

[Nov. 13 (4 Marks)]

Ans. : Adjustment of dividend provisions made by associate in consolidated financial statements:

- *Explanation* (*b*) to Para 6 of AS 23 "Accounting for Investments in Associates in Consolidated Financial Statements" requires that in case an associate has made a provision for proposed dividend in its financial statements, the investor's share of the results of operations of the associate is computed without taking in to consideration the proposed dividend.

- In the present case, the consolidated financial statements are prepared in violation of AS-23 to the extent that share of result of operations of associate is computed after taking into account the proposed dividend.

Conclusion: Auditor is required to state the matter and quality the report accordingly.

Q.7 **A Ltd. holds the ownership of 10% of voting power and control over the composition of Board of Directors of B Ltd. While planning the statutory audit of A Ltd., what factors would be considered by you for audit of financial statements? [May 15 (6 Marks)]**

Ans. : Special considerations in case of entities controlling the composition of Board of Directors of others:

- Ownership of voting power is not necessary to control the other enterprise. Control may be exercised by controlling the composition of the Board of Directors (in the case of a company) or corresponding governing body (in the case of any other enterprise) with a view to obtain economic benefits. For example, an entity holds only 10 per cent of the share capital of another entity but it has control over the composition of the Board of Directors/governing body of the second entity. In such a case, the first entity would be considered as a parent of the second entity and, therefore, it would consolidate the second entity in the consolidated financial statements as subsidiary.
- The auditor, therefore, apart from carrying out general procedures, should verify whether the parent controls the composition of the Board of Directors or corresponding governing body of any entity.
- In this regard, the auditor may verify the Board's minutes, shareholder agreements entered into by the parent, agreements with the entities to which the parent might have provided any technology or know how, enforcement of statute, as the case may be, etc.
- The auditor would have to use his professional judgment to determine whether the parent controls the composition of the Board of Directors of any other entity. If yes, whether that entity has been consolidated as a subsidiary in the consolidated financial statements.

"ICAI Examiner Comments"

Most of the candidates discussed SA 550 on Related Parties but did not mention about audit procedures. Many candidates could not identify holding subsidiary relationship thereby they did not refer to consolidation of Holding and Subsidiary company accounts. Candidates could not narrate the opinion to be made where related party transactions are not properly accounted and disclosed.

Q.8 **Parent Ltd. acquired 51% shares of Child Ltd. during the year ending 31-3-2017. During the financial year 2017-18 the 20% shares of Child Ltd. were sold by Parent Ltd. Parent Ltd. while preparing the financial statement for the year ending 31-3-2017 and 31-3-2018 did not consider the financial statements of Child Ltd. for consolidation. As a statutory auditor how would you deal with it? [May 15 (6 Marks)]**

Or

Moon Ltd. acquired 65% shares of Sun Ltd. on 28th October 2017. On 25th April 2018 they sold 25% shares of Sun Ltd. While preparing consolidated financial statements for the year ended 31st March, 2018, accountant of Moon Ltd. did not consider financial statements of Sun Ltd. for consolidation. Comment. [May 17 (5 Marks)]

Ans. : Auditor's duties in case of exclusion of subsidiaries/associates in consolidation:

- As per section 129(3) of the Companies Act, 2013, where a company has one or more subsidiaries or associate companies, it shall, in addition to its own financial statements prepare a consolidated financial statement of the company and of all the subsidiaries and associate companies in the same form and manner as that of its own and in accordance with the applicable accounting standards.
- As per Rule 6 of Companies (Accounts) Rules, 2014, the consolidation of financial statements of the company shall be made in accordance with the provisions of Schedule III to the Act and the applicable AS. However, a company which is not required to prepare consolidated financial statements under the Accounting Standards, it shall be sufficient if the company complies with provisions on consolidated financial statements provided in Schedule III of the Act.
- As per AS 21 "Consolidated Financial Statements" consolidation of a subsidiary is not required if the relationship of parent with the subsidiary is intended to be temporary or subsidiary operate under severe long term restrictions which significantly impair its ability to transfer funds to the parent.
- Where an enterprise owns majority of voting power by virtue of ownership of the shares of another enterprise and all the shares are acquired & held exclusively with a view to their subsequent disposal in the near future, the control by the first mentioned enterprise would be considered temporary and the investments in such subsidiaries should be accounted for in accordance with AS 13 "Accounting for Investments".

- The auditor should satisfy himself that the exclusion made by the management falls within these two categories.
- As per Ind AS 110, there is no such exemption for 'temporary control', or "for operation under severe long-term funds transfer restrictions" and consolidation is mandatory for Ind AS compliant financial statement in this case.
- In the given case, Parent Ltd. has acquired 51% shares of Child Ltd. during the year ending 31-03-2017 and sold 20% shares during the year 2017-18. Parent Ltd. did not consolidate the financial statements of Child Ltd. for the year ending 31-03-2017 and 31-03-2018.

Conclusion: The intention of Parent Ltd. is quite clear that the control in Child Ltd. is temporary as the former company disposed off the acquired shares in the next year of its purchase.

Parent Ltd. is not required to prepare consolidated F.S. as per AS 21. However, for compliance of Sec. 129(3), Parent Ltd. is required to made disclosures in the F.S. as per the provisions provided in Schedule III to the Companies Act, 2013.

If the Parent Ltd. is required to prepare its financial statements under Ind AS, it shall have to prepare Consolidated F.S. in accordance with Ind AS 110 as exemption for 'temporary control', or "for operation under severe long-term funds transfer restrictions" is not available under Ind AS 110.

"ICAI Examiner Comments"

Most of the candidates mentioned that as per Sec. 129(3) of the Companies Act, 2013 where a company having subsidiary, which is not required to prepare consolidated F.S. under the accounting standards, it shall be sufficient if the company complies with the provisions on consolidated F.S. provided in Schedule III to the Act. Only few candidates referred to AS 21 and AS 13.

Q.9 **H Ltd. owns 55% voting power in S Ltd. It however holds and discloses all the shares as "Stock-in-trade" in its accounts. The shares are held exclusively with a view to their subsequent disposal in the near future. H Ltd. represents that while preparing Consolidated Financial Statements, S Ltd. can be excluded from the consolidation. As a Statutory Auditor, how would you deal?**

Ans. : Consolidation of Financial Statement:

- As per section 129(3) of the Companies Act, 2013, where a company has one or more subsidiaries or associate companies, it shall, in addition to its own financial statements prepare a consolidated financial statement of the company and of all the subsidiaries and associate companies in the same form and manner as that of its own and in accordance with the applicable accounting standards.
- As per Rule 6 of Companies (Accounts) Rules, 2014, the consolidation of financial statements of the company shall be made in accordance with the provisions of Schedule III to the Act and the applicable AS. However, a company which is not required to prepare consolidated financial statements under the Accounting Standards, it shall be sufficient if the company complies with provisions on consolidated financial statements provided in Schedule III of the Act.
- There could be two reasons for exclusion of a subsidiary, associate or jointly controlled entity
  (*a*) The relationship of parent with the subsidiary, associate or jointly controlled entity is intended to be temporary, or
  (*b*) The subsidiary, associate or joint venture operates under several long-term restrictions which significantly impair its ability to transfer funds to the parent.
  The auditor should satisfy himself that the exclusion made by the management falls within these two categories.
- In the present case, H Ltd.'s intention is to dispose off the shares in the near future as shares are being held as stock in trade and it is quite clear that the control is temporary.

Conclusion: H Ltd. is not required to consolidate as per requirement of AS 21. However, for the compliance of provisions related to consolidation of financial statements given under Section 129(3) of the Companies Act, 2013 read with Companies (Accounts) Rules, 2014, H Ltd. is required to consolidate the financial statements as per the provisions on consolidated financial statements provided in Schedule III to the Act.

Q.10 **B Ltd. is the Subsidiary company of A Ltd. ABC & Associates has been appointed as auditor of A Ltd. for the Financial year 2017-2018 and XYZ & Associates has been appointed as auditor of B Ltd. for the year 2017-18. Explain the role of ABC & Associates and XYZ & Associates as auditors of the parent company and subsidiary respectively. [Nov. 16 (4 Marks)]**

Ans. : Role of Auditor of Parent Company and Subsidiary company:

SA 600 "Using the work of Another Auditor" establishes the standard when an auditor, reporting on the financial statements of a group (consolidated financial statements), uses the work of another auditor on the financial information of one or more components included in the financial statements of the entity. Accordingly, role of auditor of parent company and subsidiary are as follows:

Role of Auditor of Parent Company:

(*a*) Consider the professional competence of Other Auditor, if Other Auditor is not a member of ICAI.

(*b*) Visit component and examine books of account, if essential.

(*c*) Obtain sufficient appropriate evidence, that work of Other Auditor is adequate for Principal Auditor's purposes.

(*d*) Discuss audit procedures applied by Other Auditor.

(*e*) Review a written summary of Other Auditor's procedures and findings through questionnaires/checklist.

(*f*) Consider significant findings of Other Auditor and discuss audit findings with Other Auditor. Perform supplemental tests if necessary.

Role of Auditor of Subsidiary Company:

The auditor of subsidiary company, knowing the context in which his work is to be used by the principal auditor, should co-ordinate with the principal auditor w.r.t. following:

(*a*) Adhering to time-table.

(*b*) Bringing to the attention of PA any significant finding.

(*c*) Compliance with relevant statutory requirements.

(*d*) Respond to detailed questionnaire.

Q.11 You are appointed as an auditor of Nawab Limited, a listed company which is a main supplier to the UK building and construction market. With a turnover of ₹ 2.9 billion, the company operates through 11 business units and has nearly 180 branches across the countries.

As an auditor, how will you draft the report in case:

(*a*) When the Parent's Auditor is also the Auditor of all its Components?

(*b*) When the Parent's Auditor is not the Auditor of all its Components?

(*c*) When the Component(s) Auditor Reports on Financial Statements under an Accounting Framework Different than that of the Parent?

(*d*) When the Component(s) Auditor Reports under an Auditing Framework Different than that of the Parent?

(*e*) Where the financial statements of one or more components are not audited?

Or

You are appointed as an auditor of Najib Limited, a listed company which is a main supplier to the USA building and construction market. With a turnover of Rs. 1.9 billion, the company operates through 11 business units and has nearly 170 branches across the countries.

As an auditor, how will you draft the report in case

(*i*) When the Component(*s*) Auditor Reports on Financial Statements under an Accounting Framework Different than that of the Parent?

(*ii*) When the Component(*s*) Auditor Reports under an Auditing Framework Different than that of the Parent? [RTP-Nov. 18]

Ans. : Reporting Considerations

(*a*) **Parent Auditor is also the auditor of all of its components**

◆ Auditor should issue an audit report expressing opinion whether the consolidated financial statements give a true and fair view of the state of affairs of the Group as on balance sheet date and as to whether consolidated profit and loss statement gives true and fair view of the results of consolidated profit or losses of the Group for the period under audit.

◆ Where the consolidated financial statements also include a cash flow statement, the auditor should also give his opinion on the true and fair view of the cash flows presented by the consolidated cash flow statements.

◆ Auditor of Parent should report whether principles and procedures for preparation and presentation of consolidated F.S. as laid down in the relevant AS(s) have been followed. In case of any deviation, the auditor should make adequate disclosure in the audit report so that users of the consolidated F.S. are aware of such deviation.

(*b*) **Parent's Auditor is not the Auditor of all of its components**

- If the parent's auditor is not the auditor of the components included in the consolidated F.S., the auditor of the consolidated F.S. should also consider the requirement of SA 600.
- If the parent's auditor decides that he will make reference to the audit of the other auditors in the report, he should disclose clearly the portion of the F.S. audited by the other auditor(s). This may be done by stating the amount or %age of total assets and total revenue of subsidiary(s) included in consolidated F.S. not audited by him.
- It is to be noted that reference in the report of the auditor of consolidated F.S. to the fact that part of the audit of the group was made by other auditor(s) is not to be construed as a qualification of the opinion but rather as an indication of the divided responsibility between the auditors of the parent and its subsidiaries.

(*c*) **Component Auditor Reports on F.S. under an Accounting Framework different than that of the Parent**

- When a component's F.S. are prepared under an accounting framework that is different than that of the framework used by the parent in preparing group's consolidated F.S., the parent's management perform a conversion of the components' audited F.S. from the framework used by the component to the framework under which the consolidated F.S. are prepared.
- The conversion adjustments are audited by the principal auditor to ensure that the financial information of the component(s) is suitable and appropriate for the purposes of consolidation.
- Alternatively, component may prepare financial statements on the basis of the parent's accounting policies, as outlined in the group accounting manual. The local component auditor can then audit and issue an audit report on the components F.S. prepared in accordance with "group accounting policies".
- The Principal auditor can then decide whether or not to rely on the components' audit report and make reference to it in the auditor's report on the consolidated financial statements.

(*d*) **Component Auditor Reports under an Auditing Framework Different than that of the Parent**

- Audits of F.S., including consolidated F.S., are performed under auditing standards generally accepted in India.
- In order to maintain consistency of the auditing framework and to enable the parent auditor to rely and refer to the other auditor's audit report in their audit report on the consolidated F.S., the components' F.S. should also be audited under a framework that corresponds to Indian Auditing Standards.

(*e*) **Components Not Audited**

- F.S. of all components included in consolidated F.S. should be audited or subjected to audit procedures. Such audits and audit procedures can be performed by the auditor reporting on the consolidated F.S. or by the components' auditor.
- Where the F.S. of one or more components continues to remain unaudited, the auditor reporting on the consolidated F.S. should consider unaudited components in evaluating a possible modification to his report on the consolidated F.S.
- The evaluation is necessary because the auditor has not been able to obtain sufficient appropriate audit evidence in relation to such consolidated amounts/balances.
- Auditor should evaluate both qualitative and quantitative factors on the possible effect of such amounts remaining unaudited when reporting on the consolidated F.S. using the guidance provided in SA 705, "Modifications to the Opinion in the Independent Auditor's Report".

Q.12 C Ltd. is holding 55% shares of D Ltd. M/s. AB & Associates are statutory auditors of C Ltd. Whereas for D Ltd. there is another firm appointed as statutory auditors. What are the reporting responsibilities of M/s. AB & Associates for audit of consolidated financial statements? [May 17 (5 Marks)]

Ans.: Reporting Responsibilities of auditor of Holding Company if auditor of subsidiary company is different:

- If the parent's auditor is not the auditor of the components included in the consolidated F.S., the auditor of the consolidated F.S. should also consider the requirement of SA 600.
- If the parent's auditor decides that he will make reference to the audit of the other auditors in the report, he should disclose clearly the portion of the F.S. audited by the other auditor(s). This may be done by stating the amount or %age of total assets and total revenue of subsidiary(s) included in consolidated F.S. not audited by him.
- It is to be noted that reference in the report of the auditor of consolidated F.S. to the fact that part of the audit of the group was made by other auditor(s) is not to be construed as a qualification of the opinion but rather as an indication of the divided responsibility between the auditors of the parent and its subsidiaries.

Requirements of SA 600:

- When the principal auditor concludes, based on his procedures, that the work of the other auditor cannot be used and the principal auditor has not been able to perform sufficient additional procedures regarding the financial information of the component audited by the other auditor, the principal auditor should express **a qualified opinion or disclaimer of opinion** because there is a limitation on the scope of audit.
- When the principal auditor has to base his opinion on the financial information of the entity as a whole relying upon the statements and reports of the other auditors, his report should state clearly the **division of responsibility** for the financial information of the entity by indicating the extent to which the financial information of components audited by the other auditors have been included in the financial information of the entity, *e.g.*, the number of divisions/branches/subsidiaries or other components audited by other auditors.

Q.13 **H Co. Ltd., is a holding company with two subsidiaries R Co. Ltd. and S Co. Ltd. The H Co. Ltd., adopts straightline method of depreciation for its assets whereas S Co. Ltd., follows written down value or diminishing value method. Though R Co. Ltd., follows straightline method of depreciation, it does not give effect to component accounting of depreciation in respect of high value assets, while consolidating the financials of the R Co. Ltd., and S Co. Ltd., with those of H Co. Ltd., determine the possible issue that you have to ensure for compliance in the light of above facts. [May 18 - New Syllabus (5 Marks)]**

Ans : Consolidated Financial Statements:

- In preparing consolidated financial statements, the financial statements of the parent and its subsidiaries are combined on a line by line basis by adding together like items of assets, liabilities, income and expenses.
- Consolidated financial statements are prepared using uniform accounting policies for like transactions. If a member of the group uses different accounting policies, appropriate adjustments are made to its financial statements when they are used in preparing the consolidated financial statements. If it is not practicable to use uniform accounting policies in preparing the consolidated financial statements, that fact should be disclosed together with the proportions of the items in the consolidated financial statements to which the different accounting policies have been applied.
- As per para 60 and 61 of Ind AS 16, 'Property, Plant and Equipment', a change in the method of depreciation shall be accounted for as a change in an accounting estimate as per Ind AS 8, 'Accounting Policies, Changes in Accounting Estimates and Errors'. Therefore, the selection of the method of depreciation is an accounting estimate and not an accounting policy.
- Therefore, there can be different methods of estimating depreciation for property, plant and equipment, if their expected pattern of consumption is different. The method once selected in the individual financial statements of the subsidiary should not be changed while preparing the consolidated financial statements.
- Accordingly, in the given case, the property, plant and equipment of S Co. Ltd. (subsidiary company) may be depreciated using WDV method and property, plant and equipment of parent company may be depreciated using SLM, if such method closely reflects the expected pattern of consumption of future economic benefits embodied in the respective assets.
- However, under the provisions of Companies Act, 2013 and as per requirement of AS 10, component accounting of depreciation is mandatory. Auditor should insist the parent company to ask R Co. Ltd. (subsidiary company) to give effect to component accounting of depreciation before consolidation of financial statements.

Q.14 **H Limited is an investment company preparing its Financial Statements in accordance with Ind AS. The company obtains funds from various investors and commits its performance for fair return and capital appreciation to its investors. During the year under audit, it had been observed that the company had invested 25% in S1 Ltd., 50% in S2 Ltd. and 60% in S3 Ltd. of the respective share capitals of the Investee Companies. When checking the investment schedule of the company, an issue cropped as to whether there would arise any need to consolidate accounts of any such investee companies with those of H Limited in accordance with Section 129(3) of the Companies Act, 2013 which contains no exclusion from consolidation. Analyse the issues involved and give your views. [Nov. 18-New Syllabus (5 Marks)]**

Answer: Auditor's duties in case of exclusion of subsidiaries/associates in consolidation:

- As per section 129(3) of the Companies Act, 2013, where a company has one or more subsidiaries or associate companies, it shall, in addition to its own financial statements prepare a consolidated financial statement of the company and of all the subsidiaries and associate companies in the same form and manner as that of its own and in accordance with the applicable accounting standards.

- As per Rule 6 of Companies (Accounts) Rules, 2014, the consolidation of financial statements of the company shall be made in accordance with the provisions of Schedule III to the Act and the applicable AS. However, a company which is not required to prepare consolidated financial statements under the Accounting Standards, it shall be sufficient if the company complies with provisions on consolidated financial statements provided in Schedule III of the Act.
- As per Para 31 of Ind-AS 110, an investment entity shall not consolidate its subsidiaries. Instead, an investment entity shall measure an investment in a subsidiary at fair value through profit or loss in accordance with Ind AS 109 (Financial Instruments). As per Para 33, parent of an investment entity shall consolidate all entities that it controls, including those controlled through an investment entity subsidiary, unless the parent itself is an investment entity.
- In the given case H Limited is an investment company preparing its Financial Statements in accordance with Ind AS. Company had invested 25% in S1 Ltd., 50% in S2 Ltd. and 60% in S3 Ltd. of the respective share capitals of the Investee Companies.

Conclusion: H Ltd. is not required to consolidate accounts of investee companies as provided under Para 31 of Ind-AS 110. However, company is required to comply with the provisions on consolidated financial statements as provided in Schedule III.

Q.15 What is meant by "Group financial statements"? Give reference of relevant Auditing Standard and issues addressed concerning the audit of Group financial statements. [Nov. 18 - Old Syllabus (4 Marks)]

Answer: Meaning of Group Financial Statements:

- Group Financial Statements also known as Consolidated financial statements are the financial statements of a group presented as those of a single entity.
- Group financial statements are presented for a Group of entities under the control of a Parent.
- A group comprises a parent and its subsidiaries. A parent is an entity that has one or more subsidiaries. Group financial statements are presented, to the extent possible, in the same format as adopted by the parent for its separate Financial Statements.
- AS-21 and Ind AS-110 lays down principles and procedures for preparation and presentation of Consolidated Financial Statements.

Relevant Auditing Standard: Refer answer of Q. No. 10

Q.16 R Ltd. owns 51% voting power in S Ltd. It however, holds and discloses all the shares as "Stock-in-trade" in its financial statements since the shares are held exclusively with a view to their subsequent disposal in the near future. R Ltd. represents that while preparing Consolidated Financial Statements, S Ltd. can be excluded from the consolidation. As the Statutory Auditor of R Ltd., how would you deal when the consolidated financial statements are to be drawn up in compliance with Ind AS.

[May 19 - Old Syllabus (4 Marks)]

Or

M Ltd. acquired 51% shares of S Ltd. on 01.04.2018 and sold 25% of these shares during the financial year 2018-19. M Ltd. did not prepare Consolidated Financial Statements for the financial year 2018-19 on the plea that the control was only temporary. Do you agree with the view of M Ltd.? Decide, assuming that M Ltd. is required to prepare its financial statements under Ind As. [Nov. 19 - Old Syllabus (4 Marks)]

Ans. : Consolidation of financial statements:

- As per section 129(3) of the Companies Act, 2013, where a company has one or more subsidiaries or associate companies, it shall, in addition to its own financial statements prepare a consolidated financial statement of the company and of all the subsidiaries and associate companies in the same form and manner as that of its own and in accordance with the applicable accounting standards.
- As per Rule 6 of Companies (Accounts) Rules, 2014, the consolidation of financial statements of the company shall be made in accordance with the provisions of Schedule III to the Act and the applicable AS. However, a company which is not required to prepare consolidated financial statements under the Accounting Standards, it shall be sufficient if the company complies with provisions on consolidated financial statements provided in Schedule III of the Act.
- As per AS 21 "Consolidated Financial Statements" consolidation of a subsidiary is not required if the relationship of parent with the subsidiary is intended to be temporary or subsidiary operate under sever long term restrictions which significantly impair its ability to transfer funds to the parent.

- There is no exemption for 'temporary control', or "for operation under severe long-term funds transfer restrictions" in Ind AS 110 and consolidation is mandatory for Ind AS compliant financial statement in this case.

Conclusion: Auditor should ask the management for the consolidation of S Ltd. If Consolidation not made, auditor should modify the audit report on Consolidated Financial Statements.

Q.17 ALM Associates has been appointed as auditor of M/s Harry Ltd. which acquired 55% shares in M/s Sam Ltd. on 15th October, 2018. During audit of Harry Ltd. the auditors found that the company have not prepared consolidated financial statements because on the date of acquisition the fair value of certain assets & liabilities has not been ascertained which is significant and are accounted for on estimated basis only. Help ALM Associates in framing opinion paragraph of audit report. [May 19 - New Syllabus (4 Marks)]

Ans. : Consolidation of financial statements:

- As per section 129(3) of the Companies Act, 2013, where a company has one or more subsidiaries or associate companies, it shall, in addition to its own financial statements prepare a consolidated financial statement of the company and of all the subsidiaries and associate companies in the same form and manner as that of its own and in accordance with the applicable accounting standards.
- As per Rule 6 of Companies (Accounts) Rules, 2014, the consolidation of financial statements of the company shall be made in accordance with the provisions of Schedule III to the Act and the applicable AS. However, a company which is not required to prepare consolidated financial statements under the Accounting Standards, it shall be sufficient if the company complies with provisions on consolidated financial statements provided in Schedule III of the Act.
- In the present case, during audit, auditors found that the company have not prepared consolidated financial statements because on the date of acquisition the fair value of certain assets & liabilities has not been ascertained which is significant and are accounted for on estimated basis only.

Conclusion: Consolidation is mandatory, auditor is required to state the fact in auditor report on standalone financial statements.

Note: Answer given in the Suggested answer of ICAI is entirely different covering therein the draft of Adverse opinion and Basis for Adverse opinion.

Author's view: It is not necessary that auditor of standalone financial statements should be appointed as auditor of consolidated financial statements, so while auditing standalone financial statements, auditor is not required to modify the opinion on standalone financial statements on the ground of non-consolidation. Further, when consolidated F.S. are not available, how the auditor is issuing report on consolidated financial statements (It is specified in the suggested answer - Opinion Section - the accompanying consolidated financial statements do not give a true and fair view)

12 CHAPTER AUDIT OF DIVIDEND

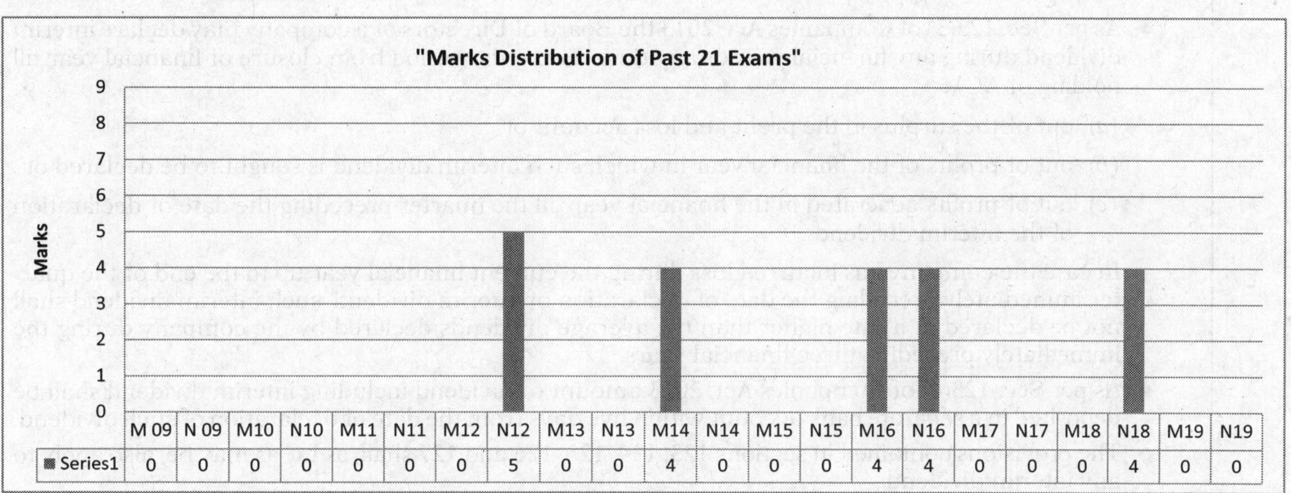

	M 09	N 09	M10	N10	M11	N11	M12	N12	M13	N13	M14	N14	M15	N15	M16	N16	M17	N17	M18	N18	M19	N19
Series1	0	0	0	0	0	0	0	5	0	0	4	0	0	0	4	4	0	0	0	4	0	0

Q.1 Write short note on: Investor Education and Protection Fund.

Ans. : Investor Education and Protection Fund:

Sec. 125 of the Companies Act, 2013 empowers the Central Government to establish a fund known as Investor Education and Protection Fund. The purpose of this fund is to utilize the money for the promotion of investor awareness and protection to the interests of the investors.

The amount that are required to be credited in this fund are:

(*a*) amount given by the C.G. by way of grants after due appropriation made by Parliament by law in this behalf;

(*b*) donations given to the Fund by the C.G., State Governments, companies or any other institution;

(*c*) amount in the Unpaid Dividend Account of companies;

(*d*) amount in the general revenue account of the C.G. which had been transferred to that account u/s 205A(5) of the Companies Act, 1956, as it stood immediately before the commencement of the Companies (Amendment) Act, 1999, and remaining unpaid or unclaimed on the commencement of this Act;

(*e*) the amount lying in the Investor Education and Protection Fund u/s 205C of the Companies Act, 1956;

(*f*) the interest or other income received out of investments made from the Fund;

(*g*) the amount received under sub-section (4) of section 38;

(*h*) the application money received by companies for allotment of any securities and due for refund;

(*i*) matured deposits with companies other than banking companies;

(*j*) matured debentures with companies;

(*k*) interest accrued on the amounts referred to in clauses (*h*) to (*j*);

(*l*) sale proceeds of fractional shares arising out of issuance of bonus shares, merger and amalgamation for seven or more years;

(*m*) redemption amount of preference shares remaining unpaid or unclaimed for seven or more years; and

(*n*) such other amount as may be prescribed:

Provided that no such amount referred to in clauses (*h*) to (*j*) shall form part of the Fund unless such amount has remained unclaimed and unpaid for a period of seven years from the date it became due for payment.

Q.2 While adopting the accounts for the year, the Board of Directors of Prima Ltd., decided to consider the Interim Dividend declared @ 12% as final dividend and did not consider transfer of profit to Reserves. As a statutory auditor, how would you deal with this? [Nov. 16 (4 Marks)]

Ans. : Declaration of Interim Dividend:

- As per Sec. 2(35) of Companies Act, 2013 dividend includes interim dividend. Therefore, the procedures which are applicable to final dividend also applies to any interim dividend.
- As per Sec. 123(3) of Companies Act, 2013 the Board of Directors of a company may declare interim dividend during any financial year or any time during the period from closure of financial year till holding of AGM

  (*a*) out of the surplus in the profit and loss account or

  (*b*) out of profits of the financial year in which such interim dividend is sought to be declared or

  (*c*) out of profits generated in the financial year till the quarter preceding the date of declaration of the interim dividend.

  In case the company has incurred loss during the current financial year up to the end of the quarter immediately preceding the date of declaration of interim dividend, such interim dividend shall not be declared at a rate higher than the average dividends declared by the company during the immediately preceding three financial years.
- As per Sec. 123(4) of Companies Act, 2013 amount of dividend including interim dividend shall be deposited in a separate bank account within five days from the date of declaration of such dividend.
- The provisions contained in sections 123, 124, 125, 126 and 127 shall, as far as may be, also apply to any interim dividend.
- First proviso to Section 123(1) provides that a company may, before the declaration of any dividend in any financial year, transfer such percentage of its profit for that financial year as it may consider appropriate to the reserves of the company. Therefore, company is not mandatorily required to transfer the profit to the reserves, it is an option available to the company to transfer a percentage of profit to reserves.

Conclusion: Assuming that the company has complied with the depreciation requirement, the interim dividend can be declared without transferring profits to reserves.

Q.3 A company has paid interim dividend at 10% based on its half-yearly performance while at the end of the year suffered a net loss. How you will deal with the matter in your audit report as a statutory auditor?

Ans. : Payment of Interim Dividend:

- As per Sec. 2(35) of Companies Act, 2013 dividend includes interim dividend. Therefore, the procedures which are applicable to final dividend also applies to any interim dividend.
- Section 123(1) of the Companies Act, 2013 provides that dividend cannot be declared or paid by a company for any financial year except out of profits of the company for that year arrived at after providing for depreciation in accordance with the provisions of Section 123(2), or out of the profits or the company for any previous financial year or years arrived at after providing for depreciation in the manner aforementioned and remaining undistributed, or out of both.
- In the present case, the company has suffered a net loss at the end of the year, which signifies that the directors have not calculated the performance of the company about the second half of the year accurately.
- Hence, if the company had a sufficient balance in the P & L Account as at the beginning of the year, the interim dividend paid may be adjusted against the same. In this situation, auditor need not report anything.
- However, if balance in P & L A/c was not available, the dividend may also be paid out of reserves, subject to compliance of conditions as prescribed in Companies (Declaration and Payment of Dividend) Rules, 2014. If, however, there is no balance in the profit and loss account nor any reserves were available, the dividend would be clearly paid out of capital.

Conclusion: Assuming that there is no balance in the profit & loss account nor any reserves were available. auditor need to qualify his report mentioning the fact that the dividend having been paid out of capital.

Q.4 For the year ended on 31st March, 2018, P Ltd. proposed to pay a dividend of 25% on its equity shares and it further proposed to transfer 20% of Net profit for that year after tax to its reserves. Its auditor objected to the same stating that 10% is the maximum permissible limit to transfer to reserves.

[May 14 (4 Marks)]

Ans. : Transfer to Reserve:

- Section 123(1) of the Companies Act, 2013 provides that dividend cannot be declared or paid by a company for any financial year except out of profits of the company for that year arrived at after providing for depreciation in accordance with the provisions of Section 123(2), or out of the profits or the company for any previous financial year or years arrived at after providing for depreciation in the manner aforementioned and remaining undistributed, or out of both.
- First proviso to Section 123(1) provides that a company may, before the declaration of any dividend in any financial year, transfer such percentage of its profit for that financial year as it may consider appropriate to the reserves of the company. Therefore, company is not mandatorily required to transfer the profit to the reserves, it is an option available to the company to transfer a percentage of profit to reserves.
- In the present case, P Ltd. has proposed to pay a dividend of 25% on its equity shares and a transfer of 20% of Net profit to its reserves.

Conclusion: Assuming that the company has complied with the depreciation requirement, the dividend can be declared by transferring any amount of profits to reserves.

Q.5 As a statutory auditor, how would you deal with the following: ABC Ltd. having a paid-up capital of ₹ 1 crore earned as total net profit of ₹ 1 crore for the years 2014-15 to 2016-17. The Company did not declare any dividend nor transferred any amount to Reserves for these years. The entire profit was retained in the Profit & Loss Account.

In 2017-18, the company made a profit of ₹ 20 lacs. The company also proposed in 2017-18 to declare dividend @ 25% of capital out of accumulated profits.

Ans. : Declaration of Dividends:

- Section 123(1) of the Companies Act, 2013 provides that dividend cannot be declared or paid by a company for any financial year except out of profits of the company for that year arrived at after providing for depreciation in accordance with the provisions of Section 123(2), or out of the profits or the company for any previous financial year or years arrived at after providing for depreciation in the manner aforementioned and remaining undistributed, or out of both.
- First proviso to Section 123(1) provides that a company may, before the declaration of any dividend in any financial year, transfer such percentage of its profit for that financial year as it may consider appropriate to the reserves of the company. Therefore, company is not mandatorily required to transfer the profit to the reserves, it is an option available to the company to transfer a percentage of profit to reserves.
- In the present case company earns a profit of ₹ 20 Lacs, but wants to declare dividend @ 25%, of capital that amounts to ₹ 25 Lacs. The deficiency of ₹ 5 Lacs may be paid out of accumulated profits.

Conclusion: The company is well within its power and right to declare the dividend of ₹ 25 lacs for the year 2017-18.

Q.6 As Auditor of Act Fast Ltd. what steps will you take to ensure that the dividend has been paid only out of profit?

[Nov. 08 (8 Marks)]

Or

AARK Ltd. is a large-sized listed company having annual turnover of INR 4000 crores. The company also has a plan to get listed on New York Stock Exchange next year. The company has paid good amount of dividend during the year to its shareholders which is significantly higher as compared to earlier years. The statutory auditors would like to focus on this aspect at the time of their statutory audit.

Please advise the relevant procedures that the statutory auditors should perform in respect of this area.

[RTP-May 19]

Ans. : Steps for verification of dividend:

To ensure that dividend is paid out of profits, auditor should take the following steps:

(*i*) Ensure that all the rules and regulations concerning the declaration or payment of dividends have been complied with.

(*ii*) Ensure that the dividends have been declared or paid only out of distributable profit i.e. profits for the current year for which dividend is declared, or accumulated profits of the previous years, or money provided by the Central or State Government as per Sec. 123(1) of the Companies Act, 2013.

(*iii*) In case of inadequacy or absence of profits in any financial years, if dividend has been paid out of accumulated profits, earned by it in previous years and transferred to the reserves, verify that the rules related to such distribution has been complied.

(*iv*) Verify that the dividend recommended by the Board has been approved by the members at the AGM.

(*v*) Verify that the dividend has been transferred to the separate scheduled bank account within 5 days from the declaration of such dividend as required by Sec. 123(4) of the Companies Act, 2013.

(*vi*) Verify that the dividend has been paid within 30 days from the declaration. If in case the dividend has not been claimed or paid within 30 days from the declaration, verify that the unpaid or unclaimed dividend amount has been transferred to a special account called unpaid dividend account as per Sec. 124(1) of the Companies Act, 2013.

(*vii*) Verify that the company has prepared a statement within a period of 90 days of making any transfer of an amount to the Unpaid Dividend Account containing the specified particulars, and have placed it on the website of the company, if any, and also on any other website approved by the C.G. for this purpose as required under Sec. 124(2) of the Companies Act, 2013.

(*viii*) Verify that, if any money transferred to Unpaid Dividend Account has remained unpaid or unclaimed for a period of 7 years from the date of such transfer then, whether it has been transferred by the company along with interest accrued, if any, thereon to the Investor Education and Protection Fund established u/s 125(1) of the Companies Act, 2013 and a statement regarding such transfer has also been sent to the authority which administers such fund.

(*ix*) In case the company has outsourced the activity to the Service Organisation, check that all the compliances with laws, regulations, accounting and disclosure related to the dividends have been made appropriately.

Q.7 **The management of limited company states that proposed dividend does not represent a liability and hence no provision need to be made. Comment.**

or

As a statutory auditor of the company, comment on the following: For the year ended 31st March 2018, the financial statements of A (Pvt) Ltd. were adopted on 30th April, 2017. At this meeting, the directors proposed a dividend for the year 2017-18 of 25% on the equity share capital amounting to ₹ 10 Lacs. No entry was passed for the proposed dividend in the books of the company, since in the view of the directors the same was not required as per Schedule III. [Nov. 12 (5 Marks)]

Ans. : Non-Provisions for proposed dividends:

- Schedule III requires disclosure of the amount of dividend proposed to be distributed to equity and preference shareholders for the period and the related amount per share to be disclosed separately. It also requires separate disclosure of the arrears of fixed cumulative dividends on preference shares.
- As per AS-4, "Contingencies and Events Occurring after the Balance Sheet Date" there are events which, although they take place after the balance sheet date, are sometimes reflected in the financial statements because of statutory requirements or because of their special nature. For example, if dividends are declared after the balance sheet date but before the financial statements are approved for issue, the dividends are not recognised as a liability at the balance sheet date because no obligation exists at that time unless a statute requires otherwise. Such dividends are disclosed in the notes.
- In the present case, no entry was passed for proposed dividend.

Conclusion: Contention of the management not to provide dividend is correct.

Q.8 **The Board of Directors of ACP Ltd. has recommended the dividend of 15% on paid up share capital of ₹ 450 crores for the year ended 31st March, 2018, at their meeting held on 1st of May, 2018 when the accounts for the financial year 2017-18 were approved. The Board of Directors when they met on 7th July, 2018 for the review of first Quarter accounts, the Board has decided to rescind their decision to recommend dividend.**

The notice for AGM to be held on 14-8-2018 was sent on 15th July, 2018 without any recommendation of dividend.

At the AGM the members asked the management how they can rescind the declaration of dividend once recommended. Comment. [May 16 (4 Marks)]

Ans. : Revocation of recommended Dividend:

- As per Regulation 80 of Table F of schedule I of the Companies Act, 2013, the company in general meeting may declare dividends, but no dividend shall exceed the amount recommended by the Board.

- Section 123 of the Companies Act, 2013, provides that the dividend shall be declared or paid by a company for any financial year out of the profits of the company for that year arrived at after providing for depreciation in prescribed manner.
- As per Sec. 127 of Companies Act, 2013, dividend after declaration has to be paid or warrant in respect thereof has to be posted within 30 days from the date of declaration.
- Dividend once declared, becomes a debt against the company and cannot be revoked except in certain situations.
- In the present case, the decision for revocation of dividend arrived before its declaration in General meeting.

Conclusion: Board of directors are well within their powers to rescind the dividend which is recommended earlier, but not yet declared in the AGM.

"ICAI Examiner Comments"

Most of the candidates failed to explain the valid reason for rescinding the dividend.

Q.9 **ABC Limited is in the practice of maintaining consistent dividend payment over a minimum of 14%. The Financial year 2017-18 was so very bad for the company that it was not possible for the company to maintain the payment of consistent dividend as above. The Management, being hopeful of recovery of its performance in next year, felt that the depreciation of the year to the extent of 75% alone be charged to the statement of profit and loss and the remaining 25% be kept in a separate account code in the balance sheet - 'Debit Balances Adjustable against Revenue Account'. The Management was of the view that it would be in fair practice of accounting if the depreciation for asset is charged before the expiry of the lifes of assets and the amount parked in asset code as above would unfailingly be adjusted to Revenue before the close of next financial year anyway. Analyse the issues involved and state how the Auditor should decide on this matter. [Nov. 18-New Syllabus (5 Marks)]**

Answer: Declaration of Dividend without providing the depreciation:

- Sec. 123(1) of Companies Act, 2013 provides that, no dividend shall be declared or paid by a company for any financial year except out of the profits of the company for that financial year arrived at after providing for depreciation in accordance with the provisions of Sec. 123(2).
- Sec. 123(2) provides that depreciation shall be provided to in accordance with the provisions of Schedule II.
- As per Schedule II to the Companies Act, 2013 depreciation is to be charged over useful lives of the assets. Useful life of an asset is the period over which an asset is expected to be available for use by an entity or the number of production or similar units expected to be obtained from the asset by the entity. The useful life of an asset shall not be longer that the useful life specified in the Part C of Schedule II. If, however where a company uses a different useful life justification for the difference shall be disclosed in the financial statement with justification supported by technical device.
- In the present case, company in order to maintain consistency in payment of dividend is willing to charge 75% of the depreciation to the statement of profit and loss and the remaining 25% be kept in a separate account code in the balance sheet - 'Debit Balances Adjustable against Revenue Account'.

Conclusion: Management view is not correct as depreciation can be paid only out of profits that is arrived at after providing the depreciation.

Auditor should ensure the compliance of provisions of section 123 and Schedule II. In case the management does not comply with the provisions and does not charge the 100% depreciation the auditor shall suggest the management for the same and if management refuses, the auditor should qualify his report accordingly.

[illegible]

[illegible]

ABC Limited is in the business of manufacturing [illegible] in financial year 2018-19 [illegible] company [illegible] the payment of [illegible] dividend [illegible] as above. [illegible] management [illegible] depreciation [illegible] charge [illegible] the statement of profit and loss [illegible] balance sheet [illegible] Management [illegible] the view that it would be [illegible] of accounting [illegible] the company [illegible] decision on the matter.

[illegible]

CHAPTER 13

AUDIT COMMITTEE AND CORPORATE GOVERNANCE

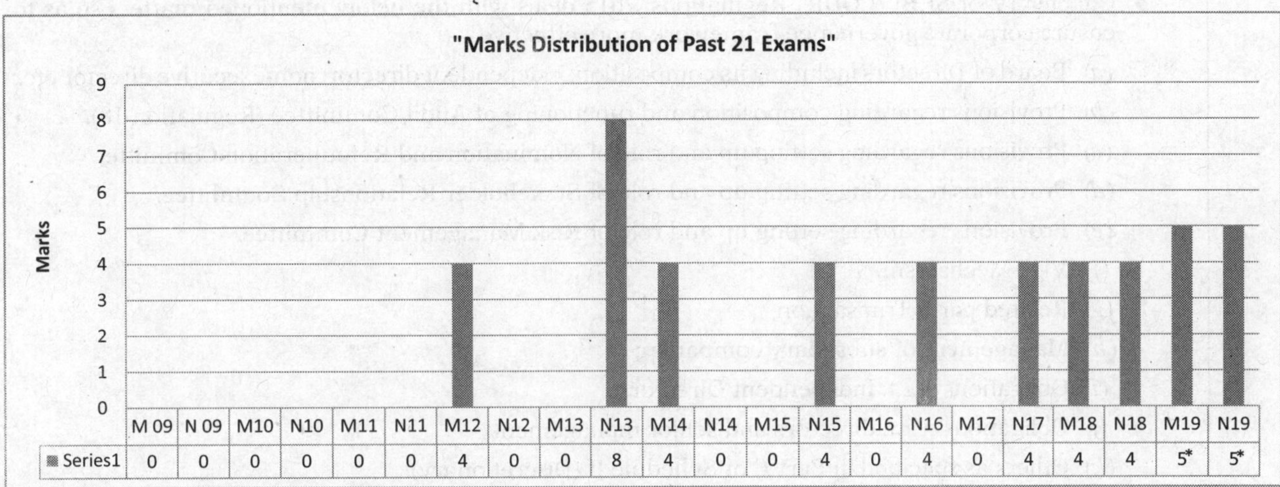

*Only Subjective Questions.

13.1 - CORPORATE GOVERNANCE

Q.1 Write short note on: Corporate Governance.

Ans. : Corporate Governance:

- Corporate Governance is the system by which companies are directed and governed by the management in the best interests of the stakeholders and others ensuring better management, greater transparency and timely financial reporting.
- Responsibility to ensure corporate Governance rests with the Board of Directors.
- In India, the legal framework of Corporate Governance is contained in Sec. 177 of the Companies Act, 2013 (relating to Audit Committee) and Chapter IV (Regulation 17 to Regulation 27) of SEBI (LODR) Regulations, 2015.
- SEBI (LODR) Regulations, 2015, issued by SEBI with the objective of streamlining and consolidating the provisions of various listing agreements in operation for different segments of the capital markets, such as equity shares, preference shares, debt instruments, units of mutual funds, Indian depository receipts, securitised debt instruments and any other securities that the SEBI may specify.
- These Regulations are divided into 2 parts - the substantive provisions are incorporated in the main body while the procedural requirements are incorporated in the form of schedules.
- It may be noted that the LODR Regulations deal with only post-listing requirements and exclude all pre-listing requirements.

Q.2 Write short note on: Matters addressed in SEBI (LODR) Regulations, 2015 regarding Corporate Governance. [Nov. 15 (4 Marks)]

Or

Enumerate the issues addressed in the SEBI (Listing Obligations and Disclosure Requirements) Regulations, 2015 regarding Corporate Governance.

Ans. : Corporate Governance:

- Corporate Governance can be defined as "the formal system of **accountability and control** for ethical and socially responsible organisational decisions and use of resources".
- Corporate Governance is the system by which companies are directed and governed by the management in the best interests of the stakeholders and others ensuring better management, greater transparency and timely financial reporting.
- Responsibility to ensure corporate Governance rests with the Board of Directors.
- In India, the legal framework of Corporate Governance is contained in Sec. 177 of the Companies Act, 2013 (relating to Audit Committee) and Chapter IV (Regulation 17 to Regulation 27) of SEBI (LODR) Regulations, 2015.
- Chapter IV of SEBI (LODR) Regulations, 2015 deals with the below mentioned matters so as to ensure corporate governance framework more effective —

(*a*) Board of Directors including its composition, independent director, non-executive director etc.;

(*b*) Provisions regarding composition and functioning of Audit Committee (Regulation 18).

(*c*) Provisions regarding setting up and role of Nomination and Remuneration Committee.

(*d*) Provisions regarding setting up and role of Stakeholder Relationship Committee.

(*e*) Provisions regarding setting up and role of Risk Management Committee.

(*f*) Vigil Mechanism.

(*g*) Related party Transaction;

(*h*) Management of subsidiary companies;

(*i*) Obligations w.r.t. Independent Directors.

(*j*) Obligations w.r.t. directors and senior management.

(*k*) Others as specified in Part E of Schedule II (Discretionary).

ICAI Examiner Comments

Most of the examinees did not highlight the matters addressed in Clause 49 (Now SEBI (LODR) Regulations regarding Corporate Governance, instead they wrote general answers on Corporate Governance. Also some examinees explained about audit committee.

13.2 - AUDIT COMMITTEE (SEC. 177 OF COMPANIES ACT, 2013)

Q.3 Explain the Constitution and Functions of Audit Committee u/s 177 of Companies Act, 2013.

Or

Write short note on: Requirement for Audit Committee as per Companies Act, 2013.

[Nov. 17 (4 Marks)]

Ans. : Constitution of Audit Committee:

Section 177(1) of Companies Act, 2013 read with Rule 6 of Companies (Meetings of Board and its Powers) Rules, 2014 requires Board of Directors of every listed public company and below mentioned class of companies to constitute an Audit Committee —

(*i*) all public companies with a paid-up capital of ₹ 10 Cr. or more;

(*ii*) all public companies having turnover of ₹ 100 Cr. or more;

(*iii*) all public companies, having in aggregate, outstanding loans and debentures and deposits exceeding fifty crore rupees or more.

Explanation to Rule 6 provides that the paid-up share capital or turnover or outstanding loans or debentures and deposits, as the case may be, as existing on the date of last audited Financial Statements shall be taken into account.

Functions of Audit Committee:

Every Audit Committee shall act in accordance with the terms of reference specified in writing by the Board which shall, *inter alia*, include:

(i) the recommendation for appointment, remuneration and terms of appointment of auditors;
(ii) review and monitor the auditor's independence and performance, and effectiveness of audit process;
(iii) examination of the financial statement and the auditors' report thereon;
(iv) approval or any subsequent modification of transactions of the company with related parties;
(v) scrutiny of inter-corporate loans and investments;
(vi) valuation of undertakings or assets of the company, wherever it is necessary;
(vii) evaluation of internal financial controls and risk management systems;
(viii) monitoring the end use of funds raised through public offers and related matters.

13.3 - AUDIT COMMITTEE (REGULATION OF SEBI (LODR) REGULATIONS, 2015)

Q.4 State the main features of the qualified and independent Audit Committee set up under regulation 18 of SEBI (LODR) Regulations, 2015. [Nov. 08 (4 Marks)]

Or

Every listed company shall constitute a qualified & Independent audit committee in accordance with the terms of reference subject to a few conditions. Explain. [MTP-Aug. 18]

Ans. : Features of Qualified and Independent Audit Committee:

(a) The audit committee shall have minimum 3 directors as members. Two-thirds of the members of audit committee shall be independent directors.

In case of a listed entity having outstanding Superior Rights (SR) equity shares, the audit committee shall only comprise of independent directors.

(b) All members of audit committee shall be financially literate and at least one member shall have accounting or related financial management expertise.

(c) The Chairperson of the Audit Committee shall be an independent director.

(d) The Chairperson of the Audit Committee shall be present at AGM to answer shareholder queries.

(e) The audit committee at its discretion shall invite the finance director or head of the finance function, head of internal audit and a representative of the statutory auditor and any other such executives, to be present at the meetings of the committee.

(f) The Company Secretary shall act as the secretary to the committee.

Q.5 The audit committee has been granted several roles under SEBI (LODR) Regulations, 2015. Oversight of the company's financial reporting process; recommendation for appointment of auditors; approval of payment to statutory auditors etc. are some of the roles that an audit committee perform. State the role of Audit Committee as provided under SEBI (LODR) Regulations.

Ans. : Role of Audit Committee under SEBI (LODR) Regulations, 2015:

1. Oversight of the company's financial reporting process and the disclosure of its financial information to ensure that the financial statement is correct, sufficient and credible.
2. Recommendation for appointment, remuneration and terms of appointment of auditors.
3. Approval of payment to statutory auditors for any other services rendered by them;
4. Reviewing with management the annual financial statements before submission to the Board, focusing primarily on:
   (a) Matters required to be included in the Director's Responsibility Statement to be included in the Board's report in terms of Sec. 134(3)(c) of the Companies Act, 2013;
   (b) Changes, if any, in accounting policies and practices and reasons for the same;
   (c) Major accounting entries involving estimates based on the exercise of judgment by management;
   (d) Significant adjustments made in the financial statements arising out of audit findings;
   (e) Compliance with listing and other legal requirements relating to financial statements;
   (f) Disclosure of any related party transactions;
   (g) Qualifications in the draft audit report.
5. Reviewing, with the management, the quarterly financial statements before submission to the board for approval;

6. Reviewing, with the management, the statement of uses/application of funds raised through an issue (public issue, rights issue, preferential issue, etc.), the statement of funds utilized for purposes other than those stated in the offer document/prospectus/notice and the report submitted by the monitoring agency monitoring the utilisation of proceeds of a public or rights issue, and making appropriate recommendations to the Board to take up steps in this matter;
7. Review and monitor the auditor's independence and performance, and effectiveness of audit process;
8. Approval or any subsequent modification of transactions of the company with related parties;
9. Scrutiny of inter-corporate loans and investments;
10. Valuation of undertakings or assets of the company, wherever it is necessary;
11. Evaluation of internal financial controls and risk management systems;
12. Reviewing, with the management, performance of statutory and internal auditors, adequacy of the internal control systems;
13. Reviewing the adequacy of internal audit function.
14. Discussion with internal auditors of any significant findings and follow up thereon;
15. Reviewing the findings of any internal investigations by the internal auditors into matters where there is suspected fraud or irregularity or a failure of internal control systems of a material nature and reporting the matter to the board;
16. Discussion with statutory auditors before the audit commences, about the nature and scope of audit as well as post-audit discussion to ascertain any area of concern;
17. To look into the reasons for substantial defaults in the payment to the depositors, debenture holders, shareholders (in case of non-payment of declared dividends) and creditors;
18. To review the functioning of the Whistle Blower mechanism;
19. Approval of appointment of CFO after assessing the qualifications, experience and background, etc. of the candidate;
20. Carrying out any other function as is mentioned in the terms of reference of the Audit Committee.
21. ***Reviewing the utilization of loans and/or advances from/investment by the holding company in the subsidiary exceeding ₹ 100 crore or 10% of the asset size of the subsidiary, whichever is lower including existing loans/advances/investments existing as on 1.4.2019.***

Q.6 State the mandatory Review areas of the audit committee. [May 12 (4 Marks)]

Or

List few documents that require mandatory review by Audit Committee.

[Nov. 18-New Syllabus (5 Marks)]

Ans. : Mandatory Review Area of Audit Committee:

1. Management discussion and analysis of financial condition and results of operations.
2. Statement of significant related party transactions submitted by management.
3. Management letters/letters of internal control weaknesses issued by the statutory auditors.
4. Internal audit reports relating to internal control weaknesses; and
5. The appointment, removal and terms of remuneration of the Chief Internal Auditor.
6. Statement of deviations:
   (*a*) Quarterly statement of deviation(s) including report of monitoring agency, if applicable submitted to stock exchange.
   (*b*) Annual statement of funds utilised for purposes other than those stated in offer document/prospectus.

Q.7 D Ltd., a company incorporated in India has six members in its Audit Committee. Due to recessionary conditions in India the revenue of the company is going down and there is showdown in other activities of the company. Therefore, it is expected that there would not be significant work for members of the Audit Committee.

Considering the overall recession in the company and the economy, the members of the Committee decided unanimously to meet only once at the year end. They reviewed monthly information system of the company and found no errors.

As an auditor of D Limited would you consider the decision taken by the Audit Committee to hold the meeting once in a year, is complying with Listing Obligation and Disclosure Requirements (LODR)? Also state the quorum requirements for such meetings.

[Nov. 13 (4 Marks), RTP-Nov. 18., Nov. 19 - New Syllabus (5 Marks)]

Ans. : Validity of Audit Committee decisions w.r.t. meetings and review area:

- Regulation 18 of SEBI (LODR) Regulations, 2015, among other things, requires the following:
  1. The audit committee should meet at least 4 times in a year and not more than 4 months shall elapse between two meetings.
  2. Audit committee should mandatorily review certain areas like management discussion and analysis, statement of significant related party transactions, letters of internal control weaknesses, internal audit reports etc.
- In the present case, members of audit committee decided to meet only once in a year and review only the monthly information system which does not meet the requirement of regulation 18 of SEBI (LODR) Regulations, 2015 as stated above.

Conclusion: Decision taken by audit committee to conduct meeting once in a year and review of only monthly information system is not in line with the requirements of Regulation 18 of SEBI (LODR) Regulations, 2015.

Quorum requirements of meetings of audit committee: The quorum shall be either 2 members or 1/3 of the members of the audit committee whichever is greater, but there should be a minimum of two independent members present.

Q.8 Mr. 'U', a respectable Chartered Accountant of international repute was requested by one of the major corporate in India to join its Board and also as a Chairman of Audit Committee. He expressed his apprehensions that he is not having the requisite experience. Mr. 'U' seeks your view on the responsibility of Audit Committees vis-à-vis the review of Financial Statements. **[May 14 (4 Marks)]**

Ans. : Responsibility of Audit Committee vis-a-vis the review of Financial statement:

As per Regulation 18 of SEBI (LODR) Regulations, 2015, audit committee is required to review with management the annual financial statements before submission to the Board, focusing primarily on:

1. Matters required to be included in the Director's Responsibility Statement to be included in the Board's report in terms of Sec. 134(3)(c) of the Companies Act, 2013.
2. Changes, if any, in accounting policies and practices and reasons for the same
3. Major accounting entries involving estimates based on the exercise of judgment by management
4. Significant adjustments made in the financial statements arising out of audit findings
5. Compliance with listing and other legal requirements relating to financial statements
6. Disclosure of any related party transactions
7. Qualifications in the draft audit report.

Note : Information to be reviewed mandatorily is covered in Q No. 6

Q.9 Write short notes on: Power of Audit Committee as stipulated under SEBI (Listing Obligations and Disclosure Requirements) Regulations.

Ans. : Power of Audit Committee:

As per SEBI (LODR) Regulations, 2015, the audit committee may exercise following powers, in addition to others:

1. To investigate any activity within its terms of reference.
2. To seek information from any employee.
3. To obtain outside legal or other professional advice.
4. To secure attendance of outsiders with relevant expertise.

Q.10 Comment on the following in the light of certificate of compliance of conditions of Corporate Governance to be issued for a listed company where the Board consists of 10 directors including a non-executive director as its chairman and further:

(i) There were 5 meetings held during the year as follows: 01/04/2017, 01/06/2017, 01/09/2017, 03/01/2018, 25/03/2018.

(ii) There are 4 independent directors. One of them resigned on 25/05/2017. A new independent director was appointed on 01/09/2017.

(iii) The chairman of Audit Committee did not attend the Annual General meeting held on 14/09/2017.

(iv) The internal audit reports were obtained by Audit Committee on quarterly basis. Quarter 1 internal audit report commented on certain serious irregularities as regards electronic online auction of scrap. The agenda of Audit Committee did not deliberate or take note of the issue.

[Nov. 18-Old Syllabus (4 Marks)]

Ans. : Compliance of conditions as to Corporate Governance:

- Regulation 18 of SEBI (LODR) Regulations, 2018, among other things provides the followings:
  - (*a*) The audit committee shall have minimum 3 directors as members. Two-thirds of the members of audit committee shall be independent directors.
  - (*b*) The Chairperson of the Audit Committee shall be an independent director. The Chairperson of the Audit Committee shall be present at AGM to answer shareholder queries.
  - (*c*) The audit committee should meet at least 4 times in a year and not more than 120 days shall elapse between two meetings.
  - (*d*) Audit committee must mandatorily review certain aspects including therein is the Internal audit reports relating to internal control weaknesses.
- Regulation 17(1) of the SEBI (LODR) Regulations, 2015 provides the following:
  - (*a*) The Board of Directors of the company shall have an optimum combination of executive and non-executive directors with at least one woman director and not less than 50% of the Board of Directors comprising non-executive directors.
  - (*b*) Where the Chairperson of the Board is a non-executive director, at least 1/3rd of the Board should comprise independent directors and in case the company does not have a regular non-executive Chairman, at least half of the Board should comprise independent directors.
- Further Sec. 149(4) of the Companies Act, 2013 read with Rule 4 of Companies (Appointment and Qualifications of Directors) Rules, 2014 provides that any intermittent vacancy of an independent director shall be filled-up by the Board at the earliest but not later than immediate next Board meeting or 3 months from the date of such vacancy, whichever is later.

Accordingly, while issuing certificate of Corporate Governance, auditor is required to make the following modifications:

(*i*) Gap between meetings held on 01.09.2017 and 03.01.2018 is more than 120 days;

(*ii*) Casual vacancy in the office is independent director was filled up after the period prescribed u/s 149(4) read with Rule 4 of Companies (Appointment and Qualifications of Directors) Rules, 2014;

(*iii*) Chairman was mandatorily required to attend AGM, which he did not.

(*iv*) Internal audit report was not reviewed by the audit committee.

Q.11 Section 177 of the Companies Act, 2013 provides that every listed company and other class of companies as prescribed shall constitute a committee of the Board known as "audit Committee". Briefly discuss the additional requirements as per Sec. 177 which are silent in Regulation 18 of SEBI (LODR) Regulations, 2015.

Ans. : Additional requirement of Sec. 177 which are silent in Regulation 18:

(*a*) Every Audit Committee shall act in accordance with terms of reference to be specified in writing by the Board.

(*b*) The Board's report u/s 134(3) shall disclose the composition of an Audit Committee and where the Board had not accepted any recommendation of the Audit Committee, the same shall be disclosed in such report along with the reasons therefor.

(*c*) The auditors of a company and the key managerial personnel shall have a right to be heard in the meetings of the Audit Committee when it considers the auditor's report but shall not have the right to vote.

Q.12 Briefly explain the role of auditor in audit committee and certification of compliance of conditions of Corporate Governance.

Ans. : Role of Auditor in Audit Committee and certification of compliance of conditions of corporate governance:

Regulation 18 of SEBI (LODR) Regulations, 2015 requires a representative of the statutory auditor, when required, shall be invited to the meetings of the Audit Committee.

Sec. 177 of Companies Act, 2013 requires that auditors of a company and the key managerial personnel has a right to be heard in the meetings of the Audit Committee when it considers the auditor's report but they shall not have the right to vote.

In relation to audit committee and certification of compliance of conditions of corporate governance, auditor is required:

(*a*) To ensure that he communicates frequently with the Audit Committee on key accounting or auditing issues that, in his judgment, give rise to a greater risk of material misstatement of the financial statements.

(*b*) To ensure that he addresses any questions or concerns voiced by the Audit Committee.

(*c*) To assist and advise the Audit Committee on improving corporate governance, oversight of financial reporting process, implementation of accounting policies and practices, compliance with accounting standards, strengthening of the internal control systems in regard to financial reporting and reporting processes.

(*d*) To assist the management and the Audit Committee to enable them to discharge their functions effectively and in certification of the requirements of corporate governance.

Note: Auditor role is not to drive corporate governance directly. It is the management's responsibility to do so and in the process, auditor may play a significant role in assisting management to ensure better standards of corporate governance.

13.4 - MATTERS COVERED BY SEBI (LODR) REGULATIONS, 2015

Q.13 Elaborate under SEBI (LODR) Regulations, 2015, who is an independent director.

Ans. : Independent Director under Clause 49:

As per Regulation 16(1) of SEBI (LODR) Regulations, 2015, 'independent director' shall mean a non-executive director, other than a nominee director of the company:

a. who, in the opinion of the Board, is a person of integrity and possesses relevant expertise and experience;

b. who is or was not a promoter of the company or its holding, subsidiary or associate company; and not related to promoters or directors in the company, its holding, subsidiary or associate company; ***or member of the promoter group of the listed entity.***

c. apart from receiving director's remuneration, has or had no material pecuniary relationship with the company, its holding, subsidiary or associate company, or their promoters, or directors, during the two immediately preceding financial years or during the current financial year;

d. none of whose relatives has or had pecuniary relationship or transaction with the company, its holding, subsidiary or associate company, or their promoters, or directors, amounting to 2% or more of its gross turnover or total income or ₹ 50 Lacs or such higher amount as may be prescribed, whichever is lower, during the two immediately preceding financial years or during the current financial year;

e. who, neither himself nor any of his relatives:

1. holds or has held the position of a key managerial personnel or is or has been employee of the company or its holding, subsidiary or associate company in any of the three financial years immediately preceding the financial year in which he is proposed to be appointed;
2. is or has been an employee or proprietor or a partner, in any of the three financial years immediately preceding the financial year in which he is proposed to be appointed, of:
   - a firm of auditors or CS in practice or cost auditors of the company or its holding, subsidiary or associate company; or

- any legal or a consulting firm that has or had any transaction with the company, its holding, subsidiary or associate company amounting to 10% or more of the gross turnover of such firm;

3. holds together with his relatives 2% or more of the total voting power of the company; or
4. is a Chief Executive or director, by whatever name called, of any non-profit organisation that receives 25% or more of its receipts from the company, any of its promoters, directors or its holding, subsidiary or associate company or that holds 2% or more of the total voting power of the company;
5. is a material supplier, service provider or customer or a lessor or lessee of the company;

f. who is not less than 21 years of age.

g. who is not a non-independent director of another company on the board of which any non-independent director of the listed entity is an independent director.

Q.14 P Limited is a listed Company in which no code of conduct is laid down for its board members and senior members. As an auditor of P Limited:

(*a*) Briefly explain the compliance requirements with respect to Code of Conduct as per Listing Order Disclosure Requirement (LODR) Regulations.

(*b*) What will be your role in compliance of above-mentioned Code of Conduct as per LODR Regulations?

Ans. : Requirements of Code of Conduct in SEBI (LODR) Regulations, 2015:

(*a*) Compliance Requirements w.r.t. Code of Conduct:

1. **Regulation 17(5):** The board of directors shall lay down a code of conduct for all members of board of directors and senior management of the listed entity. The code of conduct shall suitably incorporate the duties of independent directors as laid down in the Companies Act, 2013.
2. **Regulation 26(3):** All members of the Board and senior management shall affirm compliance with the code of conduct on an annual basis.
3. **Regulation 46(2):** Listed entity shall disseminate code of conduct on its website.
4. **Part D of Schedule V:** Annual Report of the company shall contain a **declaration** signed by the CEO stating that the members of board and senior management have affirmed compliance with the code of conduct.

(*b*) Role of auditor in compliance of code of conduct requirements:

(*i*) Ascertain whether the Board has laid down a Code of Conduct for all Board members and senior personnel of the company.

(*ii*) Obtain a copy of the code of conduct.

(*iii*) Verify whether all Board members and senior management have affirmed compliance with the code on an annual basis.

(*iv*) Verify whether the code has been posted on company's website.

Q.15 Write short note on: CEO/CFO Certification to the Board.

Ans. : CEO/CFO Certification to the Board:

Regulation 17(8) of SEBI (LODR) Regulations, 2015 requires that the CEO and CFO shall provide the compliance certificate to the Board that:

(*a*) They have reviewed financial statements and the cash flow statement for the year and that to the best of their knowledge and belief:

- These statements do not contain any materially untrue statement or omit any material fact or contain statements that might be misleading.
- These statements together present a true and fair view of the company's affairs and are in compliance with existing accounting standards, applicable laws and regulations.

(*b*) There are no transactions entered that are fraudulent, illegal and violative of the company's code of conduct.

(*c*) They accept responsibility for establishing and maintaining internal controls w.r.t. financial reporting.

(*d*) They have indicated to the auditors and the audit committee:

- Significant changes in internal control during the year.
- Significant changes in accounting policies during the year.
- Instances of significant fraud.

Q.16 Write short note on: Content of Management Discussion and Analysis. [Nov. 13 (4 Marks)]

Ans. : Management Discussion and Analysis:

Schedule V of SEBI (LODR) Regulations, 2015 requires that a Management Discussion and Analysis should form part of the Annual Report to the shareholders. This Management Discussion & Analysis should include discussion on the following matters within the limits set by the company's competitive position:

1. Industry structure and developments.
2. Opportunities and Threats.
3. Segment-wise or product-wise performance.
4. Outlook
5. Risks and concerns.
6. Internal control systems and their adequacy.
7. Discussion on financial performance with respect to operational performance.
8. Material developments in Human Resources/Industrial Relations front, including number of people employed.
9. ***Details of significant changes (i.e. change of 25% or more as compared to the immediately previous financial year) in key financial ratios, along with detailed explanations therefor, including:***
   - ***Debtors Turnover***
   - ***Inventory Turnover***
   - ***Interest Coverage Ratio***
   - ***Current Ratio***
   - ***Debt Equity Ratio***
   - ***Operating Profit Margin (%)***
   - ***Net Profit Margin (%)***
   - ***or sector-specific equivalent ratios, as applicable.***
10. ***Details of any change in Return on Net Worth as compared to the immediately previous financial year along with a detailed explanation thereof.***

Q.17 The auditor of Mould Limited made an adverse statement in his certificate as the Audit Committee of the company did not meet four times a year. Discuss few circumstances which require an adverse or qualified statement in the auditor's certificate in respect of compliance of the requirements of Corporate Governance.

[Nov. 16 (4 Marks)]

Or

Discuss any eight (8) adverse or qualified statement or disclosure, which you would like to make in respect of non-compliance with requirements Corporate Governance of a company.

[May 18 - Old Syllabus (4 Marks)]

Or

Some situations may require an adverse or qualified statement or a disclosure without necessarily making it a subject matter of qualification in the Auditors' Certificate, in respect of compliance of requirements of corporate governance. Give four examples of such situations. [MTP-Oct. 18]

Or

A listed entity has to obtain a compliance certificate from either the statutory auditors or practicing company secretaries regarding compliance of conditions of corporate governance and annex it to the Directors' Report. Discuss some situations which may require an adverse or qualified statement in respect of the above certificate. [Nov. 19 - Old Syllabus (5 Marks)]

Ans. : Circumstances requiring adverse or qualified statement in Auditor's certificate in respect of compliance of requirements of corporate governance:

1. The number of non-executive directors is less than 50% of the strength of Board of directors.
2. A qualified and independent audit committee is not set up.
3. The chairman of the audit committee is not an independent director.
4. The audit committee does not meet four times a year.
5. The necessary powers in terms of SEBI (LODR) Regulations, 2015 have not been vested by the Board in the audit committee.
6. The time gap between two Board meetings is more than four months.
7. A director is a member of more than ten committees across all companies in which he is a director.
8. The information of quarterly results is neither put on the company's website nor sent in a form so as to enable the Stock Exchange on which the entity's securities are listed to enable such Stock Exchange to put it on its own website.
9. The power of share transfer is not delegated to an officer or a committee or to the registrar and share transfer agents.

Q.18 M/s All-in-one limited is a large-sized listed Indian company with focus on design and delivery of custom made information technology applications for various business entities in India and abroad. The management wants to know whether they are required to constitute Risk Management committee as per SEBI (LODR) Regulations, 2015 and if so, required, what should be its composition? Advise.

[May 18 - New Syllabus (4 Marks)]

Ans : Requirement and Composition of Risk Management Committee:

As per Regulation 21 of SEBI (LODR) Regulations, 2015 requires the board of directors of companies to constitute a Risk Management Committee.

Composition of Risk Management Committee:

(*a*) The majority of members of Risk Management Committee shall consist of members of the board of directors.

(b) ***The majority of members of Risk Management Committee shall consist of members of the board of directors and in case of a listed entity having outstanding SR equity shares, at least 2/3rd of the Risk Management Committee shall comprise of independent directors.***

(*c*) The Chairperson of the Risk management committee shall be a member of the board of directors and senior executives of the listed entity may be members of the committee.

(*d*) The board of directors shall define the role and responsibility of the Risk Management Committee and may delegate monitoring and reviewing of the risk management plan to the committee and such other functions as it may deem fit.

(e) ***The risk management committee shall meet atleast once in a year.***

(*f*) The provisions of this regulation shall be applicable to top 100 listed entities, determined on the basis of market capitalisation, as at the end of the immediate previous financial year.

Q.19 The Directors and senior management of a listed company of which you are the statutory auditor, want to know their obligations under the SEBI Regulations in regard to Board or Non-Executive Directors. (mention any Five).

[May 19 - Old Syllabus (5 Marks)]

Ans. : Obligations of Directors and Senior Management under SEBI (LODR) Regulations, 2015:

(1) **Regulation 17(2):** The Board shall meet at least 4 times a year, with a maximum time gap of 120 days between any two meetings

(2) **Regulation 17(3):** The Board shall periodically review compliance reports pertaining to all laws applicable to the listed entity, prepared by the listed entity as well as steps taken by the listed entity to rectify instances of non-compliances.

(3) **Regulation 17(3):** The Board shall satisfy itself that plans are in place for orderly succession for appointment to the Board and senior management.

(4) **Regulation 17A**: A person shall not be a director in more than 8 listed entities with effect from April 1, 2019 and in not more than 7 listed entities with effect from April 1, 2020:

Provided that a person shall not serve as an independent director in more than 7 listed entities.

(5) **Regulation 25**: An independent director shall be held liable, only in respect of such acts of omission or commission by the listed entity which had occurred with his knowledge and with his consent or where he had not acted diligently with respect to the provisions contained in these regulations.

(6) **Regulation 26(1):** A director shall not be a member in more than 10 committees or act as chairperson of more than 5 committees across all listed entities in which he is a director.

(7) **Regulation 26(2):** Every director shall inform the listed entity about the committee positions he or she occupies in other listed entities and notify changes as and when they take place.

(8) **Regulation 26(4):** Non-executive directors shall disclose their shareholding in the listed entity in which they are proposed to be appointed as directors, in the notice to the general meeting called for appointment of such director.

(9) **Regulation 26(5):** Senior management shall make disclosures to the board relating to all material, financial and commercial transactions, where they have personal interest that may have a potential conflict with the interest of the listed entity at large.

Q.20 You have been appointed as an auditor of M/s Real Ltd. in which total number of directors in the board is 9. As an auditor, state the points to be considered in verification of composition of Board under Regulation 17 of the Securities and Exchange Board of India (Listing Obligations and Disclosure Requirements) Regulations, 2015. [May 19 - New Syllabus (6 Marks)]

Ans. : Verification regarding composition of Board of Directors:

(*i*) Ascertain whether, the Board comprises an optimum combination of executive and non-executive directors, with at least one woman director and not less than 50% of members of Board comprising non-executive directors.

The minutes of the Board meetings may be verified to ascertain whether a director is an executive director or a non-executive director.

(*ii*) ***Verify that no listed entity shall appoint a person or continue the directorship of any person as a non-executive director who has attained the age of 75 years unless a special resolution is passed to that effect, in which case the explanatory statement annexed to the notice for such motion shall indicate the justification for appointing such a person.***

(*iii*) Verify that where the Chairperson of the Board is a non-executive director and at least 1/3rd of the Board comprise of independent directors.

In case the listed entity does not have a regular non-executive Chairperson, at least ½ of the Board should comprise of independent directors.

(*iv*) ***Verify that the board of directors of the top 1000 listed entities (with effect from April 1, 2019) and the top 2000 listed entities (with effect from April 1, 2020) shall comprise of not less than six directors.***

(*v*) ***In case of listed company having outstanding SR equity shares, the auditor shall check that at least half of the board of directors comprises of independent directors.***

(*vi*) ***Ensure that the Chairperson of the board of the top 500 listed entities is - (a) a non-executive director; (b) not related to the Managing Director or the CEO as per the definition of the term "relative" defined under the Companies Act, 2013.***

(*vii*) Auditor may also examine the annual disclosure submitted by the directors to the Board.

(*viii*) Auditor should also verify that independent non-executive director, apart from receiving remuneration, should not have any material pecuniary relationship with the listed entity, its holding, subsidiary or associate company, or their promoters, or directors, during the two immediately preceding financial years or during the current financial year.

Q.21 Mr. S has been appointed as a director of CAC Ltd. You are required to state the information to be provided to the shareholders of the company in accordance with Regulation 36 of the Securities and Exchange Board of India (Listing Obligations and Disclosure Requirements) Regulations, 2015.

Ans. : Information to be provided to Shareholders under Regulation 36 of SEBI (LODR) Regulations:

The listed entity shall send annual report to the holders of securities, not less than 21 days before the AGM.

In case of the appointment of a new director or re-appointment of a director the shareholders must be provided with the following information:

(*a*) a brief resume of the director;

(*b*) nature of his expertise in specific functional areas;

(*c*) disclosure of relationships between directors *inter se*;

(*d*) names of listed entities in which the person also holds the directorship and the membership of Committees of the board; and

(*e*) shareholding of non-executive directors.

CHAPTER 14

LIABILITIES OF AUDITOR

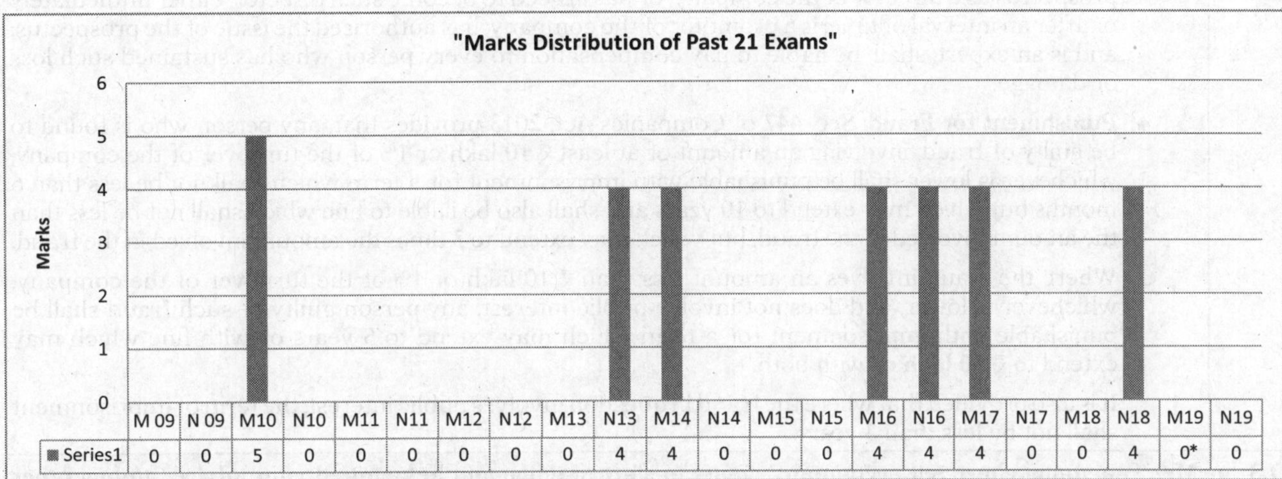

	M 09	N 09	M10	N10	M11	N11	M12	N12	M13	N13	M14	N14	M15	N15	M16	N16	M17	N17	M18	N18	M19	N19
■ Series1	0	0	5	0	0	0	0	0	0	4	4	0	0	0	4	4	4	0	0	4	0*	0

*Only Subjective Questions.

14.1- PROFESSIONAL NEGLIGENCE

Q.1 Write a short note on: Professional Negligence.

Ans. : Professional Negligence:

It connotes any failure to perform a duty according to accepted professional standards, which has resulted in some loss, damage or detriment to the party who had engaged a professional.

It is an act or omission which gives rise to a civil liability to compensate.

Elements of Professional Negligence

(*a*) **Existence of duty or responsibility**: One party is owed to another party to perform some act with due care, skill and competency.

(*b*) **Occurrence of Breach**: A breach occurs while performing the duty.

(*c*) **Loss or damages**: Loss or detriment being served by the party to whom the duty was owed as a result of breach. To establish a liability in respect of a third party, it is necessary that such third party should have suffered a loss or damage on account of the professional negligence.

Coverage: Professional negligence is necessarily restricted to the duties in a professional capacity.

14.2 - CIVIL AND CRIMINAL LIABILITIES UNDER COMPANIES ACT, 2013

Q.2 Explain the liability of the auditor under the Companies Act, 2013, for making an untrue statement in the report (as an expert forming a part of the prospectus). **[May 10 (5 Marks)]**

Or

Indicate the precise nature of auditor's liability for a misstatement that had occurred in the prospectus issued by the company.

Ans. : Liability of auditor for making untrue statements:

- **Criminal liability for misstatement in prospectus**: Sec. 34 of Companies Act, 2013 provides that where any prospectus is issued or circulated or distributed, which includes any statement which is untrue or misleading in form or context in which it is included or where any inclusion or omission of any matter is likely to mislead, then every person who authorises the issue of such prospectus shall be liable u/s 447 (fraud).
- **Civil liability for misstatement in prospectus:** Sec. 35 of Companies Act, 2013 provides that where a person has subscribed for securities of a company acting on any statement included, or the inclusion or omission of any matter, in the prospectus which is misleading and has sustained any loss or damage as a consequence thereof, the company and every person who is a director of the company at the time of the issue of the prospectus; has authorised himself to be named and is named in the prospectus as a director of the company, or has agreed to become such director, either immediately or after an interval of time; is a promoter of the company; has authorised the issue of the prospectus; and is an expert, shall, be liable to pay compensation to every person who has sustained such loss or damage.
- **Punishment for Fraud**: Sec. 447 of Companies Act, 2013 provides that, any person who is found to be guilty of fraud, involving an amount of at least ₹ 10 lakh or 1% of the turnover of the company, whichever is lower shall be punishable with imprisonment for a term which shall not be less than 6 months but which may extend to 10 years and shall also be liable to fine which shall not be less than the amount involved in the fraud, but which may extend to 3 times the amount involved in the fraud.

  Where the fraud involves an amount less than ₹ 10 lakh or 1% of the turnover of the company, whichever is lower, and does not involve public interest, any person guilty of such fraud shall be punishable with imprisonment for a term which may extend to 5 years or with fine which may extend to ₹ **50 lakh** or with both.

  It is also provided that where the fraud in question involves public interest, the term of imprisonment shall not be less than 3 years.

Q.3 Mr. X, a young chartered accountant, wants to start practice and he required your advice, among other things, on criminal liabilities of an auditor under the Companies Act, 2013. Kindly guide him.

[Nov. 13 (4 Marks)]

Or

Mr. Arjun, a newly qualified Chartered Accountant started his practice wants to specialize in Audits of corporate and required your advice on criminal liabilities of an auditor under the Companies Act, 2013. Kindly guide him. **[May 16 (4 Marks)]**

Ans. : Criminal Liabilities under Companies Act, 2013:

- **Criminal liability for misstatement in prospectus**: Sec. 34 of Companies Act, 2013 provides that where any prospectus is issued or circulated or distributed, which includes any statement which is untrue or misleading in form or context in which it is included or where any inclusion or omission of any matter is likely to mislead, then every person who authorises the issue of such prospectus shall be liable u/s 447 (fraud).
- **Punishment for false statement**: Sec. 448 of Companies Act, 2013 provides that if in any return, report, certificate, financial statement, prospectus, statement or other document required by, or for, the purposes of any of the provisions of this Act or the rules made thereunder, any person makes a statement, (*a*) which is false in any material particulars, knowing it to be false; or (*b*) which omits any material fact, knowing it to be material, he shall be liable under section 447.
- **Punishment for fraud**: Sec. 447 of Companies Act, 2013 provides that, any person who is found to be guilty of fraud, involving an amount of at least ₹ 10 lakh or 1% of the turnover of the company, whichever is lower shall be punishable with imprisonment for a term which shall not be less than 6 months but which may extend to 10 years and shall also be liable to fine which shall not be less than the amount involved in the fraud, but which may extend to 3 times the amount involved in the fraud.

  Where the fraud involves an amount less than ₹ 10 lakh or 1% of the turnover of the company, whichever is lower, and does not involve public interest, any person guilty of such fraud shall be punishable with imprisonment for a term which may extend to 5 years or with fine which may extend to ₹ **50 lakh** or with both.

  It is also provided that where the fraud in question involves public interest, the term of imprisonment shall not be less than 3 years.

ICAI Examiner Comments

Candidates lacked knowledge of sections 447 and 448 of the Companies Act, 2013 and mainly discussed about quantum of punishment and the amount of fine rather than the provisions leading to arising of criminal liability.

Q.4 **A Chartered Accountant in practice has been appointed as an auditor of a company which raised finance from the capital market on the basis of a prospectus issued a few years back. The main object for raising the finance was specified to be setting up a project on information technology. The company advanced the sum so raised to various firms and private companies in which the directors of the company were a partner or a director respectively. These parties had no standing whatsoever with information technology. In the Balance Sheet, these advances appeared as a current asset under the head "Short-term Loans and Advances - unsecured, considered good". There was no mention to the notes to accounts about nature and purpose of such advances; and the auditor has issued routine audit report without any qualifications. On the very next day to the issuance of audit report, the directors and their related parties gone disappeared. The company, in which the auditor was conducting audit, has just vanished. You are required to state whether the auditor will be held guilty for professional misconduct? Is there any liability subsists under any law?**

Ans. : Auditor's negligence in performance of duties:

- Clause 7 of Part I of Second Schedule to the CA Act, 1949 provides that a CA in practice will be deemed to be guilty of professional misconduct if he does not exercise due diligence in performance of his duties or is grossly negligent while performing his duties.
- Schedule III to the Companies Act, 2013 requires specific disclosure of loans and advances due by directors or other officers of the company or any of them either severally or jointly with any other person or amounts due by firms or private companies respectively in which any director is a partner or a director or a member.
- As per Section 188 of the Companies Act, 2013, no company shall enter into any contract or arrangement with a related party with respect to sale, purchase or supply of any goods or materials, except with the consent of the Board of Directors given by a resolution at a Board Meeting. Section 184 requires disclosure of interest by director and also lays down the procedure to be followed in this regard. Section 189 of the Companies Act, 2013 requires that every company shall keep one or more registers in which particulars of all contracts or arrangements, to which Section 184 or Section 188 applies, shall be entered separately.
- In the given case, the company has advanced the sum to the parties that are related to the Directors of the company and showed the same under the head "Short-term Loans and Advances - unsecured, considered good" rather than specific disclosure under the notes to accounts. The auditor of the company also issued clean audit report without any qualifications. It appears that the auditor did not perform his duties properly.

Conclusion: Auditor is guilty of professional misconduct under Clause 7 of part I of Second Schedule to CA Act, 1949 and is also liable to be punished u/s 147 of Companies Act 2013, due to non-observance of compliance of Schedule III and Sections 184, 188 and 189 of Companies Act, 2013.

Q.5 **Indicate the precise nature of auditor's liability in the following situation: Certain weaknesses in the internal control procedure in the payment of wages in a large construction company were noticed by the statutory auditor who in turn brought the same to the knowledge of the Managing Director of the company. In the subsequent year huge defalcation came to the notice of the management. The origin of the same was traced to the earlier year. The management wants to sue the auditor for negligence and also plans to file a complaint with the Institute.**

Ans. : Liabilities of auditor:

- SA 265 on "Communicating Deficiencies in Internal Control to TCWG and Management" requires the auditor to determine whether, on the basis of the audit work performed, he has identified one or more deficiencies in internal control. If one or more deficiencies in internal control has been identified, he shall determine whether, such deficiencies individually or in combination constitute significant deficiencies. Significant deficiencies are required to be communicated in writing to TCWG and management on a timely basis.
- In the given case, certain weaknesses in the internal control procedure in the payment of wages in a large construction company were noticed by the statutory auditor and brought the same to the knowledge of the Managing Director of the company. In the subsequent year, a huge defalcation took place, the ramification of which stretched to the earlier year. The management of the company desires to sue the statutory auditor for negligence.

- The precise nature of auditor's liability in the case can be ascertained on the basis of the following considerations:
  (*a*) Whether the defalcation emanated from the weaknesses noticed by the statutory auditor, the information regarding which was passed on to the management; and
  (*b*) Whether the statutory auditor properly and adequately extended the audit programme of the previous year having regard to the weaknesses noticed.
- If circumstances indicate the possible existence of fraud or error, the auditor should consider the potential effect of the suspected fraud or error on the financial information. If the auditor believes the suspected fraud or error could have a material effect on the financial information, he should perform such modified or additional procedures as he determines to be appropriate. Thus, normally speaking, as long as the auditor took due care in performing the audit work, he cannot be held liable.
- The fact that the matter was brought to the notice of the managing director may be a good defence for the auditor as well. In Kingston Cotton Mills Ltd., it was held that it is the duty of the auditor to probe into the depth only when his suspicion is aroused. The statutory auditor, by bringing the weakness to the notice of the managing director had alerted the management which is judicially held to be primarily responsible for protection of the assets of the company and can put forth this as defence against any claim arising subsequent to passing of the information to the management.

Q.6 **Indicate the precise nature of auditor's duties in the following situation: Based upon the legal opinion of a leading advocate, X Ltd. made a provision of ₹ 5 crores towards Income Tax liability. The assessing authority has worked out the liability at ₹ 15 crores. It is observed that the opinion of the advocate was inconsistent with legal position with regard to certain revenue items.**

Ans. : Auditor's liabilities in case of short provisions:

- SA 500 on "Audit Evidence" requires that auditor to perform appropriate procedures while using the work of management expert as audit evidence. Before relying on expert's opinion, the auditor should have seen that opinion given by the expert is *prima facie* appropriate and acceptable.
- In the present case, opinion of the management expert was inconsistent with legal position with regard to certain items. It is, perhaps, quite possible that auditor did not seek reasonable assurance as to the appropriateness of the source data, assumptions and methods used by the expert properly.
- SA 500 requires that auditor to resolve the inconsistency by discussion with the management and the expert. In case, the expert's work does not support the related representation in the financial information, the inconsistency in legal opinions could have been detected by the auditor if he had gone through the same. This seems apparent having regard to wide difference in the liability worked out by the assessing authority.

Conclusion: Auditor should reject the opinion and insisted upon making proper provision.

Q.7 **State the nature of liability as provided in the Companies Act, 2013 of an auditor for not appropriately dealing with a misstatement appearing in audited financial statements or a false statement in Audit Report.** **[Nov. 18-Old Syllabus (4 Marks)]**

Ans. : Auditor's Liability for not appropriately dealing with a misstatement appearing in audited financial statements or a false statement in Audit Report:

- Sec. 448 of Companies Act, 2013 provides that if in any return, report, certificate, financial statement, prospectus, statement or other document required by, or for, the purposes of any of the provisions of this Act or the rules made thereunder, any person makes a statement,
  (*a*) which is false in any material particulars, knowing it to be false; or
  (*b*) which omits any material fact, knowing it to be material,
  he shall be liable under section 447.
- **Punishment for fraud**: Sec. 447 of Companies Act, 2013 provides that, any person who is found to be guilty of fraud, involving an amount of at least ₹ 10 lakh or 1% of the turnover of the company, whichever is lower shall be punishable with imprisonment for a term which shall not be less than 6 months but which may extend to 10 years and shall also be liable to fine which shall not be less than the amount involved in the fraud, but which may extend to 3 times the amount involved in the fraud.

  Where the fraud involves an amount less than ₹ 10 lakh or 1% of the turnover of the company, whichever is lower, and does not involve public interest, any person guilty of such fraud shall be punishable with imprisonment for a term which may extend to 5 years or with fine which may extend to ₹ **50 lakh** or with both".

14.3 - LIABILITIES UNDER INCOME TAX ACT, 1961

Q.8 **In assessment procedure of M/s Cloud Ltd., Income Tax Officer observed some irregularities. Therefore, he started investigation of Books of Account audited and signed by Mr. Old, a practicing Chartered Accountant. While going through books he found that M/s Cloud Ltd. used to maintain two sets of Books of Account, one is the official set and other is covering all the transactions. Income Tax Department filed a complaint with the Institute of Chartered Accountants of India saying Mr. Old had negligently performed his duties. Comment.** **[May 14 (4 Marks)]**

Ans. : Liabilities of Auditor:

- It is the auditor's responsibility to audit the statement of accounts and prepare tax returns on the basis of books of account produced before him. After being satisfied with the books and documents produced to him, he can give his opinion on the basis of those documents only by exercising requisite skill and care.
- In the present case, Income-tax Officer observed some irregularities during the assessment proceeding of M/s Cloud Ltd. Therefore, he started investigation of books of accounts audited and signed by Mr. Old, a practicing Chartered Accountant. While going through the books, he found that M/s Cloud Ltd. Used to maintain two sets of Books of Account, one is the official set and other is covering all the transactions. Income Tax Department filed a complaint with the ICAI saying Mr. Old had negligently performed his duties.
- Mr. Old, the auditor was not under a duty to prepare books of account of assessee and he should, of course, neither suggest nor assist in the preparations of false accounts. He is responsible for the books produced before him for audit. He completed his audit work with official set of books only.

Conclusion: As Mr. Old, performed the auditing with due skill and diligence; and, therefore, no question of negligence arises. It is the duty of the Department to himself investigate the truth and correctness of the accounts of the assessee.

Q.9 **Write a short note on - Auditor's liability in case of unlawful acts or defaults by clients.**

Ans. : Auditor's liability in case of unlawful acts of the client:

The Institute has recommended following course of action for a member when he is not directly involved in tax frauds committed by his clients, but he discovers such fraud in the course of his professional work:

(*a*) Member is under no obligation to inform income tax authorities about taxation frauds.

(*b*) If the fraud relates to accounts or tax matters of the client for past years for which the client was not represented by the member, client should be advised to disclose. The member may however continue to act for the client in respect of current matters, but at the same time he is also required to ensure that the past fraud does not in any way affect the current tax matters.

(*c*) If the fraud relates to past years accounts examined and reported by the member himself, on the basis of which the tax assessment in the past has been made, he should advise the client for a disclosure. In case the client refuses, he should disassociate himself from the case and make a report to authorities that the accounts examined by him previously are unreliable on account of some information obtained later. (Details of information should not be communicated)

(*d*) In case of suppression of current accounts, the client should be advised to make a full disclosure. If he refuses, the accountant should make a complete reservation is his report and disassociate himself with return.

(*e*) If the services are dispensed with before completion of the assignment, there is no further duty to disclose.

Q.10 **Mr. Ram, a Chartered Accountant has appeared before the Income Tax Authorities as the authorized representative of his client and delivers to the income tax authorities a false declaration. What are the liabilities of Mr. Ram under Income-tax Act, 1961?** **[May 17 (4 Marks)]**

Ans. : Liabilities under Income-tax Act, 1961:

Section 278 of Income-tax Act, 1961 (Liability for submission of false information): Any person who acts or induces, in any manner another person to make and deliver to the Income Tax Authorities a false account, statement, or declaration relating to any income chargeable to tax which he knows to be false or does not believe to be true is punishable:

(*i*) in a case where the amount of tax, penalty or interest which would have been evaded, if the declaration, account or statement had been accepted as true, or which is wilfully attempted to be evaded, exceeds ₹ 25 Lacs, with rigorous imprisonment for a term which shall not be less than 6 months but which may extend to 7 years and with fine;

(*ii*) in any other case, with rigorous imprisonment for a term which shall not be less than 3 months but which may extend to 2 years and with fine.

ICAI Examiner Comments

Candidates showed lack of knowledge on liability of Chartered Accountants acting as authorised representative and delivering false information u/s 278 of the Income Tax Act, 1961 and most of them mistakenly related with professional misconduct under the Chartered Accountants Act, 1949.

Q.11 What are the liabilities of a Chartered Accountant under Income Tax Act, 1961 for furnishing an incorrect statement in any report or certificate required to be submitted by him under the Act?

[Nov. 18-New Syllabus (4 Marks)]

Ans. : Liabilities of a Chartered Accountant under Income Tax Act, 1961 for furnishing an incorrect statement in any report or certificate:

Liabilities u/s 271J: Sec. 271J of the Income Tax Act, 1961 provides that where the Assessing Officer or the Commissioner (Appeals), in the course of any proceedings under this Act, finds that an accountant or a merchant banker or a registered valuer has furnished incorrect information in any report or certificate furnished under any provision of this Act or the rules made thereunder, the Assessing Officer or the Commissioner (Appeals) may direct that person to pay a penalty of Rs. 10,000 for each such report or certificate.

Liabilities u/s 278: Refer Answer of Q. No. 10

CHAPTER 15

COST AUDIT

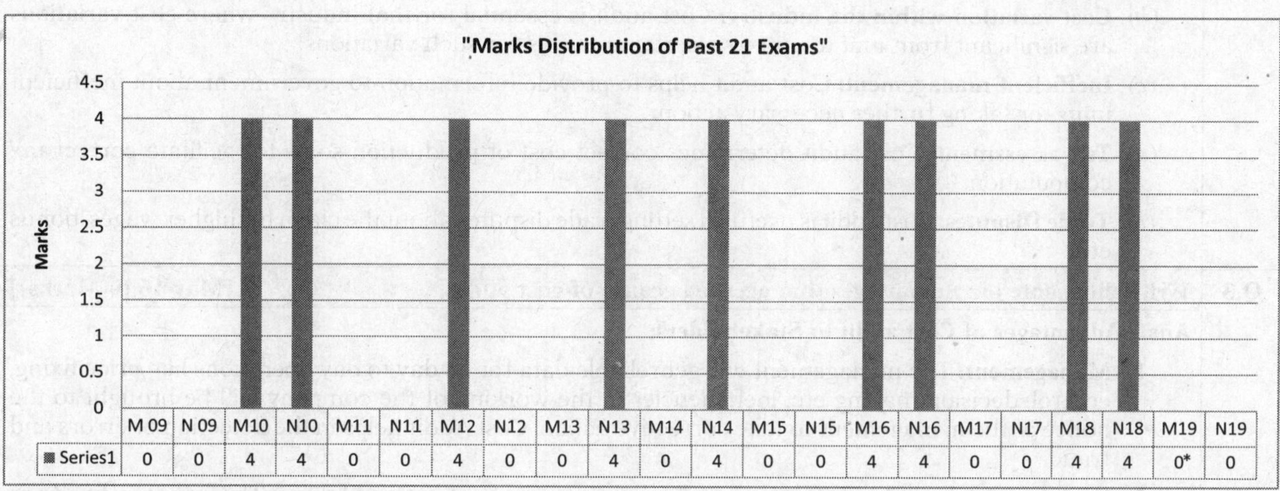

*Only Subjective Questions.

15.1 BASICS OF COST AUDIT

Q.1 Write short note on: Cost Audit **[Nov. 14 (4 Marks)]**

Ans. : Cost Audit:

Meaning and Functions of Cost Audit:

Cost audit is the specific application of auditing principles and procedure in the field of cost accounting. Cost audit performs two basic functions:

(*i*) Verification of cost accounting records such as accuracy of the cost accounts, cost reports, cost statements, cost data, costing techniques.

(*ii*) Examination of cost accounting records to ensure that they adhere to the cost accounting principles, procedures and objectives.

Statutory Provisions w.r.t. Cost Audit (Sec. 148 of Companies Act, 2013):

- If the CG is of the opinion, that it is necessary to do so, it may, by order, direct that the audit of cost records of class of companies, which are covered under Sec. 148(1) and which have a net worth of such amount as may be prescribed or a turnover of such amount as may be prescribed, shall be conducted in the manner specified in the order.
- The audit under Sec. 148 shall be conducted by a Cost Accountant in practice who shall be appointed by the Board on such remuneration as may be determined by the members in such manner as may be prescribed.
- The report on the audit of cost records shall be submitted by the Cost Accountant in practice to the Board of Directors of the company.
- A company shall within **30** days from the date of receipt of a copy of the cost audit report furnish the Central Government with such report along with full information and explanation on every reservation or qualification contained therein.

- If, after considering the cost audit report and the information and explanation furnished by the company, the CG is of the opinion that any further information or explanation is necessary, it may call for such further information and explanation and the company shall furnish the same within such time as may be specified by that Government.

Q.2 State the circumstances that may warrant the introduction of Cost audit. [May 18 (4 Marks)]

Or

What is the purpose served by introduction of cost audit? [May 10 (4 Marks)]

Ans. : Purpose served by Cost Audit:

(*a*) **Price Fixation:** Cost Audit may be required to fix price of certain materials of national importance like steel, cement etc.

(*b*) **Cost variation within the industry:** Cost audit is essential for that industry where cost variations are significant from unit to unit to ascertain reasons for such variations.

(*c*) **Inefficient management:** Cost audit helps to provide information to government about inefficient units for taking further necessary action.

(*d*) **Tax assessment:** Cost audit determines correct cost of production so as to facilitate correct tax computation.

(*e*) **Trade Disputes:** Cost audit is useful in setting trade disputes about the claim for higher wages, bonus etc.

Q.3 Write short note on: Advantages that accrue because of cost audit. [May 16 (4 Marks)]

Ans. : Advantages of Cost audit to Stakeholders:

1. **Management:** The management will get reliable data for its day to day operations like price fixing, control, decision making etc. inefficiencies in the working of the company will be brought to the notice of the management to take corrective action. Cost Audit helps in the detection of errors and fraud.
2. **Society**: Cost Audit is often introduced for the purpose of fixation of price. The prices so fixed are based on the correct costing data and so the consumers are saved from exploitation. Price increase by the industry is not allowed without proper justification as to increase in cost of production. Consumers are saved from unreasonable price hike.
3. **Shareholder**: Cost audit ensures that proper records are kept as to purchases and utilisation of material and expenses incurred on wages, overheads etc. It also ensures that the unit has been run economically and efficiently. Shareholders are assured about profitability and the return on investments.
4. **Government:** Cost Audit helps the fixation of selling prices of essential commodities and thus undue profiteering is checked. Cost audit enables the Govt. to focus its attention on inefficient units. Cost audit facilitates the settlement of trade disputes brought to the government. Since cost audit ensures efficient running of business and ensure accurate use of cost data, a healthy competition is generated among the various units and hence imposes an automatic check on inflation.

"ICAI Examiner Comments"

Some of the candidates failed to mention benefits to various stakeholders and answered in general way.

Q.4 Write a short note on: Advantages of Cost Audit to Government.

Or

Conducting Cost Audit is useful to the management, society, shareholders and the government in many ways. Briefly mention some of the advantages of cost audit to the government.

Ans. : Advantages of Cost Audit to Government:

(*a*) Where the Government enters into a cost plus contracts, cost audit helps the Government to fix the price of the contract.

(*b*) Cost Audit helps the fixation of selling prices of essential commodities and thus undue profiteering is checked.

(*c*) Cost audit enables the Govt. to focus its attention on inefficient units.

(*d*) Cost Audit enables the Government to decide in favour of giving protection to certain industries.

(*e*) Cost audit facilitates the settlement of trade disputes brought to the government.

(*f*) Since cost audit ensures efficient running of business and ensure accurate use of cost data, a healthy competition is generated among the various units and hence imposes an automatic check on inflation.

15.2 COST AUDIT PROGRAMME

Q.5 Answer the following: "Like every other audit, a systematic planning for cost audit is also necessary". Indicate the matters to be included in a Cost Audit Programme.

Ans. : Matters to be included in cost audit programme:

a. **Review of Cost Accounting Records**: This will include:

- Method of costing in use
- Method of accounting for raw material, stores and spares, wastage
- System of recording wages, salary, etc.
- Basic of allocation of overheads to cost centres
- Treatment of expenses on finance, R&D, royalty, etc.
- Method for depreciation accounting
- Method of stock-taking and valuation
- System of budgetary control

b. **Verification of Cost statement and Other Data**: This will mainly cover:

- Licensed, installed and utilized capacity
- Operating and financial ratio
- Production data
- Consumption of material and actual expenses
- Sales realization
- Abnormal non-recurring and special cost
- Reconciliation with financial books

Some other factors which need to be brought into cost audit programme includes system of cost accounting, range of products, areas to be covered etc. indicating allocation of manpower and the time to be taken for computing the audit.

Q.6 For what purposes the cost auditor refers to financial records while conducting cost audit of an entity?

Ans. : Reference to Financial Records:

- Cost auditor, while framing his opinion on cost records is required to examine various information like cost of raw materials consumed, cost of fuel and power, employee costs, provision for depreciation, etc., which is turn is available in financial records.
- Annexure to the cost audit reports (Form CRA-3) require reporting on followings:
  1. Reconciliation of profit as per cost accounts and financial accounts,
  2. Value addition and Distribution of Earnings
  3. Financial Position and Ratio analysis.
  4. Related Party Transactions.
  5. Reconciliation of Indirect Taxes.

  Such information is available only from financial records.
- Further information covered in Part II of Schedule III to the Companies Act, 2013, w.r.t. consumption of raw materials, purchases of stock-in-trade, sales of products/services, changes in inventories in respect of finished goods, work-in-progress, stock-in-trade etc. are also to be covered in cost statements. A correlation between consumption of raw materials as per cost records and financial records may help the cost auditor to identify instances of any mis-statement.

15.3 MISCELLANEOUS

Q. 7 What is meant by True and Fair Cost of Production? [Nov. 18 (4 Marks)]

Ans. : True and Fair Cost of Production:

The concept of "True and Fair Cost of Production" is used in the context of cost audit wherein the cost auditor has to state whether in his opinion the company's cost accounting records have been kept so as to give a true and fair view of the cost of production, processing and marketing of the product. A cost auditor checks the cost accounting records to verify that the cost statements are properly drawn up as per the records and that they present a true and fair view of the cost of production and marketing of various products dealt with by the undertaking.

The following are the relevant considerations in determining whether the cost of production determined by the cost auditor is true and fair:

- Determination of cost following the generally accepted cost accounting principles.
- Application of the costing system appropriate to the product.
- Materiality
- Consistency in the application of costing system and cost accounting principles.
- Maintenance of cost records and preparation of cost statements in the prescribed form and having the prescribed contents.
- Elimination of material prior-period adjustments.
- Abnormal wastage's and losses and other unusual transactions being ignored in determination of cost.

Q.8 Write a short note on - Reconciliation of cost and financial accounts. [Nov. 10 (4 Marks)]

Ans. : Reconciliation of Cost and Financial accounts:

- Form CRA-1 as prescribed by the Companies (Cost Records and Audit) Rules, 2014 requires that the cost statements shall be reconciled with the financial statements for the financial year specifically indicating the expenses or incomes not considered in the cost records or statements so as to ensure accuracy and to adjust the profit of the goods or services under reference with the overall profit of the company. The variations, if any, shall be clearly indicated and explained.
- Part D of annexure to Cost Audit Report (CRA-3) requires the cost auditor to incorporate a profit reconciliation for the company as a whole in his cost audit report.
- Reconciliation statement is to be prepared as below:

S. No.	Particulars	Current Year (₹)	Previous Year (₹)
1.	Profit as per Cost Accounting Records (*a*) For the audited product/service (*b*) For the unaudited product/service		
2.	Add: Income not considered in cost accounts		
3.	Less: Expenses not considered in cost accounts		
4.	Difference in valuation of stock between financial accounts and cost accounts		
5.	Other Adjustments, if any		
6.	Profit or Loss as per Financial Accounts		

- This reconciliation statement helps the cost auditor to identify instances of any misstatement by comparing the similar information from cost records and financial records.

Note: PM of ICAI answers this question on the basis of "Reference of Financial records in Cost Audit", instead of details of reconciliation of cost and financial accounts. In Exam, students may answer this question in accordance with that topic.

Q. 9 It is not possible to merge cost audit with financial audit to have a composite audit. State with reasons whether the above statement is true or false.

Ans. : Composite Audit:

- Combining cost audit and financial audit to produce composite audit requirements would mainly depend upon whether objectives of cost audit and financial audit are common.
- Objective of Financial Audit is to express an opinion on the true and fair information provided by the F.S. while the main objective of cost audit is to verify the cost statements and ascertain that cost of production is true and fair.
- Cost audit can be considered as a tool of internal management by a company to operate effectively by disclosing weakness in cost accounting system and disclosing inefficiencies at all levels of organization. Financial audit on the other hand is conducted on behalf of shareholders and is directed to ascertain true and fair view of financial information.

Conclusion: It would be very difficult to reconcile the audit reports because the objectives of the two audits are all together different.

Q.10 Write short note on: Cost Statement. [May 12 (4 marks)]

Ans. : Costs Statement:

Form CRA -1 as prescribed by the Companies (Cost Records and Audit) Rules, 2014 state the following requirements w.r.t. cost statements:

(*a*) Cost statements (monthly, quarterly and annually) showing quantitative information in respect of each good or service under reference shall be prepared showing details of available capacity, actual production, production as per excise records, capacity utilization (in-house), stock purchased for trading, stock and other adjustments, quantity available for sale, wastage and actual sale during current financial year and previous year.

(*b*) Such statements shall also include details in respect of all major items of costs constituting cost of production of goods or services, cost of sales of goods or services and margin in total as well as per unit of the goods or services. The goods or services emerging from a process, which forms raw material or an input material or service for a subsequent process, shall be valued at the cost of production or cost of service up to the previous stage.

(*c*) Cost Statements (monthly, quarterly and annually) in respect of reconciliation of indirect taxes showing details of total clearances of goods or services, assessable value, duties or taxes paid, CENVAT or VAT or Service Tax credit utilized, duties or taxes recovered and interest or penalty paid.

(*d*) If the company is operating more than one plant, factory or service centre, separate cost statements as specified above shall be prepared in respect of each plant, factory or service centre.

15.4 COMPANIES (COST RECORDS AND AUDIT) RULES, 2014

Q.11 Sugar Ltd. is a top sugar manufacturer and exporter in India operating from Noida Specific Economic Zone, Uttar Pradesh. Its revenue from sale/export for the immediate preceding year is given below:

Sale within India	**₹ 1157 lakhs**
Sale outside India (Export)	**₹ 1353 lakhs**
Total Revenue	**₹ 2510 lakhs**

Mr. X, the statutory auditor of Sugar Ltd., is of the view that the company is mandatorily required to include cost records in their books of account and consequently conduct cost audit. He also suggested the name of his friend, who is a Cost Accountant in Practice, for the purpose of such cost audit. However, the management is of the view that the company neither required including cost records in their books of account nor conduct cost audit.

Being an expert in cost records and audit rules, you are required to guide the management in this regard.

Ans. : Applicability of Provisions related to Cost Records and Audit:

- The provisions relating to cost records and audit are governed by section 148 of the Companies Act, 2013 read with the Companies (Cost Records and Audit) Rules, 2014. The audit conducted under this section shall be in addition to the audit conducted under section 143.
- Rule 3 of the Companies (Cost Records and Audit) Rules, 2014 provides the classes of companies (including Foreign Companies) required to include cost records in their books of account if they are having turnover ₹35 Cr. or more during immediately preceding financial year. The said rule has also divided the list of companies into regulated sectors and non-regulated sectors. Company belonging to sugar industry is one of the types of companies prescribed under the regulated sectors.

- Rule 4 of Companies (Cost Records and Audit) Rules, 2014 requires audit of cost records in case of regulated sector industries if annual turnover from all products and services in immediately preceding financial year is ₹ 50 Cr. or more and the turnover of individual product or service is ₹ 25 Cr. or more.
- Rule 4 further provides that requirement of cost audit shall not apply to a company whose revenue from exports in foreign exchange exceeds 75% of total revenue or which is operating from a SEZ.
- In the given case, Sugar Ltd., a sugar manufacturer and exporter in India, is operating from Noida Specific Economic Zone, Uttar Pradesh and its turnover for the immediate preceding year is just ₹ 25.10 Cr.

Conclusion: Sugar Ltd. is not required to include cost records in their books of account in accordance with Rule 3 of the Companies (Cost Records and Audit) Rules, 2014 and no Cost audit is required.

Q.12 **XYZ Ltd., having place of business in Delhi, is engaged in the production, trading, import and export of orthopaedic implants and pacemaker. The company's revenue from export is usually in foreign currency. Its total revenue classification for the immediate preceding financial year is as below:**

Intra-State Sale	**₹ 1400 lakhs**
Inter-State Sale	**₹ 1550 lakhs**
Export to US	**₹ 4900 lakhs**
Export to UK	**₹ 6900 lakhs**
Total Revenue	**₹ 14750 lakhs**

The management of the company is of the opinion that the company is not required to maintain cost records in their books of account. Consequently, there is no need to appoint cost auditor and conduct cost audit. Comment.

Ans. : Applicability of Provisions Related to Cost Records and Audit:

- The provisions relating to cost records and audit are governed by section 148 of the Companies Act, 2013 read with Companies (Cost Records and Audit) Rules, 2014. The audit conducted under this section shall be in addition to the audit conducted under section 143.
- Rule 3 of the Companies (Cost Records and Audit) Rules, 2014 provides the classes of companies (including Foreign Companies) required to include cost records in their books of account if they are having turnover ₹ 35 Cr. or more during immediately preceding financial year.
- Rule 4 of Companies (Cost Records and Audit) Rules, 2014 requires audit of cost records in case of non regulated sector industries if annual turnover from all products and services in immediately preceding financial year is ₹ 100 Cr. or more and the turnover of individual product or service is ₹ 35 Cr. or more.
- Rule 4 further provides that requirement of cost audit shall not apply to a company whose revenue from exports in foreign exchange exceeds 75% of total revenue or which is operating from a SEZ.
- In the given case, XYZ Ltd. is a foreign company and its total revenue for the immediate preceding financial year is ₹ 14750 lakhs, out of which, export, in foreign currency, comprises ₹ 11800 lakhs (₹ 4900 lakhs + ₹ 6900 lakhs). The proportion of the company's export to its total revenue is 80% [(₹ 11800 lakhs/₹ 14750 lakhs)×100].

Conclusion: XYZ Ltd. is required to include cost records in their books of account in accordance with Rule 3 of the Companies (Cost Records and Audit) Rules, 2014.

However, the company is not required to conduct cost audit as its revenue from exports, in foreign exchange, exceeds 75 per cent of its total revenue.

Q.13 **Electro Ltd. is engaged in generation of electricity for captive consumption through Captive Generating Plant. The Company also maintain cost records in their books of account as required under Cost Records and Audit Rules. Mr. X, friend of Managing Director of the company, suggested name of his brother, who is a Cost Accountant in Practice, for the purpose of cost audit. However, the statutory auditor of the company, is of the view that the company is not legally required to conduct cost audit. Now, the Managing Director is in dilemma about the requirement of cost audit.**

Being an expert in cost records and audit rules, you are required to guide in this regard.

Ans. : Applicability of Provisions related to Cost Records and Audit:

Provisions relating to cost records and audit are governed by section 148 of the Companies Act, 2013 read with the Companies (Cost Records and Audit) Rules, 2014.

Rule 3 of the Companies (Cost Records and Audit) Rules, 2014 provides the classes of companies, engaged in the production of goods or providing services, required to include cost records in their books of account. However, the requirement for cost audit under these rules shall not be applicable to a company which is covered under Rule 3, and,

(*i*) whose revenue from exports, in foreign exchange, exceeds 75 per cent of its total revenue; or

(*ii*) which is operating from a special economic zone.

(*iii*) which is engaged in generation of electricity for captive consumption through Captive Generating Plant.

In the given case, Electro Ltd. is engaged in generation of electricity for captive consumption through Captive Generating Plant. Electro Ltd. is not required to conduct cost audit as it is falling under the exemption criteria.

Conclusion: The opinion of statutory auditor of the company regarding non-applicability of cost audit is correct and the management should follow the same.

Q.14 X Ltd. is engaged in the production of Iron and Steel. A CA Firm 'M/s M & Co.' was appointed as the statutory auditor of X Ltd. for the current financial year. During the year, the management of the company realized that the company is required to maintain cost records in their books of account and get it audited. Therefore, in a general meeting, the members of the company appointed M/s M & Co. as the cost auditor of the company. You are required to examine the validity of appointment of M/s M & Co. as the cost auditor.

Ans. : Appointment of Statutory Auditor as Cost Auditor:

As per Section 148(3) of the Companies Act, 2013 read with Rule 6 of Companies (Cost Records and Audit) Rules, 2014 -

(*i*) in the case of companies which are required to constitute an audit committee, the Board shall appoint an individual, who is a cost accountant in practice, or a firm of cost accountants in practice, as cost auditor on the recommendations of the Audit committee;

(*ii*) in the case of other companies which are not required to constitute an audit committee, the Board shall appoint an individual who is a cost accountant in practice or a firm of cost accountants in practice as cost auditor.

Sec. 148(3) also provides that no person appointed under section 139 as an auditor of the company shall be appointed for conducting the audit of cost records.

In the given case, the members of X Ltd. in general meeting appointed M/s M & Co., the statutory auditor of the company, as the cost auditor.

Therefore, the appointment of the CA firm as cost auditor made by the company is not valid.

Conclusion: Appointment is not valid as a CA firm cannot be appointed as cost auditor. The Board shall appoint a cost accountant in practice or a firm of cost accountants in practice to conduct such cost audit.

Q.15 On 30.08.2016, the Board of SRE Ltd. proposed to appoint Mr. Elex, a Cost Accountant in practice, for conducting cost audit for the financial year 2016-17. The management came to know about the certificate which needs to be obtained from the auditor before such appointment is made. However, the management is unaware about what certification is required from the auditor. Please guide.

Ans. : Certificate to be obtained from Cost Auditor:

As per Rule 6 of Companies (Cost Records and Audit) Rules, 2014, Companies required to get the cost records audited, shall within 180 Days of the commencement of every financial year, appoint a cost auditor. Before such appointment is made, the written consent of cost auditor to such appointment and a certificate from him or it shall be obtained.

The Cost Auditor appointed shall submit certificate that-

(*a*) the individual or the firm, as the case may be, is eligible for appointment and is not disqualified for appointment under the Act, the Cost and Works Accountants Act, 1959 and the Rules or regulations made there under.

(*b*) the individual or the firm, as the case may be, satisfies the criteria provided in Sec. 141, so far as may be applicable.

(*c*) the proposed appointment is within the limits laid down by or under the authority of the Act.

(*d*) the list of proceedings against the cost auditor or audit firm or any partner of the audit firm pending with respect to professional matters of conduct, as disclosed in the certificate, is true and correct.

Q.16 Elucidate the provisions relating to submission of Cost Audit Report - to the Board and the Central Government as per the Companies Act, 2013.

Ans. : Submission of Cost Audit Report:

- Sec. 148(5) of Companies Act 2013 requires the cost auditor to submit the report on the audit of cost records to the Board of Directors of the company. Sec. 148(6) provides that the company shall within **30** days from the date of receipt of a copy of the cost audit report furnish the Central Government with such report along with full information and explanation on every reservation or qualification contained therein.
- Sec. 148(7) of Companies Act, 2013 provides that if, after considering the cost audit report and the information and explanation furnished by the company, the Central Government is of the opinion that any further information or explanation is necessary, it may call for such further information and explanation and the company shall furnish the same within such time as may be specified by that Government.
- Rule 6 of Companies (Cost Records and Audit) Rules, 2014 provides the following in this regard:
  - *a.* Every cost auditor, who conducts an audit of the cost records of a company, shall submit the cost audit report along with his or its reservations or qualifications or observations or suggestions, if any, in Form CRA-3.
  - *b.* Every cost auditor shall forward his report to the Board of Directors of the company within a period of 180 days from the closure of the financial year to which the report relates and the Board of Directors shall consider and examine such report particularly any reservation or qualification contained therein.
  - *c.* Every company covered under these rules shall, within a period of thirty days from the date of receipt of a copy of the cost audit report, furnish the Central Government with such report along with full information and explanation on every reservation or qualification contained therein, in Form CRA-4 along with specified fees.

Q.17 Write short note on: Cost records in respect of by products. [Nov. 13 (4 Marks)]

Ans. : Cost Records in respect of by products:

Form CRA -1 as prescribed by the Companies (Cost Records and Audit) Rules, 2014 state the following requirements w.r.t. cost records of by products:

- Proper records shall be maintained for each item of by-product, if any, produced showing the receipt, issues and balances, both in quantity and value.
- The basis adopted for valuation of by-product for giving credit to the respective process shall be equitable and consistent and shall be indicated in cost records.
- Records showing the expenses incurred on further processing, if any, and actual sales realisation of by-product shall be maintained.
- The proper records shall be maintained in respect of credits or recoveries from the disposal of by-products.

Q.18 Write a short note on: Records to be maintained for Related party Transactions in terms of Cost Audit. [Nov. 16 (4 Marks)]

Ans. : Cost Records in respect of Related Party Transactions:

Form CRA -1 as prescribed by the Companies (Cost Records and Audit) Rules, 2014 requires that in respect of related party transactions, records shall be maintained w.r.t. following:

(*i*) purchase and sale of raw materials, finished goods, rendering of services, process materials and rejected goods including scraps and other related materials;

(*ii*) utilisation of plant facilities and technical know-how;

(*iii*) supply of utilities and any other services;

(*iv*) administrative, technical, managerial or any other consultancy services;

(*v*) purchase and sale of capital goods including plant and machinery; and

(*vi*) any other payment related to the production of goods or rendering of services under reference.

16 CHAPTER
INTERNAL AUDIT

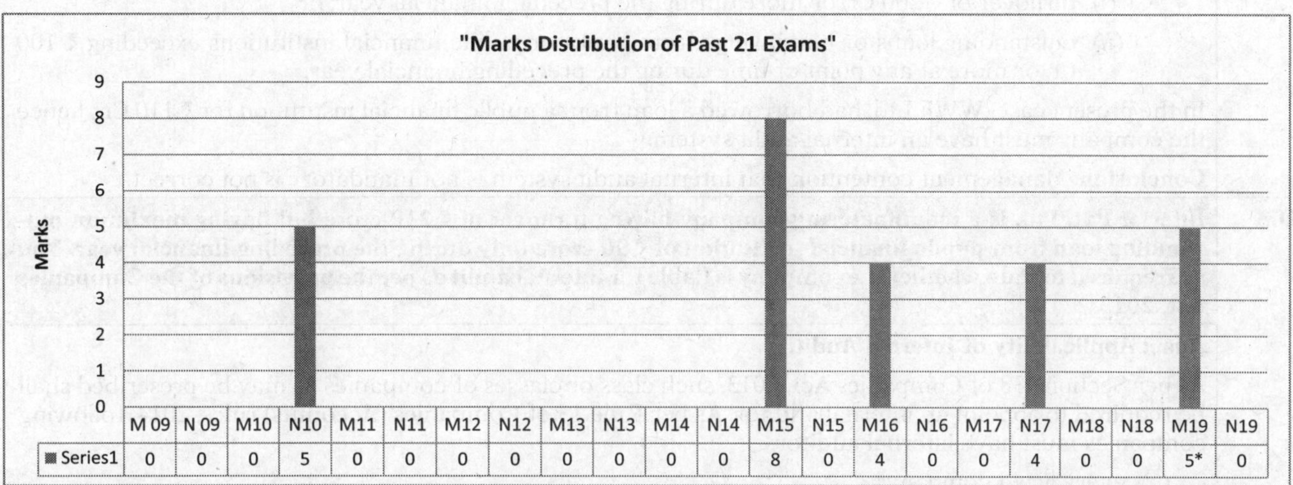

	M 09	N 09	M10	N10	M11	N11	M12	N12	M13	N13	M14	N14	M15	N15	M16	N16	M17	N17	M18	N18	M19	N19
■ Series1	0	0	0	5	0	0	0	0	0	0	0	0	8	0	4	0	0	4	0	0	5*	0

*Only Subjective Questions.

Q.1 **JKH Pvt. Ltd. who is into the business of imparting coaching to CA students did not appoint any internal auditor for the year ended 31st March, 2018. As on 31st March, 2017, the company had paid up capital of ₹ 50 lakhs and reserves of ₹ 10 crores. Its turnover for the 3 years preceding the year ended 31st March, 2018 was ₹ 75 crores, ₹ 145 crores and ₹ 260 crores respectively. As an auditor of the company for the year ended 31st March, 2018, how would you deal with the above? [Nov. 17 (4 Marks)]**

Ans. : Applicability of Provisions of Internal Audit:

As per section 138 of the Companies Act, 2013, read with rule 13 of Companies (Audit and Auditors) Rules, 2014 every private company shall be required to appoint an internal auditor or a firm of internal auditors, having—

(*i*) turnover of two hundred crore rupees or more during the preceding financial year; or

(*ii*) outstanding loans or borrowings from banks or public financial institutions exceeding one hundred crore rupees or more at any point of time during the preceding financial year:

In the instant case, JKH Pvt. Ltd. is having turnover of ₹ 260 crores during the preceding financial year which is more than two hundred crore rupees.

Conclusion: Company has the statutory liability to appoint an Internal Auditor and mandatorily conduct internal audit.

Q.2 **WWF Ltd. is a public company having ₹ 40 lacs paid up capital in previous financial year which raised to ₹ 60 lacs in current financial year under audit. The company had turnover of previous three consecutive financial years being ₹ 49 crores, ₹ 145 crores and ₹ 150 crores. During the previous year, WWF Ltd. borrowed a loan from a public financial institution of ₹ 110 crores but squared up ₹ 20 crores by the year end. The company does not have any internal audit system. In view of the management, internal audit system is not mandatory. Comment.**

Ans. : Applicability of Internal Audit:

As per Section 138 of Companies Act, 2013, such class or classes of companies as may be prescribed shall be required to appoint an internal auditor. As per Rule 13 of Companies (Accounts) Rules, 2014, following companies must have internal auditor:

1. every listed company;
2. every unlisted public company having—
   (*i*) paid up share capital of ₹ 50 Cr. or more during the preceding financial year; or
   (*ii*) turnover of ₹ 200 Cr. or more during the preceding financial year; or
   (*iii*) outstanding loans or borrowings from banks or public financial institutions exceeding ₹ 100 Cr. or more at any point of time during the preceding financial year; or
   (*iv*) outstanding deposits of ₹ 25 Cr. or more at any point of time during the preceding financial year; and
3. every private company having—
   (*i*) turnover of ₹ 200 Cr. or more during the preceding financial year; or
   (*ii*) outstanding loans or borrowings from banks or public financial institutions exceeding ₹ 100 Cr. or more at any point of time during the preceding financial year.

In the present case, WWF Ltd. had borrowed a loan from a public financial institution for ₹ 110 Cr., hence the company must have an internal audit system.

Conclusion: Management contention that internal audit system is not mandatory is not correct.

Q.3 Interior Pvt. Ltd. is a manufacturing company having turnover of ₹ 210 crore but having maximum outstanding loan from public financial institution of ₹ 90 crore only during the preceding financial year. You are required to state whether the company is liable for internal audit as per the provisions of the Companies Act, 2013

Ans. : Applicability of Internal Audit:

As per Section 138 of Companies Act, 2013, such class or classes of companies as may be prescribed shall be required to appoint an internal auditor. As per Rule 13 of Companies (Accounts) rules, 2014, following companies must have internal auditor:

(*a*) every listed company;

(*b*) every unlisted public company having—
   (*i*) paid up share capital of ₹ 50 Cr. or more during the preceding financial year; or
   (*ii*) turnover of ₹ 200 Cr. or more during the preceding financial year; or
   (*iii*) outstanding loans or borrowings from banks or public financial institutions exceeding ₹ 100 Cr. or more at any point of time during the preceding financial year; or
   (*iv*) outstanding deposits of ₹ 25 Cr. or more at any point of time during the preceding financial year; and

(*c*) every private company having—
   (*i*) turnover of ₹ 200 Cr. or more during the preceding financial year; or
   (*ii*) outstanding loans or borrowings from banks or public financial institutions exceeding ₹ 100 Cr. or more at any point of time during the preceding financial year.

In the present case, turnover of Interior Pvt. Ltd. for the immediate preceding financial year was ₹ 210 Cr. which is more than the prescribed limit.

Conclusion: Interior Pvt. Ltd. is liable for the internal audit. Statutory auditor will have to mention in his report the fact of not having internal audit system by the Company.

Q.4 PQR Ltd., a listed company and having an average annual turnover of more than ₹ 5 crores have no Internal Audit System. Give your views. [Nov. 10 (5 Marks)]

Ans. : Applicability of Internal Audit:

As per Section 138 of Companies Act, 2013, such class or classes of companies as may be prescribed shall be required to appoint an internal auditor. As per Rule 13 of Companies (Accounts) Rules, 2014, following companies must have internal auditor:

(*a*) every listed company;

(*b*) every unlisted public company having—
   (*i*) paid up share capital of ₹ 50 Cr. or more during the preceding financial year; or
   (*ii*) turnover of ₹ 200 Cr. or more during the preceding financial year; or

(*iii*) outstanding loans or borrowings from banks or public financial institutions exceeding ₹ 100 Cr. or more at any point of time during the preceding financial year; or

(*iv*) outstanding deposits of ₹ 25 Cr. or more at any point of time during the preceding financial year; and

(*c*) every private company having—

(*i*) turnover of ₹ 200 Cr. or more during the preceding financial year; or

(*ii*) outstanding loans or borrowings from banks or public financial institutions exceeding ₹ 100 Cr. or more at any point of time during the preceding financial year.

In the present case, PQR Ltd. is a listed entity which is covered under Rule 13 irrespective of its turnover.

Conclusion: PQR Ltd. is liable for the internal audit.

Q.5 **AB Pvt. Ltd. company having outstanding loans or borrowings from banks exceeding one hundred crore rupees wants to appoint internal auditor. Please guide him who can be appointed as internal auditor and what would be reviewed by him. [May 15 (4 Marks)]**

Ans. : Who can be appointed as Internal Auditor:

As per Section 138 of the Companies Act, 2013, every private limited company is required to have internal audit system if its outstanding loans or borrowings from banks or public financial institutions exceed ₹ 100 Cr. at any point of time during the preceding financial year. In present case, AB Pvt. Ltd. is under compulsion to conduct internal audit, as its loans or borrowings exceed ₹ 100 Cr.

As per Section 138, the internal auditor shall either be a chartered accountant, whether engaged in practice or not, or a cost accountant, or such other professional as may be decided by the Board to conduct internal audit of the functions and activities of the companies. The internal auditor may or may not be an employee of the company.

Work to be reviewed by Internal Auditor:

As per SA 610 "Using the work of Internal Auditor" the activities of the internal audit function may include one or more of the following:

1. **Activities Relating to Governance:** Internal audit function may assess the governance process in its accomplishment of objectives on ethics and values, accountability and communicating risk to appropriate areas of the organization.
2. **Activities Relating to Risk Management:** Internal audit function may assist the entity by identifying and evaluating significant exposures to risk and contributing to the improvement of risk management and internal control (including effectiveness of the financial reporting process).
3. **Evaluation of internal control:** Internal audit function may be assigned specific responsibility for reviewing controls, evaluating their operation and recommending improvements thereto.
4. **Examination of financial and operating information:** Internal audit function may be assigned to review the means used to identify, recognize, measure, classify and report financial and operating information, and to make specific inquiry into individual items, including detailed testing of transactions, balances and procedures.
5. **Review of operating activities:** The internal audit function may be assigned to review the economy, efficiency and effectiveness of operating activities, including non-financial activities of an entity.
6. **Review of compliance with laws and regulations:** Internal audit function may be assigned to review compliance with laws, regulations and other external requirements, and with management policies and directives and other internal requirements.

"ICAI Examiner Comments"

Many candidates could not mention either who can be appointed as an internal auditor or the work to be reviewed by internal auditor.

Q.6 **XYZ Yarns Ltd. is a manufacturing company engaged in manufacturing of different types of yarns. Its annual turnover is Rs. 100 Crores and net profit Rs. 10 crores. It has two manufacturing units. Company is facing difficulties in maintaining adequate system of internal control. Company wants to appoint Internal Auditor who would help in the above task and also various other functions including compliance. In view of above, you are required to explain the main responsibility of Internal Auditors. [MTP-Oct. 18]**

Ans. : Responsibilities of Internal Auditor:

(*i*) To maintain adequate system of internal control by a continuous examination of accounting procedures, receipts and disbursements and to provide adequate safeguards against misappropriation of assets.

(*ii*) To operate independently of the accounting staff and must not in any way divest himself of any of the responsibilities placed upon him.

(*iii*) To observe unusual facts and circumstances and bring them to notice of management.

(*iv*) To appraise policies and procedures prevailing in the entity and bring to the notice of management any deficiencies, wherever these require to be corrected.

(*v*) To perform his work with independence. He need to associate closely with management and his knowledge must be kept up to date by his being kept informed about all important occurrences and events affecting the business, as well as the changes that are made in business policies.

Q.7 The internal auditor must be regarded as part of the management and not merely as an assistant thereto. He must have authority to investigate from the financial angles every phase of the organisational activity under any circumstances. Explain.

Ans. : Role and Responsibilities of internal Auditor:

- Rule 13 of Companies (Accounts) Rules, 2014 provides that the scope, functioning, periodicity and methodology for conducting the internal audit shall be formulated by the Audit Committee of the company or the Board shall, in consultation with the Internal Auditor.
- Over a period of time, scope of internal auditing has been widened so as to cover all operations besides accounting and financial operations. To be effective, the internal auditor must be regarded as part of the management and not merely as an assistant thereto. He must have authority to investigate from the financial angles, every phase of the organisational activity under any circumstances.
- Major responsibilities that are entrusted to internal auditor are listed as below:

  (*i*) To maintain adequate system of internal control by a continuous examination of accounting procedures, receipts and disbursements and to provide adequate safeguards against misappropriation of assets.

  (*ii*) To operate independently of the accounting staff and must not in any way divest himself of any of the responsibilities placed upon him.

  (*iii*) To observe unusual facts and circumstances and bring them to notice of management.

  (*iv*) To appraise policies and procedures prevailing in the entity and bring to the notice of management any deficiencies, wherever these require to be corrected.

  (*v*) To perform his work with independence. He need to associate closely with management and his knowledge must be kept up to date by his being kept informed about all important occurrences and events affecting the business, as well as the changes that are made in business policies.

Q.8 M/s ME Ltd. is a manufacturing Company of M/s Bars and Rods. The turnover of the company for financial year 2017-18 was ₹ 870 crores. The audit committee has appointed M/s MK Associates, Chartered Accountants as an internal auditor of the company for the financial year 2018-19. As an auditor of ME Ltd., draw out the internal audit plan specifying coverage of area. [May 16 (4 Marks)]

Ans. : Internal Audit Plan specifying the coverage of Area:

While drawing internal audit plan, following specific areas may be covered:

1. Terms of audit engagement and scope of internal audit as determined by audit committee.
2. Nature and timing of reports and other communications.
3. Legal or statutory requirements.
4. Accounting policies adopted by the client and changes made therein.
5. New accounting or auditing pronouncements and their impact on the entity.
6. Identification of significant audit areas.
7. Setting up of materiality levels for purpose of audit.
8. Circumstances requiring special attention, such as the possibility of material error or fraud or related party transactions.
9. Degree of reliance to be placed on accounting system and internal control.

10. Nature, form and extent of audit evidence to be obtained.
11. Nature, timing and extent of procedures to be performed.
12. Use of expert's work.
13. Establishing and coordinating staffing requirements.
14. Attending the inventory count
15. Method of physical verification of cash and investment.
16. Verification of Assets and Liabilities.
17. Compliance of laws and Regulations.

"ICAI Examiner Comments"

Candidates, in general, failed to explain the areas to be covered in drawing an internal audit plan and rather discussed about role of internal auditor, internal control & internal check.

Q.9 **ABC Ltd. is engaged in manufacturing of Yarns and Towels. It sells its product in both domestic as well as in International Market. It has achieved turnover of 200 crores in the F.Y. 2016-17. Directors of the company realized that they are not managing the company professionally and thereby request your firm of Internal Auditors for appraisal of its organizational structure to ascertain whether it is in harmony with the objectives of ABC (P) Ltd. Comment.** **[MTP-Aug. 18]**

Or

Internal auditor makes an appraisal of organization structure to ensure that it is in harmony with the objectives of the entity, besides checking of financial truncations and operational activities of the entity. Elaborate. **[Nov. 18 - New Syllabus (4 Marks)]**

Answer: Appraisal of Organisational Structure by Internal auditor:

The internal auditor should conduct an appraisal of the organisation structure to ascertain

- whether it is in harmony with the objectives of the enterprise and
- whether the assignment of responsibilities is in consonance therewith.

For this purpose, internal auditor should:

(*a*) Review the manner in which the activities of the enterprise are grouped for managerial control so as to find out whether responsibility and authority are in harmony with the grouping pattern.

(*b*) Examine the organisation chart to find out whether the structure is simple and economical and that no function enjoys an undue dominance over the others.

(*c*) Ensure that the responsibilities of managerial staff at headquarters do not overlap with those of chief executives at operating units.

(*d*) Examine the reasonableness of the span of control of each executive (the number of subordinates that an executive controls). He should examine whether there is a unity of command *i.e.*, whether each person reports only to one superior.

(*e*) Evaluate the process of managerial development in the enterprise.

Q.10 **"Review of the internal audit function has become statutory responsibility for the statutory auditor."** **[May 15 (4 Marks)]**

Ans. : Review of internal audit Function by Statutory Auditor:

- It is obligatory for a statutory auditor to examine the scope and effectiveness of the work carried out by the internal auditor.
- For this purpose, statutory auditor should examine the Internal Audit function of the organisation, the strength of the internal audit staff, their qualification and powers.
- Besides statutory auditor should have studied the procedures adopted by internal auditor, refer audit programmes, reports submitted, points raised in audit and ascertain how these had been dealt with subsequently.
- The extent of independence exhibited by the internal auditor in the discharge of his duties and his status in the organisation are important factors for determining the effectiveness of his audit.
- In a large business, it has been increasingly recognised that, if function of internal auditor and those of statutory auditors could be integrated, it might not be necessary for the statutory auditors to go

over the same facts and figure as have been previously examined by a competent and trustworthy internal audit staff.

"ICAI Examiner Comments"

Many candidates wrote about evaluation of internal control instead of need for review of internal audit function. They also failed to explain the factors that should be considered by statutory auditor while reviewing the work of internal auditor.

Q.11 **ABC Ltd. appointed CA Mr. X, for conducting internal audit for the financial year 2015-16. Mr. X seeks your advice in drafting a good quality internal audit report. You are, therefore, required to guide him by elaborating essential features of a good internal audit report.**

Or

Webcom Ltd. a public company with a paid up share capital of Rs. 20 crores has a turnover for the financial year 2019-20 of Rs. 220 crores. X, a recently qualified Chartered Accountant, has been appointed for conducting internal audit. He seeks your advice in drafting a good quality internal audit report. Please guide him by elaborating (in brief) the essential features of good internal audit report.

[May 19 - Old Syllabus (5 Marks)]

Ans. : Essential Features of Internal Audit Report

1. **Objectivity:** Comments and opinions expressed in the report should be as objective and unbiased as possible.
2. **Clarity:** The language used should be simple and straight-forward.
3. **Accuracy:** The information contained in the report, whether quantified or otherwise, should be accurate.
4. **Conciseness:** Important information should not be omitted.
5. **Constructiveness:** Destructive criticism should carefully be avoided in the report.
6. **Readability:** The reader's interest should be captured and retained throughout. For this, appropriate paragraph heading may be used.
7. **Timeliness:** The report should be submitted promptly because if the time lag between the occurrence of an event and its reporting is considerable, the opportunity for taking action may be lost or a wrong decision may be taken in the absence of the information.
8. **Findings and conclusions:** These may be given either department-wise or in the order of importance. Each conclusion and opinion should normally follow the findings.
9. **Recommendations:** An internal audit report usually includes recommendations for potential improvements.
10. **Auditee's views:** The auditee's views about audit conclusions or recommendations may also be included in the audit report in appropriate circumstances.
11. **Summary:** A summary of conclusions and recommendations may be given at the end. This is particularly useful in long reports.
12. **Supporting information:** The internal auditor should supplement his report by such documents and data which adequately and convincingly support the conclusions. Supporting information may include the relevant standards or regulations.
13. **Draft Report:** Before writing the final report, the internal auditor should prepare a draft report. This would help him in finding out the most effective manner of presenting his reports.
14. **Writing and issuing the Final Report:** The final report should be written only when the auditor is completely satisfied with the draft report. The head of the internal auditing department, may review and approve the final report. Before issuing the final report, the auditor should discuss conclusions and recommendations at appropriate levels of management. The report should be duly signed.

17 CHAPTER MANAGEMENT AND OPERATIONAL AUDIT

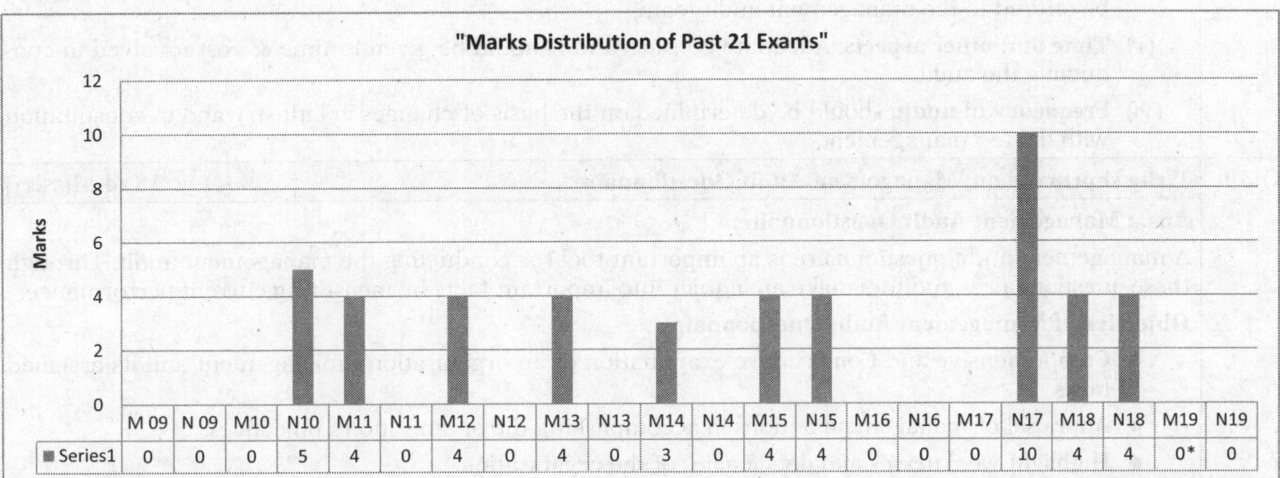

	M 09	N 09	M10	N10	M11	N11	M12	N12	M13	N13	M14	N14	M15	N15	M16	N16	M17	N17	M18	N18	M19	N19
■ Series1	0	0	0	5	4	0	4	0	4	0	3	0	4	4	0	0	0	10	4	4	0*	0

*Only Subjective Questions.

17.1 - MANAGEMENT AUDIT

Q.1 Management Audit and Operational Audit are complementary and supplementary to one another. Discuss. **[Nov. 15 (4 Marks)]**

Ans. : Management Audit and Operational Audit:

◆ Management audit and Operational Audit are complementary and supplementary to one another. Management audit is concerned with the quality of managing, whereas operational audit is concerned with the quality of operations.

◆ The basic difference between the two audits, is not in method, but in the level of appraisal. In management audit, the auditor evaluates decisions taken at the level of top management w.r.t. formulation of objectives, plans and policies whereas in operational audit auditor evaluates effectiveness, efficiency and economy of operations under management's control along with recommendations for improvement.

◆ In addition to what would normally be covered in an operational audit, management audit would also encompass the relevance and effectiveness of the aims, duties and decisions of management at various levels. Every aspect of the functions of Board of Directors should be in conformity with the objects set out in the constituting document.

Conclusion: From the above discussion which recognises management audit and operational audit as two identifiable exercises having a large area of overlapping jurisdiction, it may be convenient to consider them together to avoid duplication; and for this purpose, the expression "management and operational audit" may be acceptable as a management audit which includes within its scope all the elements of operational auditing.

"ICAI Examiner Comments"

Examinees failed to emphasize how the Operational audit and Management audit are complementary and supplementary to one another instead examinees merely wrote the meaning of Operational and Management audit.

Q.2 K Ltd. requires you to organize a Management audit program. Briefly state a plan of action.

Ans. : Management Audit Program:

Management Audit Program may be based on the following plan of action:

(*i*) **Devising a statement of policy**: in consultation with the top Management. The policy should ideally cover the scope, objective, the authority of the management audit function.

(*ii*) **Location of audit function within the organization**: The hierarchical status of management auditor and his team should be clearly defined.

(*iii*) **Allocation of personnel**: The management audit team should comprise of personnel who have adequate experience on various aspects of the organization.

(*iv*) **Staff Training**: In order to maintain qualitative standards, adequate and continuous training should be offered to the management audit team.

(*v*) **Time and other aspects**: Adequate consideration should be given to time & cost involved in conducting the audit.

(*vi*) **Frequency of audit**: should be determined on the basis of changes in industry and in consultation with the top management.

Q.3 Write short note on: Management Audit Questionnaire. [Nov. 18 (4 Marks)]

Ans. : Management Audit Questionnaire:

A management audit questionnaire is an important tool for conducting the management audit. Through these questionnaires auditors make an inquiry into important facts by measuring current performance.

Objective of Management Audit Questionnaire:

- Comprehensive and Constructive examination of an organisation's management and its assigned tasks.
- Appraisal of management actions in accomplishing the organisation's objectives.
- Highlight weaknesses and deficiencies of the organisation.
- Review of management functions of planning, organising, directing and controlling.
- Evaluation of effectiveness of decision-making process in accomplishing the organisation objectives.

Working: There are three possible answers to the management audit questions - "Yes", "No" and "N.A.". "Yes" answer indicates that the specific area or function under study is functioning in an acceptable manner; no written explanation is needed in that case. "No" answer indicates unacceptable performance and requires explanation in writing. Those questions that are not applicable and should be ignored in the audit are checked in the "N.A." column.

Importance: Management Audit Questionnaire not only serves as a management tool to analyse the current situation; but also, it enables the management auditors to identify the elements that are causing organisational difficulties and deficiencies.

Q.4 Write a short note on - Management Audit Reports.

Ans. : Management Audit Reports:

Management Audit Reports are of following types:

1. **Oral Reports:** Oral reports are required in case of emergency. But they not considered reliable as no permanent record. Oral Reports helps in taking corrective steps timely.
2. **Interim written report:** These reports are issued in case of matters requiring early consideration so as to inform management before regular report.
3. **Regular written reports:** These are the formal report submitted after completion of work.
4. **Summary written report:** Summary reports are also known as "Flash" reports. These reports summarize various individual reports on integrated approach and facilitates management by exception.

Q.5 Write short note on: Summary Written Report.

Ans. : Summary Written Report:

- Summary Reports are also known as Flash Reports. These reports summarize various individual reports on integrated approach and facilitates management by exception.
- They are significant highlights for immediate attention of top management. Generally suspected defalcations are reported briefly to the appropriate management official on the 'flash' basis, often ending up in referral for criminal investigation and legal action.

- It is common practice in number of companies of issuing a report quite frequently summarising the various individual reports issued and describing the range of their contents in a very brief and comprehensive manner where only important points are highlighted.
- Such reports are primarily issued for audit committees and other top-level managers who do not have sufficient time to go through the elaborate reports and matters which are required to be brought to their notice for immediate action.

Q.6 Briefly describe the general guidelines that may be observed while drafting a management audit report.

Ans. : General guidelines while drafting a management audit report:

Management Audit Reports may be drafted considering following guidelines:

(*i*) **Title:** Title of the management audit report needs to be short but descriptive so that its subject matter can be easily identified.

(*ii*) **Objectives:** Management audit report may describe the objectives of the audit assignment.

(*iii*) **Scope:** Management audit report may give a brief description of the activities audited.

(*iv*) **Findings, conclusions and opinions:** Findings should be discussed comprehensively. Conclusions and opinions should normally follow the findings.

(*v*) **Recommendations:** Management audit report may include recommendations for potential improvements. Management Auditor should avoid providing detailed procedures in the capacity of an auditor.

(*vi*) **Auditee's views:** Auditee's views about audit conclusions or recommendations may also be included in the audit report in appropriate circumstances.

(*vii*) **Summary:** In case of long reports, a summary of conclusions and recommendations may be given at the end.

Q.7 Explain in brief the behavioural aspects encountered in the management audit and state the ways to solve them.

Ans. : Behavioural aspects encountered in management Audit:

1. **Staff/Line conflict**: Management auditors are staff people while the members of other departments are line people. Management auditors has superiority complex and they may think their approach and solutions are the only answers. Staff do not consider the line before advising, as a result Line may not use advice of staff properly. Line does not co-operate with staff and do not provide sufficient information to staff.
2. **Control:** The management auditor is expected to evaluate the effectiveness of controls, there is an instinctive reaction from the auditee that the report of the auditor may affect them. There is a fear that the action taken based on the management audit report will affect the line people.

Solution to behavioural problems

(*i*) Demonstrate that audit is part of an overall programme of review for protective and constructive benefit.

(*ii*) Demonstrate the objective of review is to provide maximum service in all feasible managerial dimensions.

(*iii*) Perform the review to ensure minimum interference with regular operation.

(*iv*) Involve responsible officers in the process of review of the findings and recommendations before the audit report is formally released.

(*v*) Create an atmosphere of trust and friendliness.

17.2 - OPERATIONAL AUDIT

Q.8 Write short note on: Meaning and Types of Operational Audit.

Or

What are the types of Operational Audits? [Nov. 17 (6 Marks)]

Ans. : Meaning and Types of Operational Audit:

Operational Audit is the review and appraisal of operations of an organization conducted by competent independent person. It analyse the regular operations like production, purchase, sales etc. to check whether they are in tune with company's policies, objectives and goals or not. It focuses more on Qualitative aspects of operations rather than regular accounting aspects.

Types of Operational Audit:

1. **Functional Audits:** A functional audit deals with one or more functions in an organization, for example, the payroll function for a division or for the company as a whole. A functional audit has the advantage of permitting specialization by auditors. They can more efficiently spend all their time auditing in that area. A disadvantage of functional auditing is the failure to evaluate interrelated functions.
2. **Organizational Audits:** An operational audit deals with an entire organizational units, such as a department, branch, or subsidiary. It emphasizes how efficiently and effectively functions interact. The plan of organization and the methods to coordinate activities are especially important in this type of audit.
3. **Special Assignments:** In operational auditing, special assignments arise at the request of management, for example, investigating the possibility of fraud in a division, making recommendations for reducing the cost of a manufactured product, etc.

"ICAI Examiner Comments"

Examinees have explained the functional audit but could not explain the other types of operational audits namely Organizational Audits and Special Assignments. Some examinees unnecessarily explained the objectives of operational audit and various types of audits viz., management audit, internal audit, cost audit, environmental audit, energy audit, compliance audit etc.

Q.9 Briefly explain the objectives of Operational Audit. **[May 11 (4 Marks)]**

Ans. : Objectives of Operational Audit:

1. **Appraisal of Controls:** Operational auditing deals with the administrative controls and its purpose is to determine whether the controls are adequate.
2. **Evaluation of performance:** In the task of performance evaluation, an operational auditor is heavily dependent upon availability of acceptable standards. The operational auditor cannot be expected to possess technical background in so many diverse technical fields obtaining even in one enterprise.
3. **Appraisal of objectives and plans:** In performance appraisal, the operational auditor is basically concerned not so much with how well technically the operations are going on, but with accumulating information and evidence to measure the effectiveness, efficiency and economy with which the operations are being carried on.
4. **Appraisal of organisational structure:** In evaluating organisational structure, the operational auditor should consider whether the structure is in conformity with the management objectives and it is drawn up on the basis of matching of responsibility and authority.

Q.10 In evaluating the organisational structure of a company, what aspects may be considered by the operational auditor to achieve his objectives? **[May 18 - Old Syllabus (4 Marks)]**

Ans : Appraisal of Organisational Structure:

Organisational structure is an important area for appraisal by operational auditor as it provides the line of relationships and delegation of authority and tasks. In evaluating organisational structure, the operational auditor should consider the following:

(*i*) Whether the organizational structure is in conformity with the management objectives

(*ii*) Whether it is drawn up on the basis of matching of responsibility and authority.

(*iii*) Whether the line of responsibility from the top to the bottom is clearly discernible from the structure?

(*iv*) Whether the delegation of responsibility and authority at each stage is clear and overlapping are avoided?

Q.11 Mr. 'P' have been appointed as operational auditor of M/s Books & Magazine Ltd. And observed a totalling error in invoice of ₹ 1,000. He has not taken care of the same saying that this is out of scope of his work. Comment. **[May 14 (3 Marks)]**

Ans. : Scope of Operational Audit:

- Operational Audit is the review and appraisal of operations of an organization conducted by competent independent person. It analyse the regular operations like production, purchase, sales etc. to check whether they are in tune with company's policies, objectives and goals or not. It focuses more on Qualitative aspects of operations rather than regular accounting aspects.

- In carrying out his work, operational auditor will have to exercise judgment to evaluate evidence in connection with the situations and issues; he will have to get the assistance of norms and standards in every operating field to be able to objectively judge a situation.
- To a financial auditor, a loss of ₹ 1,000 caused by a wrong totalling of invoice is important, but for an auditor engaged in the review of operations, it does not assume so much importance. But simultaneously, it should not be assumed, that, an operational auditor is not concerned with the financial aspects of transaction and controls.

Conclusion: Contention of operational auditor that totalling error in invoice of ₹ 1,000 is out of scope is not correct as operational audit is being carried out to ensure that all the management functions like planning, organizing, staffing, directing and controlling are working effectively and efficiently. Such kind of error is very much in scope because such an existence of error indicates that control system (controlling function) is not sound.

Q.12 Write short note on: Operational auditing arose from the need of mangers responsible for areas beyond their direct supervision.

or

Operational Auditing is a systematic process involving logical, structured and organized series of procedures. It concentrates on effectiveness, efficiency and economy of operations and therefore it is future oriented. In this perspective, state the Need of operational auditing. [May 15 (4 Marks)]

Ans. : Need of Operational Audit:

- Operational auditing arose from the need of managers responsible for areas beyond their direct observation to be fully, objectively and currently informed about conditions in the units under control.
- Traditional sources of information remain inadequate for an effective management of the company where the management is at a distance from actual operations due to layers of delegation of responsibility, separating it from actualities in the organisation.
- Operational audit as a specialised management information tool fill the void that conventional information sources fail to fill. Conventional sources of management information are departmental managers, routine performance report, internal audit reports, and periodic special investigation and survey. These conventional sources fail to provide information for the best direction of the departments all of whose activities do not come under direct observation of managers.
- Operational auditing has filled a very significant vacuum; it has come to provide the management with inexpensive, continuous and objective appraisal of activities, operations and controls to inform the management about achievement of standards and, if otherwise, to inform the management about what has gone wrong and how it has gone wrong. Also, it enlightens the management about possible dangers, constraints and opportunities that may be of immense value to the management.

"ICAI Examiner Comments"

The need for operational auditing are not properly highlighted. Instead candidates explained operational Auditing.

Q.13 Perfect Steel Ltd. has reported a higher turnover of ₹ 560 crores in the year 2018-19 as compared to earlier years but its sales return has also increased to 10% from only 4% upto the last year. The management is concerned about the high sales returns and feels a need to get the operational audit done for sales and production department of the company. The company is also having an internal audit system in the company. Elaborate the possible reason/s, why management is getting operational audit done when internal audit has already been done for both the departments by stating the shortcomings of conventional information sources. [RTP-Nov. 19]

Ans. : Need of Operational Audit:

The need for operational auditing has arisen due to the inadequacy of traditional sources of information for an effective management of the company where the management is at a distance from actual operations due to layers of delegation of responsibility, separating it from actualities in the organisation.

Operational audit as a specialised management information tool fill the void that conventional information sources fail to fill. Conventional sources of management information are departmental managers, routine performance report, internal audit reports, and periodic special investigation and survey. These conventional sources fail to provide information for the best direction of the departments all of whose activities do not come under direct observation of managers.

The shortcomings of these sources can be stated as under:

(*i*) Executives and managers are too preoccupied with implementation of plans and achieving of targets. They are left with very little time to collect information and locate problems. They may come across problems that have come to surface but they are hardly aware of problems that are brewing and potential.

(*ii*) Managers or their aides are generally relied upon for transmitting information than for booking for information or for analysing situations.

(*iii*) The information that is transmitted by managers is not necessarily objective - often it may be biased for various reasons.

(*iv*) Conventional internal audit reports are often routine and mechanical in character and have a definite leaning towards accounting and financial information. They are also historical in nature.

(*v*) Other performance reports contained in the annual audited accounts and the routine reports prepared by the operating departments have their own limitations. The annual audited accounts are good as far as an overall evaluation is concerned in monetary terms.

(*vi*) Operations of controls in a satisfactory manner çannot be relied upon to bring to light the environmental conditions. Controls are specific and their satisfactory operation is related to the specific situation under control. Also monitoring of the breakdown or non-operation of controls is a periodic phenomenon.

(*vii*) Surveys and special investigations, no doubt, are very useful but these are at the best occasional in character. Also, they are costly, time consuming and keep the departmental key personnel busy during the period they are on. These are basically an attempt to carry out a post-mortem rather than to enlighten the management about the ways on improvement or for better performance or to give a signal for dangers and disasters to come.

Q.14 "Operational Auditing is not different from Internal Auditing" Discuss.

Ans. : Operational Audit vs. Internal Auditing:

Operational Auditing	Internal Auditing
It is concerned with the review and appraisal of operations of an organization carried on by a competent independent person	It is concerned with determining whether other internal controls are well designed and in place
It is not a part of internal control	It is a part of internal control system
It is an constructive function i.e. to provide suggestions for improvement	It is an protective function i.e. to safeguard the assets of the enterprise.
It analyses all aspects of operations whether they are in tune with management policies, objectives and Goals	It is primarily concerned with financial accounting and internal control
It mainly deals with qualitative aspects	It focuses more on quantitative aspects

NOTE: Over a period of time, scope of internal auditing has been widened so as to cover all operations besides accounting and financial operations. So in the present time, there is no difference in internal auditing and operational auditing.

Q.15 State the key differences between financial and operational audit. [May 12 (4 Marks)]

Or

The main objective of operational auditing is to verify the fulfilment of plans, and sound business requirements. While in financial auditing, the concentration is more in the financial and accounting areas to ensure that possibilities of loss, wastage and fraud are minimized or removed.

In the light of above, state the major differences between Financial and Operational Auditing.

Or

Write short note on: Financial vs. Operational Audit. [Nov. 17 (4 Marks)]

Ans. : Financial Auditing vs. Operational Auditing:

	Financial Auditing	Operational Auditing
Purpose	It concerned with the opinion that whether the historical information recorded is correct or not.	It emphasizes on effectiveness and efficiency of operations for future performance.
Area	It is restricted to the matters directly affecting the appropriateness of the presented financial statements.	It covers all the activities that are related to efficiency and effectiveness of business operations.
Reporting	Financial audit report is sent to all stockholders, bankers and other persons having interest in the organization.	Operational audit report is primarily for the management.
End Task	Financial audit reports the findings to the persons as its end objectives.	Operational audit is not limited to the reporting only, but includes suggestions for improvements also.

Q.16 Many modern enterprises have become huge and sophisticated. This has resulted in decentralisation of their activities and different type of audits. You are required to explain the difference to the management:

(*i*) Internal & Operational Audit.

(*ii*) Management Audit & Operational Audit.

(*iii*) Financial Audit & Operational Audit. [RTP-Nov. 18]

Ans. : Refer Answer of Q. No. 1, 14 & 15.

Q.17 The Operational audit is carried out effectively when the operational auditor responds with positive traits in a scenario which is blended with behavioural issues. Explain few positive traits that help to conclude an Operational Audit, a success. [May 18 - New Syllabus (4 Marks)]

Ans. : Positive traits of an Operational Auditor: Refer answer of Q. No. 18

Q.18 Employees of GIG Ltd. have to travel frequently for business purposes, so the company entered into a contract with a Simony Travels Ltd. for managing booking, cancellation and other services required by their employees. As per contract terms, Simony travels has to raise its monthly bills for the tickets booked or cancelled during the period and the same are paid by GIG Ltd. within 15 days of the bill date. The bills raised by Simony travels were of huge amount, so the management of GIG Ltd. decided to get an audit conducted of the process followed for booking/cancellation of tickets and verify the accuracy of bills raised by the travel agency. Which audit do you feel the management should opt for? Also briefly discuss the qualities the auditor should possess for such audit. [RTP-May 19]

Ans. : Audit Requirement for verification of bill raised by travel agency:

In the case mentioned in the question, management should opt for operational audit. Operational auditor will ensure verification of effectiveness, efficiency and economy of operations done by the Simony travels for the organisation.

Qualities an operational auditor should possess:

The operational auditor should possess some very essential personal attributes to be effective in his work. Such personal attributes comprise of:

1. Operational auditor should be more inquisitive as, his knowledge ordinarily would be scanty in areas beyond accounting and finance.
2. Operational auditor is required to visualise whether simpler alternative means are available to do a particular work. He should ask the who, why, how of everything.
3. Operational Auditor should possess an attitude of skepticism. He should try to see everything as to whether particular operational aspects properly fit in the business frame and organisational policy.
4. He should imbibe a constructive approach rather than a fault-finding approach and should give a feeling that his efforts are to help attaining an improved operation and not merely fault finding. If the auditor succeeds in giving a feeling of help and assistance through constructive criticism, he will be able to obtain co-operation of the persons who are involved in the operations.
5. He should try to develop a team comprised of people of different backgrounds.

17.3 - MISCELLANEOUS QUESTIONS

Q.19 In an operational audit performance evaluation, what factors can cause unsatisfactory production performance?

Ans. : Factors causing unsatisfactory production:

1. Inadequate or unskilled personnel
2. Non-availability of raw materials
3. Lack of proper supervision
4. Lack of proper machine maintenance
5. Strikes and/or lock out
6. Problems of power supply
7. Non-availability of essential machine spares
8. Lack of proper quality control
9. Poor quality of raw materials
10. Other causes like fire, earthquake etc.

Q.20 You have been appointed to carry out Management-cum-Operational Audit of a Public Ltd company. State whether the use of quantitative ratios is more effective than the use of financial ratios to gain real insight into the financial statements.

Ans. : Use of Quantitative Ratio:

- The objective of management-cum-operational audit is not only to verify compliance with the control but to suggest measures to improve operational environment & increase overall productivity.
- Financial ratios keep changing with the variations in the price level. In a dynamic economy, price levels seldom remain constant and hence comparison of financial ratios over the years becomes vitiated. Quantitative ratios and reconciliations remain unaffected by changes in price. They reflect certain basic relationships and change only if there is a change in the method of operation, technology, degree of automation, product mix, etc.
- A comparison of quantitative ratios over the years can reveal pertinent and leading indications of the real state of affairs.
- The various quantitative ratios which may be calculated are input-output ratio for a manufacturing concern, occupancy ratio for hotels, etc.
- The nature of quantitative ratios and reconciliations that an auditor can work out in a particular audit would depend upon the actual circumstances of the case. However, the auditor must keep a few general considerations in mind while using quantitative data.
- Firstly, he should analyse and use such data mainly as an evidence to support the figures in the statements under audit.
- Secondly, the auditor should try to correlate vital relationships between physical quantities. In this regard the auditor should establish the cause and effect relationship between activities.
- Thirdly, the auditor may attempt to link a physical quantity with its corresponding monetary figure through an estimated average rate.

Conclusion: Though working out quantitative ratios involves greater strain on the auditor, but it is more rewarding.

Q.21 You have been appointed Management Auditor of a large manufacturing company suffering from working capital crunch. Enlist and discuss the related areas which you would probe into to overcome the company's problem.

Ans. : Action Plan for management audit of a company facing financial crunch

(*a*) **Working Capital Estimation:** Prepare a statement of the projected working capital requirements. It should be based on the functional budgets in sales, production, expenses, capital expenditure and the master budget consisting of projected profit and loss and the balance sheet.

(*b*) **Cash Flow Statement/Cash Budget:** Month-wise cash budgets showing inflows and outflows of cash heading-wise should be prepared to analyse the major inflows and outflows affecting the entity.

(*c*) **Inventory/Stock Management:** Raw materials and inventories should be classified properly to determine the level of stock of materials. The system of inventory management needs to be looked at so as to check the avoidable wastes/scraps generated during storage and handling.

(*d*) **Credit Management:** The company should lay down a proper policy for evaluating customers, determining the credit period and offering discounts for early payment. An age-wise analysis of debtors should also be prepared so as to avoid credit to defaulters. The sale department needs to be geared up so that realisation can be made in time.

(*e*) **Funds Flow Analysis:** The company should prepare a funds flow analysis, distinguishing between long-term and short-term sources and applications.

(*f*) **Investment Management:** The idle funds of the company, if any, should be invested in short-term securities to augment the income.

(*g*) **WIP Analysis:** WIP should be monitored and for the purpose it is necessary to ensure that no bottlenecks develop at any stage during the production process.

Q.22 XYZ, a manufacturing unit does not accept the recommendations for improvements made by the Operational Auditor. Suggest an alternative way to tackle the hostile management. [Nov. 10 (5 Marks)]

Ans. : Way to tackle the Hostile Management:

- To tackle the hostile management, auditor is advised to follow participative approach. In this approach the auditor discuss the ideas for improvements with those managers that have to implement them and make them feel that they have participated in the recommendations made for improvements.
- This approach encourages the auditee to develop a friendly attitude towards the auditors and look forward to their guidance in a more receptive fashion.
- The proposed recommendations are discussed with the auditee and modifications as may be agreed upon are incorporated in the operational audit report.
- With this attitude of the auditor it becomes absolutely easy to implement the proposed suggestions as the auditee themselves take initiative for implementing and the auditor do not have to force any change on the auditee.

Q.23 The Managing Director of X Ltd is concerned about high employee attrition rate in his company. As the internal auditor of the company he requests you to analyze the cause for the same. What factors would you consider in such analysis? [May 13 (4 Marks)]

Ans. : The factors responsible for high employee attrition rate are as under:

1. Job Stress & work life imbalance
2. Wrong policies of the Management
3. Unbearable behaviour of Senior Staff
4. Safety factors
5. Limited opportunities for promotion
6. Low monetary benefits
7. Lack of labour welfare schemes
8. Whether the organization has properly qualified and experienced personnel for the various levels of works?
9. Is the number of people employed at various work centres excessive or inadequate?
10. Does the organization provide facilities for staff training so that employees and workers keep themselves abreast of current techniques and practices?

Q.24 The Board of Directors of XYZ Ltd. is concerned with decreasing operating efficiency in material consumption. As an Auditor entrusted with investigating the causes for this poor state, what may be the areas of your focus in this respect. [Nov. 18 - New Syllabus (5 Marks)]

Ans. : Focus Area while investigating the causes of decreasing operating efficiency in material consumption:

To determine the reasons for decreasing efficiency in material consumption, the auditor is required to understand the manufacturing operations from the initial stage of purchase of materials, issue of material, consumption of material and conversions into finished goods. For this purpose, auditor may focus on following aspects:

1. Obtain a list of raw materials used in the production process mentioning therein the names and detailed characteristics of each raw material.
2. Ascertain the basis of computation of normal wastage figures and its consistency as compared to previous months.

3. Obtain internal control reports, in respect of manufacturing costs incurred with reference to predetermined standards or budgets.
4. Examine the stock records so as to determine the raw material purchased, material issued to production.
5. Examine the production records so as to determine the material received from the stores and actual material consumed in the production and waste produced in the production process.
6. Study the Maintenance Programme of machinery to ensure that the machinery does not consume more raw material and quality of goods manufacture is not of sub-standard nature.
7. Ascertain whether employees engaged in production are properly trained and working efficiently.
8. Determine the existence and effectiveness of quality control techniques employed in the entity.
9. Examine inventory controls in respect of storage, pilferage, issues etc.
10. Obtain a statement showing break up of wastage figures in storage, handling and production for the period under reference and compare the results of the analysis for each of the month.
11. Consider the existence of following situations that may also cause the abnormal wastage:
    (*a*) Purchase of poor quality of raw materials.
    (*b*) Machinery breakdown or power failure.
    (*c*) High rate of rejections of finished goods
    (*d*) Deterioration of raw material lying in godowns
    (*e*) Abnormal wastages in storage and handling.
    (*f*) Commencing new production line.

18 CHAPTER AUDIT UNDER FISCAL LAWS

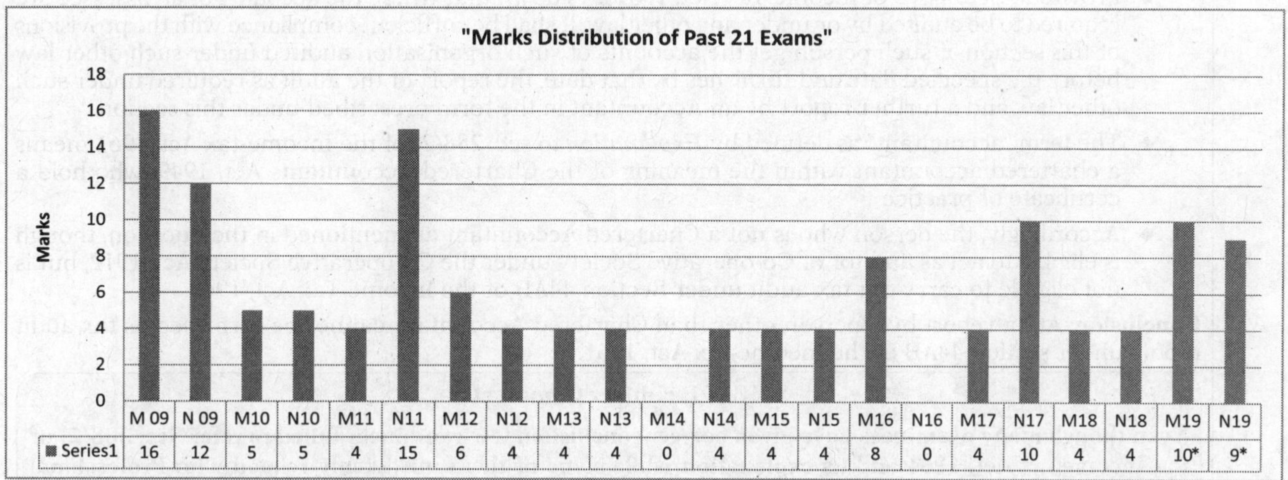

*Only Subjective Questions.

18.1 - AUDIT OF PUBLIC TRUSTS

Q.1 **Draft an Audit programme for conducting the audit of a Public Trust registered under section 12A of the Income Tax Act, 1961.** **[May 09 (8 Marks)]**

Ans. : Audit Programme for conducting audit of a public trust:

1. **Preliminary:** Obtain the following from the trust:
   - A copy of resolution from the trust so as to determine the scope of audit.
   - A list of accounting records maintained by the trust.
   - A certified true coy of trust deed.
   - Trial Balance as at end of accounting period.
   - Balance Sheet and Profit & Loss account of the trust authenticated by the trustee.
2. **Compliance and Substantive Checking**

   (*i*) Examine the system of accounting and internal control.

   (*ii*) Vouch the transactions of the trust so as to ensure the following:

   (*a*) transaction falls within the ambit of the trust;

   (*b*) transaction is properly authorized by the trustees or other delegated authority;

   (*c*) Proper accounting of all incomes and expenses on the basis of the system of accounting followed by the trust;

   (*d*) Amount applied towards the object of the trust are covered by the objects of trust as specified in the trust deed.

   (*iii*) Check whether the financial statements agrees with the trial balance.
3. **Issuing Audit Report**
   - Audit Report shall be furnished in Form No. 10B.
   - Annexure to Form 10B requires certain information to be provided by the auditor, which need to be obtained from the trustees.

18.2 - TAX AUDIT U/S 44AB

Q.2 **A Co-operative Society having receipts above ₹ 100 lakhs get its accounts audited by a person eligible to do audit under Co-operative Societies Act, 1912, who is not a C.A. State with reasons whether such audit report can be furnished as tax audit report u/s 44AB of the Income Tax Act, 1961?**

[Nov. 09 (3 Marks)]

Or

A Co-operative society having receipts over ₹ 2 crores have appointed Mr. D as the statutory auditor - Mr. D is eligible to do the same under the state Co-operative Societies Act. Mr. D is not a chartered accountant. Mr. D is also appointed to conduct the tax audit of the society under section 44AB of the Income Tax Act, 1961. Comment. **[Nov. 17 (4 Marks)]**

Ans. : Tax Audit Report in case of Co-operative society:

- Proviso to Sec. 44AB of Income Tax Act, 1961 lays down that where the accounts of an assessee are required to be audited by or under any other law, it shall be sufficient compliance with the provisions of this section, if such person get the accounts of such organisation audited under such other law before the specified date and furnishes by that date, the report of the audit as required under such other law and a further report by an Accountant in the form prescribed under this section.
- The term "accountant" as defined by *Explanation* to sec. 288(2) of the Income-tax Act, 1961 means a chartered accountant within the meaning of the Chartered Accountants Act, 1949, who hold a certificate of practice
- Accordingly, the person who is not a Chartered Accountant as mentioned in the question, though is eligible to act as auditor of Co-operative Society under the Co-operative Society Act, 1912, but is not eligible to carry out tax audit under Section 44AB of the Income Tax Act, 1961.

Conclusion: Audit report by a person other than Chartered Accountant cannot be furnished as tax audit report under section 44AB of the Income-tax Act, 1961.

"ICAI Examiner Comments"

Even though many examinees have given correct conclusion, few examinees failed to refer Sec. 288(2) of the Income tax Act, 1961 and its explanation while some of them mistakenly related with Professional misconduct under CA Act, 1949.

Q.3 **Mr. X deals in a commodity and purchase and sales of that commodity is ultimately settled otherwise than by the actual delivery. During the financial year 2018-19 he purchased the commodity worth ₹ 95 Lacs and sold the same commodity for ₹ 104 Lacs and the contract was settled otherwise than by the actual delivery. X seeks your advice whether he is liable for tax audit u/s 44AB of the Income Tax Act, 1961.**

Ans. : Liability for Tax Audit in case of Speculative Transactions:

- Mr. X deals in commodity as a speculator. A speculative transaction means a transaction in which a contract for the purchase or sale of any commodity, including stocks and shares, is periodically or ultimately settled otherwise than by the actual delivery.
- As such, in such transaction the difference amount is 'turnover'. In the given case the difference of ₹ 104 lacs and ₹ 95 lakhs i.e., ₹ 9 Lakhs is the turnover.
- In such transactions though the contract notes are issued for full value of the purchases or sales, but the entries in the books of account are made only for the differences.

Conclusion: Mr. X is not liable for Tax audit u/s 44AB of the Income Tax Act, 1961.

Q.4 **Concession Ltd. is engaged in the business of manufacturing of threads. The company recorded the turnover of ₹ 1.13 crore during the financial year 2018-19 before adjusting the following:**

Discount allowed in the Sales Invoice	**₹ 8,20,000**
Cash discount (other than allowed in Cash memo/sales invoice)	**₹ 9,20,000**
Trade discount	**₹ 2,90,000**
Commission on Sales	**₹ 6,00,000**
Sales Return (F.Y. 2016-17)	**₹ 1,60,000**
Sale of Investment	**₹ 6,60,000**

You are required to ascertain the effective turnover to be considered for the prescribed limit of tax audit and guide the company whether the provisions relating to tax audit applies.

Ans. : Computation of Turnover for the purpose of determining requirement of Tax Audit:

As per section 44AB of the Income Tax Act, 1961, audit is required in case of every person carrying on business, if his total sales, turnover or gross receipts in business exceed ₹ 1 crore and in case of every person carrying on a profession, if his gross receipts from profession exceed ₹ 50 lakhs in any previous year.

As per Guidance Note on Tax Audit issued by the ICAI, the following points merit consideration for the purpose of computing turnover:

(*i*) Discount allowed in the sales being in the nature of trade discount will be deducted from the turnover.

(*ii*) Cash discount otherwise than that allowed in a cash memo/sales invoice is in the nature of a financing charge and hence should not be deducted from the turnover.

(*iii*) Special rebate allowed to a customer can be deducted from the sales if it is in the nature of trade discount. If it is in the nature of commission on sales, the same cannot be deducted from the figure of turnover.

(*iv*) Price of goods returned should be deducted from the turnover even if the returns are from the sales made in the earlier year/s.

(*v*) Sale proceeds of any shares, securities, debentures, etc., held as investment will not form part of turnover. However, if the shares, securities, debentures etc., are held as stock-in-trade, the sale proceeds thereof will form part of turnover.

Accordingly, the turnover of concession limited may be computed as under:

Recorded turnover during the year	₹ 1,13,00,000
Less: Discount allowed in the Sales Invoice	(8,20,000)
Trade discount	(2,90,000)
Sales Return	(1,60,000)
Effective turnover	₹ 1,00,30,000

Conclusion: As the effective turnover of Concession Ltd. is more than ₹ 1 Crore, the provisions related to tax audit are applicable to the company.

Q.5 **Mr. A engaged in business as a sole proprietor presented the following information to you for the FY 18-19. Turnover made during the year ₹ 124 lacs. Goods returned in respect of sales made during FY 17-18 is ₹ 20 lacs not included in the above. Cash discount allowed to his customers ₹ 1 lac for prompt payment. Special rebate allowed to customer in the nature of trade discount ₹ 5 lacs. Kindly advise him whether he has to get his accounts audited u/s 44AB of the Income Tax Act, 1961.** **[Nov. 13 (4 Marks)]**

Ans. : Computation of Turnover for the purpose of determining requirement of Tax Audit:

As per section 44AB of the Income Tax Act, 1961, audit is required in case of every person carrying on business, if his total sales, turnover or gross receipts in business exceed ₹ 1 crore and in case of every person carrying on a profession, if his gross receipts from profession exceed ₹ 50 lakhs in any previous year.

As per Guidance Note on Tax Audit issued by the ICAI, the following points merit consideration for the purpose of computing turnover:

(*i*) Discount allowed in the sales being in the nature of trade discount will be deducted from the turnover.

(*ii*) Cash discount otherwise than that allowed in a cash memo/sales invoice is in the nature of a financing charge and hence should not be deducted from the turnover.

(*iii*) Special rebate allowed to a customer can be deducted from the sales if it is in the nature of trade discount.

(*iv*) Price of goods returned should be deducted from the turnover even if the returns are from the sales made in the earlier year/s.

Accordingly, the turnover of Mr. A may be computed as under:

Recorded turnover during the year	₹ 1,24,00,000
Less: Trade discount	(5,00,000)
Sales Return	(20,00,000)
Effective turnover	₹ 99,00,000

Conclusion: As the effective turnover of Mr. A is less than ₹ 1 Crore, the provisions related to tax audit are not applicable to Mr. A.

Q.6 **Comment with respect to computation of total sales, turnover or gross receipts in business exceeding the prescribed limit under section 44AB of Income Tax Act, 1961.**

(*i*) Discount allowed in the sales invoice

(*ii*) Cash discount

(*iii*) Price of goods returned related to earlier year

(*iv*) Sale proceeds of fixed assets. **[May 15 (4 Marks)]**

Ans. : Computation of Total Sales:

(*i*) **Discount allowed in the sales invoice**: Deducted from turnover as it reduces the sale price.

(*ii*) **Cash discount**: Not to be deducted being in the nature of financing charge.

(*iii*) **Price of goods returned related to earlier year**: Deducted from turnover.

(*iv*) **Sale proceeds of fixed assets**: Will not form part of turnover as these are not held for resale.

Q.7 Write short note on: Circumstances in which Chartered Accountant in practice or firm of Chartered Accountants cannot conduct tax audit u/s 44AB of the Income Tax Act, 1961 of the concern.

Ans. : Circumstances in which CA in Practice cannot conduct tax audit:

As per *Explanation* to Sec. 288, the following persons cannot conduct tax audit:

- In case of a company, the person who is not eligible for appointment as an auditor of as per provisions of Sec. 141(3) the Companies Act, 2013 cannot conduct tax audit.
- In case of assessee other than company, following persons cannot conduct tax audit:
  1. the assessee himself or in case of the firm or AOP or HUF, any partner of the firm, or member of the AOP or the HUF;
  2. in case of the assessee, being a trust or institution, any person referred to in Sec. 13(3);
  3. the person who is competent to verify the return in accordance with the provisions of section 140;
  4. any relative of any of the persons referred above;
  5. an officer or employee of the assessee;
  6. an individual who is a partner, or who is in the employment, of an officer or employee of the assessee;
  7. an individual who, or his relative or partner:

     (*a*) is holding any security of, or interest in, the assessee:

     Provided that the relative may hold security or interest in the assessee of the face value not exceeding ₹ 1,00,000;

     (*b*) is indebted to the assessee:

     Provided that the relative may be indebted to the assessee for an amount not exceeding ₹ 1,00,000;

     (*c*) has given a guarantee or provided any security in connection with the indebtedness of any third person to the assessee:

     Provided that the relative may give guarantee or provide any security in connection with the indebtedness of any third person to the assessee for an amount not exceeding ₹ 1,00,000;
  8. a person who, whether directly or indirectly, has business relationship with the assessee of such nature as may be prescribed;
  9. a person who has been convicted by a court of an offence involving fraud and a period of ten years has not elapsed from the date of such conviction.

Q.8 M/s. SB & Co. has been appointed as tax auditor under section 44AB of Income Tax Act, 1961 by Woodcraft Interior Consultants, a professional partnership firm, having turnover 1.25 Crores. M/s RS & Co. are the statutory auditors of the firm but they are unable to give their report on the financial statements of the firm. M/s. SB & Co., have, however, completed their tax audit and want to issue their reports. Comment. [May 17 (4 Marks)]

Ans. : Tax Audit Report in case of Partnership firm assessee:

- Proviso to Sec. 44AB of Income Tax Act, 1961 lays down that where the accounts of an assessee are required to be audited by or under any other law, it shall be sufficient compliance with the provisions of this section, if such person get the accounts of such organisation audited under such other law before the specified date and furnishes by that date, the report of the audit as required under such other law and a further report by an Accountant in the form prescribed under this section.
- There is no statutory requirement of audit of a firm under the provisions of Partnership Act, 1932. So, appointment of two auditors one as tax auditor and another as statutory auditor does not appears to be correct.
- It is also provided under section 44AB that the tax auditor should report whether in his opinion the particulars in respect of Form 3CD are true and correct. The audit report is in the form of 3CA if accounts are being examined under the requirements of provisions of any other Act, otherwise report should be in Form 3CB.

- In the present case, assessee is a partnership firm and appoints separate persons as tax auditor and statutory auditor. Statutory auditor is not able to give their report on financial statements of firm.

Conclusion: Form No. 3CA requires the tax auditor to enclose a copy of the audit report conducted by the statutory auditor. Where the report of the statutory auditor is not available for whatever reasons, it will be possible for the tax auditor to give his report in Form No. 3CB and to certify the relevant particulars in Form No. 3CD.

Note: There is no requirement of statutory audit under Partnership Act, 1932. Hence while answering the question, this fact also need to be stated.

"ICAI Examiner Comments"

Majority of candidates failed to discuss the circumstances in which Form 3CA and Form 3CB are furnished by a Tax auditor. Some candidates wrongly discussed the relationship between the statutory auditor and tax auditor and concluded wrongly that Tax auditor has to wait till statutory audit is completed.

It seems that Candidates failed to understand the requirement of the question.

Q.9 **Mr. PK is conducting the Tax audit u/s 44 AB of the Income Tax Act, 1961 of MG Ltd. for the year ended 31st March, 2019. There is a difference of opinion between Mr. PK and the Management in respect of certain information to be furnished in Form No. 3CD. As a tax auditor, Mr. PK has to report whether the statement of particulars in Form 3CD are true and correct and the same is to be annexed to the report in Form No. 3CA. Advise on the matters to be considered by Mr. PK while furnishing the particulars in Form No. 3CD.** **[Nov. 19 - New Syllabus (4 Marks)]**

Ans. : Form 3CD - Considerations for auditor while furnishing particulars in Form 3CD:

While furnishing the particulars in Form No. 3CD it would be advisable for the tax auditor to consider the following:

1. If a particular item of income/expenditure is covered in more than one of the specified clauses, care should be taken to make a suitable cross reference to such items at the appropriate places.
2. If there is any difference in the opinion of the tax auditor and that of the assessee in respect of any information furnished in Form No. 3CD, the tax auditor should state both the view points and also the relevant information in order to enable the tax authority to take a decision in the matter.
3. If any particular clause in Form No. 3CD is not applicable, he should state that the same is not applicable.
4. In computing the allowance or disallowance, he should keep in view the law applicable in the relevant year, even though the form of audit report may not have been amended to bring it in conformity with the amended law.
5. In case the prescribed particulars are given in part to the tax auditor or relevant form is incomplete and the assessee does not give the information against all or any of the clauses, the auditor should not withhold the entire audit report. In such a case, he can qualify his report on matters in respect of which information is not furnished to him.
6. The information in Form No. 3CD should be based on the books of account, records, documents, information and explanations made available to the tax auditor for his examination.
7. In case the auditor relies on a judicial pronouncement, he may mention the fact as his observations in Form No. 3CA or Form No. 3CB, as the case may be.

18.3 - METHODS OF ACCOUNTING & ICDSs (SEC. 145)

Q.10 **As the tax auditor of a non-corporate entity u/s 44AB of the Income Tax Act, 1961, how would you ensure compliance of section 145 of the Income Tax Act, 1961?** **[May 09 (8 Marks)]**

Ans. : Compliance of Section 145:

- Sec. 145(1) of Income Tax Act, 1961 requires that the income chargeable under the head 'PGBP' or 'Other sources' shall, be computed in accordance with either cash or mercantile system of accounting regularly employed by the assessee.
- Sec. 145(2) provides that the C.G. may notify in the Official Gazette from time to time Income Computation and Disclosure Standards to be followed by any class of assessee or in respect of any class of income.

- Sec. 145(3) provides that where the A.O. is not satisfied about the correctness or completeness of the accounts of the assessee, or where method of accounting provided u/s 145(1) have not been regularly followed by the assessee or income has not been computed in accordance with the Standards notified u/s 145(2), the A.O. may make an assessment in a manner provided in Sec. 144 of the Income Tax Act.
- Auditor has to therefore ensure the following:
  (*a*) That the entity follows either the cash or accrual method of accounting and same is to be reported in clause 13(a) of Form 3CD.
  (*b*) Accounting policies has been disclosed separately.
  (*c*) Provisions as stated in Income Computation and Disclosure Standards (ICDS) notified by Central Government u/s 145(2) has been complied with.

Q.11 Discuss briefly Income Computation and Disclosure Standards to be followed by assessee under the Income-tax Law. [Nov. 09 (4 Marks)]

Ans. : Income Computation and Disclosure standards to be followed by assessee under Income Tax Law:

The Central Government has prescribed the following Income Computation and Disclosure Standard:

I	Accounting Policies
II	Valuation of Inventories
III	Construction Contracts
IV	Revenue Recognition
V	Tangible Fixed Assets
VI	Effects of Changes in Foreign Exchange Rates
VII	Government Grants
VIII	Securities
IX	Borrowing Costs
X	Provisions, Contingent Liabilities and Contingent Assets

The above Standards are to be followed by all assessee following mercantile system of accounting for computation of income under the head "PGBP" and "Other Sources". Therefore, it is clear that those assessees who are following cash system of accounting need not follow the ICDSs notified above.

18.4 - FORM 3CD

Q.12 Mr. A, is a renowned lawyer. During the previous year, he collected GST of ₹ 25 lakhs but utilized it for his personal use. The department issued a show cause notice to him as to why the tax, collected by him, is not deposited to the government account. He appeared before the department and stated his inability to pay the sum due to financial crisis. The proceedings are still pending.

Mr. A instructed his tax auditor not to disclose his GST registration details, while filling particulars to be furnished in Form No. 3CD, believing that the income tax department might trace his scrutiny proceedings details pending before department which would bring disrepute to his profession.

Or

You are appointed as tax auditor of Mr. X a practicing advocate in Agra. During the previous year he collected GST of ₹ 7 lakhs but utilized for personal use. The department issued a show cause notice to him why the tax collected by him in not deposited to the Government account. He appeared before the department and stated his inability to pay the sum due to financial crisis. The proceedings are still pending. Mr. X requests you not to disclose his GST registration details while filling particulars to be furnished in Form No. 3CD.

As a tax auditor how would you deal with this? [May 16 (4 Marks)]

Ans. : Reporting Requirement of Form 3CD:

- Clause (4) of Form 3CD, requires tax auditor to mention the registration number or any other identification number, if any, allotted, in case the assessee is liable to pay indirect taxes like excise duty, service tax, sales tax, GST, customs duty, GST etc. Auditor is required to furnish the details of registration numbers as provided to him by the assessee.

◆ The reporting is however, to be done in the manner or format specified by the e-filing utility in this context. The information may be obtained and maintained in the following format:

Sr. No.	Relevant Indirect Tax Law which requires registration	Place of Business/profession/service unit for which registration is in place/ or has been applied for	Registration/Identification number

◆ In the present case Mr. X has defaulted in payment of GST for the previous year. Consequently, the department issued a show cause notice for such non-payment of tax. The arguments are still going on between the department and assessee. He also restrained his tax auditor from disclosing GST registration details in tax audit report.

Conclusion: Instruction of Mr. X is not acceptable as clause (4) of Form 3CD requires tax auditor to furnish the details of registration number or other identification number of assessee, if assessee is required to pay indirect taxes like excise duty, service tax, GST etc.

"ICAI Examiner Comments"

Most of the candidates failed to visualize the requirement of the question and answered about reporting requirement due to non-payment of GST under clause 41 instead of GST registration number under clause (4).

Q.13 BB Ltd., a non-resident company, is engaged in the business of extraction of mineral oils, having turnover of ₹ 20 lakhs during the financial year 2018-19. The company claims that its profits and gains chargeable to tax under the head "Profits and gains of business or profession" is lower than the deemed income chargeable under section 44BB of the Income Tax Act, 1961. Therefore, it decided to get its accounts audited under section 44AB of the Income Tax Act, 1961. Discuss reporting requirement of Form 3CD in this behalf.

Ans. : Reporting Requirement of Form 3CD:

◆ BB Ltd., is a non-resident company which is engaged in the business of extraction of mineral oils, hence, its income is chargeable in accordance with the provisions of section 44BB of the Income Tax Act, 1961. But as the company is claiming lower income in comparison to deemed income u/s 44BB, provisions of section 44AB in relation to audit has to be complied with.

◆ Clause (*8*) of Form 3CD, requires tax auditor to mention the relevant clause of section 44AB under which the audit has been conducted. Accordingly, auditor is required to mention clause (*c*) of Section 44AB which requires tax audit.

◆ Further, as per Clause (12) of Form 3CD, if the profit and loss account of the assessee includes any profits and gains assessable on presumptive basis, the tax auditor has to indicate the amount and the relevant sections.

Conclusion: Under Clause 8, auditor is required to indicate the relevant clause of section 44AB under which audit is to be conducted and in addition under clause 12, auditor is required to indicate the amount of profits of business covered u/s 44BB and the relevant section.

Q.14 State the reporting requirement regarding books of account (prescribed, maintained and examined) in Form No. 3CD of Tax Audit under section 44AB of the Income Tax Act, 1961.

Ans. : Reporting Requirement regarding books of account in Form 3CD:

Clause 11 of Form 3CD requires the following reporting requirements in Form 3CD w.r.t. books of account:

(*a*) Whether books of account are prescribed under section 44AA, if yes, list of books so prescribed.

(*b*) List of books of account maintained and the address at which the books of account are kept.

(In case books of account are maintained in a computer system, mention the books of account generated by such computer system. If the books of account are not kept at one location, please furnish the addresses of locations along with the details of books of account maintained at each location.)

(*c*) List of books of account and nature of relevant documents examined.

Q.15 Write a short note on: Method of Accounting in Form No. 3CD of Tax Audit.

Ans. : Method of Accounting in Form No. 3CD:

Clause 13 of Form 3CD requires the following reporting requirements w.r.t. Methods of accounting:

(*a*) Method of accounting employed in the previous year.

(*b*) Whether there had been any change in the method of accounting employed *vis-a-vis* the method employed in the immediately preceding previous year.

(*c*) If answer to (b) above is in the affirmative, give details of such change, and the effect thereof on the profit or loss.

Serial number	Particulars	Increase in profit (₹)	Decrease in profit (₹)

(*d*) Details of deviation, if any, in the method of accounting employed in the previous year from accounting standards prescribed under section 145 and the effect thereof on the profit or loss.

Q.16 A leading manufacturing concern valued its inventory following a method not in line with the provisions of Income Computation and Disclosure Standard (ICDS)- 2 'Valuation of Inventories'.

In such a situation, discuss the relevant clause of Form No. 3CD under which the tax auditor is required to report?

Or

ABC Ltd., is consistently following accounting standards as required u/s 133 of the Companies Act, 2013. During your tax audit u/s 44AB of the Income-tax Act, 1961, the board of directors informed you that profits of the company is properly arrived at and the ASs applicable to it have been followed consistently and as such, there need not be any adjustments to be made as per ICDS notified u/s 145 of Income Tax Act, 1961. Based on the requirement of Law in this regard, examine the validity of the stand of management in this regard. [May 18-New Syllabus (5 Marks)]

Ans. : Reporting for Adjustment to be made to the Profits or Loss for complying with ICDSs:

- Central Government has, in exercise of the powers conferred u/s 145(2) of Income Tax Act, 1961, notified ten Income Computation and Disclosure Standards (ICDSs) to be followed by all assessees (other than an individual or a HUF who is not required to get his accounts of one previous year audited in accordance with the provisions of section 44AB), following the mercantile system of accounting, for the purposes of computation of income chargeable to income-tax under the head "Profit and gains of business or profession" or "Income from other sources".
- Clause 13(*d*) of Form No. 3CD of the tax audit report requires the tax auditor to state whether any adjustment is required to be made to the profits or loss for complying with the provisions of income computation and disclosure standards notified under section 145(2) of the Income Tax Act, 1961.
- Further, the tax auditor is also required to report under Clause 13(*e*), if answer to Clause 13(*d*) above is in the affirmative i.e. the auditor is required to give details of such adjustments as follows:

		Increase in Profit (Rs.)	Decrease in Profit (Rs.)	Net Effect (Rs.)
ICDS I	Accounting Policies			
ICDS II	Valuation of Inventories			
ICDS III	Construction Contracts			
ICDS IV	Revenue Recognition			
ICDS V	Tangible Fixed Assets			
ICDS VI	Changes in Foreign Exchange Rates			
ICDS VII	Governments Grants			
ICDS VIII	Securities			
ICDS IX	Borrowing Costs			
ICDS X	Provisions, Contingent Liabilities & Contingent Assets			
	Total			

Conclusion: Contention of the management that they are following Accounting Standards and need not to make any adjustments as per ICDS, is not correct. Thus, ABC Ltd. is required to adjust the profits in compliance with ICDS.

Q.17 A leading jewellery merchant used to value his inventory at cost on LIFO basis. However, for the current year, in view of requirements of AS-2, he changed over to FIFO method of valuation. The difference in value of stock amounted to ₹ 55 lakhs which is higher than that under the previous method. In such a situation, what are the reporting responsibilities of a Tax Audit u/s 44AB of Income Tax Act, 1961.

Ans. : Reporting of Changes in Valuation of Inventory:

- As per the provisions of Income Tax Act, 1961, if the change in method of valuation is *bona fide*, and is regularly and consistently adopted in the subsequent years as well, such change would be permitted to be made for tax purposes.
- In the instant case, the change in the valuation of stock is pursuant to mandatory requirements of the AS-2 'Valuation of Inventories' and therefore should be viewed as *bona fide* change and allowed.
- Clause 14 of Form 3CD also requires in this regard reporting over the following:
  1. Method of valuation of closing stock employed in the previous year.
  2. In case of deviation from the method of valuation prescribed under section 145A, and the effect thereof on the profit or loss.
- In reference to section 145A, auditor is not required to change the method of valuation of purchases, sales and inventories which is regularly employed by the assessee. Auditor is required to adjust the valuation for any tax, duty, cess or fee actually paid or incurred by the assessee, if the same had not already been adjusted.

Q.18 T Ltd.'s previous year ended on 31st March 2019. During that period, it made a claim for refund of customs duty which was admitted as due by the customs authorities during April 2019. T Ltd. neither credited the claim in the profit and loss account nor reported the same in clause 16(b) of Form 3CD for the reason that this has been admitted as due by the authorities only in the next financial year. Further T Ltd. had changed the method of determination of cost formula for the purpose of stock valuation from FIFO basis to Weighted Average Cost basis, but that was also not reflected in clause 13(b) of Form 3CD which requires reporting on change in accounting method employed. Comment. [May 12 (6 Marks)]

Ans. : Reporting requirement of Claim of Custom Duty Refund and change in Accounting policy:

- As per Clause 16(b) of Form 3CD, the details of custom duty refund, if admitted as due but not reported in Profit and Loss account, are to be stated. But the claim which have been admitted as due after the relevant previous year need not be reported.
- Hence non-reporting of claim of refund of custom duty in Form 3CD is in order.
- Clause 13(b) of Form 3CD required reporting in case of change in method of accounting employed. But in the present case there is a change in accounting policy. Change in Accounting policy cannot be treated as change in method of accounting, hence does not require any reporting under clause 13(b) in Form 3CD.
- Hence non-reporting of method of valuation in Form 3CD is in order.

Q.19 While conducting the tax audit of A & Co. you observed that it made an escalation claim to one of its customers but which was not accounted as income. What is your reporting responsibility? [May 11 (4 Marks)]

Ans. : Clause 16(c) of Form 3CD:

- A tax auditor has to report under clause 16(c) of Form 3CD on any escalation claim accepted during the previous year and not credited to the profit and loss account under clause 16(c) of Form 3CD.
- The escalation claim accepted during the year would normally mean "accepted during the relevant previous year." If such amount is not credited to Profit and Loss Account the fact should be reported. The system of accounting followed in respect of this particular item may also be brought out in appropriate cases. If the assessee is following cash basis of accounting with reference to this item, it should be clearly brought out since acceptance of claims during the relevant previous year without actual receipt has no significance in cases where cash method of accounting is followed.
- Escalation claims should normally arise pursuant to a contract (including contracts entered into in earlier years), if so permitted by the contract. Only those claims to which the other party has signified unconditional acceptance could constitute accepted claims. Mere making claims by the assessee or claims under negotiations cannot constitute accepted claims. After ascertaining the relevant factors as outlined above, a decision whether to report or not, can be taken.

Q.20 While writing the audit program for tax audit in respect of A Ltd. you wish to include possible instances of capital receipt if not credited to Profit & Loss Account which needs to be reported under clause 16(e) of Form 3CD. Please elucidate possible instance. [May 13 (4 Marks)]

or

What can be the possible instance of capital receipt which, if not credited to the profit and loss account, needs to be reported in Form 3CD? [Nov. 15 (4 Marks)]

Or

In the course of your tax audit assignment u/s 44AB of the Income Tax Act, 1961 of Dream Bank Ltd. You have instructed your assistant to find out receipt of capital nature which might not have been credited to Profit & Loss Account and needs to be reported in Para 16(*e*) of Form 3CD. Your audit assistant seeks your guidance in reporting the same. Specify any four illustrative examples of such receipt.

[May 19 - New Syllabus (4 Marks)]

Ans. : Instances of Capital receipt:

(*a*) Capital subsidy received in the form of Government grants, which are in the nature of promoters' contribution i.e., they are given with reference to the total investment of the undertaking or by way of contribution to its total capital outlay. For e.g., Capital Investment Subsidy Scheme.

(*b*) Government grant in relation to a specific fixed asset where such grant is shown as a deduction from the gross value of the asset by the concern in arriving at its book value.

(*c*) Compensation for surrendering certain rights.

(*d*) Profit on sale of fixed assets/investments to the extent not credited to the profit and loss account.

Audit procedures:

Capital receipts are not generally credited to profit and loss account hence the auditor should take enough care to check out any transaction generating the capital receipts by -

- Enquiring whether the assessee is in receipt of any amount of capital nature during the previous year.
- Going through the financial statements, in particular reserve account, to ascertain whether the assessee has received any such receipts and credited them directly to reserve account.
- Enquiring whether the assessee has credited such receipts to profit and loss account.
- Checking that any such receipts is accounted for in terms of method of accounting followed by the assessee.

"ICAI Examiner Comments"

Some examinees wrote about Form No. 3CD. Also, few examinees discussed about the items of profit and loss account which was not required.

Q.21 **ABC Ltd., a manufacturing concern, sold a house property in Mumbai for a consideration of ₹ 48 lakh, to Mr. X on 1.8.2018. ABC Ltd. had purchased the house property in the year 2014 for ₹ 30 lakh. The stamp duty value on the date of transfer, i.e., 01.08.2018, is ₹ 65 lakh for the house property. How would you deal this matter in tax audit report?**

Ans. : Reporting of Sale of property at a price lower than value adopted for the purpose of stamp duty:

- Clause 17 of Form 3CD requires tax auditor to furnish certain information if land or building or both is transferred during the previous year for a consideration less than value adopted by any authority of a State Government as under:

Details of Property	Consideration Received or Accrued	Value adopted or assessee or assessable

- For this purpose, auditor should obtain a list of all properties transferred by the assessee during the previous year and furnish the amount of consideration received or accrued, as disclosed in the books of account of the assessee.
- For reporting the value adopted or assessed or assessable, the auditor should obtain from the assessee a copy of the registered sale deed. In case the property is not registered, the auditor may verify relevant documents from relevant authorities or obtain third party expert like lawyer, solicitor representation to satisfy the compliance of section 43CA/section 50C of the Act.

Conclusion: ABC Ltd. has sold the house property to Mr. X at a price lower than value adopted for stamp duty purpose, tax auditor is required to report on the same under Clause 17 of Form 3CD.

Q.22 **A is proprietor of a firm M/s ABC & Co. The firm has a turnover of ₹ 500 lakhs during the financial year ended 31.03.2019. The firm sold land and building during the year for a consideration of ₹ 15 lakhs, whose value for stamp duty purposes was ₹ 16 lakhs. As the Tax Auditor of the said firm, is the above to be reported? If yes, how will you report the same?** **[Nov. 19 - Old Syllabus (4 Marks)]**

Ans. : Reporting of Sale of property at a price lower than value adopted for the purpose of stamp duty:

- Clause 17 of Form 3CD requires tax auditor to furnish certain information if land or building or both is transferred during the previous year for a consideration less than value adopted by any authority of a State Government as under:

Details of Property	Consideration Received or Accrued	Value adopted or assessees or assessable

- For this purpose, auditor should obtain a list of all properties transferred by the assessee during the previous year and furnish the amount of consideration received or accrued, as disclosed in the books of account of the assessee.
- For reporting the value adopted or assessed or assessable, the auditor should obtain from the assessee a copy of the registered sale deed. In case the property is not registered, the auditor may verify relevant documents from relevant authorities or obtain third party expert like lawyer, solicitor representation to satisfy the compliance of section 43CA/section 50C of the Act.

Conclusion: ABC ltd. has sold the house property to Mr. X at a price lower than value adopted for stamp duty purpose, tax auditor is required to report on the same under Clause 17 of Form 3CD.

Q.23 As an auditor of a partnership firm under section 44AB of the Income Tax Act, 1961, how would you report on the following: Capital Expenditure incurred for scientific research assets. [Nov. 12 (2 Marks)]

Ans. : Reporting of Capital Expenditure incurred on Scientific Research Assets in Form 3CD:

Clause 19 of Form 3CD requires the auditor to report the following:

(*i*) Amount debited to profit and loss account.

(*ii*) Amounts admissible as per the provisions of the Income Tax Act, 1961 and also fulfils the conditions, if any specified under the relevant provisions of Income Tax Act, 1961 or Income Tax Rules, 1962 or any other guidelines, circular, etc., issued in this behalf.

Q.24 As a tax auditor how would you deal and report the following: An assessee has incurred payments to clubs. [Nov. 11 (2 Marks)]

Or

As an auditor of a partnership firm under section 44AB of the Income Tax Act, 1961, how would you report on the following: Expenditure incurred at Clubs. [Nov. 12 (2 Marks)]

Ans. : Reporting of Payment to Club in Form 3CD:

- Clause 21(a) of Form 3CD requires the tax auditor is required to furnish the details of amounts debited to the profit and loss account, being in the nature of capital, personal, advertisement expenditure etc.
- Such reporting requires the tax auditor to report on the
  (*a*) Expenditure incurred at clubs being entrance fees and subscriptions; and
  (*b*) Expenditure incurred at clubs being cost for club services and facilities used.
- The payments made may be in respect of directors and other employees in case of companies, and for partners or proprietors in other cases.
- The fact whether such expenses are incurred in the course of business or whether they are of personal nature should be ascertained.

Q.25 ABC Ltd., engaged in the manufacturing of goods carriage, appointed you as the tax auditor for the financial year 2018-19. How would you deal with the following matters in your tax audit report:

(*i*) Payments of 6 invoices of ₹ 5,000 each made in cash to Mr. X, engaged in leasing of goods carriages on 4th July, 2018.

(*ii*) Payments of 2 invoices of ₹ 18,000 each made in cash to Mr. Y, engaged in leasing of goods carriages on 5th July, 2018 and 6th July, 2018 respectively.

(*iii*) Payment of ₹ 40,000 made in cash to Mr. Z, engaged in leasing of goods carriages on 7th July, 2018 against an invoice for expenses booked in 2017-18.

Ans. : Reporting of Payments Exceeding ₹ 35,000 in Cash:

- Clause 21(d)(A) and 21(d)(B) of Form 3CD, requires tax auditor to scrutinize on the basis of the examination of books of account and other relevant documents/evidence, whether the expenditure covered under section 40A(3) and 40A(3A) respectively read with rule 6DD were made by account payee cheque drawn on a bank or account payee bank draft. If not, the same has to be reported under abovementioned clauses.
- As per section 40A(3) of the Income Tax Act, 1961, an expenditure is disallowed if the assessee incurs any expenses in respect of which payment or aggregate of payments made to a person in a day, otherwise than by an account payee cheque drawn on bank or account payee draft, exceeds ₹ 10,000. However, in case of payment made for plying, hiring or leasing of goods carriage, limit is ₹ 35,000 instead of ₹ 10,000.
- As per section 40A(3A) of the Income Tax Act, 1961, where an allowance has been made in the assessment for any year in respect of any liability incurred by the assessee for any expenditure and subsequently during any previous year the assessee makes payment in respect thereof, otherwise than by an account payee cheque drawn on a bank or account payee bank draft, the payment so made shall be deemed to be the profits and gains of business or profession and accordingly chargeable to income-tax as income of the subsequent year if the payments made to a person in a day, exceeds ₹ 10,000 (₹ 35,000 in case of plying, hiring or leasing of goods carriages).
- Based on the above-mentioned provisions, following conclusion may be drawn:
  - (*i*) Payments of 6 invoices of ₹ 5,000 each aggregating ₹ 30,000 made in cash on 4th July, 2018 need not be reported as the aggregate of payments do not exceed ₹ 35,000.
  - (*ii*) Payments of 2 invoices of ₹ 18,000 each made in cash on 5th July, 2018 and 6th July, 2018 respectively aggregating ₹ 36,000 need not be reported as the payment do not exceed ₹ 35,000 in a day.
  - (*iii*) Payment of ₹ 40,000 made in cash against an invoice for expenses booked in 2017-18 is likely to be deemed to be the profits and gains of business or profession under section 40A(3A) of the Income Tax Act, 1961. Thus, the details of such amount need to be furnished under clause 21(d)(B) of Form 3CD.

Q.26 Mr. R, the Tax Auditor finds that some payments inadmissible under section 40A(3) were made, and advised the client to report the same in form 3CD. The client contends that cash payments were made since the other parties insisted upon the same and did not have Bank Accounts. Comment.

[Nov. 10 (5 Marks)]

Ans. : Reporting for Cash payments above ₹ 10,000:

- Clause 21(d) of Form 3CD requires tax auditor to report on disallowance under section 40A(3). Disallowance u/s 40A(3) of the Income Tax Act, 1961 is attracted if the assessee incurs any expenses in respect of which payment or aggregate of payments made to a person in a day, otherwise than by an account payee cheque drawn on bank or account payee draft, exceeds ₹ 10,000.
- However, there are certain cases as specified in Rule 6DD, in which, disallowance under section 40A(3) would not be attracted. Cash payment made on insistence of other parties on the contention that they do not have bank accounts is not covered under the list of exceptions provided under Rule 6DD.
- In the present case, tax auditor is required to scrutinize on the basis of the examination of books of account and other relevant documents/evidence, whether the expenditure covered under section 40A(3) read with rule 6DD were made by account payee cheque drawn on a bank or account payee bank draft. If not, the same has to be reported under abovementioned clause.

Conclusion: Payments made by the XYZ Ltd. are inadmissible u/s 40A(3) of the Income Tax Act, 1961 and hence, needs to be reported under clause 21(d) of Form 3CD.

Q.27 XYZ Ltd. pays ₹ 90,000 for its 10 employees to a Hotel as boarding and lodging expenses of such employees for a conference. The Company pays the amount in cash to the Hotel. The Hotel gives 10 bills each amounting to ₹ 9,000. The Company contends that each bill is within the limit, so there is no violation of the provisions of the Income Tax Act, 1961. As the tax auditor, how would you deal with the matter in your tax audit report for the Assessment Year 2019-20? **[Nov. 14 (4 Marks)]**

Ans. : Reporting for Cash payments above ₹ 10,000:

- Clause 21(d) of Form 3CD requires tax auditor to report on disallowance under section 40A(3). Disallowance u/s 40A(3) of the Income Tax Act, 1961 is attracted if the assessee incurs any expenses in respect of which payment or aggregate of payments made to a person in a day, otherwise than by an account payee cheque drawn on bank or account payee draft, exceeds ₹ 10,000.
- In the given case, the tax auditor found that a hotel issued 6 bills to XYZ Ltd. Each amounting to ₹ 9,000 for boarding & lodging expenses of 6 employees. XYZ Ltd. In aggregate has paid ₹ 90,000 to the hotel in cash. Consequently, no expenditure shall be allowed for deduction as per the provisions of section 40A(3).
- Contention of the company that each bill is within the limit is not tenable since aggregate of payments need to be considered.

Conclusion: Payments made by the XYZ Ltd. are inadmissible u/s 40A(3) of the Income Tax Act, 1961 and hence, needs to be reported under clause 21(d) of Form 3CD.

Q.28 Answer the following: As the tax auditor of a Company, how would you report on payments exceeding ₹ 10,000 made in cash to a supplier against an invoice for expenses booked in an earlier year?

Ans. : Reporting of payments exceeding ₹ 10,000 in cash:

- Reporting is required under clause 21(d) of Form 3CD for the payments exceeding ₹ 10,000 made in cash against an invoice for expenses booked in an earlier year.
- Section 40A(3A) disallowed an expense payment exceeding ₹ 10,000 made in cash against an invoice booked in an earlier year.
- Claude 21(d) of Form 3CD requires furnishing of the amount inadmissible u/s 40A(3) read with rule 6DD along with computation.
- The entire amount paid, is likely to be disallowed u/s 40A(3A) of the Income-tax Act, 1961.

Q.29 You are the Tax auditor of BL & Co., a partnership firm engaged in the business of plying of Goods Carriages for the financial year 2018-19 having a turnover of Rs. 20 crores. How would you deal and report on the following:

(*i*) Payment of Rs. 50,000 in cash to Mr. R on 10th September, 2018 towards settlement of invoice for expenses accounted in financial year 2017-18.

(*ii*) Payments of 3 invoices of Rs. 15,000 each made in cash to Mr. Y on 8th, 9th, 10th, July, 2017 respectively.

[Nov. 18-Old Syllabus (4 Marks)]

Ans. : Reporting of Payments Exceeding Rs. 10,000 in Cash:

- Clause 21(*d*)(A) and 21(*d*)(B) of Form 3CD, requires tax auditor to scrutinize on the basis of the examination of books of account and other relevant documents/evidence, whether the expenditure covered under section 40A(3) and 40A(3A) respectively read with rule 6DD were made by account payee cheque drawn on a bank or account payee bank draft. If not, the same has to be reported under abovementioned clauses.
- As per section 40A(3) of the Income-tax Act, 1961, an expenditure is disallowed if the assessee incurs any expenses in respect of which payment or aggregate of payments made to a person in a day, otherwise than by an account payee cheque drawn on bank or account payee draft, exceeds Rs. 10,000. However, in case of payment made for plying, hiring or leasing of goods carriage, limit is Rs. 35,000 instead of Rs. 10,000.
- As per section 40A(3A) of the Income-tax Act, 1961, where an allowance has been made in the assessment for any year in respect of any liability incurred by the assessee for any expenditure and subsequently during any previous year the assessee makes payment in respect thereof, otherwise than by an account payee cheque drawn on a bank or account payee bank draft, the payment so made shall be deemed to be the profits and gains of business or profession and accordingly chargeable to income-tax as income of the subsequent year if the payments made to a person in a day, exceeds Rs. 10,000 (Rs. 35,000 in case of plying, hiring or leasing of goods carriages).
- Based on the abovementioned provisions, following conclusion may be drawn:

  (*i*) Reporting required under Clause 21(*d*)(B) w.r.t. payment of ₹ 50,000.

  (*ii*) Reporting required under Clause 21(*d*)(A) w.r.t. each payment as individual payment made on a day exceeds ₹ 10,000.

Note: Limit of ₹ 35,000 is not applicable as this limit is applicable when the payee is engaged in the business of plying of goods carriages. In this case, payer is engaged in the business of plying of goods carriages hence, limit of ₹ 10,000 will be applicable assuming that payee is not engaged in business of plying of goods carriages.

Q.30 Mr. Sharma carries on the business of dealing and export of diamonds. For the year ended 31st March 2019, you as the tax auditor find that the entire exports are to another firm in U.S.A. which is owned by Mr. Sharma's brother. Comment.

Ans. : Export Payments to a Relative:

- Clause 23 of Form 3CD, requires the tax auditor to specify particulars of payments made to persons specified u/s 40A(2)(b) of the Income Tax Act, 1961. Persons specified in the said section are relatives of an assessee and sister concerns, etc.
- In the instant case, however, Mr. Sharma has not made any payments to his brother. On the contrary, he must have received payments from him against exports made and, thus, this clause would **not be applicable** to him.

Auditor will nonetheless be still as a part of his normal audit planning would be required to verify whether the exports are genuine, i.e., whether the diamonds have been delivered by verifying the necessary delivery documents, relevant invoices, etc., the reasonableness of the price and whether the export realisations have been received.

Q.31 As a tax auditor how would you deal and report the following: An assessee has paid rent to his brother ₹ 2,50,000 and paid interest to his sister ₹ 4,00,000. [Nov. 11 (2 Marks)]

Or

As an auditor appointed under section 44AB of the Income Tax Act, 1961, how would you verify and report on the following: The assessee has paid rent of ₹ 5 lakhs for premises to his brother.

[Nov. 17 (3 Marks)]

Ans. : Reporting of payment of rent and interest to relative:

Clause 23 of Form 3CD requires the tax auditor to furnish the particulars of payments made to persons specified under Section 40A(2)(b) of the Income Tax Act, 1961. In relation to an individual, the specified persons include any relative of the assessee (i.e. Husband, Wife, Brother, Sister or any other Lineal Ascendant or Descendant).

In the present case, an assessee has paid rent to his brother and interest to his sister which may be disallowed if, in the opinion of the Assessing Officer, such expenditure is excessive or unreasonable having regard to:

1. the fair market value of the goods, services or facilities for which the payment is made; or
2. for the legitimate needs of business or profession of the assessee; or
3. the benefit derived by or accruing to the assessee from such expenditure.

Conclusion: Auditor is required to report the payments made to specified persons.

"ICAI Examiner Comments"

Examinees have discussed generally on vouching and verification aspects instead of mentioning the reporting requirements of Tax auditor. Some examinees failed to explain with reference to Clause 23 of Form 3CD for reporting the particulars of payments made to persons specified under section 40A(2)(b) of the Income Tax Act, 1961. Instead of explaining tax audit requirements few examinees wrongly discussed AS 18 and SA 550 on "Related parties".

Q.32 You are doing Tax Audit of Private Limited Company for the financial year ending 31st March, 2020. During audit, you notice that the company is not regular in deposit of VAT/GST and there remains pendency every year. The details of VAT/GST payable are:

(*i*) GST payable as on 31/03/2019 of FY 2018-19 was ₹ 200 Lakh and out of which ₹ 100 Lakh was paid on 15/09/2019 and ₹ 50 Lakh on 30/03/2020 and balance of ₹ 50 Lakh paid on 16/09/2020.

(*ii*) GST payable of current financial year 2019-20 was ₹ 100 lakh and out of this, 40 Lakh was paid on 25/05/2019 and balance of ₹ 60 Lakh remained unpaid till the due date of return.

The date of Tax Audit report and due date of return was 30th September.

Now as a Tax Auditor, how/where the said transaction will be reflected in Tax Audit Report under Section 43B(*a*)? [MTP-Oct. 19, RTP-Nov. 19]

Ans. : Reporting in Tax Audit Report:

- Any amount of GST/Tax payable on the last day of previous year (opening balance) as well as on the last day of current year has to be reported in Tax Audit Report under clause 26(A) and 26(B) in reference of section 43 B.
- Clause 26(A) dealt GST/VAT payable on the pre-existed of the first day of the previous year but was not allowed in the assessment of any preceding previous year and was either paid {clause 26(A)(*a*)}/or/and/not paid during the previous year {clause 26(A)(*b*)}
- The details will be as under in regard to opening balances:

Liability Pre-existed on the previous year.

Sr. No.	Sec.	Nature of Liability	Outstanding Opening balance not allowed in previous year	Amount paid/ set-off during the year	Amount written back to P&L Account	Amount unpaid at the end of the year
01	43B(*a*)	VAT/GST	100 lakh	50 lakh	0	50 lakh

It has been assumed that 50 lakh was allowed in last year as it was paid before the due date of return.

Liability incurred during the previous year

Sr. No.	Sec.	Nature of Liability	Amount incurred in previous year but remaining outstanding on last day of previous year.	Amount paid/set-off before the due date of filing return/date upto which reported in the tax audit report, whichever is earlier	Amount unpaid on the due of filing of return/ date upto which reported in the tax audit report, whichever is earlier
01	43B(*a*)	VAT/GST	100 lakh	40 lakh	60 lakh

Q.33 How will you verify the Income & Expenditure of earlier years credited/debited in current year for reporting under clause 27(*b*) of 3CD while carrying out Tax Audit u/s 44AB of the Income Tax Act, 1961? [Nov. 19 - Old Syllabus (5 Marks)]

Ans. : Reporting under Clause 27(*b*) of Form 3CD:

Clause 27(*b*) requires the tax auditor to report particulars of income or expenditure of prior period credited or debited to the profit and loss account. Information under clause 27(*b*) would be relevant only in those cases where the assessee follows mercantile system of accounting.

The tax auditor may perform following procedures for the purpose of reporting under clause 27(*b*):

(*i*) Ask the assessee to furnish a schedule indicating particulars of expenditure/income of any earlier year debited/credited to the Profit & Loss account of the relevant previous year.

(*ii*) Verify various expenses account to see whether any expenditure pertaining to any earlier year has been debited to the profit and loss account. For example, an assessee might have paid some certification fee etc., for four years in the year under audit. In that case payment of expenses for previous three years would be prior period payment.

(*iii*) Also see that all such items are properly disclosed.

(*iv*) Check while conducting the routine audit, that there is no expenditure/income relating to earlier years that has not been mentioned in the particulars furnished by the assessee.

(*v*) In case of cash system of accounting, there will be no amount to be disclosed under this head.

Q.34 ABC Pvt. Ltd. was XYZ Pvt. Ltd. are the Companies in which public are not substantially interested. During the previous year 2018-19, ABC Pvt. Ltd. received some property being shares of XYZ Pvt. Ltd. The details of which are provided below:

No. of shares	**1000**
Face Value	**₹ 10 per share**
Aggregate Fair Market Value	**₹ 1,00,000**
Consideration Value	**Nil**

As the tax auditor how would you deal with the situation? [May 16 (4 Marks)]

Ans. : Reporting requirement in Form 3CD:

- Clause 28 of Form 3CD requires the auditor to report "Whether during the previous year the assessee has received any property, being share of a company not being a company in which the public are substantially interested, without consideration or for inadequate consideration as referred to in section 56(2)(viia), if yes, please furnish the details of the same"
- Section 56(2)(viia) provides that where a firm or a company not being a company in which the public are substantially interested, receives, in any previous year any property being shares of a company (not being a company in which the public is substantially interested, without consideration, the aggregate fair value of which exceeds Rs. 50,000, the whole of the aggregate fair market value of such property shall be chargeable to income-tax under the head "Income from other sources". Finance Act, 2017 amends Sec. 56(2), in accordance with which provisions of Section 56(2)(*viia*) are not applicable for transactions taken place on or after 01.04.2017.
- This transaction now, falls under clause (*x*) of Sec. 56(2). For transactions falling u/s 56(2)(*x*), reporting is required as per Clause No. 29B, which provides as follow:

  (*a*) Whether any amount is to be included as income chargeable under the head 'income from other sources' as referred to in clause (*x*) of sub-section (2) of section 56? (Yes/No)

  (*b*) If yes, please furnish the following details:

  (*i*) Nature of income;

  (*ii*) Amount (in Rs.) thereof.

"ICAI Examiner Comments"

Candidates, in general, were not aware of Section 56(2)(viia) of the Income-tax Act, 1961 and clause 28 of Form 3CD. Quite a few treated it as capital gain instead of "Income from other sources".

Q.35 While doing Tax Audit, under section 44AB of the Income-tax Act, 1961, of the accounts of Glue Private Limited for the Assessment Year 2019-20, it was found that during the Financial Year 2018-19, Glue Private Limited had received 9,000 shares, the market value of which was Rs. 90,000 on the date of transfer, at a price of Rs. 45,000 from Stick Private Limited. The Management of Glue Private Limited maintained that the transaction was as per the terms of negotiations and there would be no cause for the Auditor to bring this matter in his Tax Audit Report-Comment. [Nov. 18 - New Syllabus (5 Marks)]

Answer: Reporting requirement in Form 3CD:

- Clause 28 of Form 3CD requires the auditor to report "Whether during the previous year the assessee has received any property, being share of a company not being a company in which the public are substantially interested, without consideration or for inadequate consideration as referred to in section 56(2)(*viia*), if yes, please furnish the details of the same."
- Section 56(2)(*viia*) provides that where a firm or a company not being a company in which the public are substantially interested, receives, in any previous year any property being shares of a company (not being a company in which the public is substantially interested, without consideration, the aggregate fair value of which exceeds Rs. 50,000, the whole of the aggregate fair market value of such property shall be chargeable to income-tax under the head "Income from other sources". Finance Act, 2017 amends Sec. 56(2), in accordance with which provisions of Section 56(2)(*viia*) are not applicable for transactions taken place on or after 1-4-2017.
- This transaction now, falls under clause (*x*) of Sec. 56(2). For transactions falling u/s 56(2)(*x*), reporting is required as per Clause No. 29B, which provides as follow:

  (*a*) Whether any amount is to be included as income chargeable under the head 'income from other sources' as referred to in clause (*x*) of sub-section (2) of section 56? (Yes/No)

  (*b*) If yes, please furnish the following details:

  (*i*) Nature of income;

  (*ii*) Amount (in Rs.) thereof.
- As per Sec. 56(2)(*x*), where any person receives, in any previous year, from any person or persons on or after the 1st day of April, 2017, any property, other than immovable property, for a consideration which is less than the aggregate FMV of the property by an amount exceeding ₹ 50,000, the aggregate FMV of such property as exceeds such consideration, shall be chargeable to income-tax under the head "Income from other sources".

Conclusion: In the present case, difference of Fair Market Value and consideration paid is lower than Rs. 50,000, auditor is required to state the answer with "No".

Q.36 AB Ltd. is a company in which public are not substantially interested. During the previous year 2018-19, the company issued shares to residents of India and provides you the following data related to such issue:

No. of shares issued	**1,00,000**
Face Value	**₹ 10 per share**
Fair Market Value (FMV)	**₹ 60 per share**
Consideration received	**₹ 80 per share**

The management of the company contends that, it is a normal issue of shares, thus, needs not to be reported. As the tax auditor of AB Ltd., how would you deal with the matter in your tax audit report?

Ans. : Reporting for Issue of Shares for Value Exceeding Fair Market Value:

- Clause 29 of Form 3CD requires tax auditor to report whether, the assessee received any consideration for issue of shares which exceeds the fair market value of the shares as referred to in section 56(2)(*viib*) of the Income Tax Act, 1961.
- Section 56(2)(*viib*) provides that where a company, not being a company in which the public are substantially interested, receives, in any previous year, from any person being a resident, any consideration for issue of shares that exceeds the face value of such shares, the aggregate consideration received for such shares as exceeds the fair market value of the shares shall be chargeable to income-tax under the head "Income from other sources".
- In the present case, AB Ltd. is a company, in which public is not substantially interested. Company has received consideration for issue of shares of ₹ 80 per share (Face value ₹ 10 per share + Premium ₹ 70 per share) which exceeds the face value of ₹ 10 per share and fair market value of the shares of ₹ 60 per share, and hence the case covered u/s 56(2)(*viib*).

Conclusion: Tax auditor of AB Ltd. is required to furnish the details of shares issued under clause 29 of Form 3CD.

Q.37 As a tax auditor how would you deal and report the following: An assessee has borrowed ₹ 50 Lakhs from various persons. Some of them by way of cash and some of them by way of Account payee cheque/ draft. [Nov. 11 (3 Marks)]

Or

As an auditor appointed under section 44AB of the Income Tax Act, 1961, how would you verify and report on the following: The assessee has borrowed ₹ 50 lakhs from various persons partly in cash and partly by account payee cheque. [Nov. 17 (3 Marks)]

Ans. : Reporting of Borrowing in Form 3CD:

Clause 31(*a*) of Form 3CD requires tax auditor to report on below mentioned particulars of each loan or deposit for an amount exceeding the limit specified in section 269SS taken or accepted during the previous year:

(*i*) name, address and permanent account number (if available with the assessee) of the lender or depositor;

(*ii*) amount of loan or deposit taken or accepted;

(*iii*) whether the loan or deposit was squared up during the previous year;

(*iv*) maximum amount outstanding in the account at any time during the previous year;

(*v*) whether the loan or deposit was taken or accepted by cheque or bank draft or use of electronic clearing system through a bank account;

(*vi*) in case the loan or deposit was taken or accepted by cheque or bank draft, whether the same was taken or accepted by an account payee cheque or an account payee bank draft.

Conclusion: Auditor should verify the compliance with the provisions of section 269SS of the Income Tax Act and report the same under Clause 31(*a*) of Form 3CD.

"ICAI Examiner Comments"

Examinees failed to explain with reference to clause 31 of Form 3CD for reporting on the mode of amount borrowed. Few examinees have discussed generally on vouching and verification aspects instead of mentioning the reporting requirements of Tax auditor. Few examinees mixed up section 40A(3) of the Income tax Act, 1961 on disallowance of cash payments exceeding ₹ 20000 instead of explaining the provisions of section 269SS.

Q.38 Discuss the reporting requirements in Form 3CD of the Tax Audit Report u/s 44AB of the Income-tax Act, 1961 for the Brought forward loss or depreciation allowance.

Ans. : Reporting requirements for Brought forward loss or depreciation allowance in Form 3CD:

Clause 32(*a*) of Form 3CD requires the following details of brought forward loss or depreciation allowance, in the following manner, to the extent available:

1	Serial Number
2	Assessment Year
3	Nature of loss/allowance (in rupees)
4	Amount as returned (in rupees)
5	Amounts as assessed (give reference to relevant order)
6	Remarks

Q.39 Tiger Ltd., is a company engaged in the production of wool. Along with its production business, it is also engaged in buying and selling of securities with the expectation of a favourable price change. During the year, its speculation loss on account of purchase and sale of securities was to the tune of ₹12 lacs.

As a tax auditor, what is the reporting requirement in Form 3CD u/s 44AB of the Income Tax Act, 1961?

[May 18 - Old Syllabus (4 Marks)]

Ans. : Reporting Requirement Under Clause (32)(e) of Form 3CD:

- Clause 32(*e*) of Form 3CD requires the auditor to furnish the details of speculation loss if any incurred during the previous year, in case of a company which is deemed to be carrying on a speculation business.
- Explanation to section 73 provides that where any part of the business of a company consists in the purchase and sale of shares of other companies, such company shall, for the purposes of this section, be deemed to be carrying on a speculation business to the extent to which the business consists of the purchase and sale of such shares.
- In the present case, SL Pvt. Ltd. is engaged in production business and side by side dealing in buying and selling of securities with the intention of speculation and during the current financial year, hence the company will be deemed to be carrying on a speculation business.

Conclusion: Tax auditor of is required to furnish the details under Clause 32(*e*) of Form 3CD with respect to the speculation loss of ₹ 12 lakhs made during the year.

Q.40 Discuss the reporting requirement in Form 3CD of Tax Audit Report under Section 44AB of the Income-tax Act, 1961 for the Tax Deducted at Source.

Ans. : Reporting requirement for Tax Deducted at Source in Form 3CD:

Clause 34(*a*) of Form 3CD requires the auditor to furnish below mentioned information if the assessee is required to deduct or collect tax as per the provisions of Chapter XVII-B or Chapter XVII-BB:

1	Tax deduction and collection Account Number (TAN)
2	Section
3	Nature of payment
4	Total amount of payment or receipt of the nature specified in (3)
5	Total amount on which tax was required to be deducted or collected out of (4)
6	Total amount on which tax was deducted or collected at specified rate out of (5)
7	Amount of tax deducted or collected out of (6)
8	Total amount on which tax was deducted or collected at less than specified rate out of (7)
9	Amount of tax deducted or collected on (8)
10	Amount of tax deducted or collected not deposited to the credit of the Central Government out of (6) and (8)

Q.41 **ABC Printing Press, a proprietary concern, made a turnover of above ₹ 103 lacs for the year ended 31.03.2019. The Management explained its auditor Mr. Z, that it undertakes different job work orders from customers. The raw materials required for every job are dissimilar. It purchases the raw materials as per specification/requirements of each customer, and there is hardly any balance of raw materials remaining in the stock, except pending work-in-progress at the year end. Because of variety and complexity of materials, it is rather impossible to maintain a stock-register. Give your comments.**

[Nov. 09 (5 Marks)]

Ans. : Non-maintenance of stock register:

- As per requirement of Para 35(b) and Para 11(b) of Form 3CD, auditor is required to report on the details of stock and account books (including stock register) maintained.
- Auditor need to verify the closing stock of raw materials and finished products and by-products of the entity. In case the details are not properly maintained, he has to specifically mention the same, with reasons for non-maintenance of stock register by the entity.
- The explanation of the entity for the use of varieties of raw materials for different jobs undertaken may be valid. But the auditor needs to verify the specified job-orders received and the different raw materials purchased for each job separately. The auditor may also enquire with the other similar printers in the locality to ensure the prevailing custom.

Conclusion: Auditor is required to report under Paras 35(b) and 11(b) about non-maintenance of stock register.

Q.42 **Discuss the reporting requirements in Form 3CD of the Tax Audit Report U/S 44AB of the Income-tax Act, 1961 for the Tax on distributed profits.**

Ans. : Reporting for tax on distributed profits in Form 3CD:

Clause 36 of Form 3CD requires the following reporting requirements in the case of a domestic company, w.r.t. tax on distributed profits under section 115-O in the following form:

(*a*) total amount of distributed profits;

(*b*) amount of reduction as referred to in section 115-O(1A)(i);

(*c*) amount of reduction as referred to in section 115-O(1A)(ii);

(*d*) total tax paid thereon;

(*e*) dates of payment with amounts.

Q.43 **ABC Ltd., having principal place of business in Delhi, is engaged in the generation, transmission, distribution and supply of electricity throughout the India. The management of the company came to know that the provisions related to maintenance of cost records and cost audit are applicable to the company. The company, therefore, appointed a cost auditor for the financial year 2018-19.**

The cost auditor reported certain disqualifications in Form CRA-3 of the cost audit report to which the management of the company disagreed.

The management of ABC Ltd. instructed its tax auditor not to reveal any of the disqualifications related to the cost audit while filling particulars to be furnished in Form No. 3CD contending that the disqualifications are not relevant and there is no correlation between tax audit and cost audit as well. As a tax auditor, how would you deal with the matter?

Ans. : Reporting Requirement for Disqualifications in Cost Audit Report:

- Clause (37) of Form 3CD requires cost auditor to comment upon whether cost audit was carried out and if yes, details of disqualification or disagreement on any matter/item/value/quantity as may be identified by the cost auditor should be reported.
- For this purpose, tax auditor should obtain the copy of cost audit report from the assessee. Tax auditor is not required to make any detailed study of such report, he is required to take note of the details of disqualification on any matter/item/value/quantity as may be reported by the cost auditor.
- In the present case, the cost auditor of ABC Ltd. has reported certain disqualifications in Form CRA-3 of the cost audit report. Tax auditor of is required to provide the details of disqualifications reported by the cost auditor as per Clause (37) of the Form 3CD.

Conclusion: Contention of management is not acceptable as auditor is required to provide the details of disqualifications on any matter/item/value/quantity as may be reported/identified by cost auditor under clause 37 of Form 3CD.

Q.44 Write a short note on - Accounting ratios in Form 3CD of Tax Audit.

Or

As a tax auditor, which are the accounting ratios required to be mentioned in the report in case of manufacturing entities? Explain in detail any one of the above ratios and how does it help the tax auditor in his analytical review.

Ans. : Accounting Ratios in Form 3CD:

Clause 40 of Form 3CD requires the details regarding turnover, gross profit, etc., for the previous year and preceding previous year as mentioned below:

Serial number	Particulars	Previous year	Preceding previous year
1.	Total turnover of the assessee		
2.	Gross profit/turnover		
3.	Net profit/turnover		
4.	Stock-in-trade/turnover		
5.	Material consumed/finished goods produced		

The details required to be furnished for principal items of goods traded or manufactured or services rendered. These ratios have to be given for the business as a whole and not product wise.

Details of Profitability Ratio: By relating sales with the Gross profit or net profit, auditor may ascertain the operating efficiency of an enterprise. Auditor is required to inquire any variations in any of these ratios. The fall in the gross profit ratio and net profit ratio alert the auditor who, in turn should ask the management for the reasons thereof and which should be carefully examined by him.

Details of Stock in trade/Turnover Ratio: The relationship of stock-in-trade to turnover over a period of time would reveal whether the entity has been accumulating stocks or there is a decline in the same. The auditor may obtain data for about 4-5 years, compute ratio of stock-in-trade/turnover and compare the change made. A study of this relationship would reveal whether stocks are being accumulated or they are dwindling over a period. Such information would provide an input to tax auditor as to whether figures of either stock or turnover are being manipulated.

Q.45 ABC Ltd. is engaged in providing certain services on which it did not pay any service tax. As per company, said services were not liable to service tax. However, Department issued a show cause notice to company demanding service tax along with interest worth ₹ 5,45,000 on the same and such demand was also confirmed. An appeal was filed to the Commissioner of Central Excise (Appeals) which passed an order which upheld the demand on company. Company, being aggrieved by the order of the Commissioner of Central Excise (Appeals), decided to file an appeal to the CESTAT against such order. ABC Ltd. has also requested the tax auditor not to report as those services were not liable for service tax and it has also filed an appeal for the same.

Ans. : Reporting of Taxation demands in Form 3CD:

- Clause 41 of Form 3CD requires auditor to furnish the details of demand raised or refund issued during the previous year under any tax laws other than Income Tax Act, 1961 and Wealth tax Act, 1957 along with details of relevant proceedings.
- In the instant case, ABC Ltd. is engaged in providing certain services on which it did not paid any service tax. Therefore, Department issued a show cause notice and demand for Service Tax along with interest thereon. ABC Ltd. has also filed an appeal mentioning that said services are not liable to service tax, but Central Excise (Appeals) has passed an order confirming the demand and ABC Ltd. being aggrieved by the order of Commissioner of Central Excise (Appeals) decided to file an appeal against the same. ABC Ltd. also requested the tax auditor not to report on the same as the concerned services were not liable for any service tax and they have also decided to file an appeal to CESTAT against the order of Commissioner of Central Excise (Appeals).
- Tax auditor should obtain a copy of all the demand/refund orders issued by the Excise Authorities. It may be noted that even though the demand/refund order is issued during the previous year, it may pertain to a period other than the relevant previous year.

Conclusion: Request of ABC Ltd. is not acceptable as clause 41 of Form 3CD requires tax auditor to furnish the details of demand raised during the previous year under any tax law other than Income Tax Act, 1961.

18.5 - GENERAL QUESTIONS

Q.46 Comment on the following: The Statutory Auditor of P. Ltd. is also appointed to undertake its Tax Audit. After the completion of Statutory Audit, he finalizes Tax Audit without referring to Standards on Auditing and Guidance Notes of Institute as he is of the opinion that Tax Audit relates only to tax matters with which the Income tax department is concerned. Moreover, the assessee furnishes to the auditor only the requisite information and records for the purpose of Tax Audit. [MTP-Aug. 18]

Answer: Applicability of Standards on Auditing and Guidance Note in case of Tax Audit:

- In the case of a statutory audit, auditor is required to express his opinion as to whether the financial statements give a true and fair view of the state of affairs in the case of the balance sheet and in the case of the profit and loss account/income and expenditure account, of the profit/loss or income/expenditure.
- While carrying out tax audit u/s 44AB, the tax auditor is required to state whether in his opinion, the particulars as stated in Form 3CD are true and correct. The audit report given u/s 44AB assist the income-tax department in ensuring compliance of provisions of Income-tax Act by the assessee. In order that the tax auditor may be in a position to explain any question which may arise later on, it is necessary that he should keep necessary working papers about the evidence on which he has relied upon while conducting the audit and also maintain all his necessary working papers.
- While carrying out the audit, auditor is required to refer the "Standards on Auditing" as well as the "Guidance Note on Audit Reports and Certificate for Special Purposes". If the statutory auditor is also appointed to undertake tax audit, it is advisable to carry out both the audits concurrently.
- SA 210, "Agreeing the Terms of Audit Engagements" requires an auditor to establish whether the precondition for an audit are present so as to accept or continue an audit engagement. Accordingly, the auditor is required to obtain agreement of management that it acknowledges and understands its responsibilities to provide the auditor with:
  - (*a*) Access to all information of which the management is aware that is relevant to the preparation of the financial statements such as records, documentation and other matters.
  - (*b*) Additional information that the auditor may request the management for the purpose of the audit, and
  - (*c*) Unrestricted access to persons within the entity from whom the auditor determines it necessary to obtain audit evidence.

Conclusion: Opinion of the auditor that Tax Audit relates only to tax matters with which the income-tax department is concerned and there is no need to refer the Standards on Auditing and Guidance Notes of Institute is not correct. Moreover, since the appointment of the tax auditor is made by assessee, it will be in the interest of the assessee to furnish all the information and explanation and produce books of account and records required by the tax auditor.

Q.47 State with reasons whether an auditor conducting tax audit 'certifies' or 'reports' on information contained in the statement of particulars attached to the tax audit report under Section 44AB of Income-tax Act, 1961.

Ans. : Tax Audit report u/s 44AB - Certification/Reporting:

- Section 44AB of the Income-tax Act, 1961 requires the auditor to submit the audit report in the Form 3CA/Form 3CB. The statement of particulars as required in Form 3CD are required to be annexed to the main audit report. In Form 3CA, auditor is required to report whether the particulars in Form 3CD are true and correct. Form 3CB, in addition, requires the auditor to give his opinion as to whether or not the accounts audited by him give a true and fair view.
- The term "certificate" is used where the auditor verifies the accuracy of facts while the term "report" is used in case the auditor is expressing an opinion. Form 3CA/Form 3CB requires the auditor to report on true and correct aspects of particulars stated in Form 3CD, it can be said that an auditor conducting tax audit "certifies" the information contained in the statement of particulars.
- However, it is significant to examine whether all 41 clauses included in the statement of particulars are capable of being simply certified on the basis of books of account or there are some clauses in respect of which different auditor(s) may hold different opinion.
- There are several matters (Clause 14/Clause 18) on which the auditor is required to exercise judgment while giving his report on various amounts included in the statement of particulars, which may at times lead to different figures by different persons reporting thereon. There can also be situations leading to difference of opinion between the tax auditor and the assessee.

Conclusion: Auditor conducting tax audit "reports" on certain information, apart from "certifying" factual information contained in the statement of particulars annexed to the tax audit report under section 44AB of the Income-tax Act, 1961.

Q.48 **State whether a Tax Audit Report can be revised and if so state those circumstances.**

[Nov. 08 (4 Marks)]

Or

You are doing the tax audit of a Limited Company. After submission of Tax Audit Report, management notices that there was apparent mistake of law and due to this mistake, revised the final accounts. As a tax auditor, company seeks your opinion whether the tax audit can also be revised or not.

[RTP-Nov. 18]

Ans. : Revision of Tax Audit Report:

Normally, the report of the tax auditor cannot be revised later. However, when the accounts are revised in the following circumstances, the tax Auditor may have to revise his Tax audit report also.

(*i*) Revision of accounts of a company after its adoption in the AGM.

(*ii*) Changes in law with retrospective effect.

(*iii*) Changes in interpretation of law through CBDT Circular, Notifications, Judgments, etc.

The Tax Auditor should state that it is a revised Report, clearly specifying the reasons for such revision with a reference to the earlier report.

18.6 - AUDIT UNDER GST LAWS

Q.49 **Define the term Audit under CGST Act. Describe the statutory requirements of audit under CGST Act based on threshold limit.**

Ans. : Meaning of Audit and Statutory Requirements of audit under CGST Act, 2017:

Sec. 2(13) of CGST Act, 2017 defines the term "Audit" as Audit means the examination of **records, returns and other documents** maintained or furnished by the registered person under this Act or the rules made thereunder or under any other law for the time being in force to verify the correctness of turnover declared, taxes paid, refund claimed and input tax credit availed, and to assess his compliance with the provisions of this Act or the rules made thereunder.

Statutory Requirements:

- **Sec. 35(5) of CGST Act, 2017**: Every registered person whose turnover during a financial year exceeds the prescribed limit shall get his accounts audited by a Chartered Accountant or a Cost Accountant and shall submit

  (*a*) a copy of the audited annual accounts

  (*b*) the reconciliation statement u/s 44(2) and

  (*c*) such other documents in such form and manner as may be prescribed.

- **Rule 80(3) of CGST Rules, 2017**: Every registered person whose aggregate turnover during a financial year exceeds ₹ 2 Cr. shall get his accounts audited and he shall furnish a copy of audited annual accounts and a reconciliation statement, duly certified, in FORM GSTR-9C.

- **Sec. 44(2) of CGST Act, 2017**: Every registered person who is required to get his accounts audited in accordance with the provisions of Sec. 35(5) shall furnish, electronically, the annual return along with a copy of the audited annual accounts and a reconciliation statement, reconciling the value of supplies declared in the return furnished for the financial year with the audited annual F.S., and such other particulars as may be prescribed.

Q.50 **XYZ Limited is looking for an auditor for getting it accounts audited as per GST. Being an expert in the indirect taxes field XYZ Limited is seeking your advice on types of audit to be envisage as per GST Law. Explain.**

[RTP-Nov. 18]

Ans. : Types of Audit under GST Law:

Under GST Law, three types of audit may be conducted:

(1) **Audit under based on turnover**: As per Sec. 35(5) of CGST Act, 2017, Every registered person whose turnover during a financial year exceeds the prescribed limit shall get his accounts audited by a Chartered Accountant or a Cost Accountant and shall submit

(*a*) a copy of the audited annual accounts,

(*b*) the reconciliation statement u/s 44(2) and

(*c*) such other documents in such form and manner as may be prescribed.

As per Rule 80(3) of CGST Rules, 2017, every registered person whose aggregate turnover during a financial year exceeds Rs. 2 Crore shall get his accounts audited and he shall furnish a copy of audited annual accounts and a reconciliation statement, duly certified, in FORM GSTR-9C.

(2) **Audit by Tax Authorities:** As per Sec. 65 of CGST Act, 2017, the Commissioner or any officer authorised by him, by way of a general or a specific order, may undertake audit of any registered person for such period, at such frequency and in such manner as may be prescribed. Audit may be conducted at the place of business of the registered person or in their office.

(3) **Special Audit:** As per Sec. 66 of CGST Act, 2017, If at any stage of scrutiny, inquiry, investigation or any other proceedings, any officer not below the rank of Assistant Commissioner, having regard to the nature and complexity of the case and the interest of revenue, is of the opinion that the value has not been correctly declared or the credit availed is not within the normal limits, he may, with the prior approval of the Commissioner, direct such registered person by a communication in writing to get his records including books of account examined and audited by a chartered accountant or a cost accountant as may be nominated by the Commissioner.

Q.51 Briefly discuss the provisions given under section 66 regarding special audit required under CGST Act.

Ans. : Provisions regarding Special Audit u/s 66:

(A) Directions for Special Audit

- If at any stage of scrutiny, inquiry, investigation or any other proceedings, any officer not below the rank of Assistant Commissioner, having regard to the nature and complexity of the case and the interest of revenue, is of the opinion that the value has not been correctly declared or the credit availed is not within the normal limits, he may, with the prior approval of the Commissioner, direct such registered person by a communication in writing to get his records including books of account examined and audited by a chartered accountant or a cost accountant as may be nominated by the Commissioner.
- Direction shall be issued in FORM GST ADT-03.

(B) Time limit for completion of Audit

The chartered accountant or cost accountant so nominated shall, within the period of 90 days, submit a report of such audit duly signed and certified by him to the said Assistant Commissioner mentioning therein such other particulars as may be specified.

(C) Extension of Time Limit

Assistant Commissioner may,

- on an application made to him in this behalf by the registered person or the chartered accountant or cost accountant

or

- for any material and sufficient reason,

extend the said period by a further period of 90 days

(D) Opportunity to the registered person

- The registered person shall be given an opportunity of being heard in respect of any material gathered on the basis of special audit which is proposed to be used in any proceedings against him under this Act or the rules made thereunder.
- The registered person shall be informed of the findings of the special audit in FORM GST ADT-04.

(E) Audit Expenses and Remuneration

Expenses of examination and audit, including the remuneration of such chartered accountant or cost accountant, shall be determined and paid by the Commissioner and such determination shall be final.

(F) Action on basis of Audit Report

Where the special audit conducted results in detection of tax not paid or short paid or erroneously refunded, or input tax credit wrongly availed or utilised, the proper officer may initiate action under section 73 or section 74.

Q.52 List the best practice that can be adopted for GST Audit.

Ans. : Best Practices for GST Audit:

Auditor should evaluate internal control so as to identify the areas to be focused. For this purpose, following practices may be adopted:

(1) Auditor may verify the following:

(*a*) Statutory Audit report which has specific disclosure w.r.t. to maintenance of record, stock and fixed assets.

(*b*) Information System Audit report and the Internal Audit Report.

(2) Internal Control questionnaire may be designed for GST compliance.

(3) Generalised audit software may be used for GST audit which would ensure adoption of modern practice of risk based audit.

(4) Reconciliation of the books of account or reports from the ERP's to the return is also useful.

(5) Trial balance should be reviewed for detecting any set off of expenses against incomes.

(6) Purchases/expenses are to be reviewed to examine applicability of reverse charge applicable to goods/services.

(7) Reconciliation of foreign exchange outgo would also be necessary to identify the liability of import of services.

(8) Ratio analysis may also provide important information on areas of non-compliance.

Q.53 In terms of Sl. No. 5G of Form GSTR 9C, the turnovers included in the audited financial statement for the period April 2017 to June 2017 shall be declared and deducted from the annual turnover to arrive at the turnover as per the GST Laws. Please specify which of the following supplies would form part of reporting under turnover for the period April 2017 to June 2017:

(*a*) Goods were manufactured and cleared from a factory on 1.6.2017 on sale or approval basis. The goods were not approved by the recipient and returned back on 25.12.2017.

(*b*) Goods were manufactured and cleared from a factory located in Bangalore on 30.4.2017. The goods were cleared to its showroom located in Hyderabad and eventually been sold from there on 30.8.2017. The audit under the GST Law will be conducted for Bangalore GSTIN.

(*c*) Continuous supply of service in the nature of telecommunication service has been provided for the period 1.6.2017 to 30.6.2017. The bill is raised on 3.7.2017. The bill is payable by the customer only on 21.7.2017. Should the revenue be recognised in the month of June 2017 and reduced from total turnover or should it form part of turnover for the period July 2017 to March 2018 since the due date for payment of consideration is 21.7.2017. The entity recognised the revenue in the month of June 2017.

(*d*) Services were provided during the period June 2017. The service was completed on 20.6.2017, but invoice for the service was raised only on 1.8.2017.

(*e*) Service has been provided in the month of May 17 amounting to ₹1,00,000. Invoice has been raised within 30 days. There was a deficiency in the provision of service. The customer has paid only ₹20,000. The company has issued credit note amounting to ₹80,000 on 31.3.2018 and closed the customer's account. Should any amount be reduced for the period April 2017 to June 2017. Are any adjustments required to be made for the period July 2017 to March 2018?

Ans. : Supplies to be reporting under turnover for the period April 2017 to June 2017 as per Table 5G of GSTR 9C:

(*a*) Since the goods were not approved and returned after the stipulated period of 6 months, the value of the said supplies would not be included in turnover in the audited financial statements. However, as per the 2nd proviso to Section 142(12) of the CGST Act since the goods were returned after 6 months from appointed date (i.e. 1.6.2017), GST would be payable for the tax period December 2017. Though the transaction originated in the period April 2017 to June 2017, the turnover will not be reflected under this Sl. No. However, one may reflect such adjustment under Part II, Sl. No. 5 Clause O - 'Adjustments in turnover due to reasons not listed above' as addition.

(*b*) The said goods are liable to excise duty since the goods have been cleared on 30.4.2017. The goods would not form part of turnover as per the financial statements since it is a branch transfer. It would stand reflected as branch transfers under the State Level VAT laws. Since audit is being conducted for Bangalore GSTIN and since supply has occurred from Hyderabad GSTIN, it would not be necessary to make adjustments for the period April 2017 to June 2017.

(c) As per proviso to Rule 3(*b*) of the Clause of Taxation Rules, 2011, the point of taxation in the impugned case would be the date on which bill has been raised i.e. 3.7.2017. Though invoice has been raised in the GST regime, service tax is payable since service has been provided during the currency of the Finance Act, 1994. The date for payment of service tax as per the machinery provision i.e. POTR, 2011 may be 3.7.2017 but the said service would be liable to service tax because the charge u/s 66B gets attracted for the period June 2017. Further as per S.142(11)(*b*) since if a transaction is *liable* for service tax, then tax would not be payable under the GST Laws. Hence the said amount should be deducted as turnover under this Sl. No. for the period April 2017 to June 2017.

(d) Since the invoice was raised after a period of thirty days, service tax is liable to be paid for the period ending June 2017 as per the proviso to Rule 3(*a*) of the Clause of Taxation Rules. Since the said transaction is liable to service tax, it is not liable to GST as per Section 142(11)(*b*) of the CGST Act, though the invoice is raised during the GST regime. Therefore, the said value of invoice must be deducted for the period April 17 to June 2017.

(e) As per Sec. 142(2)(*b*) of the GST Act, where in pursuance of contract entered into prior to the appointed date, where the price of service is revised downwards after 1.7.2017 and the provider issues a credit note within 30 days of such price revision, such credit note shall be deemed to have been issued in respect of outward supply, provided the recipient has reduced his input tax credit. Assuming the input tax credit is reduced by the recipient, the credit note shall be reduced from outward supply for the tax period March 2018. Thus ₹ 80,000 would be reduced from the GST turnover for the period of March 2018. The said amount of ₹ 80,000 would be reduced from the turnover in the month of March 2018 because credit note is issued in the month of March 2018. Thus, only ₹ 20,000 is required to be reduced for the period April 2017 to June 2017, though invoice for ₹ 1,00,000 is issued in the month of May 2017 and service tax is paid on ₹1,00,000 in the month of May 2017.

Q.54 **As the auditor appointed under the GST Act, 2017, how would you verify' Unbilled transactions at the beginning of the financial year'? [May 19 - Old Syllabus (5 Marks)]**

Ans. : Verification of Unbilled transactions at the beginning of the financial year:

- As per Table 5B of Form GSTR 9C unbilled revenue at the beginning of Financial Year is to be added to Turnover as per audited financial statements for the State/UT.
- Unbilled revenue is the revenue recognized in the books of accounts before the issue of an invoice at the end of a particular period. AS-9/IND AS-115 provides for recognition of revenue on full completion/partial completion of the services though the due date for issuing invoice as per the contract would be on a later date.
- Unbilled revenue which was recorded in the books of accounts on the basis of accrual system of accounting in the last financial year and was carried forward to the current financial year shall be declared in Table 5B. In other words, when GST is payable during the financial year on such revenue (which was recognized earlier), the value of such revenue shall be declared here.
- For example, if ₹10 Crores of unbilled revenue existed for the financial year 2016-17, and during the current financial year, GST was paid on ₹4 Crores of such revenue, then value of ₹4 Crores shall be declared in Table 5B.
- Unbilled revenue would appear in the profit and loss account of the previous year. For information of unbilled revenue at the beginning of a Financial Year, reference may be made to previous year's audited financial statements.

Q.55 **While conducting GST audit of PQR Ltd. you have observed the following:**

PQR Limited has exported goods to a Company located in USA. The value of goods is $100,000. The exchange rate on the date of filing Shipping Bill is:

CBEC notified Rs. 65 and RBI Reference rate Rs. 68.

At the time of receiving money, the bank exchanged the foreign currency at Rs. 70.

How would you report the adjustments in turnover due to foreign exchange fluctuations in Reconciliation statement in Form GSTR 9C prescribed in terms of Rule 80(3) of CGST Rules, 2017.

[May 19 - Old Syllabus (5 Marks)]

Ans. : Adjustments in turnover due to foreign exchange fluctuations (+/-)

- Table 5N of GSTR 9C requires reporting of any difference between the turnover reported in the Annual Return (GSTR 9) and turnover reported in the audited Annual Financial Statement due to foreign exchange fluctuations.

- For the purpose of GST Returns, the exchange rate would be ₹65 and the exports to be disclosed in the GST Returns would be ₹ 65,00,000. For the purpose of accounting records, the exchange rate would be ₹68 and the exports recorded in the books would be ₹68,00,000. The difference in revenue being ₹300,000 would have to be reduced from the Annual turnover as per the financials to arrive at the revenue as per GSTR 9.
- Additionally, difference in the amount booked in the accounts and actual amount received being ₹70 - ₹68 = ₹2 x $100,000 = ₹200,000 would be credited to the Profit and Loss Account as Forex Gain which again needs to be reduced from the Annual turnover as per the financials to arrive at the revenue as per GSTR 9.

Q.56 PQR Limited has exported goods to a Company located in USA. The value of goods is $100,000. The exchange rate (Rs/$) on the date of filing Shipping Bill is

CBEC Notified ₹65

RBI Reference Rate ₹68

At the time of receiving money, the bank exchanged the foreign currency at ₹66.

State the adjustment to be reported by GST Auditor as per Table 5N of GSTR 9C.

Ans. : Adjustments in turnover due to foreign exchange fluctuations (+/-)

- Table 5N of GSTR 9C requires reporting of any difference between the turnover reported in the Annual Return (GSTR9) and turnover reported in the audited Annual Financial Statement due to foreign exchange fluctuations.
- For the purpose of GST Returns, the exchange rate would be ₹65 and the exports to be disclosed in the GST Returns would be ₹65,00,000. For the purpose of accounting records, the exchange rate would be ₹68 and the exports recorded in the books would be ₹68,00,000. The difference in revenue being ₹300,000 would have to be reduced from the Annual turnover as per the financials to arrive at the revenue as per GSTR 9.
- Additionally, the difference in the amount booked in the accounts and actual amount received being ₹66 - ₹68 = (-) ₹2 x $100,000 = (-) ₹200,000 would be debited to the Profit and Loss Account as Forex Loss which again needs to be added from the Annual turnover as per the financials to arrive at the revenue as per GSTR 9.

Q.57 Please state which of the following are liable to reverse charge

(*a*) GTA issued a consignment note on 1.1.18. The consignment notes charges GST @ 12%. The consignor has booked the GTA. The recipient has paid the freight to GTA on 'to collect' basis. Would this turnover be mentioned in Table 7D?

(*b*) GTA issued a consignment note on 1.1.18. The consignment note does not charge GST. The consignor has booked the GTA. The recipient has paid the freight to GTA on 'to collect' basis. Would this turnover be mentioned in Table 7D?

(*c*) Advocate Mr. X has provided legal service and charged GST of ₹ 18 on his invoice of ₹ 100. The advocate's client has paid 118 to the advocate. The advocate has remitted ₹ 18 to government and is of the opinion that the aforesaid transaction should not be reduced in Table 7D. Is the stand taken by the advocate correct?

Ans. : Liability of Reverse Charge:

(*a*) The Consignment note contains GST @ 12%, so reverse charge does not attract as per N.No.13/17 CT (R) w.e.f. 22.8.10. Hence tax has to be paid by GTA under forward charge, and this transaction should not be entered in Table 7D.

(*b*) Since consignment note has not charged GST @ 12%, reverse charge provisions would apply. Tax is to be paid by the person liable to pay freight, that is, the recipient and not the GTA under forward charge. Because of this, the impugned transaction has to be entered in Table 7D.

(*c*) Supplies by a Registered Person, whose suppliers are liable for reverse charge, are to be inserted in Table 7D. Legal service provided by the advocate to his client is liable for reverse charge (assuming all other conditions in reverse charge notification stand satisfied). Hence the impugned transaction should be inserted in Table 7D. GST wrongly collected and paid by the advocate under forward charge will not change the fact that the aforesaid service is liable to reverse charge and hence merits insertion in Table 7D.

INVESTIGATION & DUE DILIGENCE

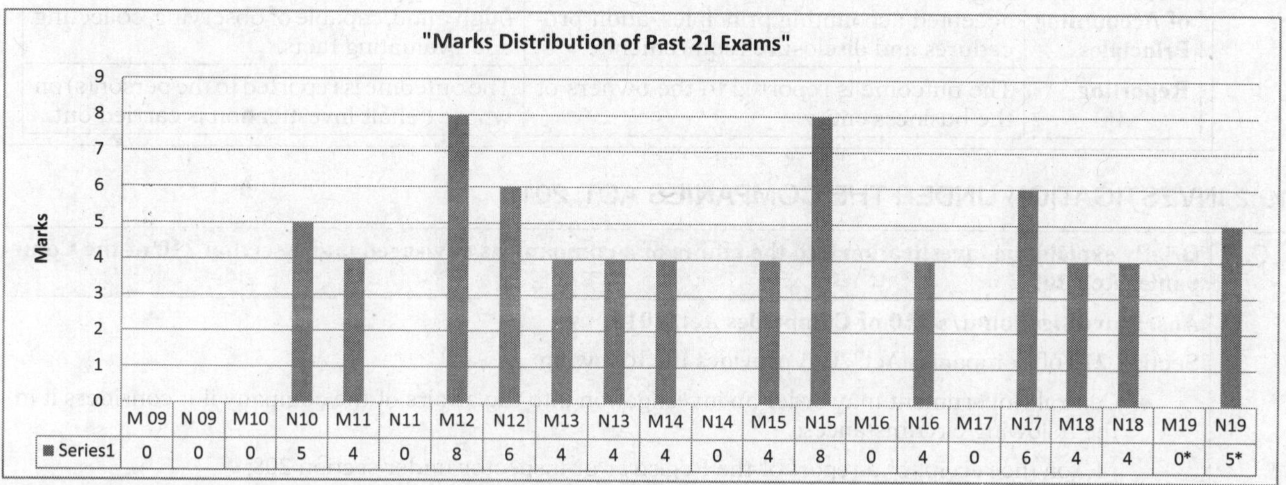

*Only Subjective Questions.

19.1 AUDIT V/S INVESTIGATION

Q.1 Write a short note on - Audit and Investigation. [Nov. 18 (4 Marks)]

Or

General objective of an audit is to find out whether the financial statements show true and fair view. On the other hand, investigation implies systematic, critical and special examination of the records of a business for a specific purpose. In view of the above, you are required to brief out the difference between Audit and Investigation.

Ans. : Audit vs. Investigation:

- Auditing involves examination of financial information contained in financial statements to express an opinion whether or not the same have been prepared properly. In essence, auditing involves independent examination of financial information prepared by the management of an entity.
- Investigation implies systematic, critical and special examination of the records of a business for a specific purpose.
- Difference between audit and investigation are given below:

Basis	Audit	Investigation
Objective	To verify whether the financial statements display a true and fair view of the state of affairs and the working results of an entity.	It aims at establishing a fact or a happening or at assessing a particular situation.
Scope	The scope of audit is wide and is determined by the provisions of relevant law in case of statutory audit.	The scope of investigation may be governed by statute or it may be non-statutory.

Basis	Audit	Investigation
Periodicity	The audit is carried on either quarterly, half yearly or yearly.	The work is not limited by rigid time frame.
Nature	Involves tests checking to collect evidences for forming a judgment.	Requires a detailed study and examination of facts and figures.
Inherent Limitations	Audit suffers from inherent limitation.	No inherent limitation owing to its nature of engagement.
Evidence	Audit is mainly concerned with *prima facie* evidence.	It seeks conclusive evidence.
Observance of Accounting Principles	Is governed by compliance with generally accepted accounting principles, audit procedures and disclosure requirements.	It is analytical in nature and requires a thorough mind, capable of observing, collecting and evaluating facts.
Reporting	The outcome is reported to the owners of the business entity.	The outcome is reported to the person(s) on whose behalf investigation is carried out.

19.2 INVESTIGATION UNDER THE COMPANIES ACT, 2013

Q.2 Briefly explain the investigation into the affairs of a company as envisaged under section 210 of the Companies Act, 2013.

Ans. : Investigation u/s 210 of Companies Act, 2013:

Section 210 of Companies Act, 2013 provides the following:

- Central Government may order an investigation into the affairs of the company if it considers it in the following circumstances:
  1. on the receipt of a report of the Registrar or inspector under section 208;
  2. on intimation of a special resolution passed by a company that the affairs of the company ought to be investigated; or
  3. in public interest,
- Central Government shall order an investigation into the affairs of that company, if an order is passed by a court or the Tribunal in any proceedings before it that the affairs of a company ought to be investigated
- For the purposes of investigation, the Central Government may appoint one or more persons as inspectors to investigate into the affairs of the company and to report thereon in such manner as the Central Government may direct.

Q.3 What will be your approach in investigation under Section 210 into the affairs of the company registered under Companies Act, 2013? [May 14 (4 Marks)]

Or

The general approach for investigation under Sections 210 and 213 of the Companies Act, 2013 is conditioned by the legal requirements in these regards. Explain the approach/Steps for pursuing the investigation.

Ans. : General approach for Investigation:

The general approach for investigation under sections 210 and 216 of Companies Act, 2013 is conditioned by the legal requirements in these regards. The affairs of the company may include everything such as goodwill, profit and loss, contracts, investments, assets, shareholding in subsidiaries, decision making, etc.

Investigation under sections 210 and 216 do not call for any special approach. The general approach for investigations should, therefore, be formulated having regard to the terms of reference, scope, the period, the programme and procedure of the investigation and the attending legal requirements as explained below:

1. **Clarity of Terms of Reference:** The inspector should ensure that the terms of reference are clear, unambiguous and in writing. If he has any doubt about any item in the terms, he should obtain clarification in writing.
2. **Scope of Investigation:** Inspector should determine scope of the investigation on the basis of the terms of reference. At this stage, it may be useful for the inspector to go into the history of the company and its affiliates or associates.

3. **Period for investigation:** Inspector should also have regard to the period over which the investigation should stretch. The evaluation of terms of reference and the consequential determination of the scope of investigation are the twin props on which the entire investigation would rest.
4. **Framing of Programme:** The next step is the investigator/inspector should frame his programme for investigation in a systematic manner. He should keep adequate working notes and papers with references and cross references in a proper and methodical way to aid him in the preparation of the report.
5. **Using the work of Experts:** He should also consider whether assistance of other experts like engineers, lawyers, etc., is necessary in the interest of a comprehensive and full proof examination of the documents and information.
6. **Legal requirements and investigation Report:** After completion of steps in the investigation programme and collection of all the information that he needed, report should be prepared. However, an interim report may be made if required. The findings should be completed and exhaustive. Before he makes his final report he should obtain and keep on record the evidences relied upon by him. By the nature of things, such evidence should be as conclusive as possible depending on circumstances of the case. He should make his report in accordance with the provisions of the Companies Act, 2013.

Q.4 The Central Government is of the view that there are certain interested members and companies who are financially interested in the success or failure of the company or who have been able to control or to materially influence the policy of the company.

Hence the Central Government wants to investigate the ownership of the company.

Describe the scope and extent of investigation by an Investigator/Chartered Accountant on behalf of Central Government under Companies Act, 2013. [Nov. 16 (4 Marks)]

Ans. : Scope and Extent of Investigation under Companies Act, 2013:

- When a CA is appointed to carry out an investigation under section 210, 213 or 216 of Companies Act, 2013, the scope and extent of enquiry, the objective of the investigation and other matters asked for investigation are specified in the order of investigation issued by the appointing authority.
- On the basis of terms of investigation, the investigating accountant should determine the areas of accounts to be investigated and the extent to which the enquiry is to be made.
- In case of a company having subsidiaries or where one or more directors are interested in one or more entities, all the dealings with these entities should be examined.
- Any breach of duty for purposes of investigation would be material only if it has resulted in a loss to the company. In such a case, the factors responsible for the losses, besides the amount thereof, shall have to be investigated. Negligence would be culpable only if it was in relation to a duty cast by the Act, Articles of Association or by a resolution of the shareholders or that of the Board of Directors.
- Any negligence in the discharge of duty of a director or any other managerial personnel must be construed very broadly. As such, it is their duty to safeguard the property of the company and protect the interest of the shareholders.
- An investigator may interrogate directors, officers, agents, and others concerned with matters under his enquiry, if appears necessary.
- If the Investigating accountant is required to report on the efficiency of the management, he should be discreet in expressing his opinion.
- The inspector must ensure that the persons who figure in the investigation get the fullest opportunity to explain their action and conduct.

19.3 INVESTIGATION ON BEHALF OF INCOMING PARTNER

Q.5 What are the important steps involved while conducting Investigation on behalf of an Incoming Partner?

Ans. : Investigation on behalf of incoming partner:

Investigation on behalf of incoming partner is carried out so as to ascertain whether the terms offered to him are reasonable having regard to the nature of the business, profit records, capital distribution, personal capability of existing partners, etc. Steps involved in investigation includes the following:

(*a*) Ascertaining the **history of the firm** since inception and growth of the firm.

(*b*) Studies of the provisions of the **Deed of Partnership**, particularly for composition of partners, their capital contribution, drawing rights, retirement benefits, job allocation, etc.

(*c*) Scrutiny of the **record of profitability** of the firm's business over a suitable number of years

(*d*) Examination of the **asset and liability position** to determine the tangible asset, investment, appraisal of the value of intangibles like goodwill, know-how, patents, etc. including contingent liabilities and those for pending tax assessment.

(*e*) Assess **position of order at hand** and the range and quality of clientele should be thoroughly examined under which the firm is presently operating.

(*f*) Scrutinize **terms of loan finance** to assess its usefulness and the implication for the overall financial position.

(*g*) Study important **contractual and legal obligations.** It may be the case that the firm has standing agreement with the employees as regards salary and wages, bonus, gratuity and other incidental benefits.

(*h*) Study the **composition and quality of key personnel** employed by the firm and any likelihood of their leaving the organisation.

(*i*) Ascertain **reasons for the offer of admission** to a new partner and it should be determined whether the same synchronizes with the retirement of any senior partner whose association may have had considerable impact having on the firm's successes.

(*j*) Appraisal of the **record of capital employed and the rate of returns.** It is necessary to have a comparison with alternative business avenues for investments.

(*k*) Ascertain **manner of computation of goodwill** on admission as also on retirement, if any.

(*l*) Examine whether any **special clause** exist in the Deed of Partnership to allow admission in future a new partner.

19.4 INVESTIGATION ON BEHALF OF THE BANK FOR ADVANCES

Q.6 A nationalized bank received an application from an export company seeking sanction of a term loan to expand the existing sea food processing plant. In this connection, the General Manager, who is in charge of Advances, approaches you to conduct a thorough investigation of this limited company and submit a confidential report based on which he will decide whether to sanction this loan or not. List out the points you will cover in your investigation before submitting your report to the General Manager.

Or

M/s. ISBN Bank Ltd. appoints you to investigate on behalf of them for advancing loan to M/s. Dust Ltd. As an investigating accountant, what information and factors you will enquire into?

[May 18 - Old Syllabus (4 Marks)]

Ans. : Points to be covered in an investigation on behalf of bank:

1. **Collection of Information:** Investigator is required to collect the information w.r.t.

   (*a*) **Purpose** for which the loan is required

   (*b*) Manner in which the borrower proposed to invest the amount of the loan.

   (*c*) **Schedule of repayment** of loan submitted by the borrower, particularly, the assumptions made therein as regards amounts of profits that will be earned in cash and the amount of cash that would be available for the repayment of loan to confirm that they are reasonable and valid in the circumstances of the case.

   (*d*) **Financial standing** and **reputation** for business integrity enjoyed by the directors and officers of the company.

   (*e*) **Authorisation** under Memorandum or the Articles of Association to borrow money for the purpose for which the loan will be used.

   (*f*) **History of growth and development** of the company and its performance during the past five years.

2. **Examination of Financial Statements:** It will cover the followings:

   (*a*) **Preparation of a condensed income statement:** It will be prepared from statement of profit & Loss for the previous five years, showing separately therein various items of income and

TAXMANN®

expenses, the amounts of gross and net profits earned and taxes paid annually during each of the five years. Purpose of condensed income statement is to ascertain strengths of profitability.

(*b*) **Computation of Relevant Ratios:**

- Sales to Average Stocks held.
- Sales to Fixed Assets.
- Equity to Fixed Assets.
- Current Assets to Current Liabilities.
- Quick Assets to Quick Liabilities.
- Equity to Long Term Loans.
- Sales to Book Debts.
- Return on Capital Employed.

(*c*) **Break-up of annual sales:** Product-wise to show their trend.

(*d*) **Schedule of assets and liabilities:** Schedule of assets is to be prepared to ensure their existence, ownership and proper valuation and to examine whether assets have been adequately insured. Schedule of liabilities will assist in determining present and future obligations and ensure completeness of recording.

19.5 INVESTIGATIONS OF FRAUDS

Q.7 In a company, it is suspected that there has been embezzlement in cash receipts. As an investigator, guide the company the areas where embezzlement is possible?

Or

In cases like holding back cash sales, collections by travelling salesmen, V.P.P receipts, or casual receipts, e.g., sales of scrap, recoveries out of debts written off earlier, etc., the amount or amounts of receipts embezzled may be subsequently covered up by the perpetrator adopting certain methods. In a company, it is suspected that there has been embezzlement in cash receipts. The company appoints you as an investigator. What are the areas you would verify?

Ans. : Areas of embezzlement of cash receipts:

(*i*) Issuing a receipt for full amount collected, entering lesser amount on the counterfoil.

(*ii*) Showing a larger cash discount than actually allowed.

(*iii*) Adjusting a fictitious credit in the account of a customer for goods returned.

(*iv*) Cash sales entered as credit sales with debit to customer.

(*v*) Writing off a good debt as bad & irrecoverable to cover up misappropriation of amount collected.

(*vi*) Short-debiting customer's ledger account and withdrawing the difference on collection of full amount.

(*vii*) Under-casting the receipts side of cash book.

(*viii*) Over-casting the payment side of the cash book.

Q.8 You have been appointed to investigate a suspected embezzlement of cash receipts in a departmental store. What are the steps you would take in this regard? [Nov. 12 (6 Marks)]

Or

What steps needs to be taken to investigate frauds of Cash Receipts. [Nov. 15 (4 Marks)]

Ans. : Steps to investigate frauds of cash receipts:

(*i*) Ascertain nature of duties of person who is suspected to have committed a fraud.

(*ii*) Examine line of responsibility among the various members of the staff.

(*iii*) Income received from different sources should be scrutinized.

(*iv*) Carbon copies of receipts marked 'duplicate' should be scrutinized.

(*v*) Examining record of small or negligible sources of income such as sales of scrap or sale of waste paper.

(vi) Review of recoveries from customers and sundry parties along with deductions on account of cash discounts.

(vii) Examine that receipts are serially numbered and all receipts have been accounted for.

(viii) In case of cancelled receipt, its original copy should be examined and verified.

(ix) Enquiries should be made for unreasonable cash discount.

> **"ICAI Examiner Comments"**
>
> **Instead of explaining about steps to be taken to investigate frauds of cash receipts, examinees wrote about verification of cash balance and cash payments.**

Q.9 Write short note on: Frauds through suppliers Ledger. [Nov. 08, May 11 (4 Marks)]

Ans. : Frauds through Supplier's Ledger:

Frauds through supplier's ledger may be committed in following ways:

(i) Adjusting fictitious or duplicate invoices as purchases in the accounts of suppliers and subsequently misappropriating the amounts when payments are made to the suppliers in respect of these invoices.

(ii) Suppressing the Credit Notes issued by suppliers and withdrawing the corresponding amounts not claimed by them.

(iii) Withdrawing amounts unclaimed by suppliers, for one reason or another by showing that the same have been paid to them.

(iv) Accepting purchase invoices at prices considerably higher than their market prices and collecting the excess amount, paid in cash, from the suppliers.

Q.10 State the points in an investigation of frauds through suppliers' ledger.

Or

In a Public Limited Company, it is suspected by the Management that there has been embezzlement in supplier's ledger. As an auditor of the Company, you have been asked to investigate the matter. What are the major areas that you would verify in this regard? [Nov. 19 - Old Syllabus (4 Marks)]

Ans. : Investigation of frauds through suppliers ledger:

(i) The Bought Journal should be vouched by reference of Goods Inward Book.

(ii) Amounts have been correctly credited in respect of goods duly received or not.

(iii) Request the supplier to furnish statements of their accounts to find out whether or not any balance is outstanding or due and

(iv) Confirm that allowances and rebates given by them is correctly adjusted.

Q.11 Mr. Sharma is reviewing the anti-fraud controls for a construction company. The company has witnessed a few frauds in the past mainly in the nature of material stolen from the sites and fake expense vouchers.

Mr. Sharma is evaluating options for verifying the process to reveal fraud and the corrective action to be taken in such cases. As an expert, you are required to brief Mr. Sharma about the inventory fraud and verification procedure with respect to defalcation of inventory? [RTP-May 19]

Or

MF Ltd., engaged in the manufacturing of various products in its factory, is concerned with shortage in production and there arose suspicion of inventory fraud. You are appointed by MF Ltd. to evaluate the options for verifying the process to reveal fraud and the corrective action to be taken. As an investigating accountant what will be your areas of verification and the procedure to be followed for verification of defalcation of inventory? [Nov. 19 - New Syllabus (4 Marks)]

Ans. : Ways of Committing Inventory Frauds:

(i) Employees may simply remove goods from the premises.

(ii) Theft of goods may be concealed by writing them off as damaged goods, etc.

(iii) Stock records may be manipulated by employees who have committed theft so that book quantities tally with the actual quantities of stocks in hand.

Verification procedure:

1. The first step towards verification is to establish the different items of inventory defalcated and their quantities by checking physically the quantities in inventory held and those shown by the Inventory Book.

2. Next step will be to verify all the receipts and issues of inventory recorded in the Inventory Book by reference to entries in the Goods Inward and Outward Registers and the documentary evidence as regards purchases and sales. This would reveal the particulars of inventory not received but paid for as well as that issued but not charged to customers.

   In addition, entries in respect of returns, both inward and outward, recorded in the financial books should be checked with corresponding entries in the Inventory Book.

3. Afterwards, the shortages observed on physical verification of inventory should be reconciled with the discrepancies observed on checking the books in the manner mentioned above.

4. Defalcations of inventory, sometimes, also are committed by the management, by diverting a part of production and the consequent shortages in production being adjusted by inflating the wastage in production; similar defalcations of inventories and stores are covered up by inflating quantities issued for production.

   For detecting such shortages, the investigating accountant should take assistance of an engineer. For that he will be more conversant with factors which are responsible for shortage in production and thus will be able to correctly determine the extent to which the shortage in production has been inflated. In this regard, guidance can also be taken from past records showing the extent of wastage in production in the past.

19.6 DUE DILIGENCE

Q.12 Write short note on: Areas in which Due Diligence can take place. [May 15 (5 Marks)]

Ans. : Areas in which Due Diligence can take place

1. **Commercial/Operational due diligence:** To evaluate whether proposed merger would create operational synergies.
2. **Financial Due Diligence:** To analyse books of account and other information pertaining to financial matters of the entity.
3. **Tax Due diligence:** To determine the tax effect of the merger or acquisition.
4. **Information Systems due diligence:** To ascertain whether information systems is providing reliable information in a timely manner.
5. **Legal due diligence:** To review legal aspects w.r.t. functioning of the entity and compliance with applicable laws.
6. **Environmental due diligence:** To study the entity's environment, its flexibility and adaptiveness to the acquirer entity.
7. **Personnel due diligence:** To ascertain that the entity's personnel policies are appropriate and suit the requirements of the restructuring.

Q.13 Mr. Q is the proprietor of a very profitable business dealing in specialty chemicals. Due to his old age, Mr. Q wants to sell his business and has approached XYZ Pvt. Ltd., a competitor, for the same. As an advisor to XYZ Pvt. Ltd., you are appointed to do a 'Due Diligence' of the business. Enumerate the points which you would look into as part of the Due diligence exercise. [Nov. 17 (6 Marks)]

or

Mr. Clean who proposes to buy the proprietary business of Mr. Perfect, engages you as investigating accountant. Specify the areas which you will cover in your investigation.

or

An American Company engaged in the business of manufacturing and distribution of industrial gases, is interested in acquiring a listed Indian Company having a market share of more than 65% of the industrial gas business in India, request you to conduct a "Due Diligence" of this Indian Company and submit your Report. As due Diligence Auditor, what key areas you will cover in your review?

Ans. : Aspects to be covered in Financial due diligence:

1. **Studying the Business History:** Examine the details of establishment of company and ascertain details about the original promoters and the history of business - products, markets, suppliers, expenses and operations.
2. **Significant Accounting Policies:** Determine Accounting policies followed and their appropriateness.

3. **Examining Profit and Loss Account:** Examine extraordinary items of income or expense that might have affected the operating results. Compare the actual figures with the budgeted figures for the period under review and those of the previous accounting period.
4. **Examining Net worth:** Evaluate the basis upon which assets have been valued and liabilities have been recognised. The net worth of the business has to be arrived at by taking into account the impact of over/under valuation of assets and liabilities.
5. **Payment of Taxes:** Check whether the business is regular in payment of taxes; both Central and State Taxes. In case taxes are in arrears, check the arrangements made to clear off the arrears.
6. **Studying the Economic environment:** Study the impact of economic forces at the business.
7. **Cash Flow:** Review historical cash flows and their pattern to determine cash generating abilities. Check whether the company is able to honour its commitments to its creditors, to the banks, to government and other stakeholders. Examine how well does the company deploy its funds.
8. **Financial Projections:** Evaluate the projections for the next five years with detailed assumptions and workings and the appropriateness of assumption used in the preparation and presentation of financial projections. If assumption used by the company appears to be are unrealistic, consider its impact on the overall valuation of the company.
9. **Human Resources:** Examine the status of work force, staff and employees and their retention. Match the job profile of the administrative and managerial staff with the requirements of the new incumbents.
10. **Statutory Compliance:** Make a list of laws that are applicable to the entity as well as to make a checklist of compliance required from the company under those laws. If the company has not been regular in its legal compliance, it could lead to punitive charges under the law. The impact on such violations be quantified and assessed in respect of entity; financial status and even on its going concern status.

Q.14 Write a short note on - Outline the contents of a due diligence report.

Or

XYZ Limited, a company engaged in the business of manufacturing and distribution of copper rods and copper wire is interested in acquiring a listed company having a market share of 38% of Insulated Copper Wires. You were appointed to conduct a "Due Diligence" of the target company and you have completed review of a few key areas. List out the contents of the Due Diligence Report which you will submit to XYZ Limited. [Nov. 15 (4 Marks)]

Ans. : Contents of a Due Diligence Report

1. Executive summary.
2. Introduction.
3. Objective of due diligence.
4. Terms of reference and scope of verification.
5. Brief history of the company.
6. Summary on capital structure and group structure of company.
7. Shareholding pattern.
8. Observations on the review.
9. Assessment of Management structure.
10. Assessment of financial liabilities.
11. Assessment of valuation of assets.
12. Assessment of operating results.
13. Assessment of taxation and statutory liabilities.
14. Assessment of possible liabilities on account of litigation.
15. Assessment of net worth.
16. Any liabilities not provided for in the books.
17. SWOT analysis comments on future projections.
18. Status on charges, liens, mortgages and assets of the company.

19. Ways and means to cover unforeseen contingent liabilities.
20. Aspects to be taken care of before/after merger.
21. Interlocking investments and financial obligations with group/associate companies amounts receivable subject to litigation.

"ICAI Examiner Comments"

Presentation of the answers regarding the contents of a due diligence report was not satisfactory. Many examinees mentioned the types of due diligence instead of contents.

Q.15 **Ekbote Co. is currently a large organisation trading in items of office furniture. The entity wants to expand and hence are looking at acquisition of Rawat Co. which deals in items of household furniture. Ekbote Co. hires a Chartered accountant to conduct a due diligence to consider whether there is the potential for additional value to be brought out of the target company by improving its operational function and also whether there are serious operational risks about which the potential buyer should be concerned (thereby allowing the buyer to consider aborting the deal or renegotiating the price). Which of the due diligence review would be helpful to achieve the above objective? You are also required to briefly discuss the contents of a due diligence report. [MTP - April 19]**

Ans. : Due Diligence:

In the instant case Operational Due Diligence is required to confirm that the business plan provided is achievable with the existing facilities plus the capital expenditure outlined in the business plan.

Contents of Due Diligence Report: Refer answer of Q. No. 14.

19.7 OTHER IMPORTANT QUESTIONS

Q.16 **Your client is contemplating taking over a manufacturing concern and desires that in the course of due diligence review, you should look specifically for any hidden liabilities and overvalued assets. State (in brief) the major areas you would examine for the above. [Nov. 10 (5 Marks)]**

Or

Z Ltd is intending to acquire A Ltd. It hires B & Co., a firm of Chartered Accountants to conduct a due diligence. B & Co., wants to reduce the risk of over valuation of assets in its due diligence exercise. Kindly guide B & Co. [May 12 (8 Marks)]

Or

M Limited is going to acquire S Limited. The purchase consideration has been decided at ₹ 4,000 Crores. M Limited is worried about hidden liabilities or overvalued assets of S Limited and approached you to examine the same. List out eight important transaction/items which you would like to investigate in the Due Diligence exercise. [Nov. 13 (4 Marks)]

Or

KDK Bank Ltd., received an application from a pharmaceutical company for takeover of their outstanding term loans secured on its assets, availed from and outstanding with a nationalized bank. KDK Bank Ltd., requires you to make a due diligence audit in the areas of assets of pharmaceutical company especially with reference to valuation aspect of assets. State what may be your areas of analysis in order to ensure that the assets are not stated at overvalued amounts. [May 18 - New Syllabus (5 Marks)]

Or

Beta Ltd. is anticipating taking over a manufacturing concern and appoints you for due diligence review. While reviewing, it requests you to look specifically for any hidden liabilities and overvalued assets. State in brief the major areas you would examine for hidden liabilities and overvalued assets. [RTP-Nov. 19]

Ans. : Investigation of Hidden Liabilities:

In order to investigate hidden liabilities, the auditor should pay his attention to the following areas:

- Any show cause notice, which have not matured into demands but may be material and important.
- Contingent liabilities not shown in books
- Company may have sold some subsidiaries/businesses and may have agreed to take over and indemnify all liabilities and contingent liabilities of the same prior to the date of transfer.
- Product and warranty liabilities, product returns & discounts, liquidated damages, etc.

- Tax liability under direct and indirect taxes.
- Long pending sales tax assessment.
- Cases of custom duty where only provisional assessment has been made and final assessment is yet to completed.
- Agreement to buy back shares at a stated price.
- Future lease liabilities.
- Claims against the company including third party claims.
- Unfunded retirement benefit of employees.
- Labour claims under negotiations.

Regularly Overvalued assets: The auditor shall have to specifically examine the following areas:

- Uncollectable receivables.
- Obsolete, slow and non-moving inventories and inventories valued above net realizable value, if any.
- Obsolete and unused plant and machinery and their spares.
- Assets value which have impaired due to sudden fall in market value.
- Assets shown in books above market value due to capitalization of expenditure/foreign exchange fluctuation or capitalisation of revenue expenditure.
- Assets under litigation.
- Investment shown at cost whose market value is much lower.
- Investment carrying very low rate of return.
- Infructuous project expenditure.
- Intangibles of no value.

Q.17 A company engaged in manufacturing of chemicals is consistently recording higher sales turnover, but declining net profits since the last 5 years. As an investigator appointed to find out the reasons for the same, what are the points you would verify?

Ans. : Decline in Net Profits Despite Increasing Sales:

As per the facts that there has been consistently high turnover but declining net profits is an anomalous situation. It may be attributed to one or more following reasons requiring further investigation:

(*i*) **Unfavourable Sales mix**: Where the company sells different chemical products with different product margins, the product with the maximum PV ratio/margin should have a higher share in the total sales. If due to revision of sales mix, more quantities of unprofitable products are sold, profits will be reduced in spite of an increase in sales.

(*ii*) **Negative Impact of Financial Leverage**: Where the company does not have sufficient own funds (equity) but has a higher debt-equity ratio, the interest commitments will be higher. As the volume of its operation increases, higher debt and interest charges would result in lower profits.

(*iii*) **Other Items Included in Sales**: The figure of sales as per Profit and Loss Account may include incidental revenues, e.g., freight, excise duty, sales-tax, etc. where the amount of excise duty goes up considerably the total sales may show an increase which is not represented by a real increase in sales quantity/value.

(*iv*) **High Administrative and Selling Expenses**: Administrative and selling costs are generally period costs which are fixed in nature. Their increase is generally not proportional to sale increase. However, a reduction in profit could also be due to increase in administrative overheads and sales overheads at a rate higher than the rate of increase in sales.

(*v*) **Cost-Price Relationship**: If the increases in cost of raw materials and labour has not been compensated by a corresponding increase in the sales price this would also result in higher sales and declining profits. In spite of same sales quantity, for the increasing cost of raw materials and other services, per unit values of the product has been increased which is however unmatched by the increase in cost.

(*vi*) **Competitive Price**: Where sales have been made at cut-throat prices in order to eliminate competition from the market, the profits would be in the declining trend in the short-run.

(*vii*) **Additions to Fixed Assets**: Where there are heavy additions to fixed assets and consequent depreciation charges in the initial years of additions, there may be reduction in profits in spite of increased sales.

Q.18 J Ltd. is interested in acquiring S Ltd. The valuation of S Ltd. is dependent on future maintainable sales. As the person entrusted to value S Ltd. what factors would you consider in assessing the future maintainable turnover? [May 13 (4 Marks)]

Or

A Ltd. who is one of the leading manufacturer of kids clothing is interested to acquire B Ltd. B Ltd. is currently a manufacturer of womens' clothing. As a professional consultant in due diligence and valuation, A Ltd. entrusted you to value B Ltd. The valuation of B Ltd. is dependent on future maintainable sales. Discuss the factors you would consider in assessing the future maintainable turnover of B Ltd.?

[MTP-March 19]

Ans. : Factors to be considered in assessing future maintainable turnover:

In assessing the turnover which the business would be able to maintain in the future, the following factors should be taken into account:

(*i*) **Trend**: Whether in the past, sales have been increasing consistently or they have been fluctuating. A proper study of this phenomenon should be made.

(*ii*) **Marketability**: Is it possible to extend the sales into new markets or that these have been fully exploited? Product wise estimation should be made.

(*iii*) **Political and economic considerations**: Are the policies pursued by the Government likely to **promote** the extension of the market for goods to other countries? Whether the sales in the home market are likely to increase or decrease as a result of various emerging economic trends?

(*iv*) **Competition**: What is the likely effect on the business if other manufacturers enter the same field or if products which would sell in competition are placed on the market at cheaper price? Is the demand for competing products increasing? Is the company's share in the total trade constant or has it been fluctuating?

20 CHAPTER

PEER REVIEW

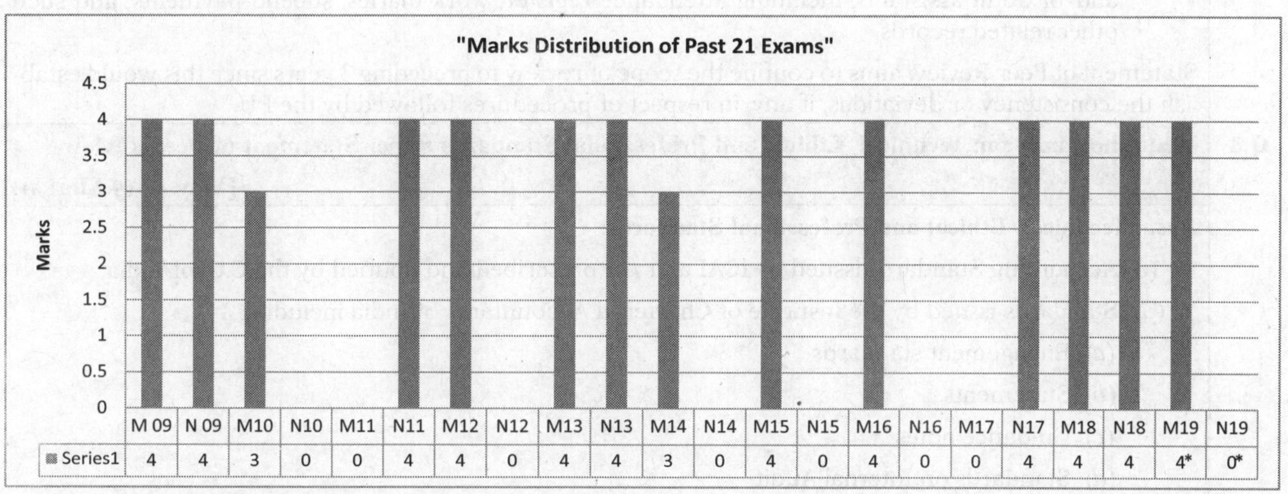

*Only Subjective Questions.

20.1 MEANING, OBJECTIVES AND SCOPE OF PEER REVIEW

Q.1 Explain the objectives of Peer Review. **[Nov. 08, Nov. 18 - New Syllabus (4 Marks)]**

Ans. : Objectives of Peer Review:

As per Statement of Peer Review issued by ICAI , objectives of peer review can be listed as below:

(1) To ensure that members while carrying out assurance service assignments comply with Technical, Professional and Ethical Standards issued by the Institute;

(2) To ensure that member has in place proper system, including documentation thereof, for maintaining the quality of assurance services;

(3) To ensure adherence to various statutory and regulatory requirements.

(4) To identify and address patterns of non-compliance with quality control standards.

Note: Primary objective of peer review is not to find out deficiencies but to improve the quality of services rendered by members of the profession.

Q.2 Write short note on: Focus of Peer Review. **[May 10 (3 Marks)]**

Or

Write short note on : Scope of Peer Review **[Nov. 11, Nov. 13, Nov. 18 - Old Syllabus (4 Marks)]**

Ans. : Scope of Peer Review:

The Peer Review process shall apply to all the assurance services provided by a Practice Unit. While carrying out review, the reviewer examines the assurance engagement records of the Practice Unit so as to cover the following:

1. Compliance with Technical, Professional and Ethical Standards:
2. Quality of reporting.
3. Systems and procedures for carrying out assurance services.
4. Training programmes for staff (including articled and audit assistants) concerned with assurance functions, including availability of appropriate infrastructure.
5. Compliance with directions and/or guidelines issued by the Council to the Members, including Fees to be charged, Number of audits undertaken, register for Assurance Engagements conducted during the year and such other related records.
6. Compliance with directions and/or guidelines issued by the Council in relating to article assistants and/or audit assistants, including attendance register, work diaries, stipend payments, and such other related records.

Statement of Peer Review aims to confine the scope of review to preceding 3 years since this would establish the consistency or deviations, if any, in respect of procedures followed by the PU.

Q.3 Write short note on: Technical, Ethical and Professional Standards as per Statement of Peer Review. **[May 13 (4 Marks)]**

Ans. : Technical, Ethical and Professional Standards:

(*i*) Accounting Standards issued by ICAI and /or prescribed and notified by the C.G. of India;

(*ii*) Standards issued by the Institute of Chartered Accountants of India including

(*a*) Engagement standards

(*b*) Statements

(*c*) Guidance notes

(*d*) Standards on Internal Audit

(*e*) Statements on Quality Control

(*f*) Notifications/Directions/Announcements/Guidelines/Pronouncements/Professional standards issued from time to time by the Council or any of its committees.

(*iii*) Framework for the Preparation and presentation of financial statements, framework of statements and Standard on Auditing, Standard on Assurance Engagements, Standards on Quality Control and Guidance Notes on related services issued, from time to time, by the Institute of Chartered Accountants of India and framework for assurance engagements;

(*iv*) Provisions of the various relevant statutes and /or regulations which are applicable in the context of the specific engagements being Reviewed including instructions, guidelines, notifications, directions issued by regulatory bodies as covered in the scope of assurance engagements.

Q.4 What are the areas excluded from the scope of Peer Review. **[May 14 (3 Marks)]**

Or

Write short note on : Areas not to be examined in Peer Review. **[Nov. 17 (4 Marks)]**

Ans. : Area excluded from the scope of peer review:

As per Statement of Peer Review by ICAI, the following services are excluded from the scope of peer review:

(*i*) Management Consultancy Engagements;

(*ii*) Representation before various Authorities;

(*iii*) Engagements to prepare tax returns or advising clients in taxation matters;

(*iv*) Engagements for the compilation of financial statements;

(*v*) Engagements solely to assist the client in preparing, compiling or collating information other than financial statements;

(*vi*) Testifying as an expert witness;

(*vii*) Providing expert opinion on points of principle, such as Accounting Standards or the applicability of certain laws, on the basis of facts provided by the client; and

(*viii*) Engagement for Due diligence

"ICAI Examiner Comments"

Some examinees were able to highlight only few of the areas that are outside the purview of Peer Review. Few examinees wrongly mentioned that tax audit and internal audit are also not to be examined by Peer Reviewer. While few other examinees discussed wrongly on the areas to be examined by Peer Reviewer.

Q.5 Write short note on: Eligibility criteria to be a Peer Reviewer. [May 18-Old Syllabus (4 Marks)]

Or

The elements of skill, experience and independence of reviews are ensured before initiating them in Peer Review process. In the above light, state few eligibility criteria fixed for a person to be empanelled and also for being appointed as a peer Reviewer. [May 18 - New Syllabus (4 Marks)]

Or

What is the eligibility to be a Peer Reviewer. [May 19 - Old Syllabus (4 Marks)]

Ans : Eligibility criteria to be a Peer Reviewer:

(a) A Peer Reviewer shall: —

- Be a member with at least 10 years of experience in practice;
- Is in Practice as per the Chartered Accountants Act, 1949.
- Should have undergone the requisite training as prescribed by the Board.
- Should furnish a declaration as prescribed by the Board, at the time of acceptance of Peer Review appointment.
- Should have signed the Declaration of Confidentiality as prescribed by the Board.
- Should have conducted audit of Level I Entities for at least 7 years to be eligible for conducting Peer Review of Level I Entities as referred to in Para II of this Statement.

(b) For being a Reviewer, a member should not have:

- disciplinary action/proceedings pending against him
- been found guilty by the Council or the Disciplinary Board or Committee at any time.
- been convicted by a Competent Court whether within or outside India, of an offence involving moral turpitude and punishable with transportation or imprisonment.
- any Obligation or conflict of interest in the Practice Unit or its Partners/Personnel.

20.2 PEER REVIEW PROCESS

Q.6 Write short note on: "Reporting stage in Peer Review". [May 09 (4 Marks)]

Or

Write a short note on: Preliminary Report under Peer Review.

Ans. : Reporting Stage in Peer Review:

As per Statement of Peer Review by ICAI, reporting stage in peer review covers the following:

1. **Preliminary Report of Reviewer**: At the end of review, the reviewer is required to send a preliminary report to the PU (before making any report to the Board) in case systems and procedures of the PU have been found to be deficient or where non-compliance with reference to any other matter has been noticed by the reviewer. No preliminary report is required in case no deficiencies or non-compliance are noticed by the reviewer.
2. **Response to Preliminary Report**: The PU has to send its representations, in writing, to the reviewer, on the areas mentioned in the preliminary report within a period of 15 days from the receipt of the preliminary report from the reviewer.
3. **Modified Report**: If the reviewer is not satisfied with the reply of the PU, the reviewer shall submit a modified report to the Board incorporating his reasons for the same. The Reviewer shall also

submit initial findings (i.e. Preliminary Report), response by the Practice Unit (Response to Preliminary Report) and the manner in which the responses have been dealt with. A copy of the modified report shall also be forwarded to the PU. In case of a modified report, the Board shall order for a "Follow On" Review after a period of one year from the date of issue of modified report. If the Board so decides, the period of one year may be reduced but shall not be less than six months from the date of issue of the report.

4. **Peer review Report**: At the end of an on-site Review if the Reviewer is satisfied with the reply received from the PU, he shall submit a Peer Review Report to the Board along with his initial findings, response by the Practice Unit and the manner in which the responses have been dealt with. A copy of the report shall also be forwarded to the PU.

Q.7 Explain the stepwise approach adopted by the Peer Reviewer. [May 15 (4 Marks)]

Ans. : Stepwise Approach adopted by the Peer Reviewer:

(*i*) **Obtain an understanding of the assignment**: The reviewer should obtain an understanding of the assignment so as to plan the review of documentation.

(*ii*) **Selection of assurance engagements**: Reviewer should ascertain the number of assurance engagements to be reviewed based on the evaluation of replies given in the questionnaire and the size of the practice unit.

(*iii*) **Examine the Policies and procedures of Practice Unit**: The reviewer should, wherever possible, examine that the policies and procedures for acceptance of audit have been complied with and necessary documentation with regard to the same exists.

(*iv*) **Review and Evaluation of records – Compliance and Substantive Checking**: The reviewer would conduct adequate compliance procedures to gain evidence that those general controls on which the reviewer intends to rely upon, actually exists and functioning effectively throughout the period of reliance. Based on the results of compliance procedures, the reviewer concludes either to rely or not to rely on the general controls. In case the reviewer decides to rely on the general controls, he would also need to determine the extent of reliance to be placed on such controls. In such a situation, the NTE of substantive procedures would be, normally, less extensive and vice-versa. The substantive approach involves application of such review procedures that provide the reviewer with the evidence as to the appropriateness of the factors on which the review is required to be focused on.

"ICAI Examiner Comments"

Most of the candidates explained the process of Peer Review instead of step-wise Approach.

20.3 COMPLIANCE REVIEW PROCEDURES

Q.8 A, a practicing Chartered Accountant is appointed to conduct the peer review of another practicing unit. What areas A should review in the assessment of independence of the practicing unit? [May 12 (4 Marks)]

Or

Write short note on: Area to be reviewed in the assessment of independence of the practicing unit, while conducting peer review. [May16 (4 Marks)]

Ans. : Assessment of Independence of the Practice Unit:

(*i*) Does the PU have a policy to ensure independence, objectivity and integrity, on the part of partners and staff? Who is responsible for this policy?

(*ii*) Does the PU communicate these policies and the expected standards of professional behaviour to all staff?

(*iii*) Does the PU monitor compliance with policies and procedures relating to independence?

(*iv*) Does the PU periodically review its association with clients to ensure objectivity and independence?

20.4 MISCELLANEOUS

Q.9 **Briefly explain: Collection of evidences by Peer reviewer.** **[Nov. 09 (4 Marks)]**

Ans. : Collection of Evidences by Peer Reviewer:

A Peer Reviewer collects evidence by applying the following methods:

(*a*) **Inspection**: It includes scrutiny of documentation and other records of the practicing unit.

(*b*) **Observation**: He observes the procedures/processes followed in the production unit.

(*c*) **Enquiries**: He enquires and collects required information from the responsible person of practice unit, even by the use of questionnaire.

Q.10 **What are the inherent limitations of Peer Review?** **[Nov. 18 - New Syllabus (4 Marks)]**

Answer: Inherent Limitations of Peer Review:

Peer review suffers from certain inherent limitations given as below;

- The reviewer conducts the review in accordance with the Statement on Peer Review.
- The review would not necessarily disclose all weaknesses in compliance of technical standards and maintenance of quality of assurance services since it would be based on selective tests.
- As there are inherent limitations in the effectiveness of any system of quality control which happens to be subject-matter of review, departure from the system may occur and may not be detected.

21
CHAPTER

AUDIT OF BANKING COMPANIES

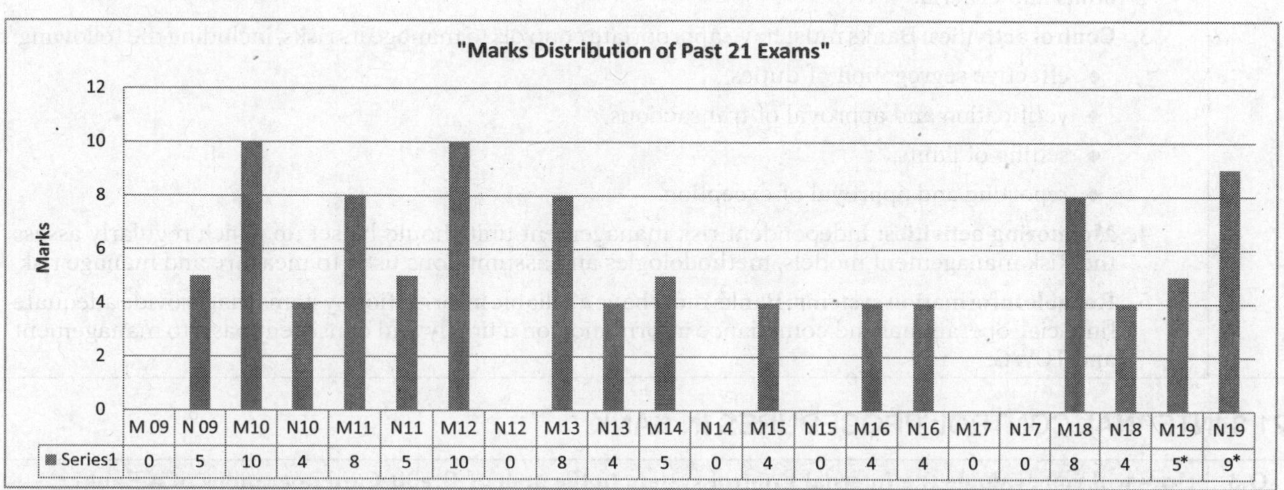

*Only Subjective Questions.

21.1 PRINCIPAL ENACTMENTS GOVERNING BANK AUDIT

Q.1 Write a short note on - Principal Enactments Governing Bank Audit.

Ans. : Principal Enactments governing Bank Audit:

1. Banking Regulation Act, 1949;
2. Reserve Bank of India Act, 1934;
3. Banking Companies (Acquisition and Transfer of Undertakings) Act, 1970;
4. State Bank of India Act, 1955;
5. State Bank of India (Subsidiary Banks) Act, 1959
6. Regional Rural Banks Act, 1976;
7. Companies Act, 2013;
8. Cooperative Societies Act, 1912 or the relevant State Cooperative Societies Acts.
9. Information Technology Act, 2000;
10. Prevention of Money Laundering Act, 2002;
11. Securitisation & Reconstruction of Financial Assets & Enforcement of Security Interest Act, 2002;
12. Credit Information Companies Regulation Act, 2005; and
13. Payment and Settlement Systems Act, 2007

21.2 RISK MANAGEMENT SYSTEM

Q.2 Management develops controls and uses performance indicators to aid in managing key business and financial risks. Explain in this reference the requirements of an effective risk management system in a bank.

Or

Write short note on: Requirements of a Risk Management Process/System in a bank.
[Nov. 16 (4 Marks)]

Ans. : Requirements of a Risk Management Process/System in a Bank:

1. **Involvement of TCWG:** Risk Management policies should be approved by TCWG. While approving the policies, TCWG should ensure that the policies should be consistent with the bank's business objectives and strategies, capital strength, management expertise, regulatory requirements and the types and amounts of risk it regards as acceptable.
2. **Identification, measurement & monitoring of risks:** Risks that may significantly affect the achievement of bank's goals and objectives should be identified, measured and monitored against pre-approved limits and criteria.
3. **Control activities:** Banks must have appropriate controls to manage its risks, including the following:
   - effective segregation of duties,
   - verification and approval of transactions,
   - setting of limits,
   - reporting and approval of exception.
4. **Monitoring activities:** Independent risk management unit should be set up which regularly assess the Risk management models, methodologies and assumptions used to measure and manage risk.
5. **Reliable information systems:** Banks must have a reliable information systems that provide adequate financial, operational and compliance information on a timely and consistent basis to management and TCWG.

21.3 INTERNAL CONTROL PROCEDURES IN BANK

Q.3 How will you evaluate the Internal Control system in the area of Credit Card operations of a Bank?
[Nov. 09 (5 Marks)]

Or

You have been appointed as an auditor of LCO Bank, a nationalized bank. LCO Bank also deals in providing credit card facilities to its account holder. The bank is aware of the fact that there should be strict control over storage and issue of credit cards. How will you evaluate the Internal Control System in the area of Credit Card operations of a Bank? **[Nov. 19 - New Syllabus (4 Marks)]**

Ans. : Evaluation of Internal Control System in the area of Credit Card Operations:

The following points should be considered so as to evaluate the internal control system in the area of credit card operations:

1. There should be effective screening of applications with reasonably good credit assessments.
2. There should be strict control over storage and issue of cards.
3. There should be a system whereby a merchant confirms the status of unutilised limit of a credit-card holder from the bank before accepting the settlement in case the amount to be settled exceeds a specified percentage of the total limit of the card holder.
4. There should be system of prompt reporting by the merchants of all settlements accepted by them through credit cards.
5. Reimbursement to merchants should be made only after verification of the validity of merchant's acceptance of cards.
6. All the reimbursements (gross of commission) should be immediately charged to the customer's account.
7. There should be a system to ensure that statements are sent regularly and promptly to the customer.
8. There should be a system of monitor and follow-up of customers' payments.
9. Items overdue beyond a reasonable period should be identified and attended to carefully. Credit should be stopped by informing the merchants through periodic bulletins, as early as possible, to avoid increased losses.
10. There should be a system of periodic review of credit card holders' accounts. On this basis, the limits of customers may be revised, if necessary. The review should also include determination of doubtful amounts and the provisioning in respect thereof.

Q.4 State the internal controls in the area of Loans and Advances of Banks.

Or

As the concurrent auditor of Z Bank Ltd you are requested by its management to draft an internal control policy in respect of loans and advances. What factors do you consider as important while drafting such a policy? [May 12 (10 Marks)]

Ans. : Internal Controls in the area of Loans and Advances:

The following points should be considered so as to evaluate the internal control system in the area of loans and advances:

1. Advances should be made only after evaluating creditworthiness of the borrowers and obtaining sanction from the proper authorities of the bank.
2. All the loan documents like promissory notes, letters of hypothecation, guarantee letter, etc should be executed by the parties before advances are made.
3. While determining the loan amount to be sanctioned, sufficient margin should be kept against securities taken so as to cover any decline in the value thereof and also to comply with RBI directives.
4. Securities should be received and returned by responsible officer and should be kept in the joint custody of atleast two responsible officers.
5. Securities requiring registration should be registered in the name of the bank.
6. In the case of physical possession of goods as security, the goods should be test checked at the time of receipts. In respect of hypothecated goods not in possession of the bank, surprise checks should be made.
7. Personal inquiries should be made so as to determine market value of goods.
8. For any increase/decrease in the value of securities, drawing power should be adjusted. All the accounts should be kept within both the drawing power and the sanctioned limit at all times.
9. All irregular accounts should be brought to the notice of the H.O. regularly.
10. The operation in each advance should be reviewed at least once every year.
11. There should exist a proper system for post disbursement supervision and follow-up.
12. Classification of advances should be made as per RBI Guidelines.
13. Ensure that the funds disbursed should be utilized only for the purpose for which advances has been granted.

Q.5 While doing the audit of a nationalized bank, your audit assistant informed you that there are a lot of irregularities in telegraphic transfers and demand drafts. What guidance would be given to audit assistant? [Nov. 13 (4 Marks)]

Ans. : Evaluation of Telegraphic Transfer and Demand Drafts operations:

The following points should be considered so as to identify the irregularities in the area of telegraphic transfers and demand drafts:

1. Codes for TT should be known only to responsible officers.
2. Coding and Decoding of telegrams should be done only by authorised officers.
3. The signatures on the documents used for TT and DD should be checked by an officer with the Signature Book.
4. All the T.Ts and D.Ds. sold by a branch should be immediately confirmed by the advices to the branches concerned.
5. If the paying branch does not receive proper confirmation of any T.T. or D.D. from the issuing branch or does not receive credit in its account with that branch, it should take immediate steps to ascertain the reasons.

21.4 VERIFICATION OF INVESTMENTS

Q.6 How are investments to be classified as per prudential norms issued by RBI in financial statements of a Bank?

Ans. : Classification of Investments as per prudential norms:

The entire investment portfolio of the bank should be classified under three categories:

(*i*) **Held to Maturity (HTM)**: The securities acquired by the banks with the intention to hold them up to maturity will be classified under Held to Maturity. The investments included under 'Held to maturity' should not exceed 25% of the bank's total investments.

(*ii*) **Held for Trading (HFT)**: The securities acquired by the banks with the intention to trade by taking advantage of the short term price/interest rate movements will be classified under Held for Trading. These securities are to be sold within 90 days.

(*iii*) **Available for sale (AFS)**: The securities which do not fall within the above two categories will be classified under Available for Sale.

Banks should decide the category of the investment at the time of acquisition and the decision should be recorded on the investment proposal/deal slip.

Q.7 Write short note on: Special purpose Certificates Relating to Investments required to be issued by Central Statutory Auditors of a bank.

Ans. : Special purpose Certificates Relating to Investments

Pursuant to RBI's circulars, issued from time to time, banks require their central auditors to issue the following certificates regarding investments of the bank (in addition to their main audit report and the LFAR):

1. Certificate on reconciliation of securities by the bank (both on its own Investment Account as well as PMS client's account). The reconciliation is to be presented in a given format.
2. Certificate on compliance by the bank in key areas of prudential and other guidelines relating to such transactions issued by the RBI.

Q.8 What are Non-performing investments in case of banking companies. How income is recognized on such investments?

Ans. : Non-Performing Investments (NPI)

A non-performing investment (NPI), is one where Interest/instalment (including maturity proceeds) is due and remains unpaid for more than 90 days and includes:

(*i*) Preference shares where the fixed dividend is not paid.

(*ii*) Unquoted Equity shares which are valued at ₹ 1 due to non-availability of the latest balance sheet.

(*iii*) Securities issued by any issuer who has been given any credit facility which is a NPA in the Bank's Books.

(*iv*) Equity, debentures, bonds, etc., received as a result of conversion of Non-Performing advances.

Income recognition on non performing investments: Income on NPI should be recognized on realisation.

Q.9 Write short note on: Income Recognition Norms of Investments in case of banking companies.

Ans. : Income Recognition Norms of Investments in case of banking companies:

1. **Performing Investments:** Banks may book interest income from all performing investments on accrual basis provided interest rates on these instruments are pre-determined.
2. **Income on Non performing investments:** Income on NPI should be recognized on realisation.
3. **Government Guarantee:** Income on securities of Corporate/PSU in respect of which the payment of interest and repayment have been guaranteed by the C. G./S.G. can be accounted for on **accrual** basis. However, where the interest is not serviced regularly and is in arrears, such income cannot be accounted for on accrual basis.
4. **Dividends:** Income from Dividend on Shares of Corporate Bodies can be booked on **accrual basis**, if the same has been declared by the Corporate Body in its AGM and the Shareholder's right to receive payment is established.
5. **Discount earned in discounted instruments :** Discount earned on discounted instruments like commercial papers, zero coupon bonds should be booked on accrual basis over the remaining period to maturity.
6. **Units of MFs:** Income from units of Mutual Funds should be accounted for only on **cash basis**.
7. **Profit/Loss on sale Investments:** Profit and loss on sale of investments including on HTM category, should be shown under Profit/Loss on sale of investments.

Q.10 Your firm has been appointed as Central Statutory Auditors of a Nationalised Bank. The bank has recognised on accrual basis income from dividends on securities and Units of Mutual Funds held by it as at the end of financial year. The dividends on securities and Units of Mutual Funds were declared after the end of financial year. Comment.

Ans. : Income Recognition w.r.t. Investments:

Prudential Norms on income recognition of investments provides the following:

- Income from dividend on shares of corporate bodies and units of mutual funds should be booked on cash basis.
- In respect of income from government securities and bonds and debentures of corporate bodies, where interest rates on these instruments are pre-determined, income could be booked on accrual basis, provided interest is serviced regularly and as such is not in arrears.
- Banks may book income from dividend on shares of corporate bodies on accrual basis, provided dividend on the shares has been declared by the corporate body in its AGM and the owner's right to receive payment is established. This is also in accordance with AS-9 as well.

Conclusion: Recognition of dividend income on securities may be recognized on accrual basis if the same has been declared by the Corporate Body in its AGM and the Shareholder's right to receive payment is established. In the present case, dividends were declared after the end of financial year. Hence, recognition of income from dividends on securities and units of mutual fund on accrual basis is not in order.

21.5 VERIFICATION OF ADVANCES

Q.11 Your firm has been appointed as auditors of a branch of a nationalised Bank. The bank is a consortium member of Cash Credit Facilities of ₹ 50 crores to X Ltd. Bank's own share is ₹ 10 crores only. During the last two quarters against a debit of ₹ 1.75 crores towards interest, the credits in X Ltd's account are to the tune of ₹ 1.25 crores only. Based on the certificate of lead bank, the bank has classified the account of X Ltd as performing.

Ans. : NPA Classification in Consortium advances:

- Prudential Norms on Asset Classification provides that in case of consortium advances, each bank may classify the advance given by it according to its own experience of recovery and other factors.
- In the present case, in the last two quarters, the amount remains outstanding and, thus, interest amount should be reversed.
- Despite the certificate of lead bank to classify the account as performing, the advance need to be classified as non-performing asset.

Conclusion: Advance to be classified as NPA.

Q.12 "An Asset, including a leased asset, becomes non-performing when it ceases to generate income for the bank." Define the criteria for classification of non-performing asset. [May 11 (8 Marks)]

Ans. : Criteria for Classification of Non-performing asset:

An Advance will be classified as NPA if:

(*a*) It ceases to generate income for a bank.

(*b*) Interest and/or instalment of principal in respect of such an advance have remain overdue or out of order for a specified period of time

- **Overdue:** An amount is said to be 'Overdue', if it is not paid on the due date fixed by the Bank.
- **Out of Order:** An account should be treated as 'Out-of-order' if the outstanding balance remains continuously in excess of the sanctioned limit/drawing power.

Or

If there are no credits continuously for 90 days as on the balance sheet date or the credits are not enough to cover the interest debited during the same period.

NPA classification w.r.t. specified advances:

1. **Term Loans:** Interest and/or Instalment of principal has remained overdue for a period exceeding 90 days.
2. **CC/OD:** The account has remained out-of-order for a period exceeding 90 days.
3. **Bills Purchased & Discounted:** The Bill remains overdue & unpaid for a period exceeding 90 days.
4. **Agricultural Advances/Loans:** Interest and/or Instalment of principal is overdue for two crop seasons, in case loans granted for Short Duration crops, one crop season, in case loans granted for Long Duration crops (i.e. more than 1 year).

5. **Credit Card Accounts:** Credit card account will be treated as nonperforming asset if the minimum amount due, as mentioned in the statement, is not paid fully within 90 days from the next statement date.
6. **Other Accounts:** Any amount to be received is **overdue** for a period of more than 90 days.

Q.13 M/s. S Ltd. is a MSME unit. The company does multiple banking. The company is availing cash credit limit from U Bank of Rs. 25 crores. The limit availed remained less than Rs. 5.00 crores during all the days of F.Y. 2018-19. The company has not done any credit in cash credit account during the year as it is operating current account in newly opened another bank branch adjoining to company premises. The company is having sufficient security of stocks and debtors and DP of Rs. 25.00 crores remains all over the year. The company is availing term loans from other bank branches. Now the Bank Manager is insisting to route the sale proceeds through U Bank, otherwise cash credit limit and term loan accounts with other banks will be treated as Non-Performing Accounts. Now company seeks your opinion.

Ans. : NPA Classification in Consortium advances:

- An Advance will be classified as NPA if:
  - (*a*) It ceases to generate income for a bank.
  - (*b*) Interest and/or instalment of principal in respect of such an advance have remain overdue or out of order for a specified period of time
- An amount is said to be 'Overdue', if it is not paid on the due date fixed by the Bank. An account should be treated as 'Out-of-order' if the outstanding balance remains continuously in excess of the sanctioned limit/drawing power or if there are no credits continuously for 90 days as on the balance sheet date or the credits are not enough to cover the interest debited during the same period.
- Prudential Norms on Asset Classification provides that in case of consortium advances, each bank may classify the advance given by it according to its own experience of recovery and other factors.
- In the present case, company is availing cash credit limit from U Bank of Rs. 25 crores. The limit availed remained less than Rs. 5.00 crores during all the days of F.Y. 2018-19. The company has not done any credit in cash credit account during the year as it is operating current account in newly opened another bank branch adjoining to company premises. The company is availing term loans from other bank branches. Now the Bank Manager is insisting to route the sale proceeds through U Bank, otherwise cash credit limit and term loan accounts with other banks will be treated as Non-Performing Accounts.

Conclusion: Cash credit facility with U bank need to be classified as NPA as there are no credit in the account to serve the interest charged in the account. Classification of term loan with other banks depends upon the payment made to that bank.

Q.14 Shy & Co. had been allotted the branch audit of a nationalized bank for the year ended 31st March, 2017. In the audit planning, the partner of Shy & Co. observed that the allotted branches are predominantly based in rural areas and major portion of the advances were for agricultural purpose. He needs your assistance in incorporating the criteria prescribed for determination of NPA norms in respect of agricultural advance, in audit plan. [May 14 (5 Marks)]

Ans. : Criteria for determination of NPA norms in respect of agricultural advances:

An agricultural advances is classified as NPA is interest and/or instalment of principal is **overdue** for

- two crop seasons, in case loans granted for Short Duration crops,
- one crop season, in case loans granted for Long Duration crops (i.e. more than 1 year)

For this purpose, the following points are to be considered:

1. Long duration crops means the crops with crop season longer than one year.
2. Short Duration Crops means the crops, other than long duration crops.
3. Crop season means the period up to harvesting of the crops, as determined by the State Level Bankers' Committee in each State.
4. The above norms should be made applicable to all direct agricultural advances as listed in the Master Circular on Lending to Priority Sectors. In respect of all other agricultural loans, identification of NPAs would be done on the same basis as non-agricultural advances, which, at present, is the 90 days delinquency norm.
5. If natural calamities impair the repaying capacity of agricultural borrowers, banks may decide on their own as a relief measure conversion of the short-term production loan into a term loan or re-schedulement of the repayment period; and the sanctioning of fresh short-term loan, subject to guidelines issued by RBI.

Q.15 Your firm has been appointed as central statutory auditors of Rustic Bank, a nationalised bank of India. In the course of audit, you observed that the accountant has classified an advance as NPA due to non-receipt of latest stock statement. You further observed that there are many other wrong classification of assets to NPA without considering RBI norms issued in this perspective.

You are therefore required to guide him by stating the exceptions to the general rule of treating advances as Non-performing Assets (NPAs).

Or

Write short note on: Exceptions to the General Rule of treating advances as Non performing Assets.

[May 16 (4 Marks)]

Ans. : Exceptions to NPA Classification norms:

RBI has laid down norms for classification of assets and provisioning norms for NPAs. However, certain exceptions to these norms are discussed below-

(*i*) **Temporary Deficiencies**: The classification of an asset as NPA should be based on the record of recovery. An account need not be classified as NPA merely due to the existence of some deficiencies, which are temporary in nature like non-availability of current drawing power due to non-receipt of latest stock statement, temporary delay in renewals of limits on due date, etc.

(*ii*) **Natural Calamities**: Where, in the wake of natural calamities, short-term agricultural loans are converted into term loans or there is rescheduling of repayment period or fresh short-term loans are sanctioned, the term loan as well as fresh short term loan may be treated as current dues and need not be classified as NPA.

(*iii*) **Facilities backed by Central Government Guarantees**: Credit facilities backed by guarantee of the Central Government though overdue should be treated as NPA only when the government repudiates its guarantee when invoked (this exemption is only for the purpose of asset classification and provisioning and not for the purpose of recognition of income).

(*iv*) **Advances to "On Lending" arrangements.**

Q.16 What is the income recognised in the case of 'non-performing' assets of bank?

Ans. : Income Recognition Norms

1. **General Rule:** Generally, banks should recognize income like interest, fees and commission on accrual basis, provided it is reasonable to expect its ultimate collection.
2. **Income from NPAs:** Banks should recognize Interest on NPA only on cash basis, i.e. when such interest is actually realized/received.
3. **Income on advances made against term deposits, NSCs, KVPs and Life policies:** Interest may be taken to income account on due date, provided adequate margin is available in the accounts.
4. **Fees and Commission on rescheduled advances:** Fees and Commission earned by the bank as a result of rescheduling of advances should be recognized on accrual basis over the period covered by the rescheduled extension of credit period.
5. **Government Guaranteed Advances:** Interest on such Advances should not be taken to Income Account unless it has been realized.

Q.17 In course of audit of Good Samaritan Bank as at 31st March, 2017 you observed the following: In a particular account there was no recovery in the past 18 months. The bank has not applied the NPA norms as well as income recognition norms to this particular account. When queried the bank management replied that this account was guaranteed by the central government and hence these norms were not applicable. The bank has not invoked the guarantee. Please respond. Would your answer be different if the advance is guaranteed by a State Government? **[May 13 (5 Marks)]**

Ans. : Classification of Government Guaranteed advances:

- The credit facilities backed by Central Government guarantee, though overdue will be classified as NPA only when the govt. repudiates its guarantee when invoked. Credit facilities backed by State Government guarantee should be classified as NPA in normal way.
- This exemption in case of Central Government is only for the purpose of asset classification and provisioning and not for the purpose of recognition of income
- Interest on government guaranteed advances should not be taken to Income Account unless it has been realized.

- In the present case, bank has not revoked the guarantee, the question of repudiation does not arise. Therefore, advance need not be classified as NPA in case of Central Government Guarantee. However, as this exemption is not available in respect of income recognition norms, the income to the extent not recovered should be reversed.

Conclusion: Bank is correct to the extent of not applying the NPA norms for provisioning purpose. But this exemption is not available in respect of income recognition norms. The situation would be different if the advance is guaranteed by State Government because this exception is not applicable for State Government Guaranteed advances.

Q.18 Write short note on: Reversal of Income under Bank audit. [Nov. 10, Nov. 19-Old Syllabus (4 Marks),]

Ans. : Reversal of Income under Bank Audit:

Provisions as per Master Circular issued by RBI w.r.t. reversal of income are as follows:

(*i*) **First time NPAs:** If a Loan/Advance is treated as NPA for the first time, interest accrued which has not been realized but credited to the Income Account should be reversed or provided for.

(*ii*) **Commission/other Income:** If Interest Income is recognized on cash basis, then Commission and other such income with respect to the same Borrower, which has been recognized on accrual basis in the Important but has not been realized, should be reversed or provided for with respect to Important.

(*iii*) **Finance Charge of leased assets:** The finance charge component of finance income [as defined in AS 19 -Leases] on the leased asset which has accrued and was credited to income account before the asset became non-performing, and remaining unrealised, should be reversed or provided for in the current accounting period.

Q.19 As a branch auditor of a Nationalised bank, how would you classify the following advances based on securities?

(*i*) Advances covered by ECGC/DISGC guarantees.

(*ii*) An account which is fully secured but the margin in which is lower than that stipulated by the bank.

(*iii*) Advances covered against cheques purchased including self cheques.

(*iv*) Advances against supply bill.

Ans. : Classification of Advances based on Securities:

An advance should be treated as secured to the extent of the value of the security on the balance sheet date. If only a part of the advance is covered by the value of the security as at the date of the balance sheet, that part only should be classified as secured; the remaining amount should be classified as unsecured.

(*i*) Advances covered by ECGC/DICGC guarantees should be treated as covered by guarantees to the extent of guarantee cover available. The amount already received from ECGC/DICGC and kept in sundry creditors account pending adjustment should be deducted from advances.

(*ii*) An account which is fully secured but the margin in which is lower than that stipulated by the bank should nevertheless be treated as fully secured for the purposes of balance sheet presentation.

(*iii*) Cheques purchased including self-cheques (i.e., where the drawer and payee are one and the same) should be treated as unsecured.

(*iv*) Advances against supply bills, unless collaterally secured, should be classified as unsecured even if they have been accepted by the drawees.

Q.20 The bank's advance portfolio comprised of significant loans against Life Insurance Policies. Write suitable audit program to verify these advances. [May 13 (3 Marks)]

Ans. : Verification of Advances against life insurance policies:

Audit program for the verification of advances against life insurance policies need to cover the following:

1. Inspect the policies and see whether they are assigned to the bank and whether such assignment has been registered with the insurer.
2. Examine whether premium has been paid on the policies and whether they are in force.
3. Obtain Certificate regarding surrender value from the insurer.
4. The auditor should particularly see that if such surrender value is subject to payment of certain premia, the amount of such premia has been deducted from the surrender value.

Q.21 As a statutory auditor, how would you verify advances against goods?

Ans. : Verification of Advances against goods:

Auditor need to verify the following:

1. **Sanctioning**: Auditor should examine the sanction letter and loan documents to ascertain important terms and conditions.
2. **Verification of Stock statements**: To ascertain the quantity and value of goods hypothecated.
3. **Inspection**: Ascertain whether the premises of the borrowers are periodically inspected by the bank officials to verify the quantity as per the stock statements.
4. **Stock Audit**: Review the stock audit report and identify whether the report contains any adverse comments.
5. **Insurance**: Ascertain whether the stock is appropriately insured and policies are in favour of the bank.
6. **Documents of title**: Inspect the documents of title to goods to ensure that they are endorsed in favour of the bank.

Q.22 During the bank audit AB & Co. a new Chartered Accountant firm, observed the sale/purchase of NPAs. Please help them by narrating the aspects, relating to sale/purchase of NPAs, to be considered.

[May 15 (4 Marks)]

Or

In the course of audit of Skip Bank Ltd., you found that the bank had sold certain of its non-performing assets. Draft the points of audit check that are very relevant to this area of checking.

[May 18 - New Syllabus (4 Marks)]

Ans. : Sale/Purchase of NPA:

- RBI issued guidelines to banks in respect of sale/purchase of NPAs which requires Board of Directors of the banks to lay down policy in respect of the aspects relating to sale/purchase of NPAs, including procedure for purchase/sale, valuation procedure, delegation of powers & accounting policy etc. Any purchase/sale of non-performing financial assets should be conducted in accordance with the policy approved by the Board.
- Banks should, while selling NPAs, work out the NPV of the estimated cash flows associated with the realisable value of the available securities net of the cost of realisation. The sale price should generally not be lower than the NPV so arrived.
- A bank may purchase/sell non-performing financial assets from/to other banks only on 'without recourse' basis.
- Banks should ensure that subsequent to sale of the non-performing financial assets to other banks, they do not have any involvement with reference to assets sold and do not assume operational, legal or any other type of risks relating to the financial assets sold.
- A non-performing asset in the books of a bank is eligible for sale to other banks only if it has remained a non-performing asset for at least two years in the books of the selling bank.
- NPAs can be sold to other banks only on cash basis. The entire sale consideration should be received upfront and the asset can be taken out of the books of the selling bank only on receipt of the entire sale consideration.
- A non-performing financial asset (NPFA) should be held by the purchasing bank in its books at least for a period of 15 months before it is sold to other banks. Banks should not sell such assets back to the bank, which had sold the NPFA.

"ICAI Examiner Comments"

Many candidates wrongly mentioned the prudential norms for classification of NPAs. They did not highlight the aspects to be considered regarding Purchase/Sales of NPAs.

Q.23 Write short note on: Verification of Provision for Non-performing assets.

Ans. : Verification of Provision for Non-Performing Assets:

- Study the latest Master Circular of RBI to get familiarise with the norms prescribed by RBI in relation to provisioning requirements for NPA. The circulars issued by RBI after the date of issue of Master Circular and till the date of audit should also be considered.

- Provisioning norms as laid down in the master circular should be construed as the minimum provisioning requirements and wherever a higher provision is warranted in the context of the threats to recovery, ensure that higher provision is made by the bank.
- Examine whether the classification made by the branch into Standard, Sub-standard, doubtful and loss assets is appropriate.
- Examine whether the secured and the unsecured portions of advances have been segregated correctly and provisions have been calculated properly.
- As per the RBI guidelines, if an account has been regularised before the balance sheet date by payment of overdue amount through genuine sources, the account need not be treated as NPA. However if an account indicates inherent weakness, the account should be deemed as a NPA. In other genuine cases, auditor need to examine satisfactory evidence about the manner of regularisation of the account to eliminate doubts on their performing status.
- Date of NPA is of significant importance to determine the classification and hence specific care be taken in this regard and ensure that the classification is made as per the position as on date and hence classification of all standard accounts be reviewed as on balance sheet date.

Q.24 Write short note on: Audit Procedure for Accounts falling under Corporate Debt Restructuring (CDR) Programme.

Ans. : Verification of Accounts falling under Corporate Debt Restructuring Programme:

(*a*) Review the present classification of the account under IRAC norms adopted by the bank and corresponding provision made in the books of account, if any.

(*b*) If the account is already treated as NPA, the same cannot be upgraded only because of the CDR package.

(*c*) Review the Debtor-Creditor Agreement (DCA) and Inter Creditor Agreement (ICA) with respect to availability of such agreements and necessary provisions in the agreement for reference to CDR cell.

(*d*) Ascertain the terms of rehabilitation along with the sacrifices, if any, assumed in the rehabilitation program to verify whether such sacrifices have been accounted in the books of account of the lender.

(*e*) Ascertain whether any additional financing/conversion of loan into equity have been envisaged in the rehabilitation/restructuring program.

(*f*) Ascertain whether account has been referred to BIFR, as such cases are not eligible for restructuring under CDR system. Large value BIFR cases may be eligible for restructuring under CDR if specifically recommended by CDR core group. Auditor has to verify the necessary approvals/recommendations by CDR core group if auditor comes across any BIFR cases.

(*g*) Ensure that accounts wherein recovery suits have been filed, the initiative to resolve under CDR system is taken by at least by 75% of the creditors by value and 60% in number.

Q.25 As the concurrent auditor of Nagpur Main Branch of XYZ Bank Ltd. state the issues which have to be considered in the audit of advances. [Nov. 08 (6 Marks)]

Or

Your firm has been appointed as branch auditor of East West Bank Ltd. In carrying out verification of advances, what are the primary evidences you will look into? [May 18 - Old Syllabus (4 Marks)]

Ans. : Verification of Advances:

Concurrent auditor is required to consider the following issues in the audit of advances:

1. Ensure that loans and advances are sanctioned properly.
2. Verify whether the sanctions are in accordance with the delegated authority.
3. Ensure that securities and documents have been received and properly charged/registered.
4. Ensure that post disbursement supervision and follow up is proper.
5. Verify whether there is any misuse of loans and advances and whether there are instances indicative of diversion of funds.
6. Check whether letters of credit issued by the branch are within the delegated power and ensure that they are genuine trade transactions.

7. Check bank guarantees issued are properly worked and recorded.
8. Ensure proper follow up of over due bills of exchange.
9. Verify the classifications of advances are as per RBI directions.
10. Verify whether the submission of claims to DICGC and ECGC is in time.
11. Verify the instances of exceeding delegated powers have been promptly reported.
12. Verify the frequency and genuineness of such exercise of authority beyond to delegated powers of the concerned officials.

Q.26 M/s Sri & Co., Chartered Accountant have been allotted the branch audit of a nationalized bank for the year ended 31st March, 2019. You are part of audit team and have been instructed by your partner to verify the following areas:

(*i*) Fulfilment of the criteria prescribed for NPA norms for the advances given for agricultural purposes.

(*ii*) Drawing power calculation from stock statements in respect of working capital accounts.

What may be your areas of concern as regards matters specified above?[May 19 - Old Syllabus (5 Marks)]

Ans. : (*i*) Criteria prescribed for NPA Norms in respect of agricultural advances:

Refer answer of Q. No. 14

(*ii*) Verification of Drawing Power Calculation from stock statements:

(*a*) Ensure that the DP is calculated as per the BOD guidelines of the respective bank and agreed upon by the concerned statutory auditors.

(*b*) Ensure that due consideration has been given to proper reporting of sundry creditors for the purposes of calculating DP.

(*c*) Ensure that bank has conducted stock audit for all accounts having exposure of more than stipulated limit. Review the report submitted by the stock auditors and consider the comments made by the stock auditors on valuation of security and calculation of drawing power.

(*d*) Special focus needs to be given in examining the DP calculation in case of working capital advances to companies engaged in construction business.

21.6 VERIFICATION OF OTHER ITEMS

Q.27 Describe the procedure for verification of balances of drafts paid without advice in the account books of a bank.

Ans. : Procedure for verification of balances of drafts paid without advice:

It represents payments made on account of drafts issued by other branches but for which the relevant advice from those branches have not been received. Auditor should perform the following procedures:

(*i*) Examine the following:

- System of verifying the genuineness of the draft by reference to specimen signature of the signing authority;
- System of co-relating drafts paid, with advices subsequently received;
- System of sending reminders, where advices are not received within a reasonable time and the recording of reasons for their non-receipt.

(*ii*) Verify the composition of the balances appearing in this account with particular reference to any long outstanding items.

(*iii*) Verify whether the items appearing in this account have been subsequently cleared on receipt of the relevant advices.

(*iv*) Verify that the bank maintain a record of names and addresses of the payees of such drafts.

Q.28 While auditing the branch of a Bank you are required to examine inter branch adjustments. What points require your special attention. [May 10 (6 Marks)]

Or

Describe the procedure for verification of Branch Adjustment Account appearing in the account books of a bank.

Ans. : Examination of Inter Branch Adjustments (Branch Adjustment Account):

It represent the balance of all inter-branch transactions of the bank. The same are to be disclosed "NET". If the inter-office adjustment (Net) is a debit, it is to be shown under "other assets" and if it is a credit, it is shown under "other Liabilities and Provisions". These can be sub-divided into segments like DD paid, Inter-branch remittances, Head Office Account, etc.

The auditor should pay special attention to the following points:

(*a*) The origin and validity of old outstanding unmatched entries, particularly debit entries. The auditor may also seek confirmation of transactions relating to outstanding.

(*b*) Whether there are any reversal entries indicating the possibilities of irregular payments or frauds.

(*c*) Whether the balances include any items in the nature of cash-in-transit, which remain pending for more than a reasonable period. This is because such items are not expected to remain outstanding beyond a very small period during which they are in transit.

(*d*) Whether transactions, other than those relating to inter-branch transactions have been included in inter-branch accounts.

(*e*) Any unusual items put through inter-branch accounts as well as old or large entries outstanding in inter-branch accounts should be carefully looked into. The auditor may also seek explanations from the management in this regard

Q.29 INDO Bank appointed your firm of Chartered Accountants as a branch auditor for the financial year 2018-19. Being head-in-charge of the assignment, while planning, you distributed the work among your team members and assigned Mr. Pary for verification of bills payable. However, Mr. Pary, being fresh to the bank audits, needs your guidance. Kindly guide. [MTP-Oct. 19]

Ans. : Verification of Bills Payable:

(*i*) Evaluate the existence, effectiveness and continuity of internal controls over bills payable. Such controls should usually include the following-

- Drafts, mail transfers, traveller's cheques, etc. should be made out in standard printed forms.
- Unused forms relating to drafts, traveller's cheques, etc. should be kept under the custody of a responsible officer.
- The bank should have a reliable private code known only to the responsible officers of its branches, coding and decoding of the telegrams should be done only by such officers.
- The signatures on a demand draft should be checked by an officer with the specimen signature book.
- All the telegraphic transfers and demand drafts issued by a branch should be immediately confirmed by advices to the branches concerned. On payment of these instruments, the paying branch should send a debit advice to the originating branch.

(*ii*) Examine an appropriate sample of outstanding items comprised in bills payable accounts with the relevant registers. Reasons for old outstanding debits in respect of drafts or other similar instruments paid without advice should be ascertained.

(*iii*) Correspondence with other branches after the year-end (e.g., responding advices received from other branches, advices received from other branches in respect of drafts issued by the branch and paid by the other branches without advice) should be examined specially in so far as large value items outstanding on the balance sheet date are concerned.

Q.30 While auditing APNA Bank, you observed that a lump sum amount has been disclosed as contingent liability collectively. You are, therefore, requested by the management to guide them about the disclosure requirement of Contingent Liabilities for Banks. Kindly guide.

Or

Briefly explain the disclosure requirements of Contingent Liabilities for banks.

Ans. : Disclosure Requirements of Contingent Liabilities:

The Third Schedule to the Banking Regulation Act, 1949, requires the disclosure of the following as a footnote to the balance sheet.

(*i*) Claims against the bank not acknowledged as debts.

(*ii*) Liability for partly paid investments.

(*iii*) Liability on account of outstanding forward exchange contracts.

(*iv*) Guarantees given on behalf of constituents-

- In India.
- Outside India.

(*v*) Acceptances, endorsements and other obligations.

(*vi*) Other items for which the bank is contingently liable.

Q.31 Describe the audit procedures to be followed by a Statutory Auditor of a bank for audit of contingent liabilities.

Ans. : Verification of Contingent Liabilities:

In respect of contingent liabilities, the auditor is primarily concerned with seeking reasonable assurance that all contingent liabilities are identified and property valued.

Auditor should generally follow the audit procedures given below:

(*a*) Ascertain whether there are adequate internal controls to ensure that transactions giving rise to contingent liabilities are executed only by persons authorised to do so and in accordance with the laid down procedures.

(*b*) Ascertain whether the accounting system of the bank provides for maintenance of adequate records in respect of such obligations and whether the internal controls insures that contingent liabilities are properly identified and recorded.

(*c*) Perform substantive audit tests to establish the completeness of the recorded obligations. Such tests include confirmation procedures and examination of relevant records in appropriate cases.

(*d*) Review the reasonableness of the year end amount of contingent liabilities in the light of previous experience and knowledge of the current year's activities.

(*e*) Obtain representation from the management that all contingent liabilities have been disclosed and that the disclosed contingent liabilities do not include any contingencies which are likely to result in a loss and which, therefore, require adjustments of assets or liabilities.

(*f*) Ensure Compliance of AS 29, "Provisions, contingent liabilities and contingent assets".

Q.32 While doing the audit of a Nationalised bank branch, your audit assistant informed you that he suspects some irregularities in Guarantees issued by the Bank. What should be your guidance in the matter to check the same? **[May 18 - Old Syllabus (4 Marks)]**

Ans : Verification points for checking irregularities in guarantees issued by the bank:

(*a*) Examine the adequacy of internal controls exercised over issuance of guarantees, for example, whether guarantees are sanctioned by appropriate authority, whether adequate margins are taken from customers before issuance of guarantees, etc.

(*b*) Examine the adequacy of controls exercised over unused guarantee forms, for example, whether unused forms are kept under the custody of a responsible official, whether a proper record of forms issued is being kept, whether stock of forms is periodically verified and reconciled with the book records, etc.

(*c*) Examine whether the prescribed procedure of marking off the expired guarantees is being followed or not.

(*d*) Examine the relevant guarantee registers with the list of outstanding guarantees to ensure that all outstanding guarantees are included in the amount disclosed.

(*e*) Examine that expired guarantees are not included in this head.

(*f*) Verify guarantees with the copies of the letters of guarantee issued by the bank and with the counter-guarantees received from the customers.

(*g*) Verify the securities held as margin.

(*h*) Ensure whether a provision is required in terms of the requirements of AS 29, "Provisions, Contingent Liabilities and Contingent Assets", in case any claim arises under these guarantees.

Q.33 How would you verify "Acceptances, Endorsements and other obligations" appearing in the Balance Sheet of a bank?

Ans. : Verification of Acceptances, Endorsements and Other Obligations:

Acceptance, Endorsements and Other Obligations includes the following balances:

(*a*) Letters of credit (LC) opened by the bank on behalf of its customers and

(*b*) Bills drawn by the bank's customers and accepted/endorsed by the bank.

Points to be examined w.r.t. Letters of credit:

1. Evaluate the adequacy of the internal controls over LC Forms e.g. custody, maintenance of records, periodical verification, reconciliation etc.
2. Verify the balance of LC from the Register maintained by the bank to ascertain the amount of LC and payments made under them.
3. Examine the guarantees of the customers, copies of the LC issued & security obtained for issuing LC.

Points to be examined w.r.t. other acceptances and endorsements:

(*i*) Examine the arrangements made by the bank with its customers.

(*ii*) Test check the amounts of bills with the register maintained by the bank.

(*iii*) Verify whether such bills are marked off in the register on payment at maturity.

Q.34 How do you examine claims against the Bank not acknowledged as debts? [May 10 (4 Marks)]

Ans. : Examination of Claims against the bank not acknowledged as debts:

The following points should be considered so as to examine the claims against the bank not acknowledged as debts:

(*i*) The auditor should examine the relevant evidence, for example correspondence with lawyers, claimants, workers/officers and workmen's/officers' unions.

(*ii*) The auditor should also review the minutes of the meeting of the Board of directors/committees of the Board, contracts, agreements and arrangements, list of pending legal cases and correspondence relating to taxes, duties etc., to identify claims against the bank.

(*iii*) The auditor should ascertain from the management the status of claims outstanding as at the end of previous year.

(*iv*) A review of subsequent events would also provide evidence about completeness and valuation of claims.

Q.35 As statutory central auditors of a Nationalised Bank, what special points are to be borne in mind in the audit of compliance with "Statutory Liquidity Ratio" (SLR) requirements?

Or

You have been appointed as a statutory central auditor of AAPKA Bank, a Nationalized bank. What special points would you borne in mind while conducting the audit of compliance with "Statutory Liquidity Ratio" (SLR) requirements?

Ans. : Audit of Compliance of SLR Requirements:

Central statutory auditors are required to verify the compliance of SLR on 12 odd dates in different months not having Fridays. The resultant report is to be sent to the management of the bank and to the RBI. To verify compliance with SLR requirements, the statutory auditor has to examine two aspects:

(*a*) The correctness of the figure of the DTL at the close of business on the reporting Friday relevant to the dates selected by the auditor, and

(*b*) Maintenance of prescribed percentage of liquid assets on the selected date.

Steps for verification

1. Obtain an understanding of the relevant circulars of the RBI so as to ascertain the items to be included in composition of DTL.
2. Request the branch auditors to verify the correctness of the trial balances and examine the cash balance at the branch on the selected dates.
3. Examine, on a test basis, the consolidations regarding DTL position prepared by the head office with reference to the related returns received from branches. Ensure that the consolidations prepared by the bank include the relevant information in respect of all the branches.

4. Examine the composition of items of DTL as per circulars/instructions of RBI.
5. Ensure that the interest accrued but not accounted for in the books is included in composition of DTL.
6. Specify number of unaudited branches and a statement that auditor has relied on the returns received from the unaudited branches in forming his opinion.

21.7 CONCURRENT AUDIT SYSTEM

Q.36 Discuss the concurrent audit system in commercial banks.

Or

Explain the scope of concurrent audit of a bank with reference to RBI guidelines.

Ans. : Scope of Concurrent Audit System:

Concurrent audit is an examination which is contemporaneous with the occurrence of transactions. It attempts to shorten the interval between a transaction and its examination by an independent person not involved in its documentation. There is an emphasis in favour of substantive checking in key areas rather than test checking. It is considered as part of bank's early-warning system to ensure timely detection of irregularities.

Coverage: Concurrent audit should cover the following:

(*a*) Branches whose total credit and other risk exposures aggregate to not less than 50% of the total credit and other risk exposures of the bank; and

(*b*) Branches whose aggregate deposits cover not less than 50% of the aggregate deposits of the Bank.

In addition to the above-mentioned parameter, bank should ensure the coverage of following:

(*a*) Exceptionally large, very large and large branches;

(*b*) Special branches handling foreign exchange business and merchant banking business.

(*c*) Branches rated as poor/very poor.

(*d*) Head Office department dealing with treasury/funds management and handling investment portfolio.

(*e*) Other branches or departments where in the opinion of the Bank concurrent audit is desirable.

Scope of Concurrent Audit

1. Daily cash transactions with reference to abnormal receipts and payments. This will include currency chest transactions, major expenses met by cash, high value receipts and disbursements.
2. Purchase and sale of shares, securities etc. Physical verification of investments and rates at which they are entered into.
3. Verification of procedure and documentation to open new current, savings, term deposit accounts, etc. Unusual operations noticed have to be thoroughly examined.
4. Verification of advances, overdrafts, temporary OD, Cash credit accounts, term loans, bills purchase, letters of credit etc. Procedure for sanction and documentation to be verified. Any deviation noticed to be examined in great detail.
5. Foreign exchange transactions to be verified with reference to RBI guidelines.
6. Verification of balancing of all ledgers and registers, inter branch reconciliation calculation and verification of interest, discount, commission etc.
7. Revenue leakage to be detected.
8. Special efforts to be made in all fraud prone areas. The attempt should be to ensure that all effective measures are taken to prevent frauds.
9. Verification of high value transactions.
10. Procedure for safe custody of security forms with the branch.
11. Whether all procedures for tax deduction at source are followed and the tax so deducted are deposited into Government Account within the time fixed.
12. Verification of returns, statements, calculation of capital adequacy ratio and compliance with requirements of government business.

13. Study of RBI and Internal Inspection reports, statutory auditor's report and compliance thereto.
14. Whether the customers' complaints are dealt with promptly.

Q.37 As the concurrent auditor of Nagpur Main Branch of XYZ Bank Ltd. state the issues which have to be considered in the audit of advances. [Nov. 08 (6 Marks)]

Or

ABC Chartered Accountants have been appointed as concurrent auditors for the branches of Effective Bank Ltd. for the year 2018-19. You are part of the audit team for Agra branch of the bank and have been instructed by your senior to verify the advances of the audit period. You are required to guide your assistant about the areas to be taken care while doing verification during the concurrent audit. [RTP-May 19]

Ans. : Areas to be taken care in verification of advances:

1. Ensure that loans and advances have been sanctioned properly.
2. Verify whether the sanctions are in accordance with delegated authority.
3. Ensure that securities and documents have been received and properly charged/registered.
4. Ensure that post disbursement supervision and follow-up is proper.
5. Verify whether there is any misutilisation of the loans and whether there are instances indicative of diversion of funds.
6. Check whether the letters of credit issued by the branch are within the delegated power and ensure that they are for genuine trade transactions.
7. Check bank guarantees issued, whether they have been properly worded and recorded.
8. Ensure proper follow-up of overdue bills of exchange.
9. Verify whether the classification of advances are as per RBI guidelines.
10. Verify whether the submission of claims to DICGC and ECGC is in time.
11. Verify that instances of exceeding delegated powers have been promptly reported
12. Verify the frequency and genuineness of such exercise of authority beyond the delegated powers by the concerned officials.

Q.38 You are the Concurrent Auditor of a Branch of Nationalized Bank which deals in foreign exchange transactions. Give focus areas of your checking in this respect. [Nov. 18-New Syllabus (4 Marks)]

Or

You have been appointed as Concurrent Auditor of a nationalized bank branch. The main business at the branch is dealing in foreign exchange. Suggest the main areas of coverage in regard to foreign exchange transactions of the said branch under concurrent audit. [Nov. 19 - Old Syllabus (5 Marks)]

Ans. : Focus area in checking of foreign exchange transactions:

Foreign exchange transactions to be verified with reference to RBI guidelines. Important points of verification in this respect are:

1. Check foreign bills negotiated under letters of credit.
2. Check Foreign Currency Non-Resident and other non-resident accounts to ensure that only permissible transactions route through these accounts.
3. Check whether inward/outward remittance have been properly accounted for.
4. Examine extension and cancellation of forward contracts for purchase and sale of foreign currency. Ensure that they are duly authorised and necessary charges have been recovered.
5. Ensure that the overbought/oversold position maintained in different currencies is reasonable considering the foreign exchange operations.
6. Ensure compliance of the guidelines issued by RBI/HO of the bank.
7. Ensure that balances in Nostro accounts in different foreign currencies are within the limit as prescribed by the bank.
8. Verify transactions of Nostro and Vostro account and their reconciliation statements.

21.8 MISCELLANEOUS QUESTIONS

Q.39 As a branch auditor of a nationalised bank, how would you verify the advances to Dot Com Companies.

Ans. : Verification of Advances to Dotcom Companies:

(1) Examine the internal control system w.r.t. determination of credit worthiness of the borrower and sanctioning of advances by appropriate authorities.

(2) Examine documents relating to compliances of regulatory provisions of Companies Act, 2013 such as resolution of board of directors and resolution of shareholders.

(3) Verify the business plan of the company.

(4) Determine the sources of funds, whether the company depends only on outside funding or can self generate funds.

(5) Review the transactions in the account to ensure the outstanding does not exceed the limit sanctioned and the account is not window-dressed by running down overdrafts at the year end and again drawing further advances in the new year.

(6) Examine whether the amount of credits in the account are commensurate with the nature and volume of business of the borrower. Any unusual items in the account should be carefully examined by the auditor.

(7) Review periodic statements, cash flow statements, latest financial statements, etc. to assess the recoverability of advances.

(8) Verify the security exist in the account and determine whether the security is legally enforceable and is in the effective control of the bank.

(9) Ensure that proper provisions has been made in case of irregular accounts.

Q.40 Write a short note on - Vostro and Nostro Accounts.

Or

Your firm has been appointed as statutory Branch auditor of a Nationalised Bank for the financial year 2017-18 which is dealing in Nostro accounts. Enumerate the audit procedures you will follow for verification of Nostro accounts. [Nov. 18-Old Syllabus (4 Marks)]

Ans. : Vostro and Nostro account:

Meaning of Vostro Account: "Vostro Account" is the opposite of Nostro accounts. Here a foreign bank in another country maintains stocks of Indian rupees with their Indian branch/correspondent/local bank.

Meaning of Nostro A/c: Foreign currency accounts maintained by Indian banks at other overseas centres is designated by it as "Nostro Account".

Examination Aspects

1. **Reconciliation:** Unreconciled Nostro Accounts, on an examination, may reveal unauthorized payments from the foreign currency account, unauthorized withdrawals.
2. **Evaluation of I.C. w.r.t. inward/outward message:** The inward/outward messages should be properly authenticated and discrepancies noticed, should be properly dealt with, in the books of account.
3. **Inter bank confirmation:** In case balance confirmation certificate have been received but the same have not been reconciled, or where confirmation has not been received the same should be reported, in respect of each Account.

Q.41 As a branch auditor of a nationalized bank, how would you verify the Balances in account of a bank situated in a foreign country.

Or

NAYA Bank appointed your firm of Chartered Accountants as a branch auditor for the financial year 2016-17. Being head in-charge of the assignment, while planning, you distributed the work among your team members and assigned Mr. Gary for verification of Balances in account of the bank situated in foreign country. However, Mr. Gary being fresh to the bank audits, needs your guidance. Kindly guide.

Ans. : Verification of Balance in account of a bank situated in foreign country:

1. Examine the ledger balances in each account with reference to the confirmation certificates obtained from the bank and reconciliation statements available.

2. Review the reconciliation statements to examine the following:
   - No debit for charges or credit for interest is outstanding and all the items which ought to have been taken to revenue for the year have been considered.
   - No cheque sent or received in clearing is outstanding.
   - All bills or outstanding cheques sent for collection and outstanding as on the closing date have been credited subsequently.
3. Examine the large transactions in the accounts, particularly near the year-end, to ensure that there is no manipulation in the account.
4. In respect of year end balance, obtain confirmation certificates from the banks and examine the original deposit receipts.
5. Ensure compliance of AS 11"Accounting for the Effects of Changes in Foreign Exchange Rates". In regard to conversion of balance into the Indian currency at the exchange rates prevailing on the balance sheet date.

Q.42 What do you understand by Long-form Audit Report? [Nov. 08 (2 Marks)]

Ans. : Long Form Audit report:

- The Long Form Audit Report has to be furnished by the auditor of a bank in addition to the audit report as per the statutory requirement.
- The matters which the banks require their auditor to deal with in the form of Long Form Audit Report have been specified by the RBI.
- The LFAR is to be submitted before 30th June every year. To ensure timely submission of LFAR, proper planning for completion of the LFAR is required. While the format of LFAR does not require an executive summary to be given, members may consider providing the same to bring out the key observations from the whole document.

Q.43 As a bank branch auditor, what aspects will be considered while reporting on credit appraisal, sanctioning/ disbursement and documentation in respect of advances in the LFAR? [Nov. 11 (5 Marks)]

Ans. : Aspects to be considered in LFAR:

Credit Appraisal: Compliance with the procedure/instructions of the controlling authorities of the bank, regarding loan applications, preparation of proposals for grant/renewal of advances, enhancement of limits etc. including adequate appraisal documentation in respect thereof.

Sanctioning/Disbursement

(*i*) Instance of credit facilities having been sanctioned beyond the delegated authority or limit fixed for the branch?

(*ii*) Instances where advances have been disbursed without complying with the terms and conditions of the sanctions?

Documentation

(*i*) Instances of credit facilities without complying without execution of necessary documents.

(*ii*) Instances of deficiencies in documentation, non-registration of charges, non-obtaining guarantees etc.

(*iii*) Making a lien on deposits in case of advances given against deposits in accordance with the guidelines of the controlling authorities of the bank?

Verification points: For the reporting of above-mentioned points in LFAR, the auditor should examine the following:

1. Whether the loan applications are complete and in prescribed form;
2. Procedural instructions regarding grant/renewal/enhancement of facilities have been complied with;
3. Sanctions are within delegated authority and disbursements are as per terms of the sanction;
4. Documentation is complete; and supervision is timely, effective and as per prescribed guidelines.

The auditor is required to collect the appropriate evidences by examining relevant documents (such as loan application forms, supporting documentation, sanction letters, security documents, etc.) and by obtaining information and explanations from the branch manager.

AUDIT OF GENERAL INSURANCE COMPANIES

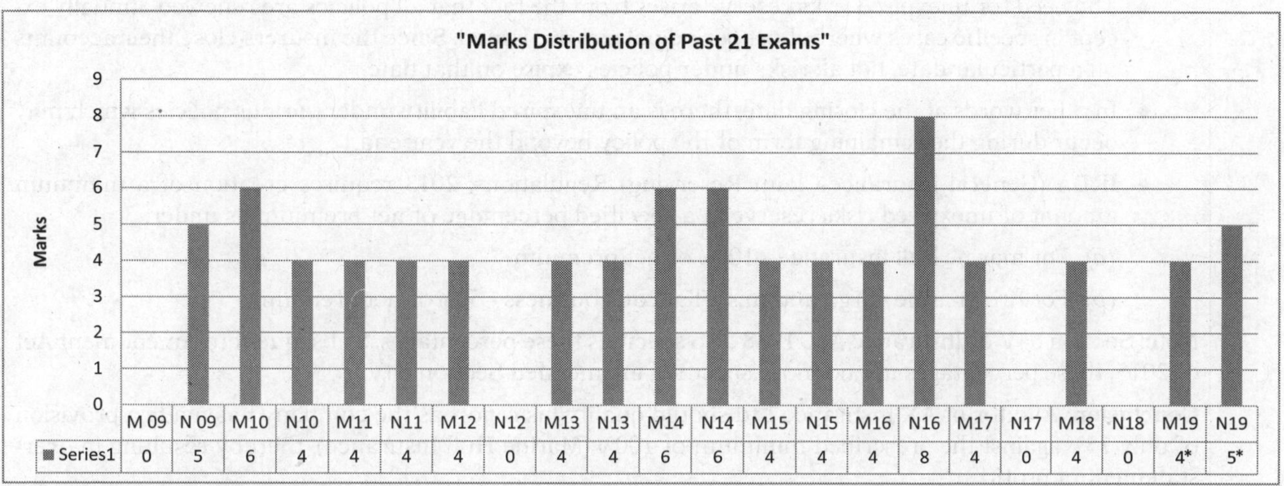

*Only Subjective Questions.

22.1 REGULATORY REQUIREMENTS OF INSURANCE ACT, 1938

Q.1 Write short note on: Solvency Margin. [May 12 (4 Marks)]

Or

Discuss Solvency Margin in case of an Insurer carrying on General Insurance Business. [May 19 - Old Syllabus (4 Marks)]

Ans. : Solvency Margin (Sec. 64VA of Insurance Act, 1938 as amended by Insurance Laws (Amendment) Act, 2015):

1. **Requirement of solvency margin**: Sec. 64VA of Insurance Act, 1938 requires that every insurer and re-insurer shall at all times maintain an excess of value of assets over the amount of liabilities of, not less than 50% of the amount of minimum capital as stated u/s 6 and arrived at in the manner specified by the regulations.

2. **Non-compliance of solvency margin**: An insurer or re-insurer, as the case may be, who does not comply with the requirement of solvency margin shall be deemed to be insolvent and may be wound-up by the court on an application made by the Authority.

3. **Power of authority to prescribe level of solvency**: The Authority shall by way of regulation made for the purpose, specify a level of solvency margin known as control level of solvency on the breach of which the Authority shall act in accordance with without prejudice to taking of any other remedial measures as deemed fit.

4. **Submission of Financial Plan**: If, at any time, an insurer or re-insurer does not maintain the required control level of solvency margin, he shall, in accordance with the directions issued by the Authority, submit a financial plan to the Authority, indicating a plan of action to correct the deficiency within a specified period not exceeding six months.

5. **Modifications to Financial Plan**: If the authority considers the financial plan submitted by an insurer inadequate, it shall propose modifications to the plan and shall give directions, as may be deemed necessary, including direction in regard to transacting any new business, or, appointment of an administrator or both.
6. **Non-submission of financial plan**: An insurer or re-insurer, as the case may be, who does not submit financial plan shall be deemed to have made default in complying with the requirements of this section.

Q.2 AX Insurance Limited has made a provision of 75% of net premium in case of marine hull insurance and 50% in case of marine cargo and miscellaneous business of net premium for unexpired risks reserve in its books. Comment. [Nov. 15 (4 Marks)]

Ans. : Reserve for Unexpired Risks:

- The need for unexpired risks reserve arises from the fact that all policies are renewed annually except in specific cases where short period policies are issued. Since the insurers close their accounts on a particular date, not all risks under policies expire on that date.
- In other words at the closing date, there is an unexpired liability under various policies which may occur during the remaining term of the policy beyond the year end.
- IRDA (General insurance-Claim Reserving) Regulations, 2013 requires creation of a minimum amount of unexpired risks reserve at a specified percentage of net premium as under:
  (*a*) For marine hull insurance - 100% of net premium
  (*b*) For fire, marine cargo and miscellaneous business - 50% of net premium.

Note: Section 64V of Insurance Act, 1938 also specifies these percentages. Subsequent to Amendment Act of 2015, these percentages are no more specified in amended Section 64V.

Conclusion: Auditor of AX Insurance Ltd should qualify his report as the company has made a provision of only 75% against the prescribed minimum of 100% (Marine Hull Insurance), thereby resulting in overstatement of profit.

Q.3 You have been appointed as an auditor of a General Insurance Company. In this context, explain Unexpired Risks Reserve and audit procedures for the same. [Nov. 19 - Old Syllabus (5 Marks)]

Ans. : Reserve for Unexpired Risks:

- The need for unexpired risks reserve arises from the fact that all policies are renewed annually except in specific cases where short period policies are issued. Since the insurers close their accounts on a particular date, not all risks under policies expire on that date.
- In other words, at the closing date, there is an unexpired liability under various policies which may occur during the remaining term of the policy beyond the year end.
- There are two methods of creating this reserve. One is based on the proportionate number of days of risk remaining to risk expired, which is called 1/365 method. The other method is by taking a URR directly on 50% of the premium amount.
- IRDA (General Insurance-Claim Reserving) Regulations, 2013 requires creation of a minimum amount of unexpired risks reserve at a specified percentage of net premium as under:
  (*a*) For marine hull insurance - 100% of net premium
  (*b*) For fire, marine cargo and miscellaneous business - 50% of net premium.

Note: Section 64V of Insurance Act, 1938 also specifies these percentages. Subsequent to Amendment Act of 2015, these percentages are no more specified in amended Section 64V.

22.2 CONTROL PROCEDURES

Q.4 Internal control functions in case of general insurance business can be categorised under main operational cycles. Since various operational cycles are inter -linked, the internal controls operating within the systems of such cycles should be reviewed simultaneously. State the specific control procedures to be evaluated in relation to general insurance business.

Ans. : Specific Control Procedures to be evaluated in relation to General Insurance Business:

1. **Underwriting:** Underwriting function comprises of examination and evaluation of applications for insurance, the rating of risks and the establishment of premiums. Prime objectives of internal control

system for underwriting is adherence to guidelines for acceptances of insurance, proper recording of insurance risk and its evaluation.

2. **Premium:** Premium is the consideration received by an insurer from the insured. Prime objectives of internal controls over premium is to ensure that correct premium is calculated and collected before acceptance of any risk, that premium is accounted for in an appropriate manner and that the premium is collected only in respect of such risks which are assumed by the company.
3. **Commission:** Commission is the consideration payable for getting the insurance business. Prime objectives of internal controls over commission is to ensure that commission is paid in accordance with the rules and regulations of the company, commission is paid to the agent who brought the business and the legal compliances, for example, tax deduction at sources.
4. **Claim:** Claim is the demand for payment of policy benefit because of the occurrence of an insured event. Prime objectives of internal controls over claim are to ensure that only *bona fide* claims are paid. Cost of claims are properly recorded and disclosed in the financial statements.
5. **Reinsurance:** Prime objectives of internal controls over reinsurance transaction is determination of correct amounts for reinsurance ceded, proper valuation of assets and liabilities arising out of reinsurance transactions and adherence to legal provisions, regulations and reinsurance agreements.

22.3 AUDIT OF REVENUE ITEMS

Q.5 What are the steps to be taken while verifying the Premium of a General Insurance Company?

Ans. : Verification of Premium of a General insurance Company:

1. **Review of Internal Control Procedure and Its compliance:**

To ensure the followings:

- Proper cover notes are issued and that no cover note/policy is omitted.
- All cover notes are serially numbered.
- Existence of adequate internal check on issue of stamps, stationery, etc.

Depending on the assurance obtained, decide the extent of substantive checking to be carried out.

2. **Accounting of Premiums**

To Ensure the followings:

- All premiums in respect of risks incepting during the relevant accounting year has been accounted as the premium income of that year.
- Premium received for fire, marine, motor and miscellaneous insurance business is recorded in relevant books of account.
- In respect of risks commencing after the year end, and the premium is received in advance, the same has been shown as "Premium Received in Advance" and see whether the similar advance of last year is accounted this year as income.

3. **Inception of Risk - Sec. 64VB**

To Ensure the followings:

- The company is not at risk in case policy documents have not been issued for any reason like dishonour of cheque and ensure that the risk has not commenced.
- The company is not under risk in respect of amounts lying at credit (Premium received in advance) and outstanding (Uncollected premium) at the year end.

4. **Co-insurance**

Examine whether the company's share of premium have been properly booked in the books of account in case the risk has commenced.

Q.6 **As at 31st March, 2017 while auditing Safe Insurance Ltd you observed that a policy has been issued on 25th March, 2017 for fire risk favouring one of the leading corporate houses in the country without the actual receipt of premium and it was reflected as premium receivable. The company maintained that it is a usual practice in respect of big customers and the money was collected on 5th April, 2017. You further noticed that there was a fire accident in the premises of the insured on 31st March, 2017 and a claim was lodged for the same. The insurance company also made a provision for claim. Please respond.**

[May 13 (4 Marks)]

Or

While auditing Suryankiran Insurance Ltd. as on 31st March, 2017, you observed that there is one policy which has been issued on 25th March, 2017 towards fire risk favouring one of the leading corporate houses in the country without the actual receipt of premium and it was reflected as premium receivable. It is the usual practice maintained by the company in respect of big customers that they would issue the policy before receiving the premium. The premium money was collected on 5th of April, 2017. It is further noticed that there was a fire accident in the premises of insured on 31st March, 2017 and a claim was lodged. The insurance company also provided for the same.

How would you respond? **[May 16 (4 Marks)]**

Ans. : Inception of Risk:

- As per Section 64VB of the Insurance Act, 1938, no insurer should assume any risk in India in respect of any insurance business on which premium is ordinarily payable in India unless and until the premium payable is received or is guaranteed to be paid by such person in such manner and within such time, as may be prescribed, or unless and until deposit of such amount, as may be prescribed, is made in advance in the prescribed manner.
- In the present case, though policy was issued on 25th March, 2017, but premium was collected only on 5th April, 2017. Applying the provisions of Sec. 64VB, company cannot be held liable for the claim arises due to fire accident happened on 31st March, 2017.

Conclusion: In view of the above, the insurance company is not liable to pay the claim and hence no provision for claim is required.

"ICAI Examiner Comments"

Very few candidates related it to Section 64VB of the Insurance Act, 1938 and explained in a general manner.

Q.7 **You have been appointed as an auditor of ABC Insurance Co. Ltd. and found that M/s PQR Ltd. got their plant & Machinery insured on 01-10-2018 but the amount of premium has been paid by them on 15-10-2018. In the meanwhile, on 10-10-2018 a fire has broken out in the factory and the company filed a claim for damages of plant & machinery with the Insurance company. Advise the insurance company in this regard.** **[May 19 - New Syllabus (5 Marks)]**

Ans. : Inception of Risk:

- As per Section 64VB of the Insurance Act, 1938, no insurer should assume any risk in India in respect of any insurance business on which premium is ordinarily payable in India unless and until the premium payable is received or is guaranteed to be paid by such person in such manner and within such time, as may be prescribed, or unless and until deposit of such amount, as may be prescribed, is made in advance in the prescribed manner.
- In the present case, though plant & Machinery insured on 01.10.2018, but premium was paid only on 15.10.2018. Applying the provisions of Section. 64VB, company cannot be held liable for the claim arises due to fire accident happened on 10.10.2018.

Conclusion: In view of the above, the insurance company is not liable to pay the claim.

Q.8 **What are the specific areas to which you will give your attention while examining "Claims paid" by a General Insurance Company.**

or

While auditing claims paid in respect of a General Insurance company what aspects need to be looked in to. **[May 10 (6 Marks)]**

Or

You are the Auditor of Good Luck General Insurance Company. You want to ensure that there exists goods system that effectively serves the requirements of true and fair accounting of claim-related expenses and liabilities. Suggest how this can be ensured. **[May 18 - New Syllabus (4 Marks)]**

Ans. : Verification of Claims Paid:

The following aspects needs to be examined in respect of claims paid:

(*a*) **Coinsurance**: In case of co-insurance arrangements, claims paid have been booked only in respect of company's share and the balance has been debited to other insurance companies.

(*b*) **Settlement Amount**: Ensure that the Claim Account is debited with all the payments including repair charges, fire fighting expenses, police report fees, survey fees, amount decreed by the Courts, travel expenses, photograph charges, etc.

(*c*) **Claims communicated after the year-end** for losses which occurred prior to the year end must be accounted for in the year of audit.

(*d*) **Accounting for salvage and letter of subrogation**: salvage recovered has been duly accounted company and a letter of subrogation has been obtained in accordance with the procedure.

(*e*) **Amount deposits with courts**: in matters under litigation/arbitration have not been treated as claims paid but are held as assets till final disposal of such claims.

(*f*) **Unqualified Discharge Note**: has been given by claimant in case of final settlement of claims.

Q.9 **ABC & Co., Chartered Accountants are the Auditors of Just Care General Insurance Company Limited. As on March 31, 2015 the Management made a provision for claims outstanding. Enumerate the steps to be taken by the Auditor while verifying the "Claims Provision".** **[Nov. 14 (6 Marks)]**

Ans. : Verification of Claims Provisions:

The auditor should satisfy himself that the estimated liability provided for by the management is adequate with reference to the relevant claim files/dockets, keeping in view the following:

(*a*) Provision has been made for all unsettled claims as at the year-end on the basis of claims lodged/communicated.

(*b*) Provision has been made for only such claims for which the company is legally liable, considering particularly, that:

- the risk was covered by the policy,
- the claims arose during the currency of the policy; and
- claim did not arise during the period the company was not supposed to cover the risk.

(*c*) Provision made should not be in excess of the amount insured.

(*d*) Application of 'average clause' in case of under-insurance.

(*e*) In case of co-insurance arrangements, provisions should be made only in respect of its own share of anticipated liability.

(*f*) Claims are provided for net of estimated salvage, wherever applicable.

Q.10 **Your audit assistant seeks your help in checking the claim liability of Bharat Insurance Co. Ltd. and wants to know the registers and records which they should obtain and review in this regard.** **[May 18 - Old Syllabus (4 Marks)]**

Ans. : Register of Claims:

(*i*) Claims intimation register.

(*ii*) Claims paid register.

(*iii*) Claims Disbursement bank book.

(*iv*) Claims Dockets, normally containing the following records:

Claim intimation, claim forms, particulars of policy, survey report, photograph showing damage, Repairer's bills, letter of subrogation, police report, fire service report, claim settlement note, claim satisfaction note, salvage report, salvage disposal note, claims discharge voucher etc.

(*v*) Report of quality assurance team and

(*vi*) Salvage register.

Q.11 While auditing Secure Insurance Ltd., you observed that the major proportion of expense of the company is the remuneration/commission paid to its insurance agents. As the auditor of the company, what audit procedure would you adopt for verification of such expense?

Or

Write short note on: Verification of payment of remuneration to an insurance agent. [May 17 (4 Marks)]

Or

You have been appointed to carry out the audit of Sky Insurance Company Ltd. for the year 2017-18. In the course of your audit, you observed that the commission paid to agents constituted a major expense in operating expenses of the company. Enumerate the audit concerns that address to the assertions required for the Auditor to ensure the continued existence of internal control as well as fairness of the amounts in accounting of commission paid to agents. [Nov. 18-New Syllabus (4 Marks)]

Ans. : Verification of Commission paid to agents:

An insurance company pays commission to its agents for business procured through them, as per Sec. 40 of the Insurance Act, 1938; no commission can be paid to a person other than its agent. In order to verify the amount of commission, the auditor should:

(*a*) Ensure that commission/brokerage is not paid in excess of the limits specified by IRDAI.

(*b*) Ensure that commission/brokerage is paid as per rates agreed with the agent and filed with IRDAI.

(*c*) Ensure that commission/brokerage is paid to the agent/broker who has solicited the business.

(*d*) Vouch disbursement entries with commission bills.

(*e*) Check whether all disbursements were properly authorized.

(*f*) Check the calculation of commission amount.

(*g*) Scrutinize agent's ledger for any abnormal entries or balance

(*h*) Examine whether commission outgo for the period has been properly accounted for.

Q.12 "In an audit of an insurance company, the Receipts and Payments Account is also subjected to audit". Comment on this statement in brief.

Ans. : Audit of receipt and Payment Account:

- Section 11(1) of the Insurance Act, 1938 provides that every insurer, should prepare at the end of each financial year, a Balance Sheet, a Profit and Loss Account, separate account of receipts and payments and a Revenue Account in accordance IRDA Regulations.
- Since receipts and payments account has been made a part of financial statements of an insurer, it is implied that the receipts and payments account is also required to be audited.
- The IRDA (Preparation of Financial Statements and Auditor's Report of Insurance Companies) Regulations, 2002 require that the auditor of an insurance company should:
  (*i*) report whether the receipts and payments account of the insurer is in agreement with the books of account and returns;
  (*ii*) express an opinion as to whether the receipts and payments account has been prepared in accordance with the provisions of the relevant statutes; and
  (*iii*) express an opinion whether the receipts and payments account give a true and fair view of the receipts and payments of the insurer for the financial year/period under audit.

22.4 AUDIT OF BALANCE SHEET ITEMS

Q.13 State the audit procedures for verification of outstanding premium and agents' balances of General Insurance companies. [Nov. 08, Nov. 10, Nov. 11 (4 Marks)]

Or

M/s ABC & Co., a CA firm was appointed as the auditor of 'Always Safe General Insurance Ltd.' Advise them how they will verify outstanding premium and agent's balances. [May 14 (6 Marks)]

Ans. : Verification aspects of outstanding premium & agents balances of General Insurance Company:

(*i*) Scrutinize and review control account debit balances and their nature should be enquired into.

(*ii*) Examine in-operative balances and treatment given for old balances with reference to company rules.

(*iii*) Enquire into the reasons for retaining the old balances.

(*iv*) Verify old debit balances which may require provision or adjustment. Notes of explanation may be obtained from the management in this regard.

(*v*) Check age-wise, sector-wise analysis of outstanding premium.

(*vi*) Verify whether outstanding premiums have since been collected.

(*vii*) Check the availability of adequate bank guarantee or premium deposit for outstanding premium.

Q.14 State the disclosure requirements in respect of contingent liabilities in the notes to the Balance Sheet of a General Insurance Company. [May 11 (4 Marks)]

Ans. : Disclosure requirements in respect of Contingent Liabilities:

The following shall be disclosed by way of notes to balance sheet in respect of Contingent Liabilities.

1. Partly paid up investments.
2. Underwriting Commitments outstanding.
3. Claims, other than those under policies, not acknowledged as debts.
4. Guarantees given by or on behalf of the Company.
5. Statutory demands/Liabilities in dispute, not provided for.
6. Reinsurance obligations to the extent not provided for in the accounts.
7. Others (to be specified).

22.5 MISCELLANEOUS

Q.15 Write a short note on: Incoming and Outgoing Co-insurance.

Ans. : Incoming and Outgoing Co-insurance:

In cases of large risks, the business is shared between more than one insurer under co-insurance arrangements at agreed percentages. The leading insurer issues documents, collects premium and settles claims. Statement of accounts is rendered by the leading insurer to the other co-insurers. The auditor should verify incoming co-insurance and outgoing co-insurance as follows:

Incoming Co-Insurance

1. Ensure that the Premium Account is credited on the basis of statements received from the Lead insurer.
2. In case, the statement is not received, the premium is accounted for on the basis of advices to ensure that all premium in respect of risks assumed in any year is booked in the same year.
3. For this purpose, the auditor may examine the communication in the post-audit period and obtain a written confirmation to the effect that all incoming advices have been accounted for.
4. The auditor should also verify claims provisions and claims paid with reference to advice received from the Lead insurer.

Outgoing Co-Insurance

1. The auditor should scrutinise the transactions relating to the outgoing business, i.e. where the company is the Lead Insurer.
2. These should be checked with reference to the relevant risks assumed under policies and correspondingly for debits arising to the co-insurer on account of their share of claims.

Q.16 Enumerate the steps to be taken by an auditor for the verification of Re-insurance inward in case of a General Insurance Company.

Ans. : Verification of Re-insurance Inward (Reinsurance accepted):

1. Evaluate internal control system in the area of reinsurance accepted to ensure determination of correct amount for reinsurance accepted, proper valuation of assets and liabilities arising out of reinsurance transaction and adherence to legal provisions and regulations.

2. Ascertain whether adequate guidelines and procedures are established with respect to granting reinsurance.
3. Reconcile reinsurance underwriting returns received from various units with the figures of premium, claims paid and outstanding claims for the company as a whole.
4. Examine whether premium received and commission paid on reinsurance accepted is as per the terms of the agreement with the Principal Insurer.
5. Examine whether claims paid have been accounted on a regular basis.
6. Examine whether remittances from foreign Principal Insurer are as per foreign exchange regulations.
7. Examine whether confirmations have been obtained regarding balances with Principal Insurer.
8. Review individual accounts of Principal Insurers.

Q.17 What are the steps to be taken by an auditor for the audit of re-insurance ceded?

or

Enumerate the steps to be taken by an auditor for the verification of Re-insurance outward in case of a General Insurance Company. **[Nov. 09 (5 Marks)]**

Ans. : Verification of Re-insurance Outward (Reinsurance ceded):

1. Evaluate internal control system in the area of reinsurance ceded to ensure determination of correct amount for reinsurance ceded, proper valuation of assets and liabilities arising out of reinsurance transaction and adherence to legal provisions and regulations.
2. Ascertain whether adequate guidelines and procedures are established with respect to obtaining reinsurance.
3. Reconcile reinsurance underwriting returns received from various units with the figures of premium, claims paid and outstanding claims for the company as a whole.
4. Examine whether commission on reinsurance ceded is as per the terms of the agreement with the re-insurers.
5. Examine the computation of profit commission for automatic treaty arrangements in the light of the periodic accounts rendered and in relation to outstanding loss pertaining to the treaty.
6. Examine whether loss recoveries have been claimed and accounted on a regular basis.
7. Examine whether outstanding losses recoverable have been confirmed by re-insurers.
8. Examine whether remittances to foreign re-insurers are as per foreign exchange regulations.
9. Examine whether confirmations have been obtained regarding balances with re-insurers.
10. Review individual accounts of re-insurers to evaluate whether any provision/write off or write back is required.

Q.18 Write a short note on: Facultative reinsurance under Insurance Act, 1938.

Ans. : Facultative Reinsurance:

It is that type of reinsurance whereby contract relates to one particular risk and is expressed in the reinsurance policy. Each transaction has to be negotiated individually. Each party has free choice i.e., ceding company to offer and re-insurer to accept. The Insurance is used when:

(*i*) Automatic cover has exhausted.

(*ii*) Risk is excluded from treaties

(*iii*) Reinsurance treaties have not to be over burdened for abnormal risks.

(*iv*) When insurer has no automatic cover.

(*v*) Where technical guidance is required at each stage of acceptance of risk.

Q.19 Explain the difference between the Proportional Treaties and Non-Proportional Treaties? **[Nov. 16 (4 Marks)]**

Ans. : Proportional Treaties and Non-Proportional Treaties:

Proportional Treaty Reinsurance

- In proportional treaty reinsurance, the reinsurer will receive a prorated share of the premiums of all the policies sold by the insurance company being covered. Consequently, when claims are made, the reinsurer will also bear a portion of the losses. The proportion of the premiums and losses that will be shared by the reinsurer will be based on an agreed percentage.
- In a proportional coverage, the reinsurance company will also reimburse the insurance company for all processing, business acquisition and writing costs. Also known as ceding commission, such costs may be paid to the insurance company upfront.

Non-proportional Treaty Reinsurance

- In a non-proportional type of coverage, the reinsurer will only get involved if the insurance company's losses exceed a specified amount, which is referred to as priority or retention limit. Hence, the reinsurer does not have a proportional share in the premiums and losses of the insurance provider.
- The priority or retention limit may be based on a single type of risk or an entire business category.

Q.20 Write short note on: "Trade credit insurance policy" and basic requirements of a trade credit insurance product. [Nov. 16 (4 Marks)]

Ans. : Trade Credit Insurance

Trade credit insurance is business of effecting contracts of insurance in respect of trade credit insurance transactions. It provides protection to suppliers against the risk of non-payment of goods or services by their buyers who may be situated in the same country (domestic risk) or in another country (export risk) against non-payment as a result of insolvency of the buyer or non-payment after an agreed number of months after due date.

Requirements

Trade credit insurance product is offered subject to following requirements:

1. Policyholder's loss arises due to non-receipt of trade receivable arising out of a trade of goods or services.
2. Policyholder is a supplier of goods or services for a consideration and does not arise out of factoring or reverse factoring arrangement or any other similar arrangement.
3. Buyer is liable to pay a trade receivable to the policyholder in return for the goods and services received by him from the policyholder, in accordance with a policy document filed with the insurer.
4. Premium for the entire Policy Period has been paid.
5. Other requirement that may be specified by the Authority from time to time.

AUDIT OF NON-BANKING FINANCE COMPANIES

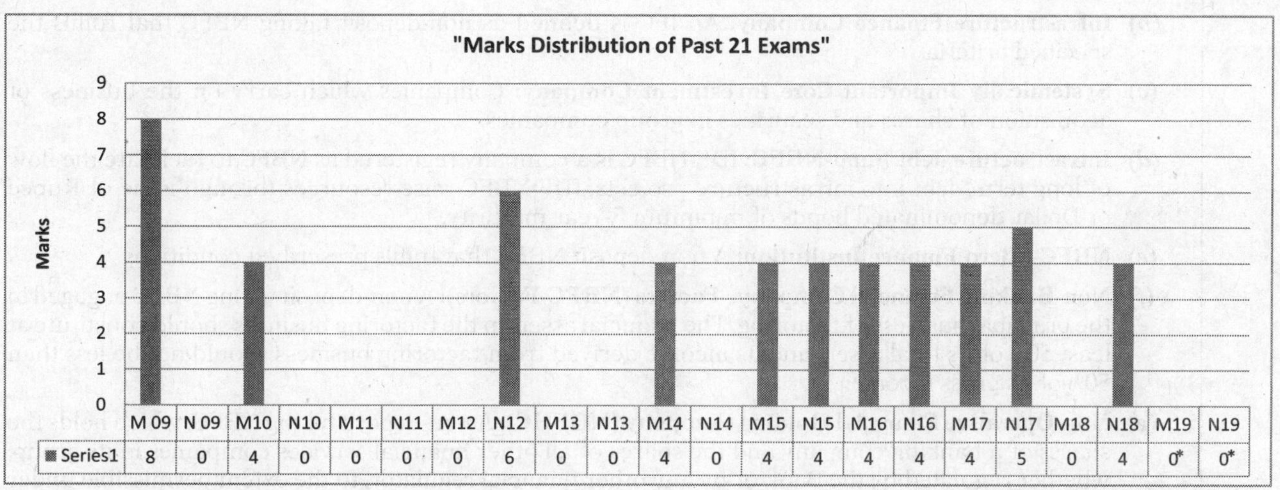

	M 09	N 09	M10	N10	M11	N11	M12	N12	M13	N13	M14	N14	M15	N15	M16	N16	M17	N17	M18	N18	M19	N19
■ Series1	8	0	4	0	0	0	0	6	0	0	4	0	4	4	4	4	4	5	0	4	0*	0*

*Only Subjective Questions.

23.1 - TYPES OF NBFC

Q.1 Shubham & Associates are going to start the audit of NBFCs. They have not performed much work for the NBFCs in the past years. You are required to explain the requirements related to registration and regulation of NBFCs which an auditor needs to keep in his mind while planning the audit of NBFC which would help this firm.

Ans. : Registration and regulation of NBFC:

- Sec. 45-IA of RBI (Amendment) Act, 1997 provides that no NBFC is allowed to commence or carry on the business of a NBFC without obtaining a certificate of registration from RBI.
- The registration is required where the financing activity is a principal business of the company.
- Financial activity will be considered as principal business if the company's financial assets constitute more than 50% of the total assets and income from financial assets constitute more than 50% of the gross income, A company which fulfils both these criteria is required to get itself registered as NBFC with RBI.
- However, to obviate dual regulation, certain categories of NBFC which are regulated by other regulators are exempted from requirement of registration with the RBI, for example: companies registered with SEBI or IRDA.
- The RBI has issued directions to NBFC on acceptance of public deposits, prudential norms, risk exposure norms & other measures to monitor financial solvency and reporting by NBFC.
- RBI also issued directions to auditors to report to the RBI, BOD and shareholders, any non-compliance with the RBI Act and regulations made by the RBI.

TAXMANN®

Q.2 What are the different types of NBFCs registered with RBI?

or

Write short notes on Categories of Non-Banking Finance Companies (NBFCs). [Nov. 05 (4 Marks)]

Ans. : Categories of NBFC:

RBI vide its circular classified the NBFC into following categories:

(*a*) **Investment and Credit Company (ICC):** Investment and Credit Company means any company which is a financial institution carrying on as its principal business - asset finance, the providing of finance whether by making loans or advances or otherwise for any activity other than its own and the acquisition of securities; and is not any other category of NBFC as defined by the RBI in any of its Master Directions.

(*b*) **Infrastructure Finance Company:** An IFC is defined as non-deposit taking NBFC that fulfils the specified criteria.

(*c*) **Systemically Important Core Investment Company:** Companies which carry on the business of acquisition of shares and securities in group companies.

(*d*) **Infrastructure debt Fund-NBFC:** IDF-NBFC is a company registered as NBFC to facilitate the flow of long term debt into infrastructure projects. IDF-NBFC raise resources through issue of Rupee or Dollar denominated bonds of minimum 5-year maturity.

(*e*) **NBFC-Micro Finance Institution:** A non-deposit NBFC that fulfils prescribed conditions.

(*f*) **Non-Banking Financial Company - Factors (NBFC-Factors):** A non-deposit taking NBFC engaged in the principal business of factoring. The financial assets in the factoring business should constitute at least 50% of its total assets and its income derived from factoring business should not be less than 50% of its gross income.

(*g*) **Non-Operative Financial Holding Company (NOFHC):** A non-deposit taking NBFC, which holds the shares of a banking company and the shares of all other financial services companies in its group, whether regulated by the Bank or by any other financial regulator, to the extent permissible under the applicable regulatory prescriptions.

Q.3 Write short note on: Infrastructure Finance Companies.

Ans. : Infrastructure Finance Companies (IFC):

An IFC is defined as non-deposit taking NBFC that fulfils the criteria mentioned below:

(*i*) a minimum of 75 per cent of its total assets should be deployed in infrastructure loans;

(*ii*) Net owned funds of ₹ 300 crores or above;

(*iii*) minimum credit rating 'A' or equivalent of CRISIL, FITCH, CARE, ICRA or equivalent rating by any other accrediting rating agencies;

(*iv*) Capital to Risk Asset Ratio (CRAR) of 15%.

23.2 - AUDIT PROCEDURES

Q.4 You are the auditor of IJK Ltd., a NBFC registered with RBI. How would you proceed to ensure the compliance of Prudential Norms directions by it. [Nov. 08 (4 Marks)]

Or

As an auditor of a non-banking financial company registered with RBI, what are the prudential norms of RBI, whose compliance is to be verified. [Nov. 12 (6 Marks)]

Or

You are the auditor of MP Ltd., a NBFC registered with RBI as an Investment Company. How would you proceed to ensure the "Compliance of Prudential Norms Directions" by MP Ltd.? [Nov. 18-Old Syllabus (4 Marks)]

Ans. : Compliance of Prudential Norms by NBFC

1. **Prudential Norms**: The auditor has to verify the compliance of prudential norms relating to (1) income recognition; (2) Income from investments; (3) Asset classification; (4) Provision for bad & doubtful debts; (5) Capital adequacy norm; (6) Prohibition of granting loans against its own shares; (7) Prohibition on loans & investments for failure to repay public deposits & (8) Norms for concentration of credit etc.

2. **Policy for demand Loans**: The auditor shall ensure that Board of the NBFC shall frame a policy for granting demand/call loans and implement the same.
3. **Classification of Advances**: The auditor should verify the classification of advances and loans as standard/substandard/doubtful/loss and that proper provision has been made in accordance with the directions.
4. **Income from NPA**: Auditor should ensure that unrealised income from non-performing assets has not been taken to profit and Loss Account.
5. **Recovery in NPA Accounts**: The auditor should check all NPAs of the previous years to verify whether during the current year any payments have been received or still they continue to be NPA during the current year also.

Additional Verification point in case of investment company:

In case of Investment Company, NBFC Prudential Norms stipulates the following:

- NBFCs should not lend more than 15% of its owned funds to any single borrower and not more than 25% to any single group of borrower.
- The ceiling on investments in shares by a NBFC in a single entity and the aggregate of investments in a single group of entities has been fixed at 15% and 25% respectively.
- Moreover, a composite limit of credit to and investments in a single entity/group of entities has been fixed at 25% and 40% respectively of the owned fund of the concerned NBFC.

Auditor is required to verify that the credit facilities extended and investments made by the concerned NBFC are in accordance with the prescribed ceiling.

Q.5 **You are the auditor of ABC Ltd., a NBFC registered with RBI. How would you proceed to ensure the compliance of Public Deposit Directions by it.**

Ans. : Compliance of Public Deposit Direction by NBFC:

1. **Credit Rating**: Obtain a copy of the credit rating assigned to NBFC and check whether the public deposits accepted/held by it are in accordance with the level of credit rating assigned to it.
2. **Interest and Brokerage payments**: Test checks the interest and brokerage calculations to ascertain that the NBFC has not paid in excess.
3. **Written Application**: Examine whether the NBFC has accepted or renewed any public deposit only after a written application form the depositor in the specified form.
4. **Deposit Register**: Verify the deposit register maintained by a NBFC and test check the particulars that have been entered therein in respect of each depositor with supporting receipts issued to the depositors.
5. **Repayment of deposits**: Check whether the NBFC is regularly paying its deposits on due dates.
6. **Custody of investments**: Check whether the investments made in approved liquid assets have been lodged in safe custody with a designated bank. Obtain a certificate from the bank to that effect.
7. **Submission of Accounts**: Ascertain whether audited statement of accounts together with a copy of the auditor's report and director's report thereon have been submitted within prescribed time limit from the date of holding the AGM.
8. **Filing of Annual return**: Check whether the NBFC has filed its annual return in specified time.
9. **Board Resolution in case of non-acceptance of public deposits**: In case, NBFC is not accepting/holding public deposits, check whether a board resolution has been passed by the NBFC to the effect that it has neither accepted any public deposits nor would it accept any public deposits during the year.

23.3 - CLASSIFICATION OF FRAUDS

Q.6 **Write short note on: Classification of Frauds by NBFC.** **[May 14 (4 Marks)]**

Or

Under what heads can the frauds committed by Non-Banking Financial Companies (NBFCs) be classified? **[Nov. 17 (5 Marks)]**

TAXMANN®

Ans. : Classification of Frauds by NBFC:

In order to have uniformity in reporting, frauds have been classified as under based mainly on the provisions of the Indian Penal Code:

(*a*) Misappropriation and criminal breach of trust.

(*b*) Fraudulent encashment through forged instruments, manipulation of books of account or through fictitious accounts and conversion of property.

(*c*) Unauthorised credit facilities extended for reward or for illegal gratification.

(*d*) Negligence and cash shortages. Reporting as fraud is required only if the intention to cheat/defraud is suspected/proved. However, if fraudulent intention is not suspected/proved, at the time of detection, cases of negligence and cash shortage will be treated as fraud and reported, if:

- Cash shortages are more than ₹ 10,000/- and
- Cash shortages are more than ₹ 5,000/- and detected by management/auditor/inspecting officer and not reported on the occurrence by the persons handling cash.

(*e*) Cheating and forgery.

(*f*) Irregularities in foreign exchange transactions. Reporting as fraud is required only if the intention to cheat/defraud is suspected/proved.

(*g*) Any other type of fraud not coming under the specific heads as above.

"ICAI Examiner Comments"

Though examinees pointed out the various classification of frauds by NBFC but few examinees failed to explain the manner of reporting in cases where fraudulent intention is suspected and proved. Some examinees wrongly mentioned general types of frauds committed by corporates.

23.4 - AUDIT CHECK LIST

Q.7 Ram and Associates, a firm of Chartered Accountants, are the auditors of NBFC (Investment and Credit Company). Some of the team members of the audit team who audited this NBFC have left the firm and the new team members are in discussion with the previous team members who are still continuing with the firm regarding the verification procedures to be performed. In this context, please explain what verification procedures should be performed in relation to audit of NBFC - Investment and Credit Company (NBFC-ICC). [MTP - Oct. 19, RTP-Nov. 19]

Ans. : Audit of NBFC - Investment and Credit Companies:

(A) Points related in Investments:

(*i*) **Physical Verification**: Auditor should physically verify the securities held by a NBFC. Where any security is lodged with an institution or a bank, a certificate from the bank/institution to that effect must be verified.

(*ii*) **Income recognition**: Verify that dividend income wherever declared by a company, has been duly received and accounted for. NBFC Prudential Norms directions require dividend income on shares of companies and units of mutual funds to be recognised on cash basis.

(*iii*) **Authorisation**: Verify the Board Minutes for purchase and sale of investments.

(*iv*) **Classification**: Ascertain from the Board resolution or obtain a management certificate to the effect that the investments so acquired are current investments or Long Term Investments.

(*v*) **Valuation**: Check whether the investments have been valued in accordance with the NBFC Prudential Norms Directions and adequate provision for fall in the market value of securities, wherever applicable, have been made there against, as required by the Directions.

(*vi*) **Compliance of AS 13**: An auditor will have to ascertain whether the requirements of AS 13 "Accounting for Investments" or other accounting standard, as applicable, (to the extent they are not inconsistent with the Directions) have been duly complied with by the NBFC.

(*vii*) **External Confirmations**: In respect of shares/securities held through a depository, obtain a confirmation from the depository regarding the shares/securities held by it on behalf of the NBFC. Obtain a confirmation from the approved intermediary regarding securities deposited with/borrowed from it as at the year end.

(B) Point related to Credit:

(*i*) **Sanctioning**: Auditor should examine whether each loan or advance has been properly sanctioned. He should verify the conditions attached to the sanction of each loan or advance *i.e.* limit on borrowings, nature of security, interest, terms of repayment, etc.

(*ii*) **Security**: Auditor should verify the security obtained and the agreements entered into, if any, with the concerned parties in respect of the advances given. He must ascertain the nature and value of security and the net worth of the borrower/guarantor to determine the extent to which an advance could be considered realisable.

(*iii*) **Loan against own shares**: Verify whether the NBFC has not advanced any loans against the security of its own shares.

(*iv*) **Compliance of prudential norms**: Check whether the NBFC has not lent/invested in excess of the specified limits to any single borrower or group of borrowers as per NBFC Prudential Norms Directions.

(*v*) **Appraisal and follow up System**: Auditor should verify whether the NBFC has an adequate system of proper appraisal and follow up of loans and advances. In addition, he may analyse the trend of its recovery performance to ascertain that the NBFC does not have an unduly high level of NPAs.

(*vi*) **Classification**: Check the classification of loans and advances (including bills purchased and discounted) made by a NBFC into Standard Assets, Sub-Standard Assets, Doubtful Assets and Loss Assets and the adequacy of provision for bad and doubtful debts as required by NBFC Prudential Norms Directions.

23.5 - NBFC AUDITOR'S REPORT (RESERVE BANK) DIRECTIONS, 2016

Q.8 Write short note on: Matters to be included in Auditor's Report in case of NBFC not accepting deposits.

[May 16 (4 Marks)]

Or

What are the specific Matters to be included in Auditor's Report in an audit of NBFC not accepting public deposits. [May 17 (4 Marks)]

Ans. : Matters to be included in Auditor's Report in case of NBFC:

In addition to the Report made by the auditor u/s 143 of the Companies Act, 2013, the auditor shall also make a separate report to the Board of Directors of the Company on the matters as specified in paragraphs 3 of the NBFCs Auditor's Report (Reserve Bank) Directions, 2016:

Matters to be reported in case of all NBFC - Para 3

1. Whether the company has obtained a Certificate of Registration (CoR) from the Bank. (Conducting Non-Banking Financial Activity without a valid CoR is an offence under the RBI Act, 1934)
2. In case of a company holding CoR issued by the Bank, whether that company is entitled to continue to hold such CoR in terms of its Principal Business Criteria (Financial asset/income pattern) as on March 31 of the applicable year.
3. Whether the NBFC is meeting the required net owned fund requirement as laid down in Directions issued by RBI.

Matters to be reported in case of NBFC not accepting public deposits - Para 3

(*i*) Whether the Board of Directors has passed a resolution for non-acceptance of any public deposits;

(*ii*) Whether the company has accepted any public deposits during the relevant period/year.

(*iii*) Whether the company has complied with the prudential norms relating to income recognition, accounting standards, asset classification and provisioning for bad and doubtful debts as applicable to it;

(*iv*) In respect of Systemically Important Non-deposit taking NBFCs:

(*a*) Whether the capital adequacy ratio as disclosed in the return submitted to the Bank, has been correctly arrived at and whether such ratio is in compliance with the minimum CRAR prescribed by the Bank;

(*b*) Whether the company has furnished to the Bank the annual statement of capital funds, risk assets/exposures and risk asset ratio within the stipulated period.

(*c*) Whether the NBFC has been correctly classified as NBFC Micro Finance Institutions (MFI).

"ICAI Examiner Comments"

Majority of candidates failed to discuss the disclosure of Capital adequacy ratio/ risk asset ratio in respect of Systemically Important Non-deposit taking NBFCs.

Q.9 What are the obligations of auditor to submit Exception Report to RBI in case of non-banking financial companies? [Nov. 16 (4 Marks)]

Ans. : Obligation of Auditor to submit exception report to RBI:

Para 5 of NBFC Auditor's Report (Reserve Bank) Directions, 2008 provides that Where, in the case of a NBFC, the statement regarding any of the items referred to in para 3, is unfavourable or qualified, or in the opinion of the auditor the company has not complied with:

(*a*) the provisions of Chapter III B of Reserve Bank of India Act, 1934; or

(*b*) the NBFC Acceptance of Public Deposits (Reserve Bank) Directions, 2016; or

(*c*) NBFC-Non-Systemically Important Non-Deposit taking Company (Reserve Bank) Directions, 2016 and NBFC-Systemically Important Non-Deposit taking Company and Deposit taking Company (Reserve Bank) Directions, 2016,

it shall be the obligation of the auditor to make a report containing the details of such unfavourable or qualified statements and/or about the non-compliance, as the case may be, in respect of the company to the concerned Regional Office of the Department of Non-Banking Supervision of the Bank under whose jurisdiction the registered office of the company is located.

Note: Duty of the Auditor to submit exception report shall be to report only the contraventions of the provisions of RBI Act, 1934, and Directions, Guidelines, instructions and such report shall not contain any statement with respect to compliance of any of those provisions.

23.6 - COMPLIANCE WITH CARO, 2016

Q.10 The RBI restrict companies from carrying on the business of a non-banking financial institution without obtaining the certificate of registration, therefore, obtaining registration under section 45-IA of the Reserve Bank of India Act, 1934 is necessary. Additionally, new clause has been inserted under CARO, 2016 for commenting whether the registration has been obtained, if required.

You are required to state the audit procedure and reporting to be followed under above mentioned circumstances.

Or

In the case of companies carrying on the business of a non-banking financial institution the auditor needs to report under CARO, 2016 whether the registration has been obtained under section 45-IA of the Reserve Bank of India Act, 1934, if required.

You are required to state in brief the audit procedure to be followed while reporting under above mentioned circumstances.

Or

Abhimanyu Finance Ltd. is a Non Banking Finance Company and was in the business of accepting public deposits and giving loans. The company was having net owned funds of Rs.1,50,00,000 (one crore fifty lakhs) and was not having registration certificate from RBI and applied for it on 30th March 2018. The company appointed Mr. Kabra as its statutory auditors for the year 2017-18. Advise the auditor with reference to auditor procedures to be taken and reporting requirements on the same in view of CARO 2016?

Ans. : Audit Procedure for reporting under CARO, 2016 w.r.t. registration u/s 45-IA of RBI Act, 1934:

Clause (xvi) of Paragraph 3 of CARO 2016 requires the company auditor to report: "Whether the company is required to be registered under Section 45-IA of the RBI Act, 1934 and if so, whether the registration has been obtained".

Sec. 45-IA of RBI (Amendment) Act, 1997 provides that no NBFC is allowed to commence or carry on the business of a NBFC without obtaining a certificate of registration from RBI. The registration is required where the financing activity is a principal business of the company.

Audit Procedure and Reporting

(*i*) Examine the transactions of the company with relation to the activities covered under the RBI Act and directions to determine whether the company is engaged in financial activity.

(*ii*) Auditor should examine the financial statements to ascertain whether company's financial assets constitute more than 50 per cent of the total assets and income from financial assets constitute more than 50 per cent of the gross income.

(*iii*) Ascertain whether the net owned funds of the company exceeds such amount so as to require the company to get itself registered as NBFC with RBI.

(*iv*) Ascertain whether the company has obtained the registration as NBFC, if not, the reasons should be sought from the management and documented.

(*v*) Auditor's Report under CARO, 2016 shall incorporate the following:

- Whether the registration is required under section 45-IA of the RBI Act, 1934.
- If so, whether it has obtained the registration.
- If the registration not obtained, reasons thereof.

23.7 - IND AS AND SCHEDULE III

Q.11 Mr. G has been appointed as an auditor of LMP Ltd., a NBFC company registered with RBI. Mr. G is concerned about whether the format of financial statements prepared by LMP Ltd. is as per notification issued by the Ministry of Corporate Affairs (MCA) dated October 11, 2018. The notification prescribed the format in Division III under Schedule III of the Companies Act, 2013 applicable to NBFCs complying with Ind-AS. Mr. G wants to know the differences in the presentation requirements between Division II and Division III of Schedule III of the Companies Act, 2013. Help Mr. G.

[Nov. 19 - New Syllabus (5 Marks)]

Ans. : Differences between Division II and Division III:

The presentation requirements under Division III for NBFCs are similar to Division II (Non NBFC) to a large extent except for the following:

(*a*) NBFCs have been allowed to present the items of the balance sheet in order of their liquidity which is not allowed to companies required to follow Division II. Additionally, NBFCs are required to classify items of the balance sheet into financial and non-financial whereas other companies are required to classify the items into current and non-current.

(*b*) An NBFC is required to separately disclose by way of a note any item of 'other income' or 'other expenditure' which exceeds 1% of the total income. Division II, on the other hand, requires disclosure for any item of income or expenditure which exceeds 1% of the revenue from operations or ₹ 10 lakhs, whichever is higher.

(*c*) NBFCs are required to separately disclose under 'receivables', the debts due from any Limited Liability Partnership (LLP) in which its director is a partner or member.

(*d*) NBFCs are also required to disclose items comprising 'revenue from operations' and 'other comprehensive income' on the face of the Statement of profit and loss instead of showing those only as part of the notes.

24

CHAPTER

AUDIT OF CO-OPERATIVE SOCIETIES

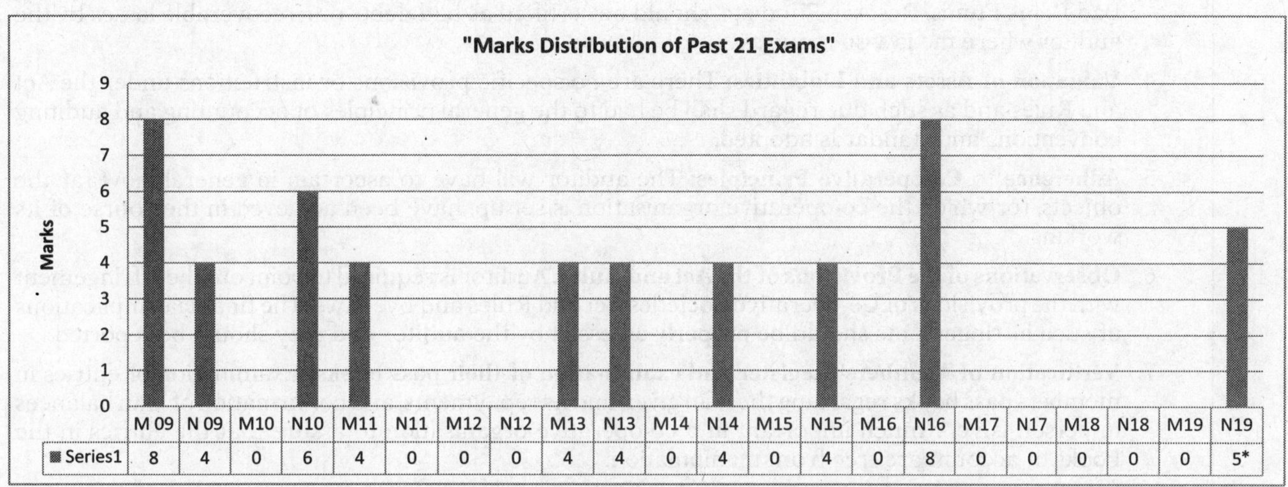

24.1 IMPORTANT PROVISIONS OF CO-OPERATIVE SOCIETIES ACT, 1912

Q.1 Write short note on: Restrictions on shareholding in a co-operative society. [Nov. 14 (4 Marks)]

Ans. : Restrictions of Shareholding:

- Section 5 of the Co-operative Societies Act, 1912 provides that in the case of a society where the liability of a member of the society is limited, no member of a society other than a registered society can hold such portion of the share capital of the society as would exceed a maximum of 20% of the total number of shares or of the value of shareholding to ₹ 1,000/-.
- The auditor of a co-operative society will be concerned with this provision so as to watch any breach relating to holding of shares.

Q.2 Write short note on: Restrictions on investments of funds of a central co-operative society. [May 13, Nov. 16 (4 Marks)]

Ans. : Restrictions in Investments of Funds:

According to Section 32 of the Central Act the modes of investment of funds of a society may be stated as follows. A society may invest its funds in any one or more of the following:

(*a*) In the Central or State Co-operative Bank.

(*b*) In any of the securities specified in Section 20 of the Indian Trusts Act, 1882.

(*c*) In the shares, securities, bonds or debentures of any other society with limited liability.

(*d*) In any co-operative bank, other than a Central or State co-operative bank, as approved by the Registrar on specified terms and conditions.

(*e*) In any other moneys permitted by the Central or State Government.

24.2 SALIENT FEATURES OF CO-OPERATIVE SOCIETIES AUDIT

Q.3 State the special features of Co-operative Societies Audit. [May 09 (8 Marks)]

Ans. : Special features of Co-operative Societies Audit:

1. **Examination of overdue debts:** Overdue debts for a period from six months to five years and more than five years will have to be classified and shall have to be reported by an auditor. The auditor will have to ascertain whether proper provisions for doubtful debts are made and whether the same is satisfactory.
2. **Overdue Interest:** Overdue interest should be excluded from interest outstanding and accrued due while calculating profit.
3. **Certification of Bad Debts:** Bad debts and irrecoverable losses before being written off against Bad Debts Funds, Reserve Fund etc. should be certified as bad debts or irrecoverable losses by the auditor where the law so requires.
4. **Valuation of Assets and Liabilities:** There are no specific provisions or instructions under the Act and Rules and as such due regard shall be had to the general principles of accounting and auditing conventions and standards adopted.
5. **Adherence to Co-operative Principles:** The auditor will have to ascertain in general, how far the objects, for which the co-operative organisation is set up, have been achieved in the course of its working.
6. **Observations of the Provisions of the Act and Rules:** Auditor is required to point out the infringement with the provisions of Co-operative Societies Act and Rules and bye-laws. The financial implications of such infringements should be properly assessed by the auditor and they should be reported.
7. **Verification of Members' Register and examination of their pass books:** Examination of entries in members pass books regarding the loan given and its repayments, and confirmation of loan balances in person is very much important in a co-operative organisation to assure that the entries in the books of account are free from manipulation.
8. **Special report to the Registrar:** During the course of audit, if the auditor notices that there are some serious irregularities in the working of the society, he may report these special matters to the Registrar, drawing his specific attention to the points.
9. **Audit classification of society:** After a judgment of an overall performance of the society, the auditor has to award a class to the society. This judgment is to be based on the criteria specified by the Registrar.
10. **Discussion of draft audit report with managing committee:** On conclusion of the audit, the auditor should ask the Secretary of the society to convene the managing committee meeting to discuss the audit draft report. The audit report should never be finalised without discussion with the managing committee.

Q.4 Mention the duties of Auditor of Co-operative Societies in regard to the following:

(*i*) Overdue interest.

(*ii*) Compliance with provisions of Co-operative Act and Rules thereunder.

(*iii*) Special Report to Registrar of Co-operative Societies.

Ans. : Duties of Auditor of Co-operative Societies:

1. **Overdue Interest:** Overdue interest should be excluded from interest outstanding and accrued due while calculating profit.
2. **Adherence to Co-operative Principles:** The auditor will have to ascertain in general, how far the objects, for which the co-operative organisation is set up, have been achieved in the course of its working. The assessment is not necessarily in terms of profits, but in terms of extending benefits to members who have formed the society. While auditing the expenses, the auditor should see that they are economically incurred and there is no wastage of funds. The principles of propriety audit should be followed for the purpose.
3. **Special report to the Registrar:** During the course of audit, if the auditor notices that there are some serious irregularities in the working of the society, he may report these special matters to the Registrar, drawing his specific attention to the points. The Registrar on receipt of such a special report may take necessary action against the society.

Circumstances in which special report is required: Refer answer of Q. No. 5

Q.5 Under what circumstances, an auditor is required to submit a special report to the registrar of Co-operative Societies? **[Nov. 09 (4 Marks)]**

Ans. : Circumstances requiring submission of Special Report:

During the course of audit, if the auditor notices that there are some **serious irregularities** in the working of the society, he may report these special matters to the Registrar. The Registrar on receipt of such a special report may take necessary action against the society.

Circumstances in which special report is required:

(*i*) Personal profiteering by members of managing committee in transactions of the society, which are detrimental to the interest of the society.

(*ii*) Detection of fraud relating to expenses, purchases, property and stores of the society.

(*iii*) Mis-management (decisions of management against co-operative principles).

(*iv*) In the case of urban co-operative banks, disproportionate advances to vested interest groups, such as relatives of management, and deliberate negligence about the recovery thereof. Cases of reckless advancing, where the management is negligent about taking adequate security and proper safe-guards for judging the credit worthiness of the party.

Q.6 Examination of overdue debts, audit classification of society, and reporting the infringements of provisions of the Act are the special features of audit of a co-operative society." Do you agree? **[Nov. 10 (6 Marks)]**

Ans. : Special Features of Audit of a co-operative society:

1. **Examination of Overdue debts:**

   Overdue debts for a period from six months to five years and more than five years will have to be classified and shall have to be reported by an auditor. A further analysis of these overdue debts from the viewpoint of chances of recovery will have to be made, and they will have to be classified as good or bad. The auditor will have to ascertain whether proper provisions for doubtful debts is made and whether the same is satisfactory.

2. **Audit Classification of the Society:**

   After a judgment of an overall performance of the society, the auditor has to award a class to the society. This judgment is to be based on the criteria specified by the Registrar. It may be noted here that if the management of the society is not satisfied about the award of audit class, it can make an appeal to the Registrar, and the Registrar may direct to review the audit classification.

3. **Reporting on Infringements of provisions of the Act:**

   Auditor of a cooperative society is required to point out the infringement with the provisions of Cooperative Societies Act and Rules and bye-laws. The financial implications of such infringements should be properly assessed by the auditor and they should be reported.

24.3 RIGHTS AND DUTIES OF AUDITOR OF CO-OPERATIVE SOCIETY

Q.7 Auditor of a cooperative society has to submit his audit report in the prescribed form specified by the Registrar or as given in the related Rules. State the matters to be covered in the audit report.

Ans. : Matters to be reported in Audit Report:

The audit report has to be submitted in the prescribed form specified by the Registrar or as given in the related Rules. According to the present prescribed form in some of the States, the auditor has to state:

(*a*) Whether he has obtained all the necessary information and explanations which to the best of his knowledge and belief were necessary for the purpose of audit.

(*b*) Whether in his opinion and to the best of his information and according to the explanations given to him, the said accounts give all the information required by the Act.

(*c*) Whether the Profit and Loss Account of the society gives a true and fair view of the Profit and Loss made by the society.

(*d*) Whether the Balance Sheet drawn up as at the end of the year gives a true and fair view of the state of affairs of the society as on the given date.

(*e*) Whether in his opinion, proper books of account as required by the Act, the Rules and the bye-laws of the society have been properly maintained.

(f) Whether the Balance Sheet and the Profit and Loss Account examined by him are in agreement with the books of account and returns of the society.

The auditor will have to give qualifying observations, if any of the answers to the above mentioned matters are negative.

Q.8 An auditor of a Co-operative Society governed by Co-operative Societies Act, 1912 is required to attach schedules giving certain information. Please list the information required to be given in the schedules.

Ans. : Schedules forming part of Audit Report:

The form of the audit report to be submitted by the auditor, as prescribed in various states, contains a number of matters which the auditor has to state or comment upon. In addition to that, the auditor will have to attach schedules to the report regarding the following information:

(1) All transactions which appear to be contrary to the provisions of the Act, the rules and bye-laws of the society.

(2) All sums, which ought to have been, but have not been brought into account by the society.

(3) Any material, or property belonging to society which appears to the auditor to be bad or doubtful of recovery.

(4) Any material irregularity or impropriety in expenditure or in the realisation or monies due to society.

(5) Any other matters specified by the Registrar in this behalf.

In the case of nil report in any of the above matters, the auditor will have to give a nil report.

24.4 MULTI STATE CO-OPERATIVE SOCIETIES ACT, 2002

Q.9 State the requirements regarding the maintenance of books of account with respect to a multi-state co-operative society. [May 11 (4 Marks)]

Or

Write short note on: Aspects to be covered in the books of account to be maintained by a multi-cooperative society. [Nov. 13, Nov. 15 (4 Marks)]

Ans. : Aspects to be covered in Books of Account:

As per the Multi State Co-operative Society Rules, 2002, every multi state co-operative society shall keep books of account with respect to:

(a) all sum of money received & expended

(b) all sales and purchases of goods.

(c) the assets and liabilities of the society.

(d) in the case of Multi State Co-operative Society engaged in production, processing and manufacturing particulars relating to utilization of materials or labour or other term of cost as may be specified in the bye laws.

"ICAI Examiner Comments"

Many examinees failed to mention the aspects to be covered in the books of account to be maintained in case of Multi-State co-operative society rather they explained features of co-operative society. Also some examinees discussed about enquiry and inspection of co-operative society. Some examinees wrote irrelevant points regarding the Registers and Bye laws.

Q.10 Write short notes on: Powers and duties of an auditor of a Multi-State Co-operative Society.

Ans. : Powers and Duties of Auditor of Multi-State Co-operative Society:

Section 73 of the Multi-State Co-operative Societies Act, 2002 provides the provisions relating to powers and duties of auditor.

Powers of Auditor [Sec. 73(1)]:

- Every auditor shall have a right of access at all times to the books, accounts and vouchers of the Multi-State Co-operative Society whether kept at the head office or elsewhere.
- Every auditor shall be entitled to require from the officers or other employees of the Multi-State Co-operative Society such information and explanation as the auditor may think necessary for the performance of the duties as an auditor.

Duties of Auditor [Sec. 73(2)]:

(*A*) To conduct Inquiry: The auditor shall make the following inquiries:

(*i*) Whether loans and advances made by the Multi-State Co-operative Society on the basis of security have been properly secured and whether the terms on which they have been made are not prejudicial to the interests of the Multi-State Co-operative or its members;

(*ii*) Whether transactions of the Multi-State Co-operative Society which are represented merely by book entries are not prejudicial to the interest of the Multi- State Co-operative Society;

(*iii*) Whether personal expenses have been charged to revenue account; and

(*iv*) Where it is stated in the books and papers of the Multi-State Co-operative Society that any shares have been allotted for cash, whether cash has actually been received in respect of such allotment, and if no cash has actually been so received, whether the position as stated in the account books and the balance sheet is correct, regular and not misleading.

(*B*) Making Report: The auditor shall make a report over the following:

- On the accounts examined by him
- On every Balance Sheet and Profit and Loss Account and
- On every other document required to be part or annexed to the balance-sheet or profit and loss account,

which are laid before the society in general meeting during his tenure of office.

The report shall state whether, in his opinion and to the best of his information and according to the explanations given to him, the said accounts give the information required by this Act in the manner so required and give a true and fair view-

(*a*) in the case of the balance-sheet, of the state of the multi-state cooperative society's affairs as at the end of its financial year; and

(*b*) in the case of the profit and loss account, of the profit or loss for its financial year.

Q.11 Under which circumstances can the Central Government appoint the special auditor of a Multi State Co-operative Society? [Nov. 16 (4 Marks)]

Ans. : Circumstances requiring Special Audit:

Sec. 77 of Multi State Cooperative Societies Act, 2002 empowers Central Government to pass an order for the special audit if they are of opinion

(*i*) that the affairs of any Multi-State co-operative society are not being managed in accordance with co-operative principles or prudent commercial practices or with sound business principles; or

(*ii*) that any Multi-State co-operative society is being managed in a manner likely to cause serious injury or damage to the interests of the trade industry or business to which it pertains; or

(*iii*) that the financial position of any Multi-State co-operative society is such as to endanger its solvency.

Q.12 On a complaint and request from a Federal Co-operative to which a Multi-State Co-operative Society is affiliated, you have been appointed by the Central Registrar to conduct an enquiry into working and financial condition of the Society. What shall be your powers in this regard? [Nov. 19 - Old Syllabus (5 Marks)]

Ans. : Powers of person conducting inquiry:

As per Sec. 78 of the Multi-State Co-operative Societies Act, 2002, the Central Registrar or the person authorized by him shall have the following powers, namely:

(*a*) Free access to the books, accounts, documents, securities, cash and other properties belonging to the multi-state cooperative society;

(*b*) Require the officers of the society to call a general meeting of the society by giving notice of not less than 7 days at such time and place at the headquarters of the society to consider such matters, as may be directed by him; and where the officers of the society refuse or fail to call such a meeting, he shall have power to call it himself; and

(*c*) Summon any person who is reasonably believed by him to have any knowledge of the affairs of the multi-state cooperative society to appear before him at any place at the headquarters of the society or any branch thereof and may examine such person on oath.

Q. 11 Where are the circumstances, on the Central Government may order for special audit of a Multi-State Co-operative Society? [Nov. 2004 (4 Marks)]

CHAPTER 25

AUDIT OF PUBLIC SECTOR UNDERTAKINGS

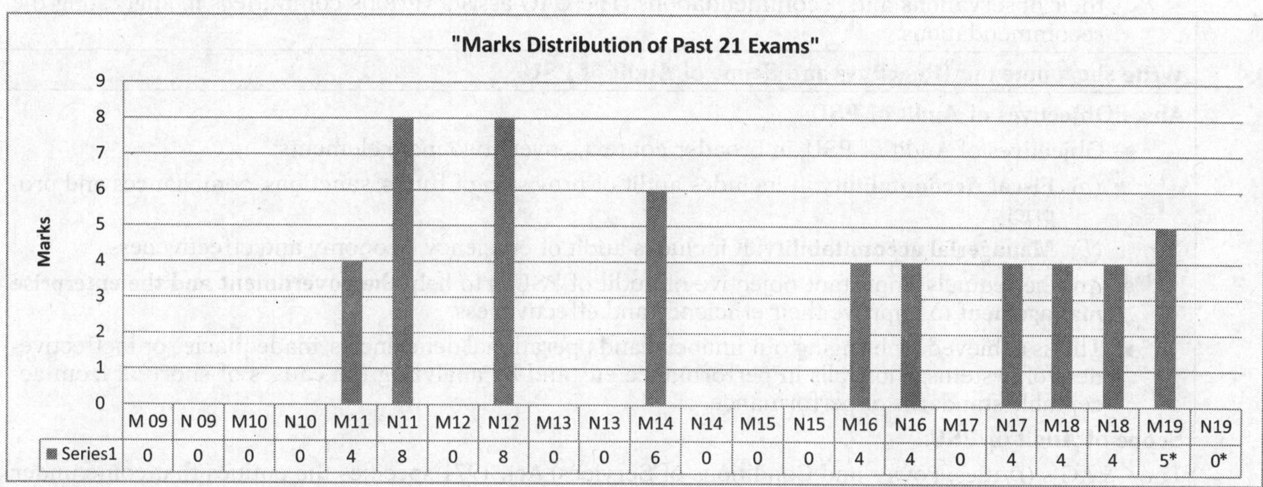

*Only Subjective Questions.

25.1 - BASICS OF AUDIT OF PSU

Q.1 Write short note on: Organisation subject to CAG Audit.

Ans. : Organisation Subject to CAG Audit:

- All the Union and State Government departments and offices including the Indian Railways, Posts and Telecommunications.
- Public commercial enterprises controlled by the Union and State governments, i.e. government companies and corporations.
- Non-commercial autonomous bodies and authorities owned or controlled by the Union or the States.
- Authorities and bodies substantially financed from Union or State revenues.

Q.2 Write short note on: Public accounts Committee

Ans. : Public Accounts Committee:

Audit Reports and Annual Accounts of entities subject to CAG audit will be referred to specialized committees constituted by Parliament and the State legislatures, i.e. Public Accounts Committee and Committee on Public Undertakings. Public Accounts Committee performs the following functions:

1. Examine that the moneys (shown in the accounts) were disbursed for the purpose to which they were applied.
2. Examine that the expenditure was authorised.
3. Examine that re-appropriation has been made in accordance with the provisions made (i.e. distribution of funds).
4. Examine the statement of accounts of autonomous and semi-autonomous bodies, the audit of which is conducted by the CAG either under the directions of the President or by a Statute of Parliament.

Q.3 The Comptroller & Auditor General of India plays a key role in the functioning of the financial committees of Parliament and the State Legislatures. He has come to be recognised as a 'friend, philosopher and guide' of the Committees. In view of above, you are required to list down role of CAG.

Ans. : C & AG Role in functioning of financial committees of Parliament and State Legislature:

(*i*) Reports of CAG form the basis of Committees' working, *i.e.* committees examine the issues raised by C & AG Reports.

(*ii*) Committees requires the assistance of C & AG for scrutinising the notes which the Ministries submit to the Committees in so far as to check the correctness of submissions to the Committees and facts and figures in their draft reports;

(*iii*) Reports of the Financial Committees are being submitted to the Parliament/State Legislature with their observations and recommendations. The CAG assists various committees in suggesting the recommendations.

Q.4 Write short note on: Objectives and Scope of Audit of PSU

Ans. : Objectives of Audit of PSU:

- Objectives of Audit of PSU, in broader context, covers two main elements:
  - (*a*) **Fiscal Accountability**: It includes audit of provision of funds, sanctions, compliances and propriety.
  - (*b*) **Managerial accountability**: It includes audit of efficiency, economy and effectiveness.
- Another equally important objective of audit of PSU is to **help the government and the enterprise management** to improve their efficiency and effectiveness.
- This is achieved by bringing out financial and operational deficiencies, inadequacies or ineffectiveness of systems, shortfalls in performance etc. and by analyzing the causes of shortfall from acceptable standards of performance.

Scope of Audit of PSU:

The C&AG's (Duties, Power and Conditions of Services) Act, 1971 specifies the entities that come under audit purview of C&AG at the Union and State level, however, the scope and extent of audit is determined by the C&AG itself.

Scope and extent of audit of PSU extends to

(*i*) Financial audit,
(*ii*) Compliance Audit,
(*iii*) Comprehensive audit,
(*iv*) Propriety Audit and
(*v*) Performance audit.

Q.5 Write short note on: Elements of PSU Audit.

Ans. : Elements of PSU Audit:

There are three elements of PSU Audit. These are:

(*a*) **Parties Involved:**

- **The auditor:** In public sector auditing the role of auditor is fulfilled by Supreme Audit Institution, India and by its personnel delegated with the task of conducting audits.
- **The responsible party**: Generally, auditable entities and TCWG of the auditable entities would be the responsible parties.
- **Intended users**: The intended user is primarily the Parliament or the Legislature which represents the citizens by determining the priorities of public finance, purpose and content of public spending and income.

(*b*) **Subject Matter, Criteria and Subject Matter Information**

- **Subject matter** refers to the information, condition or activity that is measured or evaluated against certain criteria.
- **The criteria** are the benchmarks used to evaluate the subject matter.
- **Subject matter information** refers to the outcome of evaluating or measuring the subject matter against the criteria.

(*c*) **Types of Engagement:** There are two types of engagement: Attestation Engagements and Direct Reporting Engagements.

- In attestation engagements, the responsible party measures the subject matter against the criteria and presents the subject matter information, on which the auditor then gathers sufficient and appropriate audit evidence to provide a reasonable basis for expressing a conclusion.
- In direct reporting engagements, it is the auditor who measures or evaluates the subject matter against the criteria.

Q.6 Briefly describe the various principles associated with audit of Public Sector enterprises.

Ans. : Principles associated with audit of PSU:

(*a*) **General Principles**

- Ethics & Independence
- Professional Judgment, due care and skepticism
- Quality Control
- Audit Team Management & Skill
- Audit Risk
- Materiality
- Documentation
- Communication

(*b*) Principles associated with Audit:

(*i*) Planning an Audit

1. Auditors shall obtain an understanding of the nature of the entity/programme to be audited.
2. Auditors shall conduct a risk assessment or problem analysis and revise this as necessary in response to the audit findings.
3. Auditors shall identify and assess the risks of fraud relevant to the audit objectives.
4. Auditors shall plan their work to ensure that the audit is conducted in an effective and efficient manner.

(*ii*) Conducting an Audit

1. Auditors shall perform audit procedures that provide sufficient and appropriate audit evidence to support the audit report
2. Auditors shall evaluate the audit evidence and draw conclusions

(*iii*) Reporting & Follow-up

1. Auditors shall prepare a report based on the conclusions reached.
2. Follow up on reported matter as relevant.

25.2 - AUDIT OF GOVERNMENT COMPANIES

Q.7 Write short notes on the Role of C&AG in the Audit of a Government company.

Ans. : Role of C&AG in the Audit of a Government company:

Role of C&AG is prescribed under sub-sections (5), (6) and (7) of section 143 of the Companies Act, 2013.

(*a*) **Directions to Auditor - Sec. 143(5)**: In the case of a Government company, the CAG shall appoint the auditor and direct such auditor the manner in which the accounts of the Government company are required to be audited.

(*b*) **Supplementary Audit - Sec. 143(6)**: The CAG shall within 60 days from the date of receipt of the audit report have a right to,

- conduct a supplementary audit of the financial statement of the company by such person or persons as he may authorize in this behalf; and for the purposes of such audit, require information or additional information to be furnished to any person or persons, so authorised, on such matters, by such person or persons, and in such form, as the CAG may direct, and
- Comment upon or supplement such audit report:

(*c*) **Test Audit - Sec. 143(7)**: The CAG may, in case of .government company, if he considers necessary, by an order, cause test audit to be conducted of the accounts of such company and the provisions of section 19A of the CAG (Duties, Powers and Conditions of Service) Act, 1971, shall apply to the report of such test audit.

Q.8 Write short note on: Supplementary Audit u/s 143(6) of Companies Act, 2013. [Nov. 12 (4 Marks)]

Ans. : Supplementary Audit u/s 143(6) of Companies Act, 2013:

The CAG shall within 60 days from the date of receipt of the audit report have a right to,

(*i*) conduct a **supplementary audit of the financial statement** of the company by such person or persons as he may authorize in this behalf; and for the purposes of such audit, require information or additional information to be furnished to any person or persons, so authorised, on such matters, by such person or persons, and in such form, as the CAG may direct; and

(*ii*) Comment upon or supplement such audit report:

Provided that any comments given by the CAG upon, or supplement to, the audit report shall be sent by the company to every person entitled to copies of audited financial statements u/s 136(1) i.e. every member of the company, to every trustee for the debenture holders, and to all other entitled persons and also be placed before the AGM of the company at the same time and in the same manner as the audit report.

Q.9 Comptroller & Auditor General of India were conducting supplementary audit u/s 143(6) of the Companies Act, 2013 made certain comments on the reported foreign exchange loss in the accounts of a Public-sector company. The Board of Directors failed to reply to the comments of C & AG in their report. Comment. [Nov. 11 (4 Marks)]

Ans. : Reply of Board of Directors on the comments of C & AG:

- Section 134(3)(*f*) of the Companies Act, 2013 imposes a duty on the Board of Directors of a company to give the fullest information and explanations in the Directors' Report regarding every reservation, qualification or adverse remarks contained in the auditors' report.
- The Board's remarks on the auditors' report are to be given as an addendum to the report and are to form part of the main body of the report as per Section 134(3).
- However there exists no mandatory requirement for the Board of Directors of a government company to give their reply on the reservations made by C&AG. Hence the Board of Directors of the Company is not bound to give information or explanation in respect of C&AG comments.

Conclusion: The Board of Directors has not contravened any of the provisions of the Companies Act.

Q.10 What are the relevant sections of the Companies Act, 2013 and steps involved in audit of Government Companies? [Nov. 16 (4 Marks)]

Or

"The C&AG may direct the appointed auditor the manner in which the accounts of the Government company are required to be audited and thereupon the auditor so appointed shall submit a copy of the audit report to the Comptroller and Auditor-General of India." What are the relevant sections of the Companies Act, 2013 and steps involved in auditor of Government Companies? [Nov. 19-New Syllabus (5 Marks)]

Ans. : Relevant Sections of Companies Act, 2013:

- Sec. 139(5) - Appointment of Auditor other than First Auditor
- Sec. 139 (7) - Appointment of First Auditor.
- Sec. 143(5) - Duties of Auditor of Government Companies
- Sec. 143(6) - Powers of CAG to order Supplementary Audit
- Sec. 143(7) - Powers of CAG to order Test Audit.

Steps involved in Audit of Government Companies:

In the case of a Government company, the CAG shall appoint the auditor and direct such auditor the manner in which the accounts of the Government company are required to be audited.

The auditor so appointed shall submit a copy of the audit report to the CAG which, among other things, include the following:

1. directions, if any, issued by the CAG,
2. the action taken thereon and
3. its impact on the accounts and financial statement of the company.

Q.11 On receipt of statutory audit report on 30-03-2018 of M/s Sunlight Ltd., a government company, C&AG on 25-5-2018 appointed M/s Veeru & Associates to conduct supplementary audit u/s 143(6)(*a*) of the Companies Act, 2013. They submitted their report to C&AG as per their scope of work. The Company held

its AGM on 1-9-2018 but directors did not think it necessary to discuss supplementary auditor's report and comment of the C&AG. Is the approach of the directors of Sunlight Ltd. correct? Guide the company with the provisions related to supplementary audit. [May 19 - New Syllabus (5 Marks)]

Ans. : Supplementary Audit u/s 143(6) of Companies Act 2013:

Sec. 143(6) of Companies Act, 2013 provides that the C&AG shall within 60 days from the date of receipt of the audit report have a right to,

(*i*) conduct a **supplementary audit of the financial statement** of the company by such person or persons as he may authorize in this behalf; and for the purposes of such audit, require information or additional information to be furnished to any person or persons, so authorised, on such matters, by such person or persons, and in such form, as the C&AG may direct; and

(*ii*) Comment upon or supplement such audit report:

Provided that any comments given by the C&AG upon, or supplement to, the audit report shall be sent by the company to every person entitled to copies of audited financial statements u/s 136(1) i.e. every member of the company, to every trustee for the debenture holders, and to all other entitled persons and also be placed before the AGM of the company at the same time and in the same manner as the audit report.

In the instant case, directors think that it is not necessary to discuss supplementary auditor's report and comment of the C&AG.

Conclusion: Based on the requirements of proviso to Sec. 143(6), management thinking does not seem to be proper.

25.3 - TYPES OF AUDIT CONDUCTED BY CAG AND COMPREHENSIVE AUDIT

Q.12 Write short notes on: Various Types of Audit conducted by CAG.

Ans. : Types of Audits conducted by CAG

1. **Financial Audit:** Financial audit is conducted to express an audit opinion on a set of financial statements.
2. **Compliance Audit:** Compliance audit is carried out to determine whether specified compliance requirements are met or not.
3. **Comprehensive Audit:** Comprehensive Audit involves assessing overall efficiency and effectiveness of Public Enterprises. This is done by reference to certain pre-determined standards, objectives and criteria.
4. **Propriety audit:** Propriety Audit stands for verification of transactions on the tests of public interest, commonly accepted customs and standards of conduct.
5. **Performance Audit:** Performance audit is an objective and systematic examination of evidence for the purpose of providing an independent assessment of the performance of a government organization, program, activity, or function in order to provide information to improve public accountability and facilitate decision-making by parties with responsibility to oversee or initiate corrective action.

Q.13 For facility of consideration, the reports of the Comptroller and Auditor General on the public sector undertakings of the Central Government are presented to the Parliament in several parts. Briefly describe those parts.

or

Write short note on: Contents of Audit report given by Comptroller & Auditor-General of India.

[Nov. 17 (4 Marks)]

Or

The reports of the Comptroller and Auditor General of India on the audit of PSUs are presented to the Parliament and to various state legislatures to facilitate a proper consideration. Enumerate the contents of Audit Report presented by C&AG [Nov. 19 - Old Syllabus (5 Marks)]

Ans. : Audit Report of CAG:

Reports of the CAG on the PSUs of C.G. are presented to the Parliament in following parts:

(*a*) Introduction containing a general review of the working results of Government companies, deemed Government companies and corporations.

(*b*) Results of comprehensive appraisals of selected undertakings conducted by the Audit Board.

(*c*) Resume of the company auditor's reports submitted by them under the directions issued by the CAG and that of comments on the accounts of the Government companies.

(*d*) Significant results of audit of the undertakings not taken up for appraisal by the Audit Board.

"ICAI Examiner Comments"

Majority of the examinees instead of explaining the contents of Report presented by C&AG on the public sector undertakings required in the question, wrongly discussed the Contents of General audit report like title, opening paragraph, responsibility of auditors etc., besides wrongly explaining supplementary audit and Test audit.

Q.14 What is a comprehensive audit of public enterprises? Discuss some of the areas to be examined therein.

Or

XYZ & Co., a CA. firm was appointed by C&AG to conduct comprehensive audit of ABC Public undertaking. C&AG advised to cover areas such as investment decisions, project formulation, organisational effectiveness, capacity utilisation, management of equipment, plant and machinery, production performance, use of materials, productivity of labour, idle capacity, costs and prices, materials management, sales and credit control, budgetary and internal control systems, etc. Discuss stating the issues examined in comprehensive audit.

Or

The Comptroller and Auditor General assists the legislature in reviewing the performance of public undertakings. He conducts an efficiency-cum-performance audit other than the field which has already been covered either by the internal audit of the individual concerns or by the professional auditors. He locates the area of weakness and extravagance for managements' information. Explain stating clearly the issues examined in comprehensive audit.

Or

Sun Light Limited is a public sector undertaking engaged in production of electricity from solar power. It had commissioned a new project near Goa with a new technology for a cost of Rs. 5,750 crore. The project had seen delay in commencement and cost overrun. State the matters that a Comprehensive Audit by C&AG may cover in reporting on the performance and efficiency of this project.

[Nov. 18-New Syllabus (4 Marks)]

Or

Write a short note on the following: Areas covered in Comprehensive Audit. [RTP-May 19]

Ans. : Comprehensive Audit:

Meaning: Comprehensive Audit involves assessing overall efficiency and effectiveness of Public Enterprises. This is done by reference to certain pre-determined standards, objectives and criteria.

The starting point of a comprehensive audit is the preparation of an audit programme based on the study of decisions relating to the setting up of the enterprise, its objectives, the areas of operation, organisation, financial and operational details, capital and operational budgets and other relevant available papers.

Areas to be covered in Comprehensive Audit:

The areas covered in comprehensive audit will vary from enterprise to enterprise depending on the nature of the enterprise, its objectives and operations. Some of the broad areas are listed below:

1. Comparison of overall capital cost of the project with the approved planned costs.
2. Production or operational outputs vis-a-vis under-utilisation of the installed capacity.
3. Soundness of systems of project formulation and implementation.
4. Achievement of Planned rate of return
5. Adequacies of Cost control measures.
6. Existence and performance of Research and development programmes.
7. Existence of adequate system of repairs and maintenance.
8. Effective and economical procedures
9. Inefficiency or insufficiency of Project planning.
10. Undue waste, unproductive time for men and machines, wasteful utilisation or even non utilisation of resources

25.4 - PROPRIETY AUDIT

Q.15 Write short note on: General Principles relating to Propriety Aspect. [Nov. 08, May 11 (4 Marks)]

Or

What are the principles involved regarding "Propriety audit' in the case of Public Sector Undertaking?

Or

Write a short note on - Propriety Audit.

Ans. : General Principles of propriety Aspect:

Propriety Audit stands for verification of transactions on the tests of public interest, commonly accepted customs and standards of conduct.

Instead of too much dependence on documents, vouchers and evidence, it shifts the emphasis to the substance of the transactions and looks into the appropriateness thereof on a consideration of financial prudence, public interest and prevention of wasteful expenditure. Audit against propriety seeks to ensure that expenditure conforms to these principles which have been stated as follows:

(*i*) Expenditure is not *prima facie* more than the occasion demands and that every official exercise the same degree of vigilance in respect of expenditure as a person of ordinary prudence would exercise in respect of his own money.

(*ii*) The authority exercises its power of sanctioning expenditure to pass an order which will not directly or indirectly accrue to its own advantage.

(*iii*) Funds are not utilised for the benefit of a particular person or group of persons.

(*iv*) Apart from the agreed remuneration or reward, no other avenue is kept open to indirectly benefit the management personnel, employees and others.

Q.16 Briefly describe the problems associated with the Propriety Audit.

Ans. : Problems associated with the Propriety Audit:

- The expression "propriety" is a moral term and can be understood by reference to the concept of morality accepted by the society at a given time.
- Propriety audit has an inherent element of subjectivity because it is very difficult to establish standards of public interest, commonly accepted customs, standards for conduct which are not firm basis for audit evaluation.
- The element of subjectivity has caused proper discharge of duty very delicate and demands discretion, but wisdom of taking commercial decisions under dynamic environment (the economic, social and political) must be evaluated with reference to the circumstances in which these were taken and therefore, the auditor in his field must reconstruct such circumstances.
- The judgment of the auditor must be objective as otherwise it would dampen the initiative of management and others in taking commercial decisions and propriety audit would prove itself to be counterproductive.
- To take care of this situation, the C&AG has developed the norms of propriety for expenditure of public funds in our country. By laying down the standards of propriety for Government expenditure the C&AG has really tried to tackle in a practical way the complex problem of subjectivity inherent in a situation calling for propriety consideration.

Q.17 Write a short note on - Areas of propriety audit under Section 143(1) of the Companies Act, 2013.

[Nov. 12 (4 Marks)]

Tee & Co., a firm of chartered accountants had been appointed by C&AG to conduct statutory audit of M/s. Rare Airlines Limited, a Public-Sector Company. They would like to check certain mandatory propriety points sector company. They would like to check certain mandatory propriety points as required u/s 143(1) of the Companies Act, 2013. List the areas of check to meet these requirements.

[May 18 - New Syllabus (4 Marks)]

Ans. : Areas of propriety u/s 143(1) of Companies Act 2013:

Section 143(1) of the Companies Act, 2013 requires the auditor to make an enquiry into certain specific areas. In some of the areas, the auditor has to examine the same from propriety angle as to:

(*a*) whether loans and advances made by the company on the basis of security have been properly secured and whether the terms on which they have been made are prejudicial to the interests of the company or its members;

(*b*) whether transactions of the company which are represented merely by book entries are prejudicial to the interests of the company;

(*c*) where the company not being an investment company or a banking company, whether so much of the assets of the company as consist of shares, debentures and other securities have been sold at a price less than that at which they were purchased by the company;

(*d*) whether loans and advances made by the company have been shown as deposits;

(*e*) whether personal expenses have been charged to revenue account;

(*f*) where it is stated in the books and documents of the company that any shares have been allotted for cash, whether cash has actually been received in respect of such allotment, and if no cash has actually been so received, whether the position as stated in the account books and the balance sheet is correct, regular and not misleading.

Q.18 Write short note on: Propriety Elements in CARO, 2016. [Nov. 11 (4 Marks)]

Ans. : Propriety elements in CARO, 2016:

1. Whether the company has granted any loans, secured or unsecured to companies, firms, LLPs or other parties covered in the register maintained under section 189 of the Act. If so, whether the schedule of repayment of principal and payment of interest has been stipulated and whether the repayments or receipts are regular. If the amount is overdue, state the total amount overdue for more than 90 days and whether reasonable steps have been taken by the company for recovery of the principal and interest;
2. Whether the company is regular in depositing undisputed statutory dues including provident fund, employees' state insurance, income-tax, sales-Lax, service tax, duty of customs, duty of excise, value added tax, cess and **any other statutory dues** to the appropriate authorities and if not, the extent of the arrears of outstanding statutory dues as at the last day of the financial year concerned for a period of more than six months from the date they became payable, shall be indicated.
3. Whether the company has defaulted in repayment of loans or borrowings to a financial institution, bank, government or dues to debenture holders? If yes, the period and amount of default to be reported.
4. Whether moneys raised by way of IPO/FPO and term loans were applied for the purposes for which those are raised. If not, the details together with delays or default and subsequent rectification, if any, as may be applicable, be reported.
5. Whether any fraud by the company or any fraud on the Company by its officers/employees has been noticed or reported during the year; If yes, the nature and the amount involved is to be indicated.
6. Whether managerial remuneration has been paid or provided in accordance with the requisite approvals mandated by the provisions of Sec. 197 read with schedule V to the Companies Act? If not, state the amount involved and steps taken by the company for securing refund of the same
7. Whether the company has entered into any non-cash transactions with directors or persons connected with him and if so, whether provisions of Section 192 of Companies Act, 2013 have been complied with.

25.5 - PERFORMANCE AUDIT

Q.19 Write short note on: Performance Audit

Or

"A performance audit is an objective and systematic examination of evidence for the purpose of providing an independent assessment of the performance of a government organization, program, activity, or function in order to provide information to improve public accountability and facilitate decision-making by parties with responsibility to oversee or initiate corrective action." Briefly discuss the issues addressed by Performance Audits conducted in accordance with the guidelines issued by C&AG. [RTP-Nov. 18]

Or

Write short note on: Issues addressed in Performance Audit of PSUs. [Nov. 18-Old Syllabus (4 Marks)]

Ans. : Performance Audit:

Meaning: A performance audit is an objective and systematic examination of evidence for the purpose of providing an independent assessment of the performance of a government organization, program, activity, or function in order to provide information to improve public accountability and facilitate decision-making by parties with responsibility to oversee or initiate corrective action.

Elements of Performance Audit: Performance audits include evaluation of economy, efficiency and effectiveness.

1. **Economy:** Economy stands for minimising the cost of resources used for an activity, having regard to appropriate quantity, quality and at the best price. Evaluating economy implies forming an opinion whether resources have been used economically and acquired in due time, in appropriate quantity and quality at the best price.
2. **Efficiency Audit:** Efficiency is the measurement of input-output. It is said to be achieved when the output is maximised at the minimum of inputs, or input is minimised for any given quantity and quality of output. Examining efficiency embraces aspects such as whether:
   (*a*) procurement practices followed are sound;
   (*b*) resources are properly protected, maintained and efficiently used;
   (*c*) efficient operating procedures are used; and
   (*d*) the objectives of public sector programmes are met cost-effectively.
3. **Effectiveness:** Effectiveness is the measurement of the extent to which objectives are achieved and the relationship between the intended impact and the actual impact of an activity. Examining effectiveness will cover the following:
   (*a*) determine the extent to which a program achieves a desired level of results;
   (*b*) assess the effectiveness of the program and/or of individual program components;
   (*c*) determine whether management has considered alternatives for carrying out the program that might yield desired results more effectively or at a lower cost;
   (*d*) assess the adequacy of the management control system for measuring, monitoring and reporting a programme's effectiveness;
   (*e*) ensure compliance with laws and regulations applicable to the program.

Q.20 In carrying out efficiency audit of a Public-Sector Undertaking (PSU), what important aspects are required to be looked into, to assess the efficiency? [May 18 - Old Syllabus (4 Marks)]

Ans : Aspects to be looked into to assess the efficiency of a PSU:

Efficiency is the measurement of input-output. It is said to be achieved when the output is maximised at the minimum of inputs, or input is minimised for any given quantity and quality of output. Examining efficiency embraces aspects such as whether:

(*a*) procurement practices followed are sound;
(*b*) resources are properly protected, maintained and efficiently used;
(*c*) efficient operating procedures are used; and
(*d*) the objectives of public sector programmes are met cost-effectively.

Q.21 ABG & Co., a Chartered Accountant firm has been appointed by C & AG for performance audit of a Sugar Industry. What factors should be considered by ABG & Co., while planning a performance audit of Sugar Industry? [May 14 (6 Marks)]

Or

Kalmani & Co. Chartered Accountants have been appointed by C & AG for performance audit of a sugar industry. What factors should be considered by Kalmani & Co., while planning a performance audit of a sugar industry? [May 16 (4 Marks)]

Ans. : Factors to be considered while planning performance audit:

1. Significance and the needs of potential users of the audit report.
2. Obtaining an understanding of the program to be audited.
3. Legal and regulatory requirements.
4. Management controls.
5. Identifying the criteria needed to evaluate matters subject to audit.
6. Identify significant findings and recommendations from previous audits that could affect the current audit objectives.
7. Potential sources of data that could be used as audit evidence and consider the validity and reliability of these data.
8. Consider whether the work of other auditors and experts may be used to satisfy some of the auditors' objectives.

9. Providing sufficient staff and other resources to do the audit.
10. Preparing a written audit plan.

"ICAI Examiner Comments"

Most of the Candidates failed to highlight important factors while planning the performance audit, instead treated this to be covered as internal audit of sugar industry and discussed only general points.

Q.22 You have been appointed by C & AG for performance audit of a PSU. What are the steps to be followed by you while planning the performance audit.

Ans. : Steps for planning an performance audit:

1. **Understanding the entity/programme:** Auditors should obtain an understanding of the programme to be audited to help assess, among other matters, the significance of possible audit objectives and the feasibility of achieving them.
2. **Defining Audit Objective:** These are the basic audit questions that performance auditors seek answers to. These are usually expressed in terms of questions about performance i.e., achievement of economy, efficiency and effectiveness of an entity, programme or activity under audit.
3. **Scope of Audit:** Defining scope focuses the extent, timing and nature of the audit. Answers to the following four questions help in defining the audit scope: WHAT, WHO, WHERE, WHICH PERIOD.
4. **Determining the audit Criteria:** Criteria are the standards used to determine whether a program meets or exceeds expectations. In selecting criteria, auditors have a responsibility to use criteria that are reasonable, attainable, and relevant to the matters being audited.
5. **Deciding Audit Approach:** Performance auditing generally follows one of three approaches in examining the performance of the audited entity(ies).
6. **Developing audit Questions:** Audit team should prepare a list of questions to which they would seek answers. There could be many ways to develop and frame audit questions. The performance auditors should frame a comprehensive and detailed list of questions.
7. **Assess audit team skills and requirement of outside expertise:** The performance auditor must possess the range of skills and experience necessary for effective discharge of audit mandate. The Audit team needs to decide at the planning stage on which aspect expertise is required.
8. **Audit design Matrix:** Audit Design matrix is a rigorous, structured and highly focused approach to designing a performance audit study, based around the audit objectives, associated sub-objectives and lower level detailed questions.
9. **Establish the timetable and resources:** It is important to determine the timetable and the resources needed. Selection of appropriate audit team is the most important component in planning an audit. Considerations for selection of a particular team should be recorded in the planning documents along with the proposed timelines for various activities to be undertaken as part of the audit process.
10. **Intimation of Audit:** Audited entities must be informed about the intention of taking up the planned performance audit with scope and extent of audit well before the commencement of Audit.

26 CHAPTER ACCOUNTING STANDARDS

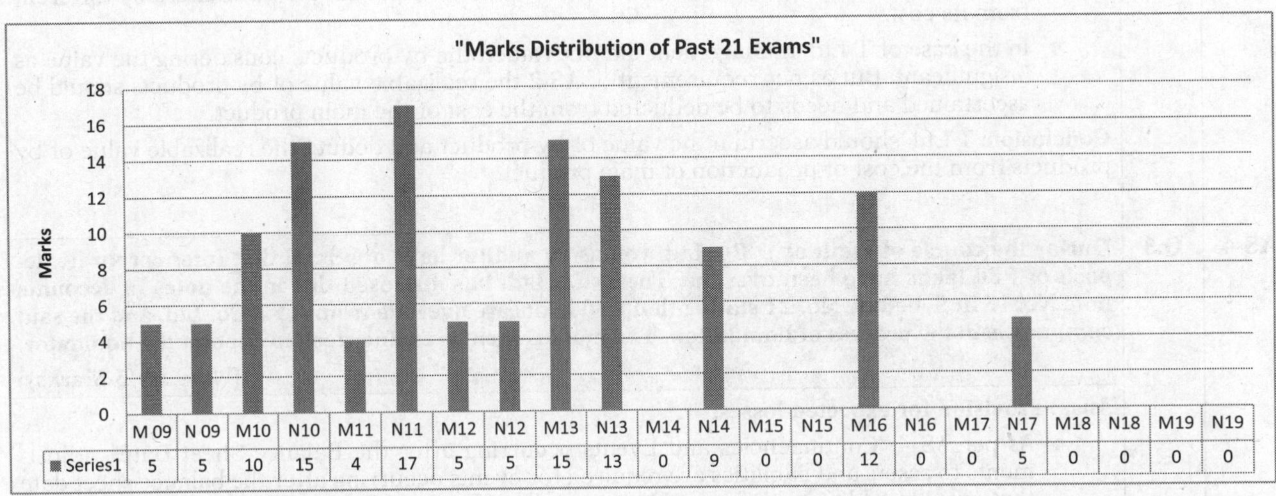

26.1 - ACCOUNTING STANDARDS

AS-2	Q.1	**Write short notes on the following: Normal Capacity for the purpose of Inventory valuation.**
		Ans. : Normal Capacity for the purpose of Inventory Valuation:

- As per AS-2 "Valuation of Inventories" the cost of inventories should comprise all costs of purchase, costs of conversion and other costs incurred in bringing the inventories to their present location and condition.
- While computing cost of conversion a systematic allocation of fixed and variable production overheads that are incurred in converting materials into finished goods is also included.
- The allocation of fixed production overheads for the purpose of their inclusion in the costs of conversion is based on the normal capacity of the production facilities.
- Normal capacity is the production expected to be achieved on an average over a number of periods or seasons under normal circumstances, taking into account the loss of capacity resulting from planned maintenance.
- The actual level of production may be used if it approximates normal capacity.
- Unallocated overheads are recognised as an expense in the period in which they are incurred.
- In periods of abnormally high production, the amount of fixed production overheads allocated to each unit of production is decreased so that inventories are not measured above cost. Variable production overheads are assigned to each unit of production on the basis of the actual use of the production facilities.

	Q.2	**T. Ltd. Commenced its manufacturing activities from 1st April, 2017. In the course of production, the company generated certain by-products. As at 31st March 18 the company did not value the by-products considering the value as insignificant. The auditor of the company is of the opinion that the by-products are inventory of the company and it should be valued and brought into books of account. Comment. [May 13 (5 Marks)]**
		Ans. : Valuation of By-Products: ◆ As per Para 10 of AS-2 "Valuation of Inventories" a production process may result in more than one product being produced simultaneously. This is the case when joint products are produced or when there is a main product and a by-product. Most of the by-products as well as scrap or waste materials, by their nature, are immaterial. In such a case, they are often measured at net realisable value and this value is deducted from the cost of the main product. As a result, the carrying amount of the main product is not materially different from its cost. ◆ In the case of T Ltd. management did not valued the by-products considering the value as insignificant. But as per requirement of AS-2 the realizable value of by products should be ascertained and needs to be deducted from the cost of the main product. **Conclusion**: T Ltd. should ascertain the value of by-product and deduct the realizable value of by products from the cost of production of main product.
AS-4	**Q.3**	**During the course of audit of D Co. Ltd. you as an auditor have observed that Inter corporate deposit of ₹ 50 lakhs have been overdue. The D Co. Ltd. has disclosed this in the notes to accounts note No. 15 in Schedule No. 21 stating that ₹ 50 lakhs are overdue from XYZ Co. Ltd. and the said company is in the process of liquidation. The management is taking steps to appoint the liquidator. [Nov. 10 (5 Marks)]**
		Ans. : Provision for expected losses: ◆ As per AS 4 "Contingencies and Events occurring after the Balance Sheet Date", adjustments to assets and liabilities are required for events occurring after the balance sheet date that provide additional information materially affecting the determination of the amounts relating to conditions existing at the balance sheet date. ◆ In the instant case, it appears from the note No. 15 that the overdue of outstanding inter corporate deposit may not be realisable in full. The company is in the process of liquidation, makes it clear that on the balance sheet date, the amount of deposit is not safe and is not likely to be realised. **Conclusion**: Company was required to provide the loss in the accounts. Accordingly, auditor should qualify the Audit Report.
	Q.4	**As a statutory auditor of a company, comment on the following: A fire broke out on 15th May, 2017, in which material worth ₹ 50 lakhs which was lying in stock since 1st March, 2017 was totally destroyed. The financial statements of the company have not been adopted till the date of fire. The management of the company argues that since the loss occurred in the year 2017-2018, no provision for the loss needs to be made in the financial statements for 2016-17. [Nov. 12 (5 Marks)]**
		Ans. : Event Occurring after the Balance Sheet Date: ◆ As per AS-4 on 'Contingencies and Events Occurring After the Balance Sheet Date', assets and liabilities should be adjusted for events occurring after the balance sheet date that provide additional evidence to assist the estimation of amounts relating to conditions existing at the balance sheet date or that indicate that the fundamental accounting assumption of going concern is not appropriate. ◆ AS-4 also requires disclosure of the non-adjusting event, in the report of approving authority. ◆ Further as per SA 560 "Subsequent Events" the auditor should ensure that all events occurring subsequent to the date of financial statements and for which applicable financial reporting framework requires adjustment or disclosure have been adjusted or disclosed. ◆ In the instant case, fire took place after the close of the accounting year and does not relate to conditions existing at the balance sheet date. **Conclusion**: The event will have no impact on items appearing at the Balance Sheet date and hence not required any adjustment, subject to satisfaction in respect of non-violation of going concern concept. Hence management is correct by not providing provision. However, auditor is required to ensure the proper disclosure in report of approving authority.

AS-5 | Q.5 **State your views as an auditor on the following: Y Ltd. provided ₹ 25 lakhs for inventory obsolescence in 2017-2018. In the subsequent years, it was determined that 50% of such stock was usable. The company wants to adjust the same through prior period adjustment account as the provision was made in the earlier year.** **[Nov. 11 (5 Marks)]**

Ans. : Prior Period Adjustment:

- As per AS 5 on "Net Profit or Loss for the Period, Prior Period Items and Changes in Accounting Policies", prior period items are income or expenses which arise in the current period as a result of errors or omissions in the preparation of the F.S. of one or more prior periods.
- The write-back of provision made in respect of inventories in the earlier year does not constitute prior period adjustment since it neither constitutes error nor omission.
- An estimate may have to be revised if changes occur regarding the circumstances on which the estimate was based, or as a result of new information, more experience or subsequent developments.
- The revision of the estimate, by its nature, does not bring the adjustment within the definitions of an extraordinary item or a prior period item.

Conclusion: Revision of the estimate does not bring the resulting amount of ₹ 12.5 lakhs within the definition either of a prior period item or of an extraordinary item. The amount, however, involved is material and requires separate disclosure to understand the financial position and performance of an enterprise. Accordingly, adjustment in the value of the inventory through prior period item would not be proper.

AS-7 | Q.6 **Comment: B Co. Ltd. is engaged in the business of developing mass scale housing projects including development of small commercial complexes. The flats/commercial spaces are booked by the public and are allotted by way of allotments letter to each allottee. Major construction activities pertaining to buildings are undertaken of flats/commercial spaces is given to allottees by executing legal document. The CEO of the B Co. says that AS 7 is not applicable to the company.** **[Nov. 10 (5 Marks)]**

Ans. : Applicability of AS-7:

- AS 7 (Revised) "Accounting for Construction contracts" states that, "This Statement should be applied in accounting for construction contracts in the F.S. of contractors. The revised AS 7 is silent about its applicability to construction activities undertaken by enterprises on their own account and not as contractors.
- The matter was considered by Expert Advisory committee of the Institute and they are of the view that the revised AS 7 is not applicable to such enterprises.

Conclusion: The activity of developing housing projects on its own account can be considered as a commercial venture by the company in the nature of production activity and, therefore, should be construed as such. Accordingly, the flats/commercial spaces should be identified as inventories in accordance with AS 2 and revenue should be recognition in accordance with AS 9.

AS-9 | Q.7 **Comment: LM Ltd. has 2 divisions L and M. The finished products of division L are transferred to division M where further processing is carried out before sale to customers. To achieve transparency and accountability between the divisions, division L raises an invoice on division M at cost plus normal margins. At the year end the unrealized profits on inter-division stocks are eliminated. However, the transfers are recorded at the invoice value as sales and purchases in the respective divisions for the purpose of preparing the Profit and Loss Account. Suitable disclosures, for this are given in then 'Notes to Accounts'.**

Ans. : Revenue recognition in case of inter division transfers:

- The recognition of inter-divisional transfers as sales is an inappropriate accounting treatment and is inconsistent with AS 9.
- In case of inter-divisional transfers, risks and rewards remain within the enterprise and also there is no consideration from the point of view of the enterprise as a whole. Thus, the recognition criteria for revenue recognition has not been fulfilled in respect of inter-divisional transfers.

Conclusion: In the instant case, LM Ltd. cannot recognise inter-division transfers from L to M as sales and the same will have to be eliminated during finalisation. If not so done, the statutory auditor will have to qualify his report.

Q.8 **In the course of audit of T Ltd., you observed that export incentives are not accounted on accrual basis. The company's management contended that these would be accounted on cash basis citing the uncertainty about its receipts as they are not admitted as due by the customs authorities. Comment.** **[May 11 (4 Marks)]**

Ans. : Revenue recognition in case of export incentives:

- As per Para 9 of AS-9 "Revenue Recognition" where the ability to assess the ultimate collection with reasonable certainty is lacking at the time of raising any claim, e.g., export incentives., revenue recognition is postponed to the extent of uncertainty involved. In such cases, it may be appropriate to recognise revenue only when it is reasonably certain that the ultimate collection will be made.
- When recognition of revenue is postponed due to the effect of uncertainties, it is considered as revenue of the period in which it is properly recognised.

Conclusion: Contention of management of T Ltd. to record the export incentive on cash basis is correct.

Alternative Ans. : Export incentives are considered due as and when the exports have been made from India, though customs authorities does not acknowledge them as due. It cannot be considered that an uncertainty arises about its receipt. If there was any objection, that might have been raised at the time of clearance of the goods for export. Hence, the only uncertainty is the timing of the receipt of such incentives, but not the incentive itself. Accordingly, T Ltd. has to account the export incentives on Accrual basis.

Q.9 **A infrastructure company has constructed a mall and entered into agreement with tenants towards licence fees (monthly rental) and variable licence fees, a percentage on the turnover of the tenant (on an annual basis). Chief Finance Officer wants to account/recognize fee as income for 12 months during current year under audit and variable licence fees as income during next year, since invoice is raised in the subsequent year. As an auditor, how would you deal and state in the statement of Accounting policies? [Nov. 11 (6 Marks)]**

Ans. : Revenue Recognition:

- AS-9 on Revenue Recognition, is mainly concerned with the timing of recognition of revenue in the statement of profit and loss of an enterprise. The amount of revenue arising on a transaction is usually determined by agreement between the parties involved in the transaction. However, when uncertainties exist regarding the determination of the amount, or its associated costs, these uncertainties may influence the timing of revenue recognition.
- Further, as per accrual concept of fundamental accounting assumptions given in AS 1 "Disclosure of Accounting Policies", revenue should be recognised as and when it is accrued i.e. recorded in the financial statements of the periods to which they relate.
- In the present case, monthly rental towards licence fees and variable licence fees as a percentage on the turnover of the tenant though on annual basis is the income related to common financial year. Therefore, recognising the fees as revenue cannot be deferred simply because the invoice is raised in subsequent period. Hence it should be recognised in the financial year of accrual.

Conclusion: The contention of the Chief Financial Officer is not in accordance with AS 9 and hence the auditor may qualify the report indicating the understatement of income/profit and that the profit and loss account does not exhibit a true and fair view of the profit or loss.

Q.10 **A Ltd. is a manufacturer of readymade garments. It sells its products to franchisees located across the country. Readymade garment industry is subject to change in trends of fashion and as such, some of the goods are returned and A Ltd accepts them back as sales returns. On the basis of past trends such returns are estimated to be at 20% of the sales of any year. For the financial year 2017-18, A Ltd. had accounted for the actual sales return made upto 31st March 2018 but has not reversed the possible expected return that are likely to happen after 31st March 2018, in respect of the sale made for the FY 17-18. Mr. X the auditor of A Ltd. wants this to be considered in the accounts of for the year ended on 31st March 2018 but the company is of the opinion that although there is a probability of some goods being returned by the franchisees, there is no significant uncertainty regarding the amount of consideration that will be derived from the sale of goods, since the goods are not in the possession of the company and risk and rewards of ownership still lie with the franchisees and the company cannot record sales returns in its books of account if respect of goods that are likely to be received after the date of balance sheet. Comment. [May 12 (5 Marks)]**

Ans. : Recognition of Revenue:

(*a*) AS-9 on "Revenue Recognition" states that revenue from sale of goods should be recognised at the time of sale of goods subject to following conditions:

- The seller has transferred to the buyer the property in the goods for a price.
- Risks and Rewards of ownership have been transferred to the buyer.
- Seller retains no effective control of the goods transferred associated with ownership.

◆ No significant uncertainty exists regarding the amount of consideration.

(*b*) In the present case, A Ltd. is bearing a risk of sales return and therefore, the company should not recognise the revenue to the extent of 20% of its sales. The company is required to make suitable disclosure of revenue recognition policy in the financial statements.

(*c*) In the absence of the above, the auditor must qualify the report.

Note: Alternatively, the answer may be given with reference to AS-29, requiring a provision.

Q.11 As a statutory auditor of a company, comment on the following: The accounting policy on Revenue Recognition for a company engaged in manufacture and sale of chemical products was stated as "Revenue is recognized only when it can be reliably measured and it is reasonable to expect ultimate collection". [Nov. 12 (5 Marks)]

Ans. : Revenue Recognition:

(*a*) AS-9 on "Revenue Recognition" states that revenue from sale of goods should be recognised at the time of sale of goods subject to following conditions:

◆ The seller has transferred to the buyer the property in the goods for a price.

◆ Risks and Rewards of ownership have been transferred to the buyer.

◆ Seller retains no effective control of the goods transferred associated with ownership.

◆ No significant uncertainty exists regarding the amount of consideration.

(*b*) If conditions mentioned above not satisfied, then revenue recognition should be postponed.

In the instant case, the company is engaged in manufacturing and sale of chemical products and made disclosure that "**Revenue is recognized only when it can be reliably measured and it is reasonable to expect ultimate collection**" is in line with AS-1 and AS-9.

Q.12 Write a short note on Effect of uncertainties on revenue recognition.

Ans. : Effect of Uncertainties on Revenue Recognition:

AS-9 "Revenue Recognition" provides the following:

◆ Recognition of revenue requires that revenue is measurable and that at the time of sale or the rendering of the service it would not be unreasonable to expect ultimate collection.

◆ Where the ability to assess the ultimate collection with reasonable certainty is lacking at the time of raising any claim, e.g., for escalation of price, export incentives, interest etc., revenue recognition is postponed to the extent of uncertainty involved. In such cases, it may be appropriate to recognise revenue only when it is reasonably certain that the ultimate collection will be made. Where there is no uncertainty as to ultimate collection, revenue is recognised at the time of sale or rendering of service even though payments are made by instalments.

◆ When the uncertainty relating to collectability arises subsequent to the time of sale or the rendering of the service, it is more appropriate to make a separate provision to reflect the uncertainty rather than to adjust the amount of revenue originally recorded.

◆ An essential criterion for the recognition of revenue is that the consideration receivable for the sale of goods, the rendering of services or from the use by others of enterprise resources is reasonably determinable. When such consideration is not determinable within reasonable limits, the recognition of revenue is postponed.

◆ When recognition of revenue is postponed due to the effect of uncertainties, it is considered as revenue of the period in which it is properly recognised.

AS-10 Q.13 In the notes to accounts of Z Co. Ltd. as on 31-03-2018 Note No. 11 states that 'Certain machinery items are lying at customs warehouses and company has paid ₹ 500 lakhs up to 30-06-2017 as detention charges, out of which a sum of ₹ 220 lakhs are written back during the year 2017-18 based on settlement with the concerned authorities in respect of a major spares of machinery. For the remaining machinery item negotiations are pending and a provision of ₹ 48 lakhs are made. As such total amount of ₹ 328 lakhs paid/provided on account of detention charges have been capitalized and included in the fixed assets/capital work in progress. The management is of the view that these expenses are directly attributable to the acquisition of the related Fixed Asset.' As the auditor, how would you respond to this? [Nov. 10, Nov. 14 (5 Marks)]

Ans. : Capitalisation of Detention Charges:

As per AS-10 "Accounting for Fixed Assets" the cost of an item of fixed assets comprises its purchase price, including import duties and other non-refundable taxes or levies and any directly attributable cost of bringing the asset to its working condition for its intended use; any trade discounts and rebates are deducted in arriving at the purchase price. Examples of directly attributable costs are:

1. site preparation;

		2. initial delivery and handling costs; 3. installation cost, such as special foundations for plant; and 4. professional fees, for example fees of architects and engineers. **Conclusion**: Detention charges, being in the nature of penalty levied by Customs for not removing the articles within specified period from custom port cannot be considered as directly attributable cost. Treatment done by the company is incorrect. The auditor should qualify the report appropriately mentioning the effect on Balance sheet and Profit and Loss Account.
	Q.14	**F Limited includes in the Schedule of Inventory, those items of Fixed Assets which have not been in active use and held for disposal, as inventory item. [May 10 (5 Marks)]**
		Ans. : Treatment of assets held for Disposal ◆ **AS-10 "Accounting for Fixed Assets"** requires that the items of fixed assets that have been retired from active use and are held for disposal be stated at the lower of their net book value and NRV and are shown separately in the financial statements. ◆ As per **AS-2 "Valuation of Inventories"**, "inventories" are assets "held for sale in the ordinary course of business, in the process of production for such sale; or in the form of materials or supplies to be consumed in the production process or in the rendering of service". **Conclusion**: Inclusion of fixed assets, not in active use and held for disposal, as inventory item in the schedule of inventory is not in line with the requirements of AS-10 and AS-2. Such fixed assets should be stated at lower of net book value and NRV and are shown separately in F.S.
AS-11	**Q.15**	**X Limited, a newly incorporated company in India commenced its business form April 1, 2017. The company purchased fixed assets costing ₹ 4,000 lakhs on 01-04-2017 and the same was fully financed by foreign currency loan (U.S. Dollars) payable in three annual equal instalments. Exchange rates were 1 Dollar = ₹ 40.00 and ₹ 42.50 as on 01-04-2017 and 31-03-2018 respectively. The company worked out foreign exchange loss as per AS 11 at ₹ 250 Lakhs and expensed the entire amount in the profit and loss account. The managing director of the company was worried about this heavy revenue loss and asked the accountant not to follow AS 11 issued by the ICAI for this particular transaction. The accountant of the company, followed the instruction of the managing director and removed exchange loss from the profit and loss account but then he added the entire exchange loss to the value of fixed asset and computed the depreciation thereon. As an Auditor of X Limited how you would deal with this particular transaction? [Nov. 13 (5 Marks)]**
		Ans. : Treatment of Exchange Difference: ◆ As per Para 46A(1) of AS 11 "The Effects of Changes in Foreign Exchange Rates" the exchange differences arising on reporting of long- term foreign currency monetary items in so far as they relate to the acquisition of a depreciable capital asset in respect of accounting periods commencing on or after the 1st April, 2011 can be added to or deducted from the cost of the asset and shall be depreciated over the balance life of the asset. ◆ So, X Ltd. has the choice to avail this option. However, the company should disclose the fact of such option and of the amount remaining to be amortized in the financial statements of the period in which such option is exercised and in every subsequent period so long as any exchange difference remains unamortized. **Conclusion**: Treatment done by the accountant is correct and auditor need to check the disclosures made in the financial statement.
AS-12	**Q.16**	**Comment on the following: XYZ Limited received a grant of ₹ 25 lakhs under the Government's Subsidy Scheme, for acquiring an imported machinery for setting up new plant. The entire grant received is credited to Profit and Loss Account. [Nov. 09 (5 Marks)]**
		Ans. : Treatment of Capital Grant: As per AS 12, "Accounting for Government Grants" grants received for acquisition of specific fixed asset maybe treated in following ways: (*a*) Deduction from the gross value of the asset; or (*b*) Treating it as deferred income which should be recognised in the P & L account on a systematic and rational basis over the useful life of the asset. By crediting the entire amount of grant to P & L account, the company has treated it as a revenue income which is not in accordance with the requirements of the AS 12. **Conclusion**: Auditor needs to qualify the report stating the fact that the income has been overstated to the extent of the amount of grant net of proportionate credit that would have been worked out.

Q.17 **XYZ Ltd. had received a grant of ₹ 50 lacs in 2012 from a State Government towards installation of pollution control machinery on fulfilment of certain conditions. The company, however, failed to comply with the said conditions and consequently was required to refund the said amount in 2016.**

The company debited the said amount to its machinery in 2017 on payment of the same. It also reworked the depreciation for the said machinery from the date of its purchase and passed necessary adjusting entries in the year 2017 to incorporate the retrospective impact of the same.

Ans. : Accounting Treatment of Refund of Government Grant:

- As per AS 12, "Accounting for Government Grants", the amount refundable in respect of a government grant related to a specific fixed asset is recorded by increasing the book value of the asset or by reducing the capital reserve or the deferred income balance, as appropriate, by the amount refundable.
- In case of first alternative, i.e., where the book value of the asset is increased, depreciation on the revised book value should be provided prospectively over the residual useful life of the asset.
- In the present case, XYZ Ltd. had received a grant of ₹ 50 lacs in 2010 from a State Government towards installation of pollution control machinery on fulfilment of certain conditions. However, the amount of grant has to be refunded since it failed to comply with the prescribed conditions.
- The accounting treatment given by XYZ Ltd. of increasing the value of the plant and machinery is quite proper, but accounting treatment in respect of depreciation given by the company of adjustment of depreciation with retrospective effect is improper and constitutes violation of AS 10, "Property, Plant & Equipment" and AS 12, "Accounting for Government Grants".

Conclusion: The auditor should discuss with the management to make necessary changes in respect of same and if management not agrees for the changes, auditor should qualify the report quantifying the impact of the same on profit as well as assets of the company.

AS-13

Q.18 **Big Ltd. has borrowed ₹ 30 lakhs from State Bank of India during the financial year 2017-18. The borrowings are used to invest in shares of Small Ltd., a subsidiary company of Big Ltd., which is implementing a new project estimated to cost ₹ 50 lakhs. As on 31st March, 2018, since the said project was not complete, the directors of Big Ltd. resolved to capitalize the interest accruing on borrowings amounting to ₹ 4 lakhs and add it to the cost of investments.**

Ans. : Capitalisation of Interest on Borrowings in respect of Investments:

- As per AS-13 "Accounting for Investments" cost of investments includes acquisition charges such as brokerage, fees and duties.
- AS-16 "Borrowing Costs" does not consider investment in shares as qualifying assets that can enable a company to add the borrowing costs to investments.
- In the instant case, X Ltd. has used borrowed funds for making investment in shares of a subsidiary company. For acquiring shares of a subsidiary company, apart from any fees, duties etc., there are no cost incurred for investing in shares.
- Any borrowing costs incurred cannot be treated as part of cost of investments and cannot be added to the cost of investments.

Conclusion: Auditor should qualify his report by stating that the borrowing costs have been wrongly added to the cost of investments rather than charging them to Profit and Loss Account. The effect of the same on the profits for the year would also have to be mentioned.

Q.19 **K Ltd. had 5 subsidiaries as at 31st March 2018 and the investments in-subsidiaries are considered as long term and valued at cost. Two of the subsidiaries net worth eroded as at 31st March 18 and the prospects of their recovery are very bleak and the other three subsidiaries are doing exceptionally well. The company did not provide for the decline in the value of investments in two subsidiaries because the overall investment portfolio in subsidiaries did not suffer any decline' as the other three subsidiaries are doing exceptionally well. Comment.** **[May 13 (5 Marks)]**

Ans. : Valuation of Long term investments:

- As per Para 17 of AS-13 "Accounting for Investments "Long-term investments are usually carried at cost. However, when there is a decline, other than temporary, in the value of a long-term investment, the carrying amount is reduced to recognise the decline.

- As per Para 18 Long-term investments are usually of individual importance to the investing enterprise. The carrying amount of long-term investments is therefore determined on an individual investment basis.

Conclusion: Considering the above, K Ltd. should provide for the decline in the value of investments in two subsidiaries despite the fact that the overall investment portfolio in subsidiaries did not suffer any decline.

AS-14 | Q.20

As a Statutory Auditor, how would you deal with the following: P Pvt. Ltd. was amalgamated with PQR Ltd. with effect from 1st April, 2017. As per the scheme of amalgamation approved by the High Court, the amalgamation was to be accounted by the "Pooling of Interests Method". The scheme further provided that the balance in Revaluation Reserve of P Pvt. Ltd. as on 31st March, 2017 was to be treated as a General Reserve on amalgamation. During the financial year 2017-18, PQR Ltd. issued bonus shares out of General Reserves (which included the amount of revaluation reserve of P Pvt. Ltd.).

Ans. : Declaration of Bonus out of General Reserves created at the time of amalgamation:

- As per AS 14, "Accounting for Amalgamations" in case of amalgamation in the nature of merger and the 'Pooling of Interest Method', the reserves appears in the financial statements of the transferee company in the same form in which they appeared in the financial statements of the transferor company.
- In the present case, P Pvt. Ltd. is amalgamated with PQR Ltd. and the amalgamation is in the nature of merger. Accordingly, Revaluation Reserves of P Pvt. Ltd. would have normally continued to remain so in PQR Ltd. However, since the scheme mentions that Revaluation Reserve is to be treated as General Reserves, the scheme will override AS 14.
- As per AS 14, "Accounting for Amalgamations", in case of any approved scheme of amalgamation if the treatment in accounting is not as per the AS, a specific disclosure of the same will have to be made along with the financial effect on the financial statements due to such deviation.

Conclusion: Auditor is required to ensure that the company complies with the requirements regarding treatment of reserves and other related disclosure requirements. In case of any non-compliance, he need to modify his report.

AS-15 | Q.21

Excellent Limited, a Company incorporated in India and Listed with SEBI, has a scheme for payment of settlement allowance to retiring employees. Under the scheme, retiring employees are entitled to reimbursement of certain travel expenses for class they are entitled to as per company rules and regulations. Employees are also entitled to claim a lump-sum payment to cover expenses on food and stay during the travel. The Company also gives option to employees that they can claim a lump-sum amount equal to three months' pay last drawn.

Excellent Limited have following accounting policies to record these travel expenses:

(*i*) Settlement allowance does not depend upon the length of service of employee. It is restricted to employee's eligibility under the travel rule of the company therefore all travel expenses fall under the category of defined contribution plans.

(*ii*) Since it is not related to the length of service of the employees, it is difficult to estimate reliably and there is no present obligation to pay employees as per AS 29 "Provisions' Contingent Liabilities and Contingent Assets", hence it is accounted for on claim basis.

You are statutory auditor of Excellent Limited. What would be your guidance to audit team?

[Nov. 13 (4 Marks)]

Ans. : Accounting Treatment of Settlement Allowance:

- AS 15 "Employee Benefits" covers the cases where payment promised to be made to an employee at or near retirement presents significant difficulties in the determination of periodic charge to the statement of profit and loss.
- The present case falls under the category of Defined Benefit Scheme. The contention of the Company that the settlement allowance will be accounted for on claim basis is not correct even if company's obligation under the scheme is uncertain and requires estimation.
- In estimating the obligation, assumptions may need to be made regarding future conditions and events, which are largely outside the company's control.
- So Accounting Treatment of the settlement allowance in this case as per AS 15 will be following points:

(1) Settlement allowance payable by the company is a defined retirement benefit, covered by AS 15.

(2) A provision should be made every year in the accounts for the accruing liability on account of settlement allowance. The amount of provision should be calculated according to actuarial valuation.

(3) Where, however, the amount of provision so determined is not material, the company can follow some other method of accounting for settlement allowances.

Q.22 Z Ltd. changed its employee remuneration policy from 1st of April 2016 to provide for 12% contribution to provident fund on leave encashment also. As per the leave encashment policy the employees can either utilize or encash it. As at 31st March 17 the company obtained an actuarial valuation for leave encashment liability.

However, it did not provide for 12% PF contribution on it. The auditor of the company wants it to be provided but the management replied that as and when the employees availed leave encashment, the provident fund contribution was made. The company further contends that this is the correct treatment as it is not sure whether the employees will avail leave encashment or utilize it. Comment.

[May 13 (5 Marks), May 16 (4 Marks)]

Ans. : Treatment of short term compensated absences:

- As per AS-15 "Employee Benefits", an enterprise should recognise the expected cost of short-term employee benefits in the form of compensated absences as follows:
  - (*a*) in the case of accumulating compensated absences, when the employees render service that increases their entitlement to future compensated absences; and
  - (*b*) in the case of non-accumulating compensated absences, when the absences occur.
- An enterprise should measure the expected cost of accumulating compensated absences as the additional amount that the enterprise expects to pay as a result of the unused entitlement that has accumulated at the balance sheet date.
- In the given case, company obtained actuarial valuation for leave encashment, it is obvious that the compensated absences are accumulating in nature. Z Ltd will accumulate the amount of leave encashment benefits as it is the liability of the company to provide 12% PF on amount of leave encashment.

Conclusion: Contention of the auditor that full provision should be provided by the company is correct

AS-16

Q.23 As a statutory auditor for the year ended 31st March 2018, how would you deal with the Following: X Ltd., has borrowed ₹ 25 crores from financial institutions during the financial year 2017-18. These borrowings are used to invest in shares of Y Ltd., a subsidiary company which is implementing a new project estimated to cost ₹ 50 crores. As on 31st March 2018, since the said project was not yet complete, the directors of X Ltd. resolved to capitalize the interest on the borrowings amounting to ₹ 3 Crores and add it to the cost of investments.

Ans. : Capitalisation of Interest on Borrowings in respect of Investments:

- AS-16 "Borrowing Costs" does not consider investment in shares as qualifying assets that can enable a company to add the borrowing costs to investments.
- In the instant case, X Ltd. has used borrowed funds for making investment in shares of a subsidiary company. For acquiring shares of a subsidiary company, apart from any fees, duties etc., there are no cost incurred for investing in shares.
- Any borrowing costs incurred cannot be treated as part of cost of investments and cannot be added to the cost of investments.

Conclusion: The statutory auditor is required to qualify his report by stating that the borrowing costs have been wrongly added to the cost of investments. It is required to Charge the borrowing cost to the profit and loss account. The effect of the same on the Profit for the year would also have to be mentioned in the audit report.

Q.24 As a Statutory Auditor, how would you deal with: ABC Ltd. commenced construction of a flyover in Mumbai in January, 2017 under BOLT scheme. The same was completed in February, 2018. Due to seasonal heavy rains in July, 2017 in the area, the work on the flyover had to be suspended for 1 month. The company accordingly suspended borrowing costs of ₹ 12.50 lakhs for that month from capitalisation.

		Ans. : Capitalization of borrowing costs: ◆ As per AS 16, "Borrowing Costs", capitalization of borrowing costs should be suspended in respect of periods in which active development is interrupted, except for the situation when temporary delay is necessary as a part of the process or substantial technical and administrative work is being carried out. ◆ Thus, the test as to whether or not to capitalize the borrowing costs depends primarily upon the nature of interruption of activities during "extended periods". ◆ In the instant case, it has been mentioned that the construction activity was interrupted due to seasonal rain and hence being regular feature. **Conclusion**: Borrowing cost of ₹ 12.50 lakhs incurred by ABC Ltd. should be capitalized. Suspension of capitalization by the company is not a correct treatment and statutory auditor should report accordingly.
AS-18	**Q.25**	**A firm of a father and a son is receiving ₹ 2 lakhs towards job work done for XYZ Ltd. during the year ended on 31.03.18. The total job work charges paid by XYZ Ltd. during the year are over ₹ 50 lakhs. The father is a Managing Director of XYZ Ltd. having substantial holding. The Managing Director told the auditor that since he is not involved in the activities of the firm and since the amount paid to it is insignificant; there is no need to disclose the transaction. He further contended that such a payment made in the last year was not disclosed. Is Managing Director right in his approach?**
		Ans. : Related party Disclosures: ◆ AS 18 "Related Party Disclosures" requires disclosure of related party relationship and transactions between a reporting enterprise and its related parties. ◆ According to AS-18, in the case of related party transactions, the reporting enterprise should disclose the following: 1. the name of the transacting related party; 2. a description of the relationship between the parties; 3. a description of the nature of transactions; 4. volume of the transactions either as an amount or as an appropriate proportion; 5. any other elements of the related party transactions necessary for an understanding of the financial statements; 6. the amounts or appropriate proportions of outstanding items pertaining to related parties at the balance sheet date and provisions for doubtful debts due from such parties at that date; and 7. amounts written off or written back in the period in respect of debts due from or to related parties. ◆ In the instant case, the managing director of XYZ Ltd. is a partner in the firm with his son, which has been paid Rs. 2 lakhs as job work charges. The managing director constitutes a substantial holding in the firm. And hence the transaction is covered by AS 18. **Conclusion**: The approach of the managing director is not tenable under the law and accordingly all disclosure requirements have to be complied. Accordingly, the approach followed by the Managing Director is not right. Under the circumstances, auditor shall apply the procedures as stated in SA 550 and modify his report accordingly.
AS-20	**Q.26**	**G Ltd. Has paid up capital of ₹ 20 crores divided into equity shares of ₹ 10 each on 31st March, 2017. During the financial year 2016-17, the company issued bonus shares in the ratio of 1:1. The net profit of the company for the financial years 2016-17 and 2017-18 was ₹ 10 Crores and ₹ 15 Crores respectively. The EPS as disclosed by the company for two years was ₹ 5 and ₹ 3.75 respectively. As the statutory auditor of G Ltd., comment on the above. [Nov. 17 (5 Marks)]**
		Ans. : Disclosure of Earnings Per Share: ◆ As per AS 20, in the case of a bonus issue, the number of equity shares outstanding before the event of a bonus issue have to be adjusted for the proportionate change in the number of equity shares outstanding as if the event had occurred at the beginning of the earliest period reported. ◆ In view of the above, the EPS for both the years will have to be calculated taking the equity share capital after the bonus issue as the denominator.

- If the same is done the EPS for 31.3.2017 will be ₹ 2.50 and that for 31.3.2018 will be ₹ 3.75. Since the above figures of EPS have not been disclosed, the company has not complied with the provisions of the AS 20.

Conclusion: As EPS reported is not in compliance with AS 20, auditor is required to qualify his report in terms of Sec. 143(3)(*e*) of the Companies Act, 2013.

Q.27 T Pvt. Ltd. is an unlisted closely held company with turnover less than ₹ 50 crores. While finalizing the accounts, Mr. M the Director (finance) disputed the applicability of AS 20 to the company.

Ans. : Applicability of AS-20:

- AS 20 "Earning Per Share", is mandatory in respect of enterprises whose equity shares or potential equity shares are listed on a recognised stock exchange in India. However, every company is required under Schedule III to the Companies Act 2013, to disclose EPS.
- Accordingly, every company, which is required to give information under Schedule III to the Companies Act, 2013, should calculate and disclose EPS in accordance with AS 20, whether or not its equity shares or potential equity shares are listed on a recognised stock exchange in India.

Conclusion: The contention of Director (Finance) is incorrect. The auditor will have to ensure that EPS is disclosed as per AS 20 or else the auditor should appropriately modify the audit report.

Q.28 X Ltd. did not follow the applicable Accounting Standard for disclosing Earnings Per Share (EPS) in the financial statements. The fact of such non-disclosure was however, mentioned in the notes forming part of accounts. As the statutory auditor of X Ltd., how would you report in the above case? **[May 09 (5 Marks)]**

Ans. : Noncompliance of AS 20:

- Section 133 of Companies Act 2013 empowers the Central Government to prescribes the accounting Standards to be complied with by the companies. Ministry of Corporate Affairs (MCA) *vide* General Circular clarified that the existing Accounting Standards notified under the Companies Act, 1956 shall continue to apply till they are prescribed by Central Government. AS 20 is also one of the AS notified by Section 133 of the Companies Act, 2013
- AS 20 "Earnings per Share" requires every company to disclose the EPS. If the disclosures required by AS 20 are not made, the auditor is required to state the fact in his report as per the requirements of Section 143(3) which requires the auditor to comment on "Whether Accounting Standards notified u/s 133 have been followed?"
- This cannot be considered as a qualification to affect the "True & Fair" position of financial results of the company.

AS-22 Q.29 Write short note on: Deferred Taxation. **[May 16 (4 Marks)]**

Ans. : Deferred Taxation:

- AS 22 "Accounting for Taxes on Income" deferred tax may be defined as the effect of timing difference.
- Taxable income is calculated in accordance with tax laws. In some circumstances, the requirements of these laws to compute taxable income differ from the accounting policies applied to determine accounting income. The effect of this difference is that the taxable income and accounting income may not be the same.
- The differences between taxable income and accounting income can be classified into permanent differences and timing differences. Permanent differences are those differences between taxable income and accounting income which originate in one period and do not reverse subsequently.
- Timing differences are those differences between taxable income and accounting income for a period that originate in one period and are capable of reversal in one or more subsequent periods.
- Timing differences arise because the period in which some items of revenue and expenses are included in taxable income do not coincide with the period in which such items of revenue and expenses are included or considered in arriving at accounting income. For example, machinery purchased for scientific research related to business is fully allowed as deduction in the first year for tax purposes whereas the same would be charged to the statement of profit and loss as depreciation over its useful life.

- AS 22 requires that deferred tax should be recognized for all the timing differences, subject to the consideration of prudence in respect of deferred tax assets.

Q.30 **As a statutory auditor for the year ended 31st March 2017, how would you deal with the following: X Ltd., a listed company, was incurring heavy losses since the last several years and the industry in which it was functioning was not expected to perform better in the next few years. While finalising the accounts for the year ended 31st March 2017, the CFO of the company decided to create a Deferred Tax Asset for the tax benefits that would arise in future years from the earlier years losses that had remained unabsorbed in Income tax.**

Or

Do you approve of the following: Shakti Pan Masala (P.) Ltd. was incurring heavy losses in the last several years since it could not withstand the competition in the market. The State in which the company had its registered office and also its major sales had moved a bill in the State Assembly to ban manufacture and sale of all kinds of Pan Masalas in the State. While finalizing the accounts for the year ended 31-03-2017, the CFO of the company created a Deferred Tax Asset for the tax benefits that would arise in future years from the earlier years losses that had remained unabsorbed in Income Tax.

Ans. : Recognition of Deferred Tax Assets:

- AS 22 on "Accounting for Taxes on Income", requires that deferred tax should be recognised for all timing differences, subject to the considerations of prudence in respect of deferred tax assets.
- The standard further states that where an enterprise has unabsorbed depreciation or carry forward of losses under the tax laws, deferred tax assets should be recognised only to the extent that there is virtual certainty supported by convincing evidence that sufficient future taxable income will be available against which such deferred tax assets can be realised.
- This implies that there is a reasonable certainty that the carry forward losses would be recouped in the future years.
- In the instant case, looking to the fact that the industry in which the company was functioning was not expected to perform well in the next few years, getting virtual certainty and convincing evidence for the same would be almost impossible.
- Hence, in the absence of virtual certainty for offset of the losses in future years, creating a deferred tax asset would not be possible for the company.

Conclusion: The statutory auditor would therefore have to qualify his report by stating that deferred tax assets have been created though there is no virtual certainty for getting the said benefit in income tax. He would also have to mention the amount by which the loss for the year has been understated and the amount by which the reserves are overstated.

Q.31 **Comment: T Ltd. an Indian company, subject to Income-tax Act, 1961, discloses advance Income-tax paid (Current tax asset) and provision for Income-tax (Current tax liability), separately in Balance Sheet for the year ended 31.03.2018, i.e., it does not offset the amount. [May 10 (5 Marks)]**

Ans. : Set off of Advance tax against Provision for tax:

As per AS 22 - Accounting for Taxes in Income, an enterprise should offset assets and liabilities representing current tax if the enterprise:

(*i*) has a legally enforceable right to set off the recognized amounts and

(*ii*) intends to settle the asset and liability on a net basis.

An enterprise will normally have a legally enforceable right to set off an asset and liability representing current tax when they relate to income taxes levied under the same governing taxation laws and the taxation laws permit the enterprise to make or receive a single net payment.

Conclusion: T Ltd. is entitled to set off the advance tax against provision for tax, and can show only the net amount in the balance sheet.

Q.32 **SRS Ltd. has drawn the financial statement as on 31.03.18 and presented to you along with additional information:**

Balance Sheet of SRS Ltd. as on 31.03.18

Liabilities	Amt.	Assets	Amt.
Share Capital	50,00,000	Fixed Assets	
Reserves & Surplus		Gross block	
Profit and Loss A/c	4,00,000	Less: Depreciation	1,00,00,000
Secured Loans	75,00,000	Investments	Nil
Current Liabilities and provisions		Current Assets Loans & Advances	
Creditors for trade	3,00,000	Debtors	25,00,000
Advance received	3,00,000	Advance Paid	10,00,000
	1,35,00,000		1,35,00,000

Additional Information:

(*a*) Entire pre-operative expenses of ₹ 7,00,000 was charged to Profit and Loss Account whereas for the purpose of Income Tax, only what is allowable is claimed.

(*b*) Depreciation as per Books ₹ 35,00,000

Depreciation as per Income Tax ₹ 50,00,000

(*c*) Losses to be carried forward as per Income Tax Act - ₹ 16,00,000

(*d*) Donation disallowed while computing tax - ₹ 50,000

Considering the additional information, Can you certify that the company has complied with the Accounting Standards and issue an unqualified report? [Nov. 11 (6 Marks)]

Ans. : Compliance of Accounting Standards:

(*a*) Based on the Additional Information provided in the question, it appears that the company had not complied with the provisions of AS 6, AS 10, AS 22.

(*b*) As per Para 28 of AS 6 "Depreciation Accounting" historical cost of each assets is required to be disclosed, which is not shown in the balance sheet.

(*c*) As per Para 39 of AS 10 "Accounting for Fixed Assets" Gross Book Value of the fixed assets should be disclosed, which is not shown in the balance sheet.

(*d*) As per requirement of AS 22 "Accounting for Taxes on income" company was required to recognise the effect of timing difference as below:

- Recognise Deferred Tax Asset for Pre-operative Expenses
- Recognise Deferred Tax Liability for Depreciation.

Conclusion: As the company had not complied with the requirements of various Accounting Standards, an Unqualified report cannot be issued.

AS-26 Q.33 **X Ltd. is engaged in the business of newspaper and radio broadcasting. It operates through different brand names. During FY 12-13 it incurred substantial amounts on external trade, business communication and branding expenses by participation in various corporate social responsibility initiatives. The company expects to benefits by this expenditure by attracting new customers over a period of time and accordingly it has capitalized the same under brand development expenses and intends to amortize the same over the period in which it expects the benefits to flow. As the statutory auditor of the company do you concur? Give reasons. [Nov. 13 (4 Marks)]**

Ans. : Recognition of Intangible Assets:

- As per AS-26 on "Intangible Assets", expenditure on an intangible item should be recognised as an expense when it is incurred unless it forms part of the cost of an intangible asset that meets the recognition criteria.
- In the given case, X Ltd. incurred substantial amounts on external trade, business communication and branding expenses by participation in various corporate social responsibility initiatives. The company expects to benefits by this expenditure by attracting new customers over a period of time and accordingly it has capitalized the same under brand development expenses. Here, no intangible assets or other asset is acquired or created that can be recognized.

Conclusion: The accounting treatment by the company to amortize the entire expenditure over the period in which it expects the benefits to flow is not correct and the same should be debited to the statement of Profit & Loss.

Q.34 B Pvt. Ltd. started stock broking activities in 2017 and for which it acquired membership of a stock exchange for ₹ 150 lakhs. While finalizing the accounts, the company disclosed the above amount under fixed assets scheduled as "Stock Exchange membership Rights". The company also did not write off any amount since the rights would enable the company to perpetually carry on its business. As a statutory auditor how would you deal with the above situation? [May 16 (4 Marks)]

Ans. : Amortization of Intangible Assets:

- As per AS 26 "Intangible Assets" an intangible asset should be recognised if, and only if:
  - (*a*) it is probable that the future economic benefits that are attributable to the asset will flow to the enterprise; and
  - (*b*) the cost of the asset can be measured reliably.
- In the given case, B Pvt. Ltd. has paid ₹ 110 lacs for acquiring membership of stock exchange. Such membership rights provide exclusive right to B Pvt. Ltd. for carrying out stock broking activities. Such membership rights acquired by B Pvt. Ltd. meet the criteria of recognition and therefore recognizing the membership rights as Fixed Assets is proper.
- AS 26 also requires that all Intangible Assets to be amortised. For this purpose, a rebuttable presumption of 10 years is to be considered.
- In the given case, the company did not write-off any amount stating that such rights would enable the company to perpetually carry on its business.

Conclusion: Contention of the company for not writing off the intangible assets is not proper and the auditor needs to qualify his report and state the fact of non-compliance with AS 26.

Q.35 Write short note on: Intangible Asset vs. Intangible Item. [Nov. 14 (4 Marks)]

Ans. : Intangible Asset vs. Intangible Item:

- As per AS 26 on "Intangible Assets", an intangible asset is an identifiable non-monetary asset, without physical substance, held for use in the production or supply of goods or services, for rental to others, or for administrative purposes.
- An intangible asset should be recognised if, and only if: (a) it is probable that the future economic benefits that are attributable to the asset will flow to the enterprise; and (b) the cost of the asset can be measured reliably.
- An enterprise frequently expends resources, or incur liabilities, on the acquisition, development, maintenance or enhancement of intangible resources such as scientific or technical knowledge, design and implementation of new processes or systems, licences, intellectual property, market knowledge and trademarks (including brand names and publishing titles). Common examples of items encompassed by these broad headings are computer software, patents, copyrights, motion picture films, etc. These expenses are known as intangible items.
- If intangible items fulfil the conditions given in the definition of an intangible asset, then only they will be recognized as intangible asset. But if any of such discussed items does not satisfy these conditions then it will not constitute intangible asset.
- Intangible assets are shown in Balance Sheet whereas intangible items which are not intangible assets are provided as expenditure in Statement of Profit and Loss.

AS-29

Q.36 V Ltd. sold 1 lakh vacuum pumps during the year 2015-16 with a condition to make good by repair/replacement any manufacturing defects reported within 6 months from the date of sale. Past experience in this regard showed that there were no replacements carried out, but minor/major repairs were necessitated to the extent of 10%/5% respectively of the units sold. The cost of such minor/major repairs would amount to ₹ 1,000/₹ 6,000 respectively. While finalizing the accounts for the year, the company does not reflect any provision, in this regard.

Ans. : Recognition of Provision in the Accounts:

- As per AS - 29, 'Provisions, Contingent Liabilities and Contingent Assets', a provision is a liability which can be measured only by using a substantial degree of estimation and should be recognised when following conditions are satisfied:
  - (*a*) An enterprise has a present obligation as a result of a past event;

(*b*) It is probable that an outflow of resources embodying economic benefits will be required to settle the obligation; and

(*c*) A reliable estimate can be made of the amount of the obligation.

- In the given case, V Ltd. fulfils all the above conditions. The sale of pumps with a warranty obligation constitutes the present obligation as a result of past event. It is probable that some outflow will be involved in setting the warranty obligation, satisfy the second condition.
- As per the details given in the question, reliable estimate can be made as under:
  = 6000 × (5% of 100000) + 1000 × (10% of 100000)
  = ₹ 400 lakhs

Conclusion: V Ltd. should make a provision for warranty obligation against sale of vacuum pumps to the extent of ₹ 400 lakhs. The auditor should insist on such provision, in the absence thereof, he should qualify his audit report.

Misc. **Q.37** **As a Statutory Auditor, how would you deal with the following: B Pvt. Ltd., implements a Voluntary Retirement Scheme (VRS) for its employees. It follows a policy of amortising the expenditure over 10 years. As at 1st April, 2017, the unamortised VRS expenditure was ₹ 15 lakhs. During the year 2017-18, it incurred further ₹ 12 lakhs as VRS. For the year ended 31st March, 2018, the company proposes to revise the period of amortisation to 5 years. It also proposes to follow the revised period for the opening balance.**

Ans. : Revision of Amortisation period of Expenditure on Voluntary Retirement:

- Voluntary Retirement Scheme (VRS) is one form of termination benefit and it is treated as per general accepted accounting practices.
- Accordingly, VRS expenditure would have to be amortised over a reasonable period.
- In the present case, company proposes to revise the period of amortisation to 5 years from 10 years. It amounts to change in accounting policy and based on the facts of the case, appears appropriate and reasonable.

Conclusion: The auditor is required to examine that the requirements of AS 5, "Net Profit or Loss for the Period, Prior Period Items and Changes in Accounting Policies" and impact of change in accounting policy is disclosed as per AS 1, "Disclosure of Accounting Policies".

Q.38 **As a Statutory Auditor, how would you deal with the following: X Ltd. is engaged in manufacture of Cement. In the Statement of Profit and Loss for the year ended 31st March, 2018, it discloses its revenue from sales transactions (turnover) net of excise duty. The excise duty collected and paid on sales transactions and that related to difference between Closing inventory and Opening inventory is, however, disclosed in the "Notes to Accounts".**

Ans. : Disclosure requirement of Excise Duty:

As per Accounting Standard Interpretation - ASI 14 'Disclosure of Revenue from Sales Transactions' (Revised) issued by ICAI, the amount of turnover should be disclosed as follows on the face of the Statement of Profit and Loss:

Turnover (Gross)	XX
Less: Excise duty	XX
Turnover (Net)	XX

Further, the excise duty shown above should be the total duty except the duty related to the difference between closing inventory & opening inventory which should be recognized separately in the Statement of Profit and Loss, with an explanatory note in the notes to accounts to explain the nature of the two amounts of excise duty.

As per Schedule II of Companies Act, 2013, in respect of a company other than a finance company revenue from operations shall disclose separately in the notes revenue from—

(*a*) Sale of products;

(*b*) Sale of services;

(*c*) Other operating revenues;

Less:

(*d*) Excise duty.

TAXMANN®

		Conclusion: X Ltd has not followed the correct accounting treatment, the auditor needs to qualify his report accordingly.

26.2 - INDIAN ACCOUNTING STANDARDS

Ind AS - 1 **Q.39** **What is 'Other Comprehensive Income' as per Ind-As? What are its components?** **[Nov. 17 (5 Marks)]**

Ans. : Other Comprehensive Income as per Ind-AS:

As per Ind-AS 1 "Presentation of Financial Statements other comprehensive income comprises items of income and expense (including reclassification adjustments) that are not recognised in profit or loss as required or permitted by other Ind ASs.

The components of other comprehensive income include:

1. changes in revaluation surplus (Ind AS 16, Property, Plant and Equipment and Ind AS 38, Intangible Asset);
2. re-measurements of defined benefit plans (Ind AS 19 - Employee Benefits);
3. gains and losses arising from translating the financial statements of a foreign operation (Ind AS 21, The Effects of Changes in Foreign Exchange Rates);
4. gains and losses from investments in equity instruments designated at fair value;
5. gains and losses on financial assets measured at fair value.
6. the effective portion of gains and losses on hedging instruments in a cash flow hedge and the gains and losses on hedging instruments that hedge investments in equity instruments measured at fair value;
7. for particular liabilities designated as at fair value through profit or loss, the amount of the change in fair value that is attributable to changes in the liability's credit risk;
8. changes in the value of the time value of options when separating the intrinsic value and time value of an option contract and designating as the hedging instrument only the changes in the intrinsic value;
9. changes in the value of the forward elements of forward contracts when separating the forward element and spot element of a forward contract and designating as the hedging instrument only the changes in the spot element, and changes in the value of the foreign currency basis spread of a financial instrument when excluding it from the designation of that financial instrument as the hedging instrument.

"ICAI Examiner Comments"

Examinees were lacking knowledge on the topic. Examinees were neither aware of the meaning of "Other Comprehensive Income" as per Ind-AS nor its Components". Many examinees mixed up "Other Comprehensive Income" with income from other sources viz., interest, dividend and capital gains etc. It seems that examinees have made poor preparation on Ind-AS.

Misc **Q.40** **As an Auditor give your comments for the following disclosures made by a company which adopted Ind-AS for compilation of financial Statements:**

(*a*) In the Balance Sheet, the sub-head inventories contained an item "goods in transit" in which a consolidated amount aggregating the cost of raw materials in transit and loose tools billed on company but delivery not made to company had been specified.

(*b*) Provision for doubtful debts of trade debtors was grouped in "Provisions" under current liabilities.

(*c*) In statement of profit and loss, prior period income was shown under "Other Income".

(*d*) Sale proceeds of scrap incidental to manufacture were included in "Other income".

(*e*) Payment towards a one time voluntary retirement scheme introduced during the year was included in "Employee Benefit Expense". **[May 18 - New Syllabus (5 Marks)]**

Ans. : Appropriateness of Disclosures made in financial statements:

(*a*) Disclosure of cost of raw material in transit and loose tools in aggregate in the financial statements is not correct. As per Division II of Schedule III of the Companies Act, 2013, cost of raw material in transit shall be disclosed as sub-head of raw material and loose tools billed on the company would be shown as separate sub-head of Loose tools under heading of Inventories *i.e.* part of Current Asset.

(*b*) Disclosure is not appropriate because as per Ind-AS 37 "Provisions, Contingent Liabilities and Contingent Assets" the term 'doubtful debts' is an adjustment to the carrying amounts of assets. Hence, provision should be shown net in trade receivable.

(*c*) Disclosure is not appropriate. As per Ind-AS 8 "Accounting Policies, Changes in Accounting Estimates and Errors", Prior Period Income should not be shown in statement of profit and loss. The entity shall adjust the opening balance of each affected component of equity for the earliest prior period presented and the other comparative amounts disclosed for each prior period presented as if the new accounting policy had always been applied.

(*d*) Disclosure is not proper. As per Ind-AS 2 "Inventories", sale proceeds of scrap incidental to manufacture should be deducted from the cost of the main product.

(*e*) Disclosure is not proper. As per Ind-AS 19 "Employee Benefits", if the termination benefits are expected to be settled wholly before 12 months after the end of the annual reporting period in which the termination benefit is recognized, the entity shall apply the requirements for short-term employee benefits, in case it is not expected to be settled before 12 months the entity shall apply the requirements for long term employee benefits. In the instant case, it should be shown as short-term employee benefits in place of Employee Benefit Expenses.

Ind-AS 24 | **Q.41** **You are the Auditor of Power Supply Corporation Limited, a Government Company for the year ended on 31st March 2018. The turnover of the Company for the period was Rs. 12,000 crores from sale of power. During your audit, you found that the Company had procured Spares for Transmitters for Rs. 850 crores from abroad through a Corporation by name Procurement and Supply India Limited which is also owned and controlled by Government of India. The Financial Statements of the Power Supply Corporation Limited, prepared in compliance with Ind AS for the year ended on 31-03-2018 did not contain any additional disclosure regarding the procurement of spares as referred to above. To your query as to whether any disclosure regarding Related Party Transaction would be required, the Management of the Corporation replied that no such disclosure would be necessary for transactions between State Controlled Enterprises. Analyse this issue in finalizing the Audit Report. [Nov. 18-New Syllabus (5 Marks)]**

Ans. : Related Party Disclosures in case of Government related Entities:

- Para 25 and Para 26 of Ind-AS 24 "Related Party Disclosures" provides the reporting requirements of related party transactions in case of government related entities.
- As per para 25, a reporting entity (Govt. entity) is exempt from the disclosure requirements in relation to related party transactions and outstanding balances, including commitments, with:

  (*a*) a government that has control or joint control of, or significant influence over, the reporting entity; and

  (*b*) another entity that is a related party because the same government has control or joint control of, or significant influence over, both the reporting entity and the other entity.
- As per Para 26, if a reporting entity applies the exemption as stated in Para 25, it shall disclose the following about the transactions and related outstanding balances referred to in Para 25:

  (*a*) the name of the government and the nature of its relationship with the reporting entity (*i.e.* control, joint control or significant influence);

  (*b*) the following information in sufficient detail to enable users of the entity's financial statements to understand the effect of related party transactions on its financial statements:

    (*i*) the nature and amount of each individually significant transaction; and

    (*ii*) for other transactions that are collectively, but not individually, significant, a qualitative or quantitative indication of their extent.

Conclusion: Management is required to ensure disclosure requirements of Para 25 of Ind-AS 24. Under the circumstances, auditor shall apply the procedures as stated in SA 550 and modify his report his necessary disclosures as discussed not provided in the financial statements.

27 CHAPTER

SCHEDULE III OF COMPANIES ACT, 2013

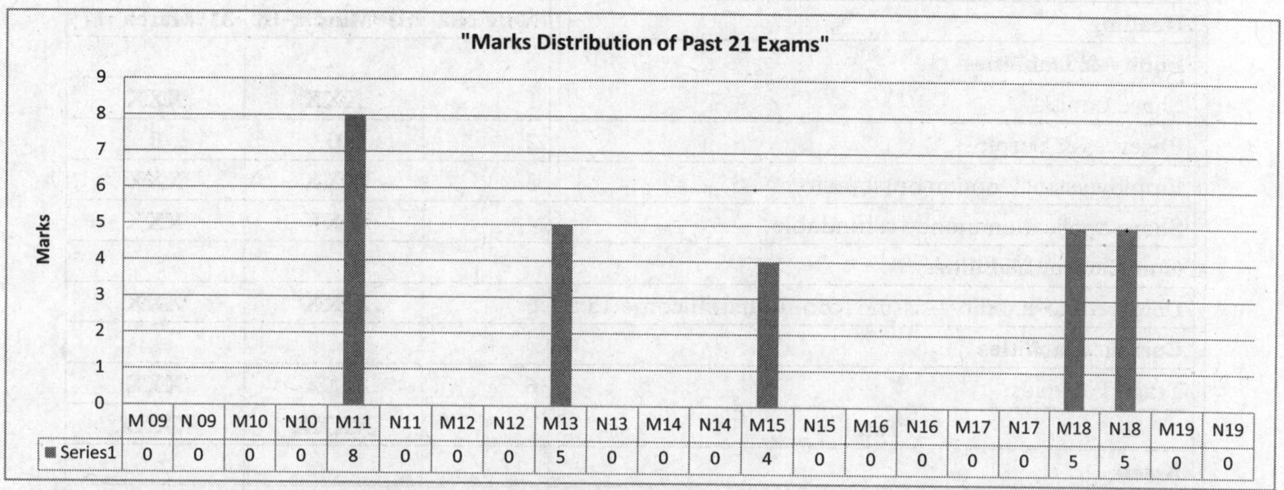

Q.1 Write short note on: Division of Schedule III to the Companies Act, 2013 w.r.t. AS and Ind AS.

Ans. : Division of Schedule III:

The Schedule III to the Companies Act, 2013 has been divided into three divisions vide notification dated 11-10-2018.

Division I

Division I deals with F.S. for a company whose F.S. are required to comply with the Companies (AS) Rules, 2006. Division I has been divided as follows:

- Part I contains the form in which the Balance Sheet of a company should be drawn up, and states the general instructions as regard to presentation of different assets and liabilities.
- Part II contains the form and states the general instructions as regard to preparation and presentation of information in the Statement of Profit and Loss.
- General instructions for preparation of Consolidated Financial Statements have also been provided in Schedule III where a company is required to prepare Consolidated Financial Statements. The company shall *mutatis mutandis* follow the requirements of this Schedule as applicable to a company in the preparation of balance sheet and statement of profit and loss.

Division II

Division II deals with F.S. for a company whose F.S. are drawn up in compliance of the Companies (Ind AS) Rules, 2015. Division II has been divided as follows:

- Part I contains the form in which the Balance Sheet of a company required to comply with Ind AS and states the general instructions as regard to preparation of Balance Sheet.
- Part II contains the form and states the general instructions as regard to preparation of Statement of Profit and Loss.
- Part III contain general instructions for preparation of Consolidated F.S.

Division III

Division III deals with F.S. for a Non-Banking Financial Company (NBFC) whose F.S. are drawn up in compliance of the Companies (Ind AS) Rules, 2015. Division III has been divided as follows:

- Part I contains the form in which the Balance Sheet of a company required to comply with Ind AS and states the general instructions as regard to preparation of Balance Sheet.
- Part II contains the form and states the general instructions as regard to preparation of Statement of Profit and Loss.
- PART III contains general instructions for preparation of Consolidated F.S.

Q.2 The Balance Sheet of G Ltd. as at 31st March, 18 is as under. Comment on the presentation in terms of Schedule III and Accounting Standards issued by NACAS.

Heading	Note No.	31st March, 18	31st March, 17
Equity & Liabilities			
Share Capital	1	XXX	XXX
Reserves & Surplus	2	0	0
Employee stock option outstanding	3	XXX	XXX
Share application money refundable	4	XXX	XXX
Non-Current Liabilities			
Deferred tax liability (Arising from Indian Income Tax)	5	XXX	XXX
Current Liabilities			
Trade Payables	6	XXX	XXX
Total		XXXX	XXXX
Assets			
Non-Current Assets			
Fixed Assets - Tangible	7	XXX	XXX
CWIP (including capital advances)	8	XXX	XXX
Current Assets			
Trade Receivables	9	XXX	XXX
Deferred Tax Asset (Arising from Indian Income Tax)	10	XXX	XXX
P & L Debit balance		XXX	XXX
Total		XXXX	XXXX

[May 13 (5 Marks)]

Ans. : Errors in presentation as per Schedule III:

1. Share Capital & Reserve & Surplus are to be reflected under the heading "Shareholders' funds", which is not shown while preparing the balance sheet.
   Although it is a part of Equity and Liabilities yet it must be shown under head "shareholders' funds". The heading "Shareholders' funds" is missing in the balance sheet given in the question.
2. Reserve & Surplus is showing zero balance, which is not correct in the given case. Debit balance of statement of profit & Loss should be shown as a negative figure under the head 'Surplus'. The balance of 'Reserves and Surplus', after adjusting negative balance of surplus shall be shown under the head 'Reserves and Surplus' even if the resulting figure is in the negative.
3. Schedule III requires that Employee Stock Option outstanding should be disclosed under the heading "Reserves and Surplus".
4. Share application money refundable shall be shown under the sub-heading "Other Current Liabilities". As this is refundable and not pending for allotment, hence it is not a part of equity.
5. Deferred Tax Liability has been correctly shown under Non-Current Liabilities. But Deferred tax assets and deferred tax liabilities, both, cannot be shown in balance sheet because only the net balance of Deferred Tax Liability or Asset is to be shown.

6. Under the main heading of Non-Current Assets, Fixed Assets are further classified as under:
   - Tangible assets
   - Intangible assets
   - Capital work-in-progress
   - Intangible assets under development.

Keeping in view the above, the Capital WIP shall be shown under Fixed Assets as Capital Work-in-Progress. The amount of Capital advances included in CWIP shall be disclosed under the sub-heading "Long term loans and advances" under the heading Non-Current Assets.

Deferred Tax Asset shall be shown under Non-Current Asset. It should be the net balance of Deferred Tax Asset after adjusting the balance of deferred tax liability.

Q.3 MG & Co. Ltd. seeks your advice while preparing financial statements the general instructions to be followed while preparing balance sheet under Companies Act, 2013 in respect of current assets and current liabilities. [May 15 (4 Marks)]

Ans. : General Instructions as to Current Assets and Current Liabilities as per Schedule III:

An asset shall be classified as current when it satisfies any of the following criteria:

(*a*) it is expected to be realized in, or is intended for sale or consumption in, the company's normal operating cycle;

(*b*) it is held primarily for the purpose of being traded;

(*c*) it is expected to be realized within twelve months after the reporting date; or

(*d*) it is cash or cash equivalent unless it is restricted from being exchanged or used to settle a liability for at least twelve months after the reporting date.

A liability shall be classified as current when it satisfies any of the following criteria:

(*a*) it is expected to be settled in the company's normal operating cycle;

(*b*) it is held primarily for the purpose of being traded;

(*c*) it is due to be settled within twelve months after the reporting date; or

(*d*) the company does not have an unconditional right to defer settlement of the liability for at least twelve months after the reporting date. Terms of a liability that could at the option of the counter-party, result in its settlement by the issue of equity instruments do not affect its classification.

Q.4 Z Ltd. has flexi deposit linked current account with various banks. Cheques are issued from the current account and as per the requirements of funds, the flexi deposits are encashed and transferred to current accounts. As of 31st March, 2018 certain cheques issued to vendors are not presented for payment resulting in the credit balance in the books of the company. The management wants to present the book overdraft under current liabilities and flexi deposits under cash & bank balances. Comment. [May 11 (8 Marks)]

Ans. : Presentation of Book Overdraft:

As per instruction given in Schedule III to the Companies Act, 2013, the "cash and cash equivalents" should be classified as:

1. Balances with banks;
2. Cheques, drafts on hand;
3. Cash on hand;
4. Others (specify nature).

The following shall be shown separately:

(*a*) Earmarked balances with banks.

(*b*) Balances with banks held as margin money or security against the borrowings, guarantees, other commitments.

(*c*) Repatriation restrictions, if any, in respect of cash and bank balances.

(*d*) Bank deposits with more than 12 months maturity.

In the present case, it appears that in substance the position is that the composite bank balance including the balance in flexi deposit accounts are positive, even though physical set-off has not been made as on the balance sheet date. Further the bank has got the right to set off the flexi deposits against the cheques issued and hence it would be more informative and useful to the readers of the financial statements to disclose the book credit balance as a set-off from the flexi deposit accounts.

Conclusion: The disclosure of the said book credit balance as book overdraft under the head current liabilities as proposed by the management is not correct.

Q.5 Comment on the following: X Ltd., paid ₹ 25 lakhs as advance to Y Ltd. towards the purchase of a printing machinery on 15-01-2017 with delivery instructions to deliver the same in the last week of June, 16. Further on 02-02-2017 X Ltd. purchased two diesel generator sets from Y Ltd. for ₹ 30 lakhs on 90 days Credit term. In the accounts for 2016-17, X Ltd. intends to adjust the advance paid against Credit purchase and show the net amount of ₹ 5 lakhs as due from them. As the statutory auditor, how would you deal with this? **[Nov. 08 (5 Marks)]**

Ans. : Adjustment of Advances:

- Advance payment by X Ltd. to the supplier of machinery (Y Ltd.) should be grouped under the head 'Capital Work-in-Progress'. This is as per requirement of Schedule III to the Companies Act, 2013 and the existing accounting practice.
- Purchase of two diesel generator sets from Y Ltd. on credit term should be disclosed separately as current liabilities.

Conclusion: Proposal of X Ltd., to show the net balance in the personal account of Y Ltd. is not correct. Such proposal will conceal the two material items in the balance sheet - one, expenditure towards capital asset and the other current liability for purchase of the generator set. Hence, the auditor should advise X Ltd. to show these two items separately. If X Ltd. does not accept the advice, the auditor should qualify his report with suitable quantification of amount involved.

Q.6 Director (Finance) of Beta Ltd. is of the opinion that total trade payables mentioned in the financial statement is sufficient disclosure in the Balance Sheet as per Part I of Schedule III to the Companies Act, 2013. They did not mention details regarding Micro, Small and Medium Enterprises (MSME). Give your view as statutory auditor of the Company and state the details required to be disclosed in notes regarding MSME. **[May 18 - Old Syllabus (4 Marks)]**

Ans : Disclosure regarding Micro, Small and Medium Enterprises:

Schedule III of Companies ACT, 2013 requires that trade payables shall be classified as:

(A) total outstanding dues of micro enterprises and small enterprises; and

(B) total outstanding dues of creditors other than micro enterprises and small enterprises."

The following details relating to Micro, Small and Medium Enterprises shall be disclosed in the notes:

(*a*) the principal amount and the interest due thereon (to be shown separately) remaining unpaid to any supplier at the end of each accounting year;

(*b*) the amount of interest paid by the buyer in terms of section 16 of the MSME Development Act, 2006, along with the amount of the payment made to the supplier beyond the appointed day during each accounting year;

(*c*) the amount of interest due and payable for the period of delay in making payment (which have been paid but beyond the appointed day during the year) but without adding the interest specified under the MSME Development Act, 2006;

(*d*) the amount of interest accrued and remaining unpaid at the end of each accounting year; and

(*e*) the amount of further interest remaining due and payable even in the succeeding years, until such date when the interest dues above are actually paid to the small enterprise, for the purpose of disallowance of a deductible expenditure u/s 23 of the MSME Act, 2006.

Q.7 Comment on the following with reference to Schedule III to the Companies Act, 2013:

(*a*) A company has disclosed performance guarantee and counter guarantees as Contingent Liabilities.

(*b*) A company has clubbed all other expenses under the head "Other Expenses" on the basis of 1% of total revenue or Rs. 5,000 whichever is higher.

(*c*) A company has shown Deferred Tax Liability under Non-Current Liabilities and Deferred tax assets under Non-Current Asset in balance sheet. **[MTP-Aug. 18]**

Ans.: Appropriateness of Disclosures as per Schedule III

(*a*) Performance guarantee and counter guarantee are not in nature of contingent liabilities, hence disclosures are not appropriate.

(*b*) Treatment is not proper as Schedule III requires that any item of expenditure which exceeds 1% of revenue from operations or Rs. 1 Lac whichever is higher, needs to be disclosed separately.

(*c*) Treatment is not proper as Schedule III requires only net balance of deferred tax liability or asset.

Q.8 **Comment on the following with reference to Schedule III to the Companies Act, 2013:**

(*a*) A company has disclosed performance guarantee and counter guarantees as Contingent Liabilities.

(*b*) The parent company has recognized in the current year's financial statement, dividend declared by its subsidiary after the balance sheet date. **[RTP-Nov. 18]**

Ans. : Appropriateness of Disclosures as per Schedule III

(*a*) Performance guarantee and counter guarantee are not in nature of contingent liabilities, hence disclosures are not appropriate.

(*b*) Dividend is to be recognized as income in the year in which right to receive dividend is established. Hence, recognition of dividend declared after balance sheet date is not proper.

Q.9 **The financial statements of MP Ltd. as on March 31, 2018 are to be prepared under Division II of Schedule III to the Companies Act, 2013. Comment on the disclosure compliances for MP Ltd. from the following information in the financial statements which are required to be drawn up in compliance with Ind AS.**

(*i*) Property, Plant and Equipment include Rs. 2.50 crore for a boiler plant under construction.

(*ii*) Cash and cash equivalents include Rs. 1.25 crore deposited with a nationalized bank on 31st March, 2018 for 18 months. It is shown under current assets.

(*iii*) Non-current assets include under caption "Biological assets other than bearer Plants" a sum of Rs. 1.50 crore being cost of cultivation for bringing to yield level, the cashewnut trees whose yield period, according to estimate shall not be less than 10 Years.

(*iv*) In the Statements of Profit and Loss, the charge due to re-measurement of defined benefit plans of employees is shown in Employee benefit Expenses.

(*v*) In the Statement of Profit and Loss, proposed dividend is shown under finance cost.

[May 18-Old Syllabus (5 Marks)]

Ans. : Appropriateness of Disclosures as per Schedule III:

(*i*) Disclosure is not appropriate. Boiler plant under construction should be reflected separately as Capital Work in progress under the heading of Non-Current Asset.

(*ii*) Disclosure is not appropriate. Amount deposited with the bank is non-current in nature being deposit period exceed 12 months.

(*iii*) Disclosure is not appropriate. Cultivation expenses cannot be capitalized under the heading Biological assets other than bearer Plants.

(*iv*) Disclosure is not appropriate. As per Ind-AS 19, charge due to re-measurement of defined benefit plans of employees should be transferred to OCI.

(*v*) Disclosure is not appropriate. As per Ind-AS 10, it cannot be shown in books of account. It is reflected in notes of accounts.

CA Final May 2019 (Old Syllabus) (Part II* - Descriptive Questions) - Suggested Answers

Q. No.		Questions	Marks	Suggested Answers	
				Chapter No.	Q. No.
1.	**Answer the following:**				
	(*a*)	As an auditor of a listed company for the year ended 31st March, 2019, how would you determine the 'Key Audit Matters'?	5	1	158
	(*b*)	As the auditor appointed under the GST Act, 2017, how would you verify 'Unbilled transactions at the beginning of the financial year'?	5	18	54
	(*c*)	Enumerate the Operating conditions of an entity that may cast significant doubt on the entity's ability to continue as a "Going Concern".	4	1	124
2.	**Answer the following:**				
	(*a*)	You have been appointed as an auditor of M/s Excellent Hotels Ltd. As a senior partner, you want to use analytical procedures in respect of room rentals as well as payroll expenses. Discuss.	5	1	94
	(*b*)	The Directors and senior management of a listed company of which you are the statutory auditor, want to know their obligations under the SEBI Regulations in regard to Board or Non-Executive Directors. (Mention any Five)	5	13	19
	(*c*)	A Chartered Accountant in practice, empanelled as an Insolvency Professional (IP) has mentioned the same on his visiting cards, letter heads and other communications also. A person residing in his neighbourhood, has filed a complaint for professional misconduct against the said member for such mention of IP. You are required to examine the same with reference to The Chartered Accountants Act 1949.	4	7	51
3.	**Answer the following:**				
	(*a*)	M/s ABC & Co, LLP are appointed auditors of Sharp Company Ltd. for the year ended 31st March, 2019. As part of the audit process, they want to use confirmation procedures as audit evidence during the course of audit. In view of the fact that positive confirmations are not responded favourably, the firm also intends to use negative confirmation requests. What are the factors to be considered for the same?	7	1	88
	(*b*)	M/s LMP Associates, Chartered Accountants while conducting the audit of PQR Ltd want to conduct an inquiry of management and those charged with governance as to whether any subsequent events have occurred which might affect the financial statements. Guide M/s LMP Associates with the matters where specific enquiry may be conducted to evaluate subsequent events.	7	1	117
4.	**Answer the following:**				
	(*a*)	Mr. Y, a practicing Chartered Accountant, has been appointed as an auditor of M/s Z Ltd. on 12th June, 2018 for the year ended 31st March, 2019. Following persons have done following transactions in securities of M/s Z Ltd.: ◆ **Daughter of Mr. Y:** Purchase of Securities on 10th September, 2018 of face value of Rs. 45,000 (market value Rs. 90,000) ◆ **Husband of daughter of Mr. Y:** Purchase of Securities on 10th December, 2018 of face value of Rs. 90,000 (Market value Rs. 1,90,000). All the above securities were sold on 10th March, 2019 for Rs. 3,00,000. Discuss the implications of the above on the appointment of Mr. Y.	5	8	38

*Part I consists of Multiple Choice Questions and are not available in public domain.

Q. No.		Questions	Marks	Suggested Answers	
				Chapter No.	Q. No.
	(*b*)	Webcom Ltd, a public company with a paid up share capital of Rs. 20 crores has a turnover for the financial year 2018-19 of Rs. 220 crores. X, a recently qualified Chartered Accountant, has been appointed for conducting internal audit. He seeks your advice in drafting a good quality internal audit report. Please guide him by elaborating (in brief) the essential features of good internal audit report.	5	16	11
	(*c*)	R Ltd. owns 51% voting power in S Ltd. It however, holds and discloses all the shares as "Stock-in-trade" in its financial statements since the shares are held exclusively with a view to their subsequent disposal in the near future. R Ltd. represents that while preparing Consolidated Financial Statements, S Ltd. can be excluded from the consolidation. As the Statutory Auditor of R Ltd, how would you deal when the consolidated financial statements are to be drawn up in compliance with Ind AS.	4	11	16
5.	**Answer the following:**				
	(*a*)	Discuss the types of Margins under stock exchange trading regulations.	5	**Topic excluded from syllabus from Nov. 2019 Exam**	
	(*b*)	M/s Sri & Co., Chartered Accountant have been allotted the branch audit of a nationalized bank for the year ended 31st March, 2019. You are part of audit team and have been instructed by your partner to verify the following areas: (*i*) Fulfilment of the criteria prescribed for NPA norms for the advances given for agricultural purposes. (*ii*) Drawing power calculation from stock statements in respect of working capital accounts. What may be your areas of concern as regards matters specified above?	5	21	26
	(*c*)	Discuss Solvency Margin in case of an Insurer carrying on General Insurance Business.	4	22	1
6.	**Answer the following:**				
	(*a*)	While conducting GST audit of PQR Ltd. you have observed the following: PQR Limited has exported goods to a Company located in USA. The value of goods is $100,000. The exchange rate on the date of filing Shipping Bill is: CBEC notified Rs. 65 and RBI Reference rate Rs. 68. At the time of receiving money, the bank exchanged the foreign currency at Rs. 70. How would you report the adjustments in turnover due to foreign exchange fluctuations in Reconciliation statement in Form GSTR 9C prescribed in terms of Rule 80(3) of CGST Rules, 2017.	5	18	55
	(*b*)	The reports of the Comptroller and Auditor General of India on the audit of PSUs are presented to the Parliament and to various state legislatures to facilitate a proper consideration. Enumerate the contents of Audit Report presented by C&AG.	5	25	13
	(*c*)	Mr. A, Chartered Accountant in practice as a sole proprietor at Mumbai has an office in the suburbs of Mumbai. Due to increase in the income tax assessment work, he opens another office near the income tax office, which is within the city and at a distance of 30 kms. from his office in the suburbs. For running the new office, he has employed a retired Income Tax Commissioner who is not a Chartered Accountant. Examine the above with respect to the Chartered Accountants Act, 1949.	4	7	14
		OR			
		What is the eligibility to be a 'Peer Reviewer'?	4	20	5

CA Final Nov. 2019 (Old Syllabus) Part II* - Descriptive Questions - Suggested Answers

Q. No.		Question	Marks	Suggested Answers: Chapter No.	Suggested Answers: Q. No.
1		**Answer the following:**			
	(*a*)	During the audit of Data Solutions Ltd., a listed company, your audit manager observed that several estimates are made by the Company. He seeks your guidance to know areas of accounting estimates that may give rise to lower level of risk of material misstatement, Guide him with examples.	5	1	108
	(*b*)	Excellent Bank Ltd. is a Public Limited Company. The said Bank has various branches all over India. The Bank appoints 3 Joint Auditors for the financial year ending 31/03/2019. All the 3 Joint Auditors divide the work with mutual consent. Verification of Consolidation, however, remained undivided. All branches and zones were divided amongst the 3 Joint Auditors. During audit of zones, CA. Z, one of the joint auditors expressed a concern about internal control in one of the large corporate branches situated in his zone. The irregularity was not reported in the final accounts as the other 2 Joint Auditors were not in favour of reporting and decision of not reporting the same was taken on the basis of majority. Subsequently, fraud has been detected in the said branch which was audited by CA. Z. The Bank seeks your advice about the responsibility of the 3 Joint Auditors in the above situation.	5	1	42
	(*c*)	A is proprietor of a firm M/s ABC & Co. The firm has a turnover of 500 lakhs during the financial year ended 31.03.2019. The firm sold land and building during the year for a consideration of Rs. 15 lakhs, whose value for stamp duty purposes was Rs. 16 lakhs. As the Tax Auditor of the said firm, is the above to be reported? If yes, how will you report the same?	4	18	22
2.		**Answer the following:**			
	(*a*)	A listed entity has to obtain a compliance certificate from either the statutory auditors or practicing company secretaries regarding compliance of conditions of corporate governance and annex it to the Directors' Report. Discuss some situations which may require an adverse or qualified statement in respect of the above certificate.	5	13	17
	(*b*)	Enumerate certain important matters which can be included in 'Emphasis of matter paragraph' in an Auditors Report.	5	1	177
	(*c*)	A, a member of the Institute of Chartered Accountants of India, not holding certificate of practice, is employed with a firm of Chartered Accountants. He recommends a particular lawyer to his firm for some client related litigation being handled by the firm. The lawyer, out of the professional fee received by him from the said client, paid a certain sum as referral fee to A. Is A guilty of misconduct under the Chartered Accountants' Act, 1949?	4	7	84

*Part I consists of Multiple Choice Questions and are not available in public domain.

<table>
<tr><th rowspan="2">Q. No.</th><th rowspan="2" colspan="2">Question</th><th rowspan="2">Marks</th><th colspan="2">Suggested Answers</th></tr>
<tr><th>Chapter No.</th><th>Q. No.</th></tr>
<tr><td>3.</td><td colspan="2">Answer the following:</td><td></td><td></td><td></td></tr>
<tr><td></td><td>(a)</td><td>You have been appointed as Concurrent Auditor of a nationalized bank branch. The main business at the branch is dealing in foreign exchange. Suggest the main areas of coverage in regard to foreign exchange transactions of the said branch under concurrent audit.</td><td>5</td><td>21</td><td>36</td></tr>
<tr><td></td><td>(b)</td><td>In a Public Limited Company, it is suspected by the Management that there has been embezzlement in supplier's ledger. As an auditor of the Company, you have been asked to investigate the matter. What are the major areas that you would verify in this regard?</td><td>5</td><td>19</td><td>10</td></tr>
<tr><td></td><td>(c)</td><td>CA. P is a newly qualified Chartered Accountant in practice and in order to increase his professional practice and client base, entered into an agreement with Mr. A, a qualified and experienced registered valuer to share 20% professional fees for all cases of valuation referred to him by CA. P. Based on this, CA. P received 1,20,000 during the year 2018-19 from Mr. A. Is CA. P guilty of misconduct under the Chartered Accountants Act, 1949?</td><td>4</td><td>7</td><td>23</td></tr>
<tr><td>4.</td><td colspan="2">Answer the following:</td><td></td><td></td><td></td></tr>
<tr><td></td><td>(a)</td><td>You have been appointed as statutory auditor of M/s Moon Ltd. for the year financial year 2018-19. As the auditor of the company you want to ensure that closing balances of previous year have been correctly brought forward as opening balances in the current year. State the audit procedures for the same to ensure that there is no misstatement.</td><td>5</td><td>1</td><td>89</td></tr>
<tr><td></td><td>(b)</td><td>The financial statements of Beta Ltd. have been prepared by the Management with due disclosures for related parties and transactions with them. However, as the auditor of the Company, you are not sure of the reliability of the said disclosures. Mention the documents and records that may be helpful in gathering information about related party relationships and transactions.</td><td>5</td><td>1</td><td>113</td></tr>
<tr><td></td><td>(c)</td><td>M/S PQR & Co. is a partnership firm of 3 partners P, Q and R. All partners are exclusively associated with the firm in practice and are not doing practice in individual capacity. For the year ended 31st March, 2019, the partners have undertaken audits and signed audit reports under section 44AB/44AD of the Income-tax Act, 1961 as under:
<table>
<tr><th></th><th>Under Section 44AB</th><th>Under Section 44AD</th></tr>
<tr><td>P</td><td>10</td><td>15</td></tr>
<tr><td>Q</td><td>60</td><td>5</td></tr>
<tr><td>R</td><td>100</td><td>5</td></tr>
</table>
Discuss whether there is any professional misconduct by the firm in regard to the aforesaid audits.</td><td>4</td><td>7</td><td>137</td></tr>
<tr><td>5.</td><td colspan="2">Answer the following:</td><td></td><td></td><td></td></tr>
<tr><td></td><td>(a)</td><td>How will you verify the Income & Expenditure of earlier years credited/debited in current year for reporting under clause 27(b) of 3CD while carrying out Tax Audit u/s 44AB of the Income-tax Act, 1961?</td><td>5</td><td>18</td><td>33</td></tr>
<tr><td></td><td>(b)</td><td>You have been appointed as an auditor of a General Insurance Company. In this context, explain Unexpired Risks Reserve and audit procedures for the same.</td><td>5</td><td>22</td><td>3</td></tr>
<tr><td></td><td>(c)</td><td>M Ltd. acquired 51% shares of S Ltd. on 01.04.2018 and sold 25% of these shares during the financial year 2018-19. M Ltd. did not prepare Consolidated Financial Statements for the financial year 2018-19 on the plea that the control was only temporary. Do you agree with the view of M Ltd.? Decide, assuming that M Ltd. is required to prepare its financial statements under Ind As.</td><td>4</td><td>11</td><td>16</td></tr>
</table>

Q. No.		Question	Marks	Suggested Answers Chapter No.	Q. No.
6.		**Answer the following:**			
	(*a*)	On a complaint and request from a Federal Co-operative to which a Multi-State Co-operative Society is affiliated, you have been appointed by the Central Registrar to conduct an enquiry into working and financial condition of the Society. What shall be your powers in this regard?	5	24	12
	(*b*)	On the advice of Management of M/s Quick Ltd., the auditor of the Company overlooked and did not report on shifting of certain current year's sales transactions to the next year. The National Company Law Tribunal (NCLT) wants to take action against you. Describe the powers of the NCLT under Section 140(5) of the Companies Act, 2013 for such action and consequences to the auditor.	5	8	19
	(*c*)	What are the factors that an auditor has to consider while using Computer Assisted Auditing Techniques (CAATs)?	4	6	19
		Or			
		Write a short note on reversal of income under bank audit.	4	21	18